World Economic and Financial Surveys

WORLD ECONOMIC OUTLOOK
April 2007

Spillovers and Cycles in the Global Economy

International Monetary Fund

©2007 International Monetary Fund

Production: IMF Multimedia Services Division
Cover and Design: Luisa Menjivar and Jorge Salazar
Figures: Theodore F. Peters, Jr.
Typesetting: Choon Lee

World economic outlook (International Monetary Fund)
  World economic outlook: a survey by the staff of the International
Monetary Fund.—1980– —Washington, D.C.: The Fund, 1980–

  v.; 28 cm.—(1981–84: Occasional paper/International Monetary
Fund ISSN 0251-6365)
  Annual.
  Has occasional updates, 1984–
  ISSN 0258-7440 = World economic and financial surveys
  ISSN 0256-6877 = World economic outlook (Washington)
  1. Economic history—1971– —Periodicals. I. International
Monetary Fund. II. Series: Occasional paper (International
Monetary Fund)

HC10.W7979   84-640155

                                        338.5'443'09048—dc19
                                                AACR 2 MARC-S

Library of Congress   8507

  Published biannually.
ISBN 978-1-58906-626-7

Price: US$57.00
(US$54.00 to full-time faculty members and
students at universities and colleges)

Please send orders to:
International Monetary Fund, Publication Services
700 19th Street, N.W., Washington, D.C. 20431, U.S.A.
Tel.: (202) 623-7430   Telefax: (202) 623-7201
E-mail: publications@imf.org
Internet: http://www.imf.org

CONTENTS

Assumptions and Conventions   ix

Preface   xi

Foreword   xii

Executive Summary   xv

Chapter 1. Global Prospects and Policy Issues   1

  Global Economic Environment   1
  Outlook and Short-Term Risks   5
  Cross-Country Spillovers: Can the Global Economy Decouple from a U.S. Slowdown?   15
  Medium-Term Challenges: Can the Productivity Boom Be Sustained?   19
  Policy Issues   27
  Appendix 1.1. Recent Developments in Commodity Markets   34
  References   46

Chapter 2. Country and Regional Perspectives   47

  United States and Canada: How Much Will the U.S. Economy Slow?   47
  Western Europe: Can Recent Vigor Be Sustained?   51
  Industrial Asia: Japan's Expansion Remains on Track   56
  Emerging Asia: How Resilient Is the Region to a U.S. Slowdown?   60
  Latin America: Boosting Productivity Is the Key to Sustaining Growth   66
  Emerging Europe: Integrating with the European Union   69
  Commonwealth of Independent States: Strong Growth but More Economic
    Diversification Needed   72
  Africa: Sustaining Recent Growth Momentum   73
  Middle East: Expanding the Benefits of the Oil Boom   77
  References   79

Chapter 3. Exchange Rates and the Adjustment of External Imbalances   81

  Past Episodes of Large External Imbalances: An Event Analysis   82
  How Responsive Are U.S. Trade Volumes to Exchange Rate Movements?   93
  Implications for Global Imbalances   104
  Conclusions   106
  Appendix 3.1. Event Analysis: Methodology and Data   107
  Appendix 3.2. Econometric Estimates of Trade Models   108
  References   118

Chapter 4. Decoupling the Train? Spillovers and Cycles in the Global Economy   121

  U.S. Economy and International Business Cycle Fluctuations   123
  Identifying Common Elements in International Business Cycle Fluctuations   139

How the United States Affects the Global Economy—A Model-Based Simulation Analysis   144
Summary and Conclusions   147
Appendix 4.1. Econometric Methodology   149
Appendix 4.2. Common Elements in International Business Cycle Fluctuations:
    Description of the Dynamic Factor Models   152
References   157

Chapter 5. The Globalization of Labor   **161**

How Globalized Is Labor?   162
How Has the Globalization of Labor Affected Workers in Advanced Economies?   166
Summary and Policy Implications   180
Appendix 5.1. Data Sources and Methods   181
References   189

Annex: IMF Executive Board Discussion of the Outlook, March 2007   **193**

Statistical Appendix   **199**

Assumptions   199
What's New   199
Data and Conventions   202
Classification of Countries   205
General Features and Composition of Countries in the *World Economic Outlook*
    Classification   205
List of Tables   209
    Output (Tables 1–6)   211
    Inflation (Tables 7–11)   222
    Financial Policies (Tables 12–19)   230
    Foreign Trade (Tables 20–24)   239
    Current Account Transactions (Tables 25–31)   247
    Balance of Payments and External Financing (Tables 32–36)   262
    External Debt and Debt Service (Tables 37–42)   272
    Flow of Funds (Table 43)   281
    Medium-Term Baseline Scenario (Tables 44–45)   285

***World Economic Outlook* and *Staff Studies for the World Economic Outlook*, Selected Topics**   **289**

Boxes

1.1 Understanding the Link Between Oil Prices and the World Economy   17
1.2 Ensuring Fiscal Sustainability in G-7 Countries   24
1.3 Oil Consumption Across Major Countries: Is the United States Different?   30
1.4 Hedging Against Oil Price Volatility   36
2.1 Housing Market Slowdowns   52
2.2 Lessons from Successful European Labor Market Reformers   58
2.3 Is China Investing Too Much?   63
3.1 External Sustainability and Financial Integration   84
3.2 Large and Persistent Current Account Imbalances   97

3.3 Exchange Rate Pass-Through to Trade Prices and External Adjustment 100
4.1 Financial Linkages and Spillovers 130
4.2 Macroeconomic Conditions in Industrial Countries and Financial Flows to
Emerging Markets 133
4.3 Spillovers and International Business Cycle Synchronization: A Broader Perspective 142
5.1 Emigration and Trade: How Do They Affect Developing Countries? 175
A1 Economic Policy Assumptions Underlying the Projections for Selected
Advanced Economies 200

Tables

1.1 Overview of the *World Economic Outlook* Projections 2
1.2 Emerging Market and Developing Countries: Net Capital Flows 8
1.3 Major Advanced Economies: General Government Fiscal Balances and Debt 29
1.4 Global Oil Demand by Region 41
1.5 Effects of Petroleum Products on Production of Selected Grains in
the United States 44
2.1 Advanced Economies: Real GDP, Consumer Prices, and Unemployment 49
2.2 Advanced Economies: Current Account Positions 51
2.3 Selected Asian Countries: Real GDP, Consumer Prices, and Current
Account Balance 61
2.4 Selected Western Hemisphere Countries: Real GDP, Consumer Prices, and
Current Account Balance 66
2.5 Emerging Europe: Real GDP, Consumer Prices, and Current Account Balance 69
2.6 Commonwealth of Independent States: Real GDP, Consumer Prices, and
Current Account Balance 72
2.7 Selected African Countries: Real GDP, Consumer Prices, and Current
Account Balance 75
2.8 Selected Middle Eastern Countries: Real GDP, Consumer Prices, and Current
Account Balance 77
3.1 Summary Statistics of Episodes of Reversals 88
3.2 Standard Trade Model: Estimates of U.S. Trade Elasticities 96
3.3 List of Reversal Episodes 109
3.4 List of Large and Persistent Episodes 111
3.5 Advanced Economies: Contractionary and Expansionary Deficit Reversals 112
3.6 Emerging Markets: Contractionary and Expansionary Surplus Reversals 112
3.7 Variable Definitions 113
3.8 Standard Empirical Trade Model: Long-Run U.S. Trade Elasticities 114
3.9 Long-Run U.S. Trade Elasticities and Aggregation Bias 115
3.10 Long-Run U.S. Import Elasticities and Vertical Integration 115
3.11 Nonlinearity Tests (p value) and Thresholds for Changes in Relative Import Prices 116
3.12 Error Correction Model for U.S. Imports, Sample 1973:Q1–2006:Q3 116
4.1 Role of Large Economies in the Global Economy 122
4.2 Export Orientation by Region 125
4.3 External Portfolio Assets and Liabilities by Region 126
4.4 U.S. Downturns and Global Growth 127
4.5 Growth and Spillovers (1) 136
4.6 Growth and Spillovers (2) 136

4.7 Contributions to Output Fluctuations 140
4.8 Consumption 156
4.9 Investment 156
4.10 Contributions to Business Cycle Fluctuations in G-7 Countries 157
5.1 Classification of Sectors by Skill Intensity 182
5.2 Impact of Labor Globalization and Technological Change on Labor Shares 187
5.3 Impact of Labor Globalization and Technological Change on Skilled and
   Unskilled Labor Shares 188

Figures

1.1 Global Indicators 1
1.2 Current and Forward-Looking Indicators 3
1.3 Global Inflation 4
1.4 Developments in Mature Financial Markets 5
1.5 Mature Financial Market Indicators 6
1.6 Emerging Market Financial Conditions 7
1.7 External Developments in Major Advanced Economies 10
1.8 External Developments in Emerging Market Countries 11
1.9 Global Outlook 12
1.10 Risks to the Global Outlook 13
1.11 Productivity and Labor Cost Developments in Selected Advanced Economies 14
1.12 Measures of the Output Gap and Capacity Pressures 15
1.13 Current Account Balances and Net Foreign Assets 16
1.14 Global Productivity Performance 20
1.15 Global Saving, Investment, and Current Accounts 21
1.16 Saving and Investment in Emerging Market and Oil-Producing Economies 22
1.17 Average Petroleum Spot and Futures Prices, and Selected Energy Product Prices 35
1.18 Demand and Prices of Petroleum Products in Selected Developing and
   OECD Countries 40
1.19 Oil Supply, OECD Inventories, and OPEC Spare Capacity 41
1.20 Actual and Expected Semiannual World Consumption and Non-OPEC
   Production Growth, and Brent Crude Oil Prices 42
1.21 Commodity Price Indices and Selected Metals and Food Price Indices 43
1.22 Semiconductor Market 45
2.1 United States: How Much Will the U.S. Economy Slow? 48
2.2 United States: Developments in the Residential and Nonresidential
   Construction Sectors 50
2.3 Western Europe: Productivity Is Failing to Catch Up 54
2.4 Western Europe: Need to Do More to Raise Labor Utilization 55
2.5 Japan: Understanding Developments in Domestic Demand 57
2.6 Emerging Asia: Assessing the Resilience to a Global Slowdown 62
2.7 Latin America: Productivity Is Lagging 68
2.8 Emerging Europe: Convergence with the European Union 70
2.9 Commonwealth of Independent States (CIS): Further Reform Needed to Raise
   Investment Levels 74
2.10 Sub-Saharan Africa: Can Recent Growth Momentum Be Sustained? 76
2.11 Middle East: Investment in Non-Oil Sectors Key to Employment Growth 78

3.1 Episodes of Deficit Reversals and Large and Persistent Deficits 83

3.2 Advanced Economies: Key Indicators During Deficit Reversals 89

3.3 Deficit Reversals in Advanced Economies: Episode Characteristics by Average
     Change in GDP Growth 90

3.4 Advanced Economies: Total Change in Real Effective Exchange Rate and Average
     Change in GDP Growth During Deficit Reversals 91

3.5 Episodes of Surplus Reversals and Large and Persistent Surpluses 92

3.6 Key Indicators During Surplus Reversals 93

3.7 Surplus Reversals in Emerging Markets: Episode Characteristics by Average
     Change in GDP Growth 94

3.8 Oil Exporters: Surplus Reversals 95

3.9 Thresholds in Relative Trade Prices, Real Effective Exchange Rate, and
     Flexibility of Markets 104

3.10 United States: Trade Flows, Real Effective Exchange Rate (REER), and
     Growth Differential with Trading Partners 105

3.11 Required Exchange Rate Change for a 1 Percentage Point Reduction in
     the Ratio of U.S. Trade Deficit to GDP 106

3.12 Sectoral Price Elasticities of Trade 114

4.1 U.S. Recessions and Real GDP Growth by Region 121

4.2 Trade Orientation 124

4.3 United States: Real Imports, Real Effective Exchange Rate, Real Stock Returns,
     and Interest Rates During Recessions and Slowdowns 128

4.4 Output Gaps and Structural Characteristics During U.S. Recessions 129

4.5 Growth Declines and Spillovers: Regional Implications 137

4.6 Impact of Growth Declines in the United States and Japan 138

4.7 Global Factor 141

4.8 Global Implications of a Disturbance to U.S. Private Demand 145

4.9 Global Growth and Inflation with Correlated Disturbances and Delayed Monetary
     Policy Response 147

4.10 Limited In-Sample Persistence of U.S. Growth Shocks 150

4.11 Impact of U.S. Growth Declines on Growth in Latin America: Effects by Country 151

4.12 Impact of Euro Area Growth Declines on Growth in Latin America: Effects
     by Country 152

4.13 Impact of U.S. Growth Declines on Growth in Emerging Asia: Effects by Country ... 153

4.14 Impact of Japanese Growth Declines on Growth in Emerging Asia: Effects
     by Country 154

5.1 Alternative Measures of Global Labor Supply 162

5.2 Immigration and Trade 163

5.3 Share of Developing Countries in Trade 164

5.4 Developing Countries: Exports of Skilled Manufacturing Goods and Services 165

5.5 Offshoring by Advanced Economies 166

5.6 Advanced Economies: Offshoring by Category of Inputs 167

5.7 Advanced Economies: Labor Income Shares 168

5.8 Advanced Economies: Labor Compensation and Employment 170

5.9 Advanced Economies: Labor Compensation and Employment in Skilled and
     Unskilled Sectors 171

5.10 Catch-Up by Emerging Markets' Manufacturing Wages 172

5.11 Information and Communications Technology (ICT) Capital, Patents, and
    Labor Market Indicators   173

5.12 Contributions to the Annual Change in Labor Share   174

5.13 Advanced Economies: Contributions to the Annual Change in the Labor Share
    by Skill Level   178

5.14 Effects of Changes in Trade Prices on Labor Share, Output, and Labor
    Compensation   179

5.15 Advanced Economies' Labor Income Share, Labor Compensation, and
    Employment: Robustness to Alternative Skill Classification   182

ASSUMPTIONS AND CONVENTIONS

A number of assumptions have been adopted for the projections presented in the *World Economic Outlook*. It has been assumed that real effective exchange rates will remain constant at their average levels during January 26–February 23, 2007, except for the currencies participating in the European exchange rate mechanism II (ERM II), which are assumed to remain constant in nominal terms relative to the euro; that established policies of national authorities will be maintained (for specific assumptions about fiscal and monetary policies in industrial countries, see Box A1); that the average price of oil will be $60.75 a barrel in 2007 and $64.75 a barrel in 2008, and remain unchanged in real terms over the medium term; that the six-month London interbank offered rate (LIBOR) on U.S. dollar deposits will average 5.3 percent in 2007 and 5.1 percent in 2008; that the three-month euro deposits rate will average 3.8 percent in 2007 and 3.7 percent in 2008; and that the six-month Japanese yen deposit rate will yield an average of 0.9 percent in 2007 and of 1.2 percent in 2008. These are, of course, working hypotheses rather than forecasts, and the uncertainties surrounding them add to the margin of error that would in any event be involved in the projections. The estimates and projections are based on statistical information available through end-March 2007.

The following conventions have been used throughout the *World Economic Outlook:*

. . .   to indicate that data are not available or not applicable;

—   to indicate that the figure is zero or negligible;

–   between years or months (for example, 2005–06 or January–June) to indicate the years or months covered, including the beginning and ending years or months;

/   between years or months (for example, 2005/06) to indicate a fiscal or financial year.

"Billion" means a thousand million; "trillion" means a thousand billion.

"Basis points" refer to hundredths of 1 percentage point (for example, 25 basis points are equivalent to ¼ of 1 percent point).

In figures and tables, shaded areas indicate IMF staff projections.

Minor discrepancies between sums of constituent figures and totals shown are due to rounding.

As used in this report, the term "country" does not in all cases refer to a territorial entity that is a state as understood by international law and practice. As used here, the term also covers some territorial entities that are not states but for which statistical data are maintained on a separate and independent basis.

This report on the *World Economic Outlook* is available in full on the IMF's Internet site, www.imf.org. Accompanying it on the website is a larger compilation of data from the WEO database than in the report itself, consisting of files containing the series most frequently requested by readers. These files may be downloaded for use in a variety of software packages.

Inquiries about the content of the *World Economic Outlook* and the WEO database should be sent by mail, electronic mail, or telefax (telephone inquiries cannot be accepted) to:

World Economic Studies Division
Research Department
International Monetary Fund
700 19th Street, N.W.
Washington, D.C. 20431, U.S.A.
E-mail: weo@imf.org   Telefax: (202) 623-6343

PREFACE

The analysis and projections contained in the *World Economic Outlook* are integral elements of the IMF's surveillance of economic developments and policies in its member countries, of developments in international financial markets, and of the global economic system. The survey of prospects and policies is the product of a comprehensive interdepartmental review of world economic developments, which draws primarily on information the IMF staff gathers through its consultations with member countries. These consultations are carried out in particular by the IMF's area departments together with the Policy Development and Review Department, the Monetary and Capital Markets Department, and the Fiscal Affairs Department.

The analysis in this report has been coordinated in the Research Department. The project has been directed by Charles Collyns, Deputy Director of the Research Department, and Tim Callen, Division Chief, Research Department.

The primary contributors to this report are Thomas Helbling, Subir Lall, S. Hossein Samiei, Peter Berezin, Roberto Cardarelli, Kevin Cheng, Florence Jaumotte, Ayhan Kose, Toh Kuan, Michael Kumhof, Douglas Laxton, Valerie Mercer-Blackman, Jonathan Ostry, Alessandro Rebucci, Nikola Spatafora, and Irina Tytell. Olga Akcadag, To-Nhu Dao, Christian de Guzman, Stephanie Denis, Nese Erbil, Angela Espiritu, Patrick Hettinger, Bennett Sutton, and Ercument Tulun provided research assistance. Mahnaz Hemmati, Laurent Meister, and Emory Oakes managed the database and the computer systems. Sylvia Brescia, Celia Burns, and Jemille Colon were responsible for word processing. Other contributors include Anthony Annett, Andrew Benito, Selim Elekdag, Robert Feenstra, Caroline Freund, Jean Imbs, George Kapetanios, Jaewoo Lee, Daniel Leigh, Jaime Marquez, Gian Maria Milesi-Ferretti, Prachi Mishra, Susana Mursula, Christopher Otrok, Cedric Tille, Shang-Jin Wei, and Johannes Wiegand. Archana Kumar of the External Relations Department edited the manuscript and coordinated the production of the publication.

The analysis has benefited from input during the early stages by Raghuram Rajan, the former Economic Counsellor, and from comments and suggestions by staff from other IMF departments, as well as by Executive Directors following their discussion of the report on March 21 and 26, 2007. However, both projections and policy assessments are those of the IMF staff and should not be attributed to Executive Directors or to their national authorities.

FOREWORD

The *World Economic Outlook* team has again done an outstanding job of pulling together both the latest key global macroeconomic developments and the three analytical issues that are highly relevant for accurately reading the current economic environment. The team continues to be ably led by Charles Collyns and Tim Callen and the cornerstone is staff at all levels in the World Economic Studies Division. My predecessor as Economic Counsellor, Raghuram Rajan, contributed key insights during the early stages of preparation. I would also like to stress the importance of inputs both from other parts of the Research Department and—critically—from other departments at the IMF.

It may surprise readers to learn that this *World Economic Outlook* sees global economic risks as having *declined* since our last issue in September 2006. Certainly this is at odds with many recent newspaper headlines and commentary, which have focused on problems related to U.S. mortgages, the potential for "disorderly" unwinding of global imbalances, and worries about rising protectionist pressures.

Nevertheless, as discussed in Chapters 1 and 2, looking at the big picture, we actually see the continuation of strong global growth as the most likely scenario. The most immediate concern is bad news from the U.S. housing market, and an associated slowing of U.S. growth. However, these developments have been evident for some months and are largely reflected in market assessments of credit quality. These assessments remain positive for most types of credit. The spreads on lower-quality BBB-rated bonds backed by subprime mortgages have indeed widened substantially, but there has been little change in the yields of lower-rated corporate bonds, let alone those of investment-grade issues. The mainstream mortgage market remains open for business to people with good credit histories.

We should be careful not to underestimate the potential spillovers from the specific problems with high-risk mortgages in the United States but, compared with six months ago and based on the information available today, there is less reason to worry about the global economy. First of all, the overall U.S. economy is holding up well despite the sharp downturn in the housing sector. Investment has slowed somewhat, but consumption remains well supported by a strong labor market and healthy household balance sheets. Unemployment remains low and—in most parts of the U.S. economy—there are good prospects for sustained job growth. Even more important, the signs elsewhere are very encouraging. The euro area is experiencing its fastest growth in six years, Japan's expansion has momentum, and emerging market and developing countries—led by China and India—continue to enjoy remarkable growth. Overall, taking the five-year period of 2003–07 as a whole, the global economy is achieving its fastest pace of sustained growth since the early 1970s.

These developments, however, do rightly focus our attention on the important issue of spillovers from the United States to the broader global economy. This is the timely focus of Chapter 4, which points out that major global growth slowdowns are generally not due to country-specific developments, even if the country in question is one of the world's largest economies. Global growth typically declines sharply only when there are events that affect many countries at the same time. The chapter finds that rising trade and financial integration of the global economy does increase the potential impact of spillovers across economies, but even if the U.S. economy were to slow further, the scale of such spillovers should be manageable, especially recognizing the strengthening of macroeconomic policy management around the world over the past 20 years. Flexible exchange rates and forward-looking monetary policies reduce the output effects from all kinds of shocks.

Turning to another risk highlighted in our September 2006 report, there has been definite progress in the right direction with regard to global imbalances. There are encouraging signs that the U.S. current account deficit is now stabilizing, albeit at a high level, helped by a real depreciation of the U.S. dollar and recent strong export performance. Moreover, policy steps have been taken, which, while small, are significant and very real. This movement in the right direction—particularly with regard to actual and intended changes in fiscal policy—is exactly what is needed at this time. However, obviously there is more to be done as the existing configuration of major current accounts is not sustainable indefinitely.

Chapter 3 reassesses the evidence on the role of exchange rates in external adjustment. It confirms that market-led real appreciations and depreciations can support macroeconomic policy changes and private sector saving and investment decisions by facilitating the reallocation of resources across sectors, and help to reduce imbalances without large fluctuations in output. In particular, the chapter pours some cold water on the "exchange rate pessimism" story, in which exchange rates move but do not contribute to current account adjustment. There is also no reason to believe that elasticities or other relevant parameters have declined recently for key countries, such as the United States. If anything, standard models may underestimate how much U.S. trade volumes are likely to respond to changes in relative prices.

Exchange rate adjustment is certainly not a panacea, but it can definitely lower the output costs that would otherwise be involved in changing current account positions. At the same time, we should never lose sight of the need to increase domestic demand in surplus countries, as well as to boost private and government net savings in the United States.

Chapter 5 continues a series of analytical pieces from previous issues of the *World Economic Outlook* on the process and consequences of the globalization of the world economy, which has been the principal wellspring of recent strong global economic performance. It focuses on the remarkable development of a bigger, more integrated worldwide market for labor. This is one of the central changes of the past 25 years and, in all likelihood, the associated changes will continue to be influential for at least another generation. In part, this global market has developed through the opening up of China, India, and the former communist bloc to the global trading system, as well as through the development of new communications and transportation technologies. But, in equal part, it has been made possible by increasing cross-border movements of financial capital that has sought out attractive skill-wage combinations even in what initially seemed to be unlikely parts of the world.

While there are some legitimate concerns about the pace and composition of those flows, it is important to put them in their proper perspective. This is not a short-run or second-order phenomenon, but rather a major secular shift in where capital finds labor. Put differently, it is the flow of capital and closely associated talent (global management and global ideas) to places where strong complementary skills (including local management and local ideas) are available at attractive prices. This "flow" into emerging markets is really a mutually beneficial set of exchanges that has made possible the creation of a larger global market for labor at low, medium, and high wages. This, in turn, has had great benefits both for the countries using better access to finance to grow faster as well as for everyone who consumes the goods that these countries produce.

The globalization of labor also has had consequences for the distribution of income, and this should not be overlooked. The labor share of income has declined over time in the advanced economies, especially in Europe, and for workers in unskilled sectors. Many factors have contributed, and the findings in Chapter 5 suggest that technological advances rather than globalization of labor is the most important element. The costs of adjustment are not small and, for the people involved, they can be truly traumatic. In fact, it is exactly the loss of jobs in some regions of the United States—due to globalization of labor as well as to technology changes—that has created the most serious reason to worry about parts of the U.S. housing market. If you lose your job, this makes it much harder to service your mortgage, and the increase in distress sales and foreclosures puts downward pressure on house prices. This makes it all the more important, from both a welfare and a macroeconomic perspective, to address the costs of adjustment, including through adequate labor market flexibility, good education and training, and safety nets that cushion but do not obstruct the process of change.

To be clear, the overall risks to global growth remain weighted to the downside, and any slow-down will further complicate people's lives. But as long as macroeconomic and structural policies are designed and implemented with these risks and real people in mind, a strong global economy should be maintained. And we need to take full advantage of the opportunity that this period provides to push ahead with deep, difficult reforms to ensure both that strong growth can be sustained despite challenges such as population aging and that the benefits of this growth can be shared across all segments of the population.

Simon Johnson
Economic Counsellor and Director, Research Department

EXECUTIVE SUMMARY

Notwithstanding the recent bout of financial volatility, the world economy still looks well set for continued robust growth in 2007 and 2008. While the U.S. economy has slowed more than was expected earlier, spillovers have been limited, growth around the world looks well sustained, and inflation risks have moderated. Overall risks to the outlook seem less threatening than six months ago but remain weighted on the downside, with concerns increasing about financial risks.

Global Economic Environment

The global economy expanded vigorously in 2006, growing by 5.4 percent (Chapter 1). In the United States, the expansion slowed in the face of headwinds from a sharp downturn in the housing market, but oil price declines since August have helped to sustain consumer spending. In the euro area, growth accelerated to its fastest pace in six years as domestic demand strengthened. In Japan, activity regained traction toward year-end, after a soft patch in mid-year. Among emerging market and developing countries, rapid growth was led by China and India, while momentum was sustained across other regions as countries benefited from high commodity prices and continued supportive financial conditions.

Strong growth and rising oil prices in the first half of 2006 raised concerns about inflation, but pressures have moderated with the decline in oil prices since August. Against the background of strong growth and reduced concerns about inflation, global financial market conditions have generally been buoyant. Despite a bout of financial volatility in February–March 2007, and rising concerns about the U.S. subprime mortgage market, equity markets remain close to all-time highs, real long-term bond yields have remained below long-term trends, and risk spreads have narrowed in most markets.

In foreign exchange markets, the U.S. dollar has weakened, mainly against the euro and pound sterling. The yen has also depreciated further, in part because prospects for continued low interest rates have encouraged capital outflows, although it recovered some ground in early 2007. The Chinese renminbi has declined modestly in real effective terms despite a mild acceleration in its rate of appreciation against the dollar. The U.S. current account deficit rose to 6½ percent of GDP in 2006, although the non-oil trade deficit declined as a percent of GDP as exports accelerated. Surpluses in Japan, China, and the Middle Eastern oil-exporting countries increased further.

The major central banks have faced differing policy challenges in recent months. The U.S. Federal Reserve has kept policy rates on hold since June 2006, seeking to balance risks from a cooling economy and lingering concerns about inflation. The European Central Bank (ECB) and other central banks in Europe have continued to remove monetary accommodation. The Bank of Japan has raised its policy rate very gradually since exiting its zero interest rate policy in July 2006. Some emerging market countries—including China, India, and Turkey—have also tightened monetary policy.

Advanced economies continued to make progress in strengthening their fiscal positions in 2006. Budget deficits were reduced substantially in Germany, Japan, and the United States. Fiscal gains largely reflected strong growth of tax revenues in the cyclical upswing.

Outlook and Risks

Global growth is expected to moderate to 4.9 percent in 2007 and 2008, some ½ percentage point slower than in 2006. In the United

States, growth is expected to come down to 2.2 percent this year, from 3.3 percent in 2006, although the economy should gather some momentum during the course of the year as the drag from the housing sector dissipates (Chapter 2). Growth is also expected to ease in the euro area, reflecting in part the gradual withdrawal of monetary accommodation and further fiscal consolidation. In Japan, the expansion is projected to continue at about the same pace as in 2006.

Emerging market and developing countries are expected to continue to grow strongly, albeit at a somewhat slower pace than in 2006. These economies will continue to draw support from benign global financial conditions and commodity prices that remain high notwithstanding recent declines. China's growth is projected to remain rapid in 2007 and 2008, albeit a little below the torrid pace in 2006, while India's economy should also continue to grow rapidly. Commodity-rich countries should continue to prosper.

The risks to the growth outlook are less threatening than at the time of the September 2006 *World Economic Outlook*, but are still tilted to the downside. Particular uncertainties include the potential for a sharper slowdown in the United States if the housing sector continues to deteriorate; the risk of a retrenchment from risky assets if financial market volatility were to rise from historically low levels; the risk that inflation pressures could revive as output gaps continue to close, particularly in the event of another spike in oil prices; and the low probability but high cost risk of a disorderly unwinding of large global imbalances.

A key question in assessing the risks to the outlook is whether the global economy would be able to "decouple" from the United States were the latter to slow down more sharply than projected. To date, the cooling of U.S. activity since early 2006 has had a limited impact abroad beyond its immediate neighbors, Canada and Mexico. As discussed in Chapter 4, this reflects a number of factors, including that the U.S. slowdown has been focused in the housing sector,

which has a relatively low import content; that spillovers from the United States are typically more muted in the context of a midcycle slowdown than in a full-blown recession; and that the shock has been a U.S.-specific event rather than a common shock. Nevertheless, were the U.S. economy to slow sharply, this would have a more substantial impact on global growth.

From a longer-term perspective, developments that undermined the buoyant productivity performance of recent years would clearly have an adverse affect on global growth. Strong productivity growth has been supported by a combination of technological progress, an increasingly open global trading system, rising cross-country capital flows, and more resilient macroeconomic policy frameworks and financial systems. It is essential that these pillars remain in place, and that trends that could pose challenges to continued strong global economic performance—such as population aging and global warming—are adequately addressed.

One particular concern is that protectionist forces could undercut trade and foreign investment. If this happens, there is a danger that some of the gains from an increasingly integrated global economy will be reversed. Chapter 5 discusses how the rapid growth of international trade and the introduction of new technologies have fostered an increasingly integrated global labor market that has produced gains in growth and incomes in both source and host countries, while at the same time affecting distributional outcomes. Against this background, more could be done to help those whose jobs may be particularly affected by recent trends in technology and trade, including through better education systems, more flexible labor markets, and welfare systems that cushion the impact of, but do not obstruct, economic change.

Policy Issues

Advanced Economies

The major central banks face varying challenges in managing monetary policy, reflecting differing cyclical positions and degrees of inflation pressure in their economies. In the United States, the Federal Reserve's approach of holding its rates steady remains appropriate for now, and the path of monetary policy should depend on how incoming data affect the perceived balance of risks between growth and inflation. In the euro area, with growth projected to remain close to or above potential and the possibility of some further upward pressure on factor utilization and prices, raising interest rates further to 4 percent by the summer would seem warranted. In Japan, monetary accommodation should be removed only gradually and on the basis of evidence confirming the continuing strength of the expansion.

Fiscal policy should be directed at achieving the necessary consolidation and reform to maintain viability in the face of aging populations, while providing room for automatic stabilizers to work as needed. Sustained progress toward fiscal consolidation will depend on fundamental reforms to contain increasing outlays as populations age, particularly in areas such as health care and pensions, and to avoid the erosion of revenue bases.

With expansions now firmly established, this is the time to further advance structural reforms aimed at sustaining potential growth. A particular challenge is to ensure that adequate employment opportunities are created within the increasingly global economy and that the less well-off share more in the prosperity created by rising trade and the introduction of new technologies. Some progress has been made in implementing productivity-enhancing reforms in the euro area and Japan, but more needs to be done, particularly in the services and financial sectors. There is also scope to improve the flexibility of the U.S. economy, including by reducing the close link between health care coverage and employment to increase labor mobility.

Emerging Market and Developing Economies

Many emerging market and developing countries face the challenge of maintaining stable macroeconomic and financial conditions in the face of strong foreign exchange inflows. Exchange rates in several Asian countries have appreciated markedly over the past six months, but China would benefit from a more flexible regime that provides a more secure basis for monetary policy management. In emerging Europe, policies need to minimize risks associated with large current account deficits and rapid credit growth. In Latin America, the task is to consolidate recent progress toward strengthening public sector balance sheets. In commodity-exporting countries, the rapid rise in export receipts and government revenues needs to continue to be carefully managed to avoid overheating.

Recent progress on structural reforms has generally been patchy and the "to do" list remains long. Further progress in liberalizing service sectors in Asia and elsewhere would help sustain and extend productivity improvements. Accelerating labor market reforms in Latin America would help boost the region's poor productivity performance. Establishing stable, transparent, and balanced regimes for infrastructure provision and for the exploitation of natural resources would help to reduce risks of bottlenecks, corruption, and lack of investment that could prove to be serious impediments to long-term growth.

Multilateral Initiatives and Policies

Cooperative policy actions are necessary to support the smooth unwinding of large global imbalances. Important elements of such an approach—which are being discussed in the context of the IMF's Multilateral Consultations—include efforts to raise saving in the United States, including through more ambitious fiscal consolidation and steps to reduce disincentives to private savings; advancing growth-enhancing reforms in the euro area and Japan; and measures to boost consumption and increase upward exchange rate flexibility in some parts of emerging Asia, especially China. Among Middle Eastern oil exporters, lower oil prices and increased spending are expected to reduce external surpluses, although there is still scope to continue to boost spending, subject to absorptive capacity constraints.

As emphasized in Chapter 3, market-led movements in real effective exchange rates could potentially play an important supportive role in the adjustment of global imbalances. Currency depreciation could help to contain the output costs that may accompany the demand rebalancing needed to lower current account deficits by encouraging a smooth shift in resources across sectors. Encouragingly, the chapter finds that concerns about "elasticity pessimism"—that U.S. trade flows are unresponsive to real exchange rate changes—are exaggerated, consistent with the view that a real effective depreciation of the dollar over the medium term could contribute to reducing the

U.S. current account deficit. To be most effective, the counterpart to this realignment of the U.S. dollar would be real exchange rate appreciations in countries with persistent current account surpluses, including China, Japan, and Middle Eastern oil exporters.

The recent revival in the Doha Round of multilateral trade negotiations is welcome. Reaching a Doha Round conclusion that achieves ambitious multilateral trade reform and further strengthens multilateral rules so as to reduce the risks of protectionism would provide an important boost to the global outlook. Prospects for a sustained global expansion and a gradual unwinding of global imbalances would also benefit from initiatives to remove obstacles to the smooth reallocation of resources in response to exchange rate movements, including through trade reform.

GLOBAL PROSPECTS AND POLICY ISSUES

Notwithstanding recent financial market nervousness, the global economy remains on track for continued robust growth in 2007 and 2008, although at a somewhat more moderate pace than in 2006 (Figure 1.1). Moreover, downside risks to the outlook seem less threatening than at the time of the September 2006 World Economic Outlook, *as oil price declines since last August and generally benign global financial conditions have helped to limit spillovers from the correction in the U.S. housing market and to contain inflation pressures. Nevertheless, recent market events have underlined that risks to the outlook remain on the downside. Particular concerns include the potential for a sharper slowdown in the United States if the housing sector continues to deteriorate; the risk of a deeper and more sustained retrenchment from risky assets if financial markets continue to be volatile; the possibility that inflation pressures may revive as output gaps continue to close, particularly in the event of another spike in oil prices; and the low probability but high cost risk of a disorderly unwinding of large global imbalances. From a longer-term perspective, a number of trends—including the aging of populations, rising resistance to increasing globalization, and the environmental consequences of rapid growth—could undermine the buoyant productivity that has underpinned recent favorable outcomes. While remaining vigilant to short-term macroeconomic risks, policymakers should take advantage of the continuing strong performance of the global economy to press ahead with more ambitious efforts to tackle deep-seated structural challenges.*

Global Economic Environment

The global economy expanded vigorously in 2006, growing 5.4 percent—¼ percentage point faster than anticipated at the time of the September 2006 *World Economic Outlook* (Table 1.1 and Figure 1.2). Activity in the United States faced strong headwinds from a sharp downturn in the housing market, while corporate investment in plant and equipment has also softened.

Figure 1.1. Global Indicators[1]
(Annual percent change unless otherwise noted)

The global expansion remains above trend, although the pace is moderating, helping to contain inflationary pressures. World trade continues to grow significantly faster than output.

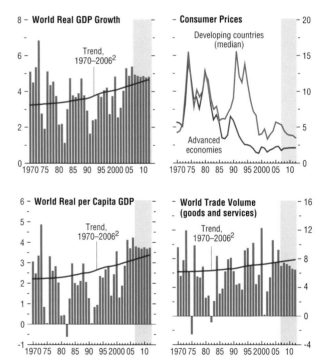

[1]Shaded areas indicate IMF staff projections. Aggregates are computed on the basis of purchasing-power-parity (PPP) weights unless otherwise noted.
[2]Average growth rates for individual countries, aggregated using PPP weights; the aggregates shift over time in favor of faster-growing countries, giving the line an upward trend.

Table 1.1. Overview of the *World Economic Outlook* Projections
(Annual percent change unless otherwise noted)

	2005	2006	Current Projections 2007	Current Projections 2008	Difference from September 2006 Projections 2007	Difference from September 2006 Projections 2008
World output	**4.9**	**5.4**	**4.9**	**4.9**	—	—
Advanced economies	2.5	3.1	2.5	2.7	–0.2	—
United States	3.2	3.3	2.2	2.8	–0.7	–0.4
Euro area	1.4	2.6	2.3	2.3	0.3	0.3
Germany	0.9	2.7	1.8	1.9	0.6	0.4
France	1.2	2.0	2.0	2.4	–0.2	—
Italy	0.1	1.9	1.8	1.7	0.5	0.3
Spain	3.5	3.9	3.6	3.4	0.6	0.3
Japan	1.9	2.2	2.3	1.9	0.2	–0.1
United Kingdom	1.9	2.7	2.9	2.7	0.1	0.2
Canada	2.9	2.7	2.4	2.9	–0.5	0.1
Other advanced economies	3.9	4.3	3.8	3.8	0.1	0.1
Newly industrialized Asian economies	4.7	5.3	4.6	4.6	0.2	0.2
Other emerging market and developing countries	7.5	7.9	7.5	7.1	0.3	0.2
Africa	5.6	5.5	6.2	5.8	0.3	0.5
Sub-Sahara	6.0	5.7	6.8	6.1	0.5	0.7
Central and eastern Europe	5.5	6.0	5.5	5.3	0.5	0.5
Commonwealth of Independent States	6.6	7.7	7.0	6.4	0.5	0.2
Russia	6.4	6.7	6.4	5.9	–0.1	–0.2
Excluding Russia	6.9	9.7	8.3	7.5	1.9	1.1
Developing Asia	9.2	9.4	8.8	8.4	0.2	0.1
China	10.4	10.7	10.0	9.5	—	—
India	9.2	9.2	8.4	7.8	1.1	0.7
ASEAN-4	5.2	5.4	5.5	5.8	–0.1	–0.2
Middle East	5.4	5.7	5.5	5.5	0.2	—
Western Hemisphere	4.6	5.5	4.9	4.2	0.6	0.4
Brazil	2.9	3.7	4.4	4.2	0.5	0.3
Mexico	2.8	4.8	3.4	3.5	–0.1	—
Memorandum						
European Union	1.9	3.2	2.8	2.7	0.4	0.3
World growth based on market exchange rates	3.3	3.9	3.4	3.5	—	—
World trade volume (goods and services)	**7.4**	**9.2**	**7.0**	**7.4**	**–0.7**	**0.2**
Imports						
Advanced economies	6.1	7.4	4.7	5.7	–1.3	0.1
Other emerging market and developing countries	12.1	15.0	12.5	12.2	0.4	1.1
Exports						
Advanced economies	5.6	8.4	5.5	5.8	–0.5	0.1
Other emerging market and developing countries	11.2	10.6	10.4	9.9	–0.2	—
Commodity prices (U.S. dollars)						
Oil[1]	41.3	20.5	–5.5	6.6	–14.6	8.2
Nonfuel (average based on world commodity export weights)	10.3	28.4	4.2	–8.8	9.0	0.3
Consumer prices						
Advanced economies	2.3	2.3	1.8	2.1	–0.6	–0.1
Other emerging market and developing countries	5.4	5.3	5.4	4.9	0.3	0.3
London interbank offered rate (percent)[2]						
On U.S. dollar deposits	3.8	5.3	5.3	5.1	–0.2	–0.4
On euro deposits	2.2	3.1	3.8	3.7	0.1	–0.1
On Japanese yen deposits	0.1	0.4	0.9	1.2	–0.2	–0.3

Note: Real effective exchange rates are assumed to remain constant at the levels prevailing during January 26–February 23, 2007. See the Statistical Appendix for details on groups and methodologies.

[1]Simple average of spot prices of U.K. Brent, Dubai, and West Texas Intermediate crude oil. The average price of oil in U.S. dollars a barrel was $64.27 in 2006; the assumed price is $60.75 in 2007 and $64.75 in 2008.

[2]Six-month rate for the United States and Japan. Three-month rate for the euro area.

However, consumption was sustained by continued employment growth (especially in the services sector) and oil prices declining from August highs. In the euro area, growth accelerated to its fastest pace in six years as domestic demand was boosted by increasing business confidence and improving labor markets, as well as special factors—including the Soccer World Cup and the boost to consumption in advance of a value-added tax (VAT) increase in Germany in January 2007. Activity in Japan slowed in the middle of the year, but regained traction toward year-end.

Rapid growth in emerging market and developing countries was led by China and India. China's growth rate reached 10¾ percent in 2006, driven by investment and export growth, notwithstanding some easing in the second half as policy tightening helped to cool the pace of fixed asset investment. India's expansion picked up momentum in the course of the year, with year-on-year growth rising to 9¼ percent. Elsewhere, growth was also generally sustained at robust rates, supported by high commodity prices and favorable financial conditions.

Strong growth and rising international oil prices in the first half of 2006 raised concerns about inflation, but pressures moderated in the second half, dampened by monetary policy tightening and the turnaround in oil markets (Figure 1.3). The oil price declines from August largely reflected some easing of security tensions in the Middle East, improved supply-demand balance in oil markets, and favorable weather conditions in the second half of 2006 (Appendix 1.1). In the advanced economies, headline CPI inflation dropped quite sharply after the summer as fuel costs fell. The core CPI inflation rate (excluding food and energy) also eased modestly in the United States, although remaining somewhat above the Federal Reserve's implicit comfort zone. The Fed has kept the Federal funds rate on hold since June, seeking to balance risks from a cooling economy and continuing concerns about inflation. In Japan, downward revision of the CPI series has left inflation readings still uncomfortably close to

Figure 1.2. Current and Forward-Looking Indicators
(Percent change from a year ago unless otherwise noted)

Industrial production and trade indicators suggest that the pace of global expansion has eased somewhat since mid-2006, although generally positive readings on confidence continue to augur well for short-term prospects.

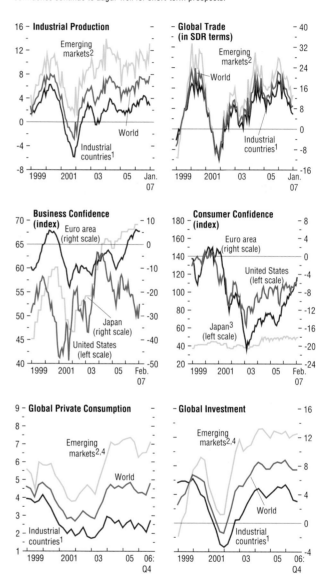

Sources: Business confidence for the United States, the Institute for Supply Management; for the euro area, the European Commission; and for Japan, Bank of Japan. Consumer confidence for the United States, the Conference Board; for the euro area, the European Commission; and for Japan, Cabinet Office; all others, Haver Analytics.
[1]Australia, Canada, Denmark, euro area, Japan, New Zealand, Norway, Sweden, Switzerland, the United Kingdom, and the United States.
[2]Argentina, Brazil, Bulgaria, Chile, China, Colombia, Czech Republic, Estonia, Hong Kong SAR, Hungary, India, Indonesia, Israel, Korea, Latvia, Lithuania, Malaysia, Mexico, Pakistan, Peru, the Philippines, Poland, Romania, Russia, Singapore, Slovak Republic, South Africa, Taiwan Province of China, Thailand, Turkey, Ukraine, and Venezuela.
[3]Japan's consumer confidence data are based on a diffusion index, where values greater than 50 indicate improving confidence.
[4]Data for China, India, Pakistan, and Russia are interpolated.

Figure 1.3. Global Inflation

(Annualized percent change of three-month moving average over previous three-month average, unless otherwise noted)

Measures of inflation and inflation expectations have generally moderated since mid-2006, helped by falling oil prices and some tightening of monetary conditions.

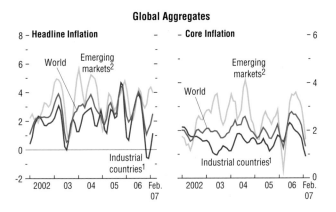

Global Aggregates

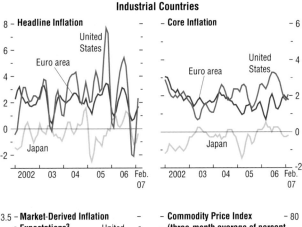

Industrial Countries

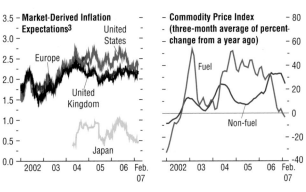

Sources: Haver Analytics; and IMF staff calculations.
[1]Australia, Canada, Denmark, euro area, Japan, New Zealand, Norway, Sweden, the United Kingdom, and the United States.
[2]Brazil, Bulgaria, Chile, China, Estonia, Hong Kong SAR, Hungary, India, Indonesia, Korea, Malaysia, Mexico, Poland, Singapore, South Africa, Taiwan Province of China, and Thailand.
[3]In percent; nominal minus inflation-indexed yields on 10-year securities.

zero, and the Bank of Japan has raised its policy interest rate only very gradually since exiting its zero interest rate policy in July 2006. The European Central Bank (ECB), the Bank of England, and other central banks in Europe have continued to remove monetary accommodation in the context of economic buoyancy. Some emerging market countries—including China, India, and Turkey—have tightened monetary conditions in the face of concerns about over-rapid growth, overheating, and (in the case of Turkey) external pressures, but, overall, inflation outcomes have continued to be favorable.

Expectations of continued solid economic growth and fading inflation concerns contributed to buoyant global financial market conditions over most of the period since mid-2006. Markets have been more volatile since late February, but this recent episode seems to be more of a modest correction after a period of rising asset prices, rather than a fundamental change in market sentiment (see the April 2007 *Global Financial Stability Report* for further details). Notwithstanding recent declines, advanced economy equity markets remain close to all-time highs, supported by strong earnings growth (Figures 1.4 and 1.5). Long-term bond yields have generally receded since mid-2006, spreads on risky assets have narrowed in most market segments, and market volatility was extremely low until recently. Emerging bond and equity markets rebounded robustly from an earlier episode of turbulence in May–June 2006 as concerns about continued tightening of monetary policy in the United States eased, and remain at close to peak levels even after the recent correction (Figure 1.6). Capital flows to emerging markets were maintained at high levels in 2006 as a whole, with Asia and emerging Europe continuing to attract a large share of the flows and corporate borrowers replacing sovereigns as the main source of demand (Table 1.2).

In foreign exchange markets, slower growth in the United States and the robust expansion in western Europe have fed expectations of narrowing interest rate differentials and contributed to a weakening of the U.S. dollar mainly against the euro and pound sterling. Over 2006 as a whole, the U.S. dollar depreciated by 4 percent in real effective terms, while the euro and pound sterling appreciated by around 7 percent (Figure 1.7). The yen also weakened further in 2006, notwithstanding Japan's rising current account surplus, as declining "home bias" among domestic investors and low interest rates continued to encourage capital outflows. However, it recovered some ground in early 2007, as heightened market volatility contributed to some unwinding of carry trade outflows. The renminbi depreciated slightly in real effective terms despite a mild acceleration in its rate of appreciation against the dollar in recent months and a further rise in China's current account surplus to 9 percent of GDP (Figure 1.8). The real effective value of Middle Eastern oil exporters' currencies depreciated moderately, although strong growth in oil exports drove the current account surplus of these countries to 21 percent of GDP.

Outlook and Short-Term Risks

The world economy is expected to continue to grow robustly in 2007 and 2008—with a modest deceleration from the rapid pace of 2006 bringing growth more in line with potential and helping to contain inflationary pressures in the fifth and sixth years of the current expansion. Specifically, global growth would moderate to 4.9 percent in 2007, around ½ percentage point less than in 2006 and in line with the rate forecast at the time of the September 2006 *World Economic Outlook*, and maintain this pace in 2008 (Figure 1.9). As discussed in more detail in Chapter 2, among the major advanced economies, the slowdown in year-over-year growth in 2007 would be most pronounced in the United States, although the U.S. economy should gather momentum in the course of the year and into 2008 as the drag from the housing sector moderates. Growth is also projected to ease in the euro area, reflecting in part gradual withdrawal of monetary accommodation and further fiscal consolidation, as well as the unwinding of spe-

Figure 1.4. Developments in Mature Financial Markets

Expectations of continued solid economic growth and moderating price concerns since mid-2006 have encouraged buoyant equity markets and declining long-term interest rates. Credit growth has eased somewhat but remains high.

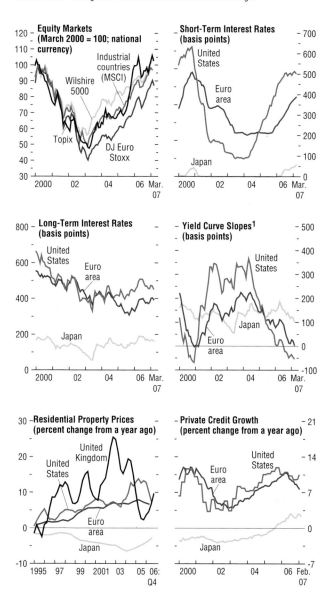

Sources: Bloomberg Financial Markets, LP; CEIC Data Company Limited; Haver Analytics; OECD; IMF, *International Financial Statistics;* national authorities; and IMF staff calculations.
[1]Ten-year government bond minus three-month treasury bill rate.

Figure 1.5. Mature Financial Market Indicators

Real interest rates are generally below long-term averages, as are price-earnings ratios in equity markets and corporate spreads. Volatility has generally remained low.

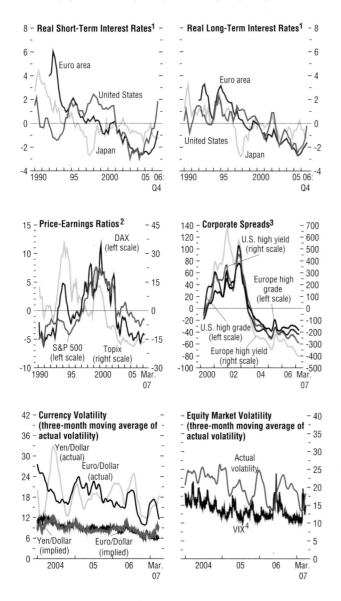

Sources: Bloomberg Financial Markets, LP; Merrill Lynch; Thomson Financial; and IMF staff calculations.

[1]Relative to headline inflation. Measured as deviations from 1990–2006 average.

[2]Twelve-month forward-looking price-earnings ratios measured as three-month moving average of deviations from 1990–2007 (January) average.

[3]Measured as three-month moving average of deviations from 2000–07 (January) average.

[4]VIX is the Chicago Board Options Exchange volatility index. This index is calculated by taking a weighted average of implied volatility for the eight S&P 500 calls and puts.

cial factors, while the expansion would continue at about the same pace in Japan.

Emerging market and developing countries would continue to grow strongly, albeit at a somewhat less torrid pace than in 2006, drawing continued support from benign global financial conditions and commodity prices that would remain high notwithstanding some recent declines. China's growth would moderate gradually in 2007 and 2008 from its very high rate in 2006, while the pace of expansion would also ease in India, reflecting in part policy tightening in response to overheating concerns. Commodity-rich countries in Africa, the Commonwealth of Independent States (CIS), the Middle East, and Latin America would continue to prosper, with growth in Africa accelerating in 2007 as new oil fields come on stream. Countries in emerging Europe and also Mexico would be somewhat more affected by spillovers from slower growth in Europe and the United States.

Risks around this "soft landing" scenario seem more evenly balanced than at the time of the September 2006 *World Economic Outlook*, but remain weighted on the downside. As shown in the fan chart (upper panel of Figure 1.10), the IMF staff see about a one in five chance of growth falling below 4 percent in 2008. The accompanying risk factor chart (lower panel of Figure 1.10) depicts the IMF staff's current assessment of the principal sources of risk to projected output growth over the next 12 months, relative to the assessment at the time of the September 2006 *World Economic Outlook*. Downside risks related to the U.S. housing sector, supply-side inflation pressures, the oil market, and from a possible disorderly adjustment of global imbalances are all seen to have receded somewhat in recent months, but they still raise concerns. Risks related to overextension of financial markets are viewed as moderately increased. There continues to be upside potential that domestic demand in emerging markets could be higher than projected, while domestic demand is also seen as a source of upside potential in western Europe.

U.S. housing market risk. The housing market downturn in the United States has, if anything, been deeper than projected at the time of the September 2006 *World Economic Outlook*, and residential investment was a substantial drag on U.S. GDP in the second half of 2006. Over the past few months, there have been some tentative signs of stabilization at least on the demand side, as sales of existing homes, mortgage applications, and potential homebuyer intentions have generally steadied or improved. However, the housing correction still has a way to run. Housing starts and permits are still heading downward, while inventories of unsold new homes are at their highest levels in 15 years. Moreover, there has been rising stress in the subprime sector of the market—which represents about 12 percent of the total mortgage market—in the form of sharp increases in delinquency and default rates. In this sector, there was clearly an excessive relaxation of lending and underwriting standards. There have also been some signs of deterioration in Alternative-A mortgages, although delinquencies in prime mortgages remain well contained. The intensifying problems in the subprime mortgage market could start having a broader impact on the housing market as rising foreclosures could add further to inventories of unsold homes, and tightening of lending standards could depress housing demand. A turnaround in residential construction is still several quarters away.

The key question is whether the continuing difficulties in the housing sector will begin to have a broader impact on the U.S. economy. House prices have continued to decelerate nationally, with outright price declines in many metropolitan areas. Nonetheless, household finances still look solid. Equity gains over the past year have brought household net worth back up to previous peaks. Moreover, household cash flows continue to be sustained by employment and income growth. With interest rates still low, debt-service obligations generally look reasonable. Overall, the baseline view remains that difficulties in the housing sector will not have major spillovers, provided that employment

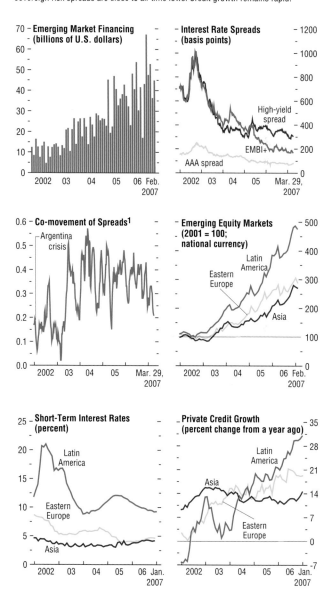

Figure 1.6. Emerging Market Financial Conditions

Emerging markets have generally remained buoyant, despite recurrent bouts of market volatility. Equity prices in many emerging markets have recorded new highs, while sovereign risk spreads are close to all-time lows. Credit growth remains rapid.

Sources: Bloomberg Financial Markets, LP; Capital Data; IMF, *International Financial Statistics;* and IMF staff calculations.
[1]Average of 30-day rolling cross-correlation of emerging market debt spreads.

Table 1.2. Emerging Market and Developing Countries: Net Capital Flows[1]
(Billions of U.S. dollars)

	1996–98	1999	2000	2001	2002	2003	2004	2005	2006	2007	2008
Total											
Private capital flows, net[2]	159.3	74.6	56.7	70.2	88.3	173.3	238.6	257.2	255.8	252.7	259.3
Private direct investment, net	142.3	177.4	168.6	182.8	152.2	165.3	190.0	266.3	266.9	283.7	288.9
Private portfolio flows, net	60.0	60.1	11.4	−80.5	−90.9	−12.1	25.0	29.4	−76.3	−62.0	−52.2
Other private capital flows, net	−43.0	−162.9	−123.4	−32.1	26.9	20.1	23.5	−38.5	65.2	30.9	22.6
Official flows, net[3]	20.2	22.4	−34.2	6.6	2.3	−44.5	−57.8	−122.6	−143.8	−96.4	−116.6
Change in reserves[4]	−72.6	−98.2	−131.2	−120.6	−198.9	−358.9	−508.2	−590.1	−738.4	−715.5	−716.4
Memorandum											
Current account[5]	−72.1	34.4	123.5	86.8	132.3	229.4	299.7	511.6	638.5	548.6	567.1
Africa											
Private capital flows, net[2]	6.5	9.0	−4.2	2.2	0.9	2.7	12.3	18.3	20.2	28.6	39.9
Private direct investment, net	5.8	8.6	7.6	23.1	13.5	15.4	16.8	27.0	19.1	21.9	29.4
Private portfolio flows, net	5.0	9.1	−1.8	−7.9	−1.6	−0.5	5.4	4.1	18.5	12.3	13.6
Other private capital flows, net	−4.3	−8.7	−10.0	−13.0	−11.0	−12.2	−9.8	−12.8	−17.4	−5.7	−3.1
Official flows, net[3]	5.0	4.1	7.7	6.5	8.6	6.4	4.3	−1.8	−3.8	10.1	10.8
Change in reserves[4]	−4.2	−0.4	−12.8	−9.7	−5.5	−11.4	−32.7	−42.3	−48.4	−44.9	−56.3
Central and eastern Europe											
Private capital flows, net[2]	27.4	36.3	38.7	10.9	54.0	52.5	74.7	117.5	121.1	109.0	117.7
Private direct investment, net	14.9	22.7	24.1	24.0	24.1	16.2	34.5	50.1	65.8	62.6	62.0
Private portfolio flows, net	1.7	5.3	3.1	0.4	1.7	6.5	26.9	20.9	8.1	12.1	14.4
Other private capital flows, net	10.8	8.3	11.6	−13.4	28.3	29.9	13.3	46.4	47.1	34.3	41.2
Official flows, net[3]	−0.5	−2.4	1.6	6.0	−7.5	−5.0	−6.6	−8.3	−4.9	−3.1	−3.3
Change in reserves[4]	−8.8	−12.1	−6.0	−3.0	−18.5	−11.5	−13.6	−48.2	−21.2	−14.9	−22.1
Commonwealth of Independent States[6]											
Private capital flows, net[2]	−5.3	−13.5	−27.6	7.2	15.8	17.9	7.7	37.6	65.7	38.0	28.6
Private direct investment, net	5.5	4.7	2.3	4.9	5.2	5.4	12.9	14.4	33.1	22.2	26.1
Private portfolio flows, net	2.2	−0.9	−10.0	−1.2	0.4	−0.5	8.1	−3.1	13.9	0.4	0.3
Other private capital flows, net	−13.0	−17.3	−19.9	3.5	10.2	13.0	−13.4	26.3	18.8	15.4	2.1
Official flows, net[3]	−1.0	−1.8	−5.8	−4.9	−10.4	−8.9	−7.3	−22.1	−32.6	−3.6	−4.3
Change in reserves[4]	5.1	−6.4	−20.3	−14.5	−15.1	−31.8	−53.8	−75.6	−126.9	−108.4	−98.7
Emerging Asia[7]											
Private capital flows, net[2]	36.9	−1.9	4.5	23.5	25.4	69.2	142.5	69.7	53.9	30.7	−5.8
Private direct investment, net	56.0	70.9	59.8	52.0	52.6	73.1	68.0	105.8	102.4	96.1	94.1
Private portfolio flows, net	16.0	54.1	19.6	−50.2	−60.1	7.8	11.2	−8.1	−99.4	−78.9	−88.8
Other private capital flows, net	−35.1	−127.0	−74.8	21.6	32.8	−11.6	63.4	−27.9	50.9	13.5	−11.1
Official flows, net[3]	5.9	8.5	−10.9	−12.0	4.1	−16.6	−7.0	−2.8	−9.8	−5.4	−7.5
Change in reserves[4]	−45.1	−84.8	−59.1	−85.4	−154.3	−234.3	−339.0	−284.1	−365.6	−410.6	−424.0

and income growth remain resilient. But there remain risks that the fallout from the housing correction could be amplified, particularly if tightening lending standards in the subprime sector were to lead to a broader reappraisal of credit availability across the economy or if household cash flows were to weaken. Such a development could imply a deeper and more prolonged slowdown or even a recession in the United States, with potential spillovers to other countries.

Domestic demand in western Europe. Western European economies ended 2006 with a robust fourth quarter, showing potential for stronger growth than projected in the *World Economic Outlook* baseline projection. The upside potential seems particularly relevant in Germany, where consumption could gather strength more commensurate with improved fundamentals and the stronger growth of employment, especially if wages pick up and the negative impact of the VAT increase on demand in early 2007 turns out to be milder than anticipated. In the United Kingdom too, domestic demand may turn out stronger than forecast despite recent monetary tightening, given the acceleration in house prices over the past year.

Table 1.2 *(concluded)*

	1996–98	1999	2000	2001	2002	2003	2004	2005	2006	2007	2008
Middle East[8]											
Private capital flows, net[2]	11.8	−3.8	−10.0	−5.5	−19.4	4.7	−12.0	−19.9	−15.5	14.4	34.8
Private direct investment, net	7.0	4.4	4.9	12.3	9.7	17.8	8.8	17.6	12.0	19.6	18.2
Private portfolio flows, net	0.5	−8.6	−1.2	−13.5	−17.4	−14.9	−14.0	−14.9	−5.0	−3.3	4.4
Other private capital flows, net	4.3	0.4	−13.7	−4.3	−11.6	1.8	−6.8	−22.5	−22.5	−1.9	12.2
Official flows, net[3]	5.2	8.0	−20.5	−14.2	−9.8	−24.6	−32.5	−57.1	−75.0	−93.2	−112.0
Change in reserves[4]	−8.1	−2.0	−31.2	−11.6	−3.1	−33.7	−45.7	−106.6	−129.7	−79.4	−75.9
Western Hemisphere											
Private capital flows, net[2]	82.0	48.5	55.2	31.9	11.5	26.2	13.3	33.9	10.4	32.0	44.2
Private direct investment, net	53.1	66.1	70.0	66.5	47.2	37.5	49.1	51.4	34.5	61.3	59.1
Private portfolio flows, net	34.6	1.0	1.7	−8.1	−13.9	−10.5	−12.5	30.5	−12.4	−4.6	3.9
Other private capital flows, net	−5.7	−18.6	−16.5	−26.5	−21.8	−0.9	−23.3	−48.0	−11.6	−24.7	−18.8
Official flows, net[3]	5.6	6.2	−6.4	25.2	17.4	4.3	−8.7	−30.4	−17.7	−1.2	−0.4
Change in reserves[4]	−11.4	7.4	−1.8	3.5	−2.4	−36.2	−23.4	−33.4	−46.5	−57.4	−39.3
Memorandum											
Fuel-exporting countries											
Private capital flows, net[2]	−5.4	−27.2	−57.0	−12.7	−11.2	12.7	−14.9	−6.8	−2.6	11.1	36.4
Other countries											
Private capital flows, net[2]	164.8	101.8	113.6	82.9	99.5	160.6	253.4	264.0	258.4	241.6	223.0

[1]Net capital flows comprise net direct investment, net portfolio investment, and other long- and short-term net investment flows, including official and private borrowing. In this table, Hong Kong SAR, Israel, Korea, Singapore, and Taiwan Province of China are included.

[2]Because of data limitations, flows listed under "private capital flows, net" may include some official flows.

[3]Excludes grants and includes overseas investments of official investment agencies.

[4]A minus sign indicates an increase.

[5]The sum of the current account balance, net private capital flows, net official flows, and the change in reserves equals, with the opposite sign, the sum of the capital account and errors and omissions. For regional current account balances, see Table 25 of the Statistical Appendix.

[6]Historical data have been revised, reflecting cumulative data revisions for Russia and the resolution of a number of data interpretation issues.

[7]Consists of developing Asia and the newly industrialized Asian economies.

[8]Includes Israel.

Domestic demand in emerging markets. IMF staff projections have consistently underpredicted emerging market growth in recent years, as China and India have continued to outperform expectations. A similar pattern could recur in 2007. It is not clear that the Chinese economy will slow consistently as a result of limited tightening measures introduced in 2006, while in India the strong momentum could be sustained despite recent interest rate increases. Both economies, as well as other emerging market oil importers more generally, will benefit significantly from recent oil price reductions. Among commodity exporters, there would seem to be some downside risk to projections in light of recent softening of their export prices. This risk however, seems contained as prices of oil and metals are still high by historical standards and recent price declines still leave significant fiscal revenue cushions. Therefore, sharp cutbacks in government spending plans seem unlikely at this point.

Inflation risk in advanced economies. Inflation pressures in the advanced economies have generally eased, and the probability that central banks may need to raise interest rates by more than now anticipated by markets seems less than last summer. That said, concerns do remain. In the United States, 12-month core inflation is still somewhat above the Federal Reserve's implicit comfort zone and some measures of wages have risen over the past year. Moreover, a gradual slowing of productivity growth is adding to cost pressures, and there is considerable uncertainty about the extent to which this is a cyclical phenomenon or reflects a moderation of potential growth (Figure 1.11). In the United Kingdom, inflation is now well above the Bank of England's target, despite policy tightening. In the euro area, price and wage increases remain subdued, but unemployment rates have fallen to cyclical lows, capacity utilization rates are high, and inflation pres-

Figure 1.7. External Developments in Major Advanced Economies

The U.S. dollar has depreciated modestly in real effective terms since late 2005, but the U.S. current account deficit has remained wide. The euro area's current account is close to balance, while the euro has appreciated. Japan retains a sizable current account surplus, while the real effective value of the yen has depreciated significantly below its long-term average.

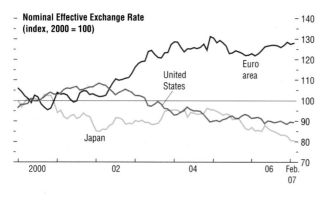

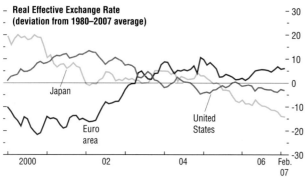

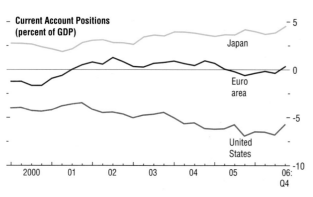

Sources: Haver Analytics; and IMF staff calculations.

sures could emerge in the year ahead if labor markets continue to tighten (Figure 1.12). More generally, after four years of strong global growth and output gaps closing in emerging markets too, there is at least a possibility that the dampening impact of global competition on price- and wage-setting behavior in the advanced economies may start to moderate, while risks remain of commodity price spikes (see discussion in Chapter 3 of the April 2006 *World Economic Outlook*).

Supply-side risk from oil markets. The overall decline in oil prices since August 2006 has provided welcome relief to the global economy, particularly by supporting household spending power and alleviating inflation concerns. However, a rebound in prices since early 2007, as geopolitical tensions have risen, has provided a reminder that the oil market remains an important source of potential volatility. Prospects for substantial price declines from recent levels should be contained as long as the present global expansion is sustained, given the commitment by the Organization of the Petroleum Exporting Countries (OPEC) to implement production cuts in response to price weakness. At the same time, spare capacity remains quite tight (notwithstanding a modest increase in recent months), and a deterioration in security in the Middle East or supply-side disruptions could still lead to another oil price spike. This concern is reflected in oil options pricing, which suggests that markets see price risk as clearly skewed upward. On April 2, options markets indicated a 1 in 6 chance that oil prices could rise above $88 a barrel by the end of 2007. Box 1.1 looks in more detail at the consequences of such a spike for the global economy, underlining that the negative economic impact from an adverse supply-side event would be significantly larger than from a demand-led surge in oil prices.

Financial stability risk. Although the recent episode of financial market turbulence in February–March 2007 appears to be contained in magnitude, it does serve as a healthy reminder of underlying financial risks. Recent years have been an unusual period for markets, with relatively low real interest rates and very low volatility, despite monetary tightening by major central banks. The concern is that, as discussed in the April 2007 *Global Financial Stability Report*, the drive for yield has led to greater risk taking in less-well-understood markets and instruments. While this strategy has been successful when markets remain buoyant, price setbacks, rising volatility, and emerging loan losses could lead to a reappraisal of investment strategies and a pull-back from positions that have become overextended. Such an unwinding could have serious macroeconomic repercussions.

The recent difficulties in the U.S. subprime mortgage market illustrate this concern. While the direct impact appears contained (in part reflecting this segment's limited size in the overall market), the indirect effect could be larger. For example, financial institutions with exposure to the U.S. subprime mortgage markets, notably as arrangers of structured credit instruments backed by subprime lending, are experiencing adverse effects. There is also concern that the emergence of loose lending practices and rising delinquencies in subprime loans foreshadow similar trends in other market segments—including prime mortgages, consumer credit, high-yield corporate paper, and other new collateralized products. A general tightening of lending standards and credit conditions in the United States would have more pervasive effects. So far, at least, there has been little contagion to either the prime mortgage market or high-yield corporate paper, but this is an area that bears close watching.

Another area of concern discussed in the April 2007 *Global Financial Stability Report* relates to the recent surge in leveraged buyouts and share buybacks, often led by private equity firms. While overall corporate leverage remains very low, leverage is rising in certain sectors, and there are concerns that a failure of one of these operations could raise doubts about these deals more generally. Also, there are concerns about the increasing role of hedge funds, whose activities are little regulated and not transpar-

Figure 1.8. External Developments in Emerging Market Countries

Movements in nominal exchange rates over the past year have generally moved real effective exchange rates in emerging market countries closer to historical averages. Current account surpluses in China and the Middle East have continued to rise.

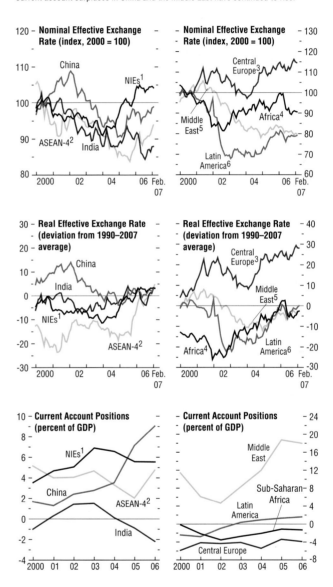

Source: IMF staff calculations.
[1]Newly industrialized economies (NIEs) include Hong Kong SAR, Korea, Singapore, and Taiwan Province of China.
[2]Indonesia, Malaysia, the Philippines, and Thailand.
[3]Czech Republic, Hungary, and Poland.
[4]Botswana, Burkina Faso, Cameroon, Chad, Republic of Congo, Côte d'Ivoire, Djibouti, Equatorial Guinea, Ethiopia, Gabon, Ghana, Guinea, Kenya, Madagascar, Mali, Mauritius, Mozambique, Namibia, Niger, Nigeria, Rwanda, Senegal, South Africa, Sudan, Tanzania, Uganda, and Zambia.
[5]Bahrain, Egypt, I.R. of Iran, Jordan, Kuwait, Lebanon, Libya, Oman, Qatar, Saudi Arabia, Syrian Arab Republic, United Arab Emirates, and Republic of Yemen.
[6]Argentina, Brazil, Chile, Colombia, Mexico, Peru, and Venezuela.

Figure 1.9. Global Outlook
(Real GDP; percent change from four quarters earlier)

Following a banner year in 2006, world growth is expected to ease in 2007 and 2008, but remain at high levels.

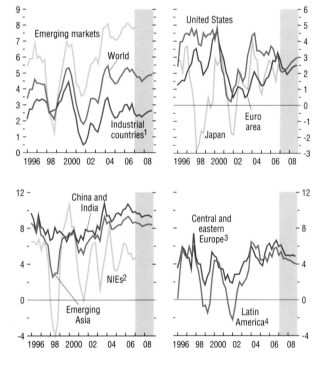

Sources: Haver Analytics; and IMF staff estimates.
[1]Australia, Canada, Denmark, euro area, Japan, New Zealand, Norway, Sweden, Switzerland, the United Kingdom, and the United States.
[2]Newly industrialized economies (NIEs) include Hong Kong SAR, Korea, Singapore, and Taiwan Province of China.
[3]Czech Republic, Estonia, Hungary, Latvia, Lithuania, and Poland.
[4]Argentina, Brazil, Chile, Colombia, Mexico, Peru, and Venezuela.

ent. To some degree, risks may be contained by structural improvements in markets, including the improved risk management made possible by the increasingly sophisticated and liquid derivatives markets, but new structures have not been fully tested under stressful financial conditions. Thus, vigilance is required to ensure that rising leverage and risk taking do not lead to the buildup of serious vulnerabilities.

Emerging market risks deserve particular attention since history offers numerous examples of boom conditions followed by devastating busts. The good news is that emerging market countries have generally continued to take advantage of the benign global environment. They strengthened public balance sheets, including further reductions in ratios of public debt to GDP; improved currency and maturity composition of debt stocks; and increased levels of international reserves. Credibility of policy management has also been enhanced through timely actions to address emerging concerns—such as steps in China to cool the rapid growth of investment, a fiscal package to lower Hungary's large fiscal deficit, and monetary tightening in Turkey in the face of rising inflationary pressures. Responsible policy management has been reflected in continued improvement of credit ratings and the decline of sovereign spreads to near all-time lows.

Nevertheless, the recent increases in asset prices and compression in risk spreads in emerging markets may not be fully justified by improving fundamentals. Potential vulnerabilities include still-high public debt ratios in some countries, especially in Latin America, and the rapid buildup of bank lending and private debt, particularly in emerging Europe and the CIS countries. Events in May–June 2006, when rising interest rates and increased volatility in the advanced economies sparked a period of turbulence in emerging markets, provided a healthy reminder of the pressures that can occur. Moreover, the possibility of a disorderly reversal of carry trade capital outflows from Japan has raised concern, although any reversal would be unlikely to be as abrupt as what occurred in

1998, given the greater currency diversification and the broadening of the investor base since that time. Countries that could come under particular pressure in a more testing external financial environment include those that remain heavily dependent on capital inflows, those where balance sheet vulnerabilities may have been allowed to build, or those where macroeconomic management may not yet have full credibility.

Risks from global imbalances. Over the past six months, there has been some welcome movement toward containing large global imbalances and the associated risk that a disorderly unwinding would have a highly disruptive impact on the world economy. Relevant developments include a further reduction in the real effective value of the U.S. dollar, some increase in flexibility in the currencies of surplus countries in Asia, lower international oil prices, and a somewhat more balanced pattern of domestic demand growth in the global economy. The U.S. non-oil trade deficit was reduced as a percent of GDP in 2006 as exports accelerated, while the U.S. net external liabilities are estimated to have again declined modestly, reflecting the depreciation of the U.S. dollar and substantial capital gains on foreign equity holdings (see discussion in Chapter 3). Against this, as mentioned earlier, the downward movement of the dollar has been largely focused against the euro and pound sterling, while currencies of the main surplus countries—China, Japan, and the Middle Eastern oil exporters—have tended to depreciate in real effective terms.

Nevertheless, the sum of these developments has not substantially changed the outlook. Projections based on the current constellation of real exchange rates and policies suggest that global imbalances would still remain large over the foreseeable future (Figure 1.13). The U.S. current account deficit is projected to be about 1 percentage point of GDP lower than at the time of the September 2006 *World Economic Outlook*, but would still remain around 6 percent of GDP in 2012, as a deteriorating net income balance offsets continued improvement on the

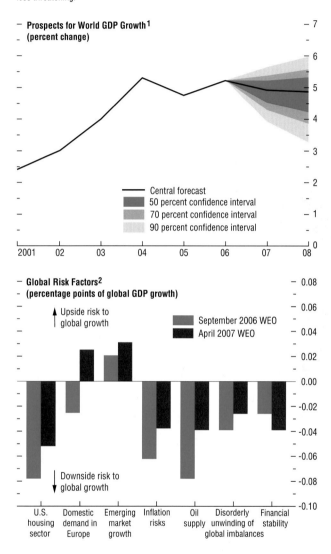

Figure 1.10. Risks to the Global Outlook

Risks to global growth now seem more balanced than six months ago, as downside risks related to the U.S. housing sector, inflationary pressures, and oil supply seem less threatening.

Prospects for World GDP Growth[1]
(percent change)

— Central forecast
■ 50 percent confidence interval
■ 70 percent confidence interval
■ 90 percent confidence interval

Global Risk Factors[2]
(percentage points of global GDP growth)

Upside risk to global growth

■ September 2006 WEO
■ April 2007 WEO

Downside risk to global growth

U.S. housing sector · Domestic demand in Europe · Emerging market growth · Inflation risks · Oil supply · Disorderly unwinding of global imbalances · Financial stability

Source: IMF staff estimates.
[1]The fan chart shows the uncertainty around the *World Economic Outlook* (WEO) central forecast with 50, 70, and 90 percent probability intervals. As shown, the 70 percent confidence interval includes the 50 percent interval, and the 90 percent confidence interval includes the 50 and 70 percent intervals. See Box 1.3 in the April 2006 *World Economic Outlook* for details.
[2]The chart shows the contributions of each risk factor to the overall balance of risks to global growth, as reflected by the extent of asymmetry in the probability density for global GDP growth shown in the fan chart. The balance of risks is tilted to the downside if the expected probability of outcomes below the central or modal forecast (the total "downside probability") exceeds 50 percent (Box 1.3 in the April 2006 *World Economic Outlook*). The bars for each forecast vintage sum up to the difference between the expected value of world growth implied by the distribution of outcomes (the probability density) shown in the fan chart and the central forecast for global GDP growth. This difference and the extent of asymmetry in the probability density in the fan chart also depend on the standard deviation of past forecast errors—which, among other factors, varies with the length of the forecasting horizon. To make the risk factors comparable across forecast vintages, their contributions are rescaled to correct for differences in the standard deviations.

Figure 1.11. Productivity and Labor Cost Developments in Selected Advanced Economies[1]
(Percent change from four quarters earlier)

Slowing productivity and rising compensation have put upward pressure on unit labor costs in the United States. However, unit labor cost increases have moderated in Europe—as productivity performance has strengthened—and continue to fall in Japan.

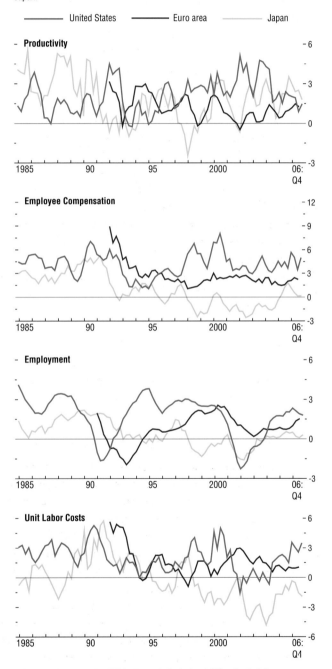

Sources: Haver Analytics; OECD, *Economic Outlook;* and IMF staff calculations.
[1]Estimates are for the nonfarm business sector for the United States, and the whole economy for the euro area and Japan.

trade balance. As a result, the U.S. net external liability position would deteriorate substantially in the absence of further valuation gains. Rapidly increasing domestic absorption and a lower oil price trajectory have lowered the path of projected surpluses in the oil-exporting countries, but China's projected surplus has risen to around 10 percent of GDP in 2012, reflecting recent rapid export growth that has continued to outpace rising imports.

Thus far, the capital inflows needed to finance the large U.S. current account deficit have been forthcoming, but over time the composition of the flows has shifted from equity to debt, and within debt away from treasuries to riskier forms. These shifts suggest an increasing vulnerability to changes in market sentiment, particularly if returns on U.S. assets continue to underperform returns elsewhere. Hence, the concern remains that at some point more substantial adjustments will be needed to ensure that the global pattern of current account positions remains consistent with the willingness of international wealth-holders to build up net claims on the United States. The challenge is to ensure that this process occurs relatively smoothly, rather than through a much more disruptive disorderly adjustment (see Box 1.3 of the September 2006 *World Economic Outlook*).

Shifting patterns of saving and investment would play an important part in an orderly adjustment process. Over time, U.S. consumption growth can be expected to moderate to allow savings out of current income to return to more normal levels after a period in which capital gains on housing and equity substituted for such saving. Elsewhere, consumption in China should rise from its present low share of GDP as consumer finance becomes more easily available and precautionary savings motives are reduced by stronger social safety nets and increasing prosperity, while absorption by oil exporters should continue to rise as investment plans are advanced.

Changes in real effective exchange rates potentially could play a substantial supportive role to facilitate a smooth unwinding in global imbalances without large cyclical swings or overshooting of aggregate output. Supporting this point, Chapter 3 presents evidence showing that exchange rate movements have been important contributors to past episodes of external adjustment, by facilitating a shift in resources across sectors. It also finds that concern about "elasticity pessimism" in the United States—that is, that trade flows are unresponsive to exchange rate changes—is exaggerated. While short-term exchange rate movements respond to conjunctural factors and are hard to predict, over a medium-term horizon market-led exchange rate movements that could support a smooth reduction of imbalances in combination with rebalancing of demand across countries would include a significant further real effective depreciation of the U.S. dollar, and real effective appreciations of the renminbi, yen, and currencies of Middle Eastern oil exporters.

Cross-Country Spillovers: Can the Global Economy Decouple from a U.S. Slowdown?

While analyzing individual sources of downside risk, it must be borne in mind that shocks can be quickly transmitted across countries through trade and financial channels, leading to a complex pattern of interactions and spillovers. The increasing integration of the global economy over the past 20 years would seem likely to increase the scope for such spillovers. Moreover, there is always particular concern about the potential for spillovers from the United States, still the dominant global economy, accounting for 20 percent of global imports and having the world's deepest, most sophisticated financial markets. The potential for such spillovers was underlined by the experience in 2000–01 when the collapse of the "hi-tech" stock market bubble in the United States quickly spread across the globe as stock market valuations and business investment dropped sharply in the context of a broader reappraisal of prospects. Thus, a key question for the present conjuncture has been whether the global economy would be able to

Figure 1.12. Measures of the Output Gap and Capacity Pressures[1]

Sustained growth has reduced output gaps and lowered unemployment rates. Tighter capacity constraints in commodities sectors have contributed to sharp increases in oil and metals prices.

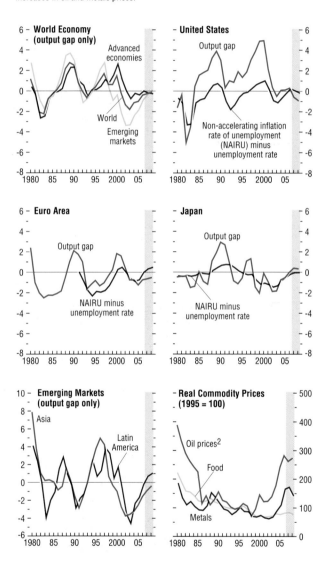

Sources: OECD, *Economic Outlook;* and IMF staff estimates.
[1]Estimates of the non-accelerating inflation rate of unemployment (NAIRU) come from the OECD. Estimates of the output gap, expressed as a percent of potential GDP, are based on IMF staff calculations.
[2]Simple average of spot prices of U.K. Brent, Dubai Fateh, and West Texas Intermediate crude oil.

Figure 1.13. Current Account Balances and Net Foreign Assets
(Percent of world GDP)

Under the baseline forecast, which assumes unchanged real effective exchange rates, global current account imbalances remain sizable through the projection period, with the U.S. current account deficit staying above 1.5 percent of world GDP. As a result, the U.S. net foreign liability position would deteriorate further in the absence of the valuation gains that have reduced U.S. net foreign liabilities in recent years.

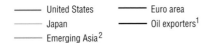

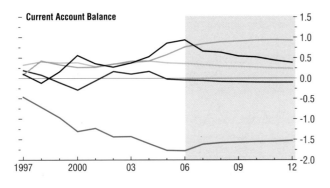

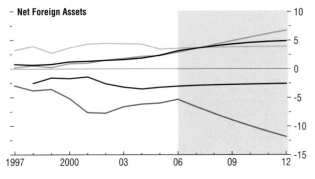

Sources: Lane and Milesi-Ferretti (2006); and IMF staff estimates.
[1]Algeria, Angola, Azerbaijan, Bahrain, Republic of Congo, Ecuador, Equatorial Guinea, Gabon, I.R. of Iran, Kuwait, Libya, Nigeria, Norway, Oman, Qatar, Russia, Saudi Arabia, Syrian Arab Republic, Turkmenistan, United Arab Emirates, Venezuela, and the Republic of Yemen.
[2]China, Hong Kong SAR, Indonesia, Korea, Malaysia, the Philippines, Singapore, Taiwan Province of China, and Thailand.

decouple from a sharper-than-projected slowdown in the United States.

So far the cooling of U.S. activity seems to have had a limited impact beyond its immediate neighbors, Canada and Mexico. As discussed in Chapter 4 of this report, which takes up the issue of cross-country spillovers in detail, the recent experience may reflect a variety of ingredients. First, the U.S. slowdown has been focused on the residential sector, which has a relatively low imported-goods content. Second, spillovers have typically been muted in the context of a midcycle slowdown, compared with the impact of a full-blown recession. Third, to date at least, the housing downturn has been a U.S.-specific event as housing markets elsewhere have remained buoyant, unlike the common disturbances across many countries (such as an oil price shock or the bursting of the IT bubble in 2000–01) that have typically been the source of previous synchronized global downturns. Fourth, the increasing strength of corporate balance sheets and improved labor market conditions in Europe have boosted domestic demand and reduced reliance on growth of net exports.

However, a further cooling of the U.S. economy that increasingly spreads to weakness in consumption and business investment in 2007 would be challenging, particularly since the euro area economy is likely to be slowing. There would also be important risks of spillovers in emerging Asia and elsewhere, particularly if growth in China were to slow more abruptly. A key message from the analysis in Chapter 4 is that in the face of such spillovers, it would be important that policymakers respond in a flexible, forward-looking, and timely fashion to help cushion the impact of weaker external demand.

A particular concern relates to possible interactions between slowing economies, exchange rate swings, and protectionist pressures. A further sharp decline in the value of the U.S. dollar in the face of weak economic data could be problematic, particularly if upward pressures were concentrated in a few currencies—as happened in late 2006. The situation would be

Box 1.1. Understanding the Link Between Oil Prices and the World Economy

While oil prices are below their August 2006 peaks, there are still concerns that unless measures are taken to curtail demand for oil and create additional capacity, oil price variability may continue to pose significant risks for the global economy. A common notion based on the experience of the 1970s is that oil price shocks trigger recessions. However, the recent past does not fit this view—oil prices are about 2½ times their 2002 levels—but this increase has apparently not had much impact on the global economy. This seeming paradox has brought attention to the need to identify the sources of the oil price increase, in particular, to distinguish the role of supply and demand factors.

This box investigates these issues using an extended version of the Global Economy Model (GEM) to analyze the causes and consequences of changes in oil prices.[1] It also looks at the global macroeconomic impact of higher taxes on petroleum products. It should be said at the outset that the analysis does not attempt to assess the relative importance of demand and supply factors in the recent run-up in oil prices. Rather, it focuses on modeling the channels through which oil prices and growth interact.[2]

Global Macroeconomic Implications of a Supply-Induced Oil Price Hike

First, consider the case where oil-exporting economies restrict the supply of oil (as in the 1970s). Oil prices rise sharply (100 percent at the peak of the simulation) and this results in a global slowdown as income is redistributed to the oil-exporting economies, which have a lower propensity to spend than the oil-importing economies. In addition, higher oil prices raise the cost

Note: The authors of this box are Selim Elekdag and Douglas Laxton, with support from Susanna Mursula. This work builds on some previous joint work with Dirk Muir, Rene Lalonde, and Paolo Pesenti.
[1]For a description of the model, see Elekdag and others (2006). The regions in the model are oil exporters, United States, emerging Asia, and a residual block of oil-importing countries.
[2]For a discussion of the role of supply and demand factors during the recent increase in oil prices, see Chapter 4 of the April 2005 *World Economic Outlook*.

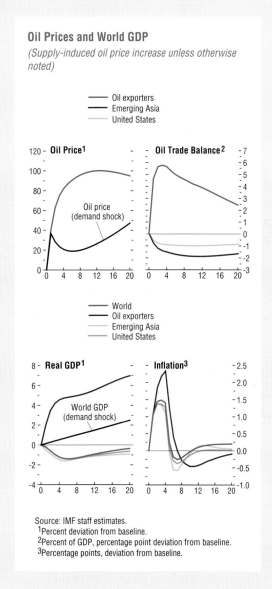

Oil Prices and World GDP
(Supply-induced oil price increase unless otherwise noted)

Source: IMF staff estimates.
[1]Percent deviation from baseline.
[2]Percent of GDP, percentage point deviation from baseline.
[3]Percentage points, deviation from baseline.

of production and put upward pressure on the aggregate price level. This would cause central banks to increase interest rates, which—together with the direct impact on production costs—would further decrease activity in the short run. As a result, world GDP falls 1.4 percent below the baseline at the trough and global inflation rises by about 1.5 percentage points (first figure).

The regional macroeconomic consequences of higher oil prices depend on whether a coun-

Box 1.1 *(concluded)*

try is a net oil exporter or importer, and on its oil intensity. Oil exporters run a large trade surplus, peaking at around 6 percent of GDP above the baseline, and also enjoy a vigorous expansion. In contrast, the oil-importing economies suffer a deterioration in their external balances and a slowdown in activity. The impact is more significant in emerging Asian economies primarily because of their higher oil intensities relative to advanced economies.

On balance, the effects on inflation and GDP in this scenario are significantly smaller than observed in many industrial countries in the 1970s. First, this partly reflects the lower oil intensities of consumption and production, which reduce both the direct effects on inflation and the medium- and long-term effects on GDP. Second, these simulations assume that forward-looking inflation targeting central banks raise interest rates promptly to prevent a ratcheting up of inflation expectations and a spillover into wages and other prices, unlike what happened in the 1970s. Third, many countries have implemented reforms that have increased flexibility in both labor and product markets, facilitating more rapid adjustment in relative prices in response to oil price shocks. Combined with credible monetary policies that have anchored longer-term inflation expectations, these structural improvements have allowed the containment of inflationary pressures caused by the higher oil prices without overly dampening output. However, the simulations do not account for possible business and consumer confidence effects or capital market disruptions, including difficulties in financing individual countries' current account deficits.[3]

Persistent Productivity Shocks with Low Oil Capacity

Macroeconomic responses are very different in a situation in which oil prices are being boosted by a demand shock. Consider

---

[3]Also, these projections do not take into full account the potential impact of higher oil prices on other energy substitutes, or the role of speculative factors that may exacerbate the associated risk premium.

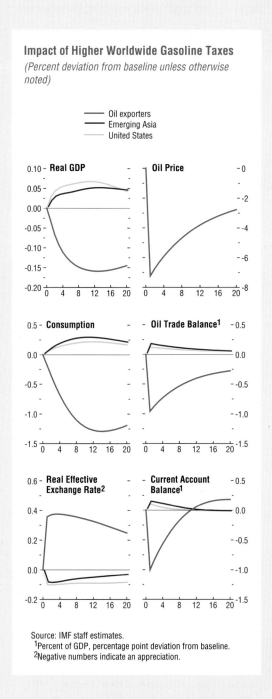

Impact of Higher Worldwide Gasoline Taxes
(Percent deviation from baseline unless otherwise noted)

Source: IMF staff estimates.
[1]Percent of GDP, percentage point deviation from baseline.
[2]Negative numbers indicate an appreciation.

a situation of low spare oil production capacity in which the responsiveness of supply to oil price changes is very limited over the short to medium term. In this case, a significant increase in productivity growth in oil-importing countries that permanently raises global growth by ½ of a percentage point generates a significant short-run surge in oil prices that is sustained over the medium term (see first figure). This response of oil prices reflects the low short-term elasticity of supply as new capacity has to be brought on stream to satisfy higher levels of current and future demand. However, the short-run path for world GDP is opposite to that resulting from a supply-induced increase in the price of oil because higher prices are being caused by stronger growth.[4]

What Difference Would Higher Gasoline Taxes Make?

Low spare capacity and higher oil prices have heightened the awareness of the consequences of growing oil usage both now and in the future. Moreover, the consumption of hydrocarbons, particularly petroleum products, is a key source of climate-changing carbon emissions—a cost that is not internalized by the market. Given these concerns, a number of observers have suggested raising taxes on oil consumption, and it is useful to look at the macroeconomic consequences of such a policy shift.

Consider the implications of a worldwide increase of gasoline taxes by 10 percentage points accompanied by a corresponding reduc-

tion in labor taxes that keeps the fiscal stance unchanged (second figure).[5] The gasoline tax encourages a gradual substitution away from energy consumption that builds steadily over time owing to the low short-run oil demand elasticities. In contrast, oil prices decline by about 7 percent on impact, creating a wealth transfer away from oil-exporting countries. The macroeconomic implications are the mirror image of the supply-induced rise in oil prices, now benefiting the oil-importing economies instead of the oil-exporting economies. The United States and emerging Asia experience improvements in growth, external positions, and consumption, which are further enhanced by an appreciation in their real exchange rates and a reduction in distortionary labor taxes made possible by higher fuel taxes.[6] In contrast, oil-exporting countries experience a deterioration in their external balances and slower growth. On balance, however, world GDP is modestly higher—as taxation has shifted from a factor of production (labor) to a less price-elastic good (gasoline)—suggesting that it may be possible to design a framework that could share the income gains from such a policy in an equitable way across regions.

[4]If the same increase in productivity is considered in a version of the model that does not include oil, world GDP expands by slightly more in the short and medium term than in the model with oil. This suggests that while high oil prices have resulted in a drag on world growth, these effects are relatively minor.

[5]The structure of GEM explicitly differentiates energy inputs (crude oil) and refined petroleum products (gasoline) directly consumed by households, allowing a thorough investigation of the impact of higher gasoline taxes.

[6]Similar medium-term effects on world GDP would be obtained if the additional tax revenue was used to finance productive government investment.

further complicated if abrupt exchange rate movements occurring in an environment of slowing activity and rising unemployment triggered a resurgence of protectionist sentiment. Such a risk is more salient given rising popular concerns about the impact of increasingly global markets on those less well-placed to take advantage of new opportunities. This issue is returned to below.

Medium-Term Challenges: Can the Productivity Boom Be Sustained?

Recent years have been a remarkable period for the world economy, as global output growth has reached its highest sustained rate since the early 1970s, with strong increases in virtually all regions. Inflation has generally been contained at the low levels achieved by the end of the 1990s, while a series of shocks

Figure 1.14. Global Productivity Performance[1]

(Annual percent increase; three-year moving average)

Global productivity has accelerated in recent years, led by emerging market and developing countries. While China's sustained performance since the early 1990s is particularly impressive, productivity growth has also been strong in emerging Asia and emerging Europe for a number of years.

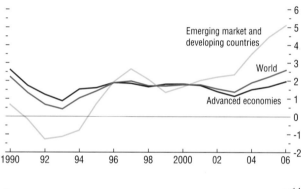

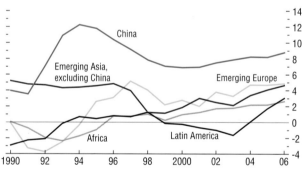

Sources: World Bank, *World Development Indicators* (2006); and IMF staff calculations.
[1]Measured as real GDP divided by working-age population.

and periods of turbulence—including sharp increases in oil and other commodity prices, and corrections in some richly valued equity and housing markets—have been largely weathered without major spillovers across sectors or regions.

What have been the sources of this global prosperity, and can the momentum be sustained? Rajan (2006) argues that a central arch of support for recent exceptional performance has been strong productivity growth. Buoyant productivity has made possible healthy growth in profits in combination with rising real wages, has allowed sharp increases in commodity prices to be absorbed without derailing inflation performance, and has contributed to rising asset values that have supported consumption and investment.

It is well known that productivity growth accelerated in the United States in the mid-1990s, in substantial part in response to increasing use of new information and communications technology (ICT), but productivity growth has also been strong and increasing in emerging market and developing countries over the same period. Figure 1.14 illustrates this point on the basis of a crude but readily available broad measure of productivity—output relative to working-age population. Detailed studies with more precise measures of total factor productivity confirm this trend, particularly for countries and regions that have undergone major structural transformations—notably China, India, and emerging Europe, which have made dramatic progress in opening their economies and advancing market reform.[1]

In turn, strong productivity growth has been supported by a combination of technological developments, an increasingly open global trading system, rising cross-country capital flows, and more resilient macroeconomic policy frameworks and financial systems. Chapter 5 of this report discusses how the rapid growth

[1]See, for example, Schadler and others (2007); the September 2006 *World Economic Outlook*; and Conference Board (2006).

of international trade and the introduction of new technologies have allowed the production process to be unbundled, with both manufacturing and services activities being offshored to lower-cost locations in an increasingly global market, thus providing productivity gains both in source and in host countries. This process has been supported by important trade liberalization initiatives, including the entry of former Eastern bloc countries in Europe into a free trade zone with the European Union in 1994, Mexico's participation in the North American Free Trade Agreement from 1994, China's entry into the World Trade Organization (WTO) in 2001, and India's progressive unilateral reduction in trade barriers since the early 1990s. The shifting production structure has also been supported by the increasing international mobility of capital, especially rising rates of foreign direct investment into emerging market countries, that has not only provided a conduit for financing but also embodied diffusion of new technologies and management skills.

Another central feature of the recent past has been that strong productivity growth has been achieved even while investment has remained relatively subdued around the world. Chapter 2 of the September 2005 *World Economic Outlook* looked at global investment and saving patterns in more detail. Since that report, there has been a modest rise in global investment relative to GDP, but this ratio remains low by historical standards (Figure 1.15). It is interesting to note that the recent increase in investment is focused almost entirely in China, where economic transformation has created such large opportunities (Figure 1.16). Meanwhile, saving outside the advanced economies has continued to rise, mainly attributable to increasing savings (public and private) in China and higher public savings in oil-producing countries, although plans to boost government spending are now well under way.

These investment and saving trends have contributed to the generally supportive global financial environment, with low long-term real interest rates and low volatilities, even as

Figure 1.15. Global Saving, Investment, and Current Accounts
(Percent of world GDP)

Global investment has risen during the present economic cycle but remains low by historical standards, particularly in the industrial countries. The corresponding rise in saving has been exclusively in emerging market and oil-producing countries, which are building up high current account surpluses.

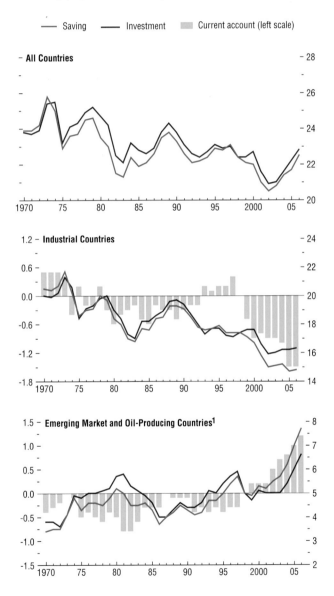

Sources: OECD Analytical Database; World Bank, *World Development Indicators* (2006); and IMF staff calculations.
[1]Includes Norway.

monetary conditions have been tightened. Thus, the U.S. expansion has continued to benefit from robust consumption growth despite the housing downturn, with the resultant widening current account deficit financed without upward pressure on long-term interest rates. Developments in the global financial system have played an important role, including the ability of the United States to generate assets with attractive liquidity and risk management features, as well as the continuing role of the U.S. dollar as an international reserve currency (see Chapter 4 of the September 2006 *World Economic Outlook*).

What factors could threaten the continuation of this benign combination of trends? There are a number of reasons to think that global productivity growth may decelerate in the period ahead. The recent slowdown in productivity growth in the United States may reflect to some degree a diminishing of the boost from advances in the ICT sector, as well as normal cyclical factors. Most other countries have lagged the United States in reaping the benefits from ICT advances, and therefore should be able to achieve continuing gains. However, doing so will depend in part on sustained reforms to reduce regulatory impediments and increase competition, particularly in service sectors such as wholesale distribution and finance, where the U.S. productivity performance has been very strong.[2]

A second source of concern is that global productivity growth may receive less support from trade liberalization in the years ahead. The recent revival in the Doha Round of multilateral liberalization is very welcome—a successful conclusion of the round could provide significant efficiency gains, particularly in agricultural sectors. The process of bilateral and regional trade liberalization may continue, but it is not a substitute: such agreements—which already cover around one-third of global trade—are

Figure 1.16. Saving and Investment in Emerging Market and Oil-Producing Economies

(Percent of each subregion's GDP)

Although investment-to-GDP ratio has risen substantially in China in recent years, the rise in the savings ratio has been even more dramatic. Elsewhere in East Asia, investment has remained generally quite low. Rising oil prices have propelled a sharp increase in savings in oil-producing countries.

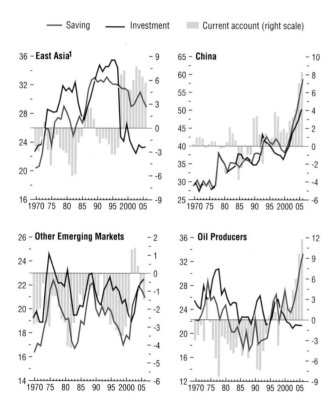

Sources: OECD Analytical Database; World Bank, *World Development Indicators* (2006); and IMF staff calculations.
[1]East Asia emerging markets excluding China.

---

[2]See, for example, a discussion of productivity performance in the services sector in western Europe (Chapter 2) and emerging Asia (Chapter 3 of the September 2006 *World Economic Outlook*).

inherently less beneficial than liberalization on a "most favored nation" basis, and can be counterproductive if not well designed.

Moreover, there is a serious danger that protectionist forces could rise in the years ahead, reversing some of the gains from an increasingly integrated global economy. Already there are concerns about recent resort to anti-dumping and "safeguards" actions around the world—and anti-trade measures could intensify in the context of a cyclical downturn and rising unemployment that would give added force to popular concerns about the impact of globalization on the distribution of income, particularly in advanced economies. Chapter 5 discusses how the rapid growth of international trade and the increasingly global labor market, combined with the introduction of new technologies, have produced important gains for income levels in both advanced and developing countries, as well as had an impact on income distribution. The chapter presents evidence suggesting that recent declines in the share of labor in advanced economies reflect more technological change than increasing competition from a burgeoning global labor force. Nonetheless, more could be done to help those whose jobs may be particularly affected by recent trends in technology and trade, including through better education systems, more flexible labor markets, and welfare systems that cushion the impact of, but do not obstruct, economic change.

Third, global environmental and resource constraints are likely to impose increasing costs. Efforts to date to address the long-term problem of global warming have been limited and partial—few countries are expected to meet the goals for control of carbon emissions over 2008–12 set out in the Kyoto Protocol. The potential long-term economic consequences of climate change are increasingly recognized, leading to rising interest across countries to take actions to control carbon emissions that would inevitably add to the costs of doing business even while averting much graver long-term consequences. For example, the recent *Stern Review on the Economics of Climate Change* estimates that

it would cost about 1 percent of GDP a year to stabilize carbon dioxide concentrations in the atmosphere, while the consequences of taking no action would be long-term damage of 5 percent or more of global consumption, concentrated in lower-income countries in the tropics.[3] Beyond such environmental consequences, the marginal costs of energy production are already rising, as easier-to-exploit oil reserves outside a few very large producers are being depleted and a rising share of non-OPEC production will take place in much more expensive offshore facilities or from low-grade, hard-to-extract deposits such as tar sands.

Fourth, aging populations, especially in advanced economies, pose challenges for maintaining productivity growth. As the share of new entrants to the labor force declines, it will become harder to continually raise the knowledge base, particularly related to the technological frontier, and there are risks of mismatches between specific labor skills and needs. A rising ratio of dependents to working-age population will also impose fiscal strains as pension and health care costs to governments rise. As discussed in Box 1.2, achieving fiscal sustainability in the face of these rising costs will require substantial adjustments of the order of 4 percent of GDP in the G-7 countries. In turn, this will put pressure to raise tax rates that will have an efficiency cost. To some degree, more open immigration policies and steps to encourage higher birth rates may help to address such concerns, but they would only be able to partially compensate for aging trends.

Slowing productivity would have implications for investment and consumption trends and the unwinding of global imbalances. Maintaining GDP growth rates in the face of slower growth

[3]See Stern (2006). While some precise numbers provided in the report may depend on particular assumptions (such as the time discount rate used to weight consequences in the future) and have been challenged, the report provides a useful framework for the assessment of the economic consequences of global warming and provides a sense of the order of magnitude of the costs that may be involved.

Box 1.2. Ensuring Fiscal Sustainability in G-7 Countries

In the coming decades, rising longevity, falling fertility rates, and the retirement of the baby boom generation will substantially raise age-related government spending in G-7 countries. By 2050, the populations in most G-7 countries are expected to be smaller and considerably older, with old-age dependency ratios projected to double. These trends will put national fiscal positions under substantial additional pressure. According to the projections submitted by national authorities, general government age-related spending in these countries is expected to rise by an average of 4 percentage points of GDP over the next 45 years with substantial cross-country variation (see the figure).[1] Estimates vary substantially across countries—from Canada at the high end, where age-related spending is projected to rise by 9 percentage points by 2050, to Italy at the low end, where such spending is projected to rise by just 2 percentage points. The bulk of the spending increase is expected to come from additional health costs, with long-term care and pension spending accounting for the remainder.

Assessing the impact of these demographic changes on the sustainability of public finances is complicated by uncertainties about long-term technological, demographic, labor supply, and productivity growth projections. A key issue is the strength of the link between aging and the cost of health care. The more traditional "expansion of morbidity" hypothesis (aging implies longer periods of illness and thus higher costs) is often contrasted with the "compression of morbidity" hypothesis (aging delays, but does

Note: The main author of this box is Daniel Leigh. The box draws on a study prepared by Hauner, Leigh, and Skaarup (2007).

[1]See Economic Policy Committee of the European Union (2006) for France, Germany, Italy, and the United Kingdom; and OECD (2001) for Canada, Japan, and the United States. More recent long-run age-related spending projections for Canada, Japan, and the United States produced by national authorities are broadly consistent with the OECD (2001) projections.

Projected Cumulative Growth in Old-Age Population and Increase in Age-Related Spending Relative to 2005

—— Age-related spending, percentage point of GDP (left scale)

—— Cumulative growth in old-age population, percent (right scale)

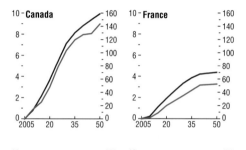

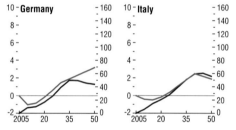

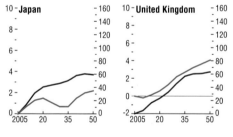

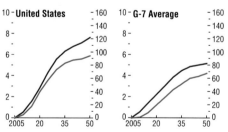

Sources: Economic Policy Committee of the European Union (2006); OECD (2001); UN (2006); and IMF staff estimates.

not extend, the periods of illness and the associated costs).

A comparison of age-related spending pressures across countries is complicated further by differences in methodology across age-related spending projections. The absence of a fully standardized projection framework is rooted in the complexity of preparing population-cohort-based long-term projections for countries with different old-age and health insurance systems. Nonetheless, there is a fairly close relationship between the projected old-age population growth rates and projected age-related expenditure (see the figure). Obtaining a more consistent set of cross-country estimates for future age-related spending pressures is an important priority for future research.

This box uses a standard indicator, the *intertemporal primary gap*, to assess the evolution of fiscal sustainability for each of the G-7 countries, and to evaluate the contribution of policy initiatives.[2] The intertemporal primary gap measures the change in the primary balance required to equate the present discounted value of future primary balances to the current level of debt. This measure thus indicates the adjustment required to stabilize debt at a level that is *permanently* sustainable (not just *attained* in a certain year).

The indicator consists of three components:
• the primary deficit component—the initial cyclically adjusted general government primary deficit;
• the debt component—the debt-servicing costs of the initial debt stock (evaluated using either gross debt or net debt data); and
• the aging component—the net present value of the projected increase in age-related expenditures times the growth-adjusted interest rate (nominal interest rate minus nominal growth), assumed, for ease of comparability,

to be 2 percent per year in the baseline scenario for all countries.[3]

The first table presents the data for the three components used to evaluate the indicator as of 2005.

The estimated fiscal adjustment required to ensure long-run fiscal sustainability is substantial for all G-7 countries. In particular, as the second table reports, closing the intertemporal primary gap would require an average adjustment estimated at 3.9 to 4.5 percentage points of GDP (depending on whether net debt or gross debt is used to evaluate the indicator).[4] Almost two-thirds of this adjustment need reflects the expected increase in age-related spending (aging component), while the remaining one-third reflects the interest on public debt (debt component). The largest primary gaps are shown for Japan and the United States. In the case of Japan, this reflects the largest primary deficit, high debt level, and the assumed interest rate–growth differential.[5] In the case of the United States, the large gap is due to a combination of high primary deficits and high projected increases in age-related spending. The smallest primary gap is shown for Canada, where a primary surplus of 5.5 percent of GDP helps to offset the impact of the very large pro-

[3]While a 2 percent interest rate–growth differential is broadly in line with the historical experience of major industrial countries, it is higher than the figure used in the debt sustainability analyses of a number of IMF Staff Country Reports. Lowering the interest rate–growth differential can substantially reduce the adjustment need for countries with high debt levels.

[4]While using net debt to evaluate fiscal sustainability is preferable in principle, methodological inconsistencies, notably in the evaluation of pension system assets, imply that net debt figures are not readily comparable across countries.

[5]The estimated adjustment need is highly sensitive to the interest rate–growth differential assumed. In the case of Japan in particular, a 10-year historical average spanning the deflation period is probably higher than the interest rate–growth differential going forward. Lowering this differential to ¾ of 1 percent would yield a required adjustment in line with the analysis and recommendations made in the context of the IMF's 2006 Article IV Consultation with Japan.

[2]This indicator belongs to the family of primary gap indicators (as discussed in Chalk and Hemming, 2000) that is based on the European Commission's (2004) approach to assessing fiscal sustainability. A similar approach is used in HM Treasury (2006).

Box 1.2 *(concluded)*

G-7: Fiscal Positions as of 2005
(In percent of GDP unless otherwise stated)

	Gross Debt (end-2005)	Net Debt (end-2005)	Structural Primary Balance (2005)	Projected Increase in Age-Related Spending, 2005–50 (in percentage points of GDP)
Canada	70.8	30.2	5.5	9.0
France	76.1	43.7	−0.2	3.3
Germany	71.1	51.5	0.1	3.2
Italy	120.4	95.1	1.4	1.9
Japan	173.1	86.4	−3.0	2.2
United Kingdom	46.7	40.0	−1.5	4.1
United States	61.8	43.5	−1.8	5.9
Average	88.6	55.8	0.1	4.2

Sources: OECD, Economic Outlook database for debt and primary balance data; and EPC (2006) and OECD (2001) for age-related spending data.

Note: All data are for general government. Differences between OECD and *World Economic Outlook* debt data may arise due to (1) different definitions of general government; (2) alternative treatment of government assets and liabilities, notably pension liabilities; and (3) alternative government account consolidating methods.

jected increase in age-related spending. Without any fiscal adjustment, the expected increases in age-related spending imply explosive debt dynamics in all seven countries.

While the overall adjustment required to achieve long-run fiscal sustainability in G-7 countries is large, there are significant growth benefits to putting public finances on a sustainable footing in the near term versus delayed adjustment. The following two scenarios illustrate this important point:

- *Near-term adjustment scenario.* This scenario involves closing the intertemporal primary gap over a period of five years.
- *Delayed adjustment scenario.* This scenario involves no changes in fiscal policy for 10 years, during which age-related spending pressures are allowed to build up. The intertemporal primary gap is then reassessed on the basis of as-of-then public debt and primary balance levels, and closed over the following five years.

G-7: Estimation Results—Primary Gaps in 2005
(Percent of GDP)

	Intertemporal Primary Gap[1]		Contributions to Intertemporal Primary Gap (Gross Debt) from:[2]			Intertemporal Primary Gap[3]	
	(Net debt)	(Gross debt)	Primary balance	Debt service	Aging costs	(Net debt)	(Gross debt)
Canada	−1.4	−2.2	5.5	−1.4	−6.3	−2.3	−2.7
France	−3.4	−4.0	−0.2	−1.5	−2.3	−3.4	−3.7
Germany	−2.7	−3.0	0.1	−1.4	−1.7	−2.8	−3.0
Italy	−1.7	−2.2	1.4	−2.4	−1.2	−1.0	−1.3
Japan	−6.2	−7.9	−3.0	−3.4	−1.6	−5.6	−6.5
United Kingdom	−4.8	−4.9	−1.5	−0.9	−2.5	−5.1	−5.1
United States	−6.9	−7.3	−1.8	−1.3	−4.2	−7.2	−7.4
Average	−3.9	−4.5	0.1	−1.8	−2.8	−3.9	−4.2

Sources: Economic Policy Committee of the European Union (2006); OECD (2001); OECD, Economic Outlook database; and IMF staff calculations.

[1]2 percent interest rate–growth differential.
[2]The contributions are presented for calculations using the baseline 2 percent interest rate–growth differential.
[3]1 percent interest rate–growth differential.

The effects of these two policy scenarios on economic activity—both in the short term and in the medium to long term—are assessed using the IMF's Global Fiscal Model (GFM), calibrated to replicate the key empirical features of each G-7 country.[6] Two main conclusions emerge from the analysis. First, delaying fiscal consolidation and allowing debt to increase implies the need to run perma-

[6]GFM is a general equilibrium model developed at the IMF to examine macroeconomic and structural fiscal policy issues, including pension reform, in a multicountry setting.

nently higher primary surpluses to service the higher interest costs. On average, the primary balance adjustment required to stabilize debt on a sustainable basis is 1.1 percentage points of GDP higher in the delayed compared with the near-term adjustment scenario. Second, early adjustment also brings significant long-run output gains. Early adjustment is estimated to deliver a total output gain of 1.8 percent of GDP on average. Given the upside risks to spending pressures, early fiscal adjustment would also provide greater fiscal space to absorb any higher-than-expected age-related expenditure needs.

of total factor productivity would require higher rates of capital accumulation than over the present expansion. At the same time, consumption growth could be dampened by lower expectations of future income growth, although aggregate consumption is likely to be boosted as a rising share of population in advanced countries retire and as populations in fast-growing countries in East Asia—especially in China—adjust to new levels of affluence and precautionary savings dwindle. The balance of these complex forces affecting saving and investment is hard to predict with any precision, but it does seem likely that the recent period of "savings glut" or "investment dearth" (depending on perspective) may come to an end, implying rising pressure on financial resources and increasing real long-term interest rates.

In this context, countries with large current account deficits, such as the United States, may face greater difficulties in attracting continuing large-scale foreign financing as needed—particularly as other countries' financial systems start closing the gap with the United States by offering a similar array of financial vehicles for savings. In such circumstances, prospects for a smooth unwinding of imbalances would benefit from trade reforms and other initiatives to remove obstacles to the smooth reallocation of

resources in response to exchange rate movements, a point supported by the findings in Chapter 3.

Anticipating and modeling these long-term forces is a complex task, and it is hard to be confident about the outcomes. Nevertheless, the potentially large costs involved in dealing with such problems as climatic change, population aging, and the unwinding of global imbalances argue for forward-looking and well-calibrated policy responses to mitigate the risks involved.

Policy Issues

The immediate challenge for policymakers is to continue to steer the global economy on a sustainable path that is consistent with low inflation as the global expansion enters its fifth year. The major central banks face distinct challenges in managing monetary policy, reflecting differing cyclical positions and degrees of inflation pressure in their economies.

- In the *United States*, the Fed continues to face a tricky task of balancing concerns of slowing activity against inflation risks, and the policy of holding rates steady remains appropriate for now. Financial markets are now pricing in a rate cut by September, following a string of weaker data. But the Fed has appropriately kept its options open, stressing that the path of monetary policy will depend on how incoming data affect the balance of risks between growth and inflation.

- Inflation in the *euro area* has been more closely aligned with objectives, and a strengthening economy has provided a context for the ECB to progressively raise short-term interest rates to more neutral levels to forestall pressures on wages and prices. With the area's growth projected to remain close to or above potential, and the possibility of some further upward pressure on factor utilization and prices, a further interest rate increase to 4 percent by the summer would seem warranted. Beyond this, additional policy action could still be required if growth momentum remains above trend and risks to wages and prices intensify.

- In *Japan*, a very easy monetary stance has been key to the country's exit from a decade-long stagnation—although it is likely to also have been a factor contributing to carry trade outflows and the weakness of the yen, which has raised some concerns about the impact on competitiveness in other countries as well as a possible disorderly reversal as policy is tightened. While the growth outlook is favorable, inflation readings have remained uncomfortably close to zero. With this background, the primary focus should remain on ensuring robust growth and a decisive departure from deflation. Thus, monetary accommodation should be removed only at a gradual pace, and on the basis of evidence confirming the continuing strength of the expansion.

The thrust of fiscal policy in the advanced economies should be directed at necessary consolidation and reform to maintain viability in the face of aging populations, while leaving room for automatic stabilizers to work as needed. Strong revenue growth has helped to strengthen fiscal positions in a number of major economies over the past three years (Table 1.3). However, it remains uncertain how much of this improvement is cyclical—boosted by high profits, rapid growth of earnings at the upper end of

the income spectrum, and rising asset prices—and how much will be permanent. Attention must be paid to containing expenditure growth, which experience has shown provides a more durable path to fiscal consolidation. Among the major advanced economies, further sustained progress toward fiscal consolidation would seem particularly important in the United States—especially in view of low private savings, concerns about the wide current account deficit, and the projected high fiscal cost of population aging; Japan, where deficit and debt levels remain particularly high and population aging is occurring rapidly; and Italy, where modest growth and weakening competitiveness reinforce concerns about fiscal sustainability.

Sustained progress toward fiscal consolidation will depend on more ambitious progress with fundamental fiscal reforms to contain increasing outlays as populations age, particularly in areas such as health care and pensions, and to avoid the erosion of revenue bases. Tax and spending policies should also be geared to dealing with the medium-term growth challenges. Price-based incentives could help to foster energy conservation and control of hydrocarbon emissions (Box 1.3). Pension system reforms could encourage longer working lives as well as ensure fiscal viability, while social safety nets could be geared to provide greater support for workers adjusting to increasingly global markets, without obstructing the process of change. Gaining support for such reforms is never easy in view of distributional consequences, but the present period of sustained growth should provide an ideal opportunity. Moreover, reform momentum could be galvanized by efforts to increase fiscal transparency and responsibility, including more intensive independent oversight, greater accountability, and fiscal frameworks to guide policy in line with clearly stated long-term objectives.

In a similar vein, the advanced economies need to make more ambitious progress with market-based reforms that would help to raise potential growth. A particular challenge is to ensure the creation of adequate employment opportunities within the increasingly global

Table 1.3. Major Advanced Economies: General Government Fiscal Balances and Debt[1]
(Percent of GDP)

	1991–2000	2001	2002	2003	2004	2005	2006	2007	2008	2012
Major advanced economies										
Actual balance	−3.0	−1.7	−4.0	−4.8	−4.2	−3.5	−2.7	−2.4	−2.4	−1.6
Output gap[2]	0.9	1.3	–	−0.8	−0.2	−0.4	−0.1	−0.4	−0.5	—
Structural balance[2]	−3.2	−2.2	−3.9	−4.4	−4.1	−3.3	−2.7	−2.3	−2.2	−1.6
United States										
Actual balance	−2.2	−0.4	−3.8	−4.8	−4.6	−3.7	−2.6	−2.5	−2.5	−1.6
Output gap[2]	2.4	2.1	0.3	−0.5	0.1	0.1	0.3	−0.6	−0.9	—
Structural balance[2]	−2.9	−1.2	−3.9	−4.6	−4.5	−3.6	−2.7	−2.4	−2.4	−1.6
Net debt	49.4	35.5	38.3	41.1	42.8	43.6	43.4	44.2	44.6	43.7
Gross debt	65.4	53.7	56.1	59.3	60.1	60.3	59.6	60.3	60.6	59.1
Euro area										
Actual balance	−3.8	−1.9	−2.6	−3.1	−2.8	−2.4	−1.6	−1.2	−1.1	−0.7
Output gap[2]	−0.2	1.4	0.3	−0.8	−0.7	−1.3	−0.6	−0.3	—	—
Structural balance[2]	−3.4	−2.3	−2.6	−2.7	−2.4	−1.9	−1.3	−1.0	−1.0	−0.7
Net debt	56.0	57.3	57.3	58.8	60.0	60.9	59.8	58.6	57.6	53.3
Gross debt	69.2	68.3	68.2	69.3	69.7	70.5	69.3	67.9	66.7	61.7
Germany[3]										
Actual balance	−2.2	−2.8	−3.7	−4.0	−3.7	−3.2	−1.7	−1.3	−1.3	−1.3
Output gap[2]	0.3	1.7	0.5	−0.9	−0.9	−1.2	0.1	0.6	1.1	—
Structural balance[2,4]	−2.0	−2.8	−3.2	−3.4	−3.4	−2.8	−1.8	−1.4	−1.4	−1.3
Net debt	43.6	52.1	54.3	57.8	60.1	62.4	62.4	62.1	61.6	61.0
Gross debt	52.4	57.9	59.6	62.8	64.8	66.4	66.8	66.5	65.9	64.9
France										
Actual balance	−3.6	−1.6	−3.2	−4.2	−3.7	−2.9	−2.6	−2.6	−2.4	−1.1
Output gap[2]	−1.4	1.0	—	−0.9	−0.9	−1.7	−1.8	−1.9	−1.6	—
Structural balance[2,4]	−2.7	−2.2	−3.2	−3.5	−3.0	−2.2	−1.4	−1.4	−1.5	−1.1
Net debt	42.0	48.2	48.5	52.6	54.8	57.0	55.0	54.2	53.7	49.5
Gross debt	51.2	56.3	58.2	62.3	64.5	66.7	64.7	63.9	63.4	59.2
Italy										
Actual balance	−6.3	−3.1	−2.9	−3.5	−3.4	−4.1	−4.4	−2.2	−2.4	−2.3
Output gap[2]	−0.9	1.2	0.3	−0.8	−0.8	−1.9	−1.4	−0.9	−0.6	—
Structural balance[2,4]	−6.0	−3.8	−3.9	−3.3	−3.4	−3.4	−3.8	−1.8	−2.0	−2.3
Net debt	107.7	107.0	103.9	103.3	102.6	105.1	105.2	104.5	103.8	101.6
Gross debt	113.4	108.7	105.6	104.3	103.8	106.2	106.8	106.0	105.3	103.1
Japan										
Actual balance	−3.8	−6.3	−8.0	−8.0	−6.2	−4.8	−4.3	−3.8	−3.5	−2.7
Excluding social security	−5.6	−6.5	−7.9	−8.1	−6.6	−5.1	−4.3	−3.8	−3.7	−3.8
Output gap[2]	—	−0.9	−1.9	−1.8	−0.7	−0.5	—	0.4	0.3	—
Structural balance[2]	−3.8	−5.8	−7.2	−7.2	−5.8	−4.6	−4.3	−3.9	−3.7	−2.7
Excluding social security	−5.6	−6.3	−7.4	−7.7	−6.4	−5.0	−4.3	−3.9	−3.8	−3.9
Net debt	31.7	66.0	72.5	77.3	81.8	93.3	96.4	98.2	99.4	99.5
Gross debt	100.3	151.6	160.8	167.7	177.8	182.9	184.8	185.0	184.3	177.8
United Kingdom										
Actual balance	−3.3	1.1	−1.6	−3.2	−3.1	−3.0	−2.5	−2.4	−2.2	−1.6
Output gap[2]	−0.6	0.6	−0.1	−0.2	0.5	−0.2	−0.2	—	—	—
Structural balance[2]	−2.9	0.6	−1.8	−3.1	−3.4	−3.0	−2.7	−2.2	−2.0	−1.6
Net debt	34.2	32.7	32.7	34.5	36.1	38.0	38.5	39.0	39.1	38.6
Gross debt	39.8	38.4	37.9	39.3	40.8	42.7	43.2	43.6	43.7	43.2
Canada										
Actual balance	−3.6	0.7	−0.1	−0.4	0.5	1.4	0.9	0.6	0.7	0.9
Output gap[2]	−0.5	0.5	0.4	−0.5	—	0.2	0.2	−0.2	−0.1	—
Structural balance[2]	−3.1	0.3	−0.2	−0.1	0.6	1.3	0.8	0.7	0.8	0.8
Net debt	61.0	43.7	42.6	38.5	34.4	30.2	27.9	26.3	24.3	17.1
Gross debt	105.2	91.5	89.4	85.2	80.2	78.6	74.1	70.7	66.5	51.9

Note: The methodology and specific assumptions for each country are discussed in Box A1 in the Statistical Appendix.
[1]Debt data refer to end of year. Debt data are not always comparable across countries.
[2]Percent of potential GDP.
[3]Beginning in 1995, the debt and debt-service obligations of the Treuhandanstalt (and of various other agencies) were taken over by general government. This debt is equivalent to 8 percent of GDP, and the associated debt service to ½ to 1 percent of GDP.
[4]Excludes one-off receipts from the sale of mobile telephone licenses (the equivalent of 2.5 percent of GDP in 2000 for Germany, 0.1 percent of GDP in 2001 and 2002 for France, and 1.2 percent of GDP in 2000 for Italy). Also excludes one-off receipts from sizable asset transactions, in particular 0.5 percent of GDP for France in 2005.

Box 1.3. Oil Consumption Across Major Countries: Is the United States Different?

Oil prices remain about 2½ times their 2002 levels. While overall demand in major countries has weakened—with OECD consumption falling in 2006 for the first time in 20 years—performance has not been even, with U.S. consumption growth less responsive. This box compares the historical response of oil demand with prices in major oil-importing advanced economies—United States, Japan, Germany, France, and Italy—and assesses recent performance in that context. The box suggests that energy policy (in particular relating to gasoline use) has likely been an important contributor to the differences in behavior between the United States and other countries.

While oil intensity (the ratio of oil consumption to real GDP) has declined dramatically in all of the five countries since 1970 (figure), it remains much higher in the United States, as does overall energy intensity. Furthermore, oil consumption has broadly retained its share of about 40 percent in total energy use in the United States, whereas in other countries there has been a substitution away from oil—albeit from generally much higher initial shares—to other energy sources, especially natural gas and (with the exception of Italy) nuclear energy. The U.S. "addiction" to oil comes largely from gasoline consumption, which as a share of GDP is nearly five times that in other major industrial countries (see figure). Its share in total U.S. oil consumption is a staggering 43 percent, compared with an average of 15 percent in other countries. (The difference is less pronounced when diesel and gasoline are lumped together: 59 percent for the United States versus an average of 38 percent for others.) Low U.S. gasoline prices and weaker fuel efficiency standards likely explain these differences. Fuel efficiency in the United States is 25 percent lower than the EU average and 50 percent lower than that of Japan (An and Sauer, 2004).

Over the past 20 years, U.S. oil consumption has grown on average by 1.4 percent a

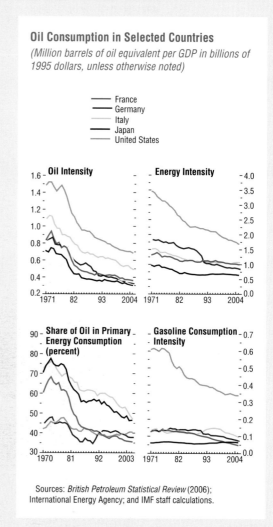

Oil Consumption in Selected Countries
(Million barrels of oil equivalent per GDP in billions of 1995 dollars, unless otherwise noted)

— France
— Germany
— Italy
— Japan
— United States

Oil Intensity

Energy Intensity

Share of Oil in Primary Energy Consumption (percent)

Gasoline Consumption Intensity

Sources: *British Petroleum Statistical Review* (2006); International Energy Agency; and IMF staff calculations.

Note: The author of this box is S. Hossein Samiei.

year, compared with a range of –0.5 percent (Italy) to 0.6 percent (Japan) in the other major advanced economies (see the table). It also remained strong during the current hike in prices until mid-2005, growing on average by 1.3 percent a year during 2003–06. By comparison, over the same period, consumption in the other countries *fell* between 0.3 percent a year (France) and 2.8 percent a year (Italy).

What explains these differences? Higher U.S. GDP growth (especially in the recent period) has clearly been a major factor. However, the

Oil Consumption in Selected Countries: Elasticities and Forecast Errors[1]

	France	Germany	Italy	Japan	United States
Oil consumption growth (average annual)					
1983–2006	0.2	−0.1	−0.5	0.6	1.4
2003–06	−0.3	−0.9	−2.8	−1.1	1.3
Long-run income elasticity	0.36*	0.26*	0.75*	1.16*	0.99*
Long-run price elasticity	−0.06*	−0.04*	−0.10*	−0.09*	−0.01
Time trend	0.0	−0.002*	−0.003*	−0.003*	−0.004*
Forecast error (in percent)					
2004	0.1	0.4	−1.6	−2.2	3.0
2005	0.4	0.1	−1.4	−0.2	2.5
2006	0.0	−0.2	0.1	−1.8	1.1

[1]The estimation utilizes the auto-regressive distributed-lag (ARDL) approach to cointegrating relationships. See Pesaran and Pesaran (1997). This method allows a simultaneous estimation of short-run and long-run coefficients. The order of lag is determined using the Schwarz-Bayesian criterion. All variables are in natural logarithms. The estimations use quarterly data over the period 1984:Q1–2003: Q4. The projection period is 2004:Q1–2006:Q4. Forecast errors are defined as excess of actual over projected in percent, averaged over four quarters. An * indicates significance at 5 percent.

much higher oil intensity in the United States suggests that other factors must be at work too. To assess this issue, individual oil demand equations are estimated using quarterly data over the period 1984:Q1–2003:Q4, with GDP, real oil prices, seasonal dummies, and time trend as explanatory variables.[1] The period 2004:Q1–2006:Q4 is used for projection to examine how performance in the recent period compares with that in the past.[2] The objective of the exercise is to illustrate differences across countries using the same simple framework rather than estimate detailed demand equations. The table shows the estimated long-run income and price elasticities, the time trend, and forecast errors for the projection period.

The remarkable result is that the United States has the lowest (and an insignificant)

estimated long-run price elasticity (−0.01) and the second highest income elasticity following Japan—although the time trend has a slightly higher coefficient. The estimated price elasticities are somewhat on the low side (especially compared with studies that use panel data sets), possibly reflecting the absence of large price movements during 1984–2003. The insignificant U.S. price elasticity since 1984 is likely explained by low U.S. gasoline prices (and taxes) and the presence of threshold effects associated with the share of consumer expenditure on fuel in total expenditure, which remains well below that of the 1970s. Indeed, large increases in prices did lower demand in the 1970s and early 1980s, in large part because they made a dent in consumer budgets.

Using the estimation results to project consumption over the 2004–06 period, the United States is the only country where actual consumption exceeds projections by a sizable margin, *despite the very low historical price elasticity used in the projections in a period of rising prices.* In other words, the projections assume little response to rising prices and still they are below actual consumption. The excess of consumption over projections is 2.5–3.0 percent during 2004–05 (well above the average U.S. oil consumption growth) and around 1 percent in 2006—notwithstanding the slight fall in actual

[1]The data on oil consumption are from the International Energy Agency and are available only from 1984. GDP and price data (real international prices) are from the World Economic Outlook database. Detailed results are not reported here but are available on request.

[2]Extending the data to cover the 1970s (which requires using annual data for estimation) did not deliver meaningful results, especially for the United States, possibly suggesting a structural break in the relationship.

Box 1.3 *(concluded)*

consumption in 2006.[3] In contrast, consumption has been mostly well below projections in Japan and Italy, and modestly different from projections in France and Germany.

Admittedly, these results should be interpreted with caution, given the relatively short duration of the available quarterly data and given that the model does not incorporate the role of factors such as weather, vehicle ownership, and geography—which contributes to higher gasoline use in the United States.[4] Nevertheless, the results are consistent with the stylized facts discussed above and the more significant efforts made in major European countries and Japan relative to the United States to reduce oil consumption, in particular in transportation. These include higher taxes on gasoline, more stringent fuel efficiency standards, a gradual switch to diesel (which has increased efficiency), and heavier investment in public transportation. In power generation, serious steps have been taken to switch to renewable energy and natural gas.[5] These policies also reflect generally stronger efforts to tackle environmental problems: all these countries have ratified the Kyoto Protocol and are acting to achieve a 6–8 percent reduction in carbon dioxide emissions relative to 1990 levels by 2012.

In contrast, in the United States, while the share of oil in power generation has become negligible, the transport sector remains heavily reliant on oil, despite efforts to increase ethanol use. Gasoline consumption taxes remain low[6]

and prices are about a third of those in major European countries. More generally, as a major producer, U.S. policies have largely focused on increasing supply—for example, through tax and royalty relief for oil exploration—rather than on efforts to curb consumption and increase fuel efficiency in automobiles, notwithstanding the declining oil reserves in the United States and the adverse environmental implications of high oil consumption. Finally, the United States is the only G-7 country that has not ratified the Kyoto Protocol at a federal level, despite accounting for about half of total OECD greenhouse gas emissions—although some states have adopted the protocol's requirements. Emissions per unit of GDP remain about 50 percent higher in the United States than the G-7 average (excluding the United States and Canada), even though they have declined more rapidly since 1990.

The U.S. administration has recently announced the objective of reducing gasoline consumption by 20 percent over the next 10 years, but most of this is expected to be achieved by raising ethanol production, which may not be feasible without significant technological advances (see Appendix 1.1). To effectively tackle the country's "addiction to oil" would require strong policy measures, including market-based incentives and judicious regulations to contain consumption (in particular, of gasoline) and increase fuel efficiency. Higher gasoline taxes (which would likely increase price responsiveness in view of the threshold effects discussed above), the introduction of a carbon tax, and strengthened Corporate Average Fuel Economy standards—which helped improve fuel efficiency during the 1970s and 1980s—could be central components of such a strategy (see also Box 1.1 for an assessment of the impact of higher gasoline taxation).[7] Continued investment in research on renewable energy and strengthened collaboration with global initiatives (such as the Kyoto Protocol) should also contribute to reduce oil consumption.

---

[3]The higher-than-projected consumption could in part reflect the strong demand for sport utility vehicles in the United States.

[4]For alternative approaches to estimating oil demand, see, for example, Gately and Huntington (2002) and Chapter 4 of the April 2005 *World Economic Outlook*.

[5]For example, in France nuclear energy is the source of 80 percent of electricity generation. Italy has greatly increased the use of natural gas. Germany has made extensive efforts to encourage renewable fuels—but also coal through undesirable heavy subsidies. Japan has taken the lead in encouraging solar energy.

[6]For evidence that U.S. gasoline taxes are likely too low, see, for example, Parry and Small (2005).

[7]Higher gasoline and carbon taxes would also contribute to lowering the fiscal and trade deficits.

economy and to ensure that the less well-off share more in the prosperity created by rising trade and new technologies. Previous issues of the *World Economic Outlook* have emphasized the scope for productivity-boosting structural reforms in the euro area and Japan, particularly in the services and financial sectors. Some progress has been made on these fronts, for example, the revised Services Directive and Financial Sector Action Plan in the European Union and steps to encourage a more flexible labor force and to reduce the government's role in the financial sector in Japan, but implementation remains a question mark and there is still considerable scope for additional measures. There would also be scope for steps to improve the flexibility of the U.S. economy, including, for example, to increase labor mobility by reducing the close links between health care coverage and employment, and to improve efficiency more generally in the health care sector.

The emerging market and developing countries face a similar set of challenges of continuing to provide a stable macroeconomic policy environment, while advancing reforms that promote growth and at the same time ensuring that the fruits of growth are well shared. As noted already, many of these countries have taken advantage of benign global financial conditions to make good progress toward consolidating the credibility of sound macroeconomic frameworks that would provide bulwarks against a return to more turbulent external conditions. Nevertheless, the following issues remain prominent:

- While exchange rates in several Asian countries have appreciated markedly over the past six months, China would benefit from a more flexible exchange rate regime that provided a more secure basis for monetary policy management in the face of large foreign exchange inflows.
- Many emerging market and developing countries around the world face the challenge of taking advantage of strong capital inflows to support investment, while avoiding large swings in competitiveness and a buildup of balance sheet vulnerabilities. There is no

simple recipe that can be uniformly applied: policymakers need to develop balanced and flexible approaches to macroeconomic management suitable for their circumstances, while avoiding steps that could undermine confidence in or distort markets. Steps to strengthen domestic financial systems and to liberalize restrictions on capital outflows could help to alleviate risks and pressures from foreign exchange inflows and allow wealth-holders to benefit from asset diversification.

- Commodity exporters—particularly large oil producers in the Middle East, Latin America, and Russia—face the challenge of using wisely the rapid buildup in revenues to build and diversify growth potential, while avoiding overheating and overcommitment.
- Countries in Latin America and elsewhere need to consolidate recent progress toward strengthening public sector balance sheets and providing a secure basis for fiscal management.

Recent progress on structural reforms in these countries has generally been patchy. Encouraging advances have been made toward market-based reform in Africa that underpin the major improvement of this region's growth performance, former Eastern bloc countries have generally made good progress in strengthening the business environment as part of joining the European Union, while a number of countries in Latin America have shown how targeted support programs can be successful in addressing poverty problems. Nevertheless, the "to-do" list remains a long one. The following particular concerns are highlighted:

- Further progress in liberalizing service sectors in Asia and elsewhere would help to sustain and extend productivity improvements (see Chapter 3 of the September 2006 *World Economic Outlook*).
- Accelerating labor reforms in Latin America and elsewhere would discourage the rapid growth of the informal sector that has lowered productivity, weakened worker protection, and reduced opportunities for improving skills.

• Establishing stable, transparent, and balanced regimes for infrastructure provision and for the exploitation of natural resources would help to reduce risks of bottlenecks, corruption, and lack of investment that could prove a serious impediment to long-term growth.

Sustaining a global environment conducive to sustained growth will also depend on joint actions across countries. An ambitious outcome of the Doha Round of multilateral trade liberalization would provide a major boost to medium-term prospects and reduce risks of protectionism. In its absence, the recent trend toward bilateral trade arrangements could provide some benefits, but this process should be subject to greater discipline to minimize costs to third countries from trade diversion and to avoid creating a spaghetti bowl of diverse regulatory requirements from such agreements, thus ensuring that it provides a stepping stone rather than a stumbling block toward global free trade. In particular, it would be important to encourage transparent rules-of-origin requirements that are easier to meet, to foster "open regionalism" that would allow the countries to join agreements on similar terms, to find ways to harmonize the multiplicity of standards and rules, and to strengthen oversight by the WTO.

Joint actions are also important to ensure an environment conducive for the smooth unwinding of global imbalances. While the necessary policy steps are in each country's long-term self-interest, concurrent actions across a range of fronts would generate synergies, since adjustment that may bring some short-term costs or have distributional consequences should be easier to advance in an environment of continued global prosperity and one in which countries are seen to be acting cooperatively toward common goals. As has been emphasized in previous issues of the *World Economic Outlook*, important elements of such an approach—which are being discussed in the context of the IMF's Multilateral Consultations—include efforts to raise saving in the United States, including through more ambitious fiscal consolidation and steps to reduce disincentives to private savings; advanc-

ing growth-enhancing reforms in the euro area and Japan; measures to boost consumption and increase upward exchange rate flexibility in some parts of emerging Asia, especially China; and continuing efforts to boost absorption by oil exporters, especially in the Middle East, consistent with absorptive capacity constraints.

Appendix 1.1. Recent Developments in Commodity Markets

The authors of this appendix are Valerie Mercer-Blackman, S. Hossein Samiei, and Kevin Cheng, with contributions from To-Nhu Dao and Nese Erbil.

Commodity price developments over the past year have been dominated by a further surge in metals prices and sharp movements in oil prices. Metals prices were the major contributor to the 22 percent increase in the IMF commodities and energy price index in 2006. Oil prices rose sharply in the first part of 2006, reaching a record nominal high in August, but then dropped significantly, showing only a moderate rise for the year as a whole. After a short-lived dip at the beginning of 2007, prices recovered and rose sharply at end-March. Food prices have also showed strength, particularly since end-2006.

This appendix assesses recent trends in oil and commodity markets. As a special topic, Box 1.4 examines the extent of hedging by oil market participants against oil price volatility, suggesting that while firms seem to do a fair amount of financial hedging, governments tend to rely largely on self-insurance. It reviews obstacles to financial hedging and measures that could lead to greater use of such instruments.

Crude Oil and Energy Products

Oil prices continue to be volatile and sensitive to geopolitical developments, and the market remains tight. The decline in oil prices in August–September 2006 reflected a combination of slowing OECD demand, a recovery in the second half of 2006 in non-OPEC supply, and some easing of geopolitical tensions in September. OPEC's production cuts since November 2006, together with a recovery in demand in the first quarter of 2007, caused OECD inventories to decline and prices to strengthen. Prices surged further in late March with the resurfacing of geopolitical tensions. Looking ahead, analysts expect a better balance in the market as both demand and non-OPEC supply growth would pick up. Nevertheless, the risks to prices remain on the upside, given the recurrent geopolitical tensions, still-limited spare capacity, and the possibility that non-OPEC supply may again fall below projections. Downside risk should be limited by active OPEC quota adjustments to price softening.

Price Developments

After reaching a record high of $76 a barrel in August 2006, the average petroleum spot price (APSP)[4] declined sharply to around $55–$60 during October–December. In early 2007, oil prices experienced a short-lived dip, falling to just over $50 a barrel, before rebounding in late March to almost $65 (Figure 1.17, top panel). The decline in the third quarter of 2006 reflected temporarily lower geopolitical tensions (in particular, tensions relating to Lebanon), the absence of a major hurricane in the fall season, more comfortable inventory levels, and rising perceptions of slowing growth in global GDP and oil demand. The short-lived drop in December–January was fostered by the warm winter weather amid initial skepticism about OPEC's ability to sustain production cuts and diminishing investor interest in oil sector derivatives (in part reflecting losses suffered during 2006).[5] Prices recovered with a strengthening of demand due to colder weather, further OPEC production cuts, and declining inventories in

---

[4]The IMF average petroleum spot price is an equally weighted average of the West Texas Intermediate, Brent, and Dubai crude oil prices. Unless otherwise noted, all subsequent references to the oil price are to the APSP.

[5]Improved returns have since brought some investors back. Note that while speculative activity may have had some influence on prices over this short period, IMF staff's analysis shows that its effect on prices is not systematic or long term (see Box 5.1 of the September 2006 *World Economic Outlook*).

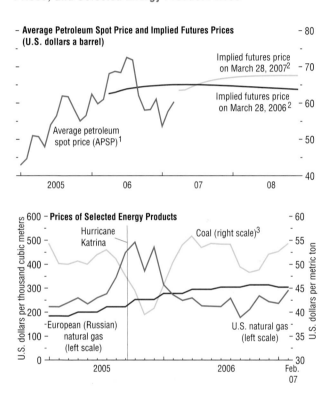

Figure 1.17. Average Petroleum Spot and Futures Prices, and Selected Energy Product Prices

Sources: Bloomberg Financial Markets, LP; and IMF staff calculations.
[1]Average unweighted petroleum spot price of West Texas Intermediate, U.K. Brent, and Dubai Fateh crude.
[2]Five-day weighted average of NYMEX light sweet crude, IPE Dated Brent, and implied Dubai Fateh.
[3]Average of Australian and South African coal prices.

Box 1.4. Hedging Against Oil Price Volatility

Volatility in oil prices—which exceeds that of other commodities (first table)—can complicate budgetary, financial, and investment plans of both companies and governments, thus providing oil market participants with obvious incentives to hedge. This box attempts to assess the extent of hedging in the oil market.

Hedging is a form of insurance, involving financial or nonfinancial activities that help reduce risks. Financial hedging involves the use of derivatives, which directly transfer risks to others. An airline company, for example, could reduce the volatility of its cash flows by locking in an agreed price for its purchase of jet fuel through a forward or swap contract.[1] An oil-exporting country could ensure a minimum stream of revenue by buying a series of put options on oil. Agents may also carry out nonfinancial hedging by adjusting their normal operations to provide some self-insurance. For example, a company could reduce the impact of price volatility by diversifying its activities. An oil-exporting government could smooth expenditure and build liquidity cushions to help reduce its vulnerability to sudden oil market shifts, thereby providing an element of self-insurance.

Do oil market participants hedge enough? Available data and anecdotal evidence may suggest that financial hedging is not used extensively. Total open positions of commercial traders in oil derivatives traded in NYMEX have increased considerably in the past 10 years, but remain low as a share of total U.S. consumption (see top panel of first figure). Furthermore, the use of oil derivatives in organized exchanges in the United States seems less extensive (as a share of global production) than some other commodities (see lower panel of first figure), in part reflecting the predominance of public sector involvement in energy production that does not favor the use of financial instruments for transactions or hedging (see discussion below).

Note: The authors of this box are Kevin Cheng, Valerie Mercer-Blackman, and S. Hossein Samiei.

[1]Notable recent examples of hedging in the airline industry include Lufthansa and Southwest.

Volatility of Commodities Prices
(January 1980–January 2007)
(In standard deviations of monthly percentage change)

Crude oil	8.25
Coal	4.03
Aluminum	5.53
Copper	5.98
Lumber	6.65
Cotton	5.03
Coffee	7.94
Fish	5.24
Soybeans	5.47
Wheat	4.78

Source: IMF staff calculations.

However, a thorough assessment of hedging activities is seriously complicated by a number of considerations, in particular the following:

- The use of derivatives in organized exchanges is only the tip of the iceberg. Over-the-counter (OTC) transactions are estimated to be five to 10 times the size of organized exchanges markets, but definitive information is limited (Campbell, Orskaug, and Williams, 2006). Moreover, the use of nonfinancial hedging is hard to observe and quantify.

- Even if information on hedging estimates were available, without knowing an agent's risk appetite and risk profile, inferring whether hedging is optimal would be a challenging task.

Subject to these limitations, the following analysis examines hedging activities by private companies and governments, obstacles to financial hedging, and measures to overcome these obstacles.

Hedging by Firms

For a risk-averse firm, hedging could reduce risks by diversifying away the risks associated with oil. Hedging may also be warranted for a risk-neutral firm if it increases the present value of its expected net cash flows. This can happen in the presence of asymmetries in the tax system or in credit markets, or large transaction costs associated with financial distress. However, a firm's shareholders may prefer exposure to the oil price risks in order to diversify their portfolios.

**Hedging in the Oil Sector and
Other Commodities**
(Percent)

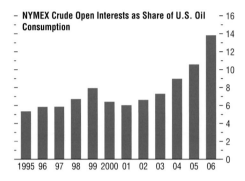

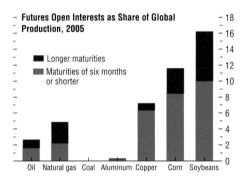

Sources: Bloomberg Financial Markets, LP; Commodities
Futures Trading Commission; International Energy Agency; World
Metal Statistics; U.S. Department of Agriculture; and IMF staff
calculations.

A number of practical considerations
underpin a firm's decision regarding financial
hedging. Firms feel more comfortable hedging short-period price risks than long-term
risks, given the likelihood of extensive shifts
(especially in technology) over the long term.
Smaller firms are more likely to use financial
hedging than larger firms, which are better able
to use their normal operations or cash reserves
to safeguard against volatility. Producers and
consumers are likely to hedge when they are
concerned about adverse movements in prices.
Furthermore, oil-producing firms are more
likely to hedge when the profit margin between
the product sale price and the marginal cost is

small. Finally, credit rating and the health of
balance sheets are important factors in hedging
decisions, because they affect the firm's ability
to borrow to smooth a volatile cash flow.

Impediments to more extensive financial
hedging range from governance issues within
firms to inadequacies of the derivatives markets.
First, a business manager's hedging activities
may often be inappropriately judged based on
whether the hedge is profitable ex post rather
than whether it was a good insurance policy ex
ante. Furthermore, the costs related to margin
requirements, transaction costs, and premiums
can be high and even prohibitive.[2] Finding a
counterparty can also be difficult, especially
at the long end, given the thinness of the oil
derivatives markets. Finally, inadequate oil market data, incomplete markets (e.g., for jet fuel),
and inappropriate hedge accounting rules can
also impede hedging activities.

In some situations, nonfinancial hedging provides a good alternative to the derivatives markets. One example is the presence of natural
hedges. An oil refinery, for example, with risk
exposures to both crude oil purchases and retail
product sales is protected by a natural hedge
to the extent that the price risks at the revenue and expenditure ends move in the same
direction. A firm can also reduce risks through
diversification of its activities, for example, by
expanding its business and taking on additional
risks that have negative correlation with its original risk profile. Finally, risks can be reduced by
issuing claims that securitize volatile cash flows
in exchange for a constant cash inflow.

Hedging by Governments

Assessing governments' hedging decisions
is even harder, given their complex incentive
structures and the political constraints they face,

[2]This is amply illustrated by the experience of the
German company, Metallgesellschaft, in the early
1990s. It attempted to offset the risks associated
with its forward contracts by using futures and swaps
but, in the face of unexpected adverse price movements, was unable to fund the margin calls and went
bankrupt.

Box 1.4 *(concluded)*

Export and Government Revenue of OPEC Members, and Average Petroleum Spot Price
(Index, 1975 = 100)

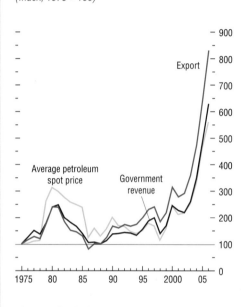

Source: IMF staff calculations.

Volatility of GDP, Exports, and Government Revenue (1976–2006)
(Standard deviations of annual percentage change)

	GDP	Export	Government Revenue
OPEC	12.7	21.3	19.7
Advanced economies	6.2	7.9	7.3
Emerging market and developing countries			
Africa (excl. OPEC countries)	9.5	11.2	10.7
Asia	7.4	9.4	10.1
Of which:			
China	10.9	12.7	14.9
India	7.7	9.2	7.9
Middle East (excl. OPEC countries)	11.0	12.6	14.9
Central and eastern Europe	10.4	12.1	16.0

Source: IMF staff calculations.

but the potential value of hedging is not any less.[3] For example, fiscal and export revenues for members of the Organization of Petroleum Exporting Countries are not only strongly correlated with oil prices (see second figure), but also are much more volatile than for other countries. Governments have, in general, tended to use nonfinancial hedging—albeit with limited success—to deal with the impact of oil price volatilities on export and fiscal revenues (see second table).[4]

Mechanisms to tackle shocks to export revenues include contingent loans from inter-

national financial institutions and commodity stabilization schemes to protect producers' incomes—though these schemes have generally failed in the past because of design flaws or bankruptcy. A flexible exchange rate regime can also in some cases serve as a mechanism to mitigate the impact of terms-of-trade volatility.[5]

To manage fiscal revenue risks, a number of oil producers have set up oil stabilization funds. The experience with these funds, however, has been mixed at best, if judged by their ability to smooth expenditures, although some (such as Norway and Russia) have been successful in increasing savings.[6] Some governments use a conservative price assumption in the budget to reduce risks, but often artificially low prices cannot be sustained and may eventually lead to

---

[3]For a discussion of hedging by governments, see Swidler, Buttimer, Jr., and Shaw (2005); and Daniel (2001).

[4]Blattman, Hwang, and Williamson (2007) find that volatility in the terms of trade of commodity exporters accounts for a substantial degree of their divergence in incomes per capita compared with other countries. The channel through which growth is affected is via a reduction in investment incentives.

[5]The choice of the exchange rate regime, of course, also depends on other considerations, in particular the extent of flexibility in domestic prices and wages. For example, allowing the exchange rate to appreciate in response to a positive shock to oil prices may adversely impact competitiveness of non-oil exports when domestic prices/wages are not flexible.

[6]See World Bank (2006). There are often several objectives for which these funds are utilized. Some funds, such as Norway's, largely act as vehicles to channel savings rather than smoothing expenditure.

spending inefficiencies when excess revenues are spent in a relatively short time period.[7]

Despite the limited success of nonfinancial hedging to protect budgeted expenditures, financial derivatives are sparsely used by oil-producing governments.[8] Of course, a large oil producer such as Saudi Arabia with plentiful liquid financial assets can withstand a negative price shock without the need to hedge. For smaller, poorer countries, in addition to the constraints faced by firms (see discussion above), they also face institutional impediments specific to governments. The ex post cost of unfavorable price movements, for example, may affect not only the hedging manager (as with

firms), but also the government in power—a risk it may not be willing to take given its short election-related planning horizon. In addition, the legislature is likely to oppose a hedging program that effectively takes away its control over a portion of the budget. Finally, because of its complexity, it may be difficult to muster public support for a hedging program.

Measures to Facilitate Greater Use of Financial Derivatives

All in all, firms appear to do a fair amount of financial hedging—subject to the constraints they face—while governments tend to rely more on nonfinancial hedging. However, scope for financial hedging is likely to expand. The recent increased interest in oil derivatives by institutional investors is providing additional liquidity in these markets and increased potential for hedging. Further deepening of these markets, an increase in the range of products they offer at reasonable costs, and improvements in the quality and reporting of data would increase their potential usefulness for hedging purposes. At the same time, as these markets expand, there would be a need for better data, especially for OTC transactions. Steps to improve the governance structure, particularly for governments, tackle the agency problem, provide sufficient safeguards, and strengthen expertise would also help improve hedging decisions.

[7]Importantly, an appropriate medium-term framework could help not only link annual budgets to longer-term policies and fiscal sustainability objectives, but also enhance risk analysis.

[8]Examples include Mexico (where Pemex is obligated to transfer a minimum amount to the budget), Norway's state oil company, the state of Texas, and the province of Alberta. Texas, for example, hedged state oil tax revenues by using a "straddled costless collar," but abandoned the program in 2000 when the state coffers became more diversified. Some U.S. municipal transport authorities have also become active hedgers as the regulatory frameworks have increasingly permitted it. Indeed, many state commissions in the U.S. require public utilities to hedge against product price risk. Information about other governments is virtually nonexistent. Chile, an oil importer, reportedly recently purchased an oil derivative.

key OECD economies. Renewed geopolitical tensions in the Middle East pushed prices up further at end-March. The correction of equity markets, which began in March, has so far not had a noticeable effect on commodity markets.

Natural gas prices have followed different trends across the Atlantic.[6] In the United States, prices in February 2007 remained only slightly above their level 13 months earlier (when prices had reverted to pre–Hurricane Katrina levels), as

warm winter weather up to January 2007 allowed inventories to return to more comfortable levels. Natural gas prices in Europe have risen steadily.[7] Coal prices rose 5 percent in 2006 and continued rising in early 2007 (Figure 1.17, bottom panel).

Oil Consumption

Global oil demand in 2006 grew by 0.8 million barrels a day (mbd), less than expected

[6]Such divergence is not abnormal given the difficulties of transporting natural gas.

[7]These refer to contractual western European prices paid in Germany and would not reflect the recent hikes in domestic prices in Belarus and Ukraine.

Figure 1.18. Demand and Prices of Petroleum Products in Selected Developing and OECD Countries

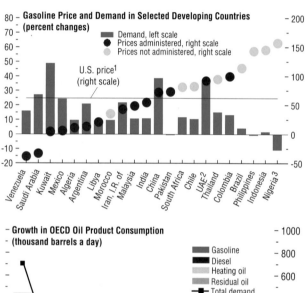

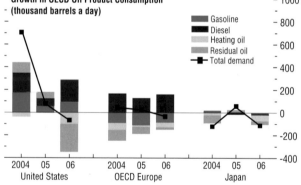

Sources: Bloomberg Financial Markets, LP; International Energy Agency; and IMF staff calculations.

[1]The U.S. gasoline price change is a good way for the market-driven price to change, given the size and competitive level of its domestic market and the relatively low taxation.
[2]United Arab Emirates.
[3]Although gasoline prices are generaly regulated, de facto many parts of the country face liberalized prices.

and below the 1.3 mbd growth in 2005. Demand growth in developing country regions rose to 1.3 mbd, but was partially offset by a 0.5 mbd fall in OECD demand (Table 1.4). Consumption was stronger than projected in China and India, and surged in many Middle Eastern oil-producing countries where growth has been strong. Demand growth in emerging markets was generally stronger in countries with administered prices, which typically have been lower than market prices in recent years (Figure 1.18, top panel).

Consumption in many OECD countries over the past year or so has been dampened by high oil prices, although temporary weather-related factors have also contributed (with the United States experiencing the warmest year ever recorded in 2006, coupled with a mild hurricane season in the Gulf of Mexico). In Europe and Japan, conservation measures and increased utilization of nuclear and coal power plants, along with some fuel switching to natural gas, have helped reduce oil demand. In the United States, while substitution to natural gas in power generation contributed significantly to a 25 percent drop in residual fuel oil demand, transportation fuel (gasoline and diesel) demand posted significant increases in the second half of 2006 and the first two months of 2007. This is in contrast with the continued weak demand for gasoline in other OECD countries (Figure 1.18, bottom panel).[8]

Medium-term consumption trends in selected advanced economies suggest that less rigorous oil conservation efforts in the United States, compared with four other advanced countries, could explain the more limited observed response of U.S. demand to higher prices (see Box 1.3).

Oil Production and Inventories

In line with weakening demand, overall oil output growth in 2006 fell to 0.8 mbd in 2006

---

[8]The move to greater use of diesel over gasoline for passenger transportation in Europe has also contributed to increase overall fuel efficiency.

Table 1.4. Global Oil Demand by Region
(Millions of barrels a day)

| | Demand | | Annual Change | | | |
| | | | mbd[1] | | percent | |
	2005	2006	2005	2006	2005	2006
OECD	49.63	49.16	0.30	−0.47	0.6	−0.9
North America	25.52	25.26	0.15	−0.26	0.6	−1.0
Of which:						
United States	21.15	21.03	0.08	−0.13	0.4	−0.6
Europe	15.52	15.45	0.05	−0.07	0.3	−0.5
Pacific	8.59	8.46	0.10	−0.13	1.2	−1.5
Non-OECD	34.06	35.32	1.01	1.26	3.1	3.7
Of which:						
China	6.69	7.16	0.27	0.47	4.2	7.0
Other Asia	8.76	8.86	0.14	0.10	1.6	1.1
Former Soviet Union	3.80	3.98	0.04	0.18	1.1	4.7
Middle East	6.12	6.45	0.32	0.33	5.5	5.4
Africa	2.88	2.94	0.09	0.06	3.2	2.1
Latin America	5.09	5.20	0.13	0.11	2.6	2.2
World	83.68	84.48	1.30	0.80	1.6	1.0

Source: International Energy Agency, *Oil Market Report*, January 2007.
[1]Millions of barrels a day.

(from 1.3 mbd in 2005). Non-OPEC supply grew by a less-than-expected 0.6 mbd in 2006, but accelerated in the second half as new capacity came on board in Brazil, Angola, and Azerbaijan. In addition, output in the United States and Russia recovered slightly, more than offsetting declines in the United Kingdom, Mexico, and Norway (Figure 1.19, top panel). OPEC's output declined in late 2006 reflecting the 0.7 mbd production cut (mostly by Saudi Arabia, Islamic Republic of Iran, and Kuwait) in the fourth quarter following OPEC's decision to cut quotas by 1.2 mbd starting in November.[9] After announcing an additional 0.5 mbd cut in quotas starting in February, in early March the group suggested that there would be no further cuts below concurrent production for the time being. Spare capacity has increased, but remains limited, despite some replenishing of facilities following the recent production cuts (Figure 1.19, middle panel).

OECD commercial inventories grew marginally in the 12 months ending in January 2007 to a near-normal level of 2.67 million barrels (mb)

[9]Angola became the twelfth member of OPEC in January 2007, but it will not need to participate in the cuts yet.

Figure 1.19. Oil Supply, OECD Inventories, and OPEC Spare Capacity

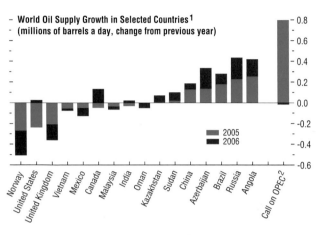

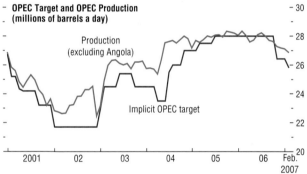

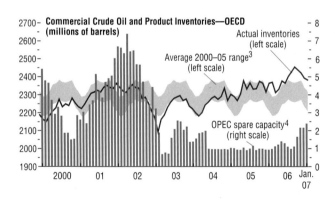

Sources: Bloomberg Financial Markets, LP; Energy Information Agency, U.S. Department of Energy; International Energy Agency; and IMF staff calculations.
[1]Includes crude oil and synthetic crude oil from tar sands, oil shale, etc.
[2]The "call on OPEC" is defined as OPEC production. Given the group's spare capacity, OPEC supplies the excess of demand not met by non-OPEC production.
[3]Average of each calendar month during 2000–05, with a 40 percent confidence interval based on past deviations.
[4]OPEC-11 spare capacity refers to production capacity that can be brought online within 30 days and sustained for 90 days.

Figure 1.20. Actual and Expected Semiannual World Consumption and Non-OPEC Production Growth, and Brent Crude Oil Prices

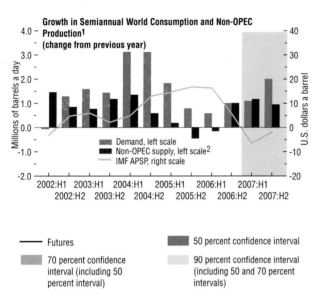

Growth in Semiannual World Consumption and Non-OPEC Production[1]
(change from previous year)

- Demand, left scale
- Non-OPEC supply, left scale[2]
- IMF APSP, right scale

Millions of barrels a day

U.S. dollars a barrel

2002:H1   2003:H1   2004:H1   2005:H1   2006:H1   2007:H1
2002:H2   2003:H2   2004:H2   2005:H2   2006:H2   2007:H2

— Futures

50 percent confidence interval

70 percent confidence interval (including 50 percent interval)

90 percent confidence interval (including 50 and 70 percent intervals)

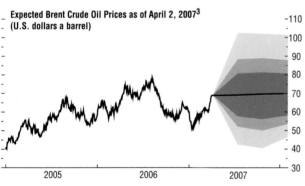

Expected Brent Crude Oil Prices as of April 2, 2007[3]
(U.S. dollars a barrel)

2005   2006   2007

Sources: Bloomberg Financial Markets, LP; International Energy Agency; and IMF staff calculations.
[1]2007:H1 and 2007:H2 supply and demand projections are from the International Energy Agency.
[2]Includes non-crude production.
[3]From futures options.

(53 days of forward cover). Stocks were built up early in 2006, reflecting precautionary demand and expectations of continuing price increases, but this trend was reversed starting in September as fears of future shortages eased (Figure 1.19, bottom panel). Preliminary data based on U.S. and Japanese inventories suggest that there has been an unseasonably large inventory draw down in the first quarter of 2007 reflecting continued strong demand and possibly a reaction to OPEC cuts.

Short-Term Prospects and Risks

Looking forward, the International Energy Agency (IEA) is projecting global consumption growth of 1.6 mbd in 2007 owing to continued robust demand from emerging markets such as China and in the Middle East, and a planned buildup of official stocks by China and the United States (Figure 1.20, top panel).[10] On the supply side, capacity growth is expected to be boosted as investment projects (such as Saudi Aramco's) come on stream by year-end. However, this projection is subject to downside risk, especially if declines in capacity in mature fields exceed expectations and costs and technical constraints delay projects further (as they have in the past few years). The IEA has already revised down its 2007 non-OPEC oil supply projections from August 2006 by about 0.3 mbd to 1.1 mbd (excluding Angola). Moreover, recent moves to increase state control of the oil sectors in Venezuela, Russia, and Ecuador, along with continued violence in Iraq and Nigeria, have further undermined prospects for a speedy global output recovery.

As of April 2, futures and options markets indicated that oil prices will average $65 a barrel in 2007 and $68 a barrel in 2008, with risks on the upside. Options markets indicated that there was a 1 in 6 chance that Brent crude

---

[10]According to the IEA, China aims to raise its reserves to 400 mb (about 4½ months of imports), purchasing 100 mb by end-2008. The United States recently announced that it aims to double its strategic reserves capacity by 2027 to almost 1,500 mb (equivalent to just under 4 months of imports).

prices could rise above $88 a barrel by end-2007 (Figure 1.20, bottom panel). The upside risks for 2007 reflect the still-limited global spare capacity, and the potential for heightened geopolitical tensions, as illustrated by developments in late March. At the same time, OPEC's commitment to defend prices through production cutbacks as necessary should limit further downward price pressures.

Nonenergy Commodities

The IMF nonfuel commodity index rose by 28 percent in 2006, ending the year at a new record high, driven by a surge in metals prices and a strengthening of agricultural prices (Figure 1.21, top panel). In the first three months of 2007, metals prices fluctuated, but generally remained strong, while agricultural prices continued to rise, albeit at a slower pace. The nonfuel commodity index is expected to increase further in 2007 as the strength of food and metals prices should carry forward. The rest of this section discusses the factors behind rising metals and selected food prices, and considers the extent to which recent high price levels are likely to be sustained.

Metals

Metals prices rose by 57 percent during 2006, by far the largest increase among the main categories in the IMF commodity index. This reflected continued strong demand growth, increased labor disputes, and unplanned disruptions to supply (Figure 1.21, middle panel). Strong growth of demand for stainless steel and automotive production, particularly in China, contributed to sharp price increases in nickel, zinc, and lead. Uranium prices rose by 71 percent, spurred by the recent revival of interest in nuclear energy. Copper prices have come down from their mid-2006 record-high levels, in part reflecting the slowdown in the U.S. housing market and weaker Chinese demand in the second half of 2006. Looking forward, copper and zinc prices are expected to weaken as new capacity comes on line. In contrast, nickel, tin, and ura-

Figure 1.21. Commodity Price Indices and Selected Metals and Food Price Indices

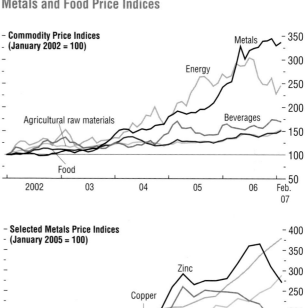

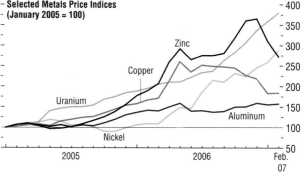

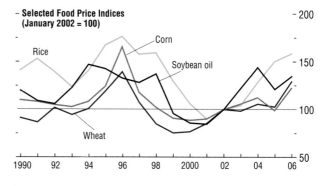

Source: IMF staff calculations.

nium still face more serious supply constraints and, therefore, higher possibility of upward price movements. Over the longer term, all base metals prices should weaken from their current highs as output continues to catch up with demand, although higher long-term production costs (wages, fuel costs, and equipment costs) are likely to keep prices above historical averages.[11]

Food and Biofuels

Food prices rose by 10 percent in 2006, driven mainly by surging prices of corn, wheat, and soybean oil in the second part of the year (Figure 1.21, bottom panel). Recent price increases have reflected a poor wheat crop in major producing countries (which pushed wheat stocks to their lowest levels in 26 years) and rising U.S. demand for ethanol (which uses corn as an input) and prospects of higher biodiesel demand (which uses soybean oil and other edible oils).[12]

Looking ahead, rising demand for biofuels will likely cause the prices of corn and soybean oil to rise further, and to move more closely with the price of crude oil, as has been the case with sugar.[13] For 2007, the United States Department of Agriculture is estimating a record corn crop, as planting areas increase by 10 percent from 2006 at the expense of soybeans and cotton. Still, demand fueled by the increase in domestic ethanol production capacity is expected to outpace the production rise. Higher prices of corn and soybean oil will also likely push up the price of partial substitutes, such as wheat and rice, and other edible oils, and exert upward pressure on meat, dairy, and poultry prices by raising

[11]The Chilean Copper Commission of experts, for example, has raised long-term copper price projections by more than 20 percent in the last year. See also Chapter 5 of the September 2006 *World Economic Outlook*.

[12]Prices of rapeseed oil (used to make biodiesel in Europe and Canada) and palm oil (used in Malaysia) have also risen.

[13]The early adoption of sugar-based ethanol in Brazil for flex-fuel cars has led to increasingly strong co-movements of sugar, ethanol, and crude oil prices. The exception was the fall in sugar prices in mid-2006, reflecting an abundant Brazilian sugar crop in combination with import protection of U.S. ethanol, which to some extent has segmented the ethanol market.

Table 1.5. Effects of Petroleum Products on Production of Selected Grains in the United States
(Percent of total)

	Wheat	Corn	Soybeans
Energy-related costs as percent of total cost—2005			
Fertilizer	12.6	13.9	3.8
Fuel, lube, and electricity	8.4	9.2	5.2
Total fertilizer and energy costs	21.0	23.1	9.0
Share of total consumption used in the production of biofuels (percent)			
2005–06 marketing year		17.6	5.6
2006–07 marketing year[1]		22.4	8.5
2009–10 marketing year (forecast)		35.3	
USDA projections for price change, 2005/06–2009/10 (percent)	24.3	87.5	29.0

Sources: U.S. Department of Agriculture (USDA); U.S. Census Bureau; and IMF staff.
[1]Estimate using the first quarter for soybeans.

animal rearing costs, given the predominant use of corn and soymeal as feedstock, particularly in the United States (more than 95 percent). Furthermore, since corn is more energy intensive than soybean in production,[14] high crude oil prices could also raise corn production costs (Table 1.5).

Recent proposals to increase biofuel production in the United States and Europe will likely put additional upward pressure on corn, wheat, and edible oil prices. Plans to double the minimum mandated biofuels consumption in the United States—the largest ethanol consumer—by 2017 would require an estimated 30 percent rise in corn production (or a corresponding reduction in exports) over the next five years to increase ethanol capacity, unless the higher demand is partially met by easing restrictions on imported ethanol—a plan that is currently not being considered.[15] In addition, the European Union's adoption of a mandate to have a mini-

[14]The most common crop rotation in the United States is between corn and soybeans, the latter providing a replenishing source of nutrients to the soil. The United States is the largest global producer of the two grains.

[15]Ethanol produced in the United States enjoys ample protection through a producer subsidy ($0.51/gallon) and a tariff ($0.54/gallon) on more efficiently produced imported ethanol. There is no such tariff on imported biodiesel.

mum of 10 percent of transport fuels replaced by biofuels by 2020 is estimated to require about 18 percent of the total agricultural land area to be set aside for rapeseed (to be used for biodiesel production), and wheat and sugar beet (to be used in ethanol), unless tariffs on imported ethanol are reduced and other financial supports continue.

While on a small scale biofuels may be beneficial by supplementing fuel supply, promoting their use to unsustainable levels under current technology is problematic, and long-term prospects for biofuels depend heavily on how quickly and efficiently second-generation substitutes (such as plant waste) can be adopted. Many energy market analysts also question the rationality of large subsidies that benefit farmers more than the environment. While new technology is being developed, a more efficient solution from a global perspective would be to reduce tariffs on imports from developing countries (for example, Brazil) where biofuels production is cheaper and more energy efficient (see Table 1.5).

Semiconductors

Global semiconductor sales revenue grew by 8.9 percent in 2006 (compared with 6.8 percent in 2005), driven by strong growth in volumes (mainly reflecting growth in demand for cell phones and other consumer electronics) amid largely stable prices (Figure 1.22, top panel). Sales growth was particularly strong in the memory segment (especially DRAM), more than offsetting a decline in microprocessor revenue as weak demand and fierce competition pushed prices lower.

Global capital spending by semiconductor producers rose by 19 percent in 2006, after declining slightly in 2005. The bulk of the expansion was in memory manufacturing and occurred mainly in Asia, which accounted for 43 percent of global capital spending. Semiconductor inventories started to build up in the second half of 2006 as new equipment came on line amid weakened demand, possibly creating some overhang. The global book-to-bill ratio for

Figure 1.22. Semiconductor Market

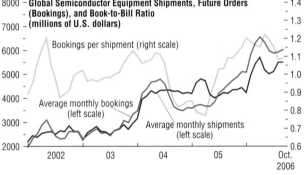

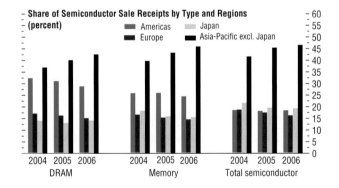

Sources: Semiconductor Industry Association; VLSI Research; and IMF staff calculations.

semiconductor equipment sales stood at over 1.1 in 2006 (Figure 1.22, middle panel).

Analysts expect semiconductor sales revenue to grow at around 10 percent in 2007, although risks are on the downside. Semiconductor demand—in particular from cell phones, MP3 players, and digital television sets—should remain strong, while the introduction of Microsoft's VISTA operating system should spur demand for memory chips, particularly DRAM (Figure 1.22, bottom panel). However, prices for chips are expected to decline in 2007 amid intensified competition and the lingering excess in inventory levels. In addition, investment expenditures should level off, while capacity utilization is expected to decline marginally.

References

An, Feng, and Amanda Sauer, 2004, "Comparison of Passenger Vehicle Fuel Economy and Greenhouse Gas Emission Standards Around the World" (Arlington, Virginia: Pew Center on Global Climate Change, December).

Blattman, Christopher, Jason Hwang, and Jeffrey Williamson, 2007, "Winners and Losers in the Commodity Lottery: The Impact of Terms of Trade Growth and Volatility in the Periphery 1870–1939," *Journal of Development Economics*, Vol. 82 (January), pp. 156–79.

Campbell, Patrick, Bjorn-Erik Orskaug, and Richard Williams, 2006, "The Forward Market for Oil," *Bank of England Quarterly Bulletin* (Spring), pp. 66–74.

Chalk, Nigel, and Richard Hemming, 2000, "Assessing Fiscal Sustainability in Theory and Practice," IMF Working Paper 00/81 (Washington: International Monetary Fund).

Conference Board, 2006, "Performance 2006: Productivity, Employment and Income in the World's Economies" (New York).

Daniel, James, 2001, "Hedging Government Oil Price Risk," IMF Working Paper 01/185 (Washington: International Monetary Fund).

Economic Policy Committee of the European Union (EPC), 2006, "Impact of Ageing Populations on Public Spending," Report No. ECFIN/CEFCPE(2006)REP/238 (Brussels).

Elekdag, Selim, René Lalonde, Douglas Laxton, Dirk Muir, and Paolo Pesenti, 2006, "Oil Price Movements and the Global Economy: A Model-Based Assessment," prepared for the Bank of Canada Workshop on Commodity Price Issues, July 10–16.

European Commission, 2004, "Public Finances in EMU," *European Economy*, No. 3/2004 (Brussels: European Commission).

Gately, D., and Huntington, H., 2002, "The Asymmetric Effects of Changes in Price and Income on Energy and Oil Demand," *The Energy Journal*, Vol. 23.

Hauner, David, Daniel Leigh, and Michael Skaarup, 2007, "Ensuring Fiscal Sustainability in G-7 Countries" (unpublished; Washington: International Monetary Fund).

HM Treasury, 2006, "Long-Term Public Finance Report: An Analysis of Fiscal Sustainability" (London).

Lane, Philip R., and Gian Maria Milesi-Ferretti, 2006, "The External Wealth of Nations Mark II: Revised and Extended Estimates of Foreign Assets and Liabilities, 1970–2004," IMF Working Paper 06/69 (Washington, International Monetary Fund).

Organization for Economic Cooperation and Deveopment, 2001, "Fiscal Implications of Age-Related Spending," OECD Economics Department Working Paper No. 305 (Paris: OECD).

Parry, I., and K. Small, 2005, "Does Britain or the United States Have the Right Gasoline Tax?" *American Economic Review*, Vol. 95, No. 4.

Peraran, M. Hashem, and Bahram Pesaran, 1997, *Working with Microfit 4: Microfit 4 User Manual* (London: Oxford University Press).

Rajan, Raghuram G., 2006, "Is There a Global Shortage of Fixed Assets?" remarks at the G-30 meetings, New York, December 1.

Schadler, Susan, Ashoka Mody, Abdul Abiad, and Daniel Leigh, 2007, *Growth in the Central and Eastern European Countries of the European Union*, IMF Occasional Paper No. 252 (Washington: International Monetary Fund).

Stern, Nicholas, 2006, *The Economics of Climate Change: The Stern Review* (London: HM Treasury).

Swidler, Steve, Richard J. Buttimer, Jr., and Ron Shaw, 2005, "Government Hedging: Motivation, Implementation, and Evaluation" (Arlington, Texas: University of Texas).

United Nations, 2006, *World Population Prospects*, UN Population Division (New York). Available via the Internet: esa.un.org/unpp/index.asp?panel=2.

World Bank, 2006, "Experiences with Oil Funds: Institutional and Financial Aspects," Energy Sector Management Assistance Program Report 321/06 (Washington).

COUNTRY AND REGIONAL PERSPECTIVES

Against the background of the global outlook discussed in Chapter 1, this chapter analyzes prospects and policy issues in the major advanced economies and in the main regional groupings of emerging market and developing countries. A consistent theme is that while the short-term outlook is generally still positive, policymakers should increase efforts to advance fiscal and structural reforms to ensure that strong growth can be sustained.

United States and Canada: How Much Will the U.S. Economy Slow?

The U.S. economy has slowed noticeably over the past year. After a strong first quarter, real GDP grew by around 2¼– 2½ percent (seasonally adjusted annualized rate) in each of the last three quarters of 2006. While private consumption spending continued to increase robustly, the housing sector remained a substantial drag on growth, with residential investment declining by around 19 percent (annualized rate) in the second half of the year and business purchases of equipment and software softening toward year-end. The manufacturing sector has been weak, particularly in autos and sectors related to construction, as demand has slowed and inventories have risen.

The central question in assessing near-term prospects for the U.S. economy is whether this weakness in growth is a temporary slowdown—a "midcycle pause" as occurred in 1986 and 1995—or the early stages of a more protracted downturn. While uncertainties remain, and recent data on retail sales and durable goods orders have been weaker than anticipated, a growth pause still seems more likely at this stage than a recession. Consistent with past "midcycle pauses," the labor market remains robust, with job losses in manufacturing and construction being offset by strong gains in the services sector, and the unemployment rate

is stable at 4½ percent (Figure 2.1). Further, corporate profitability and equity prices are at high levels, which should help support business investment, and real interest rates are still low by historical standards. And while the yield curve is inverted—which in the past has been a good leading indicator of recessions—it is less likely that this is portending a steep slowdown this time, as the inversion reflects low long-term rather than high short-term rates.[1] Lastly, the impact of the cooling housing sector on financial markets has been limited to date. While delinquency rates on subprime mortgages and spreads on associated securitized bonds have increased sharply, those on prime mortgages, other forms of consumer credit, and corporate borrowing still remain low (see the April 2007 *Global Financial Stability Report*). The financial sector is generally in good shape and credit remains readily available.

Consequently, while the growth forecast for 2007 has been lowered to 2.2 percent (0.7 percentage point lower than at the time of the September 2006 *World Economic Outlook*), the expansion is expected to gradually regain momentum, with quarterly growth rates rising during the course of 2007 and returning to around potential by mid-2008 (Table 2.1).[2] In particular, strong corporate balance sheets and high profitability should underpin a pickup in corporate investment after its recent softness, while the robust labor market should limit the negative wealth effect on consumption from weaker house prices. The downward revision to growth in 2007 largely reflects the weaker out-

[1]Ongoing structural changes, including pension fund asset reallocation and foreign demand for U.S. securities, have boosted desired holdings of long-dated U.S. securities and pushed down their yield (see Wright, 2006).

[2]The March Consensus forecast is for growth of 2.4 percent in 2007 and 3 percent in 2008 with a range of 2.1–2.9 percent in 2007 and 2.5–3.6 percent in 2008.

Figure 2.1. United States: How Much Will the U.S. Economy Slow?

(Percent change from four quarters earlier, unless otherwise noted)[1]

With employment growth steady, corporate profitability strong, and real interest rates still relatively low, it still seems likely that the current slowdown will be shallow and short lived—a midcycle pause—rather than develop into a more significant downturn.

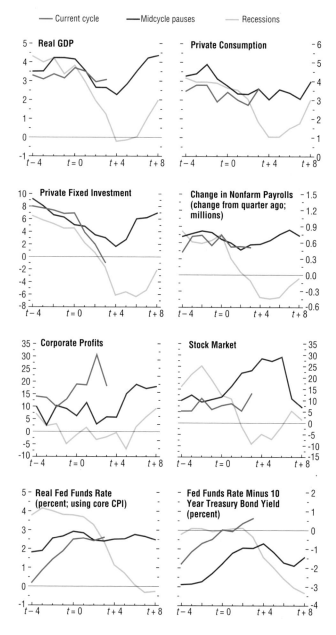

Sources: Havor Analytics; and IMF staff calculations.
[1] $t = 0$ is the peak of the GDP growth cycle. For recessions these peaks are in March 1990 and June 2000, and for midcycle pauses in March 1986 and December 1994. The peak of the current cycle is in March 2006.

look for residential investment. With the stock of new homes for sale rising to its highest level in over 15 years, home construction is falling more sharply than previously expected as home-builders move to reduce their existing inventory. While there are some very tentative signs that housing demand may be stabilizing—mortgage applications for purchase and existing home sales have risen above their September–October lows—problems in the subprime mortgage market will likely prolong the residential investment cycle. The commercial real estate market may help to partly offset the downturn in the housing sector in the near term, both in terms of investment and employment (Figure 2.2). Nevertheless, it is not clear whether the current strength of the commercial sector will be sustained in the absence of a turnaround in residential investment, particularly against the backdrop of relatively high vacancy rates. The weakness in residential investment in the forecast is partly offset by the external sector, which is expected to make its first positive contribution to growth since 1995.

The balance of risks to this less buoyant outlook remains on the downside. A sharper-than-expected slowing in house prices would pose risks to both residential investment and, through the impact on wealth and employment, consumption (see also Box 2.1). Also, the deterioration in credit quality in the subprime mortgage market could spread to other market segments in a weaker housing environment, adversely affecting the financial sector and credit availability. There are also concerns that the curent softness of business investment could be extended. On the upside of the central forecast, the depreciation of the dollar could provide a stronger spur to exports than projected.

Inflation has eased somewhat in recent months, with 12-month core CPI (excluding food and energy) inflation declining to 2.7 percent in February from 2.9 percent in September. At the same time, however, a number of measures of wage costs have been moving higher against the background of the tight labor market and slowing productivity, although strong

Table 2.1. Advanced Economies: Real GDP, Consumer Prices, and Unemployment
(Annual percent change and percent of labor force)

	Real GDP				Consumer Prices				Unemployment			
	2005	2006	2007	2008	2005	2006	2007	2008	2005	2006	2007	2008
Advanced economies	**2.5**	**3.1**	**2.5**	**2.7**	**2.3**	**2.3**	**1.8**	**2.1**	**6.0**	**5.5**	**5.4**	**5.4**
United States	3.2	3.3	2.2	2.8	3.4	3.2	1.9	2.5	5.1	4.6	4.8	5.0
Euro area[1]	1.4	2.6	2.3	2.3	2.2	2.2	2.0	2.0	8.6	7.7	7.3	7.1
Germany	0.9	2.7	1.8	1.9	1.9	1.8	2.0	1.6	9.1	8.1	7.8	7.6
France	1.2	2.0	2.0	2.4	1.9	1.9	1.7	1.8	9.7	9.0	8.3	7.8
Italy	0.1	1.9	1.8	1.7	2.2	2.2	2.1	2.0	7.7	6.8	6.8	6.8
Spain	3.5	3.9	3.6	3.4	3.4	3.6	2.6	2.7	9.2	8.5	7.8	7.7
Netherlands	1.5	2.9	2.9	2.7	1.5	1.7	1.8	2.1	4.7	3.9	3.2	3.1
Belgium	1.5	3.0	2.2	2.0	2.5	2.3	1.9	1.8	8.4	8.3	7.8	7.6
Austria	2.0	3.2	2.8	2.4	2.1	1.7	1.6	1.7	5.2	4.8	4.5	4.3
Finland	2.9	5.5	3.1	2.7	0.8	1.3	1.5	1.6	8.4	7.7	7.5	7.4
Greece	3.7	4.2	3.8	3.5	3.5	3.3	3.2	3.2	9.9	8.9	8.3	8.5
Portugal	0.5	1.3	1.8	2.1	2.1	3.1	2.5	2.4	7.6	7.7	7.4	7.3
Ireland	5.5	6.0	5.0	3.7	2.2	2.7	2.4	2.1	4.4	4.4	4.5	4.7
Luxembourg	4.0	5.8	4.6	4.1	2.5	2.7	2.1	2.1	4.2	4.4	4.6	4.8
Slovenia	4.0	5.2	4.5	4.0	2.5	2.7	2.7	2.4	6.5	6.4	6.4	6.4
Japan	1.9	2.2	2.3	1.9	−0.6	0.2	0.3	0.8	4.4	4.1	4.0	4.0
United Kingdom[1]	1.9	2.7	2.9	2.7	2.0	2.3	2.3	2.0	4.8	5.4	5.3	5.1
Canada	2.9	2.7	2.4	2.9	2.2	2.0	1.7	2.0	6.8	6.3	6.2	6.2
Korea	4.2	5.0	4.4	4.4	2.8	2.2	2.5	2.5	3.7	3.5	3.3	3.1
Australia	2.8	2.7	2.6	3.3	2.7	3.5	2.8	2.9	5.1	4.9	4.6	4.6
Taiwan Province of China	4.0	4.6	4.2	4.3	2.3	0.6	1.5	1.5	4.1	3.9	3.8	3.7
Sweden	2.9	4.4	3.3	2.5	0.8	1.5	1.8	2.0	5.8	4.8	5.5	5.0
Switzerland	1.9	2.7	2.0	1.8	1.2	1.0	0.6	1.0	3.4	3.4	2.9	2.8
Hong Kong SAR	7.5	6.8	5.5	5.0	0.9	2.0	2.1	2.3	5.7	4.8	4.4	4.2
Denmark	3.1	3.3	2.5	2.2	1.8	1.9	2.0	1.9	5.7	4.5	4.7	4.9
Norway	2.7	2.9	3.8	2.8	1.6	2.3	1.4	2.2	4.6	3.4	2.9	3.0
Israel	5.2	5.1	4.8	4.2	1.3	2.1	−0.1	2.0	9.0	8.4	7.5	7.2
Singapore	6.6	7.9	5.5	5.7	0.5	1.0	1.5	1.5	3.1	2.7	2.6	2.6
New Zealand[2]	2.1	1.5	2.5	2.6	3.0	3.4	2.3	2.6	3.7	3.8	4.2	4.4
Cyprus	3.9	3.8	3.9	4.0	2.6	2.5	2.1	2.1	5.3	4.9	4.8	4.7
Iceland	7.5	2.9	—	1.9	4.0	6.8	4.5	3.0	2.1	1.3	2.0	2.3
Memorandum												
Major advanced economies	2.3	2.8	2.2	2.5	2.3	2.3	1.7	2.0	6.0	5.6	5.5	5.5
Newly industrialized Asian economies	4.7	5.3	4.6	4.6	2.3	1.6	2.1	2.1	4.0	3.7	3.5	3.3

[1]Based on Eurostat's harmonized index of consumer prices.
[2]Consumer prices excluding interest rate components.

profitability gives corporates the scope to absorb these higher costs in their margins. Looking forward, with growth projected to remain below potential during the course of this year, inflation pressures are expected to moderate, but risks that inflation may be more persistent cannot be entirely discounted.

Against the background of weakening growth, the Federal Reserve called a halt to the monetary policy tightening cycle in August 2006, and has kept its target for the Federal funds rate unchanged at 5.25 percent. At present, after a string of weaker data, the Fed is expected by financial markets to ease rates by September. However, the Fed has appropriately kept its options open, stressing that the path of monetary policy will be determined by how the incoming data affect the perceived balance of risks between growth and inflation. If growth proves more resilient than expected, the labor market remains tight, and core inflation does not come down, expectations of monetary policy easing may not be realized.

The U.S. current account deficit is expected to narrow to close to 6 percent of GDP in 2007, about 1 percentage point of GDP less than at

Figure 2.2. United States: Developments in the Residential and Nonresidential Construction Sectors
(Percent change from a year ago, unless otherwise noted)

As the residential housing sector has slumped, investment in the nonresidential sector has boomed. Nevertheless, strong investment in nonresidential construction is unlikely to be sustained unless the housing market recovers.

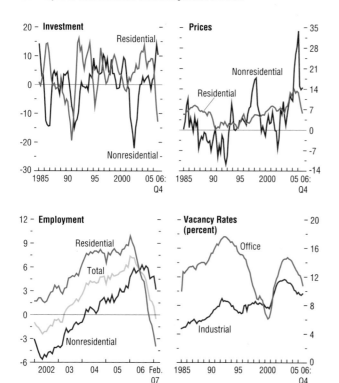

Sources: CB Richard Ellis; CEIC Data Company Limited; Haver Analytics; MIT Center for Real Estate; and IMF staff calculations.

the time of the September 2006 *World Economic Outlook,* but little further decline is anticipated over the medium term (Table 2.2). The trade deficit is set to improve, with exports benefiting from robust partner country growth and the depreciation of the dollar, but the investment income account is expected to deteriorate. Boosting national saving in the United States is an important element of the multilateral strategy to reduce global imbalances. Against this background, it is encouraging that recent fiscal performance has exceeded expectations. The federal government deficit declined to 1.9 percent of GDP in FY2006, largely because of buoyant revenues, and data for early FY2007 suggest that the strong fiscal performance is continuing. Looking to the medium term, the president has indicated that the FY2008 budget will seek to balance the federal budget by FY2012. This commitment is welcome, although a more ambitious target of aiming to achieve balance excluding the Social Security surplus would be preferable, while allowing automatic stabilizers to operate through the cycle. Policy implementation will also be critical. In particular, it will be difficult to achieve the desired adjustment based solely on additional expenditure restraint given the unprecedented compression of discretionary nondefense spending already assumed in the budget projections. Revenue measures therefore cannot be ruled out. Fiscal consolidation needs to be supported by reforms to put the Social Security, Medicare, and Medicaid systems on a sustainable long-term footing. The administration's proposal to apply "means testing" to Medicare benefits could lead to significant cost reductions over time, although broader reforms to control growth of health care costs are also likely to be needed.

While public saving has risen as fiscal consolidation has progressed, private saving out of current income, particularly by households, has continued to decline. Some increase in household saving is likely given the slowing housing market, while recent changes to pension legislation to allow "opt out" defined contribution schemes may over time also boost saving. Never-

Table 2.2. Advanced Economies: Current Account Positions

(Percent of GDP)

	2005	2006	2007	2008
Advanced economies	**–1.4**	**–1.6**	**–1.6**	**–1.6**
United States	–6.4	–6.5	–6.1	–6.0
Euro area[1]	0.1	–0.3	–0.3	–0.4
Germany	4.6	5.1	5.3	5.2
France	–1.6	–2.1	–2.2	–2.3
Italy	–1.6	–2.2	–2.2	–2.2
Spain	–7.4	–8.8	–9.4	–9.8
Netherlands	6.3	7.1	7.7	7.6
Belgium	2.5	2.5	2.4	2.5
Austria	1.2	1.8	1.9	1.6
Finland	4.9	5.3	5.1	5.2
Greece	–6.4	–9.6	–9.3	–8.7
Portugal	–9.7	–9.4	–9.1	–9.1
Ireland	–2.6	–4.1	–4.4	–3.0
Luxembourg	11.8	11.7	11.7	11.4
Slovenia	–2.0	–2.3	–2.6	–2.5
Japan	3.6	3.9	3.9	3.6
United Kingdom	–2.4	–2.9	–3.1	–3.1
Canada	2.3	1.7	0.7	0.6
Korea	1.9	0.7	0.3	—
Australia	–5.8	–5.4	–5.6	–5.5
Taiwan Province of China	4.6	7.1	7.1	7.1
Sweden	7.0	7.4	6.6	6.8
Switzerland	16.8	18.5	17.6	17.1
Hong Kong SAR	11.4	10.2	9.6	9.3
Denmark	3.6	2.0	1.7	1.9
Norway	15.5	16.7	14.9	15.9
Israel	2.9	5.2	3.6	4.3
Singapore	24.5	27.5	27.1	26.6
New Zealand	–9.0	–8.8	–8.4	–7.6
Cyprus	–5.6	–6.1	–5.2	–5.1
Iceland	–16.3	–26.3	–12.0	–11.5
Memorandum				
Major advanced economies	–2.2	–2.4	–2.3	–2.4
Euro area[2]	–0.1	–0.2	–0.3	–0.4
Newly industrialized Asian economies	5.6	5.6	5.3	5.1

[1]Calculated as the sum of the balances of individual euro area countries.

[2]Corrected for reporting discrepancies in intra-area transactions.

theless, more can be done to further strengthen the incentives for households to save, including through a greater reliance on consumption rather than on income taxes and increased transparency about possible future shortfalls in the Social Security system.

The Canadian economy has slowed, and the growth projection for 2007 has been revised down to 2.4 percent (0.5 percentage point lower than in the September 2006 *World Economic Outlook*). Domestic demand growth is expected to weaken as a result of earlier interest rate increases, although the negative contribution to growth from the external sector should ease during the course of the year as the U.S. economy rebounds and the effect of past currency appreciation dissipates. Risks to the outlook stem largely from the external sector, most notably a weaker-than-expected U.S. economy, a sharp decline in commodity prices, or a renewed appreciation of the Canadian dollar. With core CPI inflation expected to remain close to the center of the 1–3 percent target range, the Bank of Canada has kept policy interest rates on hold since May. Nevertheless, if downside risks to growth materialize, there is ample scope to cut interest rates to support activity. The recent budget has reaffirmed the government's commitment to fiscal prudence, although steps to curb increases in public health spending are also necessary to ensure long-term fiscal sustainability.

Western Europe: Can Recent Vigor Be Sustained?

Activity in western Europe gathered momentum in 2006. GDP growth in the euro area reached 2.6 percent, almost double its pace in 2005 and the highest rate since 2000. Germany was the principal locomotive, fueled by robust export growth and strong investment generated by the major improvement in competitiveness and corporate health in recent years, as well as the consumption boost from the World Cup and some spending in anticipation of the value-added tax (VAT) increase in early 2007. Growth in France and Italy was somewhat slower and more dependent on consumption, supported by a pickup in employment growth. Improved labor market performance was observed broadly across the region, and the unemployment rate in the euro area fell to 7.6 percent by the end of 2006, its lowest level in 15 years. Meanwhile, the expansion gained pace in the United Kingdom, driven by an acceleration of domestic demand, especially consumption, while investment and export performance remained solid.

Box 2.1. Housing Market Slowdowns

House price growth in the United States has slowed sharply since mid-2005. Yet, while residential investment has fallen, consumption has been little affected to date. This box seeks to understand these limited spillovers from the housing market in the context of international and U.S. experiences of previous housing market slowdowns.[1]

The two main components of expenditure linked directly with house prices are consumption and residential investment. The upper panel of the figure compares the largest and smallest declines in consumption, residential investment, and GDP across 48 episodes of real house price declines (for at least two consecutive quarters) in 13 OECD countries. It shows considerable variation across these episodes, with GDP growth on average declining by 1.5 percentage points in the lowest quartile, but actually increasing in the upper quartile. These variations can be examined by looking at what has happened to other aspects of these economies during the housing correction.

What other factors are likely to matter at a time when house prices are declining? The middle panel of the figure shows the change in the unemployment rate, the performance of equity markets, and an indicator of the stance of monetary policy, comparing occasions when relatively large and small changes in spending were experienced. The data suggest that the change in the unemployment rate is a key factor affecting the size of spillovers from a housing correction. This is because the labor market has a strong influence on household cash flows, income expectations, and thus vulnerability to distress arising from developments in the housing market.

Equity market performance, and financial wealth more generally, are also relevant factors. To the extent that households have a "buffer" of

Note: The main author of this box is Andrew Benito.

[1]See Chapter 2 of the April 2003 *World Economic Outlook* for an analysis of equity and housing market busts.

Housing Market Downturns

Cross-Country Housing Markets[1]
(change in average annual rate of growth)

■ Quartile of largest declines   ■ Quartile of smallest declines

Sources: Bank for International Settlements; Haver Analytics; and IMF staff calculations.
[1]The change in average annual rate of growth of consumption, residential investment, and GDP between the six quarters before and after the house price peak.
[2]Periods of falling house prices with the largest and smallest declines in GDP growth by quartile, for the six quarters before and after the peak. The average change in unemployment (percentage point), the average percent increase in real equity prices, and the change in short-term interest rate (percentage point) during the period of falling house prices.
[3]Median profile shows median response for a particular quarter across seven U.S. housing cycles (periods when real house prices fell) since 1969. Lower and upper quartile profiles are also shown.

financial assets at their disposal, their spending may respond more moderately to easing house prices. The figure illustrates that where households benefited from gains in equity wealth, spending was less prone to being cut back in the context of falling house prices.

Significant effects from house price falls on spending and GDP are likely to prompt a response from policymakers. The figure shows that, on average, short-term interest rates were reduced by a larger amount on those occasions when house prices were associated with larger falls in spending and activity.

Recent U.S Experience

The lower panel of the figure shows the recent profiles for U.S. consumption and residential investment compared with previous U.S. housing market slowdowns. Consistent with international experience, the panel shows that there has been a wide range of experience across housing cycles in the United States. The recent housing market downturn has seen a particularly sharp reduction in residential investment, but the impact so far on consumption has been quite mild, although previous housing market adjustments generally witnessed a delay of several quarters before consumption declined.

Consistent with the international evidence, the effect of the present U.S. house price correction on consumer spending and activity to date has been contained by other developments in the economy. In particular, the U.S. labor market has remained robust with continued gains in employment, especially in services, despite some softness in the construction and manufacturing sectors, while unemployment has declined to cyclical lows.

Growth in the euro area is projected to moderate to 2.3 percent in 2007 and 2008, still somewhat above potential. The mild deceleration would reflect both the effect of some monetary and fiscal tightening, and a lower external contribution to growth. So far, activity in early 2007 is being well sustained, although, as expected, consumption in Germany has cooled in the wake of the VAT increase. The U.K. economy is expected to continue growing robustly in 2007. Risks to the outlook seem evenly balanced, with domestic risks on the upside, given bullish confidence, rising house prices, improving employment and productivity, and record corporate profitability, but external risks are on the downside.

The drop in oil prices from August 2006 helped to bring headline CPI inflation in the euro area down to just below 2 percent by end-2006, while core inflation has risen recently, largely reflecting the VAT increase in Germany. Wage increases remain contained at low levels, despite labor market tightening. In the year ahead, inflation will be boosted by the German VAT increase, as well as continued tightening of spare capacity, but should remain close to 2 percent. With the area's growth projected to remain close to or above potential, and the possibility of some further upward pressure on factor utilization and prices, a further interest rate increase to 4 percent by the summer would seem warranted. Beyond this, additional policy action could still be required if growth momentum remains above trend and risks to wages and prices intensify. In the United Kingdom, buoyant demand and the ongoing pass-through of higher global energy prices to domestic utilities prices has pushed inflation to its highest level in five years. The combination of higher-than-targeted inflation and diminishing economic slack has prompted rate increases by the Bank of England, and inflation is expected to come down to the target by year-end. However, some further tightening may still be needed, particularly if wage pressures emerge.

The present expansion has provided a context for some progress toward needed fiscal consolidation, but concerns remain whether enough is being done. It is encouraging that the modi-

Figure 2.3. Western Europe: Productivity Is Failing to Catch Up
(Percent)

Growth in western European countries has fallen behind that of the United States over the past decade, as productivity performance has deteriorated.

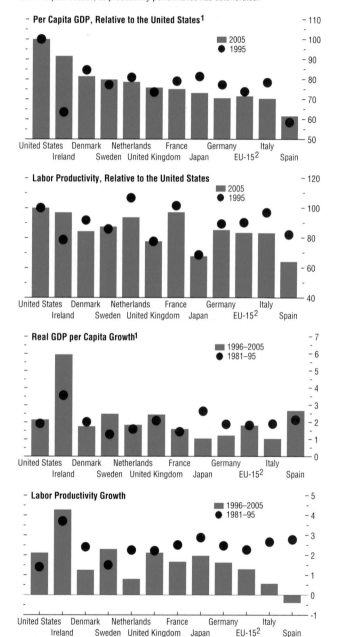

Sources: OECD, *Economic Outlook;* and IMF staff calculations.
[1]Gross domestic product at 2000 constant PPP.
[2]Austria, Belgium, Denmark, Finland, France, Germany, Greece, Ireland, Italy, Luxembourg, the Netherlands, Portugal, Spain, Sweden, and the United Kingdom.

fied Stability and Growth Pact has functioned smoothly as countries under the Excessive Deficit Procedures have lived with requirements, and almost all countries in the euro area have now lowered deficits to below 3 percent of GDP.[3] However, overall adjustment in 2006 and 2007 would still be quite slow at around ½ percent of GDP per year, largely accounted for by Germany and Italy, and rooted for the most part in buoyant revenue growth rather than tighter expenditure control. Thus, the overall ambition appears rather limited given the pace of the cyclical upturn and the looming long-term pressures from aging, with some countries distant from meeting their medium-term objectives. Against this background, some strengthening of fiscal frameworks could be helpful—to bolster national fiscal governance mechanisms and to give the preventative arm of the Stability and Growth Pact more teeth to encourage progress toward meeting the medium-term goals. In the United Kingdom, the fiscal deficit fell to 2½ percent of GDP in 2006, and tight spending control will be needed to halt the rise in public debt.

Does western Europe's strong recent economic performance portend a sustained improvement? At this point, it is too early to assess definitively to what extent the present expansion may have reflected improving underlying conditions as well as a cyclical upswing. Taking a longer perspective, after steady convergence for much of the postwar period, Europe's per capita GDP levels have fallen steadily behind those of the United States since 1995, with only a few smaller countries doing better (Figure 2.3). This widening of the income gap reflects much weaker performance in labor productivity, as productivity in Europe continued to slow broadly in line with postwar trends, while productivity in the United States accelerated. Europe has made progress in strengthening labor utilization; in fact it has reduced the differential with the United States on this front as unemployment rates have been progressively

[3]Italy's deficit was kept above 3 percent of GDP in 2006 by one-off VAT refunds and assumption of railroad debts.

lowered—but the gap with the United States nevertheless remains substantial, particularly in continental Europe (Figure 2.4). Moreover, looking ahead, aging European populations may make it harder to sustain this improvement in labor utilization, as a rising share of the population will be in upper age brackets.

A major factor behind Europe's lackluster productivity performance vis-à-vis the United States relates to the slower take-up of new technologies, particularly rapid advances in information and communications technology (ICT).[4] Recent studies by the European Central Bank (ECB) and the IMF staff find that Europe generally has smaller ICT-producing sectors, has invested less in ICT equipment, and experienced lower total factor productivity growth in ICT-using services sectors such as retail, wholesale, and finance, relative to the United States.[5] These findings underline the importance of product and labor market reforms aimed at reducing barriers to competition and innovation, and encouraging greater R&D spending. While some progress has been made in these areas, it will thus be important to accelerate implementation of the Services Directive, enhance competition in network industries, and strengthen financial integration. Commitments made under the Lisbon agenda provide a useful framework to integrate national-level plans and apply effective areawide peer pressure.

While progress has been made in improving labor utilization in Europe, further policy reforms are still needed to close the performance gap with the United States, address social concerns related to persistently high rates of unemployment, and help to offset the negative impact of population aging on the size of the labor force. To some degree, lower labor

---

[4]See Gomez-Salvador and others (2006); and Estevão (2004).

[5]Another factor may have been the pickup in labor utilization in western Europe over the past 10 years—implying a reduced rate of capital deepening and possibly a lower rate of improvement of labor quality. But this factor cannot help explain why European productivity lags the United States in absolute terms.

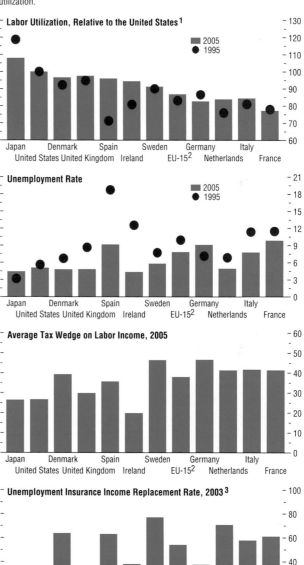

Figure 2.4. Western Europe: Need to Do More to Raise Labor Utilization
(Percent)

Labor utilization has improved in western Europe, as unemployment rates have declined, but continues to lag the United States. Countries that have a low tax wedge on labor income and tighter unemployment insurance generally have higher labor utilization.

Sources: OECD, *Economic Outlook;* OECD, Taxing Wages Database and Benefit Entitlements and Gross Replacement Rates Database; and IMF staff calculations.
[1]Labor utilization is defined as hours worked divided by population.
[2]Austria, Belgium, Denmark, Finland, France, Germany, Greece, Ireland, Italy, Luxembourg, the Netherlands, Portugal, Spain, Sweden, and the United Kingdom.
[3]Defined as the average first-year gross income replacement rate over the three different family types and two different income levels.

utilization might reflect a greater preference for leisure, but the much higher incidence of unemployment in Europe, more extensive limits on working hours, and heavy taxes on labor income all suggest that the outcome only partly reflects voluntary choices. Recent cross-country analysis by the OECD suggests that key factors that have discouraged labor utilization in western Europe include high tax wedges between employment costs and take-home pay and generous unemployment compensation schemes (see Bassanini and Duval, 2006).

Successful reformers within western Europe have taken a variety of approaches aimed at improving labor utilization (see Box 2.2). Under the so-called Anglo-Saxon model, the emphasis is on applying a low tax wedge to labor income, relatively low replacement rates to unemployed workers, and low degrees of employment protection to encourage efficient labor markets. Nordic countries have also achieved success with somewhat different policy mixes. Denmark's "flexicurity" system combines a flexible labor market—low degree of employment protection—with generous short-term income protection, but tight eligibility for longer-term benefits and extensive active labor market policies (ALMPs) to facilitate job search, while Sweden has placed greater weight on wage moderation in the context of centralized wage bargaining and a broad social compact. Recent experience has also underlined the importance of complementary product market reforms (to foster job creation) and expenditure-based fiscal consolidation (in part to provide room for reductions in labor taxation and spending on ALMPs). Countries with still-high rates of unemployment can learn from such successful examples in developing strategies consistent with national, social, and political contexts.

Industrial Asia: Japan's Expansion Remains on Track

Japan's economic expansion hit a soft patch in the middle of 2006, mainly reflecting an unexpected decline in consumption, but growth rebounded strongly in the fourth quarter. The economy's underlying momentum remains robust, with private investment expanding—supported by strong profits, improved corporate balance sheets, and the resumption of bank lending—and rising export growth. Real GDP for 2006 as a whole expanded somewhat above potential at 2.2 percent.

Near-term prospects depend crucially on whether the rebound in consumer spending in the fourth quarter is sustained. In this context, underlying fundamentals appear to be favorable (Figure 2.5). While the rate of growth of regular monthly wages has been sluggish over the past year, the increase in employment—in particular, the hiring of more full-time workers—and bonuses has contributed to a steady growth in overall employee compensation that has yet to be fully reflected in aggregate consumption. As firms continue to expand capacity and add workers, unemployment has declined to nine-year lows and the ratio of job offers to applicants has risen to the highest level since 1992. In the context of the structural upturn in the business sector following years of restructuring and limited labor demand, this tightening of the labor market is likely to be increasingly reflected in rising real wages, providing further support for household spending.

Reflecting the above considerations, real GDP growth in Japan is expected to be broadly maintained at around 2¼ percent during 2007. A recovery in consumption is expected to largely offset some cooling of exports in view of the anticipated moderation in global growth. Risks to the outlook appear broadly balanced. On the upside, the strength of business sector indicators could translate into stronger-than-anticipated investment and hiring, and a further decrease in oil prices could boost consumption through its positive impact on disposable incomes. On the downside, the underlying strength of consumer spending remains uncertain, while a sharper-than-expected slowing in the United States could weaken net exports.

Supported by strong export growth and income from foreign assets, Japan's current account surplus rose to close to 4 percent of GDP in 2006, yet the value of the yen has fallen to near 20-year lows in real effective terms. Against the background of structural shifts that support capital outflows (including a reduced "home bias" among domestic investors), an important factor underlying the weakening of the yen over the past year has been the widening interest rate differential between the yen and other key currencies and the exceptionally low volatility in foreign exchange markets. Taken together, these factors have further increased the yen's attractiveness as a funding currency for investments in other mature market currencies and within emerging Asia. While the scale of such outflows is difficult to measure, recent data suggest that the volume of such carry trades has grown. As a result, changes in the bilateral spread between yen and U.S. dollar interest rates in particular have become an increasingly important driver of the yen–U.S. dollar bilateral exchange rate. The outlook for interest rates among the major countries is therefore expected to continue to be an important determinant of exchange rate movements going forward.

The likely trajectory for interest rates in Japan is, in turn, closely tied to the outlook. With inflation still close to zero, the Bank of Japan has appropriately taken a cautious approach to raising interest rates since exiting its zero interest rate policy in July 2006, with its policy rate now standing at around ½ percent. Going forward, while interest rates will eventually have to be raised to more neutral levels, monetary accommodation should be removed only at a gradual pace and on the basis of information on the continuing strength of the expansion. The transition to a more neutral monetary stance could be supported by greater clarity regarding the Bank of Japan's medium-term inflationary goals, which would facilitate a smooth adjustment of private sector interest rate expectations. In turn, this would allow investors to unwind carry trades without sharp movements in bilateral exchange rates or abrupt shifts in the volume of

Figure 2.5. Japan: Understanding Developments in Domestic Demand

Employee compensation tends to rise during investment upturns. Rising corporate profits and tightening labor market conditions suggest that the recent softening of consumption may be temporary.

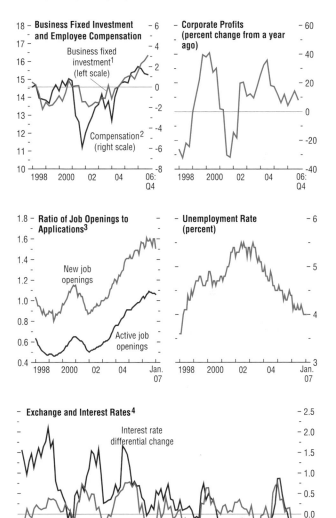

Sources: Bloomberg Financial Markets, LP; Haver Analytics; and IMF staff calculations.
[1]Measured as percent of GDP.
[2]Measured as percent change from a year earlier.
[3]Measured as ratio of new job openings to new applications and ratio of active job openings to active applications.
[4]Measured as change in eight-week moving average of yen/dollar exchange rate and change in interest rate differential of yen versus dollar one-year deposits.

Box 2.2. Lessons from Successful European Labor Market Reformers

From the early 1980s, unemployment rose precipitously in many European countries. In some cases, it remains high to this day. Other countries, however, have witnessed a remarkable turnaround, experiencing dramatic declines in unemployment rates, and corresponding steep increases in employment rates. A recent study by Annett (forthcoming) looks at the behavior of four countries—Denmark, Ireland, the Netherlands, and the United Kingdom—that stand out in terms of successful labor market performance over this period. In Europe today, these countries enjoy four of the five lowest unemployment rates, and they have also achieved the greatest reduction over two decades. Their employment gains have been equally impressive.

While the reform experiences differed across the countries, what they have in common is that they all adopted policy packages geared toward improving labor market performance in a manner that was both internally consistent and consistent over time. The outcome in all cases was *wage moderation*, in the sense of an increase in available labor supply at a given compensation rate. In a more technical sense, wage moderation corresponds to an outward shift in the labor supply (or wage) curve—more supply at a given wage, where the wage is defined as the productivity- and cyclically-adjusted real hourly compensation rate. Many factors can lead to outward shifts in the wage curve, including (1) changes in the attitudes of unions and workers, placing a greater emphasis on employment; (2) falling labor taxation, allowing workers to accept lower gross wages for the same net wage; (3) unemployment benefit reform that reduces the reservation wage (that is, the minimum at which a person would accept a new job rather than remaining unemployed and continuing a job search); and (4) reducing government employment or government wages, also reducing the reservation wage, given that government employment is an alternative to private employment. Looking across a two-decade horizon,

Note: The main author of this box is Anthony Annett.

Ireland, the Netherlands, and the United Kingdom are among the EU countries that have exhibited the biggest shifts in labor supply. Denmark's reform period came slightly later, in the mid-1990s.

In Ireland and the Netherlands, wage moderation was abetted by coordinated agreements between social partners, under which unions agreed to curb their wage claims in return for labor tax cuts. This marked a distinct structural shift in unions' approach to wage bargaining. In contrast, the United Kingdom initially relied on a less consensual approach. Again, labor tax reductions were part of the strategy. Overall, the tax wedge on labor declined markedly in these countries over the course of two decades (see the figure).

The countries in question also engaged in some form of benefit reform, reducing the level of unemployment benefits or their duration, or strengthening eligibility requirements. Reforms led to less generous benefits in the United Kingdom and the Netherlands in particular (the latter focused on sickness and disability as well as unemployment), while in Ireland, benefits failed to keep pace with after-pay income. Denmark and the Netherlands also cut the maximum duration of unemployment benefits, while three of the four countries (excluding Ireland) tightened up eligibility requirements. Much as Ireland and the Netherlands traded moderation in wage growth for tax cuts, Denmark maintained high benefit levels while tightening duration and eligibility conditions—the unemployed were required to take part in Active Labor Market Programs, and requirements on this front became progressively tougher over time. By granting this kind of "buy in" to workers and other interests, policymakers maintained broad support for the reform agenda.

One common factor was that the successful cases generally pursued government expenditure reduction in tandem with labor tax cuts. Indeed, fiscal and structural adjustment were reinforcing, as periods of extensive fiscal consolidation coincided with labor supply shifts. The four countries in question undertook substantial

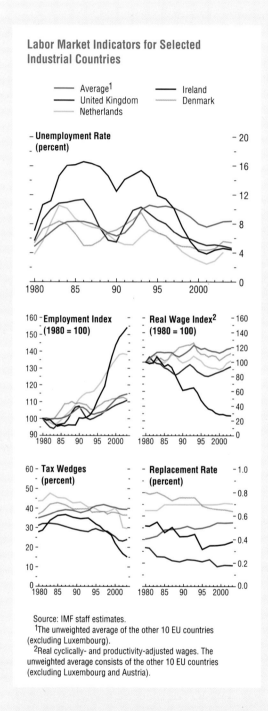

Labor Market Indicators for Selected Industrial Countries

Average[1]
Ireland
United Kingdom
Denmark
Netherlands

Source: IMF staff estimates.
[1]The unweighted average of the other 10 EU countries (excluding Luxembourg).
[2]Real cyclically- and productivity-adjusted wages. The unweighted average consists of the other 10 EU countries (excluding Luxembourg and Austria).

transfers, as well as cutting labor taxes, encouraged unions to accept lower wages, which in turn led to higher profitability, employment, and growth.

Another common factor was that these countries placed a premium on flexible labor and product markets. Unlike many of their European counterparts, they did not attempt to shield workers with stringent employment protection legislation, and product markets were relatively deregulated. Denmark's much-touted "flexicurity" model insures workers against income loss, not job loss.

Annett (forthcoming) supports this analysis with an econometric study. Two simple equations are estimated: the first relates real wages to fiscal influences and the second relates nongovernment employment to wages and underlying product and labor market rigidity. A simple panel model is estimated in first differences for 14 countries between 1980–2003, incorporating country fixed effects and year dummies. The basic findings are that fiscal adjustment and labor supply improvements are intimately entwined, and wage behavior is affected by social expenditure, government wages, and tax wedges. Interestingly, the feedback from wage moderation to employment growth depends on the degree of product and labor market regulation, with flexibility prompting greater employment gains.

These results are consistent with other recent studies. Although the empirical literature on the institutional determinants on employment and unemployment is enormous, recent work—encapsulated in an OECD study by Bassanini and Duval (2006)—suggests that most of the change in structural unemployment over the past two decades can be explained by factors such as high and long-lasting unemployment benefits, high tax wedges, and stringent product market regulation. At the same time, they also note the importance of a package of complementary reforms rather than piecemeal initiatives.

Overall, these results show that a mixture of labor supply, product market, and fiscal reforms

adjustment during various periods over the past two decades, and three of the four (excluding Denmark) reduced the size of government substantially. Reducing both government wages and

Box 2.2 *(concluded)*

that complement and reinforce each other, and that are consistent over time, can be successful in encouraging wage moderation and improving employment outcomes. Also, workers can be cushioned from the impact of reforms by reducing labor taxes or by providing generous benefits subject to strict eligibility conditions and short duration.

This experience offers clear lessons for other countries. However, the reform path in each country will ultimately depend on its own underlying institutions and circumstances. Zhou (2006), for example, shows how the Danish model may not easily transfer to other countries, in part because of the significant fiscal expenditures involved.

capital flows into emerging Asia's local currency markets.

The cyclical recovery of revenues supported a further narrowing in the fiscal deficit (excluding social security) by about 0.8 percentage point of GDP to 4.3 percent of GDP in 2006. The government's budget envisages a reduction in the primary balance by about 1 percent of GDP in FY2007. While consolidation appears to be running ahead of the government's plan to achieve a primary surplus for the central and local government by FY2011, gross and net public debt ratios continue to rise from their already-high levels (185 and 96 percent of GDP, respectively). Consequently, additional fiscal efforts beyond those contained in the current medium-term plan will be required to put the debt-to-GDP ratio on a declining trajectory. With limited room for further cuts in expenditures, future fiscal reforms will therefore need to focus on revenue measures. Consideration should be given to raising the consumption tax rate and measures to broaden the income tax base. Japan also faces important challenges in the context of a rapidly aging population, underscoring the importance of supply-side structural reforms to raise the level of potential growth. Measures to boost flexibility and productivity in the nontradables sector are of particular importance.

In Australia and New Zealand, real GDP growth weakened slightly in 2006, reflecting slower domestic demand and the impact of a severe drought in Australia. Growth is expected

to pick up during 2007–08. If inflation does not decline as expected, central banks may still need to tighten monetary policy further.

Emerging Asia: How Resilient Is the Region to a U.S. Slowdown?

Activity in emerging Asia continues to expand at a brisk pace, led by very strong growth in both China and India (Table 2.3). In China, real GDP expanded by 10.7 percent in 2006 on the strength of solid investment and export growth, although the pace of fixed asset investment cooled in the second half of the year in response to monetary policy tightening. Box 2.3 looks at the issue of whether very high levels of investment in China are efficiently allocated. In India, real GDP growth of 9.2 percent was supported by the strength of consumption, investment, and exports. The resilience of external demand, particularly in the electronics sector, has supported overall economic activity in the newly industrialized economies (NIEs), including Korea, where growth accelerated. Performance among the ASEAN-4 economies has varied. The pace of activity in Malaysia and Thailand has picked up. In Indonesia, domestic demand has begun to strengthen in response to interest rate cuts. In the Philippines, typhoon-related damage to agriculture led to temporarily weaker growth in the fourth quarter of 2006, but the economy's underlying momentum remains strong.

One question in assessing growth prospects for the region is how a sharper-than-expected

Table 2.3. Selected Asian Countries: Real GDP, Consumer Prices, and Current Account Balance
(Annual percent change unless noted otherwise)

	Real GDP				Consumer Prices[1]				Current Account Balance[2]			
	2005	2006	2007	2008	2005	2006	2007	2008	2005	2006	2007	2008
Emerging Asia[3]	**8.7**	**8.9**	**8.4**	**8.0**	**3.5**	**3.7**	**3.7**	**3.2**	**4.5**	**5.4**	**5.7**	**5.9**
China	10.4	10.7	10.0	9.5	1.8	1.5	2.2	2.3	7.2	9.1	10.0	10.5
South Asia[4]	**8.7**	**8.7**	**8.1**	**7.5**	**5.0**	**6.4**	**6.4**	**4.6**	**−0.9**	**−2.2**	**−2.5**	**−2.4**
India	9.2	9.2	8.4	7.8	4.2	6.1	6.2	4.3	−0.9	−2.2	−2.4	−2.3
Pakistan	8.0	6.2	6.5	6.5	9.3	7.9	6.5	6.0	−1.4	−3.9	−4.0	−3.6
Bangladesh	6.3	6.7	6.6	6.5	7.0	6.3	6.4	5.4	−0.3	0.9	0.7	—
ASEAN-4	**5.2**	**5.4**	**5.5**	**5.8**	**7.3**	**8.2**	**4.3**	**4.0**	**2.1**	**4.8**	**4.2**	**3.5**
Indonesia	5.7	5.5	6.0	6.3	10.5	13.1	6.3	5.3	0.1	2.7	1.8	1.3
Thailand	4.5	5.0	4.5	4.8	4.5	4.6	2.5	2.5	−4.5	1.6	1.5	0.9
Philippines	5.0	5.4	5.8	5.8	7.6	6.2	4.0	4.0	2.0	2.9	2.1	1.9
Malaysia	5.2	5.9	5.5	5.8	3.0	3.6	2.6	2.5	15.2	15.8	15.3	14.3
Newly industrialized Asian economies	**4.7**	**5.3**	**4.6**	**4.6**	**2.3**	**1.6**	**2.1**	**2.1**	**5.6**	**5.6**	**5.3**	**5.1**
Korea	4.2	5.0	4.4	4.4	2.8	2.2	2.5	2.5	1.9	0.7	0.3	—
Taiwan Province of China	4.0	4.6	4.2	4.3	2.3	0.6	1.5	1.5	4.6	7.1	7.1	7.1
Hong Kong SAR	7.5	6.8	5.5	5.0	0.9	2.0	2.1	2.3	11.4	10.2	9.6	9.3
Singapore	6.6	7.9	5.5	5.7	0.5	1.0	1.5	1.5	24.5	27.5	27.1	26.6

[1]In accordance with standard practice in the *World Economic Outlook*, movements in consumer prices are indicated as annual averages rather than as December/December changes, as is the practice in some countries.
[2]Percent of GDP.
[3]Consists of developing Asia, the newly industrialized Asian economies, and Mongolia.
[4]The country composition of this regional group is set out in Table F in the Statistical Appendix.

slowdown in the United States would affect the region. As Chapter 4 underscores, while demand for Asian exports would be affected, several factors suggest that the overall impact is likely to be relatively well contained:

- At this stage, the U.S. slowdown is being driven by the housing sector, with its effects on overall demand for exports from Asia likely to be muted. In contrast, the global demand for electronic goods, which is important for regional exports, particularly among the NIEs and the ASEAN-4 economies, has remained generally well supported despite some moderation toward late 2006.

- The importance of the United States as a destination for exports has been declining in most countries—with the important exception of China—and the role of intraregional trade has been rising (Figure 2.6).

- With the decline in inflationary pressures, there is room for countercyclical monetary policy in several countries. Fiscal policy could also play a role in cushioning a downturn in external demand in some countries, although

in others, such as India, fiscal consolidation remains an important priority.

Against this background, the near-term outlook for growth in the region remains very positive. Real GDP growth is expected to ease this year and next, but remain at a high level. This reflects some moderation in growth in China and India in response to policy tightening and slower growth among the NIEs as global demand for exports softens. A pickup in activity, however, is expected in the ASEAN-4 economies as the effects of earlier monetary tightening fade. Risks on the upside include the possibility that the slowdown projected in China may not materialize if the effect of monetary tightening on investment proves temporary, while in India, the manufacturing sector and investment could gather added momentum in the near term. On the downside, a sharper-than-anticipated slowdown in the demand for Asian exports in general, and electronic goods in particular, could undercut growth. Financial markets in the region, especially those that appear richly valued, also remain vulnerable to

Figure 2.6. Emerging Asia: Assessing the Resilience to a Global Slowdown

Regional economies have less direct exposure to the United States than at the beginning of the decade, while their exposure to China has grown. Monetary and, in some cases, fiscal policy are also cyclically well positioned to respond to a slowdown in the demand for exports.

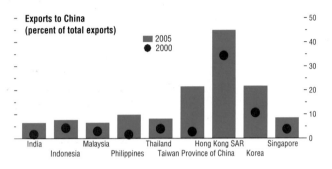

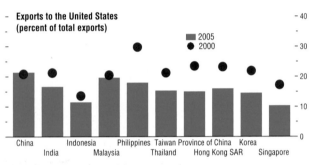

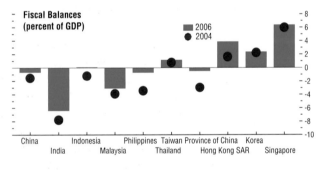

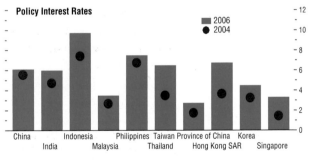

Sources: Haver Analytics; IMF, *International Financial Statistics;* and IMF staff calculations.

any unanticipated rise in global risk aversion. A related risk arises from the inflows into many regional markets stemming from the yen carry trade. These could unwind rapidly if investors were to revise their expectations of bilateral exchange rates and interest rate differentials, particularly in the context of rising volatility in foreign exchange markets. Encouragingly, the recent rise in market volatility in Thailand after the imposition of controls on capital inflows has not spread elsewhere. Avian flu also continues to pose a risk though its impact is more difficult to quantify.

Inflationary pressures across the region remain generally well contained, with monetary tightening—and currency appreciation in some countries—having limited the second round impact of the increase in oil prices last year, although rapid credit growth poses a challenge in a number of countries. In China, the People's Bank of China has responded to the rise in domestic liquidity and rapid investment growth by raising deposit and lending rates, strengthening liquidity management, and raising the reserve requirement ratio. Although investment has moderated in recent months, it remains high, and additional monetary tightening may well be needed. In India, upward inflationary pressures and rapid credit growth have prompted the Reserve Bank of India to raise policy rates and the cash reserve requirement for banks. With inflationary pressures still strong, some further tightening is likely to be needed.

The region's current account surplus rose almost a full percentage point (to 5.4 percent of GDP) in 2006, despite the rise in oil prices, underpinned by the strong growth of exports, particularly in China and among the ASEAN-4 countries. India's current account deficit widened in response to rising imports, reflecting the strength in domestic demand and the impact of higher oil prices. Looking ahead, the region's current account surplus is expected to continue to widen, but at a slower pace than has been evident in recent years, with China accounting for a substantial part of the rise. In this context, there have been some

Box 2.3. Is China Investing Too Much?

The breakneck growth rate of the Chinese economy is in large part driven by capital accumulation (and exports). The country's investment-to-GDP ratio has been high and rising in recent years, exceeding 40 percent of GDP in 2005. One concern is that some of the investment, especially that by state-owned enterprises (SOEs), may not be efficient. In other words, the same output could be achieved with less capital, thus freeing resources for other uses. Improved efficiency would result in higher profitability for the corporate sector and safeguard the balance sheet of the banks that fund the firms.

There are various reasons why SOEs may be less efficient than domestic private firms. They may face more administrative interference in terms of restrictions on hiring and laying off workers and on switching product lines in response to changing market conditions. Further, they often do not have compensation schemes that encourage management to maximize economic efficiency and deter overinvestment and "empire building," notwithstanding some progress made with SOE reforms over the years that attempt to link executive pay with performance. In addition, some SOEs also have weak corporate governance that may provide opportunities for management to divert assets for their own benefit.

The Chinese financial system, which is dominated by majority or wholly state-owned banks, may favor SOEs despite steady effort by the authorities to increase the commercial orientation of these banks. While SOEs represent a declining share of output, down to about a third in 2005, their borrowing from domestic banks accounts for more than half of the total lending by these banks (first figure). Majority state-owned firms also take up the lion's share of all publicly traded companies in China's two stock exchanges. Some of the bias may be related to the tendency for private firms to be smaller in

Note: The main author of this box is Shang-Jin Wei. The box draws on a joint research paper with David Dollar.

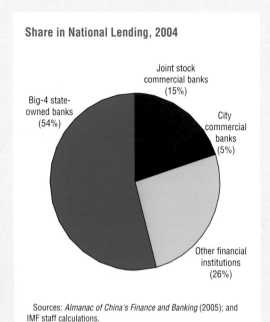

Share in National Lending, 2004

- Joint stock commercial banks (15%)
- City commercial banks (5%)
- Other financial institutions (26%)
- Big-4 state-owned banks (54%)

Sources: *Almanac of China's Finance and Banking* (2005); and IMF staff calculations.

size and take on higher risk. But it is common to hear private firms complaining about the difficulty they face in securing funding for both short-term working capital and long-term investment needs even when they have comparable size and risk profiles as their state-owned peers.

At present, approximately half of China's investment is financed out of the corporate sector's retained earnings. The reliance on bank lending by SOEs is correspondingly lower than would otherwise be the case. The high level of retained earnings in SOEs may reflect incentives for managers to increase firm size rather than to give the extra profit to the state in the form of dividends.

Research Questions

Against this background, a number of questions present themselves. Is there a significant gap in the returns to capital across firms of different ownership or firms in different locations? Has China succeeded in removing the bias in its financial sector in favor of SOEs after nearly three decades of economic reforms? What

Box 2.3 *(concluded)*

are the potential gains that could result from removing investment inefficiencies?

A new research paper by a pair of IMF and World Bank researchers investigates these questions using a data set derived from a survey carried out in 2005 covering 12,400 firms in 120 cities located all across China (Wei and Dollar, 2007).

For every firm in a given sector and location, the study computes the marginal revenue product of capital (MRPK) as value added minus payments to labor, divided by the stock of capital. Firm-level MRPK is then regressed on a set of indicator variables representing sector-time pairs and locations as well as a set of indicator variables representing firm ownership. The sector-year indicators capture the possibility that demand or supply shocks in a given sector/year could cause MRPKs in a particular sector-year to be different from others. The ownership indicators measure the MRPKs of various ownership groups relative to domestic private firms. These ownership groups are defined in a way that is mutually exclusive: wholly state-owned, majority state-owned, minority state-owned, wholly foreign-owned, majority foreign-owned (with no state shares), minority foreign-owned (with no state shares), and collectively owned.

Conceptually, managers would equate a firm's MRPK to the sum of the market interest rate, depreciation rate, and distortions in the capital market that the firm faces. If capital is efficiently allocated, then the MRPKs should be equalized across all firms, regardless of sector, location, or ownership. The difference in the MRPKs between two firms in the same sector reflects mostly the difference in the cost of capital. For example, if SOEs receive more favored treatment than domestic private firms in borrowing from banks or in obtaining government approvals to be listed in the domestic stock market, then the MRPKs for SOEs would tend to be lower than those of private firms on average. Using this framework, the study assesses three types of inefficiency, or biases, in capital allocation: at the level of ownership, location, and sector, respectively.

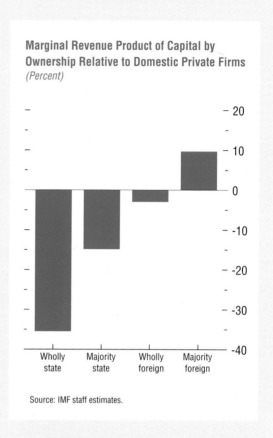

Marginal Revenue Product of Capital by Ownership Relative to Domestic Private Firms
(Percent)

Source: IMF staff estimates.

A number of interesting findings emerge. First, and most important, wholly and majority state-owned firms are found to have lower marginal returns to capital than private or foreign firms. The median MRPK for private firms is 63 percent. In contrast, the median values for wholly and majority state-owned firms are 37 percent and 52 percent, respectively. These numbers all appear large because they are computed before tax and depreciation, and reflect all other distortions to the cost of capital. The key point is that the returns to capital are not equalized across ownership types, and SOEs have substantially lower returns than private firms.

Differences in raw returns across ownership type could reflect that SOEs happen to be overrepresented in sectors or locations that have lower returns owing to temporary factors that are not related to ownership per se. To prevent this possibility from contaminating the interpretation of the results, the research uses a statistical framework that compares firms of different ownership in the same sector and same region. With these corrections, the results still suggest that private firms make substantially higher returns—on the order of 11–54 percentage points, depending on the specifications—than their state-owned counterparts (see second figure).

Second, there is a significant locational bias in returns to capital. Western provinces, specifically the Yantze River Delta region (Shanghai, Jiangsu, and Zhejiang) and Bohai Circle (encompassing Beijing and Tianjin), have higher returns to capital than northwest and southwest regions. Third, there is also an allocative bias at the sector level, though not as economically and statistically significant as the other biases.

Policy Implications

To appreciate the aggregate cost of the inefficient financial allocation, the following thought experiment could be conducted. Consider a transfer of X percent of capital currently employed by the state sector to the private firms, but leave the allocation of labor (and other inputs) fixed. The amount of capital to be transferred is chosen in such a way that

the MRPKs are equalized across ownership after the change. How much capital should be transferred? How much gain in aggregate value added could be achieved by the change? The answers depend on the estimated current gap in the MRPKs, the form of the production function, and some other parameters. In the benchmark case reported in Wei and Dollar (2007), under an efficient allocation, two-thirds of the capital currently employed by SOEs would be transferred to the private sector, which would raise GDP by 5 percent. Alternatively, with a more efficient use of capital, the country could reduce its very high investment rate substantially with no adverse effect on its growth rate. Such an improvement in investment efficiency could lead to a faster rise in household consumption and living standards.

There are a number of ways to improve the efficiency of capital usage. Besides curbing the amount of investment in the less efficient SOEs, efficiency could be raised through further reforms of the incentives for the managers of SOEs, including privatization, so that they will behave in a manner similar to their counterparts in profit-maximizing private firms. Moreover, financial sector reforms can also foster an improved allocation of capital.

---

concerns about differing degrees of exchange rate flexibility across the region. While a number of regional exchange rates have appreciated (notably the Korean won and Thai baht), in others there has been little change or even, as in China, a slight depreciation in real effective terms. A more decisive appreciation of the renminbi, in particular, would reduce competitiveness concerns from upward exchange rate movements in other countries, given increasing regional trade interdependence.

Strong private capital inflows in 2006 have complicated macroeconomic management in a few countries in the region, as net inflows remain close to historical levels. In Korea, for example, capital inflows have boosted liquidity

and put upward pressure on the won. Countries have generally responded to these inflows through a combination of a buildup in reserves while allowing some appreciation of exchange rates, and in some cases a faster liberalization of capital outflows. In Thailand, the across-the-board imposition of unremunerated reserve requirements on inflows in December 2006 led to a sharp drop in investor confidence, and subsequently the measures were partly reversed. Going forward, faster liberalization of outflows, including removal of restrictions on foreign investments by domestic financial institutions, and modest cuts in interest rates could help to alleviate the pressure from inflows while reducing distortions in resource allocation.

Table 2.4. Selected Western Hemisphere Countries: Real GDP, Consumer Prices, and Current Account Balance
(Annual percent change unless noted otherwise)

	Real GDP				Consumer Prices[1]				Current Account Balance[2]			
	2005	2006	2007	2008	2005	2006	2007	2008	2005	2006	2007	2008
Western Hemisphere	**4.6**	**5.5**	**4.9**	**4.2**	**6.3**	**5.4**	**5.2**	**5.7**	**1.4**	**1.7**	**0.5**	**−0.2**
South America and Mexico[3]	**4.5**	**5.4**	**4.8**	**4.2**	**6.2**	**5.2**	**5.2**	**5.7**	**1.7**	**1.9**	**0.6**	**—**
Argentina	9.2	8.5	7.5	5.5	9.6	10.9	10.3	12.7	1.9	2.4	1.2	0.4
Brazil	2.9	3.7	4.4	4.2	6.9	4.2	3.5	4.1	1.6	1.3	0.8	0.3
Chile	5.7	4.0	5.2	5.1	3.1	3.4	2.5	3.0	0.6	3.8	2.7	−0.2
Colombia	5.3	6.8	5.5	4.5	5.0	4.3	4.2	3.7	−1.6	−2.2	−2.3	−3.3
Ecuador	4.7	4.2	2.7	2.9	2.1	3.3	2.8	3.0	1.7	4.5	0.4	0.7
Mexico	2.8	4.8	3.4	3.5	4.0	3.6	3.9	3.5	−0.6	−0.2	−1.0	−1.4
Peru	6.4	8.0	6.0	5.5	1.6	2.0	1.0	2.0	1.3	2.6	0.7	0.4
Uruguay	6.6	7.0	5.0	3.5	4.7	6.4	6.0	5.0	—	−2.4	−3.3	−2.3
Venezuela	10.3	10.3	6.2	2.0	15.9	13.6	21.6	25.7	17.8	15.0	7.0	6.2
Central America[4]	**4.3**	**5.7**	**5.0**	**4.6**	**8.4**	**7.0**	**5.8**	**5.3**	**−4.8**	**−4.8**	**−5.0**	**−5.2**
The Caribbean[4]	**6.5**	**8.3**	**5.4**	**4.2**	**6.7**	**8.0**	**5.7**	**5.4**	**—**	**2.1**	**1.7**	**−0.3**

[1]In accordance with standard practice in the *World Economic Outlook*, movements in consumer prices are indicated as annual averages rather than as December/December changes, as is the practice in some countries. The December/December changes in the CPI for 2005, 2006, 2007, and 2008 are, respectively, for Brazil (5.7, 3.1, 3.9, and 4.3); Mexico (3.3, 4.1, 3.7 and 3.3); Peru (1.5, 1.1, 2.0, and 2.0); and Uruguay (4.9, 6.4, 6.0, and 5.0).
[2]Percent of GDP.
[3]Includes Bolivia and Paraguay.
[4]The country composition of this regional group is set out in Table F in the Statistical Appendix.

Fiscal balances are expected to continue to strengthen in most countries in the region in 2007. Nevertheless, policy priorities differ across countries. Securing sustainable fiscal positions and reducing the vulnerabilities associated with high public debt and budget deficits remain key in India, Pakistan, and the Philippines (notwithstanding substantial progress in reducing debt over the last few years in the latter two). In India, rising revenues are expected to lead to a more than 1 percent of GDP decline in the deficit (to 6.3 percent of GDP) in FY2007, but with a public debt ratio of 80 percent of GDP, further consolidation remains a priority. Comprehensive spending and revenue reforms, including removal of exemptions to corporate income taxes and excise duties and the elimination of nonessential subsidies, could help achieve consolidation goals while creating space for priority spending. In other countries, fiscal policy has more flexibility to respond to external economic developments. In China, the planned increase in spending on social services, including health care, education, and pensions, would contribute to reducing the precautionary demand for savings and increase the dynamism of consumption.

Latin America: Boosting Productivity Is the Key to Sustaining Growth

Economic growth in Latin America is projected to ease to 4.9 percent this year from 5.5 percent in 2006 (Table 2.4). This slowdown is expected to be relatively broad-based—Brazil and Chile are exceptions—although growth in Argentina is still projected at 7.5 percent. The external environment is expected to become somewhat less favorable as global growth moderates and oil and metals prices decline from the record levels of 2006. Countries and regions that have particularly close trade links with the United States (such as Mexico, Central America, and the Caribbean) or are significant exporters of oil and metals (Chile, Ecuador, Peru, and Venezuela) will be most affected. On the other hand, lower oil prices will benefit countries that are not significant exporters of commodities (including many in Central America and the Caribbean). Further, the strength of grain prices will help exporters of agricultural products such as Argentina and Brazil.

Differences in monetary policy across countries will also be an important driver of growth. In Chile, Colombia, and Peru, the central banks appropriately raised interest rates during 2006 to contain inflationary pressures (although the policy rate was cut by 25 basis points in Chile in January). Nevertheless, despite slower domestic demand, growth is still expected to rebound in Chile this year as exports recover from supply disruptions in the mining sector. However, monetary policy in Brazil has been eased substantially over the past 18 months, and with inflation well contained, there would appear scope for this easing cycle to continue. Together with recently announced initiatives to raise investment, lower interest rates should boost domestic demand, and recent data suggest that a pickup in activity is already under way. In Argentina, growth is expected to remain strong. Active sterilization by the central bank has allowed for a moderation in the growth of the targeted monetary aggregate, although short-term interest rates remain negative in real terms and fiscal policy is adding to demand pressures.

Risks to the outlook at this stage are slanted to the downside. As discussed in Chapter 4, a sharper-than-expected slowing in the United States would hit Latin America harder than other regions. A more pronounced decline in commodity prices or tighter financing conditions in international markets would also adversely affect growth prospects. Policy slippages that undermine investor confidence are another concern, particularly against the backdrop of pressures for populist fiscal measures in some countries. In Ecuador, concerns about a possible external debt restructuring saw spreads on external debt widen sharply earlier this year, although they have narrowed more recently.

Taking a longer-term perspective, 2004–06 was the strongest three-year period of growth in Latin America since the late 1970s, although growth still lagged that in other emerging market and developing country regions. The critical challenge for policymakers is to build on the

reforms that have so far been implemented to accelerate growth further, entrench macroeconomic stability, and ensure that the benefits of growth are widely distributed. Efforts to boost growth, promote stability, and achieve better social outcomes are mutually reinforcing. Improving the distribution of income is not only essential from a social perspective but is also needed to ensure broad support for economic reforms and to help sustain growth momentum.[6] And reforms that boost potential output growth make it easier to reduce public debt and maintain low inflation, contributing to greater stability and investor confidence, which in turn will have a reinforcing impact on growth.

Considerable progress has been made in strengthening macroeconomic policy frameworks in many Latin American countries and this has helped reduce vulnerabilities. The inflation targeting frameworks introduced in a number of countries are proving useful monetary policy anchors and, outside of Venezuela, inflation outcomes have been generally favorable. In Argentina, inflation declined during 2006, but the authorities continue to rely on administrative measures to keep a lid on price pressures. Important progress has been made across the region in strengthening fiscal positions, reducing public debt, and improving the structure of this debt. And the regional current account has been in surplus for four years and comfortable reserve cushions have been established. Together with more flexible exchange rates, the region should be more resilient against adverse developments than it was in the past.

Yet, the period ahead will be challenging, and difficult policy decisions will need to be made. In particular, lower commodity prices will put pressure on current account and fiscal balances and make it more difficult to meet growing calls for increased social spending within a responsible overall budgetary envelope. In this environ-

[6]Berg, Ostry, and Zettelmeyer (2006) show that a more equal distribution of income is an important factor that increases the duration of periods of strong growth.

Figure 2.7. Latin America: Productivity Is Lagging

Despite the recent pickup, growth in Latin America still lags other regions. To improve growth prospects, the region's disappointing productivity performance needs to be reversed.

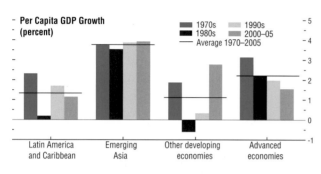

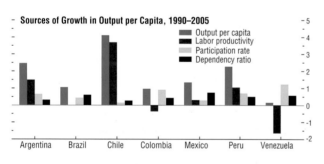

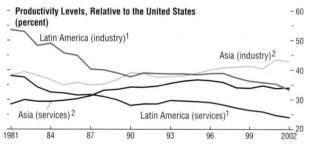

Source: IMF staff calculations.
[1]Sample includes Brazil, Chile, Costa Rica, El Salvador, Honduras, Jamaica, Panama, Trinidad and Tobago, and Venezuela for full period. For 1991–2002, Argentina, Dominican Republic, Ecuador, Guatemala, Mexico, Nicaragua, and Peru are also included.
[2]Sample includes China, India, Japan, Korea, Pakistan, the Philippines, Singapore, and Thailand.

ment, an even greater premium will need to be placed on fiscal reforms. In particular, for countries in which public sector revenues as a share of GDP are low and/or reliant on revenues from commodity exports (e.g., Mexico, Peru, and Venezuela), efforts are needed to broaden the tax base, reduce tax exemptions that benefit the better off, and improve tax administration. In others (including Brazil and Ecuador), budget rigidities in the form of revenue earmarking and mandatory expenditure requirements that are a constraint on the reallocation of resources toward priority areas need to be tackled. Such fiscal reforms would create room for increased spending on well-targeted social programs, building on the success of Oportunidades in Mexico, Bolsa Familia in Brazil, and Chile Solidario in Chile. These programs appear to be highly beneficial for the poor, but in terms of government spending, they are modest in size relative to other programs.[7] In Venezuela, efforts will be needed to rein in government spending that has grown exceptionally rapidly in recent years in response to the surge in revenues from the oil sector.

Reversing very disappointing productivity performance will be key to sustaining stronger rates of growth in Latin America (Figure 2.7; see also the IMF's April 2007 *Regional Economic Outlook: Western Hemisphere*). Labor productivity in the region has lagged considerably, falling relative to the United States and Asia in both industry and services. This relatively poor productivity performance is widespread, with Chile alone standing as an outlier. While priorities vary across countries, reforms to increase economic openness, improve the business climate, deepen the financial sector to ensure credit is available to finance investment projects at competitive interest rates, and limit the role of state-owned enterprises in the economy will all be important

---

[7]See "Latin America: Between Populism and Modernity," speech by IMF Managing Director Rodrigo de Rato at the International Foundation for Liberty Conference, Cato Institute, Washington, D.C., November 30, 2006.

Table 2.5. Emerging Europe: Real GDP, Consumer Prices, and Current Account Balance
(Annual percent change unless noted otherwise)

	Real GDP				Consumer Prices[1]				Current Account Balance[2]			
	2005	2006	2007	2008	2005	2006	2007	2008	2005	2006	2007	2008
Emerging Europe	**5.5**	**6.0**	**5.5**	**5.3**	**4.9**	**5.1**	**4.8**	**3.7**	**−5.3**	**−6.7**	**−6.6**	**−6.5**
Turkey	7.4	5.5	5.0	6.0	8.2	9.6	8.0	4.3	−6.3	−8.0	−7.3	−6.8
Excluding Turkey	4.7	6.2	5.7	4.9	3.5	3.2	3.5	3.4	−4.9	−6.2	−6.3	−6.4
Baltics	**9.0**	**9.7**	**8.7**	**7.0**	**4.2**	**4.8**	**4.9**	**4.8**	**−9.6**	**−15.3**	**−15.7**	**−14.9**
Estonia	10.5	11.4	9.9	7.9	4.1	4.4	4.8	5.3	−10.5	−13.8	−12.9	−12.2
Latvia	10.2	11.9	10.5	7.0	6.7	6.5	7.3	6.5	−12.7	−21.3	−23.0	−22.7
Lithuania	7.6	7.5	7.0	6.5	2.7	3.8	3.5	3.4	−7.1	−12.2	−12.3	−11.0
Central Europe	**4.4**	**5.7**	**5.2**	**4.7**	**2.4**	**2.1**	**3.1**	**3.0**	**−3.4**	**−3.9**	**−3.8**	**−4.0**
Czech Republic	6.1	6.1	4.8	4.3	1.8	2.5	2.9	3.0	−2.6	−4.2	−4.1	−4.2
Hungary	4.2	3.9	2.8	3.0	3.6	3.9	6.4	3.8	−6.7	−6.9	−5.7	−4.8
Poland	3.5	5.8	5.8	5.0	2.1	1.0	2.2	2.9	−1.7	−2.1	−2.7	−3.6
Slovak Republic	6.0	8.2	8.2	7.5	2.8	4.4	2.4	2.3	−8.6	−8.0	−5.7	−4.6
Southern and south-eastern Europe	**4.4**	**6.7**	**6.0**	**4.9**	**7.0**	**6.0**	**4.3**	**4.3**	**−8.7**	**−10.7**	**−10.8**	**−10.2**
Bulgaria	5.5	6.2	6.0	6.0	5.0	7.3	5.3	3.6	−11.3	−15.9	−15.7	−14.7
Croatia	4.3	4.6	4.7	4.5	3.3	3.2	2.7	2.8	−6.4	−8.1	−8.3	−7.8
Malta	2.2	2.5	2.3	2.3	2.5	2.6	2.4	2.3	−10.5	−11.2	−11.5	−11.0
Romania	4.1	7.7	6.5	4.8	9.0	6.6	4.5	5.0	−8.7	−10.3	−10.3	−9.8
Memorandum												
Slovenia	4.0	5.2	4.5	4.0	2.5	2.7	2.7	2.4	−2.0	−2.3	−2.6	−2.5

[1]In accordance with standard practice in the *World Economic Outlook*, movements in consumer prices are indicated as annual averages rather than as December/December changes, as is the practice in some countries.
[2]Percent of GDP.

to help strengthen productivity growth going forward.

Emerging Europe: Integrating with the European Union

Growth in emerging Europe accelerated to 6 percent in 2006 (Table 2.5). Export performance remained strong, boosted by the increased momentum of growth in western Europe, particularly in the main trading partner Germany, and the opening of new auto plants. At the same time, domestic demand accelerated as investment continued to benefit from heavy foreign direct investment (FDI) inflows and consumption was boosted by rising employment and real wages and by lending related to continued strong capital inflows. Current account deficits widened further, but were amply financed in most countries, while CPI inflation was generally contained at quite low levels, as falling fuel prices and some upward movements in exchange rates helped to contain pressures from

rising capacity use and tightening labor markets. However, there were two salient exceptions to this generally positive pattern. In Turkey, concerns about the widening current account deficit led to sharp downward pressure on the lira during the May–June emerging market correction, which required an abrupt tightening of monetary policy to rein in inflation, and growth subsequently decelerated. (Following the finalization of the World Economic Outlook database, the Turkish authorities released data showing that real GDP growth was 6 percent in 2006 rather than 5.5 percent as shown in Table 2.5.) In Hungary, the forint also came under pressure in May–June, with markets concerned about the sharply rising twin deficits—fiscal as well as current account—prompting the government to launch a strong multiyear fiscal consolidation effort.

Growth in emerging Europe is projected to slow moderately to 5.5 percent in 2007, largely reflecting the cooling of the expansion in western Europe and the policy tightening in Turkey

Figure 2.8. Emerging Europe: Convergence with the European Union[1]

(Unweighted averages)

Rapid GDP growth over the past 10 years has helped bring per capita incomes closer to average levels in the European Union. Inflation has also converged. Heavy reliance on foreign savings has contributed to support growth, but raises concerns if the convergence process is not sustained.

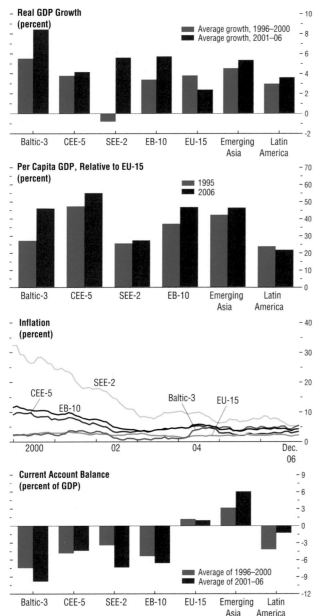

Source: IMF staff calculations.

[1]Baltic-3 includes Estonia, Latvia, and Lithuania; central and eastern Europe (CEE-5) includes Czech Republic, Hungary, Poland, Slovak Republic, and Slovenia; south and eastern Europe (SEE-2) includes Bulgaria and Romania; eastern Europe and the Baltics (EB-10) includes Bulgaria, Czech Republic, Estonia, Hungary, Latvia, Lithuania, Poland, Romania, Slovak Republic, and Slovenia; EU-15 includes Austria, Belgium, Denmark, Finland, France, Germany, Greece, Ireland, Italy, Luxembourg, the Netherlands, Portugal, Spain, Sweden, and the United Kingdom.

and Hungary. Inflation would generally edge up (Turkey being the main exception), reflecting continued pressure on domestic resources, while the pattern of large current account deficits being financed through FDI and other private capital inflows should be sustained. The principal downside risks to this continued strong performance are external: emerging Europe would be vulnerable to both a marked deceleration in western Europe—the destination for two-thirds of its exports—and a deterioration in global financial conditions that reduced investors' willingness to continue financing its large current account deficits.

A key driver of emerging Europe's sustained success over the past 10 years has been the process of integration with the European Union. With the accession of Bulgaria and Romania in January 2007, 10 former Eastern bloc countries have now joined the European Union since May 2004, while other emerging Europe countries, including Turkey, continue along a path toward membership. This enlargement process has brought large economic benefits to the new member countries, both by opening up new trade and investment opportunities and by anchoring macroeconomic and institutional reforms. Over the past 10 years, GDP growth in these countries has averaged around 5 percent, supported by rapid increases in total factor productivity, raising per capita income levels closer to the EU average (Figure 2.8; see Schadler and others, 2006).

Convergence has been particularly impressive in the three Baltic states, helped not just by their low starting positions and more dynamic trading partners, but also their strong commitment to an attractive business environment (Lithuania and Estonia rank among the top 20 in the World Bank's *Doing Business in 2006*) and sound macroeconomic policies (including lower tax burdens and early commitment to fixing exchange rates against the euro). All 10 countries have benefited from high rates of inward FDI, averaging 5 percent of GDP, as companies have taken advantage of relatively low-cost, but highly skilled labor forces in a relatively secure and familiar neighborhood, and from relatively low risk premia. These FDI flows together with heavy inflows of bank lending and EU transfers have financed substantial current account deficits, which should be sustainable provided that the convergence process continues to operate smoothly, although remaining a source of considerable vulnerability in the event of unexpected external disruptions or weakening of domestic policy frameworks.

All new member countries are committed to membership in the euro area, which would bring further benefits from trade integration and lower risk premia. However, notwithstanding generally favorable progress in bringing down inflation, so far only one country (Slovenia) has met the Maastricht criteria and joined the euro area (in January 2007). Four others (the three Baltics and the Slovak Republic) have entered the ERM II, a transitional period of at least two years during which the national currency must vary within "normal fluctuation margins" without severe tensions. These countries are well positioned to meet the fiscal criteria (maintaining a fiscal deficit of less than 3 percent of GDP and a general government debt of less than 60 percent of GDP) and the interest rate criterion (long-term interest rate on government bonds within 2 percentage points of the average in the three EU member countries with the lowest inflation rates), but satisfying the inflation criterion could be more challenging. This criterion requires that annual inflation not exceed the average of the three lowest inflation rates within the EU by more than 1½ percentage points—and is particularly demanding when it is recognized that Balassa-Samuelson effects could add 1½–2½ percentage points to inflation in an accession country as its productivity catches up to EU levels.[8] Other complicating factors include scheduled increases in administered prices, particularly

for energy products, and the heavy weight of volatile food products in the CPI.

In other new member countries, timetables for joining the euro area have been extended. In part, delays have reflected difficulties in meeting the strict Maastricht criteria, but also questions about whether adequate progress is being made to ensure sufficient flexibility to live comfortably within a currency union— concerns that have been raised particularly in the larger economies (Czech Republic, Hungary, and Poland). While such misgivings are understandable—without sufficient economic flexibility, maintaining economic competitiveness under a fixed exchange rate may require costly demand adjustments—considerable dangers would also arise from trying to make do with a slow track of sluggish reforms and hesitant steps toward currency union. Most importantly, successful transitions into the euro area provide the best route to deal with the potential currency mismatches that have arisen in economies (such as Hungary and Poland) from the rapid increases in foreign currency lending in recent years.

The recent slowing pace of reform among the new members since they entered the EU thus raises concern. While performance over the past 10 years has been impressive, to a considerable degree growth rates reflect the rebound after the dislocation following the collapse of COMECON, as well as a benign global environment that has boosted growth in other emerging market countries too. Looking ahead, continuing structural improvements are critical to facilitate continuing smooth convergence within the European Union and ensure the broader competitiveness of these countries. One key issue is the need to boost labor market flexibility and reduce sizable tax wedges that have contributed to high unemployment rates, still in excess of 10 percent in Poland and the Slovak Republic. Another priority is to control government spending, including improved targeting of social transfers and addressing pressures on pension and health care costs from rapidly aging populations.

[8]The Balassa-Samuelson effect implies a rising real exchange rate for a country with relatively rapid growth in the tradables sector compared with the nontradables sector. See Buiter and Sibert (2006).

Table 2.6. Commonwealth of Independent States: Real GDP, Consumer Prices, and Current Account Balance
(Annual percent change unless noted otherwise)

	Real GDP				Consumer Prices[1]				Current Account Balance[2]			
	2005	2006	2007	2008	2005	2006	2007	2008	2005	2006	2007	2008
Commonwealth of Independent States	**6.6**	**7.7**	**7.0**	**6.4**	**12.4**	**9.6**	**9.0**	**8.3**	**8.8**	**7.7**	**5.0**	**4.4**
Russia	6.4	6.7	6.4	5.9	12.7	9.7	8.1	7.5	10.9	9.8	6.2	5.0
Ukraine	2.7	7.1	5.0	4.6	13.5	9.0	11.3	10.0	2.9	−1.7	−4.1	−5.5
Kazakhstan	9.7	10.6	9.0	8.1	7.6	8.6	8.8	6.8	−1.3	−1.4	−0.9	−0.4
Belarus	9.3	9.9	5.5	3.9	10.3	7.0	11.4	13.7	1.6	−4.1	−8.7	−6.4
Turkmenistan	9.0	9.0	10.0	10.0	10.7	8.2	6.5	9.0	5.1	15.3	11.7	11.7
Low-income CIS countries	**12.1**	**14.6**	**14.8**	**12.8**	**12.2**	**11.8**	**12.7**	**11.9**	**2.7**	**7.4**	**11.6**	**17.0**
Armenia	14.0	13.4	9.0	6.0	0.6	2.9	4.0	4.5	−3.9	−5.0	−5.5	−5.3
Azerbaijan	24.3	31.0	29.2	23.1	9.7	8.4	21.1	17.0	1.3	15.7	27.4	36.2
Georgia	9.6	9.0	7.5	6.5	8.3	9.2	6.3	5.5	−5.4	−9.5	−15.2	−12.7
Kyrgyz Republic	−0.2	2.7	6.5	6.6	4.3	5.6	5.0	4.0	−2.3	−16.8	−12.6	−10.8
Moldova	7.5	4.0	4.5	5.0	11.9	12.7	11.4	8.9	−8.1	−8.3	−6.2	−5.7
Tajikistan	6.7	7.0	7.5	8.0	7.3	10.1	11.4	9.2	−2.5	−2.5	−15.2	−15.3
Uzbekistan	7.0	7.2	7.7	7.5	21.0	19.5	10.4	12.2	14.3	19.4	19.7	18.6
Memorandum												
Net energy exporters[3]	7.1	7.7	7.4	6.8	12.5	9.8	8.6	7.9	9.9	9.3	6.5	5.8
Net energy importers[4]	4.5	7.7	5.4	4.7	12.0	8.5	10.8	10.1	1.6	−3.2	−6.0	−6.3

[1]In accordance with standard practice in the *World Economic Outlook*, movements in consumer prices are indicated as annual averages rather than as December/December changes, as is the practice in some countries.
[2]Percent of GDP.
[3]Includes Azerbaijan, Kazakhstan, Russia, Turkmenistan, and Uzbekistan.
[4]Includes Armenia, Belarus, Georgia, Kyrgyz Republic, Moldova, Tajikistan, and Ukraine.

Commonwealth of Independent States: Strong Growth but More Economic Diversification Needed

Activity in the Commonwealth of Independent States (CIS) continues to expand briskly, reflecting the solid performance of energy exporters and a pickup in activity among energy importers, many of which have benefited from rising nonfuel commodity prices and strengthened domestic demand (Table 2.6). Looking forward, while real GDP growth is expected to moderate, its pace would be second only to emerging Asia among the major regions. In Russia, growth would remain strong, although output appears to be running close to capacity in the face of robust domestic demand. Oil production growth has slowed, however, reflecting limited past investment. In Ukraine, the rise in international steel prices and robust domestic demand are underpinning a strong growth rebound, but the pace of activity is expected to moderate in response to large increases in the price of imported natural gas and an associ-

ated overall deterioration in the terms of trade. Upside risks to the outlook for the region as a whole relate to a possible rebound in oil prices and stronger-than-anticipated demand for the region's principal non-oil commodity exports. On the downside, a sharp slowdown in global activity could adversely affect exports, although domestic demand should be resilient in most countries.

Current account positions have strengthened in energy exporters such as Turkmenistan and Azerbaijan. In other countries, current account balances have deteriorated due to a strong rise in import volumes as well as the rising costs of energy imports (Ukraine and Georgia) and the weakening demand for specific exports (Armenia). Looking ahead, the regional current account position is expected to remain strong, reflecting the continued underlying strength in demand for the region's principal exports.

Reflecting the strength of domestic demand and strong capital inflows, inflation among CIS countries remains among the highest in the world, despite some moderation in several countries. In Russia, headline inflation came down by 2 percentage points during 2006, reflecting lower administered price increases and some nominal appreciation of the ruble, but at 9 percent still remained above the official target of 8½ percent for end-2006. Bringing inflation down to the 2007 target of 8 percent will depend on allowing greater nominal appreciation of the ruble and a more restrictive fiscal stance. In Ukraine, inflation has recently accelerated into double digits following the pass-through of higher energy import prices. Monetary policy needs to play a more active role to ensure that the recent spike in inflation does not feed into higher inflationary expectations. The authorities' preliminary steps toward an inflation targeting regime are welcome, but a gradual transition to greater exchange rate flexibility will be needed to support this framework.

Fiscal balances in several countries have deteriorated as large spending increases have outpaced the increase in revenues related to higher export earnings and stronger domestic economic activity. In some others, fiscal positions have strengthened. In Russia, the primary fiscal balance has improved as a large proportion of the higher oil revenues has been placed in the stabilization fund, although spending has also accelerated. In Ukraine, spending has been held below budgeted levels while revenue growth has been strong. More generally, in the context of already strong domestic demand, governments will need to be careful to avoid excessive public spending increases, particularly in areas that boost consumption—such as on pensions and wages—and exert upward pressure on inflation. In countries where there is scope to boost public spending over the medium term, governments should ensure that expenditures are geared toward generating high-quality growth that is not linked to the commodity price cycle and are allocated efficiently in the context of often weak institutional capacity.

More generally, sustaining the recent strong growth momentum will require a diversification of the sources of growth away from exports of primary commodities. The strength of domestic demand in recent years has been driven to a large extent by consumption, fueled by capital inflows, rapid credit growth, and, in some countries, increased public sector spending in the form of wages and pensions. Despite sizable public investment in some countries, focused mainly in resource extraction industries and related transportation infrastructure, the overall ratio of investment to GDP among CIS countries remains relatively low (Figure 2.9). This underscores the need to attract greater private investment in noncommodity sectors. Foreign direct investment, in particular, is low in these sectors. Many countries in the region have a large unfinished structural reform agenda, as seen, for example, by the region's slower pace of reform relative to central Europe and the Baltics, and further progress is needed to improve the investment climate. The main priorities are broadening and deepening domestic financial markets, reforming civil services and the energy sector, making tax systems more growth- and investment-friendly, strengthening the protection of property rights, reducing corruption and state intervention, and strengthening legal and regulatory systems.

Africa: Sustaining Recent Growth Momentum

The short-term economic outlook for Africa remains very positive, against the backdrop of strong global growth, continued progress in cementing macroeconomic stability, the beneficial impact of debt relief, increased capital inflows, rising oil production in a number of countries, and strong demand for nonfuel commodities. Real GDP growth is expected to accelerate to 6.2 percent this year, from 5.5 percent in 2006, before slowing to 5.8 percent in 2008 (Table 2.7). Inflation (excluding Zimbabwe) is on a declining trend, while fiscal and current account balances are in surplus at the regional level (although this is due to large surpluses in oil-exporting countries).

Figure 2.9. Commonwealth of Independent States (CIS): Further Reform Needed to Raise Investment Levels

The CIS region attracts relatively low levels of foreign direct investment, while overall investment is still dominated by the natural resources sector and related transportation infrastructure. Further reform is needed to improve the investment climate.

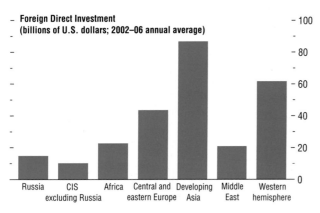

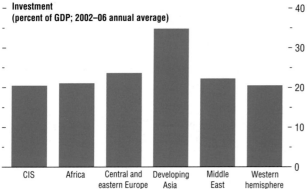

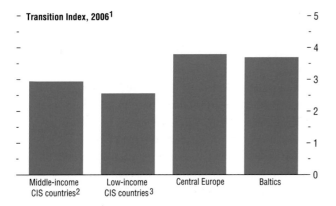

Sources: EBRD, *Transition Report;* and IMF staff calculations.
[1]The transition Index is the unweighted average of large-scale privatization index, small-scale privatization index, enterprise restructuring index, price liberalization index, trade and forex system index, competition policy index, banking reform and interest rate liberalization index, securities markets and nonbank financial institutions index, and overall infrastructure reform index.
[2]Belarus, Kazakhstan, Russia, Turkmenistan, and Ukraine.
[3]Armenia, Azerbaijan, Georgia, Kyrgyz Republic, Moldova, Tajikistan, and Uzbekistan.

In sub-Saharan Africa, the projected acceleration in growth in 2007 is driven by oil-exporting countries. (see also the IMF's April 2007 *Regional Economic Outlook: Sub-Saharan Africa*). New production facilities will come on stream in Angola and Equatorial Guinea, while oil output in Nigeria, which has been disrupted by violence in the Niger Delta, is assumed to be fully restored by midyear. Strong oil revenues are also spurring domestic demand and growth in the non-oil sector. In Nigeria, for example, non-oil GDP has grown by an average of 8 percent over the past three years. After a strong expansion in 2006, growth in oil-importing countries is projected to ease this year, driven largely by developments in South Africa, where tighter monetary policy is expected to slow domestic demand. The decline in oil prices will underpin an improvement in the terms of trade in some countries, although for others the benefit will be offset by the drop in metals prices. In the Maghreb, growth in Morocco is expected to slow (following a bumper harvest in 2006), but activity in Algeria should rebound as hydrocarbon output recovers following maintenance work in 2006 and public sector investment increases.

Despite this positive outlook, risks are tilted somewhat to the downside. While the current rotation of growth away from the United States toward the euro area is unlikely to have a significant impact on sub-Saharan Africa (each accounts for around 25 percent of exports), a sharper-than-expected slowing in global growth would hurt the region, particularly through its impact on commodity prices. Exports of the CFA franc zone countries would also be affected by a further appreciation of the euro. There are also country-specific risks. In Nigeria, violence in the Niger Delta region may prevent the restoration of oil production as assumed in the baseline forecast. In South Africa, strong domestic demand growth has pushed the current account deficit to 6½ percent of GDP and inflation has moved toward the upper end of the 3–6 percent target band. The central bank has appropriately tightened monetary policy, but further interest

Table 2.7. Selected African Countries: Real GDP, Consumer Prices, and Current Account Balance
(Annual percent change unless noted otherwise)

	Real GDP				Consumer Prices[1]				Current Account Balance[2]			
	2005	2006	2007	2008	2005	2006	2007	2008	2005	2006	2007	2008
Africa	**5.6**	**5.5**	**6.2**	**5.8**	**8.4**	**9.5**	**10.7**	**10.4**	**1.8**	**2.2**	**0.1**	**—**
Maghreb	**4.0**	**4.5**	**4.4**	**5.0**	**1.5**	**3.1**	**4.0**	**4.1**	**11.9**	**14.4**	**8.6**	**8.1**
Algeria	5.3	2.7	4.5	4.1	1.6	2.5	5.5	5.7	20.7	24.4	15.3	15.2
Morocco	1.7	7.3	3.5	5.8	1.0	3.3	2.0	2.0	1.7	3.9	2.1	0.5
Tunisia	4.0	5.3	6.0	6.0	2.0	4.5	3.0	2.9	–1.0	–2.8	–2.2	–2.1
Sub-Sahara	**6.0**	**5.7**	**6.8**	**6.1**	**10.5**	**11.5**	**12.7**	**12.2**	**–1.1**	**–1.3**	**–2.2**	**–2.1**
Horn of Africa[3]	**9.3**	**11.5**	**9.1**	**8.7**	**7.7**	**9.3**	**12.4**	**8.8**	**–9.7**	**–13.6**	**–11.2**	**–7.0**
Ethiopia	10.3	10.6	6.5	6.6	6.8	12.3	17.0	12.9	–8.6	–11.6	–10.0	–6.6
Sudan	8.6	12.2	11.1	10.2	8.5	7.2	9.2	6.0	–10.5	–14.5	–11.5	–7.0
Great Lakes[3]	**6.2**	**5.5**	**6.4**	**6.5**	**11.5**	**9.7**	**8.2**	**5.4**	**–4.5**	**–5.8**	**–7.0**	**–7.2**
Congo, Dem. Rep. of	6.5	5.1	6.5	6.9	21.4	13.2	17.4	8.9	–10.0	–7.5	–10.3	–9.3
Kenya	5.8	6.0	6.2	5.8	10.3	14.1	4.1	3.5	–3.0	–3.3	–4.1	–3.9
Tanzania	6.8	5.9	7.3	7.6	4.4	5.8	5.5	5.0	–5.2	–9.3	–11.0	–11.2
Uganda	6.7	5.4	6.2	6.5	8.0	6.6	5.8	4.2	–2.1	–4.1	–4.4	–7.9
Southern Africa[3]	**7.0**	**6.6**	**12.6**	**7.6**	**31.1**	**47.7**	**55.5**	**60.2**	**3.4**	**5.0**	**2.0**	**0.9**
Angola	20.6	15.3	35.3	16.0	23.0	13.3	10.2	5.9	13.5	10.5	4.0	2.8
Zimbabwe	–5.3	–4.8	–5.7	–3.6	237.8	1,016.7	2,879.5	6,470.8	–11.2	–3.9	–0.8	0.2
West and Central Africa[3]	**5.6**	**4.4**	**5.8**	**6.0**	**11.5**	**7.4**	**6.8**	**6.7**	**2.5**	**5.1**	**3.5**	**2.4**
Ghana	5.9	6.2	6.3	6.9	15.1	10.9	9.4	8.8	–7.0	–8.2	–8.4	–7.9
Nigeria	7.2	5.3	8.2	6.7	17.8	8.3	7.9	9.1	9.2	12.2	9.7	7.6
CFA franc zone[3]	**4.5**	**3.0**	**4.2**	**5.3**	**4.4**	**3.5**	**2.8**	**2.7**	**–1.9**	**–0.4**	**–1.4**	**–1.9**
Cameroon	2.0	3.5	4.0	4.1	2.0	5.3	1.5	1.9	–3.4	–0.5	–2.1	–3.0
Côte d'Ivoire	1.5	1.4	1.7	3.3	3.9	1.6	2.0	3.0	–0.1	1.2	1.1	0.7
South Africa	**5.1**	**5.0**	**4.7**	**4.5**	**3.4**	**4.7**	**5.5**	**4.9**	**–3.8**	**–6.4**	**–6.4**	**–6.0**
Memorandum												
Oil importers	4.8	5.3	4.8	5.2	8.2	11.1	12.3	12.1	–3.4	–4.2	–4.4	–4.2
Oil exporters[4]	7.6	5.9	9.5	7.3	8.9	5.9	7.1	6.5	11.1	12.6	7.6	6.8

[1]In accordance with standard practice in the *World Economic Outlook*, movements in consumer prices are indicated as annual averages rather than as December/December changes, as is the practice in some countries.

[2]Percent of GDP.

[3]The country composition of this regional group is set out in Table F in the Statistical Appendix.

[4]Includes Chad and Mauritania in this table.

rate increases may still be needed to counter inflationary pressures, which could result in a sharper growth slowdown. Given the importance of South Africa, particularly for the rest of southern Africa, any such slowing could negatively affect other countries.[9]

Since the beginning of this decade, real GDP growth in sub-Saharan Africa has averaged a little over 4½ percent a year, the strongest seven-year period since the beginning of the 1970s, while output variability has declined

(Figure 2.10). These developments have raised hopes that Africa has entered a period of strong and sustained growth that will begin to make deeper inroads into the extremely high poverty rates that still plague the continent.[10] Yet, the strong growth of the early 1970s was followed by two decades of stagnation as the region struggled to cope with a deteriorating terms of trade, high inflation, and bouts of conflict and political instability. Indeed, Africa

[9]Arora and Vamvakidis (2005) estimate that a 1 percentage point slowing in South African growth is associated with a ½–¾ percentage point slowing in the rest of sub-Saharan Africa.

[10]Despite the improved growth performance, only a few African countries will reach the target set by the Millennium Development Goals (MDGs) of halving extreme poverty by 2015 on current trends (see the *Global Monitoring Report 2006*).

Figure 2.10. Sub-Saharan Africa: Can Recent Growth Momentum Be Sustained?

Sub-Saharan Africa is currently witnessing a period of strong growth. While this is partly due to positive terms-of-trade developments, oil importers are also growing robustly. The key now is to sustain the recent growth momentum, something the region has been unable to do in the past. A more stable political climate should help sustain high growth rates.

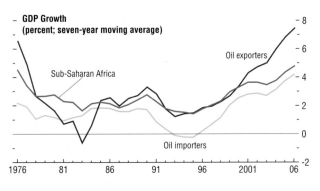

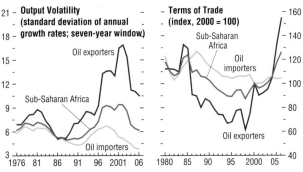

Sources: Berg, Ostry, and Zettelmeyer (2006); and IMF staff calculations.
[1]AE: advanced economies; DA: developing Asia; LA: Latin America; SSA: sub-Saharan Africa; ODE: other developing economies.
[2]From Berg, Ostry, and Zettelmeyer (2006). A growth spell is defined as a statistically significant upbreak in growth followed by a period during which per capita growth averages at least 2 percent.

has been replete with examples of countries where growth has accelerated for short periods of time. Empirical evidence suggests that growth episodes in sub-Saharan Africa start with broadly the same frequency as other regions, but the duration of these episodes is considerably shorter, and they tend to end in painful output collapses (Berg, Ostry, and Zettelmeyer, 2006).[11]

Against this background, the question is how current growth momentum in sub-Saharan Africa can be sustained, and indeed accelerated, going forward. While armed conflicts and political instability continue to undermine prospects in a number of countries, the frequency of such events in the region as a whole has declined over the past decade. This suggests that economic policies, rather than sociopolitical developments, will be the main determinant of whether strong growth continues or not. To this end, sustaining the recent improvement in macroeconomic stability will be crucial, but challenging, particularly in oil-exporting countries where the increase in oil revenues has created strong pressures for government spending.[12] An increasing focus will also need to be placed on implementing the structural reforms that will help foster vibrant market-based economies.

Further trade liberalization is key to these efforts, because of both its direct effect on competition in the domestic economy and its impact on improving institutional quality (see the September 2005 *World Economic Outlook*). Trade reforms have increased the openness of sub-Saharan African economies since the mid-1990s, but trade regimes in the region generally remain more restrictive than in the dynamic economies of Asia.[13] Steps are

---

[11]Becker and Mauro (2006) find that large output losses in developing countries are most frequently triggered by large declines in the terms of trade.
[12]See Chapter 3 of the April 2007 *Regional Economic Outlook: Sub-Saharan Africa* for a discussion of the macroeconomic challenges facing African oil exporters.
[13]For example, Johnson, Ostry, and Subramanian (2007) show that the bureaucratic costs in terms of the number of documents and days it takes to undertake import and export activity are particularly high in sub-Saharan Africa.

Table 2.8. Selected Middle Eastern Countries: Real GDP, Consumer Prices, and Current Account Balance
(Annual percent change unless noted otherwise)

	Real GDP				Consumer Prices[1]				Current Account Balance[2]			
	2005	2006	2007	2008	2005	2006	2007	2008	2005	2006	2007	2008
Middle East	**5.4**	**5.7**	**5.5**	**5.5**	**7.1**	**7.9**	**10.6**	**8.7**	**18.8**	**18.1**	**12.1**	**10.7**
Oil exporters[3]	**5.7**	**5.5**	**5.3**	**5.2**	**6.8**	**8.9**	**10.4**	**8.5**	**21.7**	**20.9**	**14.4**	**12.9**
Iran, I.R. of	4.4	5.3	5.0	5.0	12.1	14.6	17.8	15.8	7.4	6.7	6.0	4.7
Saudi Arabia	6.6	4.6	4.8	4.0	0.7	2.3	2.8	2.0	29.3	27.4	19.7	17.1
Kuwait	10.0	5.0	3.5	4.8	4.1	3.0	2.8	2.6	40.5	43.1	34.4	32.3
Mashreq	**4.2**	**5.9**	**5.9**	**6.1**	**7.8**	**5.3**	**10.7**	**9.0**	**−1.1**	**−1.9**	**−2.5**	**−3.8**
Egypt	4.5	6.8	6.7	6.6	8.8	4.2	12.3	10.7	3.2	0.8	0.7	−1.5
Syrian Arab Republic	2.9	3.0	3.3	4.7	7.2	10.0	8.0	5.0	0.8	−1.2	−3.4	−3.0
Jordan	7.2	6.0	6.0	6.0	3.5	6.3	5.7	3.5	−17.8	−16.0	−14.6	−15.0
Lebanon	1.0	—	1.0	3.5	−0.7	5.6	3.5	2.5	−11.7	−6.8	−11.0	−10.0
Memorandum												
Israel	5.2	5.1	4.8	4.2	1.3	2.1	−0.1	2.0	2.9	5.2	3.6	4.3

[1]In accordance with standard practice in the *World Economic Outlook*, movements in consumer prices are indicated as annual averages rather than as December/December changes during the year, as is the practice in some countries.
[2]Percent of GDP.
[3]Includes Bahrain, Islamic Republic of Iran, Kuwait, Libya, Oman, Qatar, Saudi Arabia, Syrian Arab Republic, United Arab Emirates, and the Republic of Yemen.

also needed by the international community to improve market access for regional exports. Delivery on aid commitments by the advanced economies would also help sustain growth momentum and support progress toward achieving the MDGs.

Strengthening institutions and improving the business climate would help to spur private sector activity and diversify economies away from excessive reliance on commodities (see also Box 2.5 in the April 2007 *Regional Economic Outlook: Sub-Saharan Africa*). At present, sub-Saharan African countries generally rank toward the bottom in the World Bank's Doing Business surveys, although reforms are under way in some countries.[14] Development of the non-commodity-producing sectors would not only generate much-needed employment, but would also reduce the region's vulnerability to terms-of-trade movements. Increased spending to address infrastructure bottlenecks

[14]In the 2007 survey, Ghana and Tanzania were ranked among the top 10 reformers in the world, while it was noted that 11 other countries have also started to simplify business regulations and this would be reflected in the Doing Business indicators next year.

and improve education and health care is also necessary, with the increase in oil wealth and recent debt relief making such options possible. Nevertheless, spending needs to be consistent with absorptive capacity and macroeconomic objectives, and to be accompanied by improved financial management to avoid wasteful spending.

Middle East: Expanding the Benefits of the Oil Boom

Middle Eastern oil exporters enjoyed another year of solid growth in 2006, accompanied by strong current account and fiscal balances (Table 2.8). Oil revenues continued to grow rapidly although the pace was tempered by the decline in oil prices since August and some cuts in output late last year among Organization of the Petroleum Exporting Countries (OPEC) members. The strong overall momentum of the non-oil sector has been maintained, with little discernible impact from the sharp correction in regional equity markets in early 2006. Inflationary pressures among oil exporters continue to remain generally well contained, although expansionary fiscal policies have contributed

Figure 2.11. Middle East: Investment in Non-Oil Sectors Key to Employment Growth

With rapidly rising working-age populations, meeting the challenge of the employment generation will require an expansion of investment in the non-oil sector.

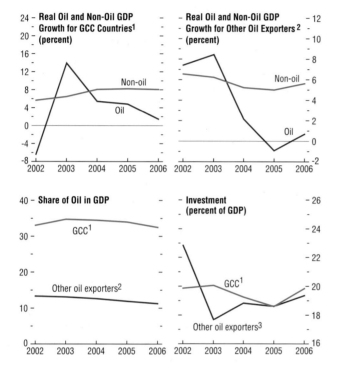

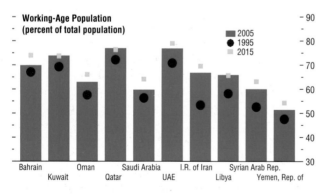

Sources: United Nations Common Database; and IMF staff calculations.
[1]The Cooperation Council of the Arab States of the Gulf (GCC) includes Bahrain, Kuwait, Oman, Qatar, Saudi Arabia, and United Arab Emirates (UAE).
[2]Consists of I.R. of Iran, Libya, Syrian Arab Republic, and the Republic of Yemen.
[3]Excludes I.R. of Iran.

to a further increase in inflation in the Islamic Republic of Iran.

In the non-oil-exporting countries of the Mashreq region, growth accelerated in 2006 in the context of an upturn in foreign direct investment and an overall favorable external environment. In Egypt, growth and exports in the non-oil sector have picked up strongly, although underlying demand pressures have contributed to rising inflation over the course of the year. In Lebanon, the mid-2006 conflict and monthlong blockade led to an economic slowdown accompanied by a further deterioration in the fiscal deficit and rising public debt and inflation.

The outlook for the region as a whole remains favorable, with some moderation of growth among oil exporters. The region's current account surplus is expected to decline from its 2006 level of 18 percent of regional GDP to around 10¾ percent of GDP over the next two years as a result of the decline in oil prices and stronger import growth. Risks to the outlook appear broadly balanced at this juncture. On the upside, oil prices could rebound after their recent decline. Beyond geopolitical uncertainties, downside risks stem from a further decline in oil prices, although the prudent management of oil revenues during the current upturn leaves oil exporters in the region in a much stronger position than in previous cycles to smooth public spending, given significantly reduced external and public debt vulnerabilities.

Following Oman's announcement of its decision not to join the Cooperation Council of the Arab States of the Gulf (GCC) monetary union at the scheduled date of 2010, it is reported that the six GCC monetary authorities are considering possible alternatives, including closer monetary policy coordination, during the transition to a full monetary union. While efforts to enhance policy coordination would be beneficial to the GCC countries, important preconditions remain to be fulfilled, including the need to better define monetary policy objectives, the use of more uniform monetary instruments, the establishment of the institutional framework required to improve the coordination of monetary policies, and formation of the planned customs union.

Despite the recent high growth and rise in real per capita incomes in the region, Middle Eastern oil exporters remain heavily dependent on the hydrocarbon sector. At the same time, rapid population growth has contributed to some of the highest levels of unemployment in the world and relatively low employment-to-population ratios (Figure 2.11).[15] While increased public sector employment has helped cushion the impact of rising labor supply in a number of GCC countries in the past, the demand for jobs is outpacing economy-wide supply by increasing margins. The current favorable conjuncture provides a unique opportunity for the region's oil exporters to implement policies that can address the twin challenges of diversifying oil-dependent economies and providing employment to a rapidly expanding labor force. In this context, the ambitious investment plans of the members of the GCC (totaling over $700 billion during 2006–10) should make a major contribution.

For the region's oil exporters more generally, a greater role for private investment in the non-oil sector will be key to balancing growth and providing increased employment opportunities. While a stable macroeconomic environment remains an important precondition, a number of other reforms could play an important role in increasing private investment in the region. The main priorities are improvements in the business environment, including the reduction of complex regulations and barriers to entry and exit, better access to finance for small and medium enterprises, improved trade facilitation (including increased efficiency in customs and ports, and document processing) to complement trade liberalization measures already undertaken, and better overall institutional frameworks. In addition, measures to improve the quality of educa-

tion in schools and vocational training programs could help align the skills mix of the labor force with the needs of the private sector.

References

Annett, Anthony, forthcoming, "Lessons from Successful Labor Market Reformers in Europe," Policy Discussion Paper (Washington: International Monetary Fund).

Arora, Vivek, and Athanasios Vamvakidis, 2005, "The Implications of South African Economic Growth for the Rest of Africa," IMF Working Paper 05/58 (Washington: International Monetary Fund).

Bassanini, Andrea, and Romain Duval, 2006, "Employment Patterns in OECD Countries: Reassessing the Role of Policies and Institutions," OECD Economics Department Working Paper No. 486 (Paris: Organization for Economic Cooperation and Development).

Becker, Törbjörn, and Paolo Mauro, 2006, "Output Drops and the Shocks That Matter," IMF Working Paper 06/172 (Washington: International Monetary Fund).

Berg, Andrew, Jonathan D. Ostry, and Jeromin Zettelmeyer, 2006, "What Makes Growth Sustained?" paper presented at the International Monetary Fund Western Hemisphere Department Workshop, "Economic Growth and Latin America: What Have We Learned?" Washington, November 17.

Buiter, Willem H., and Anne C. Sibert, 2006, "Eurozone Entry of New EU Member States from Central Europe: Should They? Could They?" (unpublished; London: London School of Economics).

de Boer, Kito, and John M. Turner, 2007, "Beyond Oil: Reappraising the Gulf States," *McKinsey Quarterly* (January), pp. 7–17.

Estevão, Marcello M., 2004, "Why Is Productivity Growth in the Euro Area So Sluggish?" IMF Working Paper 04/200 (Washington: International Monetary Fund).

Gomez-Salvador, Ramon, Alberto Musso, Marc Stocker, and Jarkko Turunen, 2006, "Labour Productivity Developments in the Euro Area," ECB Occasional Paper No. 53 (Frankfurt: European Central Bank).

International Labor Organization, 2007, "Global Employment Trends Brief" (Geneva, January). Available via the Internet: http://www.ilo.org/public/english/employment/strat/global.htm.

[15]Although data on unemployment are updated infrequently in most countries of the region, estimates of underlying trends are discussed in International Labor Organization (2007) and de Boer and Turner (2007).

International Monetary Fund, 2007a, *Regional Economic Outlook: Sub-Saharan Africa*, April (Washington).

———, 2007b, *Regional Economic Outlook: Western Hemisphere*, April (Washington).

Johnson, Simon, Jonathan Ostry, and Arvind Subramanian, 2007, "The Prospects for Sustained Growth in Africa: Benchmarking the Constraints," IMF Working Paper 07/52 (Washington: International Monetary Fund).

Schadler, Susan, Ashoka Mody, Abdul Abiad, and Daniel Leigh, 2006, *Growth in Central and Eastern European Countries of the European Union,* IMF Occasional Paper No. 252 (Washington: International Monetary Fund).

Wei, Shang-Jin, and David Dollar, 2007, "Das (Wasted) Kapital: Firm Ownership and Investment Efficiency in China," IMF Working Paper No. 07/9 (Washington: International Monetary Fund).

World Bank, 2006, *Doing Business in 2006: Creating Jobs* (Washington: World Bank).

———, and International Monetary Fund, 2006, *Global Monitoring Report 2006: Strengthening Mutual Accountability—Aid, Trade, and Governance* (Washington: World Bank and International Monetary Fund).

Wright, Jonathan, 2006, "The Yield Curve and Predicting Recessions," Federal Reserve Board Finance and Economics Discussion Paper No. 2006-7 (Washington: Board of Governors of the Federal Reserve System).

Zhou, Jianping, 2006, "Danish for All? Balancing Flexibility with Security: The Flexicurity Model," in *Denmark: Selected Issues*, IMF Country Report No. 06/342 (Washington: International Monetary Fund).

EXCHANGE RATES AND THE ADJUSTMENT OF EXTERNAL IMBALANCES

In recent years, few subjects have attracted more attention from the research, financial, and policy communities than the causes of the large U.S. current account deficit—which now absorbs about three-fourths of available world surpluses—and its implications for the global economy. Yet, there is still little consensus on either how long current imbalances may be sustained or the channels through which adjustment could take place, and in particular on the role of exchange rates in the unwinding of the imbalances.

Some argue that the current imbalances can be sustained for a relatively long period, as they are a reflection of secular changes in the global economy, including the integration into world markets of countries with a large and underutilized labor force, such as China and India; the comparative advantage of the United States in producing marketable securities in the context of increasing financial integration across countries; and relatively benign U.S. demographic trends compared with those of many surplus economies.[1] This view of global imbalances often assumes that their eventual narrowing will depend on a rebalancing of the differential saving and investment behavior between the United States and the surplus economies, with only a minor role for a realignment of exchange rates.

Others have emphasized that the narrowing of external imbalances is unlikely to occur exclusively through a rebalancing of demand between the United States and the surplus economies. Given the imperfect global integration of markets for goods and services and the rigidities that constrain the reallocation of resources to tradables sectors, the redistribution of world spending is likely to require considerable movements in real exchange rates to avoid a prolonged U.S. recession. The experience of the late 1980s—when the U.S. external deficit narrowed by about 3½ percentage points of GDP over a three-year period—suggests that these changes could be large. During that episode, the real effective value of the U.S. dollar depreciated by about 40 percent, despite a substantial decline in the U.S. GDP growth differential with trading partners. A number of recent studies also conclude that the U.S. current account deficit cannot be reduced without a major real exchange rate depreciation.[2]

Previous issues of the *World Economic Outlook* have looked at saving and investment behaviors underlying global imbalances and described alternative scenarios for their unwinding, using the IMF's Global Economy Model.[3] This chapter complements this analysis by looking more directly at the role of real exchange rates in the process of adjusting external imbalances, with the aim of answering the following questions:

- Looking at the past 40 years and across a broad range of countries, how many episodes of large external imbalances can be identified? How long have these episodes lasted and, when the adjustment occurred, what were the relative contributions of changes in growth differentials and changes in real exchange rates?

Note: The main authors of this chapter are Roberto Cardarelli and Alessandro Rebucci, with support from Angela Espiritu and Olga Akcadag. Caroline Freund, Jaime Marquez, Jean Imbs, and George Kapetanios provided consultancy support.

[1]See Dooley, Folkerts-Landau, and Garber (2005); Greenspan (2004); and Cooper (2006).

[2]Typical econometric estimates suggest that a real U.S. dollar depreciation of between 10 and 20 percent is required to achieve a 1 percent improvement in the ratio of current account to GDP in the United States (see Krugman, 2006; and Mussa, 2004). See Edwards (2005) for a survey of selected studies on U.S. current account adjustment.

[3]See the April 2005, September 2005, and September 2006 issues of the *World Economic Outlook*.

- Are there reasons to believe that U.S. trade volumes may be more reactive to changes in relative international prices than generally assumed, so that a trade balance correction in the United States could be achieved with smaller real movements in the U.S. dollar exchange rate than sometimes considered necessary?

The main findings are twofold. First, a clear lesson from cross-country experience is that movements of real exchange rates can play an important supportive role in facilitating the smooth unwinding of external imbalances. Real depreciation helps contain the costs in terms of slower GDP growth that are associated with large reversals of current account deficits. Fiscal consolidation and a significant increase in national savings are also typical of episodes where adjustment has been achieved without serious damage in terms of growth. The likelihood of such a benign adjustment decreases with the size of the external deficit and increases with the degree to which a country is open to trade. As for surplus countries, periods in which current account surpluses have narrowed have often involved real exchange rate appreciation, though an increase in domestic demand has usually also played a key role in these cases.

Second, the chapter finds that external adjustment in the United States may involve a smaller real depreciation of the U.S. dollar than sometimes claimed in the recent policy and academic debates. To start, standard empirical trade models may underestimate U.S. trade volume responses to relative prices if they fail to account for large differences in response across sectors (aggregation bias) and for the degree to which imports embody domestically produced intermediate products (vertical integration bias). Correcting for these biases significantly increases the estimated impact of real depreciation on the U.S. trade balance. Further, trade volumes seem to have become more reactive to changes in relative international prices over the past two decades, reflecting greater competition among firms in an increasingly globalized economy, and seem to

react more strongly to larger changes in relative international prices.

The chapter also shows that the more flexible the economy, that is, the smaller the obstacles to the reallocation of resources, the more responsive trade will be to changes in real exchange rates. An important corollary is that changes in real exchange rates that are consistent with a given amount of external adjustment will be larger for economies where it is more difficult for firms to enter and exit trade—either because of rigidities in product and labor markets or because of trade protectionism.

What do these results suggest for the present constellation of global imbalances? A consistent theme that emerges from this chapter is that a market-led real depreciation of the U.S. dollar and a real appreciation of the currencies of surplus countries could potentially play a helpful role in narrowing global imbalances. At the same time, the adjustment process will involve a rebalancing of domestic demand toward surplus economies, including a rising private saving rate and further fiscal consolidation in the United States. Policies that remove obstacles to the reallocation of resources and to international trade would help lower the dislocation in economic activity that might accompany this adjustment process.

Past Episodes of Large External Imbalances: An Event Analysis

Several explanations have been advanced that rationalize the large U.S. external deficit as the consequence of economic characteristics specific to the United States in the context of an increasingly globalized economy and greater international capital mobility (Greenspan, 2004). While these factors could make the current constellation of imbalances sustainable for a long period, standard sustainability analysis—which looks at the implications of large and persistent current account deficits for the ratio of net foreign assets to GDP—suggests that this position cannot be sustained forever without a trade balance correction (Box 3.1).

Against this background, it is helpful to revisit the experience of past episodes of large external imbalances. Although several papers have analyzed episodes of external adjustment in advanced economies and emerging markets, they have focused only on current account deficit reversals.[4] The main innovations of this chapter are in expanding the range of reversals to cover those that are most relevant for the current conjuncture—namely, the deficits of advanced economies and surpluses of advanced, emerging market, and oil-exporting economies—and in analyzing episodes of large imbalances that have persisted for a long period.

Large and sustained reversals are defined as swings in the current account balance of at least 2.5 percent of GDP and at least 50 percent of the initial current account imbalance that are sustained for at least five years.[5] Large and persistent imbalances are defined as episodes where the current account balance remained above 2 percent of GDP (in absolute value) for at least five years.[6]

Deficit Reversals in Advanced Economies: Do Real Exchange Rates Matter?

Based on these criteria, the chapter identifies 42 episodes of large and sustained external deficit reversals over the past 40 years in advanced economies (Figure 3.1). The magnitude of the reversals ranges from the 2.7 percent of GDP adjustment in Italy beginning in 1981 to the

[4]The literature on advanced economies includes Freund (2000); Freund and Warnock (2005); Croke, Kamin, and Leduc (2005); Goldman Sachs (2005); Debelle and Galati (2005); and de Haan, Schokker, and Tcherneva (2006). Papers on emerging market countries include Milesi-Ferretti and Razin (1998); Edwards (2005); and the September 2002 *World Economic Outlook*.

[5]The size of the adjustment is the difference between the trough of the current account balance and its value at the end of the reversal. In contrast with previous studies, this chapter also considers reversals that start from small initial levels (less than 2 percent of GDP) and explicitly estimates the duration of the episodes, rather than looking at adjustment over a fixed (e.g., two-year) period.

[6]See Appendix 3.1 for a detailed description of the data and methodology used in this section.

Figure 3.1. Episodes of Deficit Reversals and Large and Persistent Deficits[1]
(1960–2006; current account deficit in percent of GDP)

The chapter identifies 42 episodes of large and sustained deficit reversals in advanced economies, 60 episodes in emerging markets, and 17 episodes in oil-exporting countries. Moreover, 29 cases of large and persistent deficits were identified in the entire sample.

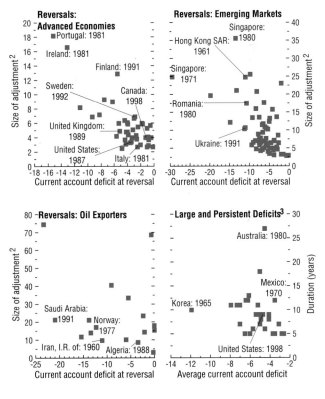

Sources: IMF, *International Financial Statistics;* OECD, *Economic Outlook* (2006); World Bank, *World Development Indicators* (2006); and IMF staff calculations.
[1]See Appendix 3.1 for the definition of deficit reversals and large and persistent deficit episodes, and information on country group composition.
[2]Change in current account deficit, in percent of GDP, from the trough to the end of the reversal episode.
[3]The x-axis refers to the average current account deficit, in percent of GDP, during the episode. The y-axis refers to the number of years the large current account deficit was sustained.

Box 3.1. External Sustainability and Financial Integration

Despite massive net external borrowing, U.S. net foreign assets have remained broadly stable for the past five years as a share of GDP. This, together with the ease with which the United States has financed its large trade and current account deficits, has led to suggestions that in an increasingly financially integrated world such deficits are sustainable without the need for exchange rate adjustment. In particular, some point to the U.S. dollar's role as a reserve currency and to the depth and liquidity of U.S. financial markets to explain high demand for U.S. assets, while others argue that intangible exports and assets make the U.S. external account much stronger than currently measured.[1]

Over the medium term, external sustainability requires that a country's net external position not increase or decrease without bound, relative to the size of the economy. To highlight how financial integration influences this requirement for sustainability, this box considers the cases of three countries that have run large and protracted current account deficits over the past few years—Australia, Spain, and the United States—and investigates the implications of these deficits for their net foreign asset positions. As the figure shows, these deficits had very different implications for the path of net foreign assets of the three countries: Spain's net foreign liabilities increased substantially, relative to its GDP; the U.S. liabilities remained broadly stable despite its large current account deficit; and Australia's experience fell in between. What accounts for these striking differences?

The balance of payments identity says that changes in net foreign assets (*NFA*) can originate from net external lending or borrowing (*FL*)—which, abstracting from statistical discrepancies and other factors such as reclassifications of claims or liabilities, is broadly equal to the

Note: The authors of this box are Jaewoo Lee and Gian Maria Milesi-Ferretti.

[1]On the first point, see Caballero, Farhi, and Gourinchas (2006); on the latter, see Hausmann and Sturzenegger (2006).

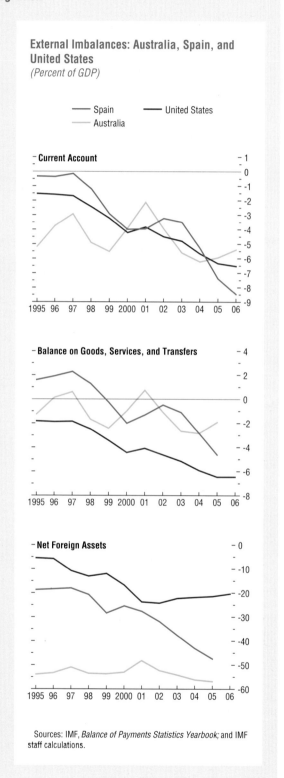

External Imbalances: Australia, Spain, and United States
(Percent of GDP)

Sources: IMF, *Balance of Payments Statistics Yearbook;* and IMF staff calculations.

current account balance (CA)—and changes in the value of external assets and liabilities due to fluctuations in exchange rates or asset prices (KG).[2] In turn, the current account is equal to the balance on goods, nonfactor services, and transfers ($BGST$) plus the investment income earned on assets ($i_t^A A_{t-1}$) minus the income paid out on liabilities ($i_t^L L_{t-1}$):

$$NFA_t - NFA_{t-1} = FL_t + KG_t$$

$$FL_t \cong CA_t = BGST_t + i_t^A A_{t-1} - i_t^L L_{t-1}. \qquad (1)$$

Dividing both sides of the equation by GDP and rearranging terms, changes in a country's net foreign asset position can be described as follows:

$$nfa_t - nfa_{t-1} = bgst_t + \frac{r_t^L - g_t}{1 + g_t} nfa_{t-1} + \frac{r_t^A - r_t^L}{1 + g_t} a_{t-1}, \qquad (2)$$

where lowercase letters denote ratios to GDP; r_t^A and r_t^L denote the nominal rate of return on foreign assets and liabilities, respectively—inclusive of the yields i_t^A and i_t^L and of capital gains; and g_t denotes the growth rate of nominal GDP. When the returns on external assets and liabilities are the same, equation (2) reduces to the standard debt accumulation equation. If this is the case, and if the rate of return is higher than the GDP growth rate, a debtor country will need to run a trade surplus to prevent its net external position from deteriorating. The equation also shows that in a world with much larger stocks of external assets and liabilities than a decade ago, differences in rates of return have potentially grown in importance as factors explaining the evolution of net foreign assets.

Equation (2) helps us understand the differential experiences of Australia, Spain, and the United States. The table illustrates the role played by the three factors driving changes in net

Evolution of Net External Position
(In percent of GDP unless otherwise noted)

	United States (2001–06)	Australia (2001–05)	Spain (2001–05)
Changes in net foreign assets	3.4	−8.7	−19.8
Cumulative effects of:			
Trade deficit	−28.2	−8.5	−8.7
Return–growth rate differential	1.5	1.0	3.1
Asset-liability return differential	30.0	−1.4	−14.2
Differential in returns on assets and liabilities average (in percent)	8.0	−0.5	−3.5
Correlation with change in the real effective exchange rate (over 1995–2005)	−0.74	−0.54	−0.34

Source: IMF staff estimates.

foreign assets in equation (2) between end-2001 and end-2005 (2006 for the United States).[3]

- Australia ran a trade deficit during this period, averaging 2 percent of GDP. The rate of return on its liabilities and the GDP growth rate were similar for this period, as were returns on assets and on liabilities. Consequently, the external position deteriorated in proportion to the size of the trade deficit.
- Spain ran a similar trade deficit of just over 2 percent of GDP, but the return on its external liabilities was much higher than the return on its assets. As a consequence, and despite a high growth rate, its net external position deteriorated much more sharply than did Australia's position.
- The U.S. trade deficit averaged over 5 percent of GDP, more than twice as large as that of Australia or Spain. However, a very large

[2]There are differences across countries in the measurement of *NFA*—in particular, most countries (including Spain) estimate foreign direct investment (FDI) at book value, while others (including Australia and the United States) estimate it at market value. These differences will be reflected in the calculation of capital gains, and hence of rates of return.

[3]Data on *NFA* for the United States in 2006 are based on staff estimates. If *NFA* was scaled by exports of goods and services, to reflect the different degree of trade openness between the three countries, the trends within countries would be similar, but net external liabilities would be lower in Spain than in the United States and Australia.

Box 3.1 *(concluded)*

positive differential between returns on external assets and on liabilities kept the external position from deteriorating at all.

Which factors can help explain differences in rates of return between external assets and liabilities?

- *Relative currency and stock price movements* play an important role. For example, in a country with liabilities denominated in domestic currency and assets in foreign currency, an unexpected exchange rate depreciation will raise the domestic currency return on assets. In a country with high net liabilities denominated in foreign currency, an unexpected depreciation would instead have unfavorable balance sheet effects, by raising the return on liabilities measured in domestic currency. Obviously, higher price increases in foreign stock markets relative to the domestic market would generate a favorable return differential.

- The *composition of the external portfolio* also matters. For example, since returns have on average been higher on equity instruments than on debt instruments, countries with a larger share of equity-type assets (FDI and portfolio equity) in total assets than of equity-type liabilities in total liabilities could have a favorable return differential.

These factors played an important role in the countries under consideration:[4]

- *Exchange rate movements.* Australia, Spain, and the United States have significant net external liabilities denominated in domestic currency but positive net foreign currency holdings. As a result, a currency depreciation will, other things being equal, raise domestic currency returns on external assets by more than returns on liabilities. During the period

under consideration, the U.S. dollar depreciated in real effective terms, while the euro appreciated, consistent with the observed return differentials.[5] The Australian dollar also appreciated, but its adverse effect on the domestic currency value of external assets was mitigated by widespread currency hedging.

- *Relative stock price movements.* Spain's stock prices increased faster than stock prices of its financial trading partners, raising the return on Spain's external liabilities, while the opposite happened for the United States. Australian stock prices also increased more rapidly than stock prices elsewhere, raising returns on Australian equity liabilities, but the effect on the overall return differential was muted by the higher weight of equity on the asset side of the balance sheet.

- *Portfolio composition.* During the sample period, the United States and Australia had a higher share of equity-type instruments (FDI and portfolio equity) in their asset portfolios (around 60 percent) than in their liability portfolios (around 40 percent), with Spain also showing a modest positive difference between the asset and liability share of equity instruments. In light of the higher returns on equity than on debt during the period under consideration, this composition effect helps explain the behavior of return differentials in Australia and especially the United States.

Of course the overall size of the net external position also matters—if overall returns rise, net external liabilities will increase faster in countries that start off with larger imbalances.

Should one extrapolate these trends for the future? Do the large favorable return differentials in the United States obviate the need for trade balance and exchange rate adjustment? Extrapolating these trends would be unwise—as

---

[4]Measured return differentials can also be affected by other factors, such as the method for estimating FDI (see footnote 2 in this box), the riskiness of assets, and incentives for transfer pricing driven by differences in corporate tax policy. Box 1.2 in the September 2005 *World Economic Outlook* discusses the role of these factors in explaining differences between returns on U.S. FDI assets and liabilities.

[5]The real effective depreciation of the U.S. dollar since early 2002 was much sharper vis-à-vis its "financial" trading partners than its commercial trading partners, thus increasing its effect on return differentials.

specified in investment prospectuses, "past performance is no guarantee of future returns." And return differentials would not indefinitely obviate the need for U.S. trade balance and exchange rate adjustment. More specifically:

- Return differentials induced by exchange rate movements require *unexpected* exchange rate depreciation period by period—hence, they are inconsistent with a stable exchange rate. The effect of exchange rate depreciation on return differentials in debtor countries with significant domestic currency liabilities can help the adjustment process, but it would disappear once the exchange rate stabilizes, or when investors require higher returns to compensate for exchange rate risk.

- Similarly, it is not realistic to project persisting differentials in stock returns (indeed, there is no evidence that the U.S. stock market has significantly underperformed world markets over the past three decades).

- Return differentials explained by differences in portfolio composition, risk, liquidity, and other factors may well persist, but they are likely to fall well short of those witnessed recently for the United States. For example, with the current differences in portfolio composition for the United States and Australia, a hefty 5 percent extra return on equity instruments relative to debt would imply a positive return differential between external assets and liabilities of about 1 percent. In addition, a return differential of 2 percent between U.S. FDI assets and liabilities would widen the overall return differential by about ½ percent. Under this illustrative scenario, the need for U.S. trade balance adjustment would be reduced by about 1½ percent of GDP, well short of the 6 percent adjustment that would be needed to stabilize the external position.

In sum, while international financial integration allows for a diversification of risk, with balance sheet effects cushioning external adjustment, it does not provide a permanent flow of "free lunches." Changes in asset prices and returns can generate large valuation effects on a year-to-year basis, but would likely play a more modest role over a longer period. Hence, in a debtor country running a large trade deficit, a correction in the trade balance is eventually inevitable to ensure external sustainability. Of course, the point in time at which this correction will actually take place, its size, and the means through which it would occur would depend on the specific circumstances of the country as well as international macroeconomic and financial market conditions more generally.

18 percent of GDP adjustment that began in Portugal in the same year. Moreover, 13 cases of large and persistent deficits were identified, including the most recent U.S. episode and Australia's two-decade-long period of current account deficit starting in 1980, and are described in detail in Box 3.2. The rest of this section focuses on the reversal episodes.

Examining the reversal episodes reveals the following common patterns:

- The current account deficit averaged 4 percent of GDP at the start of the adjustment, with an average correction of about 6 percent of GDP over a period of four to five years (Table 3.1).

- Consistent with the literature on deficit reversals, the process of current account adjustment was generally accompanied by both a real depreciation of the domestic currency (an average 12 percent total real depreciation)[7] and a slowdown of growth (an average 1½ percentage point decline in annual average GDP growth after the reversal compared with before the reversal). Figure 3.2 shows that the real currency depreciation has typically started in advance of the external adjustment.

[7]Defined as the maximum (peak-to-trough) change in the real effective exchange rate in the period surrounding the reversal.

Table 3.1. Summary Statistics of Episodes of Reversals[1]

| | Number | Current Account at Year of Reversal (percent of GDP) | Size of Adjustment (percent of GDP) | GDP Growth | | REER: Total change (percent)[4] |
				Duration of reversals (years)[2]	Average change (percent)[3]	
		Deficit reversals				
Advanced economies	42	−4.1 (−3.5)	5.7 (4.9)	4.6 (4.0)	−1.4 (−1.0)	−12.2 (−12.5)
Preceded by large and persistent deficits	7	−6.9 (−6.2)	7.4 (6.9)	5.0 (4.0)	−0.2 (−0.9)	−10.2 (−6.2)
		Surplus reversals				
Advanced economies	36	2.4 (1.9)	5.0 (4.6)	4.7 (4.0)	0.6 (0.3)	15.6 (12.1)
Emerging markets	49	4.7 (3.2)	10.1 (9.1)	4.0 (4.0)	1.4 (1.2)	23.1 (16.6)
Oil exporters	15	18.9 (12.3)	20.7 (11.7)	4.4 (4.0)	−2.4 (−1.6)	71.6 (36.0)

Sources: IMF, *International Financial Statistics;* OECD, *Economic Outlook* (2006); World Bank, *World Development Indicators* (2006); and IMF staff calculations.

[1]Average values. Medians are in parentheses.

[2]Number of years between year 0, the trough (peak) year of the current account deficit (surplus), and year *T* (the end year of the episode). See Appendix 3.1 for further details.

[3]Average after the reversal (between year 1 and *T*, where 1 is the first year of the reversal and *T* is the year when the episode ends) less average before the reversal (between −*T* and −1).

[4]Maximum change in real effective exchange rate (REER) within the period surrounding the reversal (−*T*. . .*T*). An increase represents a real appreciation of a country's domestic currency relative to its trading partners.

- Deficit reversals tended to be preceded by a positive output gap, with the difference between actual and potential output peaking one year before the start of the adjustment and declining considerably afterward. This observation is consistent with the proposition that the slowdown in economic activity associated with deficit reversals is a consequence of the business cycle (Goldman Sachs, 2005). However, the size and persistence of the average swing in the output gap during a reversal episode suggests that while the business cycle may indeed have played a role in these episodes, it does not fully account for the output costs associated with the reversals (Edwards, 2005; and Freund and Warnock, 2005).

The magnitude of the exchange rate correction and of the GDP growth slowdown varies considerably across episodes. To shed light on this, the reversal episodes were ordered based on the average change in GDP growth after the reversal. Consistent with Croke, Kamin, and Leduc (2005), two groups of episodes were identified (Figure 3.3):

- A group of "contractionary" deficit reversals, characterized by a significant growth deterioration (a median 3½ percentage point slowdown). These episodes were also associated with a strong reduction in GDP growth relative to trading partners and a widening of the output gap, following a strong decline in investment rates.[8] Relatively large initial external deficits and low openness to trade were also observed. In these cases, the degree of real effective depreciation was modest (median of about 8 percent), often reflecting limited flexibility of the exchange rate regime.[9]

---

[8]A typical case in this group is Spain, whose external deficit increased to 3.5 percent of GDP in 1991 following an economic boom after its accession to the European Union (EU) in 1986, and then returned to zero as the Spanish economy fell into recession along with the economies of the other EU member states in the early 1990s.

[9]Indeed, in 9 of the 11 episodes in this group, the exchange rate was under a narrow peg at the time of reversals, according to the classification of exchange rate systems in Reinhart and Rogoff (2004).

- A group of "expansionary" reversals, in which growth did not slow down and in fact some pickup was generally observed (a median increase in GDP growth of about ¾ percentage point). These episodes were associated with both a larger-than-average total real depreciation (median of about 18 percent), which corrected a somewhat more overvalued currency and spurred export growth, and a strong increase in saving rates, associated with substantial fiscal consolidation, which allowed investment rates to be sustained much closer to their pre-reversal values.[10]

While the contractionary episodes conform to an adjustment occurring largely through a rebalancing of demand differentials with trading partners in the context of limited exchange rate flexibility, the expansionary episodes reflect a stronger role for relative price adjustment. In these cases, real depreciation played a key role by either offsetting an expenditure-reducing shock (e.g., fiscal consolidation) or correcting a competitiveness problem.

The main conclusions from this analysis of deficit reversals in advanced economies are that while changes in growth differentials clearly play a role in the adjustment, real depreciation can help smooth the impact of slowing domestic demand. Indeed, among historical episodes of deficit reversals in advanced economies over the past 40 years, there has been a clear trade-off between the growth slowdown after the reversal and total real effective exchange rate depreciation (Figure 3.4). Simple regression analysis suggests that a 10 percent total real effective depreciation has been associated with a ½ percentage point lower average decline in GDP growth after the reversal.

[10]Episodes in this group include Finland in 1991, Sweden in 1992, and Canada in 1998. For Finland and Sweden, the depreciation helped smooth the effect of negative external shocks (the decline of prices of key commodities such as pulp and paper, the vanishing of Russia as a major export market, and the world recession) and of the banking system crisis (Dornbusch, 1996). In Canada, both the reversal and the real exchange rate depreciation occurred in the context of a significant process of fiscal consolidation.

Figure 3.2. Advanced Economies: Key Indicators During Deficit Reversals[1]

(Medians across episodes; t = 0 is the trough year of the ratio of current account deficit to GDP; x-axis in years before and after t = 0)

The real effective exchange rate (REER) starts depreciating around two years before the trough of the current account deficit. Total domestic demand growth is above that of trading partners before the reversal but falls below after the reversal. Output is above potential before the trough but the output gap widens and remains low afterwards.

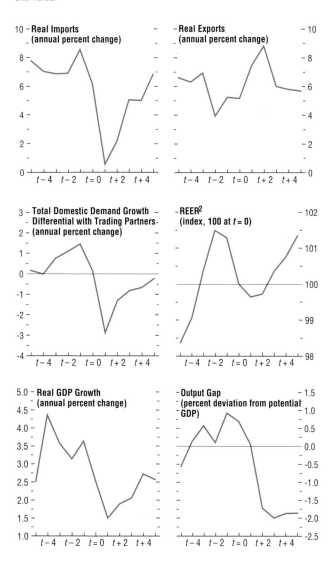

Sources: IMF, *International Financial Statistics;* OECD, *Economic Outlook* (2006); World Bank, *World Development Indicators* (2006); and IMF staff calculations.
[1]See Appendix 3.1 for the definition of deficit reversals and information on country group composition.
[2]An increase in the index represents a real appreciation while a decrease represents a real depreciation of a country's currency relative to its trading partners.

Figure 3.3. Deficit Reversals in Advanced Economies: Episode Characteristics by Average Change in GDP Growth

(Medians across the two groups of episodes; asterisks show that the difference between the medians in the contractionary and expansionary deficit reversals is statistically significant at the 10 percent confidence level)

Total depreciation of real effective exchange rate (REER) is much higher in the expansionary reversals. These cases are also characterized by higher openness to trade and smaller current account deficits.

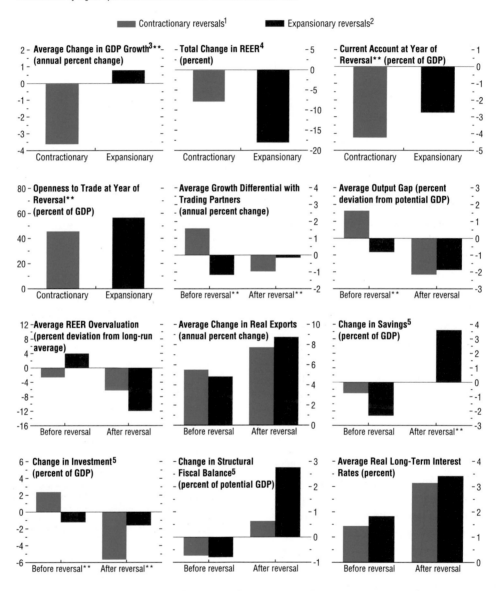

Sources: IMF, *International Financial Statistics;* OECD, *Economic Outlook* (2006); World Bank, *World Development Indicators* (2006); and IMF staff calculations.

[1]Contractionary deficit reversals are the 11 deficit reversals with the largest average decline in GDP growth (the bottom quartile in the sample ordered by the change in growth).

[2]Expansionary deficit reversals are the 10 deficit reversals with the smallest average decline in GDP growth (the top quartile in the sample ordered by the change in growth).

[3]Average of GDP annual growth rates in the period after the reversal (1 . . . T) less average annual growth rates in the period before the reversal ($-T$ . . . -1).

[4]Maximum change in REER within the period surrounding the reversal ($-T$ . . . T). A decrease represents a real depreciation of a country's currency relative to its trading partners.

[5]"Before reversal" is the change in the variable between $-T$ and 0. "After reversal" is the change in the variable between 0 and T.

Surplus Reversals: What Is the Role of Real Exchange Rate Appreciation?

This chapter identifies 36 episodes of large and sustained reversals of external surpluses in advanced economies, 49 episodes in emerging markets, and 15 episodes among oil exporters (Figure 3.5). Moreover, 20 cases of large and persistent surpluses were identified for all countries, including the two-decade-long current account surplus of Switzerland (see Box 3.2).

The following common patterns emerged from the reversal episodes:

- At the start of the reversal, the current account surplus averaged 2½ percent of GDP for advanced economies, and had higher ratios to GDP for emerging markets and oil exporters (about 5 percent and 20 percent of GDP, respectively). The average size of the adjustment was also much larger in emerging markets and for oil exporters than in advanced economies, although the reversal occurred over a similar time frame—four to five years (see Table 3.1).

- Surplus reversals in advanced economies and emerging markets have been associated with both an acceleration of GDP growth and a real appreciation (see Table 3.1). In particular, in both advanced economies and emerging markets, real effective exchange rates appreciated strongly and real GDP growth tended to accelerate when the reversals occurred (Figure 3.6).

- While these findings indicate symmetry between surplus and deficit reversals, only for advanced economies was it possible to find some weak evidence of a trade-off between the increase in GDP growth after the reversal and real exchange rate appreciation. For emerging markets, a stronger real appreciation did not reduce the magnitude of the increase in output growth associated with the reversal.

To shed further light on the relative role of GDP growth and real appreciation for emerging markets during surplus reversals, expansionary episodes (in which the surplus decline was accompanied by a strong increase in GDP

Figure 3.4. Advanced Economies: Total Change in Real Effective Exchange Rate and Average Change in GDP Growth During Deficit Reversals

Depreciation in real effective exchange rate (REER) has helped reduce the output costs associated with a deficit reversal (the larger the depreciation of the currency, the lower the output costs of the reversal).

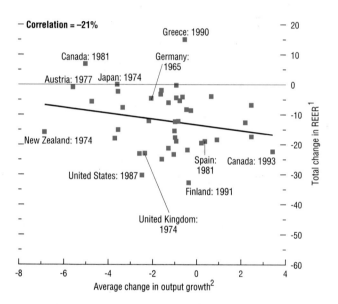

Sources: IMF, *International Financial Statistics;* OECD, *Economic Outlook* (2006); World Bank, *World Development Indicators* (2006); and IMF staff calculations.
[1]Maximum change in REER within the period surrounding the reversal (−T...T). A decrease represents a real depreciation of a country's currency relative to its trading partners.
[2]Average real GDP growth after the reversal (1...T) less average real GDP growth before the reversal (−T...−1).

Figure 3.5. Episodes of Surplus Reversals and Large and Persistent Surpluses[1]

(1960–2006; current account surplus in percent of GDP)

The chapter identifies 36 episodes of large and sustained surplus reversals in advanced economies, 49 episodes in emerging markets, and 15 episodes in oil-exporting countries. Moreover, 20 cases of large and persistent surpluses were identified in the sample.

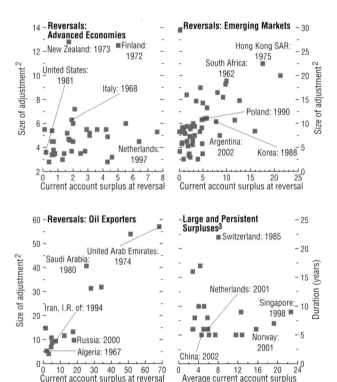

Sources: IMF, *International Financial Statistics;* OECD, *Economic Outlook* (2006); World Bank, *World Development Indicators* (2006); and IMF staff calculations.

[1]See Appendix 3.1 for the definition of surplus reversals and large and persistent surplus episodes, and information on country group composition.

[2]Change in current account surplus, in percent of GDP, from the peak to the end of the reversal episode.

[3]The x-axis refers to the average current account surplus, in percent of GDP, during the episode. The y-axis refers to the number of years the large current account surplus was sustained.

growth) were distinguished from contractionary reversals (in which the surplus decline was accompanied by a substantial fall in GDP growth) (Figure 3.7):

- In the expansionary cases, the surplus reversals were characterized by a strong acceleration in GDP growth relative to trading partners and a reduction of the output gap. The turnaround in the investment cycle and the strong increase in import volumes led to a rapid narrowing of the surplus.[11]

- In the contractionary cases, the surplus buildup was associated with a period of faster growth relative to trading partners and a relatively undervalued currency. The reversal of these surpluses was then characterized by a more significant real appreciation and, especially, a sizable increase in domestic demand (in particular, consumption) accompanied by more expansionary monetary and fiscal policies. Still, GDP growth slowed somewhat during the reversal as the increase in domestic demand did not offset the smaller contribution to growth from net exports.[12]

Overall, an increase in domestic demand appears to play a key role in both types of surplus reversals—either from an increase in investment that drives the growth acceleration in the expansionary episodes or from an increase in consumption that marks the shift from net exports to domestic demand as the main engine

[11]The modest median real appreciation for these episodes masks a vast dispersion in exchange rate changes within this group, with cases of both large appreciation (Argentina in 1978) and large depreciation (China in 1982). Such heterogeneity is probably responsible for the lack of a clear trade-off between the roles of GDP growth and real appreciation in the adjustment process for emerging markets.

[12]Clearly, despite lower output growth, the increase in consumption could enhance welfare. In addition, in the majority of the episodes in this group, the slowdown in GDP growth associated with the decline of the surplus is only a temporary phenomenon, as over the medium term GDP growth tends to return to its pre-reversal average. Typical cases are Korea in 1977 and Poland in 1990; in these episodes, GDP growth returned to its pre-reversal rate after four and six years, respectively.

of growth in the contractionary cases. Real appreciation seems to have played a larger role in the contractionary cases, in particular by correcting an initial undervaluation of the real exchange rate.

Surplus reversals in oil-exporting countries do not fit the above patterns, as the deterioration of the external position has occurred with both a substantial slowdown in GDP growth and a large total real appreciation of their currencies. For these countries, the initial buildup of external surpluses owes much to the positive terms-of-trade effect from a surge in commodity prices (Figure 3.8). In turn, this leads to an increase in domestic demand and inflation, which drives up the real value of the currency. While the sharp decline of the external surplus is related to the reversal of the terms-of-trade increase (causing a sharp decline in export revenues), the currency continues appreciating in real terms, as domestic demand growth and inflation are sustained even after the decline in the terms of trade.

In sum, this analysis of surplus reversal episodes suggests that while surplus reversals for oil exporters have followed a decline of commodity prices, reversals in advanced and emerging market economies have been associated with some real appreciation of domestic currencies and, even more importantly, an increase in domestic demand.

How Responsive Are U.S. Trade Volumes to Exchange Rate Movements?

The analysis of the historical episodes suggests that changes in real exchange rates have been important in the reversal of external imbalances, with a clear role in helping to sustain growth during deficit reversals. The conventional wisdom for the United States, however, is that large exchange rate changes are needed because of the low price elasticities of trade volumes and the partial response of trade prices to changes in nominal exchange rates.

The case for elasticity pessimism can be illustrated by looking at the standard "workhorse"

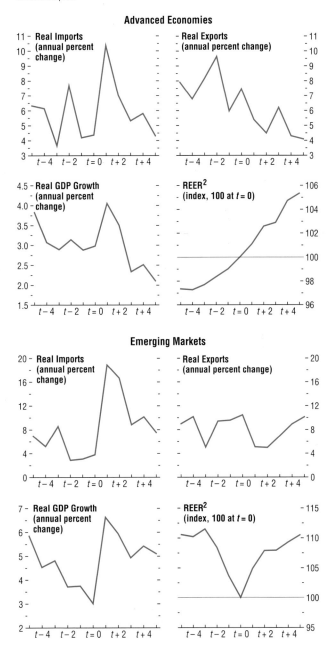

Figure 3.6. Key Indicators During Surplus Reversals[1]
(Medians across episodes; t = 0 is the peak year of the ratio of current account surplus to GDP; x-axis in years before and after t = 0)

In both advanced economies and emerging markets, real effective exchange rate (REER) appreciates and GDP growth increases after the peak year of the current account surplus.

Sources: IMF, *International Financial Statistics;* OECD, *Economic Outlook* (2006); World Bank, *World Development Indicators* (2006); and IMF staff calculations.
[1]See Appendix 3.1 for the definition of surplus reversals and information on country group composition.
[2]An increase in the index represents a real appreciation while a decrease represents a real depreciation of a country's currency relative to its trading partners.

Figure 3.7. Surplus Reversals in Emerging Markets: Episode Characteristics by Average Change in GDP Growth

(Medians across the two groups of episodes; asterisks show that the difference between the medians in the contractionary and expansionary surplus reversals is statistically significant at the 10 percent confidence level)

Reversals of current account surpluses were characterized by an increase in investment in the expansionary reversals and an increase in consumption (decrease in savings) in the contractionary reversals.

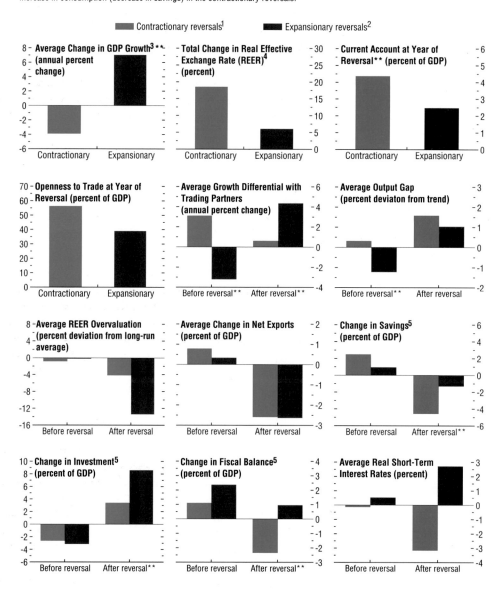

Sources: IMF, *International Financial Statistics;* OECD, *Economic Outlook* (2006); World Bank, *World Development Indicators* (2006); and IMF staff calculations.

[1]Contractionary surplus reversals are the 13 surplus reversals with the largest average decline in GDP growth (the bottom quartile in the sample ordered by the change in growth).

[2]Expansionary surplus reversals are the 12 surplus reversals with the smallest average decline in GDP growth (the top quartile in the sample ordered by the change in growth).

[3]Average of GDP annual growth rates in the period after the reversal (1 . . . *T*) less average annual growth rates in the period before the reversal (−*T* . . . −1).

[4]Maximum change in REER within the period surrounding the reversal (−*T* . . . *T*). An increase represents a real appreciation of a country's currency relative to its trading partners.

[5]"Before reversal" is the change in the variable between −*T* and 0. "After reversal" is the change in the variable between 0 and *T*.

empirical trade model—relating the volume of exports and imports to real foreign and domestic incomes and relative export and import prices. A vast empirical literature exists on this model for the United States and elsewhere, with estimates of trade elasticities varying greatly depending on the methodology, time period, and choice of variables.[13] A general result is that price elasticities tend to be quite small, especially in the short run, and at times too low to satisfy the Marshall Lerner condition.[14] Thus, an exchange rate depreciation would weaken the trade balance as its negative effect on the terms of trade would outweigh its positive effect on trade volumes.

This chapter revisits the standard empirical trade model to correct for biases that may lower estimates of trade elasticities. To provide a benchmark for this exercise, the standard model has been re-estimated for the United States over the post–Bretton Woods period (1973–2006).[15]

The results of the estimation conform to the elasticity pessimism view. In particular, the long-run estimates of U.S. import and export elasticities are quite low—indeed too low to satisfy the traditional Marshall Lerner condition (Table 3.2). Moreover, the U.S. income elasticity of imports is about 0.5 higher than the income elasticity of the trading partners' demand for U.S. exports (as in Houthakker and Magee, 1969). This suggests that foreign GDP growth would need to be about double that in the United States to start reducing the U.S. trade deficit from its 2005 level—a seemingly unrealistic condition as historically

[13]See Goldstein and Khan (1985); Hooper, Johnson, and Marquez (2000); and IMF (2006).

[14]The Marshall Lerner condition is that when changes in exchange rates are fully passed through to import prices at home and abroad, the import and export price elasticities (in absolute value) must sum to greater than one for a depreciation to improve the trade balance.

[15] See Appendix 3.2 for details on the econometric methodology and a full set of tables with the results of this section.

Figure 3.8. Oil Exporters: Surplus Reversals[1]

(Medians across episodes; t = 0 *is the peak year of the ratio of current account surplus to GDP; x-axis in years before and after* t = 0*)*

Current account surpluses for oil exporters mainly reflect large shifts in the terms of trade.

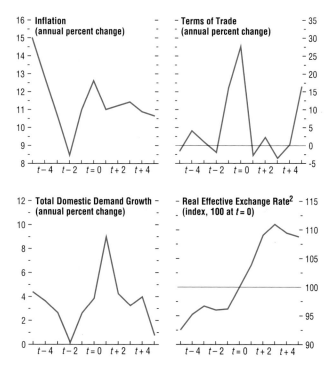

Sources: IMF, *International Financial Statistics;* OECD, *Economic Outlook* (2006); World Bank, *World Development Indicators* (2006); and IMF staff calculations.

[1]See Appendix 3.1 for the definition of surplus reversals and information on country group composition.

[2]An increase in the index represents a real appreciation while a decrease represents a real depreciation of a country's currency relative to its trading partners.

Table 3.2. Standard Trade Model: Estimates of U.S. Trade Elasticities

| | Estimated over 1973–2006 | | | | Estimated over 1986–2006 | |
| | Without correcting for biases | | Correcting for aggregation bias | Correcting for vertical integration bias[3] | Without correcting for biases | |
	RP[1]	REER[2]	RP[1]	RP[1]	RP[1]	REER[2]
Imports						
Price elasticity	−0.69	0.37	−1.45	−1.48	−0.82	0.48
Income elasticity	2.03	2.46	1.68	0.64	1.86	2.46
Exports						
Price elasticity	0.02	−0.49	−0.26	. . .	−1.06	−0.60
Income elasticity	1.85	1.82	1.60	. . .	0.76	1.97

Source: IMF staff calculations based on estimates in Appendix 3.2.
[1]Price elasticities with respect to relative prices (RP).
[2]Price elasticities with respect to real effective exchange rate (REER). Increase in REER denotes real appreciation.
[3]The correction for vertical integration bias is based on estimates on the 1979–2006 sample.

the United States has grown at about the same pace as the rest of the world.[16]

Before looking at two possible sources of misspecification of the standard empirical model, two caveats should be made about these results. First, the traditional Marshall Lerner condition is based on the assumption of complete pass-through of exchange rate movements to import prices. In the context of limited exchange rate pass-through, however, a U.S. dollar depreciation could still improve the nominal trade balance even with the low trade price elasticities estimated in the standard empirical model. The reason is that with partial pass-through, a U.S. dollar depreciation reduces the U.S. terms of trade by less than when exchange rate movements are fully transmitted to trade prices, making it easier for an improvement in real net exports to generate an adjustment in the nominal trade balance (Box 3.3).

Second, restricting the sample to the past two decades yields higher estimates of the U.S. trade price elasticities. This finding is consistent with

the view that globalization is likely to have increased the responsiveness of trade volumes to changes in real exchange rates (Obstfeld, 2002). In particular, the increasing importance of out-sourcing and of trade in intermediate products should induce firms to respond more strongly to changes in relative prices by switching between domestic and imported inputs, or by shifting tasks across borders.

Does the Standard Empirical Trade Model Underestimate the Response of Trade Volumes to Relative Prices?

The U.S. trade equations estimated above represent a basic, "stripped-down" version of the standard empirical trade model. Several efforts have been made over the years to improve upon this model and find more plausible values for trade elasticities in the long run. This subsection explores two particular variations on the standard empirical model, both of which yield larger estimates of long-run trade price elasticities and smaller (and less divergent) estimates of income elasticities of imports and exports, thus providing some ground for greater elasticity optimism.

First, low measured long-run price elasticities of U.S. trade volumes may reflect an aggregation bias. It is well known that estimates of trade price elasticities using microeconomic data (that is, at the level of individual goods or sectors) yield a wide range of values across sectors and

[16]One puzzling implication of the higher estimated income elasticities of imports than of exports is that if U.S. growth is the same or faster than its trading partners, the U.S. trade deficit will keep expanding, with unchanged relative prices. Counter to this prediction, however, is the finding that fast-growing countries tend to have higher income elasticities of exports than of imports, which explains why they have not experienced a trend depreciation or an exploding trade deficit (Krugman, 1989).

Box 3.2. Large and Persistent Current Account Imbalances

The size and persistence of the U.S. current account deficit has raised concerns about the possibility of an abrupt and disorderly adjustment.[1] However, as a number of observers have argued, large and protracted external imbalances may be a reflection of investors' decisions to allocate their savings toward the most profitable uses.[2] Even if a correction is eventually required, large and persistent deficits may not need to end in a more severe adjustment than do shorter-lived imbalances.

This box discusses the experiences that countries have had with large and persistent current account imbalances, focusing on current account deficits for advanced economies and on current account surpluses for advanced economies, emerging markets, and oil exporters. It first examines 13 episodes of large and persistent deficits in advanced economies, especially their experience with deficit reversals. It then examines 20 episodes of large and persistent surpluses for all countries in the sample, looking for common patterns during these episodes.[3]

Large and Persistent Current Account Deficits in Advanced Economies

While the criteria chosen to identify *large and persistent current account deficits*—a deficit amounting to more than 2 percent of GDP for more than five years—may seem undemanding, the actual current account deficit across the 13 episodes identified for the advanced economies averaged about 5 percent of GDP and lasted about 11 years. Seven of these episodes eventually ended with a reversal, while the remaining six are still ongoing (Australia, Greece, New Zealand, Portugal, Spain, and the United States).[4]

On average, during the 13 episodes of *large and persistent current account deficits*, GDP growth tended to be slower and consumption growth faster than outside these periods (for both variables, the difference between the cross-country medians is statistically significant at 10 percent or better; see first figure). Moreover, these episodes were characterized by faster growth in private credit and a stronger stock market performance. Taken together, these findings appear consistent with an intertemporal smoothing view of current account imbalances—that the persistent external deficits were an optimal response to a permanent increase in productivity.[5]

If these deficits reflect appropriate saving and investment decisions, one could expect their reversal to occur smoothly and without a large growth slowdown (driven by the return of investment and saving ratios to their new long-run levels). Indeed, the experience with the reversal of *large and persistent current account deficits* in advanced economies shows that the correction of these deficits has not been characterized by a larger decline in GDP growth or by a greater real effective exchange rate depreciation than the other reversal episodes identified and discussed in the main text (see Table 3.1).[6] Moreover, reversals after large and persistent deficits, on average, occurred over a similar time frame as the other reversal episodes (between four and five years). These results suggest that the adjustment of *large and persistent current account deficits in advanced economies* have generally reflected macroeconomic developments within the economy, rather than following externally driven events where the size and persistence of the current account deficit

---

Note: The main author of this box is Roberto Cardarelli.

[1]See, among others, Roubini and Setser (2004).

[2]See, among others, Backus and Lambert (2005).

[3]Clearly, the relatively small number of large and persistent episodes of external imbalances suggests caution in drawing general conclusions from these patterns.

[4]See Appendix 3.1 for a list of all episodes.

[5]Following an increase in productivity, expected future income increases more than current income, as the capital stock takes time to adjust. At the same time, consumption ratios increase in anticipation of higher future income. Both lower saving rates and higher investment ratios lead to a deficit in the current account balance (Ghosh and Ostry, 1995).

[6]See also Freund and Warnock (2005) for a similar finding.

Box 3.2 *(concluded)*

Advanced Economies: Key Indicators of Large and Persistent Deficits[1]

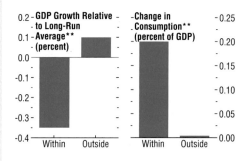

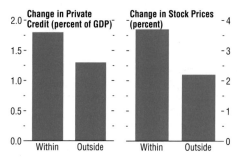

Sources: IMF, *International Financial Statistics;* OECD, *Economic Outlook* (2006); World Bank, *World Development Indicators* (2006); and IMF staff calculations.

[1]"Within" refers to the cross-country median of the average value of the variable during episodes of large and persistent imbalances. "Outside" refers to the cross-country median of the average value of the variable for the same countries but in different periods. Asterisks show that the difference between the two medians is statistically significant at the 10 percent confidence level.

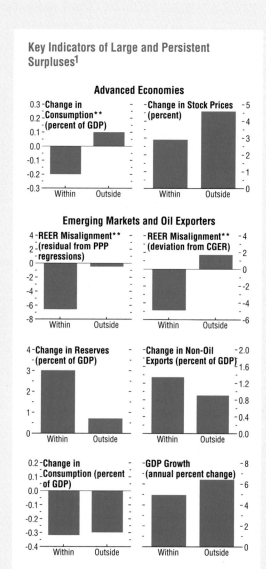

Key Indicators of Large and Persistent Surpluses[1]

Sources: IMF, *International Financial Statistics;* OECD, *Economic Outlook* (2006); World Bank, *World Development Indicators* (2006); and IMF staff calculations.

[1]"Within" refers to the cross-country median of the average value of the variable during episodes of large and persistent imbalances. "Outside" refers to the cross-country median of the average value of the variable for the same countries but in different periods. Asterisks show that the difference between the two medians is statistically significant at the 10 percent confidence level. REER stands for real effective exchange rate, PPP for purchasing power parity, and CGER for Consultative Group on Exchange Rate issues. See footnote 8 in Box 3.2 for more information.

itself has precipitated the adjustment (see also Debelle and Galati, 2005).[7]

Large and Persistent Current Account Surpluses in Advanced Economies and Emerging Market Countries

As in the deficit episodes, the average size and duration of the episodes of *large and per-*

[7]The findings that the nature of capital flows does not seem to vary prior to a current account adjustment for advanced economies (Debelle and Galati, 2005) and that the extent of the adjustment in advanced economies (the changes in GDP and currency values) does not seem to be related to the level of foreign debt (Freund and Warnock, 2005) are consistent with this interpretation.

sistent current account surpluses were well above the thresholds required—at least 2 percent of GDP for at least five years. In particular, across the eight episodes of *large and persistent current account surpluses* identified for the advanced economies, the current account surplus averaged about 6 percent of GDP and lasted on average about 12 years. Across the 12 episodes identified for emerging markets and oil exporters, the current account surpluses averaged about 9 percent of GDP and lasted six years on average.

The experiences during the eight episodes of *large and persistent current account surpluses in the advanced economies* identified in the chapter again appear consistent with the intertemporal smoothing view of current account imbalances. In particular, these cases were associated with slower growth in consumption and a weaker performance of the stock market during the episodes (see second figure).

A key characteristic of the 12 episodes of *large and persistent current account surpluses in emerging markets and oil exporters* has been a relatively undervalued real effective exchange rate

(see second figure).[8] Moreover, these episodes have been characterized by faster accumulation of foreign reserves, faster export growth, and slower consumption growth. However, for these variables, the difference with the averages outside these periods is not statistically significant. Interestingly, GDP growth was not faster on average when these countries experienced a large and sustained surplus, suggesting that currency undervaluation is not likely to result in permanently higher growth.[9]

---

[8]The difference in medians is significant at a 10 percent or better confidence interval for the two measures of currency misalignment shown in the figure, namely, the residuals from the regressions of real exchange rates on PPP-adjusted relative per capita incomes (from Johnson, Ostry, and Subramanian, 2007) and the deviation of real exchange rates from the medium-term equilibrium values estimated by the Consultative Group on Exchange Rate issues.

[9]Johnson, Ostry, and Subramanian (2007) document the role of currency undervaluation in past growth episodes in developing countries.

---

goods, most of which are much higher than the range typically found in the macroeconomic literature.[17] The large heterogeneity in these estimates raises the possibility that trade elasticities estimated on the basis of aggregate data could be different from the average of sector- or goods-specific estimates. For example, goods with relatively low price elasticities could be exposed to stronger price variations and thus exert a dominant effect on the estimated aggregate price elasticities, which would then underestimate the average response of trade volumes to relative prices (Goldstein and Khan, 1985; and Orcutt, 1950).

Second, measured long-run import price elasticities may be biased by vertical integra-

tion. Conventional empirical estimates of U.S. import price elasticities do not recognize that goods imported into the United States often are produced using intermediate goods exported from the United States (the share of U.S.-made intermediate goods in U.S. imports is estimated at about 30 percent).[18] Thus, data on U.S. imports used in econometric estimates can be interpreted as the sum of two components, the imported foreign value added and the U.S. exports of intermediate goods. As a result, measured U.S. import price elasticities will also be the sum of two components, the "true" price elasticity of imports and the effect of exchange rates on U.S. exports of intermediate products. As real exchange rate depreciation will reduce the demand for imports but increase the

---

[17]See, among others, Broda and Weinstein (2006) and Broda, Limão, and Weinstein (2006) for estimated elasticities of substitution for U.S. imports and exports at different levels of aggregation.

[18]See Appendix 3.2. There are no reliable estimates of the share of U.S. imports in U.S. exports (see National Research Council, 2006).

Box 3.3. Exchange Rate Pass-Through to Trade Prices and External Adjustment

The extent to which changes in nominal exchange rates pass through to changes in export and import prices—in short, exchange rate pass-through—affects the role of exchange rates in the process of external adjustment through two channels.[1] First, a limited pass-through at home and abroad can mute the expenditure-switching effect of exchange rate changes on trade volumes, as it forestalls movements in relative trade prices. Second, different degrees of pass-through at home and abroad affect the impact of exchange rate movements on the domestic terms of trade—the ratio between domestic-currency-denominated export and import prices—with a high pass-through at home and abroad associated with a worsening of the domestic terms of trade. It is the combination of the two effects, that is, the response of nominal trade balances, that ultimately matters for external adjustment.

Against this background, this box first reviews the available empirical evidence on exchange rate pass-through. It then discusses the implications of this evidence for nominal external adjustment. Finally, it draws some implications on the potential for a depreciation of the U.S. dollar to spur a change in the U.S. trade imbalance.

Evidence on Exchange Rate Pass-Through

A vast body of research shows that exchange rate movements are only partially transmitted to import prices—on average for OECD countries between 1975 and 2003, only 64 percent of the change in exchange rates has been transmitted to import prices after one year (see the table). Moreover, pass-through into prices at the border varies considerably across sectors—being lower for highly differentiated manufacturing products—and across countries, likely reflecting differences in the sectoral composition of

imports as well as in market size. In particular, the United States tends to have a much lower pass-through to import prices than do other advanced economies—about 0.5—while smaller, more open economies have rates closer to one.[2] This difference may be related to the stronger domestic competition for imported goods in the United States and may also reflect the international use of the dollar in invoicing export and import transactions (Goldberg and Tille, 2005).

While there is broad consensus on the fact that pass-through to U.S. import prices is lower than in most other economies, it is not clear whether pass-through has declined in advanced economies over the recent past, with several studies reaching different conclusions depending on the methodology and data used.[3] For emerging markets, pass-through coefficients have declined considerably in recent years, following the decline in inflation rates, and are now comparable to those in advanced countries (Frankel, Parsley, and Wei, 2005; and IMF, 2006).

The literature on pass-through of exchange rate movements into domestic-currency-denominated export prices is considerably less extensive. Most studies assume pass-through coefficients for exports derived as the average of the coefficients of pass-through to import prices of partner countries. For the United States, this gives an export pass-through of about 0.8.

Note: The author of this box is Cedric Tille.

[1]This box focuses on pass-through to trade prices at the border. Pass-through to retail prices of traded goods is further limited by distribution costs (Campa and Goldberg, 2005).

[2]These estimates, however, may underestimate the degree of pass-through as they fail to take into account the compositional effect associated with firms' entry and exit following exchange rate movements (Rodríguez-López, 2006).

[3]Campa and Goldberg (2005) find some decline of pass-through between 1975 and 2003 that primarily reflects a change of the import mix toward goods with low pass-through. Marazzi and others (2005) argue that the pass-through to U.S. import prices has declined further in recent years. Hellerstein, Daly, and Marsh (2006) find no evidence of a declining pass-through, while Thomas and Marquez (2006) argue that the measurement of foreign prices is central to the results and find that pass-through to import prices has remained constant at about 0.5 for the United States.

Exchange Rate Pass-Through into Import Prices After One Year

Country	
United States[1]	0.42
Euro area[2]	0.81
Japan[3]	0.53–1.00
Open advanced economies[4]	0.60
Developing countries and emerging markets[5]	0.66
Average excluding the United States[6]	0.66–0.77
Average including the United States[6]	0.61–0.70
Average for OECD countries[1]	0.64

Source: Campa and Goldberg (2005) unless otherwise noted.
[1]Campa and Goldberg (2005).
[2]Faruqee (2006).
[3]Faruqee (2006); Campa and Goldberg (2005); and Otani, Shiratsuka, and Shirota (2006).
[4]Campa and Goldberg (2005). Average of Australia, Canada, Denmark, New Zealand, Norway, Sweden, Switzerland, and the United Kingdom.
[5]Frankel, Parsley, and Wei (2005).
[6]Average of the estimates above with low and high estimates for Japan.

Pass-Through and Nominal Trade Adjustment

An important implication of the incomplete exchange rate pass-through to import prices is that the traditional Marshall Lerner condition—which states that for an exchange rate depreciation to increase the nominal trade balance, the sum of the export and import price elasticities must be greater than one ($\eta_x + \eta_m > 1$)—no longer holds.[4]

Indeed, the Marshall Lerner condition is based on the assumption of complete pass-through to import prices at home and abroad.[5] With complete pass-through, an exchange rate depreciation is fully transmitted to a country's

[4]Both elasticities are with respect to relative prices and are taken in absolute value.

[5]Defining the coefficient of pass-through to import prices at home as β_m and the coefficient of pass-through to export prices as $1 - \beta_x$, the adjusted Marshall Lerner condition can be expressed as $\eta_m \beta_m + \eta_x \beta_x > \beta_m + \beta_x - 1$, where the left-hand side is the impact of a 1 percent depreciation on real net exports and the right-hand side is the impact of a 1 percent depreciation on the terms of trade. The traditional Marshall Lerner condition follows from assuming a complete pass-through to import prices at home ($\beta_m = 1$) and to import prices abroad ($\beta_x = 1$) (Gust and Sheets, 2006).

domestic terms of trade, since, as expressed in domestic currency, import prices increase by the full amount of the depreciation while export prices remain constant (though they decrease in foreign currency).[6] In this case, the nominal trade balance improves only if the expenditure-switching effect from the changes in relative prices is sufficiently strong, that is, if the sum of trade price elasticities is larger than one. Moreover, if trade volumes respond more slowly than prices, the improvement will come with a lag and the trade balance will initially deteriorate (J-curve effect).

With zero pass-through at home and abroad, however, an exchange rate depreciation still improves the nominal trade balance even if price trade elasticities are low—and the traditional Marshall Lerner condition is not satisfied. In this case, expressed in domestic currency, import prices do not move with the exchange rate depreciation while export prices increase, as they are held constant in the currency of the destination market.[7] In this environment, the exchange rate depreciation improves the nominal trade balance, thanks to more favorable terms of trade, even though the expenditure-switching channel on trade volumes is neutralized as relative trade prices do not change with the exchange rate.

The empirical evidence suggests that the pass-through environment for the United States is a combination of the two cases described above—with low pass-through of exchange rate changes into U.S. import prices and higher pass-through into foreign-market prices of U.S. exports. Hence, both U.S.-dollar-denominated export and import prices tend to be relatively insensitive to movements of the U.S. dollar (Goldberg and Tille, 2005).

In this context, a U.S. exchange rate depreciation is likely to improve the trade balance even if the trade price elasticities are low, as

[6]This is the traditional case of producer-currency pricing (e.g., Obstfeld and Rogoff, 1996 and 2000).

[7]This is the case of local-currency pricing (e.g., Devereux and Engel, 2002).

Box 3.3 *(concluded)*

limited pass-through to the terms of trade reduces the burden of the adjustment on export and import volumes. Specifically, considering a pass-through to U.S. import prices of 0.5 and a pass-through to the foreign-market price of U.S. exports of 0.8,[8] a 10 percent depreciation of the U.S. dollar would imply a 0.3 percent deterioration in the U.S. terms of trade. Even with the low U.S. trade price elasticities estimated in the standard empirical trade model (see Table 3.2), a depreciation of

[8]As stressed by Dillon and Goldberg (2006), however, using this coefficient as a measure of the pass-through to U.S. export prices is valid only as a first approximation, as this estimate applies to all the imports of those countries, not just those from the United States. Faruqee's (2006) direct estimates of pass-through to U.S. export prices in U.S. dollars are consistent with a pass-through to foreign-currency prices of U.S. exports of about 0.85 after 18 months.

the U.S. dollar would narrow the trade deficit. This reduction would be mainly associated with stronger export volumes, following the decline in the foreign-currency-denominated price of U.S. export goods. However, as U.S. imports exceed exports by about 50 percent, this scenario would lead to only a partial narrowing of the trade deficit in the absence of other changes, such as a decline in the domestic demand for imports or an increase in foreign demand for U.S. products.

Overall, the main implication from this analysis is that given the particular pass-through environment for the United States, a U.S. dollar depreciation could contribute to some narrowing of the U.S. trade deficit even if trade price elasticities are relatively low. This contribution would take the form of an improvement in the real trade balance, with the terms of trade deteriorating less than with full pass-through.

demand for U.S. intermediate exports, ignoring vertical integration will cause the measured import price elasticities to be underestimated.[19]

Against this background, the basic standard empirical model was re-estimated controlling for the heterogeneity in individual sector price elasticities and for vertical integration:

- To control for the presence of heterogeneity in elasticities across sectors, the standard model was estimated for 17 categories of U.S. imports and 16 categories of U.S. exports, and aggregate trade price elasticities were calculated as the simple averages of individual elasticities.[20] This methodology yields much higher estimates of U.S. trade price elasticities—import price elasticities more

[19]See Chinn (2005) and Khatri and Oguro (2007) for other studies that estimate the impact of vertical integration on trade elasticities.

[20]These averages are consistent estimates of the aggregate relation in the presence of heterogeneity in the parameters (Pesaran and Smith, 1995). However, these estimates do not take into account the possibility that individual elasticities are affected by other sectors' relative trade prices.

than double while export price elasticities increase from zero to about 0.3 (in absolute value)—and the Houthakker-Magee asymmetry in income elasticities disappears (see Table 3.2).

- To correct for vertical integration, the basic model for U.S. imports was re-estimated adding U.S. exports of key intermediate products as an additional explanatory variable. This specification yields estimates of U.S. import price elasticities that are about twice as high as in the standard empirical model and have a much lower income elasticity (see Table 3.2).

Finally, the standard trade model was adapted to allow for the possibility that the responsiveness of trade to relative price changes depends on the size of the relative price changes—owing to the existence of fixed costs of entry into trade emphasized in the "new trade theory." In particular, the standard trade model for the United States was re-estimated using a nonlinear error correction specification that allows trade volumes to return to their long-run level at a faster pace when the change in relative trade prices is above a certain threshold.[21] The results show strong evidence of a nonlinear dynamic adjustment for U.S. import volumes. Specifically, they indicate that when relative import prices change by more than 2 percent per quarter (in absolute value), U.S. import volumes return to their long-run level much more rapidly, that is, after 5 quarters compared with 11 quarters when the changes are slower than the threshold.[22]

Applying the same methodology to other OECD countries generally confirms that import and export volumes tend to react more strongly to changes in relative prices above a certain threshold. These thresholds varied considerably across countries, however, raising the question of whether the effectiveness of real exchange rate changes depends on structural differences across these economies.

Exchange Rate Effectiveness and Flexibility of Markets

Does the effectiveness of changes in real exchange rates increase with the flexibility of labor and product markets? In the traditional macroeconomic approach to trade modeling, countries expand their exports by exporting more "existing" goods, while the "new trade theory" has long emphasized the importance of trade in new varieties and new markets (Krugman, 1989). A growing body of empirical evidence supports the notion that fast-growing countries tend to increase their market share essentially by expanding the range of goods that they export.[23]

This finding carries important implications for the role of exchange rate movements in external adjustment. As entry and exit into export markets require firms to sustain fixed costs, only large and persistent changes in relative prices may induce firms to incur such costs—consistent with the evidence of nonlinearities in trade responsiveness discussed above. Moreover, more flexible production structures (that is, with lower fixed costs of entry and exit) could help firms take advantage of new opportunities when relative prices change permanently, and thus enhance a country's aggregate trade responsiveness to exchange rate movements.

Two pieces of evidence point to a correlation between the effectiveness of real exchange rates and economic flexibility. First, there is a negative correlation between the thresholds in relative price changes found in the nonlinear model of trade volumes described above and an index of flexibility of product and labor markets (Figure 3.9).[24] This suggests that relative prices may need to change less to generate a faster adjustment of trade volumes in countries in which labor and product market rigidities are smaller. Second, separating the reversal episodes analyzed earlier based on the degree of flexibility of the economies in which they occurred suggests that changes in real effective exchange rates during adjustment have been smaller in relatively more flexible economies. Moreover, the negative trade-off between total real exchange rate depreciation and the average change in GDP after the reversal is found only for the more flexible economies, suggesting that only for them have the exchange rate movements been effective in cushioning (other things being equal) the output costs associated with adjustment (see Figure 3.9).

[21]Clarida, Goretti, and Taylor (2007) find evidence of threshold behavior in current account adjustment for the G-7 countries so that the dynamics of adjustment depend upon whether the current account balance breaches estimated, country-specific current account balance thresholds.
[22]Over the 1973–2006 sample period, U.S. relative import prices have exceeded the threshold level only 25 percent of the time.
[23]Several papers show that the measured U.S. import income elasticity is lower—and the puzzling Houthakker-Magee result disappears—when the classic workhorse trade model takes into account a "varieties term" in import demand. See, among others, Marquez (2003); Gagnon (2002); Mann and Plück (2007); and Justiniano and Krajnyák (2005).

[24]The index is constructed using indicators of the cost of starting and closing a firm, and of hiring and firing labor, from the Cost of Doing Business database (World Bank). For each indicator, the values for each country were re-scaled between 0 and 1 (with 1 indicating a higher degree of flexibility), and the overall flexibility index was constructed as a simple average of these values.

These findings suggest that changes in real exchange rates needed for a given amount of external adjustment will likely be larger for economies where rigidities in product and labor markets make it more difficult for firms to enter and exit trade.[25] Moreover, increased protectionism, by reducing effective flexibility in economies, would tend to raise the growth costs associated with deficit reversals for any given adjustment in relative prices.

Implications for Global Imbalances

The findings in the previous sections support the view that real exchange rate changes are likely to help reduce the output costs associated with a narrowing of external imbalances. What are the implications for the present conjuncture?

To be sure, the unprecedented scale of the U.S. deficit should make one cautious about drawing strong conclusions from the historical experience for a range of countries. Nevertheless, the 1987 deficit reversal in the United States is consistent with the more general cross-country evidence that a realignment of real exchange rates matters for external adjustment (Krugman, 1991). The adjustment of the late 1980s partially reflected a cyclical weakening in domestic demand, particularly of investment. While the gyration in growth differentials with trading partners was primarily induced by stronger growth abroad, rather than lower growth in the United States, the large real exchange rate depreciation contributed to the surge in real export growth and helped stabilize economic activity (see Kamin, Reeve, and Sheets, 2006).

The 15 percent real effective depreciation of the U.S. dollar since mid-2002 (17 percent

Figure 3.9. Thresholds in Relative Trade Prices, Real Effective Exchange Rate, and Flexibility of Markets

Countries with higher values of the flexibility index tend to have lower thresholds in the growth rate of relative prices of imports and exports. More flexible economies have experienced smaller movements in real effective exchange rate (REER) during reversal episodes. Only for these economies does there appear to be a trade-off between REER depreciation and GDP growth during deficit reversals.

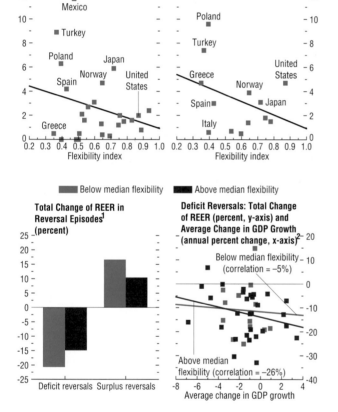

Sources: IMF, *International Financial Statistics;* OECD, *Economic Outlook* (2006); World Bank, *World Development Indicators* (2006); World Bank, Cost of Doing Business database; and IMF staff calculations.
[1]Maximum change in REER within the period surrounding the reversal (–*T* . . . *T*), median across episodes. An increase represents a real appreciation while a decrease represents a real depreciation of a country's currency relative to its trading partners.
[2]Advanced economies only. Average real GDP growth after the reversal (1 . . . *T*) less average real GDP growth before the reversal (–*T* . . . –1) on the x-axis. Maximum change in REER within the period surrounding the reversal (–*T* . . . *T*) on the y-axis. Median across episodes.

[25]This evidence is consistent with Burgess and Knetter (1998), who consider the interaction between real exchange rate changes and labor markets across the G-7 countries (with the more flexible U.S. economy more responsive than Germany and Japan), and Gourinchas (1998), who shows that U.S. import-competing sectors seem to be more responsive to exchange rates than other less flexible sectors, including nontradables sectors.

in nominal terms) is now starting to have an impact on the non-oil trade deficit as a ratio to GDP, although the impact on the current account has been obscured by rising oil prices and a deteriorating net income position (Figure 3.10). Consistent with the finding of low pass-through of exchange rate movements to U.S. import prices and high pass-through to import prices abroad (see Box 3.3), the effect of the dollar depreciation came mainly through a strong acceleration in export volumes. Import volumes, meanwhile, have continued growing, reflecting not only the modest increase in U.S. import prices but also the faster growth of the U.S. economy relative to that of its trading partners until very recently.[26]

How much would the U.S. dollar need to decline in the long run to reduce the current account deficit? Typical estimates from the standard econometric models of the U.S. economy suggest that narrowing the ratio of current account deficit to GDP by 1 percentage point would require a real depreciation ranging from 10 percent to 20 percent. The evidence on trade elasticities presented in this chapter is consistent with estimates at the lower end of this range. Incorporating estimates that correct for either aggregation or vertical integration biases into a partial equilibrium analysis of trade adjustment suggests that a real depreciation of between 10 percent and 15 percent is needed to lower the trade deficit by 1 percent of GDP. Using elasticities that correct for both biases brings the required real dollar depreciation down to below 10 percent (Figure 3.11).[27]

These estimates are based on a partial-equilibrium analysis of trade balance adjustment and thus do not take into account other changes in the U.S. economy, particularly policy shifts and changes in consumption and investment behavior. Historical evidence suggests

[26]The U.S. terms of trade have deteriorated over the past four years (cumulatively by about 8 percent), even if less than one-for-one with the U.S. dollar, reflecting the peculiar U.S. pass-through environment described in Box 3.3.

[27]See Appendix 3.2 for details of the calculations.

Figure 3.10. United States: Trade Flows, Real Effective Exchange Rate (REER), and Growth Differential with Trading Partners

The U.S. dollar REER depreciation since 2002 has positively affected export volumes. Import volume growth has remained strong though, partly reflecting positive growth differential with trading partners until 2005.

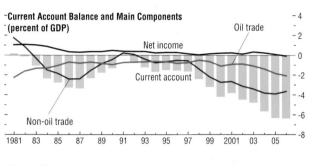

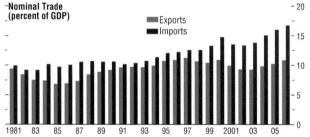

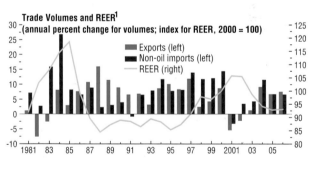

Sources: IMF, *International Financial Statistics;* OECD, *Economic Outlook* (2006); OECD, Analytical Database; World Bank, *World Development Indicators* (2006); and IMF staff calculations.
[1]An increase in the REER index represents a real appreciation while a decrease represents a real depreciation of the U.S. dollar relative to its trading partners.

Figure 3.11. Required Exchange Rate Change for a 1 Percentage Point Reduction in the Ratio of U.S. Trade Deficit to GDP[1]
(Percent)

Correcting for aggregation and vertical integration biases increases the impact of the real effective exchange rate (REER) depreciation on the U.S. trade balance.

(1) Based on the standard empirical trade model discussed in the main text (1986–2006)
(2) Based on model (1) adjusted for vertical integration bias
(3) Based on model (1) adjusted for aggregation bias
(4) Based on model (1) adjusted for both aggregation and vertical integration biases

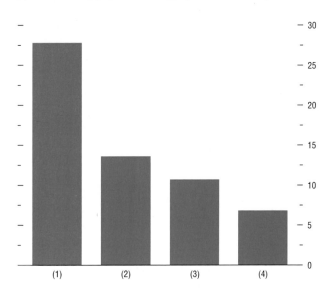

Source: IMF staff calculations.
[1]All scenarios are based on price elasticities with respect to REER, an import-to-export ratio of 1.56, and no growth differential with trading partners. Details of the calculations are in Appendix 3.2.

that in addition to movements in real exchange rates, successful and smooth external adjustments have been characterized by significant increases in saving rates and strong fiscal consolidation in deficit countries. Moreover, according to the evidence presented earlier, the narrowing of surplus positions seems to be associated with a pickup in domestic demand in surplus countries. As discussed in other recent analysis (see the September 2006 *World Economic Outlook*), the adjustment of global imbalances will likely involve a combination of exchange rate movements with a rebalancing of domestic demand—rising rates of absorption in surplus countries and a slower pace of demand growth in the United States. In part, this demand rebalancing will follow from a reversion of U.S. household saving rates to levels closer to historical averages, following the steep decline since the late 1990s in the context of strong capital gains from asset price increases. Fiscal consolidation aimed at ensuring that the U.S. economy is well placed to face the fiscal cost of population aging would also make a significant contribution.

Conclusions

The causes and implications of global imbalances have become an increasingly controversial subject in recent years. Different views exist on whether imbalances can be sustained for a long period of time, the conditions under which they could narrow, and the role of exchange rate movements in this adjustment.

The analysis in this chapter of historical episodes of large and sustained imbalances and their reversal clearly suggests that a market-led realignment of real exchange rates can play an important complementary role to demand rebalancing across countries to facilitate a smooth unwinding of external imbalances. Advanced economies have tended to experience a smaller impact on growth during deficit reversals when changes in real exchange rates have contributed to the adjustment. For both advanced economies and emerging market countries, reversals of external surpluses have tended to involve real appreciations of their currencies.

Historical evidence also suggests that while exchange rate changes may help to contain the output costs associated with deficit reversals, the role of other macroeconomic and structural policies is also very important. Episodes where deficit reversals have been achieved without serious damage to growth have typically involved fiscal consolidation and a significant increase in saving rates, which allowed investment rates to continue near pre-adjustment values. On the side of surplus countries, increases in domestic demand—associated with more expansionary monetary and fiscal policies—have played a key role in narrowing imbalances. More flexible economies have also helped by facilitating producers' response to relative price changes occurring through exchange rate movements. The evidence also suggests that the larger the initial imbalances, the lower the chance that a benign resolution can be achieved.

This chapter finds that the U.S. trade balance may be more responsive to changes in the real value of the U.S. dollar than often assumed. First, aggregate estimates have tended to underestimate the responsiveness of U.S. trade volumes, as they failed to account for aggregation and vertical integration biases—that is, differences in trade responsiveness across goods and the export content of imports. Second, long-run U.S. trade price elasticities have tended to increase over time, reflecting greater competition among firms in an increasingly globalized economy. Accounting for these channels significantly increases estimates of the impact of a real exchange rate depreciation on the U.S. external imbalance.

The implications of these findings for the current conjuncture are that market-led movements of real exchange rates—involving a real U.S. dollar depreciation and a real appreciation of the currencies of countries with persistent surpluses—would support a broader rebalancing of domestic demand across key regions that could facilitate the unwinding of the imbalances. The rebalancing of demand is likely to involve a reversion of the U.S. private saving rate to more

normal levels, further fiscal consolidation in the United States, and rising absorption in both oil-exporting and key emerging market countries. A major role for policy in this context is to make sure that structural factors do not impede the associated shifting of productive resources between sectors and the realignment of real exchange rates.

Appendix 3.1. Event Analysis: Methodology and Data

The main author of this appendix is Roberto Cardarelli.

The event analysis, which covered 1960–2006, comprised those 47 countries that had the largest GDP per capita (in PPP exchange rates against the dollar) in 2004. They were divided into three groups:

- 20 advanced economies: Australia, Austria, Belgium, Canada, Denmark, Finland, France, Germany, Greece, Ireland, Italy, Japan, the Netherlands, New Zealand, Portugal, Spain, Sweden, Switzerland, the United Kingdom, and the United States;
- 21 emerging market economies: Argentina, Brazil, Chile, China, Colombia, Czech Republic, Hong Kong SAR, Hungary, Israel, Korea, Malaysia, Mexico, Poland, Romania, Singapore, Slovak Republic, South Africa, Taiwan Province of China, Thailand, Turkey, and Ukraine; and
- 6 oil exporters: Algeria, Islamic Republic of Iran, Norway, Russia, Saudi Arabia, and the United Arab Emirates.

To identify large and sustained reversals of ratios of current account to GDP (defined as *ca*), four criteria were adopted: one for the identification of the year when the reversal began, one for the identification of the year when it ended, one to make sure the correction was sufficiently large, and the final one to make sure the correction was relatively persistent.

- The beginning of the reversal (year 0): a nonnegligible correction must be starting at year 0, as the average reduction of the imbalance over the next three years must be at least ½ percentage point of GDP. This serves to exclude very slow starts.

- The end of the reversal (year T): the episode finishes when a local maximum (for deficit reversals) or minimum (for surplus reversals) is reached. This happens when
  - $|ca_t|$ remains below $|ca_T|$ for three consecutive years; and
  - ½ percent or more of the reversal is overturned, that is,
    $$\frac{|ca_T - ca_{T-1}|}{|ca_0 - ca_{T-1}|} \geq 0.5.$$

- The size criterion: compared with the initial year, the current account ratio in T must change by at least $|2.5|$ percentage points of GDP, and by at least one-half of the initial level ca_0.

- The persistence criterion: in each of the five years after the beginning of the episode, the current account ratio must be larger (in absolute values) than ca_0.

Large and persistent imbalances were identified as episodes where the current account ratio is larger than $|2|$ percent of GDP for at least five years in which no reversal has occurred.

Tables 3.3–3.6 list the episodes of external imbalances identified in this chapter. Table 3.7 describes the variables analyzed in the event analysis and in the annual econometric estimates discussed in Appendix 3.2.

Appendix 3.2. Econometric Estimates of Trade Models

The main author of this appendix is Alessandro Rebucci.

This appendix provides further details on the econometric methodology and results discussed in the main text, and on the results shown in Figure 3.11.

Standard Empirical Trade Model

The standard empirical trade model relates import volumes to relative import prices and domestic income, and export volumes to relative export prices and foreign income.[28] The log-linear specification of the model is therefore

$$
\begin{aligned}
\mu(L)\ln M_t &= \alpha + \eta(L)\cdot\ln Y_t \\
&\quad + \varepsilon_t(L)\cdot\ln\!\left(\frac{Pm_t}{Py_t}\right) + u_{Mt} \\
\mu(L)\ln X_t &= \delta + \varphi(L)\cdot\ln Y_t^* \\
&\quad + \xi_t(L)\cdot\ln\!\left(\frac{Px_t}{Py_t^*}\right) + u_{Xt},
\end{aligned}
\tag{1}
$$

where M and X denote real imports and exports, Y and Y^* denote real home and foreign GDP, Pm and Px denote the aggregate import and export deflators (in local currency), Py and Py^* denote the domestic and foreign GDP deflators (in local currency), and u_{Mt} and u_{Xt} are the error terms.[29]

An alternative specification includes the real effective exchange rate, rather than relative trade prices, as the price variable in the model. The elasticities with respect to the real exchange rate take into account the incomplete degree of pass-through from exchange rates to relative prices.

The analysis focused on the long-run elasticities: $\eta = \eta(L)/\mu(L), \varepsilon = \varepsilon(L)/\mu(L)$ and $\varphi = \varphi(L)/\mu(L), \xi = \xi(L)/\mu(L)$. These elasticities were obtained by estimating, with ordinary least squares (OLS), the static version of the equations above, which can be interpreted as the first stage of the two-step cointegration procedure of Engle and Granger (1987).

This model was first estimated for U.S. imports and exports of goods and services for the period 1973–2006 using the annual data described in Table 3.7 (from the *World Economic Outlook* and the *World Development Indicators*). The main results (discussed in the text) were a higher estimated income elasticity of imports than of exports, and relatively low price

---

[28]This is the empirical counterpart of the standard imperfect substitution model, with constant elasticity and perfectly elastic supply of domestic and foreign-produced goods (e.g., Armington, 1969).

[29]Y^* and P_y^* are weighted averages of trading partners' GDP and GDP deflators, respectively, and are expressed in local currency. The weights used are as described in Table 3.7.

Table 3.3. List of Reversal Episodes
(Percent of GDP)

		Deficits				Surpluses	
Country	Year	Deficit at $t = 0$	Size of adjustment[1]	Country	Year	Surplus at $t = 0$	Size of adjustment[1]
			Advanced economies				
Australia	1968	−3.30	4.0	Australia	1972	0.7	3.8
Austria	1977	−4.22	3.1	Austria	1990	0.7	3.8
Austria	1980	−2.02	3.0	Belgium	1972	1.7	4.7
Austria	1999	−3.16	5.1	Belgium	2002	4.6	3.2
Belgium	1980	−2.98	6.7	Canada	1970	0.6	5.4
Canada	1975	−4.79	2.5	Canada	1982	0.6	4.5
Canada	1981	−4.16	4.8	Denmark	1993	2.8	3.7
Canada	1993	−3.86	4.4	Finland	1972	5.0	12.5
Canada	1998	−1.25	4.0	Finland	1978	1.8	4.6
Denmark	1970	−4.34	3.7	Finland	1984	0.1	5.5
Denmark	1986	−6.20	9.0	Finland	2002	7.6	5.3
Denmark	1998	−0.89	4.1	France	1978	1.4	3.5
Finland	1975	−7.46	9.3	France	1999	2.9	5.5
Finland	1991	−5.44	12.9	Germany	1978	1.3	3.0
France	1990	−0.79	3.7	Germany	1989	4.2	5.5
Germany	1965	−0.83	2.9	Ireland	1993	3.6	5.5
Germany	1980	−1.69	5.9	Italy	1968	1.9	6.3
Germany	2000	−1.78	6.0	Italy	1978	2.0	4.5
Greece	1985	−9.30	6.9	Italy	1986	0.4	2.8
Greece	1990	−5.61	4.2	Italy	1996	3.1	5.2
Ireland	1981	−13.02	16.6	Japan	1971	2.5	3.5
Italy	1974	−4.38	6.4	Japan	1986	4.3	2.8
Italy	1981	−2.47	2.7	Netherlands	1973	4.3	4.9
Italy	1992	−2.39	5.5	Netherlands	1997	6.4	4.5
Japan	1967	−0.15	2.7	New Zealand	1973	1.7	12.8
Japan	1974	−1.04	2.7	Portugal	1986	3.1	5.0
Japan	1980	−1.03	5.3	Spain	1971	0.7	4.5
Netherlands	1980	−0.41	4.0	Spain	1978	0.8	3.5
New Zealand	1974	−11.13	8.2	Spain	1986	1.6	5.2
New Zealand	1984	−8.22	7.2	Sweden	1973	1.9	3.7
Portugal	1981	−15.13	18.2	Sweden	1978	0.7	3.4
Spain	1965	−5.26	6.0	Sweden	1986	0.6	3.4
Spain	1976	−3.98	4.8	Switzerland	1976	5.5	6.0
Spain	1981	−2.67	4.3	United Kingdom	1971	2.0	6.0
Spain	1991	−3.56	3.3	United Kingdom	1981	2.1	6.0
Sweden	1982	−2.58	3.8	United States	1981	0.2	3.6
Sweden	1992	−2.83	6.9				
Switzerland	1980	−0.53	5.7				
United Kingdom	1967	−3.92	5.9				
United Kingdom	1974	−3.99	6.1				
United Kingdom	1989	−5.12	4.9				
United States	1987	−3.39	3.4				
			Emerging markets				
Argentina	1980	−6.20	5.1	Argentina	1967	2.3	3.0
Argentina	1987	−3.81	7.0	Argentina	1978	3.2	9.4
Argentina	1998	−4.84	13.3	Argentina	1990	3.2	7.5
Brazil	1974	−7.16	4.3	Argentina	2002	8.5	7.5
Brazil	1982	−5.79	5.8	Brazil	1992	1.6	6.3
Brazil	1986	−1.98	3.3	Chile	1969	2.6	9.4
Brazil	2001	−4.57	6.5	Chile	1976	1.5	16.0
Chile	1984	−10.98	10.7	China	1982	2.8	6.5
Chile	1998	−4.94	5.0	China	1997	3.9	2.6
China	1979	−0.18	3.0	Colombia	1979	1.6	9.4
China	1985	−3.74	7.2	Colombia	1991	5.7	11.1
China	1993	−2.64	6.5	Colombia	2000	0.9	2.6
Colombia	1971	−5.80	7.7	Czech Republic	1993	1.2	7.9
Colombia	1983	−7.75	8.9	Hong Kong SAR	1975	17.5	22.5
Colombia	1997	−5.39	6.3	Hong Kong SAR	1989	8.2	15.5
Czech Republic	1996	−6.71	4.6	Hungary	1973	0.7	8.2
Hong Kong SAR	1961	−10.93	24.8	Hungary	1984	0.1	4.2
Hong Kong SAR	1980	−4.97	12.4	Hungary	1991	0.9	9.2
Hong Kong SAR	1995	−6.28	17.7	Israel	1986	4.3	8.3

Table 3.3 *(concluded)*

		Deficits				Surpluses	
Country	Year	Deficit at $t = 0$	Size of adjustment[1]	Country	Year	Surplus at $t = 0$	Size of adjustment[1]
			Emerging markets (continued)				
Hungary	1978	−7.47	7.6	Israel	1989	0.5	5.8
Hungary	1986	−4.11	5.0	Korea	1977	0.0	8.3
Hungary	1994	−8.26	4.8	Korea	1988	7.7	10.4
Israel	1975	−14.77	12.2	Korea	1998	11.7	10.7
Israel	1982	−9.19	13.5	Malaysia	1969	4.7	9.1
Israel	1987	−3.97	4.5	Malaysia	1979	4.4	17.5
Israel	1996	−5.30	4.1	Malaysia	1987	8.0	16.5
Israel	2001	−1.45	3.3	Malaysia	1999	15.9	8.4
Korea	1974	−19.74	19.7	Mexico	1983	4.8	5.8
Korea	1980	−8.32	16.0	Mexico	1987	2.9	10.0
Korea	1996	−4.15	15.8	Poland	1990	4.7	10.8
Malaysia	1974	−5.33	10.3	Poland	1994	0.9	8.3
Malaysia	1982	−13.14	21.1	Romania	1988	9.7	18.2
Malaysia	1995	−9.73	25.6	Singapore	1966	0.1	29.5
Mexico	1981	−6.09	10.9	Slovak Republic	1994	4.9	14.3
Mexico	1994	−7.06	6.6	South Africa	1962	9.9	18.9
Mexico	1998	−3.81	3.1	South Africa	1979	5.3	11.0
Poland	1981	−6.75	11.5	South Africa	1987	4.9	3.7
Poland	1993	−6.15	7.0	South Africa	1993	2.1	3.7
Poland	1999	−7.43	5.9	South Africa	2002	0.6	6.0
Romania	1980	−10.66	17.5	Taiwan Province of China	1964	2.8	5.6
Romania	1990	−8.50	7.1	Taiwan Province of China	1972	5.8	13.3
Singapore	1971	−29.45	24.9	Taiwan Province of China	1986	21.2	20.0
Singapore	1980	−13.34	35.6	Thailand	1986	0.6	9.1
Slovak Republic	1975	−3.11	5.3	Thailand	1998	12.7	14.8
Slovak Republic	1996	−9.41	5.9	Turkey	1973	2.2	7.3
South Africa	1965	−9.02	6.6	Turkey	1988	1.8	5.3
South Africa	1971	−7.53	6.6	Turkey	1994	2.0	3.4
South Africa	1975	−6.49	11.8	Turkey	2001	2.3	8.9
South Africa	1981	−5.73	10.6	Ukraine	1984	3.5	14.7
Taiwan Province of China	1960	−6.61	9.4				
Taiwan Province of China	1968	−2.76	8.6				
Taiwan Province of China	1974	−7.50	13.6				
Taiwan Province of China	1980	−1.93	23.1				
Thailand	1983	−7.18	7.8				
Thailand	1996	−8.09	20.8				
Turkey	1980	−4.96	3.5				
Turkey	1983	−2.94	4.7				
Ukraine	1975	−0.64	2.9				
Ukraine	1991	−11.18	10.4				
Ukraine	1998	−3.09	13.7				
			Oil exporters				
Algeria	1978	−13.43	14.0	Algeria	1967	2.0	5.3
Algeria	1988	−3.45	8.7	Algeria	1974	1.4	14.8
Algeria	1998	−2.35	23.4	Algeria	1991	5.2	8.8
Iran, I.R. of	1960	−11.04	9.8	Iran, I.R. of	1974	28.0	31.4
Iran, I.R. of	1969	−5.46	33.5	Iran, I.R. of	1982	4.6	7.0
Iran, I.R. of	1991	−13.78	21.1	Iran, I.R. of	1994	7.3	9.4
Iran, I.R. of	1998	−2.09	14.4	Iran, I.R. of	2000	12.3	11.7
Norway	1977	−12.32	17.1	Norway	1985	4.8	10.8
Norway	1986	−5.96	10.2	Russia	1984	3.2	4.1
Norway	1998	0.01	15.4	Russia	2000	18.0	9.8
Russia	1992	−0.26	3.1	Saudi Arabia	1974	51.2	54.0
Russia	1997	−0.02	18.0	Saudi Arabia	1980	25.3	40.7
Saudi Arabia	1968	−23.29	74.5	United Arab Emirates	1974	68.1	57.1
Saudi Arabia	1984	−15.42	11.8	United Arab Emirates	1980	34.1	31.9
Saudi Arabia	1991	−20.95	21.3	United Arab Emirates	2000	17.4	13.3
Saudi Arabia	1973	−0.60	68.7				
United Arab Emirates	1973	−0.60	68.7				

Source: IMF staff calculations.
[1]Change in current account from $t = 0$ to the end of the reversal episode.

Table 3.4. List of Large and Persistent Episodes

	Deficits				Surpluses		
Country	Year	Duration (years)	Average current account surplus (percent of GDP)	Country	Year	Duration (years)	Average current account surplus (percent of GDP)
Advanced economies							
Australia	1964	5	−2.8	Belgium	1986	17	4.3
Australia	1980	27	−4.5	Denmark	2001	6	2.8
Canada	1989	5	−3.7	Japan	1991	16	2.8
Denmark	1964	7	−3.1	Netherlands	1988	10	4.0
Denmark	1979	8	−4.1	Netherlands	2001	6	5.9
Greece	1975	11	−5.2	Sweden	1997	10	5.1
Greece	1995	12	−6.4	Switzerland	1985	22	8.0
Ireland	1969	13	−6.1				
New Zealand	1978	7	−5.0				
New Zealand	1989	18	−5.0				
Portugal	1996	11	−7.3				
Spain	1999	8	−4.9				
United States	1998	9	−4.7				
Emerging markets							
Argentina	1994	5	−3.5	China	2002	5	4.6
Brazil	1970	5	−3.6	Hong Kong SAR	1967	9	12.6
Brazil	1977	6	−4.5	Hong Kong SAR	1985	5	7.4
Czech Republic	1998	9	−4.1	Malaysia	2002	5	12.8
Hungary	1996	11	−7.0	Romania	1984	5	6.1
Israel	1965	11	−7.9	Singapore	1998	9	22.6
Israel	1977	6	−5.7	Taiwan Province of China	1999	8	5.8
Korea	1965	10	−11.9	Ukraine	1979	6	2.9
Malaysia	1991	5	−6.5				
Mexico	1970	12	−3.5				
Poland	1973	9	−5.0				
Romania	1995	12	−6.2				
South Africa	1967	5	−6.0				
Thailand	1975	9	−5.4				
Thailand	1990	7	−7.0				
Ukraine	1994	5	−2.6				
Oil exporters							
				Algeria	2000	7	19.2
				Norway	2001	6	15.6
				Russia	1977	8	3.2
				United Arab Emirates	1994	6	5.0
				United Arab Emirates	2002	5	11.6

Source: IMF staff calculations.

elasticities with respect to both relative trade prices and real exchange rates (Table 3.8). Restricting the sample period to 1986–2006 yielded higher estimates of trade price elasticities, even if the difference was statistically significant only for U.S. exports. The implied pass-through to U.S. import prices—obtained from comparing price elasticities with respect to relative prices and those with respect to the real exchange rate—was about 0.5, similar to that measured directly in the literature reported in Box 3.3. Moreover, it was stable over time.

Aggregation Bias

To explore the potential for aggregation bias, the standard empirical trade model was estimated for 17 categories of import of goods and services and 16 categories of export of goods and services, using quarterly data from the Bureau of Economic Analysis (BEA) from 1973: Q1 to 2006:Q3. Figure 3.12 shows trade price elasticities for individual groups.

Given that price elasticities differ considerably across groups, an OLS estimate of the benchmark aggregate model may yield

Table 3.5. Advanced Economies: Contractionary and Expansionary Deficit Reversals

Country	Contractionary Deficit Reversals[1]		Expansionary Deficit Reversals[2]		
	Year	Average change in GDP growth[3]	Country	Year	Average change in GDP growth
Spain	1965	−3.35	Japan	1967	0.66
Italy	1974	−2.59	Switzerland	1980	2.19
Japan	1974	−3.60	Spain	1981	0.37
New Zealand	1974	−6.84	Sweden	1982	2.46
Finland	1975	−4.74	Greece	1985	0.92
Austria	1977	−5.58	Finland	1991	−0.37
Canada	1981	−5.02	Sweden	1992	0.21
Italy	1981	−3.56	Canada	1993	3.42
Portugal	1981	−3.70	Canada	1998	2.46
United States	1987	−2.48	Austria	1999	−0.26
Spain	1991	−3.55			

Source: IMF staff calculations.
[1]Contractionary deficit reversals are the 11 deficit reversals with the largest average decline in GDP growth (the bottom quartile in the sample ordered by the change in GDP growth).
[2]Expansionary deficit reversals are the 10 deficit reversals with the smallest average decline in GDP growth (the top quartile in the sample ordered by the change in growth).
[3]Average of GDP annual growth rates in the period after the reversal (1...T) less average annual growth rates in the period before the reversal (−T...−1).

Table 3.6. Emerging Markets: Contractionary and Expansionary Surplus Reversals

Country	Contractionary Surplus Reversals[1]		Expansionary Surplus Reversals[2]		
	Year	Average change in GDP growth[3]	Country	Year	Average change in GDP growth[3]
Chile	1969	−5.15	Singapore	1966	7.27
Taiwan Province of China	1972	−5.08	Chile	1976	8.67
			Argentina	1978	4.73
Hungary	1973	−5.18	China	1982	6.33
Korea	1977	−3.04	Thailand	1986	6.21
Colombia	1979	−3.37	Malaysia	1987	5.88
Malaysia	1979	−1.88	Argentina	1990	8.91
Mexico	1983	−4.60	Czech Republic	1993	8.69
Ukraine	1984	−3.93	South Africa	1993	4.75
Romania	1988	−7.30	Poland	1994	6.78
Hong Kong SAR	1989	−3.09	Slovak Republic	1994	11.21
Poland	1990	−3.39	Argentina	2002	9.94
China	1997	−3.97			
Thailand	1998	−1.90			

Source: IMF staff calculations.
[1]Contractionary surplus reversals are the 13 reversals with the largest average decline in GDP growth (the bottom quartile in the sample ordered by the change in growth).
[2]Expansionary surplus reversals are the 12 surplus reversals with the smallest average decline in GDP growth (the top quartile in the sample ordered by the change in growth).
[3]Average of GDP annual growth rates in the period after the reversal (1...T) less average annual growth rates in the period before the reversal (−T...−1).

inconsistent estimates of the "true" aggregate relations both in the short and in the long run, with the sign and magnitude of the bias depending on the specific characteristics of the data (Pesaran and Smith, 1995).[30] Following Pesaran and Smith (1995), simple averages of the individual estimates were therefore calculated as they generally provide consistent estimates of the true aggregate relations.[31] The results, reported in Table 3.9, show that the average of individual trade price elasticities is much higher than the aggregate estimate from the standard empirical trade model (over the same period and using the same data), and that not only does the gap between the income elasticity of import and that of export disappear but also the value of these elasticities is much smaller. This is particularly notable given that the relatively small level of

[30]In particular, the inconsistency reflects the fact that the difference between the aggregate and the individual relations ends up in the regression residuals.
[31]See Imbs and others (2005) for the application of this analysis to exchange rate dynamics.

disaggregation used in this chapter is probably insufficient to uncover the full scope for aggregation bias.

In addition to the simple average of individual price elasticities, weighted averages were also computed, using relative trade shares at end-2005 as weights. Compared with simple averages, they yielded a similar estimate of the price elasticity for exports but a lower estimate of the price elasticity of imports (−0.25 and −0.63, respectively), even if the latter is still above the estimated elasticity in the standard empirical model. The result for imports, though, is driven by two categories (automotive and petroleum products) with a relatively imprecise estimate of the import price elasticities. Indeed, using a generalized least square estimator (which amounts to weighting the individual estimates using the inverse of the standard errors) yielded a higher price elasticity of imports (at about −1.13).

Table 3.7. Variable Definitions

Variable	Sources	Notes
Current account balance	(1) OECD, *Economic Outlook* (OECDEO), (2) *World Development Indicators* (WDI), (3) *World Economic Outlook* (WEO), and (4) *International Financial Statistics* (IFS)	Percent of GDP
Net foreign assets	(1) Lane and Milesi-Ferretti (2006)	Percent of GDP
Private credit	(1) Lane and Milesi-Ferretti (2006)	Percent of GDP
Stock prices	(1) WEO (2006)	Annual percent change
Reserves	(1) Lane and Milesi-Ferretti (2006)	Percent of GDP
Nominal and real exports and imports	(1) WDI and (2) WEO	
Fiscal balance	(1) WDI and (2) WEO	Percent of GDP
Structural fiscal balance	(1) OECDEO and (2) WEO	Percent of GDP
Consumption	(1) OECDEO, (2) WDI, and (3) WEO	Total consumption, as percent of GDP
Investment	(1) WEO (2006), (2) WDI, and (3) WEO	Gross total investment, as percent of GDP
Nominal and real exports and imports	(1) OECDEO, (2) WDI, and (3) WEO	From balance of payment data
Nominal and real GDP	(1) OECDEO, (2) WDI, and (3) WEO	
Output gap	(1) OECDEO, (2) WEO, and (3) Derived	Percent; spliced OECDEO data with WEO and deviation from Hodrick-Prescott (HP)-filtered GDP series
Savings	(1) WEO (2006), (2) WDI, and (3) WEO	National savings
Terms of trade	(1) WEO	Ratio of export and import price deflators
Real total domestic demand	(1) WEO	
Trade balance	See exports and imports	Exports – imports, as percent of GDP
Inflation	(1) WEO, (2) OECDEO, and (3) WDI	Annual changes in CPI index
Openness to trade	See nominal exports and imports	(Exports + imports) / GDP
Overvaluation (deviations from CGER)	Derived	100*(REER – CGER) / CGER
Overvaluation (deviation from long-run average)	Derived	100*(REER – average of REER over the whole sample) / average of REER over the whole sample
Overvaluation (deviation from trend)	Derived	100*(REER – HP-filtered REER) / HP-filtered REER
Overvaluation, residual from PPP regressions	Johnson, Ostry, and Subramanian (2007)	Residuals of cross-sectional regressions of real exchange rate (measured as the price level of GDP relative to the United States from the Penn World Tables) on the log PPP-adjusted per capita income (from Penn World Tables)
Real effective exchange rate (REER)	(1) OECDEO and (2) IMF staff calculations	CPI-based (higher values = appreciation)
Real long-term interest rates	(1) IFS and (2) IMF staff calculations	Nominal rates deflated by same year changes in CPI
Real short-term interest rates	(1) WEO (2006), (2) IFS, and (3) IMF staff calculations	Nominal rates deflated by same year changes in CPI
Differentials with trading partners	Derived	Estimated as the difference between the variable (GDP) for a country and the weighted average of the same variable for its trading partners. The weights are the same ones used for the construction of the IMF real effective exchange rate indices and vary over time (three sets of weights cover the whole sample of 1960–2006).

Note: Numbers in the "Sources" column refer to the priority given to the relative data sets, that is, sources denoted with 1 were used when data were available; when data from source 1 were not available or missing, data from source 2 were used instead or the series was extended by splicing it using data from source 2. PPP = purchasing power parity; CGER = Consultative Group on Exchange Rates.

Figure 3.12. Sectoral Price Elasticities of Trade
(Coefficients)

Estimating the standard empirical model on individual sectors yields very different estimates of trade price elasticities. Averages of these elasticities are higher than the aggregate estimates from the standard empirical model.

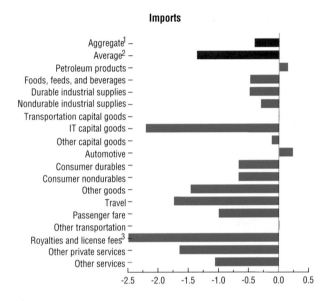

Imports

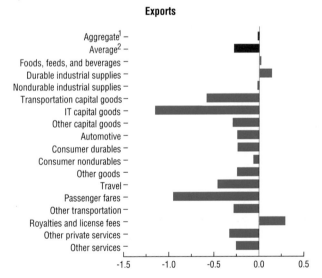

Exports

Sources: U.S. Bureau of Economic Analysis, *Survey of Current Business* (2006); and IMF staff calculations.
[1]Estimates from the standard empirical model over the 1973–2000 sample.
[2]Simple averages of sectoral price elasticities.
[3]Out of scale.

Table 3.8. Standard Empirical Trade Model: Long-Run U.S. Trade Elasticities

	Estimated over 1973–2006		Estimated over 1986–2006	
	RP[1]	REER[2]	RP[1]	REER[2]
Imports				
Prices	−0.69	0.37	−0.82	0.48
	(0.12)	(0.08)	(0.19)	(0.09)
Income	2.03	2.46	1.86	2.46
	(0.07)	(0.03)	(0.08)	(0.04)
Exports				
Prices	0.02	−0.49	−1.06	−0.60
	(0.10)	(0.12)	(0.31)	(0.24)
Income	1.85	1.82	0.76	1.97
	(0.18)	(0.04)	(0.32)	(0.10)

Source: IMF staff calculations.
Note: Exports and imports of goods (excuding oil) and services. Variables in logarithms. Standard errors in parentheses.
[1]Price elasticities with respect to relative prices (RP).
[2]Price elasticities with respect to real effective exchange rate (REER). Increase in REER denotes real appreciation.

Vertical Integration and U.S. Imports

Data on U.S. gross imports (M) can be expressed as the sum of two components, both function of the real exchange rate (R): the foreign value added $m(R)$ and U.S. exports of intermediates $X^e(R)$:

$$M = m(R) + \alpha \cdot X^e(R),$$

where α is the fraction of U.S. intermediate exports used in the assembly of products that are shipped back to the United States (a phenomenon also known as "round tripping"). Assuming that $m(R)$ and $X^e(R)$ depend linearly on R, with ε and ξ denoting the long-run price elasticity of imported value added and intermediate exports, respectively, the total estimated elasticity of gross imports with respect to the real exchange rate would be $(-\varepsilon + \alpha \cdot \xi)$, which is lower than ε (in absolute value).

One way to control for this bias is to add U.S. exports of intermediate products as an explanatory variable in the standard empirical trade model of import volumes:

$$\ln M_t = \alpha + \eta \cdot \ln Y_t + \varepsilon \cdot \ln\left(\frac{Pm_t}{Py_t}\right) + \alpha_j \cdot \ln X^e_{jt}, \quad (2)$$

Table 3.9. Long-Run U.S. Trade Elasticities and Aggregation Bias

	Aggregate Estimates[1]		Average Estimates[2]	
	Imports	Exports	Imports	Exports
Relative prices	−0.49 (0.05)	−0.06 (0.04)	−1.25 (0.63)	−0.34 (0.10)
Income	1.93 (0.03)	1.77 (0.03)	1.68 (0.35)	1.60 (0.16)

Source: IMF staff estimates.
Note: Exports and imports of goods and services. Variables in logarithms. Standard errors in parentheses.
[1]Ordinary least square estimates of the standard trade model over 1973:Q1–2006:Q3.
[2]Simple averages of individual sectors' estimates of price and income trade elasticities (from the standard empirical model estimated over 1973:Q1–2006:Q3).

Table 3.10. Long-Run U.S. Import Elasticities and Vertical Integration

	No Control for Vertical Integration[1]		Controlling for Vertical Integration[2]	
	(1979–2006)	(1986–2006)	(1979–2006)	(1986–2006)
Relative prices	−0.82 (0.16)	−1.16 (0.32)	−1.61 (0.16)	−1.52 (0.09)
Income	1.98 (0.13)	1.70 (0.29)	0.64 (0.02)	0.64 (0.02)

Source: IMF staff estimates.
Note: Imports of goods (excluding oil). Variables in logarithms. Standard errors in parentheses.
[1]Results from the standard trade model applied to U.S. non-oil imports.
[2]Results from equation (2) in Appendix 3.2.

where X_{jt}^{e} represents the jth category of U.S. exports of intermediate products. In particular, five categories of exports were considered, as they are the ones that are most likely subject to a large degree of round tripping: parts (engines, engine parts, and other parts) for autos; parts (engines, engine parts, and other parts) for planes; chemical products—excluding medicines; semiconductors; and metal products. The initial specification included five lags and was estimated based on quarterly data on U.S. imports of goods (excluding oil) from the BEA, from 1978:Q1 to 2006:Q3 (the initial date corresponds to the earliest observation for disaggregated exports) and from 1986:Q1 to 2006:Q3 (the choice of 1986 was motivated by the anticipatory effects of the adoption of the U.S.-Canada free trade agreement in 1987). The sum of the α_j across the five categories of imports—the round-tripping "elasticity"—was 0.3 and stable in the two periods. This estimate suggests that nearly ⅓ of U.S. exports of intermediates come back in the form of imports. The estimated elasticities, reported in Table 3.10, show that for both sample periods, the estimated price elasticity of imports increased substantially compared with the standard empirical model (estimated over the same periods and using the same data). Moreover, the income elasticity of imports was much lower than in the standard model.

Nonlinear Dynamics

The presence of nonlinear dynamics was tested for all OECD countries for which quarterly data were available over the whole sample period of 1973–2006. The tests used were the higher-order Taylor expansion tests of Teräsvirta, Lin, and Granger (1993) and Blake and Kapetanios (2003).

The specific nonlinear dynamic considered in the chapter took the form of a threshold effect in an error-correction representation of the standard empirical trade model (with one lag only). In particular, the existence of threshold effects were estimated within the following model:

$$T_t = I(|Q(t)|\leq\theta)\,Z_t + I(|Q(t)|>\theta)\,Z_t + e_t, \qquad (3)$$

where T_t is the growth rate of import (export) volumes; Z_t includes all variables in the error-correction specification, that is, the constant, the error-correction term, and the first lag of import (export) growth, and domestic (trading partner) GDP growth and relative import (export) price growth; $Q(t)$ is the triggering variable, the growth rate of relative import (export) prices; and I is an indicator function, with value of one if the absolute value of the growth rate of relative import (export) prices is above the threshold level θ, zero otherwise.

The results of the nonlinearity tests on import and export volumes are reported in Table 3.11,

Table 3.11. Nonlinearity Tests (*p* value) and Thresholds for Changes in Relative Import Prices

Country	Nonlinearity Test[1] Imports	Nonlinearity Test[1] Exports	Threshold for Relative Import Price Growth[2] (in percent) Imports	Threshold for Relative Import Price Growth[2] (in percent) Exports
Australia	0.11	0.86	0.8	0.2
Austria	0.00	0.00	1.6	0.7
Belgium	0.01	0.24	2.0	2.9
Canada	0.00	0.15	2.4	0.6
Denmark	0.09	0.00	1.2	1.8
France	0.32	0.48	1.6	3.4
Germany	0.62	0.89	1.2	1.3
Greece	0.00	0.09	0.5	4.7
Hungary	0.00	0.20	0.5	0.9
Ireland	0.00	0.15	0.3	1.8
Italy	0.89	0.00	1.3	0.6
Japan	0.00	0.09	5.9	3.1
Korea	0.00	0.95	2.7	0.7
Mexico	0.00	0.25	11.7	2.7
Netherlands	0.00	0.05	1.3	1.4
New Zealand	0.01	0.26	1.6	5.1
Norway	0.02	0.04	4.7	3.9
Poland	0.01	0.00	6.3	9.6
Portugal	0.00	0.21	2.1	2.5
Spain	0.00	0.09	4.2	3.0
Sweden	0.00	0.06	3.1	0.5
Switzerland	0.07	0.63	0.4	2.9
Turkey	0.00	0.03	8.9	7.4
United Kingdom	0.00	0.07	1.5	1.5
United States	0.01	0.91	2.0	4.7

Source: IMF staff calculations.

[1]Probability values of Teräsvirta, Lin, and Granger (1993) test for nonlinearity (values below 0.05 denote evidence of nonlinearity at a 5 percent confidence level).

[2]Values of thresholds in relative import price growth (import volumes react more strongly for growth rates larger than these thresholds).

Table 3.12. Error Correction Model for U.S. Imports, Sample 1973:Q1–2006:Q3

	Linear Model	Nonlinear Model Lower regime	Nonlinear Model Upper regime
Constant	−0.002 (0.00)	0.008 (0.00)	−0.011 (0.01)
Error correction	−0.139 (−0.13)	−0.121 (0.05)	−0.252 (0.09)
(Import volumes growth)_{−1}	0.229 (0.24)	0.256 (0.10)	0.212 (0.18)
(GDP growth)_{−1}	1.254 (1.34)	1.048 (0.31)	2.448 (0.77)
(Change in relative import prices)_{−1}	−0.085 (−0.14)	−0.192 (0.21)	−0.141 (0.12)
Error correction term coefficients			
Constant	42.2		
Relative prices	0.7		
GDP	−1.9		

Source: IMF staff calculations.
Note: Imports of goods (excluding oil). Standard errors in parentheses.

U.S. Trade Balance and the U.S. Real Effective Exchange Rate

To quantify the implications on trade balance adjustment of the different estimates of trade elasticities, the standard partial equilibrium condition for the trade balance (see, for example, Krugman, 1989) was modified to take into account an unbalanced initial trade position and the presence of vertical integration on the import side.

In particular, the ratio of trade balance to GDP was defined as

$$nx = \frac{X(R,Y^*)}{Y} - R\frac{M(R,Y,X)}{Y},$$

where R is the real exchange rate (defined in such a way that an increase is a depreciation). Total differentiating this equation yields

$$\hat{nx} = \left[\frac{X}{X-RM} \cdot (\varepsilon_x \cdot \hat{R} + \eta_x \cdot \hat{Y}^*) - \frac{R \cdot M}{X-RM} \right.$$
$$\cdot \left(-\varepsilon_m \cdot \hat{R} + \eta_m \cdot \hat{Y} + \alpha \cdot (\varepsilon_x \cdot \hat{R} + \eta_x \cdot \hat{Y}^*) \right)$$
$$\left. - \frac{R \cdot M}{X-RM} \cdot \hat{R} \right] - \hat{Y},$$

where $\hat{Z}$ denotes the growth rate of variable Z; the price elasticities for exports and imports are

together with the threshold values on the growth rates of relative import and export prices. The table shows strong evidence of nonlinearity for the vast majority of OECD countries, and a large dispersion in the values of the thresholds. The results for the threshold model of U.S. imports are reported in Table 3.12, together with the results from the (nonlinear) error correction model, and show a significant increase in the speed of adjustment in U.S. import volumes when the change in relative import prices is above the threshold level (the upper regime) compared with when the change in relative import prices is below the threshold level (the lower regime).

$$\varepsilon_x = \frac{R}{X} \cdot \frac{\partial X}{\partial R} \text{ and } \varepsilon_m = -\frac{R}{M} \cdot \frac{\partial M}{\partial R},$$

respectively; the income elasticities for exports and imports are

$$\eta_x = \frac{Y^*}{X} \cdot \frac{\partial X}{\partial Y^*} \text{ and } \eta_m = \frac{Y}{M} \cdot \frac{\partial M}{\partial Y},$$

respectively; the "vertical integration" elasticity is

$$\alpha = \frac{X}{M} \cdot \frac{\partial M}{\partial X};$$

and $\hat{Y}$, $\hat{Y}^*$ are the rate of growth of domestic and of foreign GDP, respectively.

If $X - RM \neq 0$, the equation above implies

$$\hat{R} = \frac{\hat{n}x + \left[\left(\frac{\gamma}{1-\gamma}\right)\cdot\eta_m + 1\right]\hat{Y} - \left[\left(\frac{1}{1-\gamma}\right)-\left(\frac{\gamma}{1-\gamma}\right)\cdot\alpha\right]\cdot(\eta_x\cdot\hat{Y}^*)}{\left[\left(\frac{1}{1-\gamma}-\frac{\gamma}{1-\gamma}\alpha\right)\cdot\varepsilon_x + \left(\frac{\gamma}{1-\gamma}\right)\cdot\varepsilon_m - \left(\frac{\gamma}{1-\gamma}\right)\right]}, (4)$$

where γ denotes the ratio of real imports to real exports $\left(\gamma = \frac{R\cdot M}{X}\right)$.

This expression gives the cumulative change in the real exchange rate that is consistent with any percent change in the ratio of trade balance to GDP ($\hat{n}x$), for a given set of elasticities (ε_x, ε_m, η_x, η_m), an initial trade imbalance (γ), a degree of vertical integration (α), and a cumulative growth differential during the adjustment period ($\hat{Y} - \hat{Y}^*$).

Figure 3.11 in the main text plots different values of $\hat{R}$ associated with a 1 percentage point of GDP decline of the U.S. trade deficit from its end-2005 level. In this calculation, the following parameters and assumptions were used:

- *Trade price elasticities* (ε_x, ε_m). The results shown in the first column of Figure 3.11 are based on the elasticities with respect to real exchange rates from the standard empirical model (equation (1)), estimated over the 1986–2006 period (Table 3.8). The results shown in the other columns of Figure 3.11 are based on these elasticities corrected for the aggregation and vertical integration biases. For example, the size of the aggregation bias for U.S. import price elasticity was estimated as the difference between the third and first columns in Table 3.9. This difference was multiplied by the ratio between the estimated elasticities with respect to the real

exchange rate and that with respect to relative trade prices from the standard trade empirical model (the ratio between the fourth and third column in Table 3.8), and added to the elasticities with respect to real exchange rates from the standard empirical model.

- *Trade income elasticities* (η_x, η_m). The results shown in the first column in Figure 3.11 are based on the income elasticities from the standard empirical model estimated over the 1986–2006 period (Table 3.8). The results shown in the other columns in Figure 3.11 are based on these elasticities corrected for the aggregation and vertical integration biases in a similar manner.
- *Initial ratio between import and export volumes* (γ). This was set at 1.56, the ratio of U.S. import and export volumes at end-2005.
- *Degree of vertical integration* (α). Following the results from estimating equation (2), this was set at 30 percent.
- *Cumulative growth differential* ($\hat{Y} - \hat{Y}^*$). For a period of five years, the GDP growth rate was set at 3 percent a year for both the United States and its trading partners, so the cumulative growth differential was set at zero.
- *Exchange rate pass-through*. In equation (4), the incomplete pass-through of exchange rate changes to relative trade prices is taken into account by considering trade price elasticities with respect to real exchange rates. In addition, the last term in the denominator of equation (4) (the change in the terms of trade after 1 percent exchange rate depreciation, adjusted for the unbalanced initial trade position) was multiplied by 0.5 to take into account the partial response of terms of trade under incomplete pass-through (see also Box 3.3).

In equation (4), only import volumes have been adjusted for the vertical integration bias. As, in principle, vertical integration could affect export price elasticities in a similar manner, the impact of vertical integration on the U.S. trade deficit has also been estimated by assuming that the downward bias on export price elasticities is the same as that on import prices, and the share of foreign intermediate products incorporated in U.S. exports is also 30 percent. Modifying equation (4) accordingly yields very similar estimates of the required depreciation rate.

References

Armington, Paul, 1969, "A Theory of Demand for Products Distinguished by Place of Production," *IMF Staff Papers*, International Monetary Fund, Vol. 16, pp. 159–78.

Backus, David, and Frederic Lambert, 2005, "Current Account Fact and Fiction" (unpublished; New York: New York University). Available via the Internet: http://pages.stern.nyu.edu/~dbackus/CA/BHLT%20latest.pdf

Blake, Andrew, and George Kapetanios, 2003, "Testing for ARCH in the Presence of Nonlinearity of Unknown Form in the Conditional Mean," Department of Economics Working Paper No. 496 (London: Queen Mary College, University of London).

Broda, Christian, Nuno Limão, and David Weinstein, 2006, "Optimal Tariffs: The Evidence," NBER Working Paper No. 12033 (Cambridge, Massachusetts: National Bureau of Economic Research).

Broda, Christian, and David Weinstein, 2006, "Globalization and the Gains from Variety," *Quarterly Journal of Economics*, Vol. 121 (May), pp. 541–85.

Bureau of Economic Analysis, 2006, *Survey of Current Business*, U.S. Department of Commerce, Vol. 86 (October).

Burgess, Simon, and Michael Knetter, 1998, "An International Comparison of Employment Adjustment to Exchange Rate Fluctuations," *Review of International Economics*, Vol. 6 (February), pp. 151–63.

Caballero, Ricardo, Emmanuel Farhi, and Pierre-Olivier Gourinchas, 2006, "An Equilibrium Model of 'Global Imbalances' and Low Interest Rates," NBER Working Paper No. 11996 (Cambridge, Massachusetts: National Bureau of Economic Research).

Campa, José Manuel, and Linda Goldberg, 2005, "Exchange Rate Pass-Through into Import Prices," *Review of Economics and Statistics*, Vol. 87, pp. 679–90.

Chinn, Menzie, 2005, "Supply Capacity, Vertical Specialization and Tariff Rates: The Implications for Aggregate U.S. Trade Flow Equations," NBER Working Paper No. 11719 (Cambridge, Massachusetts: National Bureau of Economic Research).

Clarida, Richard, Manuela Goretti, and Mark Taylor, 2007, "Are There Thresholds of Current Account Adjustment in the G7?" in *G7 Current Account Imbalances: Sustainability and Adjustment*, ed. by Richard Clarida (Chicago: University of Chicago Press).

Cooper, Richard, 2006, "Understanding Global Imbalances," paper presented at the Boston Federal Reserve Economic Conference, "Global Imbalances—As Giants Evolve," Chatham, Massachusetts, June 14–16.

Croke, Hilary, Steven Kamin, and Sylvain Leduc, 2005, "Financial Market Developments and Economic Activity During Current Account Adjustments in Industrial Economies," International Finance Discussion Paper No. 827 (Washington: Board of Governors of the Federal Reserve System).

Debelle, Guy, and Gabriele Galati, 2005, "Current Account Adjustment and Capital Flows," BIS Working Paper No. 169 (Basel: Bank for International Settlements).

de Haan, Leo, Hubert Schokker, and Anastassia Tcherneva, 2006, "What Do Current Account Reversals in OECD Countries Tell Us About the US Case?" DNB Working Paper No. 111 (Amsterdam: De Nederlandsche Bank).

Devereux, Michael, and Charles Engel, 2002, "Exchange Rate Pass-Through, Exchange Rate Volatility, and Exchange Rate Disconnect," DNB Staff Reports 77 (Amsterdam: De Nederlandsche Bank).

Dillon, Eleanor Wiske, and Linda Goldberg, 2006, "How Effective Is Dollar Depreciation at Reducing U.S. Trade Deficits?" (unpublished; New York: Federal Reserve Bank of New York).

Dooley, Michael, David Folkerts-Landau, and Peter Garber, 2005, *International Financial Stability: Asia, Interest Rates, and the Dollar* (New York: Deutsche Bank Securities, Inc.).

Dornbusch, Rudi, 1996, "The Effectiveness of Exchange-Rate Changes," *Oxford Review of Economic Policy*, Vol. 12, No. 3, pp. 26–38.

Edwards, Sebastian, 2005, "Is the Current Account Deficit Sustainable? And If Not, How Costly Is Adjustment Likely to Be?" NBER Working Paper No. 11541 (Cambridge, Massachusetts: National Bureau of Economic Research).

Engle, Robert, and Clive Granger, 1987, "Co-Integration and Error Correction: Representation, Estimation, and Testing," *Econometrica*, Vol. 55 (March), pp. 251–76.

Faruqee, Hamid, 2006, "Exchange Rate Pass-Through in the Euro Area," *IMF Staff Papers*, Vol. 53 (April), pp. 63–88.

Frankel, Jeffrey, David Parsley, and Shang-Jin Wei, 2005, "Slow Passthrough Around the World: A New Import for Developing Countries?" NBER Working Paper No. 11199 (Cambridge, Massachusetts: National Bureau of Economic Research).

Freund, Caroline, 2000, "Current Account Adjustment in Industrialized Countries," International Finance Discussion Paper No. 692 (Washington: Board of Governors of the Federal Reserve System).

———, and Frank Warnock, 2005, "Current Account Deficits in Industrial Countries: The Bigger They Are, The Harder They Fall?" NBER Working Paper No. 11823 (Cambridge, Massachusetts: National Bureau of Economic Research).

Gagnon, Joseph, 2003, "Productive Capacity, Product Varieties, and the Elasticities Approach to the Trade Balance," International Finance Discussion Paper No. 781 (Washington: Board of Governors of the Federal Reserve System).

Ghosh, Atish, and Jonathan Ostry, 1995, "The Current Account in Developing Countries: A Perspective from the Consumption-Smoothing Approach," *World Bank Economic Review*, Vol. 9 (May), pp. 305–33.

Goldberg, Linda, and Cedric Tille, 2005, "Vehicle Currency Use in International Trade," NBER Working Paper No. 11127 (Cambridge, Massachusetts: National Bureau of Economic Research).

Goldman Sachs, 2005, "Do Current Account Adjustments Have to Be Painful?" *Global Economic Weekly*, Issue No. 05/04.

Goldstein, Morris, and Mohsin Khan, 1985, "Income and Price Effects in Foreign Trade," in *Handbook of International Economics*, Vol. II, ed. by Ronald W. Jones and Peter B. Kenen (Amsterdam: North-Holland), pp. 1041–105.

Gourinchas, Pierre-Olivier, 1998, "Exchange Rates and Jobs: What Do We Learn from Job Flows?" NBER Working Paper No. 6864 (Cambridge, Massachusetts: National Bureau of Economic Research).

Greenspan, Alan, 2004, "The Evolving U.S. Payments Imbalance and Its Impact on Europe and the Rest of the World," *Cato Journal*, Vol. 24 (Spring/Summer).

Gust, Christopher, and Nathan Sheets, 2006, "The Adjustment of Global External Balances: Does Partial Exchange Rate Pass-Through to Trade Prices Matter?" International Finance Discussion Paper No. 850 (Washington: Board of Governors of the Federal Reserve System).

Hausmann, Ricardo, and Federico Sturzenegger, 2006, "Global Imbalances or Bad Accounting? The Missing Dark Matter in the Wealth of Nations," CID Working Paper No. 124 (Cambridge, Massachusetts: Center for International Development, Harvard University, January).

Hellerstein, Rebecca, Deirdre Daly, and Christina Marsh, 2006, "Have U.S. Import Prices Become Less Responsive to Changes in the Dollar?" *Current Issues in Economics and Finance*, Federal Reserve Bank of New York, Vol. 12 (September).

Hooper, Peter, Karen Johnson, and Jaime Marquez, 2000, "Trade Elasticities for the G-7 Countries," Princeton Studies in International Economics, Vol. 87 (Princeton, New Jersey: Princeton University, August).

Houthakker, Hendrik S., and Stephen P. Magee, 1969, "Income and Price Elasticities in World Trade," *Review of Economics and Statistics*, Vol. 51 (May), pp. 111–25.

Imbs, Jean, Haroon Mumtaz, Morten Ravn, and Hélène Rey, 2005, "PPP Strikes Back: Aggregation and the Real Exchange Rate," *Quarterly Journal of Economics*, Vol. 120 (February), pp. 1–43.

International Monetary Fund, *Balance of Payments Statistics Yearbook* (Washington, various issues).

———, *International Financial Statistics* (Washington, various issues).

———, 2006, "Exchange Rates and Trade Balance Adjustment in Emerging Market Economies" (Washington).

Johnson, Simon, Jonathan Ostry, and Arvind Subramanian, 2007, "The Prospect for a Sustained Growth in Africa: Benchmarking the Constraints," IMF Working Paper 07/52 (Washington: International Monetary Fund).

Justiniano, Alejandro, and Kornélia Krajnyák, 2005, "Why Has the U.S. Trade Balance Widened So Fast?" in *United States: Selected Issues*, IMF Country Report No. 05/258 (Washington: International Monetary Fund), pp. 30–45.

Kamin, Steven, Trever Reeve, and Nathan Sheets, 2006, "U.S. External Adjustment: Considering the Historical Experience" (unpublished).

Khatri, Yougesh, and Yoko Oguro, 2007, "Trade Sensitivity to Exchange Rates in the Context of Intra-Industry Trade" (unpublished).

Krugman, Paul, 1989, "Differences in Income Elasticities and Trends in Real Exchange

Rates," *European Economic Review*, Vol. 33 (May), pp. 1031–46.

———, 1991, *Has the Adjustment Process Worked?* (Washington: Institute for International Economics).

———, 2006, "Will There Be a Dollar Crisis?" (unpublished). Available via the Internet: http://www. econ.princeton.edu/seminars/WEEKLY%20SEM INAR%20SCHEDULE/SPRING_05-06/April_24/ Krugman.pdf.

Lane, Philip, and Gian Maria Milesi-Ferretti, 2006, "The External Wealth of Nations Mark II: Revised and Extended Estimates of Foreign Assets and Liabilities, 1970–2004," IMF Working Paper 06/69 (Washington: International Monetary Fund).

Mann, Catherine, and Katharina Plück, 2007, "Understanding the U.S. Trade Deficit: A Disaggregated Perspective," in *G7 Current Account Imbalances: Sustainability and Adjustment*, ed. by Richard Clarida (Chicago: University of Chicago Press).

Marazzi, Mario, and others, 2005, "Exchange Rate Pass-Through to U.S. Import Prices: Some New Evidence," International Finance Discussion Paper No. 833 (Washington: Board of Governors of the Federal Reserve System).

Marquez, Jaime, 2002, *Estimating Trade Elasticities* (Boston: Kluwer Academic Publishers).

Milesi-Ferretti, Gian Maria, and Assaf Razin, 1998, "Current Account Reversals and Currency Crises: Empirical Regularities," IMF Working Paper 98/89 (Washington: International Monetary Fund).

Mussa, Michael, 2004, "Exchange Rate Adjustments Needed to Reduce Global Payments Imbalances," in *Dollar Adjustment: How Far? Against What?* ed. by C. Fred Bergsten and John Williamson (Washington: Institute for International Economics).

National Research Council, 2006, *Analyzing the U.S. Content of Imports and the Foreign Content of Exports* (Washington: National Research Council of the National Academies).

Obstfeld, Maurice, 2002, "Exchange Rates and Adjustment: Perspectives from the New Open-Economy Macroeconomics," *Monetary and Economic Studies*, Vol. 20, No. S-1 (December), pp. 23–46.

———, and Kenneth Rogoff, 1996, *Foundations of International Macroeconomics* (Cambridge, Massachusetts: MIT Press).

———, 2000, "New Directions for Stochastic Open Economy Models," *Journal of International Economics*, Vol. 50 (February), pp. 117–53.

Orcutt, Guy, 1950, "Measurement of Price Elasticities in International Trade," *Review of Economics and Statistics*, Vol. 32 (May), pp. 117–32.

Organization for Economic Cooperation and Development (OECD), 2006, *OECD Economic Outlook* (Paris).

Otani, Akira, Shigenori Shiratsuka, and Toyoichiro Shirota, 2006, "Revisiting the Decline in the Exchange Rate Pass-Through: Further Evidence from Japan's Import Prices," *Monetary and Economic Studies*, Vol. 24, No. 1 (March), pp. 61–75.

Pesaran, M. Hashem, and Ronald Smith, 1995, "Estimating Long-Run Relationships from Dynamic Heterogeneous Panels," *Journal of Econometrics*, Vol. 68 (July), pp. 79–113.

Reinhart, Carmen, and Kenneth Rogoff, 2004, "The Modern History of Exchange Rate Arrangements: A Reinterpretation," *Quarterly Journal of Economics*, Vol. 119 (February), pp. 1–48.

Rodríguez-López, José Antonio, 2006, "Trade, Prices, and the Exchange Rate with Heterogeneous Producers and Endogenous Markups" (unpublished; Berkeley, California: University of California, Berkeley). Available via the Internet: http://socrates. berkeley.edu/~jarodrig/antonio/JMP_Rodriguez_ Lopez.pdf.

Roubini, Nouriel, and Brad Setser, 2004, "The U.S. as a Net Debtor: The Sustainability of the U.S. External Imbalances" (unpublished; New York: Stern School of Business, New York University). Available via the Internet: http://pages.stern.nyu. edu/~nroubini/papers/Roubini-Setser-US-External-Imbalances.pdf.

Teräsvirta, Timo, Chien-Fu Lin, and Clive W. J. Granger, 1993, "The Power of the Neural Network Linearity Test," *Journal of Time Series Analysis*, Vol. 14, pp. 209–20.

Thomas, Charles, and Jaime Marquez, 2006, "Measurement Matters for Modeling U.S. Import Prices," International Finance Discussion Paper No. 883 (Washington: Board of Governors of the Federal Reserve System).

World Bank, 2006, *World Development Indicators* (Washington).

CHAPTER 4

DECOUPLING THE TRAIN? SPILLOVERS AND CYCLES IN THE GLOBAL ECONOMY

Over the past year, there has been considerable debate about how the slowing of the U.S. economy could affect other countries. The concerns of investors and policymakers alike must be seen against the history of past U.S. recessions usually coinciding with significant reductions in global growth (Figure 4.1). This experience is often summed up by the saying, "If the United States sneezes, the rest of the world catches a cold."

So far, however, the U.S. slowdown has had little discernible effect on growth in most other countries. Observers have suggested a number of reasons to explain this outcome. First, the slowdown has been related to U.S.-specific sectoral developments—corrections in the housing and manufacturing sectors—rather than to broad-based, common factors such as oil price or equity market developments that were often behind earlier downturns. Second, implications for global demand may have diminished because trade linkages with the United States have become progressively less important for many countries. Third, some commentators have suggested that with the strengthening momentum of domestic demand in both advanced economies other than the United States and emerging markets, global growth should be more resilient at present than during earlier U.S. downturns.

Nevertheless, concerns about possibly larger spillover effects remain for a number of reasons. First, growth slowdowns often are the precursors to turning points in economic activity. As is well known, cyclical turning points are difficult to forecast, and the risk remains that the correction in the U.S. housing market could

Note: The main authors of this chapter are Thomas Helbling, Peter Berezin, Ayhan Kose, Michael Kumhof, Doug Laxton, and Nikola Spatafora, with support from Ben Sutton and Patrick Hettinger. Christopher Otrok provided consultancy support.

Figure 4.1. U.S. Recessions and Real GDP Growth by Region[1]
(Periods of U.S. recessions shaded, annual change in percent)

U.S. recessions have usually coincided with significant reductions in growth in other regions.

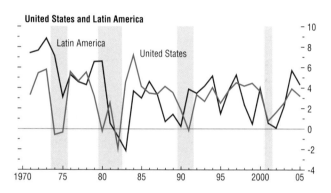

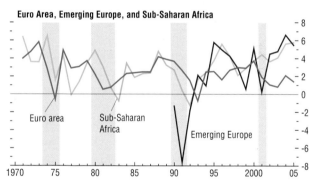

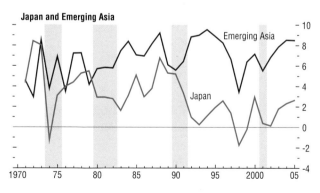

Sources: World Bank, *World Development Indicators;* and IMF staff calculations.
[1]Recession as defined by the National Bureau of Economic Research.

Table 4.1. Role of Large Economies in the Global Economy
(Ten largest economies, in percent of world total; period averages)

	GDP						Merchandise Trade		
	At PPP exchange rates			At market exchange rates			Exports		
	1971–75	1986–90	2001–05	1971–75	1986–90	2001–05	1971–75	1986–90	2001–05
United States	22.5	21.5	20.5	27.9	27.0	30.1	15.7	13.2	11.6
Euro area[1]	21.3	18.4	15.7	20.2	22.0	21.9	21.2	20.1	18.5
Japan	8.0	8.4	6.7	7.5	14.0	11.6	8.5	10.9	7.4
United Kingdom	4.3	3.5	3.1	3.7	4.1	4.9	6.9	6.2	4.7
China[2]	3.0	5.8	14.0	2.6	1.9	4.6	1.2	2.0	7.2
Canada	2.1	2.0	1.9	2.7	2.5	2.4	5.7	4.7	4.4
Mexico	1.7	1.9	1.8	1.3	1.0	1.8	0.5	0.9	2.7
Korea	0.6	1.1	1.6	0.3	1.0	1.7	0.7	2.3	3.1
India	3.5	4.0	5.7	1.7	1.5	1.6	0.7	0.6	1.0
Brazil	2.7	3.2	2.7	1.2	1.9	1.5	1.3	1.3	1.2

Sources: IMF, *Direction of Trade Statistics*, and World Economic Outlook database.
[1]Excluding intra–euro area trade.
[2]Data in 1971–75 column are for 1976–80.

be deeper than expected and the current U.S. slowdown could intensify, with likely larger spillovers into other countries.[1] Second, the relative decline in trade linkages with the United States must be balanced against the rapidly increasing cross-border financial linkages and the fact that the United States remains at the core of the global financial system. Third, the U.S. economy remains the world's largest, and while other advanced economies, in particular in Europe, have gained cyclical momentum, there remain questions about their underlying dynamism. Fourth, while the five largest emerging market economies now account for one-fourth of global GDP on a purchasing power parity (PPP) basis, their role in global trade is not yet commensurate (about one-seventh), and it is difficult to argue that they could entirely replace the U.S. economy as an engine for global growth.

Against this background, the chapter asks the broad question of how far other countries can "decouple" from the U.S. economy and sustain strong growth in the face of a U.S. slowdown. The main goal is to (1) pinpoint what factors would likely determine the magnitude of the spillovers—the effects on the output of other countries from weaker U.S. growth—in present circumstances; and (2) provide an understanding of the risks and policy challenges that apply not just at this conjuncture but also to future cycles.

The chapter has two main parts. The first part analyzes recent evidence on how the U.S. economy has affected (and been affected by) international business cycle fluctuations. Specifically, it addresses the following questions.

- What have been the global repercussions of past U.S. recessions and slowdowns, and how have these repercussions changed over time?

- How much do disturbances in the United States affect macroeconomic conditions elsewhere, and how do these effects compare with those from disturbances in other major currency areas? Has the strength of these business cycle linkages changed over time with the rapid increases in international trade and financial integration?

- How much have synchronized cycles in economic activity across the major economies been driven by common factors?

The second part of the chapter uses a model-based simulation approach to analyze how the global repercussions of a U.S. slowdown depend on the specific underlying disturbances. This section also considers the role that monetary and exchange rate policies could play in reducing the extent of adverse spillovers from a U.S. slowdown.

[1]See, among others, Artis (1996) and Timmermann (2006) on forecasting turning points.

Merchandise Trade			Stock Market Capitalization		
Imports					
1971–75	1986–90	2001–05	1971–75	1986–90	2001–05
15.6	18.6	19.7	. . .	32.8	44.4
21.2	19.0	16.9	. . .	11.3	15.3
7.9	7.4	5.8	. . .	34.4	9.4
7.9	7.3	5.6	. . .	7.9	7.5
1.3	2.1	6.2	. . .	. . .	1.9
5.5	4.7	4.0	. . .	2.6	2.8
0.8	0.9	2.9	. . .	0.2	0.5
0.9	2.1	2.7	. . .	0.8	1.1
0.8	0.8	1.2	. . .	0.3	0.8
1.9	0.8	0.9	. . .	0.3	0.8

This chapter argues that the limited global impact of the current U.S. slowdown so far reflects that it has been driven mainly by U.S.-specific sectoral corrections in housing and manufacturing, rather than broader global developments that are highly correlated across the major industrial countries. Moreover, the aggregate impact of these sectoral corrections has been contained even in the United States. That said, there are still risks at this stage of the housing downturn permeating to other sectors and private consumption, with correspondingly larger spillovers into other countries. More generally, the chapter finds that the potential size of spillovers from the United States has increased with greater trade and financial integration, but that the importance of these links should not be overestimated. Spillovers are most important for countries with close trade and financial ties with the United States, particularly Latin America and some industrial countries, and they tend to be larger during recessions, when import growth turns sharply negative, than during midcycle slowdowns. Fundamentally, however, the chapter finds that past episodes of highly synchronized growth declines across the globe were not primarily the result of developments specific to the United States, but rather were caused by factors that affected many countries at the same time. Examples of such episodes include the first oil price shock in 1974–75 and the bursting of the information technology (IT) bubble in 2000. With increasingly flexible macroeconomic policy frameworks in many countries, forward-looking monetary policy management should be able to help cushion the spillover effects of weaker growth in the United States or other large economies.

U.S. Economy and International Business Cycle Fluctuations

As a starting point, it is useful to establish some basic facts about the relative size of the U.S. economy and its linkages with other regions.

- The United States remains by far the world's largest economy (Table 4.1). When measured at PPP exchange rates, the U.S. economy accounts for about one-fifth of global GDP. In terms of market exchange rates, it accounts for slightly less than one-third of global GDP. These ratios have not changed much in the past three decades.
- The United States is the largest importer in the global economy. It has been importing, on average, about one-fifth of all internationally traded goods since 1970. It is the second largest exporter after the euro area.
- In line with the generally rapid growth in intraregional trade,[2] the share of trade with the United States has greatly increased in the Western Hemisphere region, including in neighboring countries—Canada and Mexico—and some others in Central and South America (Figure 4.2). Compared with the euro area and Japan, the United States has seen a larger increase in trade with emerging market and other developing countries in general, not just with countries in the Western Hemisphere.

[2]This development reflects, to an important extent, factors such as geographic proximity, similarities in economic structure, and historical and cultural ties (variables common to the standard gravity models of trade). Regional integration at the policy level, including, for example, through regional trade agreements and other forms of cooperation, has also helped.

Figure 4.2. Trade Orientation

(Trade with indicated areas as percent of total trade)

With the rapid growth in intraregional trade, the importance of trade with the United States has generally decreased. In Latin America, however, the trade share with the United States has increased.

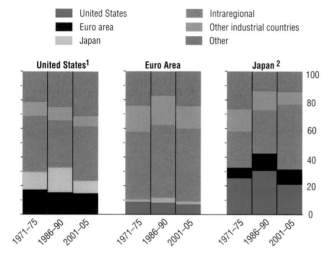

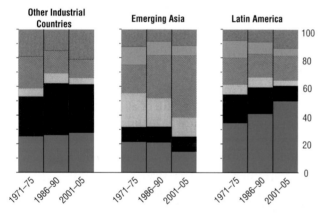

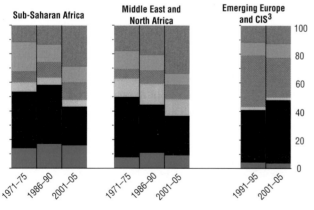

Sources: IMF, *Direction of Trade Statistics* (2006); and IMF staff calculations.
[1] Intraregional trade covers trade with countries in the Western Hemisphere.
[2] Intraregional trade covers trade with emerging Asia.
[3] Commonwealth of Independent States.

- Export exposure to the United States—the share of exports to the United States as a percent of GDP—has generally continued to increase, even for countries where the U.S. share of total exports has declined, as trade openness has increased everywhere (Table 4.2). Export exposure to the United States also tends to be larger than that to the euro area and Japan, except in neighboring regions.

- Overall, U.S. financial markets have been and remain by far the largest, reflecting not only the size of the economy but also their depth. Changes in U.S. asset prices tend to have strong signaling effects worldwide, and spillovers from U.S. financial markets have been important, especially during periods of market stress. In particular, correlations across national stock markets are highest when the U.S. stock market is declining (Box 4.1).

- Reflecting the size and depth of its financial markets, as well as its increasing net external liabilities, claims on the United States typically account for the lion's share of extra-regional foreign portfolio assets of the rest of the world (Table 4.3). At the same time, the share of foreign portfolio liabilities held by U.S. investors typically also exceeds the holdings of investors elsewhere, except for the euro area, where intraregional holdings are more important. This illustrates the extent of important international financial linkages with U.S. markets.

Spillovers During Past U.S. Recessions and Slowdowns: An Event Study

Since 1970, the United States has experienced five recessions and two midcycle slowdowns.[3] An important reason to study the global repercus-

---

[3]Following the quarterly business cycle chronology of the National Bureau of Economic Research (NBER), the five recessions covered in the event study are 1974–75, 1980, 1981–82, 1991, and 2001. Midcycle slowdowns are defined as periods during which U.S. output was below potential (as determined by a Hodrick-Prescott filter) and which were not considered recessions by the NBER. Specifically, the periods covered are 1986 and 1995.

Table 4.2. Export Orientation by Region
(Merchandise exports to indicated destinations as a percent of GDP)

	Destination							
	United States		Euro area		Japan		Intraregional	
Exports from	1981–85[1]	2001–05[1]	1981–85[1]	2001–05[1]	1981–85[1]	2001–05[1]	1981–85[1]	2001–05[1]
Industrial countries								
United States	. . .	. . .	1.0	1.1	0.6	0.5	. . .	. . .
Euro area	1.5	2.4	. . .	. . .	0.2	0.4	8.3	15.5
Japan	4.0	2.9	1.1	1.3	. . .	. . .	. . .	. . .
Other industrial countries	6.0	7.9	6.0	7.6	1.0	0.9	3.6	3.3
Emerging markets and other developing countries								
Emerging Asia	4.8	7.1	1.7	4.5	3.5	3.9	5.2	16.2
China	0.8	5.9	0.8	3.8	2.1	3.6	3.5	9.1
NIEs and ASEAN-4[2]	10.5	10.3	3.2	6.1	6.6	5.6	9.7	29.0
Latin America	4.5	11.8	2.4	2.0	0.7	0.4	2.4	3.6
Argentina	1.1	2.1	2.1	3.0	0.3	0.2	1.7	7.7
Brazil	2.4	3.1	2.2	2.6	0.6	0.4	1.3	3.2
Mexico	6.7	23.0	1.8	0.8	0.8	0.2	0.9	1.0
Sub-Saharan Africa	3.0	5.9	5.9	6.2	0.3	1.1	0.9	3.1
Nigeria	8.6	18.7	17.0	8.8	0.1	1.2	1.1	3.6
South Africa	. . .	2.1	. . .	4.9	. . .	1.8	. . .	3.0
Emerging Europe and CIS[3]	0.6	1.3	6.0	14.5	0.3	0.3	6.1	8.8
Hungary[3]	1.0	1.8	15.5	34.9	0.3	0.3	5.8	9.0
Poland[3]	0.5	0.6	9.4	14.4	0.1	0.1	2.9	5.5
Russia[3]	0.7	1.4	3.8	10.1	0.5	0.6	5.4	9.6

Sources: IMF, *World Economic Outlook*; World Bank, *World Development Indicators*; and IMF staff calculations.
[1]Period average.
[2]The countries in the group of newly industrialized economies (NIEs) comprise Hong Kong SAR, Korea, Singapore, and Taiwan Province of China. The countries in the group ASEAN-4 comprise Indonesia, Malaysia, the Philippines, and Thailand.
[3]Values in the columns for 1981–85 are period averages for 1991–95. CIS = Commonwealth of Independent States.

sions of such U.S. downturns is that international business cycle linkages tend to be particularly visible during these events (e.g., Zarnowitz, 1992). Broadly speaking, past U.S. recessions have been accompanied by declining GDP growth rates in most other countries (Table 4.4). In industrial countries, growth rates have, on average, declined by 2 percentage points, roughly half of the U.S. average decline in growth. Among emerging market economies, Latin America has tended to experience the largest declines in growth, with median growth declines of 1.7 percent during U.S. recessions. Growth in Asia has also tended to decline during U.S. recessions while the impact on growth in Africa and the Middle East has been fairly small.

However, there has been significant variation in growth performance across recessions, and across and within regions. For example, the 2001 recession was accompanied by growth declines in most industrial economies, as well as in all major Latin American economies, almost all Asian economies, and most of emerging Europe. During the 1991 recession, on the other hand, other industrial countries only experienced a modest growth decline, and, in most emerging market economies, growth actually increased. This contrast largely reflects differences in the nature of the two recessions. The 1991 recession was partly attributable to a disturbance that was U.S.-specific in nature—the aftermath of the Savings and Loan Crisis and the associated credit crunch—and its impact on many other economies was partly offset by the expansionary effects of German reunification. The 2001 recession may have initially been most visible in the United States, but it had a clear global component associated with the bursting of the IT bubble, including the sharp declines in most major stock market indices and drops in business investment around the world.

Table 4.3. External Portfolio Assets and Liabilities by Region
(Percent of GDP)

| | Destination (Assets) and Origin (Liabilities) | | | | | | | |
| | United States | | Euro area | | Japan | | Intraregional | |
	1997	2004	1997	2004	1997	2004	1997	2004
	Assets							
Industrial countries								
United States	. . .	. . .	5.9	8.1	2.0	3.2	. . .	. . .
Euro area	3.1	14.1	. . .	. . .	0.7	2.5	7.7	57.8
Japan	7.8	15.0	5.2	12.9	. . .	. . .	. . .	. . .
Other industrial countries	11.9	21.7	13.2	31.0	3.8	4.1	5.4	10.1
Emerging markets and other developing countries								
Emerging Asia	0.2	2.3	0.1	1.8	0.0	0.4	0.5	2.4
China	0.0	0.0	0.0	0.0	0.0	0.0	. . .	. . .
NIEs and ASEAN-4	0.4	5.7	0.1	4.5	0.1	1.0	0.9	4.1
Latin America	0.4	1.8	0.0	0.9	0.0	0.0	0.0	0.3
Sub-Saharan Africa	0.0	1.4	0.0	1.3	0.0	0.2	0.0	0.3
Emerging Europe	0.0	0.4	0.0	2.0	0.0	0.0	0.0	0.6
	Liabilities							
Industrial countries								
United States	. . .	. . .	2.5	11.5	4.1	5.9	. . .	. . .
Euro area	7.4	9.9	. . .	. . .	3.4	6.2	7.7	57.8
Japan	3.8	8.0	1.1	5.2	. . .	. . .	. . .	. . .
Other industrial countries	19.4	28.8	6.2	26.9	5.7	5.1	5.4	10.1
Emerging markets and other developing countries								
Emerging Asia	3.3	5.1	0.5	2.6	1.0	0.6	0.5	2.4
China	0.6	0.7	0.1	0.5	0.5	0.2	. . .	. . .
NIEs and ASEAN-4	5.5	10.8	0.9	5.4	1.5	1.3	0.9	4.1
Latin America	9.4	9.5	1.8	4.3	0.5	0.4	0.0	0.6
Sub-Saharan Africa	4.3	4.9	0.6	2.9	0.3	0.3	0.0	0.3
Emerging Europe	3.5	2.3	0.9	10.5	1.6	0.4	0.0	0.6

Sources: Coordinated Portfolio Investment Survey; IMF, *World Economic Outlook*; World Bank, *World Development Indicators*; and IMF staff calculations.

Note: The countries in the group of newly industrialized economies (NIEs) comprise Hong Kong SAR, Korea, Singapore, and Taiwan Province of China. The countries in the group ASEAN-4 comprise Indonesia, Malaysia, the Philippines, and Thailand.

Similar variations can be seen across the recessions of the early 1970s and 1980s. The 1974–75 recession was associated with large growth declines across much of the world in the wake of the first oil price "shock"—a so-called common disturbance since it affected all countries at the same time.[4] The 1982 recession was unique in that Asian and Latin American economies generally suffered larger declines in growth rates than did other industrial economies. The growth decline in Latin America was particularly

[4]The fact that the first oil shock affected all countries at the same time does not mean that it affected all countries in the same way because the impact depends on factors such as the energy intensity in production and the pass-through of world market prices to end-user prices.

severe, owing in part to the adverse impact that rising interest rates in the major industrial countries had on debt sustainability in the region, which ultimately led to the Latin American debt crises of the 1980s.

The two midcycle growth slowdowns (in 1986 and 1995) were associated with negligible slowdowns elsewhere. The median growth decline in industrial countries was 0.1 percent, while median growth in emerging market economies increased slightly. This pattern appears to apply in the current U.S. slowdown, which has thus far not generated significant growth declines in the rest of the world.

Overall, the considerable variation over time and across countries suggests that the question

Table 4.4. U.S. Downturns and Global Growth

	Recessions[1]					Slowdowns[2]		All Recessions	All Slowdowns
	1974–75	1980	1982	1991	2001	1986	1995		
Change in GDP growth (median for region)									
United States	–6.1	–3.4	–4.5	–2.1	–2.9	–0.7	–1.5	–3.8	–1.1
Other industrial countries	–5.4	–1.5	0.4	–1.3	–2.0	–0.1	–0.3	–2.0	–0.1
Latin America	–3.2	–0.8	–3.9	1.1	–1.8	1.9	—	–1.7	0.9
Middle East and North Africa	1.2	–1.0	–3.3	0.8	–0.7	–0.2	0.7	–0.6	0.3
Emerging Asia	–3.5	–0.3	–1.5	–0.1	–1.1	0.9	0.3	–1.3	0.6
Sub-Saharan Africa	–0.5	—	1.0	—	0.6	–0.6	1.9	0.2	0.7
Emerging Europe and CIS	. . .	. . .	. . .	–6.9	–0.3	. . .	3.8	–3.6	3.8
Ratio of median growth changes to U.S. growth changes (percent)									
Other industrial countries	90	44	–10	61	69	–17	20	51	1
Latin America	52	22	87	–53	61	–279	–1	34	–140
Middle East and North Africa	–20	30	74	–38	24	28	–47	14	–9
Emerging Asia	57	10	33	4	37	–131	–16	28	–74
Sub-Saharan Africa	9	–1	–23	0	–19	83	–123	–7	–20
Emerging Europe and CIS	. . .	. . .	. . .	335	11	. . .	–250	173	–250
Percent of countries experiencing growth declines									
Other industrial countries	91	64	45	73	91	45	55	73	50
Latin America	77	62	90	37	83	33	47	70	40
Middle East and North Africa	40	57	60	40	53	53	47	50	50
Emerging Asia	72	56	78	53	84	47	42	68	45
Sub-Saharan Africa	53	50	46	50	35	58	25	47	41
Emerging Europe and CIS	. . .	. . .	. . .	93	60	. . .	17	76	17

Source: IMF staff calculations.

Note: CIS = Commonwealth of Independent States.

[1]Year during which most of the impact on U.S. growth was recorded. Actual National Bureau of Economic Research (NBER) recession data may slightly differ.

[2]Midcycle slowdowns are defined as periods during which U.S. output was below potential (as determined by a Hodrick-Prescott filter) and which were not considered recessions by the NBER. Specifically, the periods covered are 1986 and 1995.

of how U.S. recessions and slowdowns affect other economies can only be answered after discerning the underlying set of factors causing the U.S. recessions and taking into account initial conditions, economic vulnerabilities, and policy responses in other regions. To this end, the section now turns to a more detailed event study based on quarterly data.[5]

Past U.S. recessions and slowdowns have affected other economies through two primary channels: (1) trade linkages and (2) financial market linkages between the United States and the rest of world. With respect to trade linkages, an important feature of past U.S. recessions has been that import growth turned sharply negative during every recession (Figure 4.3). In fact, U.S. imports are strongly procyclical, with a sensitivity that even exceeds that of private fixed investment. This reflects the relatively high import share of cyclically sensitive components of domestic final demand such as consumer durables and investment goods.[6] Not surprisingly, countries with the greatest export exposure to the United States suffered the largest declines in output gaps (Figure 4.4).

[5]While use of quarterly data reduces the sample to only those countries for which quarterly data are available, it does provide the advantage of better aligning the output behavior in other countries with the standard NBER business cycle chronology (which specifies the end and beginning of recessions by months and quarters rather than only by years).

[6]The share of imports of consumer durables and capital goods in total U.S. imports during 2005 was 48.9 percent, as compared with a share of these goods in domestic final demand of 7.9 percent during this period. Moreover, imports also include 31.3 percent of industrial raw materials, the demand for which is also cyclically sensitive.

Figure 4.3. United States: Real Imports, Real Effective Exchange Rate, Real Stock Returns, and Interest Rates During Recessions and Slowdowns

U.S. imports fell sharply in every recession while U.S. stock prices tended to decline, reflecting higher risk premia and declining corporate profitability. In contrast, imports registered a moderation in growth during slowdowns while stock prices remained relatively unaffected.

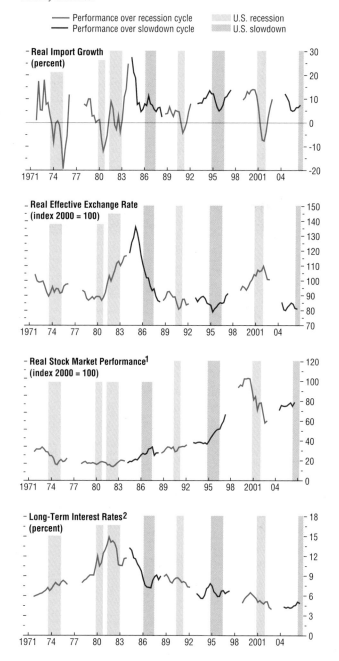

Sources: U.S. Bureau of Economic Analysis; Board of Governors of the Federal Reserve System; *The Wall Street Journal;* and IMF staff calculations.
[1]S&P 500 index deflated by consumer price index.
[2]Yield on 10-year treasury bonds at constant maturity.

For the transmission through trade channels, the behavior of the U.S. dollar during recessions also mattered. For example, the decrease in U.S. import growth during the 1982 recession was similar to that observed during the 1990–91 and 2001 recessions even though the 1982 recession was significantly deeper. This partly reflected the strong appreciation of the U.S. dollar in 1982, as monetary policy was tightened sharply to curb inflation. As a result, the competitiveness of U.S. trading partners improved, thereby buffering these economies from the U.S. recession and from the adverse effects of higher global real interest rates.

Industrial countries whose exchange rates depreciated during U.S. recessions tended to experience small growth declines while the opposite was true for emerging economies. This contrast is partly explained by the currency crises experienced by some emerging market economies during U.S. recessions, reflecting not only the external debt sustainability issues that emerged with terms-of-trade losses during these episodes (noted below), but also some-times higher U.S. interest rates and concurrent reversals of capital flows to emerging markets (Box 4.2). A related aspect is that most emerging markets have external debt liabilities that are denominated in a foreign currency, typically in U.S. dollars, which can make them vulnerable to the increase in the debt-service burden associated with currency devaluations or depreciations. Such "balance sheet" effects also help explain why emerging economies with high ratios of public debt to GDP, which tend to be highly correlated with the external debt burden, experienced greater declines in output gaps than countries with lower debt ratios. These observations highlight the important role of economic vulnerabilities in determining how other countries are affected by U.S. recessions.

The evidence from the event study also suggests that exchange rate flexibility was helpful in mitigating adverse external effects during U.S. recessions, as countries with flexible exchange rate regimes, on average, experienced smaller growth declines than those with fixed exchange rate regimes (excluding countries that experienced currency crises).[7]

While export exposure to the United States appears to be an important determinant of the severity of the response to U.S. recessions, "openness" in general seems to be more of a factor for emerging market economies. More open emerging market economies, in terms of both trade and financial openness (as defined in Appendix 4.1), consistently show larger declines in output gaps during U.S. recessions. Not surprisingly, countries that experienced terms-of-trade declines also had the largest output responses, partly reflecting the adverse effects on commodity prices of slowing global growth during U.S. recessions.

The event study suggests that countries that already suffered from large and negative output gaps at the beginning of a U.S. recession tended to perform better than countries that were closer to their cyclical peaks. This finding runs counter to the intuition that countries whose output is already below potential at the onset of a U.S. recession would be more vulnerable to adverse external shocks because these may amplify adverse confidence effects and increase risks of debt deflation. This suggests that when growth is below trend, there is also a tendency for self-correcting forces to lift growth back to trend, and it appears that this effect was the dominant one.[8]

Past U.S. recessions were generally preceded and, to some extent, accompanied by stock market declines. Given strong equity price linkages, especially during periods of market stress, stock prices also tended to fall in other economies during these episodes. In contrast, U.S. stock market indices did not decline on a quarterly basis during U.S. midcycle slowdowns, including the current one. Similarly, the weakness of U.S. stocks in the lead-up to recessions generally coincided with

[7]Countries were sorted into fixed and floating regimes based on the Reinhart-Rogoff classification (2004). See Appendix 4.1 for details.

[8]The self-correcting forces include, for example, deceleration in the growth of prices and wages in response to increasing unemployment and falling capacity utilization, which tend to stimulate demand.

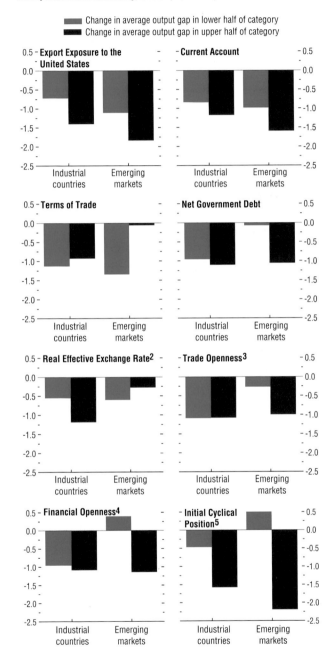

Figure 4.4. Output Gaps and Structural Characteristics During U.S. Recessions[1]
(Change in average output gaps, percent of trend GDP)

The output response to U.S. recessions differs substantially across a number of country characteristics, including, for example, trade exposure to the United States.

■ Change in average output gap in lower half of category
■ Change in average output gap in upper half of category

Sources: Lane and Milesi-Ferretti (2006); and IMF staff calculations.
[1]Output gaps estimated as the difference between real GDP and trend GDP from a Hodrick-Prescott filter.
[2]Countries in the upper half saw a real appreciation or less of a depreciation.
[3]Total exports in percent of GDP when the United States enters a recession.
[4]Gross external assets plus gross external liabilities, percent of GDP.
[5]Average output gap when the United States enters a recession.

Box 4.1. Financial Linkages and Spillovers

Asset prices are highly correlated across countries, which suggests that financial linkages are an important source of global spillovers. Moreover, since the 1970s, cross-border financial linkages have increased significantly, with gross external assets of industrial countries rising from 28 percent of GDP in 1970 to 155 percent in 2004. Gross external assets of emerging market countries increased from 16 percent of emerging market and developing country GDP to 57 percent over the same period. As global financial linkages have increased over time, the scope for financial spillovers has grown accordingly. This box reviews recent evidence on financial linkages as a conduit for the transmission of financial disturbances from one country to another.

It is widely acknowledged that the impact of a disturbance in one financial market on other markets abroad depends on the nature of financial linkages across countries and whether the disturbance affects any of the major advanced economies (Kaminsky and Reinhart, 2003). For example, the sharp devaluation of the Thai baht in 1997 and associated contraction in output and corporate distress in Thailand led to an increase in nonperforming loans among already weak Japanese banks, contributing to a more cautious attitude to lending across the region. Additionally, financial integration may also lead to increased co-movement in risk premia across markets, in part because an investor in one market is likely to be exposed to other markets as well. Thus, for example, the Russian debt default in 1998 increased market volatility, causing credit risk spreads to widen, and triggering a general "flight to quality" toward low-risk, highly liquid securities such as U.S. treasuries.

While the impact of financial disturbances depends on a number of factors, there are nevertheless two broad channels that are of particular relevance.

- Prices for similar assets across countries have become more correlated with increasing financial linkages. In particular, for industrial countries, correlations among stock market indices and bond yields have increased.[1] As for emerging markets, their asset price correlations with the United States and most other industrial countries except Japan have increased over the past 15 years. Correlations among emerging markets have also increased compared with the early 1990s.

- While much of the literature has focused on cross-country correlations of asset price changes, it is important to note that price volatility is also highly correlated across countries (Engle and Susmel, 1993). While the reasons have been widely debated, it seems that asymmetric and incomplete information is the key factor (Goodhart, 1999). Uncertainty about the conduct of monetary policy in the United States, for example, is likely to generate higher volatility in all markets. Additionally, herding behavior among investors may increase when asset prices move significantly in one direction or another, which could amplify price shocks.

There is a clear asymmetry in cross-country asset price correlations, with correlations increasing significantly during bear markets and recessions. This may help explain why global contractions tend to be more highly synchronized across countries than global expansions. Some recent research suggests that the United States plays a key role in the dissemination and propagation of financial shocks (Fung, Leung, and Xu, 2001). This is not surprising given that the United States accounts for over 40 percent of global stock market capitalization and nearly half of the private debt outstanding. The importance of the United States appears to

Note: The main author of this box is Peter Berezin.

[1]For example, among the G-7 economies, the median stock market correlation coefficient (among 21 country pair-wise correlations) increased from 0.55 to 0.69 between the periods 1995–99 and 2000–06. The median long-term bond yield correlation coefficient increased from 0.54 to 0.8 over the same period. Stock market correlation coefficients increased for all G-7 countries, while bond market correlations increased for all countries except Japan.

increase substantially during periods of market stress. For example, correlations across national stock markets are highest when the U.S. stock market is declining, which explains why months in which the U.S. stock market has declined are almost universally associated with declines in other stock markets (top panel of the figure). Thus, it would seem that from the standpoint of U.S. investors, the benefits of global diversification tend to decline just when they are needed most.

In practice, distinguishing between spillovers from a shock in one country and a common shock that simultaneously affects many countries can be a challenge, since, unlike growth spillovers, asset price spillovers typically occur with little or no lag. For example, when one observes that the U.S. and European stock markets move together, is this mainly because both markets are affected by common shocks or is it because an idiosyncratic shock to one market instantaneously spills over to the other market? One approach to overcoming this problem is to isolate the spillover effect by running regressions that control for country-specific and global common shocks through appropriate explanatory variables. Using this methodology, Ehrmann, Fratzscher, and Rigobon (2005) calculate that about 26 percent of the variation in European financial asset prices is attributable to developments in the United States, while about 8 percent of the price variation in U.S. financial markets are caused by European developments. The U.S. spillover into Europe is particularly striking for equity markets, where 50 percent of a shock to U.S. equity prices is transmitted to Europe after controlling for common shocks in both regions.

Another approach is to look at price movements in markets that are open during different times of the day (Karolyi and Stulz, 1996). This is useful for analyzing specific events such as market crashes. For example, daily price movements in the days around the 1987 stock market crash clearly show how the U.S. stock market influenced Asia and vice versa, with declines in the United States causing Asian markets to open

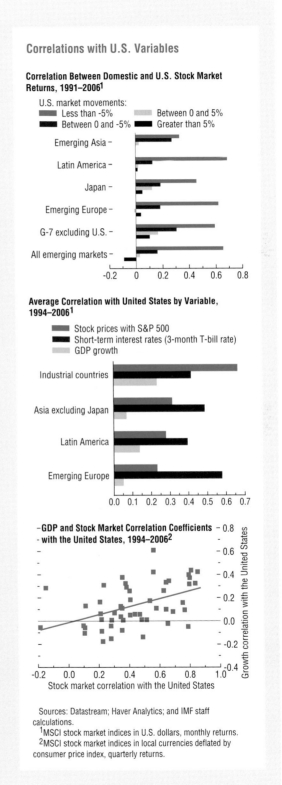

Correlations with U.S. Variables

Correlation Between Domestic and U.S. Stock Market Returns, 1991–2006[1]

U.S. market movements:
Less than -5% Between 0 and 5%
Between 0 and -5% Greater than 5%

Emerging Asia
Latin America
Japan
Emerging Europe
G-7 excluding U.S.
All emerging markets

Average Correlation with United States by Variable, 1994–2006[1]

Stock prices with S&P 500
Short-term interest rates (3-month T-bill rate)
GDP growth

Industrial countries
Asia excluding Japan
Latin America
Emerging Europe

GDP and Stock Market Correlation Coefficients with the United States, 1994–2006[2]

Growth correlation with the United States
Stock market correlation with the United States

Sources: Datastream; Haver Analytics; and IMF staff calculations.
[1]MSCI stock market indices in U.S. dollars, monthly returns.
[2]MSCI stock market indices in local currencies deflated by consumer price index, quarterly returns.

131

Box 4.1 *(concluded)*

lower and intraday movements in Asian markets strongly influencing the following day's open in New York.

Comparing financial market linkages and business cycle linkages, stock prices and interest rates have tended to be more correlated across countries than GDP growth rates (see the figure). There is also a positive relationship between how synchronized a country's stock market is with the United States and how synchronized its business cycle is with the United States. Additionally, countries that are more

financially open tend to have stock markets that are more synchronized with the United States. These facts suggest that financial linkages do indeed play an important role in transmitting shocks that affect real variables, and that continued financial integration over time may amplify financial spillovers across countries. This may be particularly true for emerging market economies as their financial sectors continue to become larger and more integrated with the global financial system (Cuadro Sáez, Fratzscher, and Thimann, 2007).

significant declines in corporate earnings while, during slowdowns, corporate earnings generally have not declined, including at present.

An event analysis was also performed for slowdowns. Unlike for recessions, however, no clear-cut patterns emerged. This finding does not mean that the factors that shape the global spillovers during recessions are irrelevant during slowdowns. It would seem more plausible that the underlying U.S. disturbances were small in scale during slowdowns, which makes the identification of such factors through simple descriptive analysis more difficult, as spillovers have been overshadowed by other developments.

Growth Fluctuations in Major Currency Areas and Spillovers: Two Econometric Assessments

Moving beyond the event analysis, econometric estimates of the effects on output elsewhere of disturbances to growth in major advanced economies, including in particular the United States, can provide a more rigorous assessment of the cross-border growth spillovers. In approaching this exercise, it is necessary to recognize that any analysis at the global level faces trade-offs between the sophistication of the modeling framework—notably, the extent to which the disturbances have a precise economic interpretation attached to them—and availability of data. This section employs two different mod-

eling frameworks to arrive at robust conclusions while maintaining some coverage for a large number of countries.

A Broad Cross-Country Analysis

To start with an approach that can be applied to a broad cross-section of countries, a series of panel regressions was estimated relating growth in domestic output per capita to various combinations of U.S. growth, euro area growth, and Japanese growth. The coefficients on these foreign growth variables provide a measure of the magnitude of spillovers. To reduce the likelihood that the estimated spillovers reflect common unobserved shocks, the set of explanatory variables was expanded to include several controls: terms-of-trade changes; a short-term interest rate (the U.S. dollar London Interbank Offered Rate, or LIBOR); controls for the Latin American debt and Tequila crises, the Asian financial crises of 1997–98, and the Argentine crisis of 2001–02; country fixed effects; initial GDP; and population growth. The sample includes up to 130 advanced economies and developing countries, covering all *World Economic Outlook* regions, and uses annual data over 1970–2005 (see Appendix 4.1 for details).

Even the simplest specification finds significant cross-country spillovers from growth in the United States, the euro area, and Japan (Table 4.5, column 1). On average, the United

Box 4.2. Macroeconomic Conditions in Industrial Countries and Financial Flows to Emerging Markets

Over the past 30 years, business cycles in industrial countries and emerging market economies have been only partially synchronized (first figure). While there are common patterns—such as the growth decelerations in the early 1980s and 1990s—other developments have been specific to emerging markets, such as the late 1990s recession, modest growth in the late 1980s when industrial countries were booming, and a stellar growth performance in recent years.

Even casual observation suggests that these differences may at least partly be related to capital flows. Since the mid-1970s, emerging markets have gone through two cycles of surging inflows followed by a painful "sudden stop" (Calvo, 1998). The first cycle began in the mid-1970s and ended with the Latin American debt crisis of 1981–83. The second cycle took off in the early 1990s and came to a halt with the Asian and Russian crises of 1997–99. In both cases, financial flows to the private sector—that is, bank loans and portfolio flows—collapsed (first figure). Understanding the forces driving these flows is therefore crucial to understanding business cycles in emerging markets and how they are affected by developments in advanced economies.

A popular hypothesis relates flows into emerging markets to global liquidity conditions. According to this reasoning, abundant liquidity in industrial countries, triggered by loose monetary policy, pushes up industrial country asset prices and reduces yields. Part of the liquidity therefore flows into riskier emerging markets assets in a "search for yield."

One difficulty in assessing the merits of this hypothesis is that there is no accepted measure of "global liquidity."[1] *The Economist* magazine tracks a measure that adds global foreign currency reserves to U.S. base money, interpreting

Note: The main author of this box is Johannes Wiegand.

[1]Matsumoto and Schindler (forthcoming) discuss various liquidity concepts. For studies of liquidity spillovers between industrial countries, see Rüffer and Stracca (2006); Sousa and Zaghini (2004); and Baks and Kramer (1999).

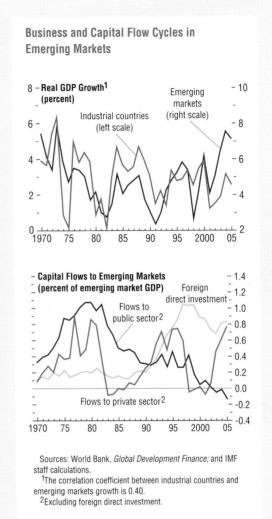

Business and Capital Flow Cycles in Emerging Markets

Sources: World Bank, *Global Development Finance;* and IMF staff calculations.
[1]The correlation coefficient between industrial countries and emerging markets growth is 0.40.
[2]Excluding foreign direct investment.

the change in this aggregate as the world supply of U.S. dollars. However, this index has little predictive power for flows to emerging markets (see second figure). In part this is due to the inclusion of changes in reserves, which tend to move concurrently with flows rather than leading them.[2] In addition, however, measures that refer only to the United States seem inadequate, as flows may also react to liquidity conditions in other industrial countries, including through their impact on "carry trade" invest-

[2]Reserves accumulation is often used to absorb capital inflows, hence this property is unsurprising.

Box 4.2 *(concluded)*

Global Liquidity and Financial Flows to Emerging Markets

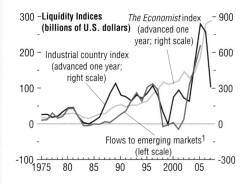

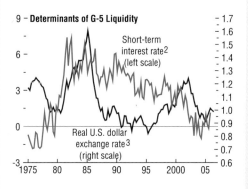

Sources: *The Economist;* IMF, *International Financial Statistics;* World Bank, *Global Development Finance;* and IMF staff calculations.
[1]Financial flows to the private sector, excluding foreign direct investment.
[2]Average real short-term interest rate in G-5 countries.
[3]Real U.S. dollar exchange rate against other G-5 country currencies.

ment strategies—borrowing in a currency with relatively low interest rates and investing in a high-return currency.

The second figure therefore also displays an alternative industrial country liquidity index, computed as the change (over three years) in base money (measured in U.S. dollars) in the five major industrial countries.[3] This index is a

[3]The United States, the euro area (member countries prior to 1999), Japan, the United Kingdom, and Canada.

surprisingly strong leading indicator for emerging market flows, and is especially successful at anticipating contractions, falling well in advance of the Latin American debt crisis and the Asian and Russian crises.[4] The relationship is less close *after* a sudden stop, when the recovery in financial flows lags the pickup in liquidity by several years. This delay may reflect a period of increased investor caution following a crisis.

The usefulness of the industrial country liquidity index as a leading indicator suggests that two factors originating in industrial countries have been important for emerging markets flows.

- *Shifts in industrial countries' monetary policy stance.* In particular, the G-5 central banks tightened policy before the 1982 Latin American debt crisis, raising the average short-term real interest rate by 8 percentage points within two years.
- *Exchange rate variations among industrial country currencies.* As most flows to emerging markets are denominated in U.S. dollars, a dollar appreciation tends to increase the debt burden of emerging markets relative to their exports earnings, which raises the riskiness of their assets relative to expected returns.[5]

[4]The industrial country index leads financial flows by one year. As it measures base money changes over three years, this implies an average lag of two years between liquidity changes and flows. A more formal analysis fitting a vector error correction model shows that the industrial country index and emerging market flows are cointegrated, and that the index is strongly exogenous for flows (hence it can be used to forecast flows). These results are robust to changes in the underlying monetary aggregate (M1 instead of base money), the types of flows considered (including flows to the public sector), and the period length over which money changes are measured (the annual change in the base money of the five major industrial countries, for example, is a noisy two-year-ahead predictor of flows).

[5]A dollar appreciation also implies that the same amount of funds denominated in non–U.S. dollar currencies buys a smaller amount of dollar-denominated assets. While this should also dampen the demand for emerging market assets in principle, the empirical importance of this channel is unclear.

Large U.S. dollar appreciations preceded both the Latin American and Asian crises. In 1995, for example, the dollar surged, especially against the Japanese yen, after depreciating for almost a decade. Hence, East Asian economies—whose currencies were mostly pegged to the dollar—lost competitiveness without a compensating drop in their refinancing costs.[6]

Looking forward, growth in the industrial country liquidity index started to slow in 2005, reflecting monetary tightening by the major central banks. Taken at face value, this would suggest a reduction in emerging market flows going forward. However, more than half of the fall owes to the phasing out of the Bank of Japan's "quantitative easing" policy. This high-

lights the question of how important Japan's highly accommodating monetary stance has been for emerging markets recently. While private outflows from Japan have been large in the past three years, little is known about the extent to which they have been channeled to emerging markets, either directly or indirectly by promoting carry trades.[7]

Among recipient regions, emerging Europe, which has received about half of financial flows to emerging markets since 2003, seems most vulnerable to a flow reversal.[8] Importantly, in many of these countries, external liabilities are denominated in euros rather than in dollars. A stronger euro could therefore be more of a concern going forward than a stronger U.S. dollar.

[6]See Ueda (1998), for example, for a more detailed discussion.

[7]See the April 2007 *Global Financial Stability Report*.
[8]See Box 1.1 of the September 2006 *World Economic Outlook*.

States exerts the greatest impact. In particular, a 1 percentage point decline in U.S. growth is associated with an average 0.16 percentage point drop in growth across the sample, substantially larger than the spillovers from the euro area or Japan.

Following the analysis in the previous section, a natural hypothesis is that the magnitude of spillovers will be closely linked to the strength of trade linkages among economies. Indeed, the results confirm that growth in both the United States and the euro area lead to spillovers into other countries precisely to the extent that these other countries trade with, respectively, the United States and the euro area (Table 4.5, column 2).[9] Quantitatively, the results imply that, if a country's total trade with the United States

rises by 10 percentage points of GDP, then the impact of a 1 percentage point increase in U.S. growth on domestic growth rises by about 0.1 percentage point. There is also some evidence that the magnitude of spillovers from U.S. growth is significantly larger into those countries that are more financially integrated with the United States (Table 4.5, column 3).[10]

Given the rapid, ongoing increases in trade and financial integration over the period, the above findings imply that spillovers should rise over time. Indeed, complementary results confirm that spillovers from growth in at least the United States were significantly higher in the post-1987 half of the sample (Table 4.5, column

[9]Trade intensity with any of the three major currency areas was measured as the ratio of total trade (exports plus imports with that area) to a country's GDP. Growth in the United States, euro area, and Japan, respectively, was then interacted with these trade ratios. Controlling for these interactions, the level terms proved statistically insignificant.

[10]Financial integration between any two countries, i and j, is measured by $|(NFA_i/GDP_i) - (NFA_j/GDP_j)|$. Imbs (2004, p. 728) argues that "pairs of countries with intense capital flows should display different (or even opposite) net external positions. Two countries with massively positive (negative) net foreign assets holdings will both tend to be issuers (recipients) of capital flows, and should experience less bilateral flows than two countries where one is structurally in surplus and the other in deficit." See Appendix 4.1 for details of other measures used.

Table 4.5. Growth and Spillovers (1)
(Panel regression coefficients)

Specification	Dependent Variable: Growth in All Countries[1]			
	(1)	(2)	(3)	(4)
Explanatory variables				
Growth in United States	0.16***		−	+
Trade ratio with United States[2]		0.92**		
Financial integration with United States[2]			0.31*	
Post-1987 indicator[2]				0.29**
Growth in euro area	0.10*		0.40*	0.34*
Trade ratio with euro area[2]		1.1***		
Financial integration with euro area[2]			−	
Post-1987 indicator[2]				−
Growth in Japan	0.11*		0.18*	+
Trade ratio with Japan[2]		+		
Financial integration with Japan[2]			−	
Post-1987 indicator[2]				−

Source: IMF staff calculations.
Note: See Appendix 4.1 for details. *, **, and *** denote statistical significance at the 10 percent, 5 percent, and 1 percent level, respectively. For coefficients that are statistically insignificant, only the sign (+ or −) is shown. Other regressors include country fixed effects; initial GDP; population growth; growth in the terms of trade; the LIBOR; and controls for the Latin American debt and Tequila crises, the East Asian crises of 1997–98, and the Argentine crisis of 2001–02. Number of countries = 130, 125, 111, 130; number of observations = 3,741, 3,312, 2,900, 3,741.
[1]Except for the United States, the euro area, and Japan.
[2]Interacted with indicated growth rate.

Table 4.6. Growth and Spillovers (2)
(Panel regression coefficients)

Specification	Dependent Variable: Growth in All Other Countries[1]		
	(1)	(5)	(6)
Explanatory variables			
Growth in United States	0.16***	0.22***	0.23*
Floating exchange rate[2]		−	
Large debt[2]			−
Growth in euro area	0.10*	0.24*	−
Floating exchange rate[2]		−0.40*	
Large debt[2]			+
Growth in Japan	0.11*	0.19*	0.25*
Floating exchange rate[2]		−	
Large debt[2]			−

Source: IMF staff calculations.
Note: See Appendix 4.1 for details. *, **, and *** denote statistical significance at the 10 percent, 5 percent, and 1 percent level, respectively. For coefficients that are statistically insignificant, only the sign (+ or −) is shown. Other regressors include country fixed effects; initial GDP; population growth; growth in the terms of trade; the LIBOR; and controls for the Latin American debt and Tequila crises, the East Asian crises of 1997–98, and the Argentine crisis of 2001–02. Number of countries = 130, 107, 96; number of observations = 3,741, 2,935, 1,454.
[1]Except for the United States, the euro area, and Japan.
[2]Interacted with indicated growth rate.

4). This evidence is consistent with recent empirical studies that find that stronger trade linkages lead to increased synchronization of business cycles across countries[11] and that increased financial integration leads to higher cross-country output (and consumption) correlations.[12]

It is worthwhile asking how the magnitude of spillovers depends on the policy environment in place. In particular, a natural hypothesis is that a floating exchange rate regime may help insulate countries from some external shocks. The results confirm that spillovers from growth in the euro area are much smaller (indeed, statistically insignificant) in countries with floating exchange rates (Table 4.6, column 2). Results for spillovers from growth in the United States and Japan point in the same direction (although they are not statistically significant).[13]

Countercyclical fiscal policy could also help to reduce the effects of large external shocks. In this context, countries with large public sector debts (or deficits) may have less fiscal room for maneuver, leading to larger spillovers. However, the empirical evidence does not point to clear links between the magnitude of spillovers and

[11]See Kose and Yi (2006). This effect is especially large in countries with strong intra-industry trade linkages and more similar sectoral structures (see Imbs, 2004; and Calderón, Chong, and Stein, 2007). Other studies report that increased intraregional trade volumes, especially in the form of intra-industry trade, have been an important factor in explaining the degree of business cycle synchronization within North America (Kose, Meredith, and Towe, 2005), Asia (Shin and Wang, 2003), and Europe (Böwer and Guillemineau, 2006).

[12]See Imbs (2004 and 2006). However, this effect appears much smaller in developing than in industrial countries (Kose, Prasad, and Terrones, 2003). Jansen and Stokman (2004) also find that countries with stronger FDI linkages had more correlated business cycles in the second half of the 1990s.

[13]An alternative interpretation of these results, however, is that those countries whose underlying shocks display greater correlation may choose to peg for "optimal currency area" reasons. Thus, greater output co-movements in fixed exchange rate countries may at least partly reflect greater correlation in the underlying shocks, rather than any inability of policy to offset the impact of external shocks.

the size of debts or deficits (Table 4.6, column 3). One potential explanation is that fiscal policy may in fact have been procyclical in most developing countries over the sample period (Kaminsky, Reinhart, and Végh, 2004).

How does the magnitude of spillovers differ across regions? The previous findings on the link between spillovers and the structure of trade linkages were used to calculate spillovers for different regions. The result shows that Canada, Latin America, and the Caribbean are most strongly influenced by U.S. growth (Figure 4.5), reflecting their sizable trade links with the United States. On average, a 1 percentage point decline in U.S. growth is associated with a slowing in growth of almost ¼ percentage point in Latin America as a whole, about 0.4 percentage point in Mexico, and about 0.5 percentage point in Canada. Emerging Asia is also affected significantly by U.S. growth, but (perhaps surprisingly) not by growth in Japan. Africa is influenced most clearly by growth in the euro area. Finally, growth in the United States and the euro area are also positively associated with growth in other advanced economies.

A More Dynamic Analysis

A key limitation of the cross-country regression approach is that it only allows for relatively simple interactions across countries. A more sophisticated analysis using a cross-country and cross-region set of vector auto regression (VAR) models allows more precise disentangling of the separate spillover effects of unexpected changes in growth—growth disturbances, in other words—in different major currency areas. In particular, they cast light on the dynamic profile of spillovers on other economies.

Specifically, a separate six-variable structural VAR model is estimated for each country (or region) in the sample. This VAR is partitioned into an exogenous foreign block and a country-specific block.[14] The foreign block includes growth in the United States, the euro area, and

[14]The analysis builds on Hoffmaister and Roldos (2001) and Genberg (2006).

Figure 4.5. Growth Declines and Spillovers: Regional Implications
(Impact of a 1 percentage point decline in growth rates of euro area, Japan, and the United States)

Growth declines from the United States exert their largest impact on Canada and Latin America. Spillovers from euro area growth are felt most strongly in Africa and smaller advanced economies. The impact of Japan's growth can be detected only in Asia.

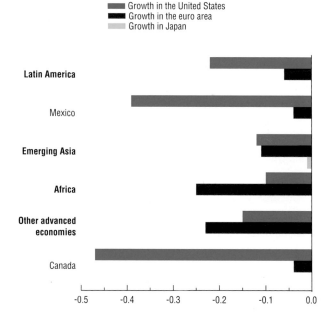

Sources: World Bank, *World Development Indicators* (2006); and IMF staff calculations.

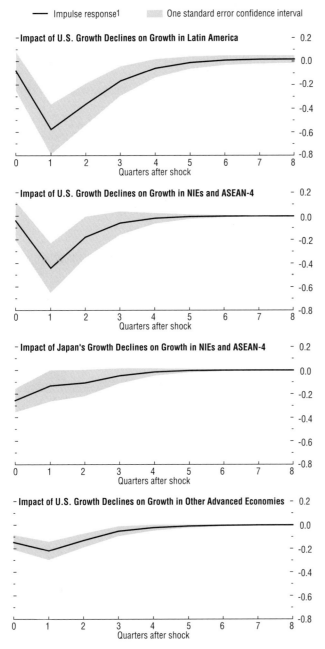

Figure 4.6. Impact of Growth Declines in the United States and Japan

Changes in U.S. growth exert a clear impact on growth in Latin America. Shocks to growth in the United States and (to a lesser extent) in Japan exert a significant effect on the newly industrialized economies (NIEs) and ASEAN-4. Growth disturbances in the United States are also positively associated with growth in other advanced economies. The spillovers peak after at most one quarter, and are estimated to die out after three to four quarters, slightly later than the underlying growth shocks.

—— Impulse response1   One standard error confidence interval

Impact of U.S. Growth Declines on Growth in Latin America

Quarters after shock

Impact of U.S. Growth Declines on Growth in NIEs and ASEAN-4

Quarters after shock

Impact of Japan's Growth Declines on Growth in NIEs and ASEAN-4

Quarters after shock

Impact of U.S. Growth Declines on Growth in Other Advanced Economies

Quarters after shock

Sources: Haver Analytics; World Bank, *World Development Indicators;* and IMF staff calculations.
[1]In all these impulse responses, the underlying shocks to growth in the United States (or Japan) are normalized to yield a cumulative decline in U.S. (or Japanese) growth after four quarters amounting to 1 percentage point.

Japan, which are interrelated given the linkages among them but are assumed not to be significantly affected by developments elsewhere. The country-specific block includes (country-specific) growth, inflation, and the percentage change in the real effective exchange rate. In addition, the equations in this block include the following control variables: the terms of trade; the LIBOR; and controls for the Latin American debt and Tequila crises, the Asian financial crises of 1997–98, and the Argentine crisis of 2001–02. The sample includes 46 countries, both advanced and developing, as well as the corresponding regional averages,[15] and uses quarterly data, typically available for 1991–2005 (see Appendix 4.1 for details).

Overall, changes in U.S. growth have a clear impact on growth in Latin America (Figure 4.6). The spillovers peak after one quarter, and are estimated to die out after three to four quarters, slightly later than the underlying growth shocks. The dynamic effects of U.S. growth disturbances only explain about 20 percent of the variation in Latin American growth at horizons of four or more quarters ahead.[16]

Disturbances to U.S. growth also have a significant but, again, short-lived effect on the newly industrialized economies (NIEs) and ASEAN-4 countries. In comparison, growth disturbances in Japan have a smaller impact on these countries. The dynamic effects of these external growth disturbances typically explain 10 percent or less of the overall variation in growth at horizons of four or more quarters ahead.[17]

Finally, shocks to U.S. growth are also positively associated with growth in other advanced economies, and the magnitude of the spillovers is roughly consistent with that observed in the panel regressions. The impact, as might be expected, is particularly large in Canada and

[15]The regional averages are constructed as weighted averages of the values for the individual countries, where the weights correspond to U.S. dollar GDP, evaluated at PPP exchange rates.

[16]Hoffmaister and Roldos (2001) obtained similar results.

[17]Genberg (2006), using a different specification, finds larger effects of foreign disturbances.

in commodity exporters such as Australia and Norway. In general, the qualitative results from this dynamic analysis are fully consistent with the results from the panel regressions. That said, the precise quantitative estimates differ, reflecting differences in the methodologies, sample composition, and sample periods.

Four important messages emerge from the panel regressions and VAR analysis. First, growth in the United States (and other large economies) can exert important spillovers on both advanced and developing economies. While generally moderate in magnitude (but statistically significant), the spillovers can be substantial for regional trading partners. Second, the panel regression analysis indicates that the magnitude of the spillovers may have increased over time. Third, for many countries, external growth disturbances nevertheless seem less important than domestic factors in explaining overall volatility. Fourth, the analysis suggests that a flexible exchange rate regime can in some cases help insulate economies from external shocks.

Identifying Common Elements in International Business Cycle Fluctuations

How important are common elements in driving international business cycles and what are the underlying forces? The answer to this question has important implications for the interpretation of past episodes of strong business cycle synchronization—that is, episodes of strong co-movements in economic activity across countries—and for the prospects of such episodes occurring again. There could be three basic, not mutually exclusive, reasons accounting for these episodes. First, such episodes could primarily reflect common shocks, such as abrupt, unexpected changes in oil prices or sharp movements in asset prices in the major financial centers. Second, they could reflect the global spillovers from disturbances originating in one of the large economies. Third, these episodes could reflect correlated disturbances that could arise for a number of reasons, including, for example, the implementation of similar policies.

The approaches pursued so far in the chapter are not suited to identifying such common elements in national business cycles. To address this issue, a dynamic factor model was estimated that captures common factors in the fluctuations of real per capita output, private consumption, and investment over the 1960–2005 period in 93 countries.[18] Specifically, the model decomposes fluctuations in these variables into four factors (see Appendix 4.2 for details):

- A *global factor* captures the broad common elements in the fluctuations across countries.
- *Regional factors* capture the common elements in the cyclical fluctuations in the countries in a particular region. For the purposes of this chapter, the world was partitioned into seven regions: North America, Europe, Oceania, Asia, Latin America, Middle East and North Africa, and sub-Saharan Africa.
- *Country-specific factors* capture factors common to all variables in a particular country.
- *Residual ("idiosyncratic") factors* capture elements in the fluctuations of an individual variable that cannot be attributed to the other factors.

Table 4.7 shows the relative contributions of the global, regional, country-specific, and idiosyncratic factors to the cyclical fluctuations in each region. The main findings are as follows:

- The global factor generally plays a more important role in explaining business cycles in industrial countries than in emerging market and developing countries. In industrial countries, this factor on average explains more than 15 percent of output fluctuations, with the contribution in the relatively larger industrial countries typically exceeding 20 percent. In contrast, in emerging market and other developing countries, the global factor explains less than 10 percent of the output fluctuations.
- Regional factors are most important in North America, Europe, and Asia, where they explain more than 20 percent of the output fluctuations. The regional factors capture well-

---

[18]This model builds on Kose, Otrok, and Whiteman (2003).

Table 4.7. Contributions to Output Fluctuations
(Unweighted averages for each region; percent)

	Factors			
	Global	Regional	Country	Idiosyncratic
1960–2005				
North America	16.9	51.7	14.8	16.6
Western Europe	22.7	21.6	34.6	21.1
Oceania	5.6	3.9	61.8	28.7
Emerging Asia and Japan	7.0	21.9	47.4	23.7
Latin America	9.1	16.6	48.6	25.7
Sub-Saharan Africa	5.3	2.7	40.7	51.3
Middle East and North Africa	6.3	6.3	53.8	33.6
1960–85				
North America	31.4	36.4	15.7	16.5
Western Europe	26.6	20.5	31.6	21.3
Oceania	10.7	5.9	50.5	32.9
Emerging Asia and Japan	10.6	9.5	50.5	29.4
Latin America	16.2	19.4	41.2	23.2
Sub-Saharan Africa	7.2	5.1	39.7	48.0
Middle East and North Africa	8.9	5.1	49.1	36.9
1986–2005				
North America	5.0	62.8	8.2	24.0
Western Europe	5.6	38.3	27.6	28.5
Oceania	9.4	25.9	31.1	33.6
Emerging Asia and Japan	6.5	34.7	31.1	27.7
Latin America	7.8	8.7	51.7	31.8
Sub-Saharan Africa	6.7	4.7	37.3	51.3
Middle East and North Africa	4.7	6.6	52.8	35.9

Source: IMF staff calculations.
Note: The table shows the fraction of the variance of output growth attributable to each factor.

known regional developments, including, for example, the 1997–98 Asian financial crises.

- Country-specific and idiosyncratic factors appear to play the most important role in the Middle East and North Africa and in sub-Saharan Africa, where they explain more than 80 percent of output variation.[19]

Figure 4.7 shows the estimated global factor and illustrates how closely this factor matches the major peaks and troughs observed in global GDP growth over the past 45 years, including the recessions in 1974–75 and the early 1980s, the slowdown in the early 2000s, and the recent global recovery. Moreover, there is considerable overlap in the evolution of the global factor and U.S. growth, especially during U.S. recessions. In the early 1990s, however, the global factor reached a trough later than did U.S. output.

[19]See Chapter 2 of the April 2005 *World Economic Outlook* for a more detailed analysis.

This is consistent with the interpretation that the 1990–91 U.S. recession reflected more U.S.-specific developments than usual, which were then transmitted to other countries, as noted earlier.

How has the importance of the global, regional, and country factors changed over time? To answer this question, the dynamic factor model was estimated over two periods, 1960–85 and 1986–2005.[20] The results suggest that the global factor has, on average, played a less important role in the later period (see Table 4.7). At the same time, regional factors have become more important in regions where trade and financial linkages have increased substantially. In particular, in the later period, the regional factor has accounted for more than half of the output fluctuations in North America, and 38 and 41 percent of output fluctuations in Europe and Asia, respectively, compared with roughly 20 and 10 percent during the first period. In Latin America, however, the regional factor explains a lower share of output fluctuations in the second period than in the first one, suggesting that the region-specific common factors were primarily related to the buildup in external debt and subsequent debt crises during the earlier period.

The total contribution of global and regional factors together to output fluctuations has, on average, remained similar between the two periods, except in emerging Asia, where it has increased.[21] Since this total contribution of global and regional factors is a measure of the extent of co-movement across national business cycles, these results show that overall, national business cycles have not necessarily become more synchronized in general (Box 4.3).

[20]These subperiods capture a structural break in output volatility in several industrial countries. In addition, this break point is intuitively appealing in the sense that there has been a substantial increase in international trade and financial flows since the mid-1980s.

[21]In Asia, the regional factor also appears to pick up the influence of the East Asian financial crisis. When the model is estimated excluding the crisis years (1997 and 1998) in East Asia, the role of the regional factor in the second period appears to be less prominent, although it still explains a larger share of output fluctuations than in the first period.

Complementary analysis for the G-7 countries using quarterly data confirms that the common factor among these countries explained a higher share of output fluctuations during 1973–86 than during 1960–72 or 1987–2006 (see Appendix 4.2).[22] At the same time, though, the results of this analysis also suggest that the common factor was relatively more important during 1987–2006 than during 1960–72, which would corroborate the interpretation that spillovers have become larger with increased trade and financial integration. Another noteworthy finding is that the global factor exhibited more persistence during 1973–86 than during 1987–2006, suggesting that the effects of disturbances for all G-7 countries were longer lived and were larger in their overall impact.

Overall, these results are consistent with the interpretation that the strong business cycle synchronization observed during the 1970s and early 1980s reflected large common disturbances—the two oil price shocks—and the effects of correlated disturbances in the major industrial countries, notably the disinflationary monetary policy stance in the early 1980s and the associated increase in real interest rates in the industrial countries.[23] From the mid-1980s onward, common global disturbances have become a less important influence in explaining international business cycle fluctuations. Since the increasing importance of regional factors from the mid-1980s was found primarily for the regions where intraregional trade and financial linkages have risen the most, a natural interpretation is that larger spillovers have begun to contribute more to

---

[22]See also Canova and de Nicoló (2003); Nadal-De Simone (2002); Helbling and Bayoumi (2003); Monfort and others (2003); Canova, Ciccarelli, and Ortega (forthcoming); and Stock and Watson (2005).

[23]Recent research shows that the implementation of similar macroeconomic policies can lead to a higher degree of business cycle synchronization. For example, Darvas, Rose, and Szapáry (2005) document that countries with similar government budget positions, proxied by the ratio of government surplus/deficit to GDP, exhibit more correlated business cycles.

Figure 4.7. Global Factor[1]
(Periods of U.S. recessions shaded; de-meaned; annual change in percent)

The global factor closely matches the major peaks and troughs in global GDP growth since 1960. There is also considerable overlap in the evolution of the global factor and U.S. growth, particularly during U.S. recessions.

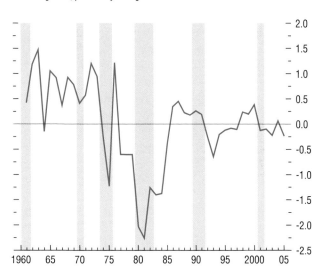

Sources: World Bank, *World Development Indicators;* and IMF staff calculations.
[1]The estimate of the global factor picks up the key peaks and troughs in the growth of U.S. output. Shading indicates recessions as defined by the National Bureau of Economic Research.

Box 4.3. Spillovers and International Business Cycle Synchronization: A Broader Perspective

Against the background of rapid increases in trade and financial linkages, which tend to amplify spillover effects, a substantial body of recent economic research has analyzed the issue of whether national business cycles have become more internationally synchronized. Since some of the forces emphasized in the chapter—spillover effects on other countries from U.S. cyclical developments or global shocks that affect all economies—also underpin business cycle synchronization, the chapter's theme is clearly related to this broad issue. To put the analysis in this chapter in a broader context, this box reviews recent evidence on the evolution of synchronization and its relationship with increased trade and financial linkages.

Recent research has typically relied on two measures of synchronization. The first one is bilateral output correlations, which capture co-movements in output fluctuations of two countries. The second one is based on the share of output variances that can be attributed to synthetic (unobservable) common factors, as discussed in the chapter.[1] Unlike the first measure, common factors capture the extent of co-movements across a larger number of countries.

Research based on bilateral output correlations has found that international business cycle synchronization increased during the 1970s and early to mid-1980s, reflecting the large common shocks observed during this period, and has moderated somewhat subsequently (see the figure).[2] The decline since the mid-1980s was largely due to decreased synchronization

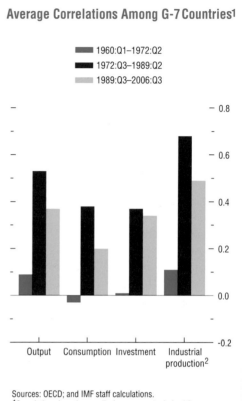

Average Correlations Among G-7 Countries[1]

■ 1960:Q1–1972:Q2
■ 1972:Q3–1989:Q2
▨ 1989:Q3–2006:Q3

Sources: OECD; and IMF staff calculations.
[1]Correlations based on cyclical components derived from a Hodrick-Prescott filter.
[2]Data for industrial production are through 2006:Q1.

Note: The main authors of this box are Thomas Helbling and Ayhan Kose.
[1]Other measures include (1) the concordance statistics (Harding and Pagan, 2002), which measures the synchronization of turning points, and (2) coherences (the equivalent of correlations in the frequency domain, although, unlike static correlations, they allow for lead-lag relationships between two variables).
[2]As a caveat, it should be noted that changes in bilateral output correlations often are not significant, a point emphasized by Doyle and Faust (2005). Nevertheless, as Stock and Watson (2005) have argued, there is some evidence of significant changes in the output persistence and volatility in the G-7

with Japan and, to a lesser extent, Germany (except for continental European countries). This observation highlights how country-specific events, such as the bursting of the asset price bubble in Japan or the reunification in Germany, can overshadow the impact of increased economic and financial linkages. In contrast, correlations among emerging market and developing countries or those between industrial countries and emerging market and developing countries have been generally stable over the past four decades.

The average correlations among many industrial countries since the late 1980s are still higher

countries, with corresponding implications for output co-movements.

than in the 1960s.[3] This increase is seen as a reflection of the substantial increase in cross-border trade and financial flows over the past 40 years (e.g., Kose, Otrok, and Whiteman, 2005). This interpretation is supported by studies that examine whether cross-sectional differences in bilateral output correlations are systematically related to differences in the strength of trade and financial linkages. In general, these studies find that increased trade and financial linkages coincide with a higher degree of synchronization. For example, based on cross-country or cross-region panel regressions, several studies find that pairs of countries that trade more with each other exhibit a higher degree of business cycle co-movement (e.g., Frankel and Rose, 1998; and Baxter and Kouparitsas, 2005, and the references therein). In addition, financial linkages are an important factor in explaining higher degrees of synchronization of both output and consumption fluctuations (Imbs, 2004 and 2006). While the latter is to be expected, as financial integration should reduce country-specific income risk through asset diversification, the former comes as a surprise since increases in financial integration between two countries could, in principle, reduce the correlation between their outputs because of increased specialization.[4]

Research based on the common factor approach has found consistent evidence that common international factors have been important drivers of business cycles in industrial countries and, to a lesser extent, in emerging market and other developing countries. There is evidence that the share of output fluctuations that can be attributed to common factors has increased in some of the G-7 countries (e.g., Canada, France, Italy, the United Kingdom, and the United States, as reported by Stock and Watson, 2005).[5]

The issue of whether there are important region-specific factors explaining the high degree of business cycle synchronization observed within certain regions has been another area of intensive research, given the emergence of regional trading blocks and common currency areas during the past two decades. Indeed, the rapid increase in intraregional trade flows appears to have underpinned the high synchronization of business cycles in the euro area and East Asia (see Böwer and Guillemineau, 2006; and Shin and Wang, 2003).[6] More generally, the notion of a common European business cycle that reflects the high and still-rising economic and financial integration in the region is widely accepted.[7] More recently, the North American Free Trade Agreement has led to a substantial increase in the degree of business cycle synchronization between Canada, Mexico, and the United States (Kose, Meredith, and Towe, 2005).

In sum, while it is difficult to derive strong conclusions about the extent of synchronization, there is some evidence that national business cycles among industrial countries are now more synchronized than in the 1960s, although less so than during the 1970s and the first half of the 1980s. This pattern seems to reflect a combination of rising cross-border trade and financial linkages, which tends to increase synchronization; the reduced incidence of truly global shocks; and the increased importance of country-specific shocks.

---

[3]Using a long sample of annual data (1980–2001) of 16 industrial countries, Bordo and Helbling (2004) find a trend toward increased synchronization.

[4]See, among others, Kalemli-Ozcan, Sorenson, and Yosha (2003).

[5]Stock and Watson (2005) compare the extent of synchronization in 1984–2002 with that in 1960–83. Kose, Otrok, and Whiteman (2005) find that a com-

mon G-7 factor, on average, explains a larger share of business cycle variations in the G-7 countries since the mid-1980s compared with 1960–72.

[6]Moneta and Rüffer (2006) find evidence of increased synchronization in East Asia (except for China and Japan), with the synchronization reflecting primarily export synchronization and common disturbances, including oil prices and the yen-dollar exchange rate.

[7]See, among others, Artis and Zhang (1997); Lumsdaine and Prasad (2003); and Artis, Krolzig, and Toro (2004) for their analysis of the implications of integration for the synchronization of business cycles in the industrial countries of Europe. Recently, however, Artis (2004) and Canova, Ciccarelli, and Ortega (forthcoming) have argued that since the 1990s, the empirical evidence does not suggest a specific European cycle.

concurrent cyclical fluctuations than common disturbances.[24]

How the United States Affects the Global Economy—A Model-Based Simulation Analysis

The analysis so far has shown that international spillover effects have been moderate on average. This average, however, hides a considerable diversity of experiences, with very large spillovers in some periods. There are two possible reasons for this. First, the extent of spillovers depends not only on the overall magnitudes of the underlying disturbances but also on their nature because this determines the relative importance of the various transmission channels. And, second, the transmission channels themselves may have changed over time, in part because the conduct of monetary policy has changed considerably in recent decades. For a fuller assessment of the potential spillovers from the current U.S. slowdown, it is thus useful to complement the earlier analysis with simulation results based on a structural model. Specifically, this section traces the likely global effects of a U.S. demand disturbance using simulations of the IMF's Global Economy Model (GEM), and attempts to isolate the factors that are likely to affect the size of spillovers.

GEM incorporates many trade linkages with an explicit microeconomic foundation and is thus well suited to analyze the effects of shocks that primarily involve the propagation through trade-related channels.[25] It also provides the basis to analyze how such shocks can affect the nexus of interest rates, exchange rates, and monetary policy. GEM divides the world into several regions, which also allows for the analysis of how responses differ across regions. The simulations were conducted with a new five-block version of GEM that involves the following countries/currency areas and regions: (1) the United States; (2) the euro area; (3) Japan; (4) emerging Asia; and (5) the remaining countries. Each region is assumed to have flexible exchange rates, and to follow "inflation targeting," specifically, a forward-looking policy rule for nominal interest rates that targets expected inflation.[26] The simulations are illustrative and should not be interpreted as forecasts.

Demand Shocks and Trade Linkages

A first simulation explores the impact of a "pure" country-specific shock to U.S. private demand. In the United States, this results in a slowdown in growth below the long-run trend for about two years, the lowest point of the contraction being reached after six quarters with a 1.4 percent decline in GDP compared with the baseline (Figure 4.8, first two rows). The reduction in domestic demand leads to a more than proportional fall in import demand, reflecting the high import content in the cyclically sensitive parts of domestic demand noted earlier. As a result, the ratio of U.S. current account to GDP improves by almost 1 percentage point.

Lower U.S. import demand is the source of *trade-related spillover effects*, as it reduces final demand outside the United States. But compared with the decline in output in the United States, these effects are relatively small (Figure 4.8, lower two rows). This primarily reflects the small share in GDP of exports to the United States in all regions. The differences in the output responses across regions mirror the differences in their trade exposure to the U.S. economy (see Table 4.2).

---

[24]Another possibility is that regional integration is more likely to lead to more common disturbances (or correlated disturbances because of similar developments in macroeconomic policies) at the regional level.

[25]See Laxton and Pesenti (2003) and Faruqee and others (2005) for details on the basic structure of GEM.

[26]Technically, the monetary reaction function in GEM is an inflation-forecast-based (IFB) rule in which interest rates are adjusted in response to the forecast of inflation three quarters ahead. The weight on expected inflation has been calibrated to bring the forecast of inflation gradually back to the target and in a way that is cognizant of the implications for the real economy (see Laxton and Pesenti, 2003, for a discussion of IFB rules and the related literature).

The trade-related quantity effects are accompanied by changes in relative prices. The relatively greater worldwide reduction in the demand for U.S. goods means that the U.S. real exchange rate depreciates. This effect is sizable, but not of an order of magnitude that would be expected to cause a major disruption in currency and financial markets. The other countries' currencies tend to appreciate *against the U.S. dollar* in real terms in the early stages. With several regions, the extent of the real *effective* appreciation is inversely related to the trade exposure to the United States. In fact, the currencies of the regions that are most exposed to the United States and that therefore suffer the largest decline in worldwide demand for their goods when U.S. import demand drops (emerging Asia and remaining countries) may actually initially depreciate in real terms against the other regions. The real exchange rate response also depends on the monetary policy framework. Under inflation targeting and flexible exchange rates, most, if not all, of the initial real appreciation against the U.S. dollar arises from nominal appreciation, as exchange rates adjust to the shifts in cross-country interest differentials.

Sources of Additional Spillover Effects

Overall, the simulation results suggest that the spillovers from a temporary, U.S.-specific demand shock would be moderate, and roughly of the same magnitude as the average spillovers estimated in the earlier empirical analysis. This result is primarily driven by the relatively low trade exposure of many regions to the United States, and is similar to results obtained with other multicountry models.[27] Such results underpin the frequently voiced opinion that demand shocks operating through trade linkages alone cannot account for the considerably larger extent of output co-movements observed during important historical episodes, such as the 1970s oil crises, and the early 1980s and 2001 reces-

[27]See, for example, Masson, Symansky, and Meredith (1990); and Bryant and others (1988).

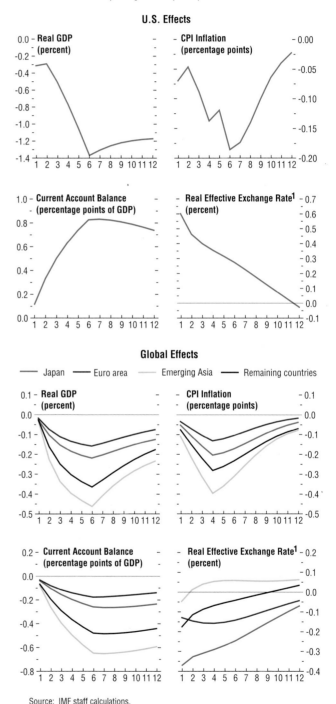

Figure 4.8. Global Implications of a Disturbance to U.S. Private Demand
(Deviations from control; x-axis in calendar quarters)

A temporary reduction in U.S. private demand lowers U.S. GDP, with a more than proportional fall in imports. The trade-related spillovers reduce GDP elsewhere, with the extent of the decline depending on the export exposure.

Source: IMF staff calculations.
[1]Increasing values represent depreciating real effective exchange rates.

sions. To model such large spillover effects, disturbances that have stronger effects on domestic spending decisions would need to be included.

An alternative simulation was built around a scenario in which disturbances are correlated around the world. Disturbances in the United States could lead to disturbances elsewhere for a number of reasons. First, they often appear to have important signaling effects, as suggested by the strong cross-country linkages in business and consumer confidence. It would seem likely that with stronger trade linkages, such spillovers across countries have been increasing. Second, with tightly integrated capital markets, some financial market shocks will tend to be highly correlated, including, for example, disturbances to risk premia on similar asset classes.[28] Finally, while perhaps less relevant at the current conjuncture, policy decisions have also frequently been synchronized across countries, with the synchronized disinflation in the early 1980s being a case in point. To illustrate the case of correlated disturbances, the previous simulations are repeated, assuming a U.S. demand shock of the same size as before, but introducing demand shocks elsewhere that are correlated with the U.S. shock. The correlation coefficients are determined by the share of exports to the United States in a region's total exports (Figure 4.9, second row). The result is a much stronger contraction outside the United States, both in absolute terms and relative to the United States (the first simulation is shown in the first row of Figure 4.9). Through some spillover effects back to the United States, the contraction there would also be deeper, but not dramatically so.

Monetary Policy Matters

Another reason why spillover effects in some past episodes may have been larger than shown

in Figure 4.8 is that the GEM simulations were constructed assuming an inflation targeting framework in all regions of the world economy. Under inflation targeting, monetary policy helps to reduce the output response to adverse demand shocks, be they foreign or domestic, through monetary accommodation that speeds up the price adjustment and thereby reduces the necessary output adjustment. The exchange rate response contributes to this process and thereby lowers the spillovers from demand shocks.

Monetary policy frameworks were different during the 1970s and 1980s and, with the benefit of hindsight, often ill-suited to meet the macroeconomic challenges at the time, which may have contributed to larger and more correlated output gaps at that time. To illustrate this, the simulations of internationally correlated demand shocks are repeated (Figure 4.9, second row) under the assumption that monetary policy in all regions (including the United States) responds much more slowly to the U.S. demand shock, by keeping nominal interest rates unchanged for a period of four quarters (Figure 4.9, third row). The contraction in demand lowers inflation, which under unchanged nominal interest rates dramatically increases real interest rates. This exacerbates the contraction in demand everywhere, with the United States now experiencing a 2.5 percent rather than 1.5 percent decline in GDP relative to the baseline after six quarters, and with similar deteriorations in the other regions. Measured by GDP responses relative to U.S. GDP, spillovers are very much stronger for this case than for all previous simulations.

Exchange rate pegs can also exacerbate the spillovers from output disturbances elsewhere. The reason is that countries adopting such a regime import the monetary policy of the anchor country, which is unlikely to always fit the circumstances of the pegging country.

In the current context, pegging to the U.S. dollar when U.S. monetary policy is eased in response to a U.S. domestic demand shock is likely to result in an excessive easing of monetary conditions in the pegging country unless the adverse trade-related spillover effects are

---

[28]With increasing cross-border integration, such disturbances then also tend to cause larger spillovers. For example, in the 2001 global slowdown, the sharp decline in equity prices led to a concomitant reduction in investment spending in the financially integrated economies, which in turn led to a sharp slowdown in global manufacturing.

very strong. With excessive monetary policy easing, output in the pegging country would rise initially, given the fall in the real interest rate and the real exchange rate, but decrease subsequently (below its medium-term path) as higher inflation would lead to an appreciation of the real exchange rate. In the case of stronger trade spillovers, however, the easing of monetary conditions implied by the peg for the particular disturbance at hand may be closer to the easing implied by an inflation targeting rule.[29]

The preceding arguments illustrate the fundamental point that forward-looking monetary policy rules coupled with exchange rate flexibility help to reduce the output effects of adverse demand shocks in many situations. In this sense, the GEM simulations reflect the major changes in macroeconomic policy frameworks that have occurred during the past decade. From a global perspective, it is worth emphasizing that monetary policy frameworks that are geared toward domestic price stability can also contribute to reducing fluctuations in world growth.

Summary and Conclusions

This chapter has analyzed how the U.S. economy affects international business cycle fluctuations, with a view to identifying the factors that influence the extent of U.S. spillovers into other countries. The analysis suggests that the limited global impact of the current U.S. slowdown so far is not surprising since the slowdown has been driven by U.S.-specific developments—primarily in housing and manufacturing—rather than by broader factors that are highly correlated across the major industrial countries.

Given the characteristics of the U.S. slowdown to date, the transmission to other countries operates primarily through demand channels, that is, through the effects on other countries'

---

[29]This explains why, for the type of disturbances explored in this section, the choice of monetary policy rule makes less of a difference for the case of emerging Asia than it would for some of the other regions. For simplicity, the simulations therefore assume the same policy rule in all regions.

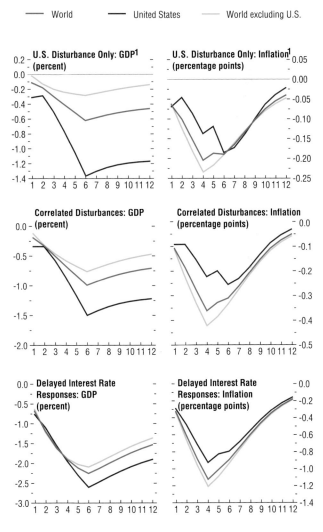

Figure 4.9. Global Growth and Inflation with Correlated Disturbances and Delayed Monetary Policy Response
(Deviations from control; x-axis in calendar quarters)

Disturbances to U.S. private demand that are associated with disturbances elsewhere have a much larger impact on global growth. The slowing in growth is exacerbated if the monetary policy response is not appropriately forward looking.

Source: IMF staff calculations.
[1]See simulation results in Figure 4.8.

exports to the United States, which, by themselves, tend to be modest. In this respect, the fact that the import content in the housing sector is relatively small has helped to mitigate the spillover effects on other countries. In contrast, if the transmission had also involved asset price spillovers or confidence channels, the impact would likely have been larger.

Overall, these factors suggest that most countries should be in a position to "decouple" from the U.S. economy and sustain strong growth if the U.S. slowdown remains as moderate as expected, although countries with strong trade linkages with the United States in specific sectors may experience some drag on their growth. However, if the U.S. economy experienced a sharper slowdown because of a broader-than-expected impact of the housing sector difficulties, the spillover effects into other economies would be larger, and decoupling would be more difficult. Nevertheless, with increasingly flexible macroeconomic policy frameworks in many countries, monetary policy should be well positioned to cushion the potential contractionary effects on economic activity.

In addition to these conclusions about the global implications of the current slowdown, the chapter's other main findings about the role of the U.S. economy in international business cycle fluctuations are as follows.

- The old saying, "If the United States sneezes, the rest of the world catches a cold," remains relevant since the analysis shows that recessions in the United States (and, to a lesser extent, in other large economies) can exert significant spillovers on both advanced and developing economies. However, it also is an exaggeration because the estimated spillovers, as measured by the declines in output growth, are generally considerably smaller than the output decrease in the United States itself, particularly in the context of midcycle slowdowns.

- The influence of the U.S. economy on other economies does not appear to have diminished. On the contrary, indications are that the magnitudes of spillovers have increased

over time, particularly in neighboring countries and regions, which is consistent with the notion that greater trade and financial integration tends to magnify the cross-border effects of disturbances.

- More generally, the analysis highlights that past episodes with large synchronized declines in global growth were characterized by common disturbances that were either truly global in nature (e.g., abrupt oil price changes), were correlated across countries (e.g., disinflationary policies during the early 1980s), or involved global movements in asset prices (e.g., the synchronous equity price declines during 2000–01). In other words, past episodes of highly synchronized growth declines were not primarily the result of spillovers as defined in this chapter, but of common (or correlated) disturbances.

- During the past two decades, common global factors have become somewhat less important drivers of national business cycle fluctuations. At the same time, the importance of regional factors among the highly integrated economies in North America, western Europe, and emerging Asia appears to have increased. These contrasting developments reflect that global disturbances have become less frequent and smaller, while intraregional trade and financial linkages have, in general, risen more rapidly than extraregional ones. Overall, compared with the 1970s and early 1980s, the world economy may thus continue to see less synchronized international business cycles at the global level unless it is subjected to the common disturbances that were the hallmark of earlier episodes.

- Policy responses can moderate or amplify the spillover effects of disturbances in the United States (or other large economies). Forward-looking monetary policy responses in the context of an inflation targeting framework have tended to reduce the output response to adverse demand disturbances, be they foreign or domestic. In contrast, monetary policy responses that are not sufficiently forward looking or flexible risk magnifying the spillover effects. To the extent that the strong international business cycle linkages in the early 1980s reflected the adjustment to disinflationary monetary policies, this episode may not prove relevant today.

Appendix 4.1. Econometric Methodology

The main author of this appendix is Nikola Spatafora.

This appendix provides details of the econometric methodology used to estimate the effects of disturbances in major economies on output and other variables elsewhere.

A Broad Cross-Country Analysis

The analysis in this subsection, based on panel growth regressions, most closely resembles Arora and Vamvakidis (2006). One crucial difference is that it is carried out using annual data, rather than five-year averages; the approach here seems more relevant to the shorter-run business cycle spillovers that are the focus of this chapter. The focus of this analysis is similar to that of other studies that have analyzed the determinants of cross-country output correlations, though it adopts a different methodology from theirs.[30]

In the panel regressions, the dependent variable is growth in domestic output per capita, measured in PPP-adjusted dollars; this variable is drawn from the Penn World Tables. The independent variables include the following:
- growth in U.S., euro area, and Japanese output per capita, measured in PPP-adjusted dollars (source: Penn World Tables);
- trade linkages with the United States, the euro area, and Japan; as defined in the text (source: IMF, *Direction of Trade Statistics*);
- financial linkages with the United States, the euro area, and Japan. In addition to the measure defined in the text, two alternative measures were created: (1) a country's total Gross Foreign Assets plus total Gross For-

eign Liabilities, as a ratio to GDP; and (2) a country's gross holdings of U.S., euro area, or Japanese assets, as appropriate, plus its gross liabilities to U.S., euro area, or Japanese residents, again as a ratio to GDP. The second measure, drawn from the Coordinated Portfolio Investment Survey of portfolio assets, is only available for 1997, 2001, 2003, and 2004. Neither of these two alternative measures proved significant;
- exchange rate regime. This was classified as "fixed" if it corresponded, in the Reinhart-Rogoff (2004) classification, to a currency board; peg; crawling peg; band; pre-announced crawling band; or de facto crawling band narrower than or equal to +/− 2 percent. All other exchange rate regimes were classified as "floating." On average, over the full sample period, 66 countries (including 61 developing countries) were deemed to have fixed exchange rates; 43 countries (including 37 developing countries) were deemed to have floating exchange rates;
- public sector debt stock; public sector deficit. Debt stocks were classified as "large" if they exceeded 40 percent of GDP, and "small" otherwise. For deficits, the threshold was set at 3 percent of GDP. In both cases, the threshold roughly corresponds to the sample mean;
- initial GDP; population growth (source: Penn World Tables);
- the (log) change in the terms of trade; the six-month LIBOR (source: World Economic Outlook database); and
- indicators denoting the Latin American debt crisis of 1982, the Latin American Tequila crises of 1995, the East Asian crises of 1997–98, and the Argentine crisis of 2002.[31]

All estimates are based on the Arellano-Bond fixed effects estimator. For comparison, Arora and Vamvakidis (2006) find much larger

---

[30]Including, for instance, Calderón, Chong, and Stein (2007); and Imbs (2004 and 2006).

[31]To the extent that these crises themselves reflected a spillover from developments in advanced economies, any procedure that controls separately for their impact will understate the true magnitude of spillovers. However, none of the estimates presented are in fact sensitive to excluding the crisis indicators.

Figure 4.10. Limited In-Sample Persistence of U.S. Growth Shocks

(Percentage points)

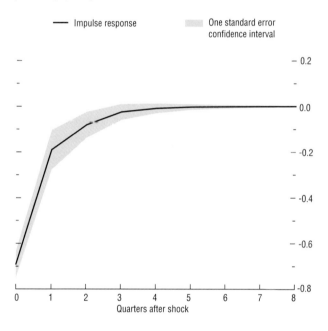

Sources: Haver Analytics; World Bank, *World Development Indicators;* and IMF staff calculations.

spillovers. In most specifications, a 1 percentage point increase in U.S. and EU growth is associated with, respectively, a roughly 1 percentage point and a ⅔ percentage point increase in other countries' growth (while Japan has an insignificant effect).

A More Dynamic Analysis

For each country (or region) in the sample, a six-variable quarterly structural VAR model is estimated. This VAR is partitioned into an exogenous foreign block and a country-specific block. The foreign block includes three variables: growth in U.S., euro area, and Japanese output per capita, measured in PPP-adjusted dollars. The country-specific block includes three (country-specific) variables: growth in domestic output per capita, measured in PPP-adjusted dollars; CPI inflation; and the (log) change in the real effective exchange rate. All are drawn from the World Economic Outlook database.

In addition, the country-specific equations include the following exogenous regressors:

- the (log) change in the terms of trade; the LIBOR (source: World Economic Outlook database); and
- indicators denoting the Latin American debt crisis of 1982:Q3–Q4, the Latin American Tequila crises of 1995:Q1–Q2, the East Asian crises of 1997:Q4–1998:Q1, and the Argentine crisis of 2002:Q1.

The identifying restrictions are as follows:

- the foreign block is strictly exogenous, reflecting the assumption that any feedback from small advanced economies and/or developing economies to the United States, euro area, and Japan is economically insignificant;
- shocks to U.S. growth affect contemporaneously growth in the euro area and in Japan, and this is the only contemporaneous linkage among the three regions; and
- each country-specific block follows a Cholesky ordering, with growth and inflation as the first and second variables.

All data are seasonally adjusted. Lag length is selected using Schwarz's Bayesian information criterion; in almost all cases, this points to just one lag, likely reflecting the short sample periods available.

The analysis of the results focuses on the dynamic effects of growth shocks in the United States, the euro area, and Japan by analyzing the cross section of impulse response functions (IRF). In all these IRF, the (structural) shocks to growth in the United States are normalized to yield a cumulative decline in U.S. growth after four quarters amounting to 1 percentage point. Analogous comments apply regarding growth shocks in the euro area and Japan. Importantly, in the sample, the effects of all these shocks on a country's own growth display little average persistence, dying out after two quarters (Figure 4.10). This suggests the need for caution regarding the potential impact of future, potentially longer-lasting, growth shocks.

The country-by-country effects of adverse U.S. growth shocks on growth in Latin America are displayed in Figure 4.11. As a general caveat, the relatively short samples available for some countries, combined with the need for a comparable specification across a broad range of economies, limit the accuracy with which individual effects can be estimated. Hence, it would be unwise to place excessive emphasis on country-specific results. That said, the spillover effects appear especially large in Mexico and Brazil. The effects broadly peak after one quarter. This extremely rapid transmission is consistent with the estimates of Canova (2003). Shocks to growth in the euro area instead have no clear impact on growth in Latin America (Figure 4.12). The country-by-country effects of U.S. and Japanese growth shocks on growth in emerging Asia are displayed in, respectively, Figure 4.13 and Figure 4.14. Spillovers from the United States appear particularly sizable in Hong Kong SAR, Korea, and Taiwan Province of China, while Japan exerts an especially large influence on Malaysia and Thailand.

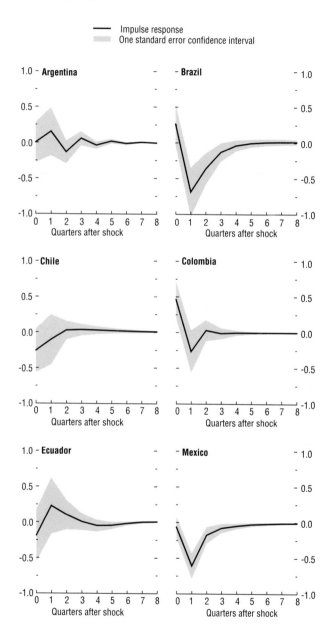

Figure 4.11. Impact of U.S. Growth Declines on Growth in Latin America: Effects by Country
(Percentage points)

Sources: Haver Analytics; World Bank, *World Development Indicators;* and IMF staff calculations.

Figure 4.12. Impact of Euro Area Growth Declines on Growth in Latin America: Effects by Country
(Percentage points)

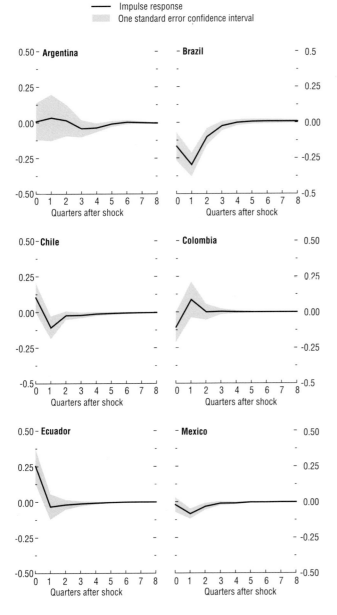

Sources: Haver Analytics; World Bank, *World Development Indicators;* and IMF staff calculations.

As a check on robustness, alternative specifications were also tried, with (1) among the endogenous regressors, short-term domestic interest rates instead of the change in the real exchange rate; and (2) among the exogenous regressors, the spread on emerging market bonds, as measured by the EMBI. The key qualitative results were unaffected.

Appendix 4.2. Common Elements in International Business Cycle Fluctuations: Description of the Dynamic Factor Models

The main authors of this appendix are Ayhan Kose and Christopher Otrok (consultant).

This appendix provides additional information about the dynamic factor models used in the chapter. The motivation for using such models in the context of the chapter is that they are designed to extract a small number of unobservable common elements from the covariance or co-movement between (observable) macroeconomic time series across countries. The unobservable common elements—typically referred to as factors—can be thought of as the main forces driving economic activity, or, in other words, indices of common economic activity, across the entire data set (e.g., global activity) or across subsets of the data (e.g., activity in a particular region or country).[32]

To quantify both the extent and the nature of international business cycle co-movement, two different dynamic factor models were estimated. The first one is an annual model for 93 countries. The second one is a quarterly model for the G-7 countries.

Annual Model for 93 Countries

The annual model has 93 blocks of equations, one for each country. The sample of 93 countries are partitioned into seven regions: North

[32]The popularity of these models has risen as some new estimation methods have been developed to perform factor analysis in large data sets (e.g., Stock and Watson, 2003; Forni and others, 2000; and Otrok and Whiteman, 1998).

Figure 4.13. Impact of U.S. Growth Declines on Growth in Emerging Asia: Effects by Country

(Percentage points)

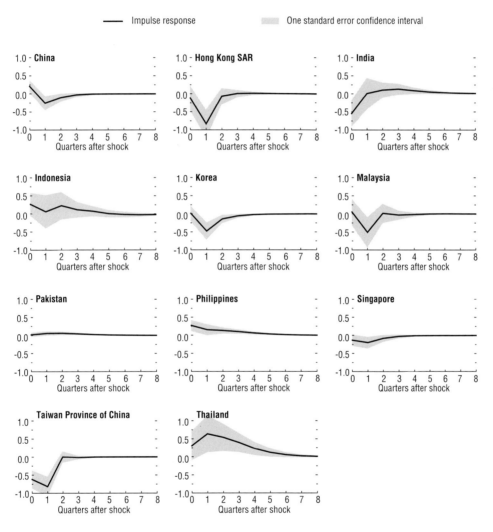

Sources: Haver Analytics; World Bank, *World Development Indicators;* and IMF staff calculations.

Figure 4.14. Impact of Japanese Growth Declines on Growth in Emerging Asia: Effects by Country
(Percentage points)

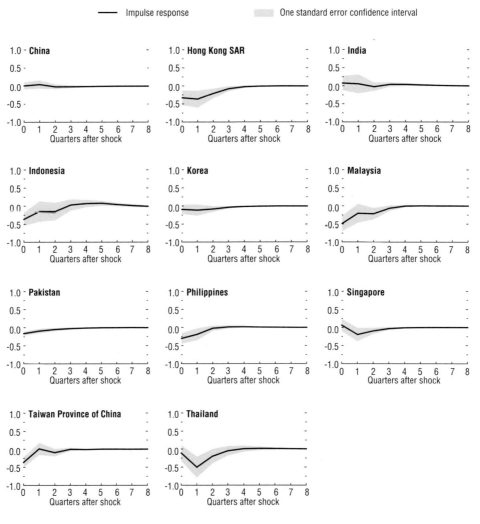

Sources: Haver Analytics; World Bank, *World Development Indicators;* and IMF staff calculations.

America, Western Europe, Oceania, Asia, Latin America, Middle East and North Africa, and sub-Saharan Africa. The grouping of countries by region is useful in identifing a "regional factor" because countries that are geographically close to each other are likely to be directly affected by some regional shocks, including, for example, weather-related shocks. Each country block contains three equations, one for output growth (Y), one for private consumption growth (C), and one for growth of private fixed investment (I). Each equation decomposes growth in Y, C, or I into a global factor, a regional factor, a country-specific factor, and a residual (idiosyncratic) component. For example, the block of equations for the first country, the United States (US), in the first region, North America (NA), is

$$Y_{US,t} = b_{US}^{Y,G} f_t^{Global} + b_{US}^{Y,NA} f_t^{NA} + b_{US}^{Y} f_t^{US} + c_{US,t}^{Y},$$

$$C_{US,t} = b_{US}^{C,G} f_t^{Global} + b_{US}^{C,NA} f_t^{NA} + b_{US}^{C} f_t^{US} + c_{US,t}^{C},$$

$$I_{US,t} = b_{US}^{I,G} f_t^{Global} + b_{US}^{I,NA} f_t^{NA} + b_{US}^{I} f_t^{US} + c_{US,t}^{I}.$$

The same block of equations is repeated for each country in the seven regions in the system.

The global factor is the component common to all countries in this system. The sensitivity of output growth in each country j in the system to the global factor depends on $b_j^{Y,G}$, the factor loading. There is also a regional factor, which captures co-movement across the countries in a region.

The model captures dynamic co-movement by allowing the factors and the series-specific terms (the c terms in the above equations) to be (independent) autoregressive processes. That is, each factor or country-specific term depends on lags of itself and an independent and identically distributed innovation to the variable (u_t). For example, for the global factor, the autoregressive processes are

$$f_t^{Global} = \phi(L) f_{t-1}^{Global} + u_t^{Global},$$

where $\phi(L)$ is a lag polynomial and u_t is normally distributed. All of the factor loadings (b coefficients in the first set of equations) and the lag polynomials are independent of each other. The model is estimated using Bayesian techniques as described in Kose, Otrok, and Whiteman (2003) and Otrok, Silos, and Whiteman (2003).[33]

To measure the importance of each factor, so-called variance decompositions that decompose the total volatility of output growth into volatility components due to each factor are calculated. The formula for the variance decomposition is derived by applying the variance operator to each equation in the system. For example, for the first equation,

$$\mathrm{var}(Y_{US}) = (b_{US}^{Y,G})^2 \, \mathrm{var}(f^{Global}) + (b_{US}^{Y,NA})^2 \, \mathrm{var}(f^{NA}) + (b_{US}^{Y})^2 \, \mathrm{var}(f^{US}) + \mathrm{var}(c_{US}^{Y}).$$

There are no cross-product terms between the factors because they are orthogonal to each other. The variance in real per capita output growth attributable to the global factor then follows as

$$\frac{(b_{US}^{Global})^2 \, \mathrm{var}(f^{Global})}{\mathrm{var}(Y^{US})}.$$

The model was estimated for the period 1960–2005 and for two subperiods, 1960–1985 and 1986–2005.

The list of countries included in the estimation is as follows (by region):

- North America: United States and Canada;
- Oceania: Australia and New Zealand;
- Western Europe: United Kingdom, Austria, Belgium, Denmark, France, Germany, Italy, Luxembourg, Netherlands, Norway, Sweden, Switzerland, Finland, Greece, Iceland, Ireland, Portugal, and Spain; and
- Latin America: Argentina, Bolivia, Brazil, Chile, Colombia, Costa Rica, Dominican Republic, Ecuador, El Salvador, Guatemala, Honduras, Mexico, Nicaragua, Panama, Paraguay, Peru, Uruguay, and Venezuela.

[33]The innovation variance of the factors (error term in the factor autoregressive equation) is normalized. This normalization is based on the variance of the underlying series and determines the scale of the factor (0.1 versus 0.01). This dependency on scaling is the reason for looking only at variance decompositions or appropriately scaled versions of the factors (factor times factor loading, as in the computation of variance shown below). The model is estimated using de-meaned output growth data allowing for a break in 1986.

Table 4.8. Consumption
(Unweighted averages for each region; percent)

	Factors			
	Global	Regional	Country	Idiosyncratic
1960–2005				
North America	20.1	45.1	14.5	20.4
Western Europe	24.3	9.1	33.0	33.7
Oceania	3.9	6.0	35.4	54.7
Emerging Asia and Japan	6.7	12.8	30.0	50.6
Latin America	6.2	11.6	39.8	42.4
Sub-Saharan Africa	2.5	3.2	39.2	55.1
Middle East and North Africa	0.9	4.0	39.0	56.1
1960–85				
North America	38.7	23.9	17.4	20.0
Western Europe	26.0	10.2	31.4	32.5
Oceania	4.6	4.7	34.6	56.2
Emerging Asia and Japan	7.9	8.2	37.2	46.8
Latin America	11.8	16.2	35.2	36.9
Sub-Saharan Africa	5.0	6.5	40.4	48.1
Middle East and North Africa	1.2	7.5	35.4	55.9
1986–2005				
North America	10.1	53.2	8.0	28.7
Western Europe	6.8	29.5	22.3	41.4
Oceania	5.9	9.2	35.5	49.4
Emerging Asia and Japan	4.9	26.4	24.5	44.2
Latin America	4.0	5.6	41.6	48.8
Sub-Saharan Africa	3.1	4.8	36.0	56.1
Middle East and North Africa	4.5	6.6	41.2	47.8

Source: IMF staff calculations.
Note: The table shows the fraction of the variance of consumption growth attributable to each factor.

Table 4.9. Investment
(Unweighted averages for each region; percent)

	Factors			
	Global	Regional	Country	Idiosyncratic
1960–2005				
North America	2.9	38.9	37.0	21.2
Western Europe	8.8	22.5	34.5	34.2
Oceania	0.3	8.4	64.3	27.0
Emerging Asia and Japan	3.9	11.9	38.6	45.5
Latin America	3.8	13.3	40.1	42.9
Sub-Saharan Africa	3.6	1.6	16.1	78.7
Middle East and North Africa	1.4	3.6	36.9	58.0
1960–85				
North America	9.2	32.0	34.9	23.9
Western Europe	10.0	21.3	34.2	34.5
Oceania	0.7	8.3	58.4	32.6
Emerging Asia and Japan	5.3	8.6	37.6	48.6
Latin America	6.8	13.0	35.0	45.1
Sub-Saharan Africa	4.9	3.2	18.8	73.1
Middle East and North Africa	3.6	5.4	33.9	57.2
1986–2005				
North America	7.1	44.8	22.8	25.3
Western Europe	6.2	35.4	28.1	30.3
Oceania	4.9	39.0	34.5	21.7
Emerging Asia and Japan	5.8	29.0	31.5	33.7
Latin America	3.2	3.8	51.8	41.2
Sub-Saharan Africa	4.1	4.2	23.4	68.4
Middle East and North Africa	6.4	4.1	42.5	47.0

Source: IMF staff calculations.
Note: The table shows the fraction of the variance of investment growth attributable to each factor.

- Middle East and North Africa: Islamic Republic of Iran, Israel, Jordan, Syrian Arab Republic, Egypt, Algeria, Morocco, Tunisia, and Turkey.
- Asia: Japan, Bangladesh, Sri Lanka, Hong Kong SAR, India, Indonesia, Korea, Malaysia, Pakistan, Philippines, Singapore, Thailand, and China.
- Africa: South Africa, Botswana, Cameroon, Chad, Comoros, Republic of Congo, Benin, Equatorial Guinea, Ethiopia, Gabon, The Gambia, Ghana, Guinea-Bissau, Guinea, Côte d'Ivoire, Kenya, Lesotho, Madagascar, Malawi, Mali, Mauritania, Mauritius, Mozambique, Niger, Nigeria, Seychelles, Senegal, Tanzania, Togo, Uganda, and Burkina Faso.

Tables 4.8 and 4.9 report the results for the variance decomposition of private consumption and fixed investment (see Table 4.7 in the main text for the results for output growth).

Quarterly Model for G-7 Countries

The quarterly model has seven blocks of equations, one for each country. As described above, each country block contains three equations, one for output growth (Y), one for private consumption growth (C), and one for growth in private fixed investment (I). For example, the block of equations for the first country, the United States (US), is

$$Y_{US,t} = b_{US}^{Y,G} f_t^{G-7} + b_{US}^Y f_t^{US} + c_{US,t}^Y,$$
$$C_{US,t} = b_{US}^{C,G} f_t^{G-7} + b_{US}^C f_t^{US} + c_{US,t}^C,$$
$$I_{US,t} = b_{US}^{I,G} f_t^{G-7} + b_{US}^I f_t^{US} + c_{US,t}^I.$$

The same form is repeated for each country in the system. The basic assumptions regarding the factor processes are identical to those above.

The model was estimated for the period 1960:Q1–2006:Q3 and for three subperiods: 1960:Q1–1972:Q2, 1972:Q3–1986:Q2, and 1986:

Table 4.10. Contributions to Business Cycle Fluctuations in G-7 Countries

(Unweighted averages for the G-7 countries; percent)

	Factors		
	G-7	Country	Idiosyncratic
Output[1]			
Full sample	24.7	45.7	29.6
1960:Q1–1972:Q2	6.7	63.9	29.4
1972:Q3–1986:Q2	32.6	41.3	26.1
1986:Q3–2006:Q3	23.7	40.9	35.4
Consumption[1]			
Full sample	13.9	31.5	54.6
1960:Q1–1972:Q2	6.7	39.3	53.9
1972:Q3–1986:Q2	17.6	29.2	53.3
1986:Q3–2006:Q3	12.3	36.8	50.9
Investment[1]			
Full sample	17.4	29.6	53.0
1960:Q1–1972:Q2	7.7	46.3	46.0
1972:Q3–1986:Q2	17.4	34.8	47.8
1986:Q3–2006:Q3	21.5	34.1	44.4

Source: IMF staff calculations.

Note: The table shows the fraction of the variance of each variable that is attributable to each factor.

[1]In constant prices; variables in log differences.

Q3–2006:Q3.[34] The first subperiod corresponds to the Bretton Woods regime of fixed exchange rates. The end of the second subperiod is consistent with the break date used in the estimations of the annual data. In addition, the second subperiod witnessed a set of common shocks associated with sharp fluctuations in the price of oil and contractionary monetary policy in major industrial countries. During the third subperiod, there were dramatic increases in the volume of cross-border trade and financial flows.

The findings—in addition to those reported in the chapter—are as follows (Table 4.10).

- The G-7 factor plays an important role in explaining business cycles for the full sample accounting for roughly one-fourth of output variation. However, country-specific factors are the main drivers of business cycle variation in the G-7 countries. These factors, on

---

[34]Kose, Otrok, and Whiteman (2005) provide details of this model and an extended discussion about the selection of the break dates defining the subperiods, including references to the related literature.

average, explain more than 45 percent of output volatility over the full sample.

- Across the subperiods, the global factor has been the most influential in the middle period. In particular, the global factor has on average accounted for more than 30 percent of output variation during the period 1972:Q3–1986:Q2. As discussed in the main text, this result is due to the relatively large common shocks and their prolonged effects observed in this period.

- From the first to the third period, there has been a fourfold increase in the variance of output attributed to the global factor. This finding is possibly driven by more potent channels of business cycle spillovers in the last period relative to the first, as the last period has been associated with much stronger trade and financial linkages. Over these two periods, there has been a decline in the importance of country-specific factors, while idiosyncratic factors have appeared to become more relevant.

References

Arora, Vivek, and Athanasios, Vamvakidis, 2006, "The Impact of U.S. Growth on the Rest of the World: How Much Does It Matter?" *Journal of Economic Integration*, Vol. 21, No. 1 (March), pp. 21–39.

Artis, Michael J., 1996, "How Accurate Are the IMF's Short-Term Forecasts? Another Examination of the World Economic Outlook," IMF Working Paper 96/89 (Washington: International Monetary Fund).

———, 2004, "Is There a European Business Cycle?" in *Macroeconomic Policies in the World Economy*, ed. by H. Siebert (Berlin-Heidelberg: Springer Verlag).

———, Hans-Martin Krolzig, and Juan Toro, 2004, "The European Business Cycle," *Oxford Economic Papers*, Vol. 56, No. 1, pp. 1–44.

Artis, Michael J., and W. Zhang, 1997, "International Business Cycles and the ERM: Is There a European Business Cycle?" *International Journal of Finance and Economics*, Vol. 2 (January), pp. 1–16.

Baks, Klaas, and Charles Kramer, 1999, "Global Liquidity and Asset Prices: Measurement, Implications, and Spillovers," IMF Working Paper 99/168 (Washington: International Monetary Fund).

Baxter, Marianne, and Michael A. Kouparitsas, 2005, "Determinants of Business Cycle Comovement: A Robust Analysis," *Journal of Monetary Economics*, Vol. 52 (January), pp. 113–57.

Bordo, Michael D., and Thomas Helbling, 2004, "Have National Business Cycles Become More Synchronized?" in *Macroeconomic Policies in the World Economy*, ed. by H. Siebert (Berlin-Heidelberg: Springer Verlag).

Böwer, Uwe, and Catherine Guillemineau, 2006, "Determinants of Business Cycle Synchronisation Across Euro Area Countries," ECB Working Paper No. 587 (Frankfurt: European Central Bank).

Bryant, Ralph, and others, 1988, *Empirical Macroeconomics for Interdependent Economies* (Washington: Brookings Institution Press).

Calderón, César, Alberto Chong, and Ernesto Stein, 2007, "Trade Intensity and Business Cycle Synchronization: Are Developing Countries Any Different?" *Journal of International Economics*, Vol. 71 (March), pp. 2–21.

Calvo, Guillermo, 1998, "Capital Flows and Capital-Market Crises: The Simple Economics of Sudden Stops," *Journal of Applied Economics*, Vol. 1 (November), pp. 35–54.

Canova, Fabio, 2003, "The Transmission of U.S. Shocks to Latin America," CEPR Discussion Paper No. 3963 (London: Centre for Economic Policy Research).

———, Matteo Ciccarelli, and Eva Ortega, forthcoming, "Similarities and Convergence in G-7 Cycles," *Journal of Monetary Economics*.

Canova, Fabio, and Gianni de Nicoló, 2003, "On the Sources of Business Cycles in the G-7," *Journal of International Economics*, Vol. 59 (January), pp. 77–100.

Cuadro Sáez, Lucía, Marcel Fratzscher, and Christian Thimann, 2007, "The Transmission of Emerging Market Shocks to Global Equity Markets," ECB Working Paper No. 724 (Frankfurt: European Central Bank).

Darvas, Zsolt, Andrew K. Rose, and György Szapáry, 2005, "Fiscal Divergence and Business Cycle Synchronization: Irresponsibility Is Idiosyncratic," NBER Working Paper No. 11580 (Cambridge, Massachusetts: National Bureau of Economic Research).

Doyle, Brian M., and Jon Faust, 2005, "Breaks in the Variability and Comovement of G-7 Economic Growth," *Review of Economics and Statistics*, Vol. 87 (November), pp. 721–40.

Ehrmann, Michael, Marcel Fratzscher, and Roberto Rigobon, 2005, "Stocks, Bonds, Money Markets and Exchange Rates: Measuring International Financial Transmission," NBER Working Paper No. 11166 (Cambridge, Massachusetts: National Bureau of Economic Research).

Engle, R.F., and R. Susmel, 1993, "Common Volatility in International Equity Markets," *Journal of Business and Economic Statistics*, Vol. 11 (April), pp. 167–76.

Faruqee, H., D. Laxton, D. Muir, and P. Pesenti, 2005, "Smooth Landing or Crash? Model-Based Scenarios of Global Current Account Rebalancing," NBER Working Paper No. 11583 (Cambridge, Massachusetts: National Bureau of Economic Research).

Forni, Mario, Marc Hallin, Marco Lippi, and Lucrezia Reichlin, 2000, "The Generalized Dynamic-Factor Model: Identification and Estimation," *Review of Economics and Statistics*, Vol. 82 (November), pp. 540–54.

Frankel, Jeffrey A., and Andrew K. Rose, 1998, "The Endogeneity of the Optimum Currency Area Criteria," *Economic Journal*, Vol. 108 (July), pp. 1009–25.

Fung, Hung-Gay, Wai K. Leung, and Xiaoqing Eleanor Xu, 2001, "Information Role of U.S. Futures Trading in a Global Financial Market," *Journal of Futures Markets*, Vol. 21 (November), pp. 1071–90.

Genberg, Hans, 2006, "External Shocks, Transmission Mechanisms, and Deflation in Asia," BIS Working Paper No. 187 (Basel, Switzerland: Bank for International Settlements).

Goodhart, Charles, 1999, "Central Bankers and Uncertainty," Keynes Lecture to the British Academy, in *Proceedings of the British Academy*, Vol. 101 (Oxford: Oxford University Press).

Harding, Don, and Adrian Pagan, 2002, "Dissecting the Cycle: A Methodological Investigation, *Journal of Monetary Economics*, Vol. 49, No. 2, pp. 365–81.

Helbling, Thomas, and Tamim Bayoumi, 2003, "Are They All in the Same Boat? The 2000–2001 Growth Slowdown and the G-7 Business Cycle Linkages," IMF Working Paper 03/46 (Washington: International Monetary Fund).

Hoffmaister, Alexander W., and Jorge E. Roldos, 2001, "The Sources of Macroeconomic Fluctuations in Developing Countries," *Journal of Macroeconomics*, Vol. 23 (Spring), pp. 213–39.

Imbs, Jean, 2004, "Trade, Finance, Specialization, and Synchronization," *Review of Economics and Statistics*, Vol. 86 (August), pp. 723–34.

———, 2006, "The Real Effects of Financial Integration," *Journal of International Economics*, Vol. 68 (March), pp. 296–324.

Jansen, W. Jos, and Ad. C.J. Stokman, 2004, "Foreign Direct Investment and International Business Cycle Comovement," ECB Working Paper No. 401 (Frankfurt: European Central Bank).

Kalemli-Ozcan, Sebnem, Bent E. Sorensen, and Oved Yosha, 2003, "Risk Sharing and Industrial Specialization: Regional and International Evidence," *American Economic Review*, Vol. 93 (June), pp. 903–18.

Kaminsky, Graciela L., and Carmen Reinhart, 2003, "The Center and the Periphery: The Globalization of Financial Turmoil," NBER Working Paper No. 9479 (Cambridge, Massachusetts: National Bureau of Economic Research).

———, and Carlos A. Végh, 2004, "When It Rains, It Pours: Procyclical Capital Flows and Macroeconomic Policies," NBER Working Paper No. 10780 (Cambridge, Massachusetts: National Bureau of Economic Research).

Karolyi, G. Andrew, and René M. Stulz, 1996, "Why Do Markets Move Together? An Investigation of U.S.-Japan Stock Return Comovements," *Journal of Finance*, Vol. 51 (July), pp. 951–86.

Kose, M. Ayhan, Guy Meredith, and Christopher Towe, 2005, "How Has NAFTA Affected the Mexican Economy? Review and Evidence," in *Monetary Policy and Macroeconomic Stabilization in Latin America*, ed. by Rolf J. Langhammer and Lúcio Vinhas de Souza (Kiel, Germany: Kiel Institute for the World Economy), pp. 35–81.

Kose, M. Ayhan, Christopher Otrok, and Charles H. Whiteman, 2003, "International Business Cycles: World, Region, and Country-Specific Factors," *American Economic Review*, Vol. 93 (September), pp. 1216–39.

———, 2005, "Understanding the Evolution of World Business Cycles," IMF Working Paper 05/211 (Washington: International Monetary Fund).

Kose, M. Ayhan, Eswar Prasad, and Marco Terrones, 2003, "How Does Globalization Affect the Synchronization of Business Cycles?" *American Economic Review, Papers and Proceedings*, Vol. 93 (May), pp. 56–62.

Kose, M. Ayhan, and Kei-Mu Yi, 2006, "Can the Standard International Business Cycle Model Explain the Relation Between Trade and Comovement?" *Journal of International Economics*, Vol. 68 (March), pp. 267–95.

Lane, Philip R., and Gian Maria Milesi-Ferretti, 2006, "The External Wealth of Nations Mark II: Revised and Extended Estimates of Foreign Assets and Liabilities, 1970–2004," IMF Working Paper 06/69 (Washington: International Monetary Fund).

Laxton, D., and P. Pesenti, 2003, "Monetary Rules for Small, Open, Emerging Economies," *Journal of Monetary Economics*, Vol. 50 (July), pp. 1109–46.

Lumsdaine, R.L., and E.S. Prasad, 2003, "Identifying the Common Component of International Economic Fluctuations: A New Approach," *Economic Journal*, Vol. 113 (January), pp. 101–27.

Masson, Paul R., Steven Symansky, and Guy Meredith, 1990, *MULTIMOD Mark II: A Revised and Extended Model*, IMF Occasional Paper No. 71 (Washington: International Monetary Fund).

Matsumoto, Akito, and Martin Schindler, forthcoming, "Global Monetary Conditions and Liquidity: Measurement and Implications" (Washington: International Monetary Fund).

Moneta, Fabio, and Rasmus Rüffer, 2006, "Business Cycle and Synchronisation in East Asia," ECB Working Paper No. 671 (Frankfurt: European Central Bank).

Monfort, A., J. Renne, R. Rüffer, and G. Vitale, 2003, "Is Economic Activity in the G7 Synchronized? Common Shocks Versus Spillover Effects," CEPR Discussion Paper No. 4119 (London: Centre for Economic Policy Research). Available via the Internet: http://www.cepr.org/pubs/dps/DP4119.asp.

Nadal-De Simone, Francisco, 2002, "Common and Idiosyncratic Components in Real Output: Further International Evidence," IMF Working Paper 02/229 (Washington: International Monetary Fund).

Otrok, Christopher, and Charles H. Whiteman, 1998, "Bayesian Leading Indicators: Measuring and Predicting Economic Conditions in Iowa," *International Economic Review*, Vol. 39 (November), pp. 997–1014.

Otrok, Christopher, Pedro Silos, and Charles H. Whiteman, 2003, "Bayesian Dynamic Factor Models for Large Datasets: Measuring and Forecasting Macroeconomic Data" (unpublished; Charlottesville, Virginia: University of Virginia).

Reinhart, C., and K. Rogoff, 2004, "The Modern History of Exchange Rate Arrangements: A Reinterpretation," *Quarterly Journal of Economics*, Vol. 119 (February), pp. 1–48.

Rüffer, Rasmus, and Livio Stracca, 2006, "What Is Global Excess Liquidity, and Does It Matter?" ECB Working Paper No. 696 (Frankfurt: European Central Bank).

Shin, Kwanho, and Yunjong Wang, 2003, "Trade Integration and Business Cycle Synchronization in East Asia," *Asian Economic Papers*, Vol. 2 (Fall), pp. 1–20.

Sousa, João, and Andrea Zaghini, 2004, "Monetary Policy Shocks in the Euro Area and Global Liquidity Spillovers," ECB Working Paper No. 309 (Frankfurt: European Central Bank).

Stock, James H., and Mark W. Watson, 2002, "Forecasting Using Principal Components from a Large Number of Predictors," *Journal of the American Statistical Association*, Vol. 97 (December), pp. 1167–79.

———, 2003, "Understanding Changes in International Business Cycle Dynamics," NBER Working Paper No. 9859 (Cambridge, Massachusetts: National Bureau of Economic Research).

———, 2005, "Understanding Changes in International Business Cycle Dynamics," *Journal of the European Economic Association*, Vol. 3 (September), pp. 968–1006.

Timmermann, Allan, 2006, "An Evaluation of the World Economic Outlook Forecasts," IMF Working Paper 06/59 (Washington: International Monetary Fund).

Ueda, Kazuo, 1998, "The East Asian Economic Crisis: A Japanese Perspective," *International Finance*, Vol. 1 (December), pp. 327–38.

Zarnowitz, Victor, 1992, *Business Cycles: Theory, History, Indicators, and Forecasting*, NBER Studies in Business Cycles, Vol. 27 (Chicago: University of Chicago Press).

THE GLOBALIZATION OF LABOR

Over the past two decades, labor markets around the world have become increasingly integrated. Political changes and economic reforms have transformed China, India, and the former Eastern bloc countries, effectively involving their large labor forces in open market economies. At the same time, the development of technology, combined with the progressive removal of restrictions on cross-border trade and capital flows, has made it possible for production processes to be unbundled and located farther from target markets for a growing universe of goods and services. The location of production has become much more responsive to relative labor costs across countries. There have also been increasing flows of migrants across borders, through both legal and informal routes.

This ongoing globalization of the labor market has drawn increasing attention from policymakers and the media, particularly in the advanced economies. The most asked question is whether the addition of this unprecedentedly large pool of labor from emerging market and developing countries is adversely affecting compensation and employment in the advanced economies.

This chapter addresses this important and emotive question. In contrast with most previous studies, which focus on one country or a single channel of transmission, it takes a broad approach, considering a large sample of advanced economies and a full range of transmission channels (competing imports of final products, offshoring of intermediate products, and immigration). The chapter focuses on the following issues:

Note: The main authors of this chapter are Florence Jaumotte and Irina Tytell, with support from Christian de Guzman and Stephanie Denis. Robert Feenstra provided consultancy support.

- How rapidly has the global labor supply grown, and which channels of labor globalization have been most important?
- To what extent can recent trends in labor shares and labor compensation in advanced economies be explained by the changing global labor supply relative to other factors such as technological change and labor market reform? Has the impact been different in skilled and unskilled sectors?
- What policies can help the advanced economies meet the challenges of further labor market globalization?

This chapter finds that the effective global labor force has risen fourfold over the past two decades. This growing pool of global labor is being accessed by advanced economies through various channels, including imports of final goods, offshoring of the production of intermediates, and immigration. The ongoing globalization of labor has contributed to rising labor compensation in advanced economies by boosting productivity and output, while emerging market countries have also benefited from rising wages. Nevertheless, globalization is one of several factors that have acted to reduce the share of income accruing to labor in advanced economies, although rapid technological change has had a bigger impact, especially on workers in unskilled sectors. The analysis finds that countries that have enacted reforms to lower the cost of labor to business and improve labor market flexibility have generally experienced a smaller decline in the labor income share. Looking ahead, it is important for countries to maximize the benefits from labor globalization and technological change, while also working to address the distributional impact. To this end, policies should seek to improve the functioning of labor markets; strengthen access to education and training; and ensure adequate social safety nets that cushion the impact on those adversely

Figure 5.1. Alternative Measures of Global Labor Supply

East Asia's marked rise in working-age population and increasing trade openness have contributed to about half of the quadrupling of the effective global labor supply, while South Asia and the former Eastern bloc accounted for smaller increases.

Sources: United Nations, Population Prospects: The 2004 Revision Population database; World Bank, *World Development Indicators;* and IMF staff calculations.

[1] National labor forces scaled by export-to-GDP ratios.
[2] Includes Western Hemisphere, Middle East and North Africa, and sub-Saharan Africa.
[3] More educated labor force is defined by persons with university-level education. Less educated is defined by labor force with primary and secondary education plus the uneducated.

affected, without obstructing the process of adjustment.

How Globalized Is Labor?

A first question to address is how the opening up of China, India, and the former Eastern bloc countries, together with ongoing demographic developments, has affected the global labor supply. This is not easy to answer because much depends on the assumptions made about how much of a country's labor force is in, or could potentially compete in, the global market. One simple approach is to weigh each country's labor force by its export-to-GDP ratio.[1] By this measure, the effective global labor supply quadrupled between 1980 and 2005, with most of the increase taking place after 1990 (Figure 5.1).[2] East Asia contributed about half of the increase, due to a marked rise in working-age population and rising trade openness, while South Asia and the former Eastern bloc countries accounted for smaller increases. While most of the absolute increase in the global labor supply consisted of less-educated workers (defined as those without higher education), the relative supply of workers with higher education increased by about 50 percent over the last 25 years, owing mostly to advanced economies, but also to China.

Advanced economies can access this increased pool of global labor both through imports of goods and services and through immigration. Trade has been the more important channel and has grown more rapidly, not least because

---

[1] This approach, which follows Harrigan and Balaban (1999), is more accurate for developing countries specialized in labor-intensive activities than for advanced economies whose exports are relatively capital intensive. In order to capture the export of labor through emigration, emigration weights could be added to the trade weights. However, these weights are generally very small.

[2] This compares to estimates in Freeman (2006) that the integration of China, India, and the former Eastern bloc countries doubled the number of workers in the global economy. The difference is due to the weighing of national labor forces by export-to-GDP ratios in this chapter's estimates.

immigration remains highly restricted in most countries (Figure 5.2). A similar picture emerges for developing and emerging market countries, where the export-to-GDP ratio is in general much higher than the ratio of emigrants to the domestic labor force.[3] Nevertheless, immigration has expanded significantly over the past two decades in some large European economies (Germany, Italy, and the United Kingdom) and in the United States. The share of immigrants in the U.S. labor force is now close to 15 percent and hence comparable to the share of imports in GDP. Elsewhere the share of immigrants is still substantially less than the share of imports in GDP, but it is not negligible.

Focusing on trade, the share of developing country products in the manufacturing imports of advanced economies has doubled since the early 1990s (Figure 5.3). This owes much to China. Developing countries have also been capturing an increasing share of world markets. At the aggregate level, however, trade is a win-win game. As China, India, and the Eastern bloc countries have opened up, world markets and opportunities to export have expanded considerably for advanced economies and developing countries alike. Developing countries' imports have been growing faster than those of advanced economies and the share of advanced economies' exports going to developing countries has been rising (though not as rapidly as the share of developing countries in their own imports). Further, while both import and export prices have been on a declining trend relative to output prices, the terms of trade of advanced economies have improved by a cumulative 7 percent since 1980. Most notably, there was a substantial improvement in the terms of trade of Japan in the first half of the 1980s. However, the large fall in import prices at this time was mainly the result of the strong appreciation of the yen at a time when oil prices were falling, and was not directly related to globalization.

[3]The stock of emigrants is limited to those emigrating to OECD economies.

Figure 5.2. Immigration and Trade
(Percent of labor force and GDP, respectively)

Although immigration has expanded significantly over the past two decades in some large European countries and the United States, trade remains as the more important channel for accessing the large global labor force.

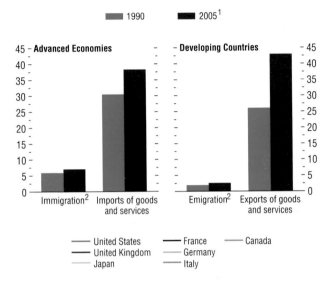

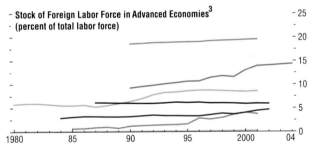

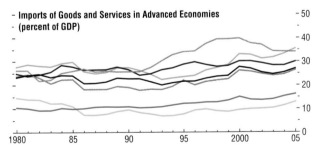

Sources: Docquier and Marfouk (2005); OECD, International Migration Data; U.S. Census Bureau; and IMF staff calculations.
[1]2000 data for immigration and emigration.
[2]Hong Kong SAR, Greece, Israel, New Zealand, Singapore, and Taiwan Province of China are not included in average immigration due to data limitations. Russia and Slovak Republic are not included in average emigration due to data limitations.
[3]Foreign-born labor force for Australia, Canada, and the United States. For Italy, the Netherlands, Norway, and the United Kingdom, the data refer to the share of foreign employment in total employment.

Figure 5.3. Share of Developing Countries in Trade

As China, India, and the Eastern bloc have opened up, world markets and opportunities to export have expanded considerably for advanced economies and developing countries alike.

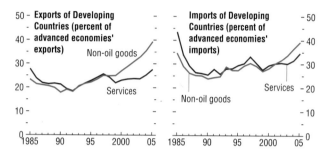

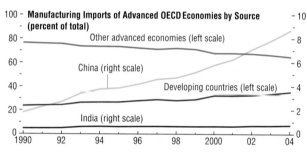

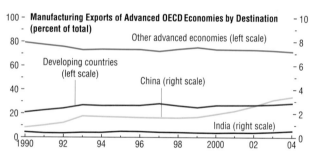

Sources: OECD, STAN Bilateral Trade Database; and IMF staff calculations.

As can be seen in Figure 5.4, the strong export dynamism of emerging market and developing countries is in skilled as well as unskilled products: developing countries' share in world exports of skilled goods and services has been on the rise in recent years.[4] China has led the way, reflecting its very strong growth and a move toward more skill-intensive goods in its export basket. India's export basket is also changing rapidly toward skill-intensive services, but the country's weight in world trade remains small.

One category of trade that has received much attention in recent years is trade in intermediates. The reduction of barriers to cross-border trade and capital flows, combined with technological progress in transport and communication, has made it easier for firms to move parts of their production to less costly foreign locations—a process referred to as offshore outsourcing or, more simply, offshoring. Nevertheless, and contrary to some popular perceptions, offshored inputs, which account for about half of total imports (the rest being imports of final products), have grown somewhat more slowly than total trade (see also OECD, 2006a). Moreover, the scale of offshoring is still quite limited in the overall economy (Figure 5.5). Imports of intermediate manufacturing and services inputs (excluding energy) accounted for about 5 percent of gross output and about 10 percent of total intermediate inputs in advanced economies in 2003, the latest year for which data are available.[5] These shares have

[4]Skilled exports are measured as exports of goods and services produced in skilled sectors, that is, sectors with a higher share of skilled workers in their labor force. The results are generally robust to excluding medium-skill sectors and focusing instead on low-skill and high-skill sectors (see Appendix 5.1 for details). Using a more refined classification of products by skill intensity, Rodrik (2006) concludes that China's export basket is much more skill intensive than would be expected given China's level of development.

[5]It is common to scale imported intermediates by total intermediate inputs to estimate the intensity of offshoring. However, it seems more appropriate to scale imported intermediates by total inputs (including labor and capital), since imported intermediates can substitute not only for domestic intermediate inputs but also for in-house labor and capital.

increased only moderately since the early 1980s.[6] The share of offshored inputs in gross output ranges from 12 percent in the Netherlands to about 2–3 percent in the United States and Japan. Offshoring is thus relatively limited in the United States and Japan, in the same way that trade openness is usually low in large economies.

The manufacturing sector has been most affected by offshoring because it is more tradable. For the countries for which long data series are available (G-7, Australia, and the Netherlands), the share of imported manufacturing inputs in gross manufacturing output increased from 6 percent in 1980 to 10 percent in 2003, with the rise being somewhat stronger in the latter years of the sample (Figure 5.6). In 2003, the offshoring intensity in manufacturing ranged from 4 percent in Japan to a high of about 25 percent in Canada. Imports of services inputs by the overall economy remain low at 1 percent of gross output, although the offshoring intensity in services has increased in recent years in a number of countries, including Canada, Germany, and the Netherlands.[7]

Interestingly, the rise in offshoring in advanced economies has been driven mostly by imports of skilled rather than unskilled inputs. Several factors may help explain this finding. First, in line with advanced economies' comparative advantage in skill-intensive production, goods traditionally produced in unskilled sectors (e.g., textiles) are more likely to be imported as final goods rather than intermediates.[8] Sectors involved in the rise in the imports of intermediaries are electronic equipment; other machinery and equipment; and chemical, rubber, and plastic products. It should be noted, however,

---

[6]The flattening in 2001–02 is temporary and reflects the slowdown in world trade associated with the global recession.

[7]See Jensen and Kletzer (2005) and Amiti and Wei (2005) for more details on offshoring of services. The latter also find that offshoring of services remains very limited, although it has grown in recent years.

[8]The share of imported intermediates in total imports of unskilled products is lower than the comparable share for skilled products, at 37 percent and 68 percent, respectively.

Figure 5.4. Developing Countries: Exports of Skilled Manufacturing Goods and Services

(Percent)

The recent robust growth in developing countries' share in world exports, particularly in skilled products, owes much to China.

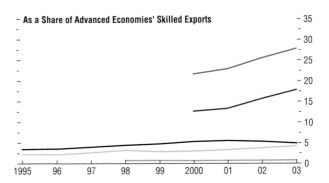

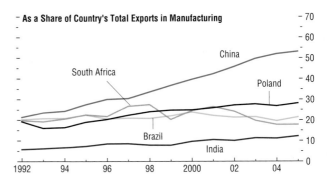

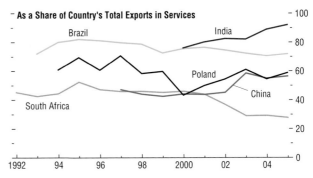

Sources: OECD, International Trade in Services Database and STAN Industrial Database; World Bank, World Integrated Trade Solution database; and IMF, *Balance of Payments Statistics.*
[1]Bangladesh, China, India, Malaysia, the Philippines, and Thailand.
[2]Czech Republic, Hungary, Poland, Romania, Slovak Republic, and Turkey.
[3]Argentina, Brazil, Chile, Colombia, Mexico, Peru, and Venezuela.
[4]Egypt, Ethiopia, Morocco, South Africa, Sudan, and Tanzania.

Figure 5.5. Offshoring by Advanced Economies[1]

The extent of offshoring is still quite limited in advanced economies. In 2003, the offshoring of nonenergy manufacturing and services inputs averaged about 5 percent of gross output and roughly 10 percent of total intermediate inputs. The low level of offshoring is particularly pronounced in the world's largest economies, the United States and Japan.

—— Share of gross output (long time series)[2]
—— Share of total intermediate inputs (long time series)[2]
—— Share of gross output (short time series)[3]
—— Share of total intermediate inputs (short time series)[3]

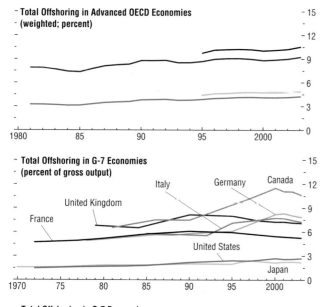

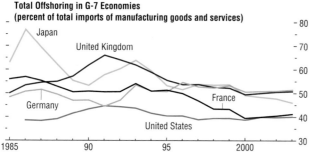

Sources: OECD, Input-Output Tables (1995, 2002, and 2006 editions), International Trade in Services Database, and STAN Industrial Database; Groningen Growth and Development Centre, 60-Industry Database (September 2006); and IMF staff calculations.

[1]Offshoring measures calculated using Input-Output Tables from OECD; resulting series extended from 2001 to 2003 by estimating extent of offshoring using a combination of data from the OECD STAN Industrial Database and the Groningen 60-Industry Database; only offshoring of nonenergy manufacturing and services inputs considered.

[2]Advanced OECD economies used in calculations for long time series include Australia, Canada, France, Germany, Japan, the Netherlands, the United Kingdom, and the United States; weighted using series on GDP at current U.S. dollars from the World Economic Outlook database.

[3]Advanced OECD economies used in calculations for short time series include Australia, Austria, Canada, Finland, France, Germany, Greece, Italy, the Netherlands, Japan, Korea, Portugal, Spain, Sweden, the United Kingdom, and the United States; weighted using series on GDP at current U.S. dollars from the World Economic Outlook database.

that offshoring is likely to involve the least skill-intensive stages of production in these skilled sectors, although the available data do not allow confirmation of this. Second, the bulk of advanced economies' imports (of both final and intermediate products) still comes from other advanced economies and likely includes more skilled rather than unskilled products. Third, as mentioned earlier, the global supply of labor with higher education has increased relative to labor with lower education.

How Has the Globalization of Labor Affected Workers in Advanced Economies?

The rapid growth of the global labor supply and its manifestation through increasing exports of emerging market and developing countries leads to the question of how these trends have affected workers in advanced economies. With exports from emerging market and developing countries being intensive in labor, especially unskilled labor, traditional trade theory would predict that the integration of these countries into the world economy would exert downward pressure on the wages (corrected for productivity) of workers in advanced economies. Hence, the share of national income received by labor—the so-called labor share—would be expected to decline. To see this, it is worth noting that the labor share can be expressed as the ratio of labor compensation per worker to average worker productivity.

Nevertheless, workers in advanced economies could still be better off if the positive effects from enhanced trade and productivity on the economy's income (the size of the total "pie") are larger than the negative effect on the share of this income that accrues to labor. The vast literature documenting gains from trade (see, for example, Lewer and Van den Berg, 2003; Berg and Krueger, 2003) suggests that the increase in the economy's income may indeed be substantial. Recently, Grossman and Rossi-Hansberg (2006) have argued that the productivity-enhancing effect from trade in intermediates could be even larger than from trade in final goods because, in addition to a competition effect for producing sectors, trade in intermediates also reduces the costs of production of using sectors. The empirical evidence on the productivity effects of offshoring is, however, mixed.[9]

What do the data show? Looking first at the labor share, there has been a clear decline since the early 1980s across the advanced economies (Figure 5.7).[10] The decline is stronger for the labor share than for the share of employees' compensation, reflecting a reduction in the share of other categories of workers in the total workforce (other categories of workers include self-employed, employers, and family workers).[11] A part of this decline is a reversal of the rise in labor shares that took place in the 1970s, especially in Europe and Japan (Blanchard, 1998).[12]

[9]There is little empirical evidence on the productivity effects of offshoring to date (see Olsen, 2006). There are some indications that positive productivity effects of manufacturing offshoring depend on the degree to which firms are already globally engaged. However, their global engagement may be already close to optimal levels in advanced economies, suggesting that the potential for productivity gains from services offshoring may be larger. Positive productivity effects of services offshoring to date appear to be generally small in manufacturing plants, but somewhat bigger in service-sector firms. Amiti and Wei (2006) find a significant positive effect of services offshoring and a somewhat smaller positive effect of manufacturing offshoring on productivity in the United States.

[10]National accounts provide the share of employees' compensation in total income but do not identify separately the labor income of other categories of workers (self-employed, employers, and family workers). Several correction procedures are available (Gollin, 2002) and, for data availability reasons, the employees' compensation was augmented with compensation of other categories of workers by assuming that the latter command similar wages per worker as employees. The results are robust if other procedures are used (see Appendix 5.1).

[11]Focusing on the United States, for which data are available since 1930, the share of employees' compensation in national income does not appear to be at a historical low (though this may be partly related to the rise in the share of employees in the total workforce).

[12]Blanchard (1998) argues that the rise of the labor share in Europe in the 1970s was driven by a negative shift in labor supply as wages did not adjust fast enough to the slowdown in underlying factor productivity growth. Over time, though, employment adjusted downward, exerting downward pressure on wages and returning the labor share toward its previous level (though at a higher unemployment rate). The further decline that has taken

Figure 5.6. Advanced Economies: Offshoring by Category of Inputs[1]

The manufacturing sector has been more affected by offshoring because it is more tradable, although there are considerable differences across countries (the vertical line shows the range of country outcomes). Skilled inputs have also played a more significant role in the growth of offshoring in advanced economies than unskilled inputs.

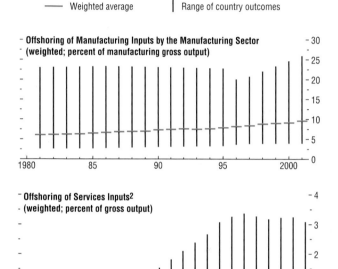

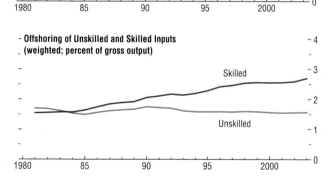

Sources: OECD, Input-Output Tables (1995, 2002, and 2006), International Trade in Services Database, and STAN Industrial Database; Groningen Growth and Development Centre, 60-Industry Database (September 2006); and IMF staff calculations.
[1]Offshoring measures calculated using Input-Output Tables from OECD; resulting series extended from 2001 to 2003 by estimating extent of offshoring using a combination of data from the OECD's STAN Industrial Database and the Groningen 60-Industry Database; only offshoring of nonenergy manufacturing and services inputs considered. Advanced OECD economies used in calculations for long time series include Australia, Canada, France, Germany, Japan, the Netherlands, the United Kingdom, and the United States; weighted using series on GDP at current U.S. dollars from the World Economic Outlook database.
[2]Excludes the United States since import data are reported as inclusive of "cost, insurance, and freight"; thus, values that normally accrue to business services are included in associated goods sectors.

Figure 5.7. Advanced Economies: Labor Income Shares
(Percent of GDP unless otherwise noted)

Over the past two decades, there has been a continued decline in the share of income that accrues to labor, especially in Europe and Japan. The income share of workers in unskilled sectors has dropped strongly while that of workers in skilled sectors has generally made small gains.

The decline in the labor share since 1980 has been much more pronounced in Europe and Japan (about 10 percentage points) than in Anglo-Saxon countries, including the United States (about 3–4 percentage points).[13] Within Europe, the strongest decline is observed in Austria, Ireland, and the Netherlands. Further, most of the decline in the labor share can be attributed to the fall in unskilled sectors, which was more pronounced in Europe and Japan than in the Anglo-Saxon countries. This decline reflects a combination of the reduction in the within-sector labor share and the shift of output from unskilled toward skilled sectors (see Figure 5.7). The income share of labor in skilled sectors, on the other hand, has been on the rise, especially in Anglo-Saxon countries where it has increased by about 5 percentage points. It is important to emphasize that due to the nature of the available data, these results relate to income shares of workers in skilled and unskilled sectors, rather than to income shares of skilled and unskilled workers themselves.

Despite the fall in the overall labor share, real labor compensation has expanded robustly in all advanced economies since 1980, with growth accelerating since the mid-1990s. This trend reflects both employment growth and increases in real compensation per worker, with a stronger weight on employment in the Anglo-Saxon countries and on real compensation per worker in Europe (Figure 5.8). Since the mid-1990s, however, employment growth has picked up in Europe, outpacing the growth in real compensation per worker. Growth in labor compensation of unskilled sectors, however, has been very sluggish (Figure 5.9). While unskilled employment has held steady in the United States, increases

_____

place in the labor share since the mid-1980s is the result of an adverse labor demand shock: at a given wage and capital stock, firms have steadily decreased employment. Such a shift may have various sources: the adoption of technologies biased against labor and toward capital or a shift in the distribution of rents away from workers.

[13]For the purpose of this chapter, Europe includes the euro area countries, Denmark, and Norway, while Anglo-Saxon countries include Australia, Canada, the United Kingdom, and the United States.

in real compensation per worker have been meager in unskilled sectors and the earnings gap between skilled and unskilled sectors has widened by 25 percent. In Europe, real compensation per worker in unskilled sectors grew broadly in line with that in skilled sectors, but employment in unskilled sectors lost ground to employment in skilled sectors (and actually contracted by a cumulative 15 percent).[14]

Turning to emerging market countries, theory would predict that the globalization of labor would bring large benefits for workers in the form of wage convergence toward the levels in advanced economies. Data from the manufacturing sector confirm that real wages in emerging market countries, particularly in Asia, have been catching up with those in the United States (Figure 5.10). Real wages (corrected for purchasing power) have been converging rapidly and are relatively high in Asian countries that started developing earlier (Hong Kong SAR, Korea, Singapore, and Taiwan Province of China). Wages in other Asian countries, including China, have been converging at a slower pace, though this has accelerated in recent years.[15] Studies confirm that both trade and emigration have contributed to rising incomes of nationals of developing countries, although the evidence on their impact on inequality is mixed (see Box 5.1 for a discussion of the evidence on the implications of globalization for labor markets in developing countries).

Labor Compensation and the Globalization of Labor: An Empirical Examination

While striking, the globalization of labor is but one of the forces that has been affecting the labor markets of advanced economies over the past two decades. Rapid technological change is another central development with potentially important implications for labor market

[14]Katz and Autor (1999) find similar changes in the gap between high- and low-income earners for the United States and European countries.

[15]Asia's labor productivity has also been converging toward the U.S. level (see the September 2006 *World Economic Outlook*).

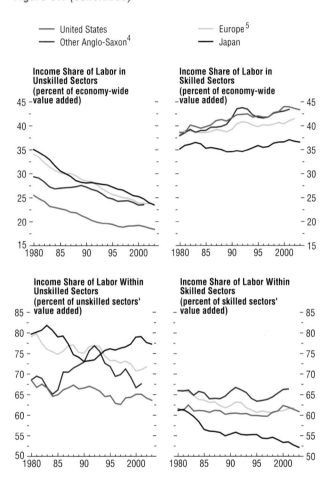

Figure 5.7 (concluded)

— United States
— Other Anglo-Saxon[4]
— Europe[5]
— Japan

Sources: Haver Analytics; International Labor Organization, Labor Statistics Database; OECD, Employment and Labor Market Statistics, National Accounts Statistics, and STAN Industrial Database; United Nations, *National Accounts Statistics* (2004); and IMF staff calculations.
[1] Income share of employees is the ratio of employees' labor compensation to value added.
[2] The income share of labor estimates the share of labor compensation of employees and "nonemployee" workers in value added.
[3] Advanced economies include Australia, Austria, Belgium, Canada, Denmark, Finland, France, Germany, Ireland, Italy, Japan, the Netherlands, Norway, Portugal, Spain, Sweden, the United Kingdom, and the United States; weighted using series on GDP in U.S. dollars from the World Economic Outlook database.
[4] Anglo-Saxon economies include Australia, Canada, and the United Kingdom. Australia is excluded from the analysis by skill level due to lack of data.
[5] Europe includes Austria, Belgium, Denmark, Finland, France, Germany, Ireland, Italy, the Netherlands, Norway, Portugal, Spain, and Sweden. Ireland, the Netherlands, and Spain are excluded from the analysis by skill level due to lack of data.

Figure 5.8. Advanced Economies: Labor Compensation and Employment

(Index, 1980 = 100)

Despite the fall in the overall labor share, real labor compensation has grown robustly in advanced economies, with a stronger weight on employment in Anglo-Saxon economies.

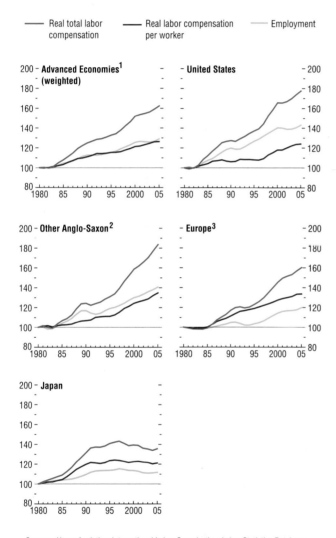

Sources: Haver Analytics; International Labor Organization, Labor Statistics Database; OECD, Employment and Labor Market Statistics, National Accounts Statistics, and STAN Industrial Database; United Nations, *National Accounts Statistics* (2004); and IMF staff calculations.

[1] Advanced economies include Australia, Austria, Belgium, Canada, Denmark, Finland, France, Germany, Ireland, Italy, Japan, the Netherlands, Norway, Portugal, Spain, Sweden, the United Kingdom, and the United States; weighted using series on GDP in U.S. dollars from the World Economic Outlook database.

[2] Anglo-Saxon economies include Australia, Canada, and the United Kingdom.

[3] Europe includes Austria, Belgium, Denmark, Finland, France, Germany, Ireland, Italy, the Netherlands, Norway, Portugal, Spain, and Sweden.

outcomes (Figure 5.11). The information and communications technology (ICT) revolution, an all-purpose technological revolution that Blinder (2006) has compared to the third industrial revolution, has stimulated capital accumulation (see the September 2001 *World Economic Outlook*) and favored skilled labor—with which it is more complementary—over unskilled labor. Technology has also progressed in other areas as reflected in the strong rise in patent applications in OECD economies, especially since the early 1990s.

There have also been changes in labor and product market policies. Reforms have proceeded in several areas, but generally in the direction of lowering the cost of labor to business and enhancing the flexibility of markets. Four main developments in labor market policies are particularly worth noting (see Figure 5.11): (1) a marked increase in the generosity of unemployment benefits in Europe (as measured by average replacement rate of income), in contrast with a slight decline in Anglo-Saxon countries; (2) a general decline in the tax wedge, especially in the United States where it has fallen by about 10 percentage points since 1995; (3) substantial declines in legislated employment protection and product market regulation, especially in Europe and Japan, both of which started with particularly restrictive stances; and (4) persisting large cross-country differences in the degree of employment protection, with low protection in the United States and other Anglo-Saxon countries and relatively high protection in Europe and Japan. Recent studies (Bassanini and Duval, 2006; and Annett, 2006) have highlighted reductions in the tax wedge, reductions in unemployment benefits, deregulation of product markets, and more limited employment protection as the main factors that have contributed to employment growth and declining unemployment.[16] Disentangling

---

[16] Some of these variables may also affect the labor share in similar ways, especially if the elasticity of substitution between labor and capital is high. For instance, an increase in the unemployment benefit replacement rate increases the reservation wage of workers and leads in the very short run to a rise in the labor share. But as employment adjusts downward, the labor share declines and can

the influence of these variables is difficult, in particular because technological change and the globalization of labor may be expected to affect compensation and the labor share in similar ways. The influence of policy variables is complex, particularly because they may also affect the labor share indirectly by facilitating or obstructing the adjustment of the economy to labor globalization and technological progress.

This section uses an econometric model to analyze the relationship between labor compensation and labor globalization—measured in terms-of-trade prices, offshoring, and immigration—controlling for technological progress and changes in labor market policies. The basic model, which has solid microeconomic foundations and is widely used in the recent trade literature (see, for instance, Feenstra, 2004; Harrigan, 1998; and Kohli, 1991), relates the labor share to the capital-labor ratio and import and export prices (expressed relative to domestic prices).[17] The two latter variables capture the effects of globalization of trade: declines in import prices are expected to decrease the labor share, as imports that come increasingly from developing countries are labor intensive; in contrast, declines in export prices should benefit labor relative to capital because of the high capital intensity of advanced economies' exports. The basic model is augmented to include the intensity of offshoring, the share of immigrants in the domestic labor force, the share of ICT capital in total capital, measures of labor market policies, and country fixed effects.[18] The model

---

fall below its initial level if the elasticity of substitution between capital and labor is high enough (Blanchard, 1998). Other shocks that increase the cost of labor, such as an increase in the tax wedge or an increase in employment protection, can be expected to have similar effects. Although strict product market regulation creates rents, it is not clear that it should affect the distribution of these rents between labor and capital and hence the labor share.

[17]The factor share equations are derived from the maximization of an (economy-wide) revenue function, taking as given the factor endowments and sectoral prices (import, export, and absorption). See Appendix 5.1 for more details.

[18]The theoretical rationale for including these variables is that they may act as shift factors in the revenue (GNP) function (Feenstra, 2004).

Figure 5.9. Advanced Economies: Labor Compensation and Employment in Skilled and Unskilled Sectors
(Index, 1980 = 100)

Despite strong growth of labor compensation overall, the growth in labor compensation of unskilled sectors has been very slow. In the United States, the earnings gap between skilled and unskilled workers has widened by about 25 percent since 1980, while in Europe, employment in unskilled sectors has contracted.

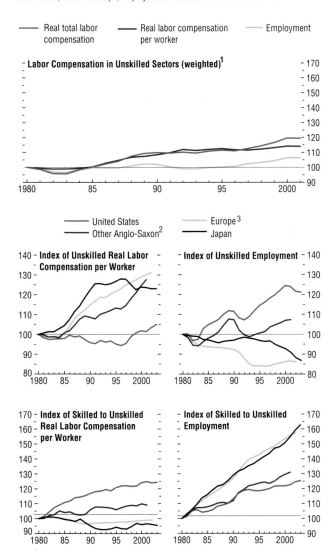

Sources: Haver Analytics; International Labor Organization, Labor Statistics Database; OECD, Employment and Labour Market Statistics, National Accounts Statistics, and STAN Industrial Database; United Nations, *National Accounts Statistics* (2004); and IMF staff calculations.

[1]For analysis by skill level, advanced economies include Austria, Belgium, Canada, Denmark, Finland, France, Germany, Italy, Japan, Norway, Portugal, Sweden, the United Kingdom, and the United States; weighted using series on GDP in U.S. dollars from the World Economic Outlook database.

[2]For analysis by skill level, Anglo-Saxon economies include Canada and the United Kingdom.

[3]For analysis by skill level, Europe includes Austria, Belgium, Denmark, Finland, France, Germany, Italy, Norway, Portugal, and Sweden.

Figure 5.10. Catch-Up by Emerging Markets' Manufacturing Wages
(Percent of U.S. manufacturing wages in constant PPP dollars)

While relative manufacturing wages in emerging Asia are generally increasing, catch-up has been most evident in the newly industrializing economies, such as Korea, Singapore, and Hong Kong SAR. In contrast, Latin American economies have not experienced much convergence.

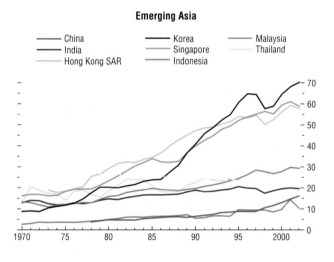

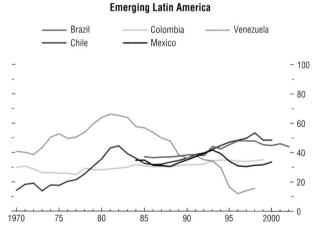

Sources: UNIDO, Industrial Statistics Database (2006); CEIC Asia Database; Instituto Brasileiro de Geografia e Estatística, *Pesquisa Industrial Mensal;* and IMF staff calculations.

was estimated on a panel of 18 advanced OECD economies over 1982–2002, for the overall labor share and for the income shares of labor in skilled and unskilled sectors (see Appendix 5.1 for more details). At the outset, it should be noted that the effects of globalization can only be imperfectly disentangled from those of technology, especially for technological progress in transport and communication, which vastly expands the opportunities for globalized production. Similarly, part of the decline in import (and, in some cases, export) prices may be attributable to productivity improvements in the production of information and communications technology.

The results from estimating this model suggest that labor globalization, technological change, and labor market policies have all affected labor shares over the past two decades (Figure 5.12).[19] Both labor globalization and technological progress have acted to reduce the labor share, with the impact of technological progress being somewhat larger, while changes in labor market policies have generally had a smaller but positive impact on the labor share.[20]

[19]The contribution of a factor to the average annual change in the labor share over the sample period is the product of its coefficient and of its own average annual change over the same period.

[20]Most studies have focused on explaining the decline in the relative wage (or labor share) of unskilled workers in the United States (see Freeman, 1995; and Feenstra, 2004, for a survey). Studies that attempt to explain the evolution of the overall labor share are more scarce. Most studies conclude that skill-biased technological change is a more important cause of wage inequality than trade (e.g., Harrigan, 1998; and Harrigan and Balaban, 1999). Feenstra (2004 and 2007) finds that the role of trade and technological progress are equally important in explaining rising wage inequality. In a recent contribution, Guscina (2006) finds that labor shares across countries are equally affected by technological progress and openness. Harrison (2002) also finds that globalization tends to reduce the labor share. Another strand of the literature examines whether globalization increases the elasticity of labor demand to wages and finds mixed results (see, for instance, Slaughter, 2001; and OECD, 2006a). Studies of immigration tend to find that its effects on wages and employment of natives are small (Greenwood, Hunt, and Kohli, 1996; and OECD, 2006b).

Each channel of labor globalization (trade prices, offshoring, and immigration) individually plays a relatively small role in explaining the decline in the labor share.

Labor globalization contributed to the decline in labor shares in most countries, with broadly similar effects in both Anglo-Saxon countries and Europe.[21] Nevertheless, the labor globalization effect in the Anglo-Saxon countries and Europe is driven by different factors. Europe's labor share has been affected both by offshoring and immigration, while, in the Anglo-Saxon countries, offshoring was a somewhat less important factor. Similarly, within Europe, large economies were affected more by immigration than by offshoring, while the opposite holds for small economies. Another component of globalization—the change in trade prices—generally had only a small net effect on the labor share. Hence, while globalization exerted downward pressure on the labor share through declines in import prices, this effect has been broadly compensated by similar declines in export prices, which have boosted the labor share since exports of advanced economies are capital intensive. In large European countries and Japan, the net effect from changes in trade prices was actually to boost the labor share, likely reflecting a stronger concentration of exports in capital-intensive goods.

The reasons for the milder decline of the labor share in the Anglo-Saxon countries than in Europe are found in the role of technological change and labor market policies rather than in the differences in the impact of labor globalization. Technological change has contributed to the reduction of the labor share in both groups, but less so in the Anglo-Saxon countries. In particular, in the United States, ICT capital even contributed to raising the labor share, possibly reflecting the fact that the United States is most

[21]Some caution is needed when interpreting these results, since they are based on the regression coefficients that are the same for all the countries and average annual changes in variables that are country specific.

Figure 5.11. Information and Communications Technology (ICT) Capital, Patents, and Labor Market Indicators

The globalization of labor is but one of the forces that have influenced labor markets in advanced economies over the past two decades. Rapid technological change and changes in labor and product market policies are other significant developments with potentially important implications for labor market outcomes.

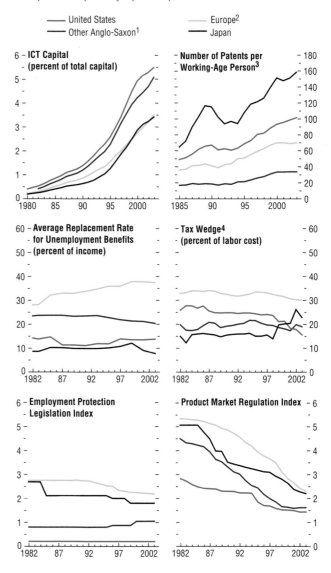

Sources: Bassanini and Duval (2006); Jorgenson and Vu (2005); OECD, Science and Technology Statistics; and IMF staff calculations.
[1] Australia, Canada, New Zealand, and the United Kingdom.
[2] Austria, Belgium, Denmark, Finland, France, Germany, Ireland, Italy, the Netherlands, Norway, Portugal, Spain, Sweden, and Switzerland. Greece is not included due to data limitations.
[3] Patents that have been filed at the European Patent Office, Japanese Patent Office, and granted by the United States Patent and Trademark Office (measured by priority year, that is, year of first application).
[4] Difference between the labor cost to the employer and the net take-home pay of the employee, in percent of the labor cost.

Figure 5.12. Contributions to the Annual Change in Labor Share[1]
(Percentage points)

Labor globalization and technological progress have acted to reduce the labor share, with the impact of technological progress being somewhat larger, while changes in labor market policies have generally had a smaller but positive impact on the labor share. Trade prices, offshoring, and immigration individually play a relatively small role in explaining the decline in the labor share.

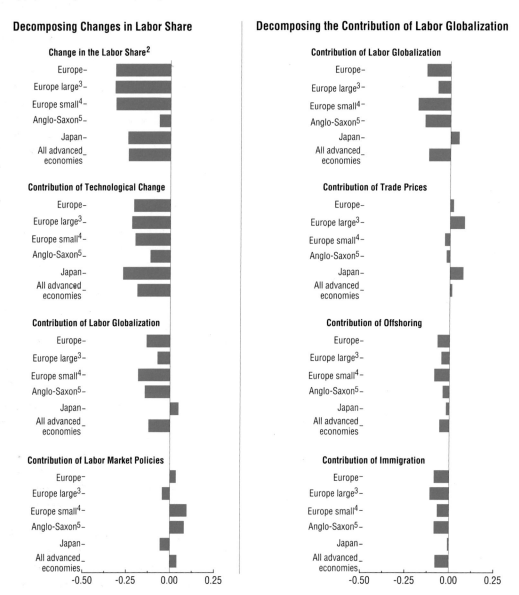

Source: IMF staff calculations.

[1]1982–2002 or longest period available. 1986–2001 for Japan, as changes in the relative import price in earlier years reflected the yen's strong appreciation rather than globalization. The contributions are based on estimated regression coefficients and average annual changes in the respective variables by country (see Appendix 5.1).

[2]The annual change in the labor share in this figure corresponds to the sample period for which all the regression variables were available and may thus differ from the one shown in Figure 5.7.

[3]Europe large includes France, Germany, Italy, and Spain.

[4]Europe small covers Austria, Belgium, Denmark, Finland, Ireland, the Netherlands, Norway, Portugal, and Sweden.

[5]Anglo-Saxon countries include Australia, Canada, the United Kingdom, and the United States.

Box 5.1. Emigration and Trade: How Do They Affect Developing Countries?

This box reviews the evidence on the effects of emigration and trade on labor markets and incomes in developing countries.

Emigration

While a vast theoretical and empirical literature considers the impact of immigration on destination countries, little work has been done on emigration and its impact on source countries.[1] This is surprising because the shares of the labor force leaving many individual source countries as emigrants are considerably higher than the proportionate changes in the labor force of many receiving countries due to immigration. To cite a few examples, the labor force in Barbados, Belize, El Salvador, Guyana, and Jamaica has been reduced by 20 percent or more due to emigration to the OECD countries.[2] Meanwhile, immigrants constitute about 15 percent of the U.S. labor force, and the share is considerably lower in most other OECD countries.

In general, source countries do not record information on those who emigrate. However, Mexico and other Latin American countries—from where immigration is mostly to the United States—offer ideal case studies because U.S. data sources can be used to analyze the impact on the source countries. Along these lines, Cardarelli and Ueda (2004) assess the impact of migration to the United States on the welfare of source countries. Using as a yardstick the income produced by the nationals of the country irrespective of where they live, they estimate that the well-being of Mexican-born people was, on average, 20 percent higher than the country's GDP alone would suggest over 1994–2003. Cardarelli and Ueda also conclude that immi-

gration opportunities to the United States have raised the well-being of nationals born in several other developing countries, particularly in Latin America and the Caribbean (e.g., Jamaica, Haiti, Nicaragua, and El Salvador) and in the Philippines and Vietnam. One channel of income gains for developing country residents, included in these calculations, is the large flow of remittances back into the country from emigrants living abroad (see the April 2005 *World Economic Outlook*). While in Mexico annual remittances were about 3 percent of GDP over 1990–2003, they amounted to over 10 percent of GDP in El Salvador and Jamaica over the same period.

Focusing on workers who have stayed home, Mishra (2007) examines the effect of emigration to the United States on wages in Mexico, using data from the Mexican and U.S. censuses for 1970–2000. She finds a strong and positive effect of emigration on Mexican wages: a 10 percent decrease in the number of Mexican workers in a given skill group (defined by schooling and experience) increases the average wage in that skill group by about 4 percent (Aydemir and Borjas, 2006, find a similar result). The impact on wages differs dramatically across schooling groups, with the greatest increase being for the higher wage earners (those with 12–15 years of schooling) owing to the higher emigration rate of this group. Hence, while all categories of workers who stay home benefit in terms of higher wages, emigration could serve as a partial explanation for the increasing wage inequality in Mexico.[3]

The positive effect of emigration on wages in Mexico is confirmed by Hanson (forthcoming). He examines changes in the distribution of labor income across regions of Mexico during the 1990s, a period of rapid globalization of the Mexican economy. He finds that over the decade, average hourly earnings in high-

Note: The main author of this box is Prachi Mishra.
[1]See Borjas (1994 and 1995) for surveys of the empirical literature on immigration.
[2]The outflow of workers is largely to the United States, and took place between 1970 and 2000. In 1965, the United States implemented the Immigration and Nationality Act, which changed the basis of entry into the United States from country quotas to family-based reunification. This brought about a drastic change in the composition of immigration, increasing the share of migrants from developing countries.

[3]Emigration accounts for approximately 37 percent of the increase in relative wages of high school graduates (12 years of schooling) and 14 percent of the increase in relative wages of those with some college education (13–15 years of schooling) between 1990 and 2000.

Box 5.1 *(concluded)*

migration states rose by 6–9 percent relative to low-migration states.

While workers benefit from higher wages and families from remittance inflows, capital owners who hire these workers lose. Overall, however, estimates suggest that there is a small aggregate annual welfare gain in the case of Mexico. Nevertheless, emigration can lead to loss of welfare if the fact that emigration of high-skilled workers leads to a decline in the productivity of those who have stayed behind is taken into account. For example, qualified doctors, researchers, and engineers confer a positive externality on the rest of the population, and this is lost when they emigrate. Mishra (2006) estimates substantial productivity losses for those who stay behind because of the very high rates of high-skilled emigration from the Caribbean countries. Gupta, Pattillo, and Wagh (2007) also report a high rate of migration of skilled workers from sub-Saharan African countries. One consequence of this is a human resource shortage in the health sector of these countries, as skilled health care professionals get hired in the high-demand OECD countries.

Trade

A large body of research shows that trade openness in developing countries has raised aggregate incomes and growth rates (see Berg and Krueger, 2003, for a survey). Using cross-country and panel regressions, many studies have found that openness to trade is a significant explanatory variable for the level or growth rate of real GDP per capita, with the weight of evidence suggesting that this result holds even when the endogeneity of trade openness is taken into account and after controlling for other important determinants, such as the quality of institutions and geography.

In contrast, the internal distributional consequences of trade reform in developing countries are still the subject of intense debate (see Goldberg and Pavcnik, forthcoming, for a survey). The workhorse model to analyze the labor market consequences of trade liberalization—the Stolper-Samuelson theorem—predicts that trade

liberalization will shift income toward a country's abundant factor.[4] For developing countries, this suggests that liberalization will principally benefit the abundant unskilled labor. Yet many developing countries, including Argentina, Brazil, Colombia, China, India, and Mexico experienced a widening wage gap between skilled and unskilled labor during periods of trade reform during the 1980s and 1990s.[5]

Of course, rising wage inequality does not necessarily imply a causal impact of trade reforms (since typically trade reforms were accompanied by significant domestic reforms in most countries).[6] Hence, the literature in the past decade has focused on trying to identify the causal link between trade liberalization and distributional outcomes. Two key methodologies used are the industry-level and the regional approaches that examine whether industries or regions that were more exposed to trade liberalization experienced larger changes in labor market outcomes. However, a drawback of both these approaches is that they can directly

---

[4]Davis and Mishra (2007) discuss a variety of reasons for why the assumptions underlying the Stolper-Samuelson model may be too simplistic to hold in the real world. One possible reason is that the pattern of trade depends on a country's "local" rather than global factor abundance: a country's factor abundance needs to be compared with that of others that produce the same set of goods. For example, Mexico is less skill abundant relative to the United States but more skill abundant relative to China. When Mexico joined the General Agreement on Tariffs and Trade in the mid-1980s, it opened its borders to the less-skill-abundant world, which could explain the rising wage inequality in the late 1980s.

[5]The definition of skill varies across specific country studies. Studies using household survey data define skill based on education of the household head, whereas studies using plant- or firm-level data typically differentiate between production and nonproduction, or blue-collar and white-collar, workers.

[6]Other explanations of the rising wage gaps include skill-biased technological change or increased offshoring of activities that are relatively skill intensive from the point of view of developing countries (though offshoring may itself be triggered by a free trade agreement with an advanced economy, leading to reduced tariffs) (Feenstra, 2007).

identify only relative differences across regions or industries and not identify the impact on the nation as a whole.[7]

The econometric evidence from different countries is mixed on how trade reforms affect relative labor market outcomes across regions or industries. Topalova (2005) and Edmonds, Pavcnik, and Topalova (2007) find that districts in India that were more exposed to import liberalization experienced a slower reduction in poverty, which was coupled with lower investment in human capital and a lower decline in child labor. On the other hand, using a broader measure of openness, Hanson (2007) finds that states in Mexico with high exposure to globalization (measured by the shares of foreign direct investment, imports, and exports assembly in state GDP) experienced a rise in labor incomes relative to low-exposure states in the 1990s.

The empirical evidence on the effect of trade liberalization on wages at the industry level is

also mixed.[8] For example, studies find no significant relationship between trade policy and industry wages in Brazil and Mexico (Pavcnik and others, 2004; and Feliciano, 2001), while the reduction in tariffs within a sector is found to be associated with a significant reduction in wages in that sector in Colombia (Goldberg and Pavcnik, 2005) but with an increase in wages in Poland (Goh and Javorcik, 2007). The evidence from India on the effects of changes in tariffs on wages is mixed (see Topalova, 2005; Dutta, 2004; and Kumar and Mishra, forthcoming). Given that the sectors that experienced the largest tariff reductions were those with the largest share of unskilled workers, the industry-level studies thus suggest mixed effects of trade liberalization on the overall wage gap between skilled and unskilled workers: trade reforms were associated with a higher wage gap in Colombia, possibly with an unchanged wage gap in Brazil and Mexico, and with lower wage inequality in Poland.

In conclusion, on the one hand, emigration and trade both increase the aggregate incomes of developing countries (once the income of emigrants is included). On the other hand, the existing evidence on the impact of globalization on inequality is mixed, particularly in the case of trade. Further research efforts are needed to fully understand these important issues.

---

[7]Porto (2006) is one study that uses a general equilibrium model of trade to answer the ambitious question of the overall effect of trade liberalization on inequality, in the context of Argentinean trade reforms. The model is used to *simulate* the effect of trade policy changes on the distribution of household welfare (household expenditure per capita). He finds evidence of a pro-poor bias caused by the reform. On average, poor households gained more from reforms than did middle-income households. However, the drawback of this approach is that predictions of the model depend crucially on parameter estimates that are typically not known (e.g., wage-price elasticities) and are difficult to estimate consistently with time-series data on wages and prices when many other policies changed along with trade (see Goldberg and Pavcnik, forthcoming, for a discussion of this paper).

[8]These studies use a two-step methodology. First, they use household survey data to estimate "industry wage premia," defined as the part of worker wages that is explained by a worker's industry affiliation after controlling for observable worker characteristics (e.g., schooling, experience, and so on). Second, the estimated industry wage premia are regressed on measures of trade reform by industry.

---

advanced in the use of ICT. The adverse labor demand effects of ICT appear to be stronger at the early stages of ICT adoption, before the needed adjustments in workers' education have taken place.

Changes in labor market policies have had a positive effect on the labor share in Anglo-

Saxon countries, but a much more modest effect on average in Europe, particularly in large European economies where labor policies are estimated to have actually contributed to a decline in the labor share. The contribution of labor market policies is driven primarily by the changes in the tax wedge and unemployment

Figure 5.13. Advanced Economies: Contributions to the Annual Change in the Labor Share by Skill Level[1]
(Percentage points)

While technological change affected mostly the income share of labor in unskilled sectors, the labor income share in skilled sectors was more affected by labor globalization.

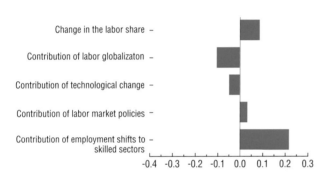

Labor in Skilled Sectors

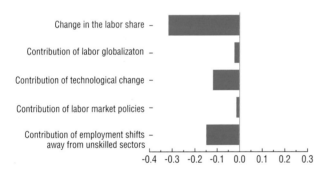

Labor in Unskilled Sectors

Source: IMF staff calculations.
[1]1982–2002 or longest period available. 1986–2001 for Japan, as changes in the relative import price in earlier years reflected the yen's strong appreciation rather than globalization. The contributions are based on estimated regression coefficients and average annual changes in the respective variables by country (see Appendix 5.1).

benefit replacement.[22] The decline in the tax wedge in Anglo-Saxon countries, especially in the United States, benefited the labor share, while in Europe the labor share was hurt by a rise in unemployment benefit replacement rates.

Turning to look at the skilled and unskilled sectors separately, the main factor affecting the income share of labor in unskilled sectors over the sample period, beyond the shift of employment toward skilled sectors, is technological change (Figure 5.13). This result is consistent with the belief that computers and other ICT equipment act as a substitute for unskilled labor, but they tend to complement skilled labor. On the other hand, labor globalization contributed to a decline in the income share of labor in skilled sectors, much more so than in unskilled sectors. This is in line with earlier findings that the increase in offshoring was mostly driven by the offshoring of skilled inputs rather than unskilled inputs. However, this was more than offset by the shift of employment from unskilled sectors to skilled sectors and the income share of labor in skilled sectors actually increased moderately.[23]

Of course, the effects on labor shares do not by themselves give the full picture of how workers' well-being is affected by forces of globalization and technological change. These factors also influence output and total labor compensa-

[22]The other variables, namely, employment protection legislation, product market regulation, and union density, did not have significant effects. The analysis was expanded to investigate whether some labor market institutions tend to amplify or attenuate the impact of labor globalization and technological progress. Although strict employment protection legislation does not appear to have any effect on its own, there is some evidence that it tends to increase the adverse effects of labor globalization on labor shares. A more flexible labor market may thus contribute to limiting the decline in the overall labor share caused by globalization.

[23]Workers in unskilled sectors have also benefited somewhat less from labor market policy changes. Although product market regulation has a negligible impact on the overall labor share, it seems to benefit the income share of labor in unskilled sectors. Hence, the reduction in product market regulation over the sample period had a negative effect on this income share.

tion. The model results imply that on average, in advanced economies, the decline in traded goods prices yielded about a 6 percent increase in both output and total labor compensation, in real terms, over 25 years.[24] Thus, although the labor share went down, globalization of labor as manifested in cheaper imports in advanced economies has increased the "size of the pie" to be shared among all citizens, resulting in a net gain in total workers' compensation in real terms (Figure 5.14).[25]

In sum, the econometric analysis suggests that both labor globalization and technological change have been important factors behind the observed decline in labor shares in advanced economies. The rapid progress in ICT has had a particularly strong effect on the unskilled sectors. The role of labor market policies has differed across countries, with positive effects largest in the United States and much more modest on average in Europe (and negative in some countries). Finally, global competition has brought down international trade prices. Cheaper imports have increased the size of real total labor compensation, implying that workers have participated in the benefits of the bigger economic "pie," although their share of it has declined.

[24]This result was calculated as follows. The model allows for deriving elasticities of labor compensation to trade prices: on average, a 1 percent decline in the relative price of imports raises real total labor compensation by 0.5 percent, while a 1 percent decline in the relative price of exports lowers it by a somewhat smaller 0.4 percent. Combining these elasticities with the actual average changes in relative export and import prices implies an average annual increase in labor compensation of about 0.2 percent on average in advanced economies (or about 6 percent if compounded over 25 years). The increase in output implied by the change in trade prices is just the difference between the percent change of total labor compensation and the percent change of the labor share (which is very small in this case).

[25]It should also be noted that a comprehensive evaluation of the impact of globalization on workers' financial means needs to go beyond labor compensation and to take into account an increase in direct and indirect asset ownership (see the September 2006 *World Economic Outlook*).

Figure 5.14. Effects of Changes in Trade Prices on Labor Share, Output, and Labor Compensation[1]
(Percent)

Although on the whole the labor share went down, the globalization of labor increases the size of the pie to be shared among all citizens, resulting in a net gain in workers' compensation in most countries.

Impact of Change in Trade Prices on Annual Change in Labor Share

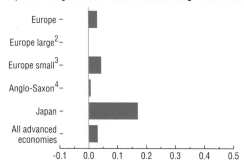

Impact of Change in Trade Prices on Annual Change in Output

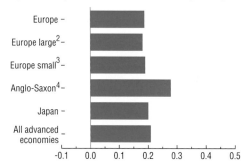

Impact of Change in Trade Prices on Annual Change in Labor Compensation

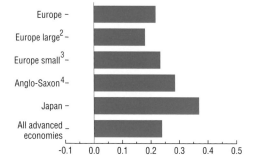

Source: IMF staff calculations.
[1]1980–2004 or longest period available. 1986–2004 for Japan, as changes in the relative import price in earlier years reflected the yen's strong appreciation rather than globalization. The effects are based on estimated regression coefficients and average annual changes in the respective variables by country (see Appendix 5.1).
[2]Europe large includes France, Germany, Italy, and Spain.
[3]Europe small covers Austria, Belgium, Denmark, Finland, Ireland, the Netherlands, Norway, Portugal, and Sweden.
[4]Anglo-Saxon countries include Australia, Canada, the United Kingdom, and the United States.

Summary and Policy Implications

There has been a dramatic increase in the size of the effective global labor force over the past two decades, with one measure suggesting it has risen fourfold. This expansion is expected to continue in the coming years. The UN projects a 40 percent rise in the world's working-age population by 2050, and trade openness will continue to grow, especially in services. Indeed, tentative projections suggest that the effective global labor supply could more than double again by 2050.[26]

The global pool of labor can be accessed by advanced economies through imports and immigration. Trade is the more important and faster-expanding channel, in large part because immigration remains very restricted in many countries. Contrary to popular perceptions, the intensity of offshoring of the production of intermediates is still small in the overall economy, although the manufacturing sector is more affected because of its greater tradability. Imports of offshored intermediates have also been growing somewhat more slowly than total trade.

The integration of workers from emerging market and developing countries into the global workforce has produced important benefits for advanced economies. Export opportunities have expanded considerably. It has provided access to cheaper imported goods and has enabled companies to operate more efficiently. This has boosted productivity and output, and contributed to rising real labor compensation. For emerging market economies, the ongoing integration of labor into the global marketplace has benefited workers, with manufacturing wages rising rapidly.

[26]This projection is based on the medium variant of the UN projections of working-age population and on the assumption that the ratio of non-oil exports to GDP will continue expanding at the rate observed in recent years (see Appendix 5.1). World Bank (2006) also provides projections of the world's workforce until 2030 and projects that although the vast majority of the world's workforce will remain unskilled, the supply of skilled workers is likely to grow faster than that of unskilled workers.

Nevertheless, labor globalization has negatively affected the share of income accruing to labor in the advanced economies (the labor share). It is, however, only one of several factors that have affected the labor share over the past two decades. Rapid technological change—especially in the information and communications sectors—has had a bigger impact, particularly on the labor share in unskilled sectors. This is broadly consistent with findings highlighted in a recent joint study by the International Labor Office and the World Trade Organization (2007).

Against this background, the increasing globalization of labor and ongoing technological changes raise important challenges for policymakers in the advanced economies. They must seek to harness the benefits that the growing pool of global labor is creating. This means continuing along the path of trade liberalization, while ensuring that domestic economies are sufficiently flexible to be able to adjust and respond to the pressures of globalization. At the same time, it is important to be fully cognizant of adjustment costs, and policies do need to support those people who are negatively affected by labor market globalization and technological changes. In broad terms, policies need to respond along three dimensions:

- *Improve the functioning of labor markets.* Steps to reduce tax wedges to enable workers to take home a larger proportion of their gross pay and to ensure that unemployment benefit replacement rates do not deter workers from seeking employment have helped a number of countries adjust to the pressures of globalization. The duration of unemployment benefits and the work availability requirements are also important (see Annett, 2006; and Bassanini and Duval, 2006). Moreover, policies that increase the flexibility of the economy and thereby enable workers to move more easily from declining to expanding areas of the economy help the process of adjustment. A variety of country-specific approaches are possible, as demonstrated by the range of experience of successful reformers in western Europe (see Box 2.2). Reform packages also have to be designed with fiscal consequences in mind.

- *Improve access to education and training.* Developing workers' skills is necessary for keeping up with rapid technological change and for continuing innovation. Skilled sectors have been better able to adapt to changing conditions caused by the ICT revolution than unskilled sectors. Further, countries that started adopting ICT and training workers in this area earlier experienced less decline in their labor share. Workers must also be ready to compete with the growing pool of skilled workers in emerging markets, especially those in Asia. Beyond increases in spending on education and training, the quality of this spending is crucial. Experience shows that evaluation and targeting of training are important to maximize its impact.

- *Ensure adequate social protection for workers during the adjustment period.* This includes providing adequate income support to cushion, but not obstruct, the process of change, and also making health care less dependent on continued employment and increasing the portability of pension benefits in some countries. The latter would also enhance the flexibility of the economy by facilitating the move of workers from declining sectors to expanding sectors. Whether measures specifically targeted at workers who have been displaced by international trade are desirable is less clear (see, e.g., OECD, 2005). The fact that these workers may face special hurdles reintegrating into the labor market as they are often older and less educated, and their skills are specific to declining industries or occupations, argues in favor of such measures. Also, minimizing losses for such workers may increase support for the international economic integration process. However, it may be difficult (even conceptually) to differentiate between job losses caused by globalization and those caused by other factors, since most labor markets are characterized by high rates of turnover and year-to-year earnings vari-

ability. If trade-displaced workers are treated more generously, including, for instance, by being provided supplementary wage subsidies, such compensation should be structured to avoid dulling incentives to search actively for new jobs.

Appendix 5.1. Data Sources and Methods

The main authors of this appendix are Florence Jaumotte and Irina Tytell.

Variable Definitions and Data Sources

This section provides further details on the construction of the variables used in this chapter and the sources of the data.

Sectoral Classification

Throughout the chapter, the analysis is carried out both for the aggregate economy and for a disaggregation of the economy by skill category. The classification of trade and labor into skill categories is based on the skill intensity of the sector. Hence skilled exports are exports of goods and services typically produced by skill-intensive sectors. The skilled labor share is the share of national income that accrues to workers in skill-intensive sectors. One drawback of this approach is that it does not capture changes that occur between skilled and unskilled workers within sectors. A more refined approach was, however, not feasible because of the lack of cross-country data on the wages of production (unskilled) and nonproduction (skilled) workers, which would have been needed to calculate labor shares and labor compensation of skilled and unskilled workers.

The classification of sectors into skilled and unskilled is based on the share of skilled workers in the labor force of the sector, where a person is considered skilled if he or she has at least upper secondary education. Data on the average fraction of skilled labor in each sector (across 16 OECD economies from 1994 to 1998) are from Jean and Nicoletti (2002). The chapter classifies 18 sectors (from the International Standard

Figure 5.15. Advanced Economies' Labor Income Share, Labor Compensation, and Employment: Robustness to Alternative Skill Classification[1]

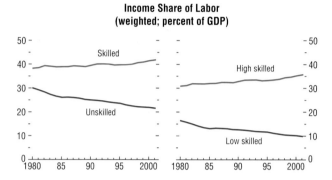

Income Share of Labor
(weighted; percent of GDP)

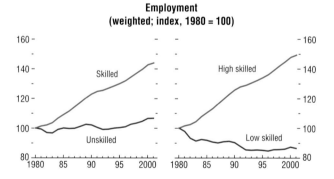

Real Labor Compensation per Worker
(weighted; index, 1980 = 100)

Employment
(weighted; index, 1980 = 100)

Sources: Haver Analytics; International Labor Organization, Labor Statistics Database; OECD, Employment and Labour Market Statistics, National Accounts Statistics, and STAN Industrial Database; United Nations, *National Accounts Statistics* (2004); and IMF staff calculations.
[1]For the analysis by skill level, advanced economies include Austria, Belgium, Canada, Denmark, Finland, France, Germany, Italy, Japan, Norway, Portugal, Sweden, the United Kingdom, and the United States; weighted using series on GDP in U.S. dollars from the World Economic Outlook database.

Table 5.1. Classification of Sectors by Skill Intensity

Main Classification	Alternative Classification
Unskilled	Low skilled
Agriculture	Agriculture
Mining	Mining
Food and tobacco	Food and tobacco
Textiles, apparel, and leather	Textiles, apparel, and leather
Wood	Wood
Other nonmetal products	Other nonmetal products
Metals and metal products	Metals and metal products
Transport equipment	Construction
Other manufacturing	
Construction	Medium skilled
Trade, hotels, and restaurants	Paper and publishing
	Transport equipment
Skilled	Other manufacturing
Paper and publishing	Utilities
Fuel, chemicals, and rubber	Trade, hotels, and restaurants
Machinery and equipment	Transport and communications
Utilities	
Transport and communications	High skilled
Business services	Fuel, chemicals, and rubber
Social and personal services	Machinery and equipment
	Business services
	Social and personal services

Sources: OECD; and IMF staff estimates.

Industrial Classification, Revision 3) into two broad aggregates, namely, unskilled and skilled sectors, as reported in Table 5.1. In order to test the robustness of the results, an alternative three-category split was also used, which distinguishes between low-skill, medium-skill, and high-skill sectors. Figure 5.15 shows that the patterns of the labor shares (and real labor compensation per worker and employment) for the narrower high- and low-skilled aggregates are similar to those for the broader skilled and unskilled aggregates.

Labor Compensation and Labor Shares

Labor compensation was calculated by augmenting the compensation of employees for the income of other categories of workers (self-employed, employers, and family workers). Following Gollin (2002) and for data availability reasons, it was assumed that other categories of workers earn the same average wage as employees. Labor compensation is hence the product of the compensation of employees and the ratio of total employment and employees.[27] Other correction procedures (see Gollin, 2002, for a review), for which the data are not widely available, yield similar patterns over the subset of the sample used in this chapter for which the data are available. This correction was applied at both the aggregate and the sectoral level of data. When sectoral data on employees or total employment were not available, the following procedure was used:

- the ratio of total employment to total employees was assumed to be the same as in previous years or, if it was not available for any year, it was assumed to be equal to the average for this sector across other OECD economies; and
- the sum of "nonemployee" workers across sectors was constrained to add up to the total for the aggregate economy by scaling the imputed number of nonemployee workers proportionately.

The variables are defined as follows. Real labor compensation is labor compensation deflated by the CPI index from the World Economic Outlook database. The labor share is calculated as the ratio of labor compensation and value added at basic prices.[28] The share of labor in skilled (unskilled) sectors is the ratio of labor compensation in skilled (unskilled) sectors to the economy-wide value added.

The main data source is the OECD's Structural Analysis (STAN) Database. However, several other sources were used to fill in missing data and extend the series to the most recent year possible. For employees' compensation and value added, these include the OECD's National Accounts Statistics, the UN's *National Accounts Statistics*, and Haver Analytics (for Japan). For data on total employment and employees, the additional sources were the OECD's Employment and Labor Market Statistics Database and the ILO Labor Statistics Database. Due to data

availability reasons, the calculations were limited to advanced OECD economies.

Manufacturing Wages

Manufacturing wages for advanced and developing economies are from the UNIDO Industrial Statistics Database. They were converted into constant purchasing power parity (PPP) dollars using CPI indices and PPP exchange rates from the World Economic Outlook database. The data for China are from the CEIC Asia database.

Immigration

The data on foreign labor force are from the OECD's *Trends in International Migration* (2003 edition for all countries except the United States). For the United States, the data are from the U.S. Census Bureau and the U.S. Bureau of Labor Statistics. Data for Italy, the Netherlands, Norway, and the United Kingdom are for foreign employment instead of labor force. Data for Australia, Canada, and the United States refer to foreign-born labor force instead of foreign labor force. The available series were extended backward using growth rates from the stock of foreign (or foreign-born, in the case of Australia, Canada, and the United States) population when available, and the missing years were interpolated.

Data on emigration for 1990 and 2000 are from Docquier and Marfouk (2005) and refer to the stock of emigrants to the OECD economies.

Trade and Offshoring

Data on trade used in the chapter are from a variety of sources. Aggregate data on trade quantities and prices are from the World Economic Outlook database, including for the non-oil goods and services aggregates. Sectoral trade data for advanced economies (used to construct skilled and unskilled trade) are from the OECD STAN Industrial Database (for manufacturing) and from the OECD International Trade in Services Database (for services). For developing countries, sectoral trade data were obtained from the World Integrated Trade Solution (for

---

[27]Korea was excluded from the sample because some of the income of the self-employed is already in the employees' compensation, making it impossible to apply the correction (see also Young, 1995 and 2003).

[28]The exceptions are Japan, where value added is measured at producer prices, and the United States, where it is measured at market prices.

manufacturing) and from the IMF's *Balance of Payments Statistics* (for services). Data on manufacturing trade of advanced OECD economies by source country are from the OECD STAN Bilateral Trade Database. The services data for India were extended using the CEIC Asia database.

Offshore outsourcing is the outsourcing of intermediate production to companies in locations outside the country, which can be foreign affiliates or independent companies. It is measured by the imports of intermediate inputs, as provided in the OECD Input-Output Tables (1995, 2002, and 2006 editions). These tables assume that an industry uses an import of a particular product in proportion to its total use of that product ("the import proportionality assumption"), and this proportion is the economy-wide share of imports in domestic demand. The measure used in the chapter only includes nonfuel manufacturing and services inputs. Imported intermediate inputs of a sector are scaled by either the sector's gross output or its total use of intermediates. Sectoral offshoring intensities are then aggregated based on sectoral gross output weights. Finally, the data on the overall offshoring intensity are interpolated for missing years.

For years beyond 2000, the OECD data were extended using the latest input-output table available (2000 for most countries) and updating the data on the import proportions for each category of intermediate input. The latter was approximated by the share of imports in domestic absorption (consumption and investment) for that category of products (sector). Data on imports by sectors are from the OECD STAN Industrial Database for manufacturing and from the OECD International Trade in Services Database for services. Data on value added by sector (used to calculate absorption) are from a combination of the OECD STAN Industrial Database and the Groningen 60-Industry Database.[29]

---

[29]Sectoral offshoring intensities were aggregated using sectoral value-added weights, due to the lack of data on sectoral gross output for the later years. The historical and extended series were then spliced using growth rates.

Imports of final goods and services are constructed as a residual by subtracting imported intermediate inputs from total imports.

Global Labor Supply

Several measures of the global labor supply are calculated, including the world's working-age population, the world's labor force, and an export-weighted world's labor force. The latter attempts to measure the presence of the countries' labor supply in the international market and is calculated as the sum across countries of national labor forces, each weighted by the country's ratio of non-oil exports to GDP (Harrigan and Balaban, 1999). The export-to-GDP ratio is capped to one to limit the weight of countries specialized in re-export trade. Data on working-age population and labor force are from various sources, including the World Economic Outlook, the World Bank's World Development Indicators, the United Nations Population Projections, and the CEIC Asia databases. The global labor supply by education level is calculated using the Barro-Lee (2000) data set on educational attainment of the population aged 15 or more. It is assumed that the share of the labor force with higher education is about the same as the share of the population aged 15 or more with higher education. For the years 2001–05, this share was extrapolated linearly for each country.

The projections of the global labor supply for 2006–50 are based on the UN projections of the working-age population. The labor force participation rate in each country is assumed to converge by 2050 to the current rate of labor force participation in the United States. Assuming instead that labor force participation rates remain at their current levels does not have much effect on the global labor supply projections. Projections for the export-to-GDP ratio are based on country-specific *World Economic Outlook* projections until 2012, and on the trend increase observed in the world export-to-GDP ratio for later years. Under these assumptions, the cumulative growth in the export-weighted global labor force over 2005–50 could range from a low of 120 percent (under the low variant of the population projections) to a high of 190 percent (under the high variant).

Capital Stock and ICT Capital

Fajnzylber and Lederman (1999) are the source of the capital stock series for the entire economy. This data set extends the capital stock series estimated by Nehru and Dhareshwar (1993) by adding the annual flow of gross fixed capital formation and assuming a 4 percent depreciation rate to the preexisting stock of capital.

Jorgenson and Vu (2005) provide series on IT investment using national expenditure data for computer hardware, software, and telecommunications equipment. A perpetual inventory method applies varying depreciation rates to estimate IT capital stock. This method assumes a geometric depreciation rate of 31.5 percent and a service life of 7 years for computer hardware, 31.5 percent and 5 years for software, and 11 percent and 11 years for telecommunications equipment.

Labor Market Policy Indicators

The indicators of labor and product market policies were provided by Bassanini and Duval (2006). The indicators are defined as follows:

- Average unemployment benefit replacement rate is the average of the unemployment benefit replacement rates corresponding to multiple income, family, and unemployment duration situations. These include two income situations (100 percent and 67 percent of the average production worker earnings), three family situations (single, with dependent spouse, with spouse in work), and three unemployment durations (1st year, 2nd and 3rd years, and 4th and 5th years of unemployment). The original data are from the OECD's Benefits and Wages Database.
- Labor tax wedge is the difference between the labor cost to the employer and the corresponding net take-home pay of the employee for a single-earner couple with two children earning 100 percent of the average production worker earnings. It is thus the sum of personal income tax and all social security contributions expressed as a percentage of the total labor cost. The original data are from the OECD Taxing Wages Database.
- Employment protection legislation is the OECD summary indicator of the stringency of Employment Protection Legislation. The original data are from the *OECD Employment Outlook* (2004).
- Product market regulation is the OECD summary indicator of regulatory impediments to product market competition in seven nonmanufacturing industries (gas, electricity, post, telecom, passenger air transport, railways passenger and freight services, and road freight). The original data are from Conway and others (2006).
- Union density measures the share of workers affiliated with a trade union. The original data are from the *OECD Employment Outlook* (2004).

Econometric Approach

This section presents the model used to examine the relationship between globalization and labor shares and reports the results from the estimations.

Methodology

The econometric approach used in this chapter is based on a model used frequently in the trade literature (see Feenstra, 2004; Harrigan, 1998; and Kohli, 1991). The model uses a revenue function with fixed factor quantities (of labor and capital) and exogenous product prices (of exports, imports, and domestic absorption). It assumes that firms are maximizing profits, all markets are competitive, and factors can move freely between firms. The revenue function is linearly homogeneous and concave in factor quantities and convex in product prices. It is typically specified as a flexible translogarithmic, or translog, form (Christensen, Jorgenson, and Lau, 1975).

Using the translog revenue function, product and factor shares can be obtained as

$$S_i = \frac{p_i y_i}{G} = \alpha_i + \Sigma\alpha_{ij}\ln p_j + \Sigma\gamma_{ij}\ln v_j + \Sigma\varphi_{ij}z_j$$

$$R_i = \frac{w_i v_i}{G} = \beta_i + \Sigma\gamma_{ij}\ln p_j + \Sigma\beta_{ij}\ln v_j + \Sigma\phi_{ij}z_j,$$

where S are product shares, R are factor shares, p are product prices, v are factor quantities, and z are shift variables. The shift variables capture any factors that could be expected to shift the revenue function, for example, measures of technological progress or offshoring, as suggested by Feenstra (2004). The share equations are subject to a number of cross-equation restrictions that follow from symmetry and linear homogeneity of the corresponding revenue function.

Given the theme of this chapter, the estimations focused primarily on the labor share equations. The following equation was adopted as the basic specification for the analysis:

$$R_L = \beta_L + \gamma_{EL}\ln\frac{p_E}{p_A} + \gamma_{ML}\ln\frac{p_M}{p_A} + \beta_{LL}\ln\frac{L}{K}$$
$$+ \phi_{LX}X + \phi_{LM}\frac{L_M}{L} + \phi_{LC}\frac{K_{ICT}}{K} + \phi_{LC2}\left(\frac{K_{ICT}}{K}\right)^2 + \varepsilon_L,$$

where P_E, P_M, and P_A are prices of exports, imports, and absorption; L is labor; K is capital; X is offshoring; L_M is immigrant employment; and K_{ICT} is ICT capital. The relative prices and quantities are used to impose the necessary homogeneity restrictions. Labor shares are corrected for the income of other (nonemployee) categories of workers, prices and the capital stock variables are measured in 2000 U.S. dollars, and labor stock variables are represented by employment. Offshoring is measured as a share of imported intermediate inputs in total intermediate inputs, immigration is captured as a share of immigrant employment in total domestic employment, and ICT capital is modeled as a share of ICT capital in the total capital stock (more detail on these measurements is provided above). The effect of ICT capital is represented by a quadratic function

to reflect potential nonlinearities associated with the need for learning the new technology: the adverse effect on wages and employment is likely to be greatest before workers acquire the skills necessary to effectively handle the new equipment. The model was estimated on a panel of 18 countries over 1982–2002 using country fixed effects. The basic specification was extended to include several measures of labor market policies, including the tax wedge, the replacement rate of unemployment benefits, indices of product market regulation, employment protection legislation, and union density.[30]

A potential concern with the accuracy of the estimation is that the variables related to labor globalization—trade prices, offshoring, and immigration—may be endogenous. Trade prices are unlikely to be exogenous for countries whose economic size is sufficiently large.[31] Reverse causality or common third factors may bias the effects of offshoring and immigration on the labor share. To address this concern, an instrumental variables estimation was used with variables reflecting domestic and foreign supply and demand conditions, as well as lags of the potentially endogenous variables as instruments. Specifically, the list of instruments included the share of government consumption in GDP; the consumption tax rate; the (log of) total population; the (log of) export-weighted real GDP of trading partners; the distance-weighted export-adjusted employment in the rest of the world (a measure of the global labor supply); and lags of (logs of) relative trade prices, offshoring, and immigration.

In addition to the aggregate labor share equation, a system of labor share equations for skilled and unskilled workers was also estimated as follows:

---

[30]A specification including interaction terms between these policy variables and measures of labor globalization and technological progress was also explored.

[31]The price of absorption could also be affected by changes in the labor share, which reflect changes in unit labor costs.

$$R_S = \beta_S + \sum_{k=E,M} \gamma_{kS} \ln \frac{p_k}{p_A} + \sum_{k=S,U} \beta_{Sk} \ln \frac{L_k}{K} + \phi_{SX} X$$
$$+ \phi_{SM} \frac{L_M}{L} + \phi_{SC} \frac{K_{ICT}}{K} + \phi_{SC2} \left(\frac{K_{ICT}}{K}\right)^2 + \varepsilon_S$$

$$R_U = \beta_U + \sum_{k=E,M} \gamma_{kU} \ln \frac{p_k}{p_A} + \sum_{k=S,U} \beta_{kU} \ln \frac{L_k}{K} + \phi_{UX} X$$
$$+ \phi_{UM} \frac{L_M}{L} + \phi_{UC} \frac{K_{ICT}}{K} + \phi_{UC} \left(\frac{K_{ICT}}{K}\right)^2 + \varepsilon_U,$$

where S and U denote skilled and unskilled, respectively, and the other variables are the same as above. A symmetry restriction postulates that the coefficients on the (log of) labor-capital ratio of the unskilled in the first equation and the skilled in the second equation are the same. This system was augmented to include country fixed effects and the measures of labor market policies, and was estimated by iterated three-stage least squares using the instruments listed above.

Estimation Results

The estimation results from the aggregate labor share equation are shown in Table 5.2. Most of the variables are statistically significant and have expected signs:

- Higher relative export prices and lower relative import prices are associated with the lower labor share. This is consistent with advanced economies' exports being relatively capital intensive and their imports, which increasingly come from developing countries, being relatively labor intensive.
- Offshoring and immigration are negatively related to the labor share, consistent with the rising global labor supply exerting a negative effect on domestic labor demand. The coefficients on these variables in the instrumental variables regression are somewhat larger in absolute value, suggesting the presence of reverse causality: a lower labor share, which reflects lower unit labor costs, makes offshoring less appealing for domestic firms and makes immigration less attractive for foreign workers.
- Technological progress appears to have a nonlinear effect on the labor share, consistent with

Table 5.2. Impact of Labor Globalization and Technological Change on Labor Shares

Dependent Variable: Labor Share	Fixed Effects Estimation (excluding labor market policies)	Fixed Effects Estimation	Instrumental Variables Estimation
Relative export price (log of)	−0.117***	−0.113***	−0.165***
Relative import price (log of)	0.076**	0.087***	0.138***
Labor-capital ratio (log of)	0.055**	0.015	−0.025
Offshoring	−0.196*	−0.156*	−0.285***
Immigration	−0.627***	−0.553***	−0.746***
ICT capital	−2.871***	−2.643***	−3.517***
ICT capital squared	56.407***	44.962***	55.598***
Tax wedge	...	−0.002*	−0.002***
Unemployment benefits	...	−0.001***	−0.001***
Fixed effects	Yes	Yes	Yes
Observations	231	225	208
R-squared	0.61	0.62	
Anderson test	...	...	151.63***
Hansen test	...	...	6.61

Source: IMF staff calculations.
Note: * denotes statistical significance at the 10 percent level; ** denotes statistical significance at the 5 percent level; and *** denotes statistical significance at the 1 percent level. Standard errors are heteroscedasticity and autocorrelation robust. ICT = information and communications technology.

the idea that labor-saving innovations initially create the need for extra learning on the part of workers, but enhance their productivity later on as the necessary skills are acquired.

- Among the policy variables, only higher tax wedges and unemployment benefit replacement rates are associated with a lower labor share, reflecting labor market rigidities stemming from these policies.[32] A nonlinear specification including interaction terms with labor globalization and technological progress variables suggested, in addition, that employment protection legislation tends to increase the effects of these variables on the labor share.

---

[32]Other labor and product market variables, specifically, the index of employment protection legislation, the index of product market regulation, and the union density measure, were not statistically significant and were, therefore, excluded from the final specification.

Table 5.3. Impact of Labor Globalization and Technological Change on Skilled and Unskilled Labor Shares

Dependent Variable	Fixed Effects Estimation		Instrumental Variables Estimation		Three-Stage Least Square Estimation	
	Skilled labor share	Unskilled labor share	Skilled labor share	Unskilled labor share	Skilled labor share	Unskilled labor share
Log of:						
Relative export price	−0.072***	−0.049***	−0.117***	−0.060***	−0.115***	−0.058***
Relative import price	0.053***	0.031**	0.089***	0.041***	0.097***	0.044***
Skilled labor-capital ratio	0.093**	−0.203***	0.075**	−0.210***	0.156***	−0.163***
Unskilled labor-capital ratio	−0.089***	0.181***	−0.098***	0.177***	−0.163***	0.143***
Offshoring	−0.134*	−0.016	−0.203***	−0.052	−0.191***	−0.043
Immigration	−0.507***	−0.162**	−0.678***	−0.225**	−0.663***	−0.216***
ICT capital	−0.808	−0.922*	−1.413*	−1.099**	−2.046***	−1.409***
ICT capital squared	22.358*	10.458	29.792***	13.346*	38.688***	17.860***
Tax wedge	−0.001	−0.001**	−0.002***	−0.001***	−0.002***	−0.001***
Unemployment benefits	−0.001**	−0.000*	−0.001***	−0.000**	−0.001***	−0.000***
Product market regulation	0.000	0.002	0.001	0.002**	0.000	0.002**
Fixed effects	Yes	Yes	Yes	Yes	Yes	Yes
Observations	219	219	202	202	202	202
R-squared	0.53	0.94	. . .	. . .	. . .	. . .
Anderson test	. . .	. . .	140.83***	140.83***	. . .	. . .
Hansen test	. . .	. . .	7.7	8.4	. . .	. . .

Source: IMF staff calculations.

Note: * denotes statistical significance at the 10 percent level; ** denotes statistical significance at the 5 percent level; and *** denotes statistical significance at the 1 percent level. Standard errors are heteroscedasticity and autocorrelation robust. ICT = information and communications technology.

The findings are generally robust to the exclusion of outliers (identified in terms of their influence on predicted values and the variance-covariance matrix of the estimates) and of individual countries.[33] They are also robust to splitting the import price into that of oil and non-oil imports (while the oil price has a statistically significant effect on the labor share, it is small in magnitude). The coefficients on the ICT capital stock, its square, and offshoring become statistically insignificant when time effects are included. This is not surprising since time effects are often used in empirical studies to capture the effect of worldwide technological progress and other broad global trends. The time effects show a declining pattern over time, consistent with the negative effect of the growth

in the ICT capital stock and offshoring on the labor share. The coefficients on the share of ICT capital are more robust to the inclusion of time effects when measured as a share of investment, rather than of capital stock. Similarly, the coefficient on offshoring of skilled inputs is more robust to the inclusion of time effects than that on total offshoring.

The estimation results from the labor share equations for skilled and unskilled sectors are shown in Table 5.3. The first two columns contain independent fixed effects estimations of the two equations, the middle two columns present independent instrumental variables estimations, and the last two columns show the system estimation with the cross-equation restriction imposed. Labor globalization and technological progress appear to have somewhat different effects on the labor shares of workers in skilled and unskilled sectors. Labor globalization has a somewhat stronger effect on the skilled sectors, in line, for example,

[33]Partial correlation plots, showing the correlation between the labor share and each regressor after controlling for the other explanatory variables, confirm that the estimated relationships are quite robust.

with more offshoring occurring in the skilled sectors. Technological change affects both skill groups negatively, but the effect is less strong for the skilled, consistent with the nonlinearity due to learning requirements, as suggested above. These results should be treated as somewhat more tentative, however, given that the classification by skill is based on broad economic sectors.

The contributions of the various factors to the change in the labor shares shown in the main text are calculated as the average annual change in the respective variable multiplied by the corresponding coefficient estimate. The averages across country groups are weighted by the number of years of data available for each country, so that countries with more data receive a larger weight in these averages. These contributions allow introducing cross-country differences in the role of various factors, although they do not fully reflect cross-country heterogeneity, since the estimated coefficients are the same for all countries in the sample.

Elasticity Calculations

The econometric model used in this chapter allows going beyond the effects of various factors on the labor share by computing the elasticities of labor compensation per worker and employment to these factors (Kohli, 1991).

The elasticities of labor compensation per worker to trade prices (given employment) are obtained as follows:

$$\varepsilon(W,p_i) = \frac{\gamma_{iL}}{R_L} + S_i,$$

where $i = E, M,$ and the output shares R_L and S_i are evaluated at the mean for each country.

The employment elasticities with respect to trade prices (given labor compensation per worker) are obtained as follows:

$$\varepsilon(L,p_i) = -\frac{\varepsilon(W,p_i)}{\varepsilon(W,L)},$$

where $\varepsilon(W,L) = \dfrac{\beta_{LL}}{R_L} + R_L - 1$ and $i = E, M.$

Combining these elasticities gives the elasticity of the total labor compensation to trade prices:

$$\varepsilon(WL,p_i) = \varepsilon(W,p_i) + \varepsilon(L,p_i),$$

where $i = E, M.$ It is important to point out that these elasticities are derived from the model that assumes fixed prices, hence possible price adjustments are not taken into account in these calculations.[34]

To compute the actual percent changes in the total labor compensation resulting from changes in trade prices, these elasticities are multiplied by the average percent changes in relative trade prices in each country. The averages across country groups are weighted by the number of years of data available for each country, so that countries with more data receive a larger weight in these averages. The results are shown in the main text.

References

Amiti, Mary, and Shang-Jin Wei, 2005, "Fear of Service Outsourcing: Is It Justified?" *Economic Policy*, Vol. 20 (April), pp. 308–47.

———, 2006, "Service Offshoring and Productivity: Evidence from the United States," NBER Working Paper No. 11926 (Cambridge, Massachusetts: National Bureau of Economic Research).

Annett, Anthony, 2006, "Lessons from Successful Labor Market Reformers in Europe," in *Euro Area Policies: Selected Issues*, IMF Country Report No. 06/288 (Washington: International Monetary Fund).

Aydemir, Abdurrahman, and George J. Borjas, 2006, "A Comparative Analysis of the Labor Market Impact of International Migration: Canada, Mexico, and the United States," NBER Working Paper No. 12327 (Cambridge, Massachusetts: National Bureau of Economic Research).

Barro, Robert J., and Jong-Wha Lee, 2000, "International Data on Educational Attainment: Updates

[34]Further, the elasticities of the total labor compensation to import and export prices might be somewhat overestimated since the elasticity of the wage (employment) assumes constant employment (wage). However, the net effect of trade prices on total labor compensation should not be affected much.

and Implications," CID Working Paper No. 42 (Cambridge, Massachusetts: Center for International Development).

Bassanini, Andrea, and Romain Duval, 2006, "Employment Patterns in OECD Countries: Reassessing the Role of Policies and Institutions," OECD Economics Department Working Paper No. 486 (Paris: Organization for Economic Cooperation and Development).

Berg, Andrew, and Anne O. Krueger, 2003, "Trade, Growth, and Poverty: A Selective Survey," IMF Working Paper 03/30 (Washington: International Monetary Fund).

Blanchard, Olivier, 1998, "Revisiting European Unemployment: Unemployment, Capital Accumulation and Factor Prices," NBER Working Paper No. 6566 (Cambridge, Massachusetts: National Bureau of Economic Research).

Blinder, Alan S., 2006, "Offshoring: The Next Industrial Revolution?" *Foreign Affairs,* Vol. 85 (March/April).

Borjas, George J., 1994, "The Economics of Immigration," *Journal of Economic Literature,* Vol. 32 (December), pp. 1667–717.

———, 1995, "The Economic Benefits from Immigration," *Journal of Economic Perspectives,* Vol. 9 (Spring), pp. 3–22.

Cardarelli, Roberto, and Kenichi Ueda, 2004, "Domestic and Global Perspectives of Migration to the United States," in *United States: Selected Issues,* IMF Country Report No. 04/228 (Washington: International Monetary Fund).

Christensen, Laurits R., Dale W. Jorgenson, and Lawrence J. Lau, 1975, "Transcendental Logarithmic Utility Functions," *American Economic Review,* Vol. 65 (June), pp. 367–83.

Conway, Paul, Donato de Rosa, Giuseppe Nicoletti, and Faye Steiner, 2006, "Regulation, Competition and Productivity Convergence," OECD Economics Department Working Paper No. 509 (Paris: Organization for Economic Cooperation and Development).

Davis, Donald R., and Prachi Mishra, 2007, "Stolper-Samuelson Is Dead, and Other Crimes of Both Theory and Data," in *Globalization and Poverty,* ed. by Ann Harrison (Chicago: University of Chicago Press and National Bureau of Economic Research).

Docquier, Frédéric, and Abdeslam Marfouk, 2005, "International Migration by Educational Attainment, 1990–2000," in *International Migration, Remit-*

tances and the Brain Drain, ed. by Ç. Özden and M. Schiff (Washington: World Bank).

Dutta, Puja Vasudeva, 2004, "Trade Protection and Inter-Industry Wages in India," PRUS Working Paper No. 27 (Sussex: Poverty Research Unit, Department of Economics, University of Sussex).

Edmonds, Eric, Nina Pavcnik, and Petia Topalova, 2007, "Trade Adjustment and Human Capital Investments: Evidence from Indian Tariff Reform," NBER Working Paper No. 12884 (Cambridge, Massachusetts: National Bureau of Economic Research).

Fajnzylber, Pablo, and Daniel Lederman, 1999, "Economic Reforms and Total Factor Productivity Growth in Latin America and the Caribbean (1950–95)—An Empirical Note," Policy Research Working Paper No. 2114 (Washington: World Bank).

Feenstra, Robert C., 2004, *Advanced International Trade: Theory and Evidence* (Princeton, New Jersey: Princeton University Press).

———, 2007, "Globalization and Its Impact on Labor," Global Economy Lecture 2007, Vienna Institute for International Economic Studies, Vienna, February 8. Available via the Internet: http://www.econ.ucdavis.edu/faculty/fzfeens/papers.html.

Feliciano, Zadia M., 2001, "Workers and Trade Liberalization: The Impact of Trade Reforms in Mexico on Wages and Employment," *Industrial and Labor Relations Review,* Vol. 55 (October), pp. 95–115.

Freeman, Richard B., 1995, "Are Your Wages Set in Beijing?" *Journal of Economic Perspectives,* Vol. 9 (Summer), pp. 15–32.

———, 2006, "Labor Market Imbalances: Shortages, or Surpluses, or Fish Stories?" paper presented at the Boston Federal Reserve Economic Conference, "Global Imbalances—As Giants Evolve," Chatham, Massachusetts, June 14–16.

Goh, Chor-Ching, and Beata S. Javorcik, 2007, "Trade Protection and Industry Wage Structure in Poland," in *Globalization and Poverty,* ed. by Ann Harrison (Chicago: University of Chicago Press and the National Bureau of Economic Research).

Goldberg, Pinelopi, and Nina Pavcnik, 2005, "Trade, Wages, and the Political Economy of Trade Protection: Evidence from the Colombian Trade Reforms," *Journal of International Economics,* Vol. 66 (May), pp. 75–105.

———, forthcoming, "Distributional Effects of Globalization in Developing Countries," *Journal of Economic Literature.*

Gollin, Douglas, 2002, "Getting Income Shares Right," *Journal of Political Economy*, Vol. 110 (April), pp. 458–74.

Greenwood, Michael J., Gary Hunt, and Ulrich Kohli, 1996, "The Short-Run and Long-Run Factor-Market Consequences of Immigration to the United States," *Journal of Regional Science*, Vol. 36 (February), pp. 43–66.

Grossman, Gene M., and Esteban Rossi-Hansberg, 2006, "The Rise of Offshoring: It's Not Wine for Cloth Anymore," paper presented at Federal Reserve Bank of Kansas City symposium, "The New Economic Geography: Effects and Policy Implications," Jackson Hole, Wyoming, August 24–26. Available via the Internet: http://www.kc.frb.org/PUBLICAT/SYMPOS/2006/PDF/Grossmanand-Rossi-Hansberg.paper.0831.pdf.

Gupta, Sanjeev, Catherine Pattillo, and Smita Wagh, 2007, "Impact of Remittances on Poverty and Financial Development in Sub-Saharan Africa," IMF Working Paper 07/38 (Washington: International Monetary Fund).

Guscina, Anastasia, 2006, "Effects of Globalization on Labor's Share in National Income," IMF Working Paper 06/294 (Washington: International Monetary Fund).

Hanson, Gordon, forthcoming, "Emigration, Labor Supply, and Earnings in Mexico," in *Mexican Immigration to the United States*, ed. by George Borjas (Chicago: University of Chicago Press and National Bureau of Economic Research).

———, 2007, "Globalization, Labor Income, and Poverty in Mexico," in *Globalization and Poverty*, ed. by Ann Harrison (Chicago: University of Chicago Press and National Bureau of Economic Research).

Harrigan, James, 1998, "International Trade and American Wages in General Equilibrium, 1967–1995," Staff Report No. 46 (New York: Federal Reserve Bank of New York).

———, and Rita A. Balaban, 1999, "U.S. Wages in General Equilibrium: The Effects of Prices, Technology, and Factor Supplies, 1963–1991," NBER Working Paper No. 6981 (Cambridge, Massachusetts: National Bureau of Economic Research).

Harrison, Anne E., 2002, "Has Globalization Eroded Labor's Share? Some Cross-Country Evidence" (unpublished; Berkeley, California: University of California at Berkeley).

International Labor Office and World Trade Organization, 2007, *Trade and Employment: Challenges for Policy Research* (Geneva: International Labor Organization).

Jean, Sébastien, and Giuseppe Nicoletti, 2002, "Product Market Regulation and Wage Premia in Europe and North America: An Empirical Investigation," OECD Economics Department Working Paper No. 318 (Paris: Organization for Economic Cooperation and Development).

Jensen, J. Bradford, and Lori G. Kletzer, 2005, "Tradable Services: Understanding the Scope and Impact of Services Outsourcing," IIE Working Paper No. 05-9 (Washington: Institute for International Economics).

Jorgenson, Dale W., and Khuong Vu, 2005, "Information Technology and the World Economy," *Scandinavian Journal of Economics*, Vol. 107 (December), pp. 631–50.

Katz, Larry F., and David H. Autor, 1999, "Changes in the Wage Structure and Earnings Inequality," in *Handbook of Labor Economics*, Vol. 3A, ed. by Orley C. Ashenfelter and David Card (Amsterdam: North-Holland).

Kohli, Ulrich, 1991, *Technology, Duality, and Foreign Trade: The GNP Function Approach to Modeling Imports and Exports* (Ann Arbor: University of Michigan Press).

Kumar, Utsav, and Prachi Mishra, forthcoming, "Trade Liberalization and Wage Inequality: Evidence from India," *Review of Development Economics*.

Lewer, Joshua J., and Hendrik Van den Berg, 2003, "How Large Is International Trade's Effect on Economic Growth?" *Journal of Economic Surveys*, Vol. 17 (July), pp. 363–96.

Mishra, Prachi, 2006, "Emigration and Brain-Drain: Evidence from the Caribbean," IMF Working Paper 06/25 (Washington: International Monetary Fund).

———, 2007, "Emigration and Wages in Source Countries: Evidence from Mexico," *Journal of Development Economics*, Vol. 82 (January), pp. 180–99.

Nehru, Vikram, and Ashok Dhareshwar, 1993, "A New Database on Physical Capital Stock: Sources, Methodology, and Results," *Revista de Análisis Económico*, Vol. 8, No. 1, pp. 37–59.

Olsen, Karsten Bjerring, 2006, "Productivity Impacts of Offshoring and Outsourcing: A Review," OECD Science, Technology and Industry Working Paper No. 2006/1 (Paris: Organization for Economic Cooperation and Development).

Organization for Economic Cooperation and Development (OECD), 2004, *OECD Employment Outlook* (Paris).

————, 2005, "Trade-Adjustment Costs in OECD Labour Markets: A Mountain or a Molehill?" in *OECD Employment Outlook* (Paris).

————, 2006a, "The Internationaliation of Production, International Outsourcing and OECD Labour Markets" (Paris).

————, 2006b, "Migration in OECD Countries: Labour Market Impact and Integration Issues" (Paris).

Pavcnik, Nina, Andreas Blom, Pinelopi Goldberg, and Norbert Schady, 2004, "Trade Liberalization and Industry Wage Structure: Evidence from Brazil," *World Bank Economic Review*, Vol. 18, No. 3, pp. 319–44.

Porto, Guido, 2006, "Using Survey Data to Assess the Distributional Effects of Trade Policy," *Journal of International Economics*, Vol. 70 (September), pp. 140–60.

Rodrik, Dani, 2006, "What's So Special About China's Exports?" NBER Working Paper No. 11947 (Cambridge, Massachusetts: National Bureau of Economic Research).

Slaughter, Matthew J., 2001, "International Trade and Labor-Demand Elasticities," *Journal of International Economics*, Vol. 54 (June), pp. 27–56.

Topalova, Petia, 2005, "Factor Immobility and Regional Impacts of Trade Liberalization: Evidence on Poverty and Inequality from India" (unpublished; Cambridge, Massachusetts: Massachusetts Institute of Technology). Available via the Internet: http://www.isid.ac.in/~planning/Topalova.pdf.

Young, Alwyn, 1995, "The Tyranny of Numbers: Confronting the Statistical Realities of the East Asian Growth Experience," *Quarterly Journal of Economics*, Vol. 110 (August), pp. 641–80.

————, 2003, "Gold into Base Metals: Productivity Growth in the People's Republic of China During the Reform Period," *Journal of Political Economy*, Vol. 111 (December), pp. 1220–61.

World Bank, 2006, *Global Economic Prospects 2007: Managing the Next Wave of Globalization* (Washington).

IMF EXECUTIVE BOARD DISCUSSION OF THE OUTLOOK, MARCH 2007

The following remarks by the Acting Chair were made at the conclusion of the Executive Board's discussion of the World Economic Outlook *on March 26, 2007.*

Executive Directors welcomed the continued strong, broad-based expansion of the global economy during 2006, and noted that activity in most regions met or exceeded expectations. Looking forward, Directors believed that the global expansion would slow only modestly in 2007 and 2008 and inflationary pressures would remain contained. Directors noted that the composition of demand is expected to be more balanced among the major advanced economies in 2007, with the United States, the euro area, and Japan all expanding slightly above 2 percent. Directors also saw continued strong, albeit somewhat less rapid, growth among emerging market and developing countries.

Risks around this central scenario appear to be more evenly balanced than at the time of the last *World Economic Outlook* (WEO) discussion in September 2006, but still tilted to the downside. In this context, Directors generally were of the view that the recent market turbulence represented a correction after a period of asset price buoyancy that does not require a fundamental revision in the positive global economic outlook. Some Directors were less sanguine about the risks to the outlook, pointing to heightened concerns about the stability of financial markets, slowing productivity and its implications for growth, and continuing uncertainties regarding oil and other commodity price developments. All Directors underscored the need for continued vigilance.

Directors discussed the downside risks facing the global economy. Most emphasized that the ongoing correction in the U.S. housing market could have a growing impact on the broader economy. Directors underscored that persistently higher financial market volatility could prompt a further retrenchment from riskier assets and markets—with several noting the potential for increased market volatility—and called for careful monitoring of market developments. Directors also recognized the possibility that inflationary pressures could revive as resource utilization constraints start to bind, and stressed the risk of a reversal of the recent decline in oil prices—given continuing geopolitical tensions and limited spare production capacity. They also noted continued risks that the existing large global imbalances could unwind in a disorderly way.

Directors considered that a key question in assessing risks to the outlook relates to the extent to which the world economy will remain on a sound growth trajectory even if the U.S. economy slows more sharply—or whether global prospects may decouple from the United States, especially in light of the limited impact of the recent cooling of U.S. activity. In this context, Directors welcomed the staff's analysis of cross-country growth spillovers, and attributed the limited global impact so far to several factors. In particular, the U.S. slowdown has been focused on the housing sector, which has a relatively low import content. Also, the causes of the slowing have been specific to the U.S. economy, rather than a common event simultaneously affecting many countries. Nevertheless, a number of Directors observed that the greater integration fostered by globalization has increased the potential magnitude of spillovers, and that a sharp further slowing in the U.S. economy would likely have a substantial impact on global growth. Directors recognized, however, that the strength of spillovers experienced by individual countries would vary both with the extent of their trade and financial linkages with the United States and with the degree of domestic vulnerabilities.

Advanced Economies

Directors noted that the U.S. economy has slowed noticeably over the past year, largely owing to the correction in the housing sector, while private consumption has so far remained robust. Nevertheless, activity in the United States is expected to regain momentum in the period ahead with growth rates rising during the course of 2007 and returning to potential in 2008. Directors expressed concern, however, about the recent evidence of intensifying difficulties in the subprime mortgage market, which could start to impose a broader drag on the economy, particularly if the housing downturn deepens and credit standards are tightened more generally. In this vein, some Directors considered that the impact of the weakening housing sector may not yet have played out fully, and that a deeper-than-anticipated downturn in the United States should not be ruled out. Although inflationary pressures have eased somewhat following the decline in oil prices from last year's highs, core inflation remains elevated. Directors supported the Federal Reserve's approach in recent months of holding the policy rate steady, while appreciating that the Fed stands ready to respond to shifts in the balance of risks between growth and inflation. Directors welcomed the indications that the FY2008 budget will seek to balance the federal budget by FY2012, while expressing a preference for the more ambitious target of aiming to achieve balance excluding the social security surplus. Fiscal consolidation will need to be supported by reforms to put the Social Security, Medicare, and Medicaid systems on a sustainable long-term footing.

Directors welcomed the acceleration in real GDP growth in the euro area in 2006, and saw the risks to the outlook as evenly balanced. They considered that further cautious withdrawal

of monetary accommodation by the European Central Bank would be warranted to forestall inflationary pressures, contingent on the recovery progressing as expected. Directors welcomed the progress made toward needed fiscal consolidation, but felt that more ambitious efforts are warranted given the strong cyclical upswing and the looming pressures from the aging of the population. Directors also underscored the importance of further policy reforms under the Lisbon agenda to bolster prospects for a sustained long-term expansion, particularly steps to boost productivity and increase labor utilization. Recent experience has also underlined the importance of complementary product and services market reforms to foster job creation and expenditure-based fiscal consolidation.

Directors welcomed the emergence of the Japanese economy from its mid-2006 soft patch. With inflation still close to zero, Directors generally supported the Bank of Japan's cautious approach to raising interest rates since exiting its zero interest rate policy last year, and suggested that monetary accommodation should be removed only if the expansion remains strong, and then only gradually. Directors suggested that greater clarity regarding the Bank of Japan's medium-term inflation goals would also help to anchor private sector expectations, while reducing risks of an abrupt unwinding of yen carry trades with sharp movements in exchange rates or the volume of capital flows. Fiscal consolidation appears to be running ahead of the government's plans to achieve a primary surplus by FY2011, but additional fiscal efforts beyond those contained in the current medium-term plan will be needed to put net debt on a declining trajectory. Further progress on structural reforms will also be important to enhance growth with spillover benefits to the world economy.

Emerging Market and Other Developing Countries

Directors welcomed the strong performance of the economies in emerging Asia, with the vibrant expansions in China and India leading the way. Most Directors were confident that the region is well positioned to withstand a U.S. slowdown, although some others cautioned that spillovers could still be sizable, as growing intra-regional trade in part represents shipments of intermediate goods ultimately destined for the United States. Against the background of widening current account surpluses in some countries in the region, Directors took note of the differing degrees of exchange rate flexibility observed within the region. Many Directors considered that greater flexibility of the renminbi would help provide a more secure base for monetary policy management in China, while also helping to contain China's widening current account surplus.

Directors observed that growth in Latin America exceeded 5 percent in 2006, supported by a strong external environment and generally sound economic policies. Although the pace of growth is likely to ease somewhat in the next two years, Directors commented that strengthened fundamentals and improved macroeconomic policy frameworks should enable countries in Latin America to maintain growth rates even in the face of a sharper-than-expected U.S. slowdown. Nevertheless, the region remains vulnerable to a softening of commodity prices, which would pose policy challenges in several countries by putting pressure on current account and fiscal balances. Directors also noted that fiscal reforms will be important to create more room for increased spending on well-targeted social programs. Reforms to improve the region's disappointing productivity performance are also a priority.

Directors welcomed the strong growth in emerging Europe, noting that the expansion is likely to moderate in 2007 in response to slower growth in western Europe. While the widening current account deficits should be comfortably financed in most countries, Directors cautioned that a deterioration in global financial conditions could reduce capital inflows in the future. Directors also drew attention to the slowing pace of reform among the new European Union

members, which again underscores the importance of structural reforms to facilitate continuing smooth convergence within the European Union.

Directors observed that economic activity in the Commonwealth of Independent States has continued to be boosted by high commodity prices, and growth prospects appear generally positive. They expressed concern that strong capital inflows and robust domestic demand growth, driven in part by large public spending increases that have outpaced revenue growth, have kept inflation high in many countries. Consequently, Directors saw a need for greater spending restraint as well as for tighter monetary policy and, in some cases, greater exchange rate flexibility, to contain inflationary pressures. Sustaining the recent strong growth momentum will also require reforms aimed at attracting greater private investment to diversify the sources of growth away from the export of primary commodities.

While recognizing the variety of challenges facing countries in sub-Saharan Africa, Directors welcomed the continued strong expansion seen in the region as a whole, as well as the prospects for a further acceleration in growth in 2007. At the same time, Directors highlighted the vulnerabilities of the non-oil-exporting economies in the region to commodity price shocks or further increases in oil prices. Sustained macroeconomic stability and structural reforms will be necessary to foster vibrant market-based economies and sustain the recent improvement in the region's growth performance. Directors underscored that most countries in the region would benefit from further trade liberalization, improved market access for their exports, and delivery on aid commitments by advanced economies to support progress toward achieving the Millennium Development Goals. Measures to strengthen institutions and the business environment will also help spur private sector activity, and reduce the region's still-high reliance on commodity exports.

In the context of continued high oil prices, Middle Eastern oil exporters enjoyed another year of solid growth, accompanied by strong current account and fiscal balances. Directors viewed the outlook for the region as a whole as favorable, and welcomed the public investment plans among the GCC countries. Nonetheless, the region remains heavily dependent on the hydrocarbon sector, while rising populations are contributing to high unemployment rates. In this context, Directors underscored the importance of fostering greater private investment in the non-oil sector in order to balance the sources of growth and increase employment opportunities. Also important will be measures to improve the business environment and adapt education systems to align the skills mix of the labor force with the needs of the private sector. In the non-oil-exporting countries of the Mashreq region, growth accelerated in 2006 in the context of an upturn in foreign direct investment and the overall favorable external environment.

Directors noted that many emerging market and developing countries around the world face the challenge of taking advantage of strong capital inflows to support investment, while avoiding large swings in competitiveness and a buildup of balance sheet vulnerabilities. Noting that there is no simple recipe that can be uniformly applied, Directors highlighted the importance of balanced and flexible approaches to macroeconomic management that suit the circumstances of each country, while avoiding steps that could undermine confidence or distort markets. Several Directors also recognized that even countries with credible policy frameworks and strong institutions and financial systems may be vulnerable to large and volatile capital flows, and could benefit from Fund advice on policy options tailored to their circumstances in the context of Article IV consultations.

Multilateral Issues

Underscoring the shared responsibility among policymakers for maintaining the foundations for strong global growth, Directors emphasized the importance of policy actions across key

countries to support the smooth unwinding of large global imbalances. Important elements of such an approach include efforts to raise national saving in the United States, including through further fiscal consolidation; advancing growth-enhancing reforms in the euro area; further structural reforms, including fiscal consolidation, in Japan; and initiatives to encourage consumption and greater exchange rate flexibility in some parts of emerging Asia, especially China. Directors were of the view that lower oil prices and increased spending would reduce external surpluses among Middle Eastern oil exporters, but saw scope for continuing to boost spending—subject to absorptive capacity constraints. A few Directors also considered that an increase in energy taxation in the United States could help reduce the country's high levels of oil consumption, thereby contributing to a reduction in global imbalances as well as to reducing environmental consequences. In this context, Directors took note of the U.S. administration's recently announced objective of curbing gasoline consumption.

Directors took note of the staff's analysis—based on historical episodes of reversals of current account imbalances and a closer look at U.S. trade behavior—that real exchange rates can play a potentially important role in the adjustment process in countries with large and persistent current account surpluses and deficits. However, they emphasized that exchange rate changes, while supportive of adjustment, must be accompanied by policy actions to rebalance domestic demand. In this vein, several Directors considered that the analysis usefully complements earlier WEO studies on the importance of domestic policy adjustments and exchange rate movements in the resolution of imbalances. Directors generally acknowledged that a shared willingness of authorities across key regions to allow real exchange rates to adjust—particularly where they are not freely floating—could prove to be a crucial ingredient of policies to promote a smooth resolution of the large global imbalances. While the staff's analysis suggests that the U.S. trade deficit could be more responsive to real exchange rate changes than is commonly found in the macroeconomic literature, many Directors were not convinced by this finding and felt that additional research and analysis in this area, using alternative methodologies, should be undertaken before firm conclusions can be drawn. Some other Directors emphasized, however, that the staff's finding is an important result.

Directors welcomed the staff's analysis on how the rapid growth of international trade and the introduction of new technologies are beginning to forge an increasingly integrated global labor market. This integration is contributing to growth and incomes in both source and host countries, but at the same time it is affecting distributional outcomes and may thus be contribut-ing indirectly to protectionist sentiment. Steps to do more to help those who are adversely affected by developments in technology and trade should include better education systems, more flexible labor markets, and welfare systems that cushion the impact of—but do not obstruct—economic change.

Directors welcomed the revival of the Doha Round of multilateral trade negotiations. A successful outcome would, by further strengthening multilateral rules and reducing the risks of protectionism, boost medium-term global prospects. Prospects for a gradual unwinding of global imbalances would also benefit from initiatives to remove obstacles to the smooth reallocation of resources in response to exchange rate movements, including through trade reform.

STATISTICAL APPENDIX

The statistical appendix presents historical data, as well as projections. It comprises five sections: Assumptions, What's New, Data and Conventions, Classification of Countries, and Statistical Tables.

The assumptions underlying the estimates and projections for 2007–08 and the medium-term scenario for 2009–12 are summarized in the first section. The second section presents a brief description of changes to the database and statistical tables. The third section provides a general description of the data, and of the conventions used for calculating country group composites. The classification of countries in the various groups presented in the *World Economic Outlook* is summarized in the fourth section.

The last, and main, section comprises the statistical tables. Data in these tables have been compiled on the basis of information available through end-March 2007. The figures for 2007 and beyond are shown with the same degree of precision as the historical figures solely for convenience; since they are projections, the same degree of accuracy is not to be inferred.

Assumptions

Real effective *exchange rates* for the advanced economies are assumed to remain constant at their average levels during the period January 26 to February 23, 2007. For 2007 and 2008, these assumptions imply average U.S. dollar/SDR conversion rates of 1.495 and 1.500, U.S. dollar/euro conversion rate of 1.30 and 1.31, and yen/U.S. dollar conversion rates of 120.4 and 119.2, respectively.

It is assumed that the *price of oil* will average $60.75 a barrel in 2007 and $64.75 a barrel in 2008.

Established *policies* of national authorities are assumed to be maintained. The more specific policy assumptions underlying the projections for selected advanced economies are described in Box A1.

With regard to *interest rates*, it is assumed that the London interbank offered rate (LIBOR) on six-month U.S. dollar deposits will average 5.3 percent in 2007 and 5.1 percent in 2008, that three-month euro deposits will average 3.8 percent in 2007 and 3.7 percent in 2008, and that six-month Japanese yen deposits will average 0.9 percent in 2007 and 1.2 percent in 2008.

With respect to *introduction of the euro*, on December 31, 1998, the Council of the European Union decided that, effective January 1, 1999, the irrevocably fixed conversion rates between the euro and currencies of the member states adopting the euro are as follows.

1 euro	= 13.7603	Austrian schillings
	= 40.3399	Belgian francs
	= 1.95583	Deutsche mark
	= 5.94573	Finnish markkaa
	= 6.55957	French francs
	= 340.750	Greek drachma[1]
	= 0.787564	Irish pound
	= 1,936.27	Italian lire
	= 40.3399	Luxembourg francs
	= 2.20371	Netherlands guilders
	= 200.482	Portuguese escudos
	= 239.640	Slovenia tolars[2]
	= 166.386	Spanish pesetas

See Box 5.4 in the October 1998 *World Economic Outlook* for details on how the conversion rates were established.

What's New

On January 1, 2007, Slovenia became the thirteenth country to join the euro area and is

---

[1]The conversion rate for Greece was established prior to inclusion in the euro area on January 1, 2001.

[2]The conversion rate for Slovenia was established prior to inclusion in the euro area on January 1, 2007.

Box A1. Economic Policy Assumptions Underlying the Projections for Selected Advanced Economies

The short-term *fiscal policy assumptions* used in the *World Economic Outlook* are based on officially announced budgets, adjusted for differences between the national authorities and the IMF staff regarding macroeconomic assumptions and projected fiscal outturns. The medium-term fiscal projections incorporate policy measures that are judged likely to be implemented. In cases where the IMF staff has insufficient information to assess the authorities' budget intentions and prospects for policy implementation, an unchanged structural primary balance is assumed, unless otherwise indicated. Specific assumptions used in some of the advanced economies follow (see also Tables 12–14 in the Statistical Appendix for data on fiscal and structural balances).[1]

United States. The fiscal projections are based on the Administration's FY2008 budget proposal submitted to Congress on February 5, 2007. Adjustments are made to account for differences in macroeconomic projections as well as staff assumptions about (1) additional defense spending based on analysis by the Congressional Budget Office; (2) slower compression in the growth rate of discretionary spending; and (3) continued AMT relief beyond FY2008. The projections also assume that personal retirement accounts are not introduced.

Japan. The medium-term fiscal projections assume that expenditure and revenue of the general government (excluding social security) are adjusted in line with the current government target to achieve primary fiscal balance by the early 2010s.

Germany. The projections reflect the measures announced in the government's coalition agreement. These aim to reduce the overall fiscal balance to below 1.5 percent of GDP in 2007. Projections include a loss in revenue due to corporate tax reform, and no change in the path of health expenditures, since the health care reform discussions have been postponed for 2007.

France. The estimates for 2006 are based on latest official estimates and the projections for 2007 on the initial budget law. Medium-term projections incorporate the authorities' tax revenue projections as outlined in the 2008–10 Stability Program Update, but assume different spending (less deceleration) and nontax revenue profiles, consistent with an unchanged policy assumption. For 2011–12, the IMF staff assumes unchanged tax policies and real expenditure growth as in the 2010 projection. All fiscal projections are adjusted for the IMF staff's macroeconomic assumptions.

Italy. Fiscal projections for 2007 are based on the IMF staff's estimate of the impact of the budget measures, adjusted for the better-than-expected 2006 fiscal outcome. From 2008, a constant primary structural balance net of one-off measures is assumed.

United Kingdom. The fiscal projections are based on information provided in the 2006 Pre-Budget Report. Additionally, the projections incorporate the most recent statistical releases from the Office for National Statistics, including provisional budgetary outturns through the third quarter of 2006.

Canada. Projections are based on the 2006 Budget and IMF staff estimates, and incorporate the most recent data releases from Statistics Canada, including provincial and territorial budgetary outturns through the third quarter of 2006.

Australia. The fiscal projections through 2009/10 are based on the Mid-Year Economic and Fiscal Outlook published in December 2006. For the remainder of the projection period, the IMF staff assumes unchanged policies.

Austria. Fiscal figures for 2006 are based on the authorities' estimated outturn. Projections for 2007 and beyond are IMF staff projections based on current policies in place.

Belgium. The projections for 2007 are based on the information provided in the 2007 Budget

---

[1]The output gap is actual less potential output, as a percent of potential output. Structural balances are expressed as a percent of potential output. The structural budget balance is the budgetary position that would be observed if the level of actual output coincided with potential output. Changes in the structural budget balance consequently include effects of temporary fiscal measures, the impact of fluctuations in interest rates and debt-service costs, and other noncyclical fluctuations in the budget balance. The computations of structural budget balances are based on IMF staff estimates of potential GDP and revenue and expenditure elasticities (see the October 1993 *World Economic Outlook*, Annex I). Net debt is defined as gross debt less financial assets of the general government, which include assets held by the social security insurance system. Estimates of the output gap and of the structural balance are subject to significant margins of uncertainty.

Report and adjusted for IMF staff's macroeconomic assumptions. For 2007, in particular, the IMF staff's fiscal projections exclude one-off measures not explicitly outlined in the budget (representing 0.3 percent of GDP). For the remainder of the projection period, the IMF staff assumes unchanged policies.

Denmark. For 2007–11, the projections incorporate the June 2006 welfare agreement as well as key features of the prior medium-term fiscal plan, and are adjusted for the IMF staff's macroeconomic assumptions. The projections imply continued budget surpluses in line with the authorities' objectives of long-term fiscal sustainability and debt reduction.

Greece. Projections are based on the 2007 budget, adjusted for IMF staff's assumptions for economic growth. For 2008 and beyond, tax revenues as a percent of GDP are assumed to be constant, while social insurance contributions are assumed to continue their trend increase and EU transfers are assumed to decline. Total expenditure is assumed to remain broadly constant as a percent of GDP.

Hong Kong SAR. Fiscal projections for 2007–10 are consistent with the authorities' medium-term strategy as outlined in the 2007/08 budget, with projections for 2011–12 based on the assumptions underlying the IMF staff's medium-term macroeconomic scenario.

Korea. Projections for 2007 are based on the authorities' budget, with some adjustment for the IMF staff's assumptions. For 2008–12, projections are in line with the authorities' budget plans.

Netherlands. The fiscal projections build on the 2006 and 2007 budgets, the latest Stability Program, and other forecasts provided by the authorities, adjusted for the IMF staff's macroeconomic assumptions.

New Zealand. The fiscal projections through 2010/11 are based on the Half Year Economic and Fiscal Update (HYEFU) of December 2006. For the remainder of the projection period, the IMF staff assumes unchanged policies.

Portugal. Fiscal projections for 2007 build on the authorities' budget. Projections for 2008 and beyond are based on the current Stability and Growth Program of the authorities.

Singapore. For the 2006/07 fiscal year, budget projections on the expenditure side are mostly based on the authorities' budget and fiscal projections, while revenues grow in line with economic activity. Thereafter, the projections assume a constant budget balance (in percent of GDP).

Spain. Fiscal projections through 2009 are based on the 2007 budget, policies outlined in the authorities' updated Stability Program 2006–09, adjusted for the IMF staff's macroeconomic assumptions, information from recent statistical releases, and official announcements. In subsequent years, the fiscal projections assume unchanged policies.

Sweden. The fiscal projections are based on information provided in the budget presented on October 16, 2006. Additionally, the projections incorporate the most recent statistical releases from Statistics Sweden, including provisional budgetary outturns through December 2006.

Switzerland. Projections for 2007–12 are based on IMF staff calculations, which incorporate measures to restore balance in the Federal accounts and strengthen social security finances.

Monetary policy assumptions are based on the established policy framework in each country. In most cases, this implies a nonaccommodative stance over the business cycle: official interest rates will therefore increase when economic indicators suggest that prospective inflation will rise above its acceptable rate or range, and they will decrease when indicators suggest that prospective inflation will not exceed the acceptable rate or range, that prospective output growth is below its potential rate, and that the margin of slack in the economy is significant. On this basis, the LIBOR on six-month U.S. dollar deposits is assumed to average 5.3 percent in 2007 and 5.1 percent in 2008. The projected path for U.S. dollar short-term interest rates reflects the assumption implicit in prevailing forward rates. The rate on three-month euro deposits is assumed to average 3.8 percent in 2007 and 3.7 percent in 2008. The interest rate on six-month Japanese yen deposits is assumed to average 0.9 percent in 2007 and 1.2 percent in 2008. Changes in interest rate assumptions compared with the September 2006 *World Economic Outlook* are summarized in Table 1.1.

now included in the advanced economy group; also on January 1, 2007, Bulgaria and Romania became members of the European Union, enlarging the group to a total of 27 countries; the Netherlands Antilles has been excluded from the World Economic Outlook database following the decision by its five constituent islands to abandon the federation and will cease to exist in July 2007; the country composition of the fuel-exporting group has been revised to reflect the periodic update of the classification criteria; and the purchasing power parity (PPP) weights have been updated to reflect the most up-to-date PPP conversion factor provided by the World Bank.

Data and Conventions

Data and projections for 182 countries form the statistical basis for the *World Economic Outlook* (the World Economic Outlook database). The data are maintained jointly by the IMF's Research Department and area departments, with the latter regularly updating country projections based on consistent global assumptions.

Although national statistical agencies are the ultimate providers of historical data and definitions, international organizations are also involved in statistical issues, with the objective of harmonizing methodologies for the national compilation of statistics, including the analytical frameworks, concepts, definitions, classifications, and valuation procedures used in the production of economic statistics. The World Economic Outlook database reflects information from both national source agencies and international organizations.

The comprehensive revision of the standardized *System of National Accounts 1993 (SNA)*, the IMF's *Balance of Payments Manual, Fifth Edition (BPM5)*, the *Monetary and Financial Statistics Manual (MFSM)*, and the *Government Finance Statistics Manual 2001 (GFSM 2001)* represented important improvements in the standards of economic statistics and analysis.[3] The IMF was

actively involved in all these projects, particularly the *Balance of Payments, Monetary and Financial Statistics,* and *Government Finance Statistics* manuals, which reflects the IMF's special interest in countries' external positions, financial sector stability, and public sector fiscal positions. The process of adapting country data to the new definitions began in earnest when the manuals were released. However, full concordance with the manuals is ultimately dependent on the provision by national statistical compilers of revised country data, and hence the *World Economic Outlook* estimates are still only partially adapted to these manuals.

In line with recent improvements in standards of reporting economic statistics, several countries have phased out their traditional *fixed-base-year* method of calculating real macroeconomic variables levels and growth by switching to a *chain-weighted* method of computing aggregate growth. Recent dramatic changes in the structure of these economies have obliged these countries to revise the way in which they measure real GDP levels and growth. Switching to the chain-weighted method of computing aggregate growth, which uses current price information, allows countries to measure GDP growth more accurately by eliminating upward biases in new data.[4] Currently, real macroeconomic data for Albania, Australia, Austria, Azerbaijan, Belgium, Canada, Cyprus, Czech Republic, Denmark, euro area, Finland, Georgia, Germany, Greece, Iceland, Ireland, Italy, Japan, Kazakhstan, Lithuania, Luxembourg, Malta, the Netherlands, New Zealand, Norway, Poland, Portugal, Russia, Slovenia, Spain, Sweden, Switzerland, the United Kingdom, and the United States are based on chain-weighted methodology. However,

---

[3]Commission of the European Communities, International Monetary Fund, Organization for Economic Cooperation and Development, United Nations, and

World Bank, *System of National Accounts 1993* (Brussels/Luxembourg, New York, Paris, and Washington, 1993); International Monetary Fund, *Balance of Payments Manual, Fifth Edition* (Washington, 1993); International Monetary Fund, *Monetary and Financial Statistics Manual* (Washington, 2000); and International Monetary Fund, *Government Finance Statistics Manual* (Washington, 2001).

[4]Charles Steindel, 1995, "Chain-Weighting: The New Approach to Measuring GDP," *Current Issues in Economics and Finance* (Federal Reserve Bank of New York), Vol. 1 (December).

data before 1996 (Albania), 1994 (Azerbaijan), 1995 (Belgium), 1995 (Cyprus), 1995 (Czech Republic), 1995 (euro area), 1991 (Germany), 2000 (Greece), 1990 (Iceland), 1995 (Ireland), 1994 (Japan), 1995 (Kazakhstan), 1995 (Luxembourg), 2000 (Malta), 1995 (Poland), 1995 (Russia), 1995 (Slovenia), and 1995 (Spain) are based on unrevised national accounts and subject to revision in the future.

The members of the European Union have adopted a harmonized system for the compilation of the national accounts, referred to as ESA 1995. All national accounts data from 1995 onward are presented on the basis of the new system. Revision by national authorities of data prior to 1995 to conform to the new system has progressed, but has in some cases not been completed. In such cases, historical *World Economic Outlook* data have been carefully adjusted to avoid breaks in the series. Users of EU national accounts data prior to 1995 should nevertheless exercise caution until such time as the revision of historical data by national statistical agencies has been fully completed. See Box 1.2, "Revisions in National Accounts Methodologies," in the May 2000 *World Economic Outlook.*

Composite data for country groups in the *World Economic Outlook* are either sums or weighted averages of data for individual countries. Unless otherwise indicated, multiyear averages of growth rates are expressed as compound annual rates of change.[5] Arithmetically weighted averages are used for all data except inflation and money growth for the other emerging market and developing country group, for which geometric averages are used. The following conventions apply.

- Country group composites for exchange rates, interest rates, and the growth rates of monetary aggregates are weighted by GDP converted to U.S. dollars at market exchange

rates (averaged over the preceding three years) as a share of group GDP.
- Composites for other data relating to the domestic economy, whether growth rates or ratios, are weighted by GDP valued at purchasing power parities (PPPs) as a share of total world or group GDP.[6]
- Composites for data relating to the domestic economy for the euro area (13 member countries throughout the entire period unless otherwise noted) are aggregates of national source data using weights based on 1995 ECU exchange rates.
- Composite unemployment rates and employment growth are weighted by labor force as a share of group labor force.
- Composites relating to the external economy are sums of individual country data after conversion to U.S. dollars at the average market exchange rates in the years indicated for balance of payments data and at end-of-year market exchange rates for debt denominated in currencies other than U.S. dollars. Composites of changes in foreign trade volumes and prices, however, are arithmetic averages of percentage changes for individual countries weighted by the U.S. dollar value of exports or imports as a share of total world or group exports or imports (in the preceding year).

For central and eastern European countries, external transactions in nonconvertible currencies (through 1990) are converted to U.S. dollars at the implicit U.S. dollar/ruble conversion rates obtained from each country's national currency exchange rate for the U.S. dollar and for the ruble.

All data refer to calendar years, except for the following countries, which refer to fiscal years: Australia (July/June), Bangladesh (July/June), Egypt (July/June), Islamic Republic of

---

[5]Averages for real GDP and its components, employment, per capita GDP, inflations, factor productivity, trades, and commodity prices are calculated based on compound annual rate of change except for the unemployment rate, which is based on simple arithmetic average.

[6]See Box A2 of the April 2004 *World Economic Outlook* for a summary of the revised PPP-based weights and Annex IV of the May 1993 *World Economic Outlook.* See also Anne-Marie Gulde and Marianne Schulze-Ghattas, "Purchasing Power Parity Based Weights for the *World Economic Outlook*," in *Staff Studies for the World Economic Outlook* (International Monetary Fund, December 1993), pp. 106–23.

Table A. Classification by World Economic Outlook Groups and Their Shares in Aggregate GDP, Exports of Goods and Services, and Population, 2006[1]

(Percent of total for group or world)

	Number of Countries	GDP		Exports of Goods and Services		Population	
		Advanced economies	World	Advanced economies	World	Advanced economies	World
Advanced economies	**30**	**100.0**	**52.0**	**100.0**	**67.3**	**100.0**	**15.3**
United States		37.8	19.7	14.5	9.8	30.6	4.7
Euro area	13	28.2	14.7	43.1	29.0	32.3	5.0
Germany		7.4	3.9	13.2	8.9	8.4	1.3
France		5.6	2.9	6.4	4.3	6.4	1.0
Italy		5.2	2.7	5.2	3.5	6.0	0.9
Spain		3.5	1.8	3.2	2.2	4.5	0.7
Japan		12.1	6.3	7.4	5.0	13.0	2.0
United Kingdom		6.2	3.2	6.8	4.6	6.2	0.9
Canada		3.4	1.7	4.7	3.1	3.3	0.5
Other advanced economies	13	12.4	6.4	23.5	15.8	14.5	2.2
Memorandum							
Major advanced economies	7	77.6	40.4	58.3	39.2	74.0	11.3
Newly industrialized Asian economies	4	6.5	3.4	13.7	9.2	8.4	1.3
		Other emerging market and developing countries	World	Other emerging market and developing countries	World	Other emerging market and developing countries	World
Other emerging market and developing countries	**143**	**100.0**	**48.0**	**100.0**	**32.7**	**100.0**	**84.7**
Regional groups							
Africa	48	7.0	3.4	7.7	2.5	15.3	12.9
Sub-Sahara	45	5.4	2.6	5.8	1.9	13.9	11.8
Excluding Nigeria and South Africa	43	2.9	1.4	2.8	0.9	10.2	8.7
Central and eastern Europe	14	7.1	3.4	13.2	4.3	3.4	2.9
Commonwealth of Independent States[2]	13	8.0	3.8	10.1	3.3	5.2	4.4
Russia		5.4	2.6	6.9	2.3	2.6	2.2
Developing Asia	23	56.3	27.0	38.6	12.6	61.7	52.3
China		31.4	15.1	21.9	7.2	24.3	20.5
India		13.1	6.3	4.1	1.3	20.6	17.4
Excluding China and India	21	11.7	5.6	12.6	4.1	16.9	14.3
Middle East	13	5.9	2.8	14.5	4.7	4.4	3.7
Western Hemisphere	32	15.7	7.6	15.9	5.2	10.1	8.5
Brazil		5.4	2.6	3.3	1.1	3.4	2.9
Mexico		3.7	1.8	5.5	1.8	1.9	1.6
Analytical groups							
By source of export earnings							
Fuel	23	13.3	6.4	26.5	8.7	11.0	9.3
Nonfuel	120	86.7	41.6	73.5	24.0	89.0	75.3
of which, primary products	21	1.7	0.8	2.3	0.7	4.1	3.5
By external financing source							
Net debtor countries	121	54.1	26.0	48.5	15.9	64.6	54.7
of which, official financing	34	6.1	2.9	3.8	1.2	13.8	11.7
Net debtor countries by debt-servicing experience							
Countries with arrears and/or rescheduling during 2001–05	51	10.2	4.9	7.6	2.5	19.0	16.1
Other net debtor countries	70	43.9	21.1	40.9	13.4	45.6	38.6
Other groups							
Heavily indebted poor countries	30	2.0	1.0	1.2	0.4	8.3	7.0
Middle East and North Africa	19	7.8	3.8	16.6	5.4	6.5	5.5

[1]The GDP shares are based on the purchasing-power-parity (PPP) valuation of country GDPs. The number of countries comprising each group reflects those for which data are included in the group aggregates.

[2]Mongolia, which is not a member of the Commonwealth of Independent States, is included in this group for reasons of geography and similarities in economic structure.

Table B. Advanced Economies by Subgroup

Major Currency Areas	Euro area		Other Subgroups			
			Newly industrialized Asian economies	Major advanced economies	Other advanced economies	
United States	Austria	Ireland	Hong Kong SAR[1]	Canada	Australia	Korea
Euro area	Belgium	Italy	Korea	France	Cyprus	New Zealand
Japan	Finland	Luxembourg	Singapore	Germany	Denmark	Norway
	France	Netherlands	Taiwan Province	Italy	Hong Kong SAR[1]	Singapore
	Germany	Portugal	of China	Japan	Iceland	Sweden
	Greece	Slovenia		United Kingdom	Israel	Switzerland
		Spain		United States		Taiwan Province
						of China

[1]On July 1, 1997, Hong Kong was returned to the People's Republic of China and became a Special Administrative Region of China.

Iran (March/February), Mauritius (July/June), Myanmar (April/March), Nepal (July/June), New Zealand (July/June), Pakistan (July/June), Samoa (July/June), and Tonga (July/June).

Classification of Countries

Summary of the Country Classification

The country classification in the *World Economic Outlook* divides the world into two major groups: advanced economies, and other emerging market and developing countries.[7] Rather than being based on strict criteria, economic or otherwise, this classification has evolved over time with the objective of facilitating analysis by providing a reasonably meaningful organization of data. Table A provides an overview of these standard groups in the *World Economic Outlook*, showing the number of countries in each group and the average 2006 shares of groups in aggregate PPP-valued GDP, total exports of goods and services, and population.

A few countries are presently not included in these groups, either because they are not IMF members and their economies are not monitored by the IMF, or because databases have not yet been fully developed. Because of data

[7]As used here, the term "country" does not in all cases refer to a territorial entity that is a state as understood by international law and practice. It also covers some territorial entities that are not states, but for which statistical data are maintained on a separate and independent basis.

limitations, group composites do not reflect the following countries: the Islamic Republic of Afghanistan, Bosnia and Herzegovina, Brunei Darussalam, Eritrea, Iraq, Liberia, Serbia, Somalia, and Timor-Leste. Cuba and the Democratic People's Republic of Korea are examples of countries that are not IMF members, whereas San Marino, among the advanced economies, and Aruba, Marshall Islands, Federated States of Micronesia, Palau, and Republic of Montenegro, among the developing countries, are examples of economies for which databases have not been completed.

General Features and Composition of Groups in the *World Economic Outlook* Classification

Advanced Economies

The 30 advanced economies are listed in Table B. The seven largest in terms of GDP—the United States, Japan, Germany, France, Italy, the United Kingdom, and Canada—constitute the subgroup of *major advanced economies*, often referred to as the Group of Seven (G-7) countries. The 13 members of the euro area and the four *newly industrialized Asian economies* are also distinguished as subgroups. Composite data shown in the tables for the euro area cover the current members for all years, even though the membership has increased over time.

In 1991 and subsequent years, data for *Germany* refer to west Germany *and* the eastern

Table C. European Union

Austria	Finland	Latvia	Romania
Belgium	France	Lithuania	Slovak Republic
Bulgaria	Germany	Luxembourg	Slovenia
Cyprus	Greece	Malta	Spain
Czech Republic	Hungary	Netherlands	Sweden
Denmark	Ireland	Poland	United Kingdom
Estonia	Italy	Portugal	

Länder (i.e., the former German Democratic Republic). Before 1991, economic data are not available on a unified basis or in a consistent manner. Hence, in tables featuring data expressed as annual percent change, these apply to west Germany in years up to and including 1991, but to unified Germany from 1992 onward. In general, data on national accounts and domestic economic and financial activity through 1990 cover west Germany only, whereas data for the central government and balance of payments apply to west Germany through June 1990 and to unified Germany thereafter.

Table C lists the member countries of the European Union, not all of which are classified as advanced economies in the *World Economic Outlook.*

Other Emerging Market and Developing Countries

The group of other emerging market and developing countries (143 countries) includes all countries that are not classified as advanced economies.

The *regional breakdowns* of other emerging market and developing countries—*Africa, central and eastern Europe, Commonwealth of Independent States, developing Asia, Middle East, and Western Hemisphere*—largely conform to the regional breakdowns in the IMF's *International Financial Statistics.* In both classifications, Egypt and the

Table D. Middle East and North Africa Countries

Algeria	Jordan	Morocco	Syrian Arab Republic
Bahrain	Kuwait	Oman	Tunisia
Djibouti	Lebanon	Qatar	United Arab Emirates
Egypt	Libya	Saudi Arabia	Yemen, Rep. of
Iran, I.R. of	Mauritania	Sudan	

Table E. Other Emerging Market and Developing Countries by Region and Main Source of Export Earnings

	Fuel	Nonfuel, of Which Primary Products
Africa	Algeria Angola Congo, Rep. of Equatorial Guinea Gabon Nigeria Sudan	Botswana Burkina Faso Burundi Chad Congo, Dem. Rep. of Guinea Guinea-Bissau Malawi Mauritania Namibia Niger Sierra Leone Zambia Zimbabwe
Commonwealth of Independent States	Azerbaijan Russia Turkmenistan	Mongolia Tajikistan Uzbekistan
Developing Asia		Papua New Guinea Solomon Islands
Middle East	Bahrain Iran, I.R. of Kuwait Libya Oman Qatar Saudi Arabia Syrian Arab Republic United Arab Emirates Yemen, Rep. of	
Western Hemisphere	Ecuador Trinidad and Tobago Venezuela	Chile Suriname

Libyan Arab Jamahiriya are included in the *Middle East* region rather than in Africa. In addition, the *World Economic Outlook* sometimes refers to the regional group of Middle East and North Africa countries, also referred to as the MENA countries, whose composition straddles the Africa and Middle East regions. This group is defined as the Arab League countries plus the Islamic Republic of Iran (see Table D).

Other emerging market and developing countries are also classified according to *analytical criteria.* The analytical criteria reflect countries' composition of export earnings and other

Table F. Other Emerging Market and Developing Countries by Region, Net External Position, and Heavily Indebted Poor Countries

	Net External Position		Heavily Indebted Poor Countries		Net External Position		Heavily Indebted Poor Countries
	Net creditor	Net debtor[1]			Net creditor	Net debtor[1]	
Africa				**Central and eastern Europe**			
Maghreb				Albania		*	
Algeria	*			Bulgaria		*	
Morocco		*		Croatia		*	
Tunisia		*		Czech Republic		*	
Sub-Sahara				Estonia		*	
South Africa	*			Hungary		*	
Horn of Africa				Latvia		*	
Djibouti		*		Lithuania		*	
Ethiopia		•	*	Macedonia, FYR		*	
Sudan		*		Malta		*	
Great Lakes				Poland		*	
Burundi		•	*	Romania		*	
Congo, Dem. Rep. of		*	*	Slovak Republic		*	
Kenya		*		Turkey		*	
Rwanda		•	*	**Commonwealth of Independent States**[2]			
Tanzania		•	*	Armenia		*	
Uganda		*	*	Azerbaijan		*	
Southern Africa				Belarus		*	
Angola		*		Georgia		*	
Botswana	*			Kazakhstan		*	
Comoros		•		Kyrgyz Republic		*	
Lesotho		*		Moldova		*	
Madagascar		•	*	Mongolia		•	
Malawi		•	*	Russia	*		
Mauritius		*		Tajikistan		•	
Mozambique, Rep. of		•	*	Turkmenistan	*		
Namibia	*			Ukraine	*		
Seychelles		*		Uzbekistan	*		
Swaziland		*		**Developing Asia**			
Zambia		*	*	Bhutan		•	
Zimbabwe		*		Cambodia		•	
West and Central Africa				China	*		
Cape Verde		*		Fiji		*	
Gambia, The		*	*	Indonesia		*	
Ghana		•	*	Kiribati	*		
Guinea		*	*	Lao PDR		*	
Mauritania		*	*	Malaysia	*		
Nigeria	*			Myanmar		*	
São Tomé and Príncipe		*	*	Papua New Guinea		*	
Sierra Leone		•	*	Philippines		*	
CFA franc zone				Samoa		*	
Benin		*	*	Solomon Islands		•	
Burkina Faso		•	*	Thailand		*	
Cameroon		*	*	Tonga		•	
Central African Republic		•		Vanuatu		*	
Chad		*	*	Vietnam		•	
Congo, Rep. of		•	*	**South Asia**			
Côte d'Ivoire		*		Bangladesh		•	
Equatorial Guinea		*		India		*	
Gabon		•		Maldives		*	
Guinea-Bissau		*	*	Nepal		•	
Mali		*	*	Pakistan		•	
Niger		•	*	Sri Lanka		•	
Senegal		*	*				
Togo		•					

Table F (concluded)

	Net External Position		Heavily Indebted Poor Countries		Net External Position		Heavily Indebted Poor Countries
	Net creditor	Net debtor[1]			Net creditor	Net debtor[1]	
Middle East				Peru		•	
Bahrain	*			Uruguay		•	
Iran, I.R. of	*			Venezuela	*		
Kuwait	*			**Central America**			
Libya	*			Costa Rica		*	
Oman	*			El Salvador		•	
Qatar	*			Guatemala		*	
Saudi Arabia	*			Honduras		*	*
United Arab Emirates	*			Nicaragua		*	*
Yemen, Rep. of	*			Panama		*	
Mashreq				**The Caribbean**			
Egypt		*		Antigua and Barbuda		*	
Jordan		*		Bahamas, The		*	
Lebanon		*		Barbados		*	
Syrian Arab Republic		*		Belize		*	
				Dominica		*	
Western Hemisphere				Dominican Republic		•	
Mexico		*		Grenada		•	
South America				Guyana		*	*
Argentina		*		Haiti		*	*
Brazil		*		Jamaica		*	
Bolivia		•	*	St. Kitts and Nevis		*	
Chile		*		St. Lucia		*	
Colombia		*		St. Vincent and the Grenadines		•	
Ecuador		*		Suriname		*	
Paraguay		•		Trinidad and Tobago	*		

[1]Dot instead of star indicates that the net debtor's main external finance source is official financing.
[2]Mongolia, which is not a member of the Commonwealth of Independent States, is included in this group for reasons of geography and similarities in economic structure.

income from abroad, exchange rate arrangements, a distinction between net creditor and net debtor countries, and, for the net debtor countries, financial criteria based on external financing source and experience with external debt servicing. The detailed composition of other emerging market and developing countries in the regional and analytical groups is shown in Tables E and F.

The analytical criterion, by *source of export earnings*, distinguishes between categories: *fuel* (Standard International Trade Classification— SITC 3) and *nonfuel* and then focuses on *nonfuel primary products* (SITC 0, 1, 2, 4, and 68).

The financial criteria focus on *net creditor, net debtor countries*, and *heavily indebted poor countries (HIPCs)*. Net debtor countries are further differentiated on the basis of two additional financial criteria: by *official external financing* and by *experience with debt servicing*.[8] The HIPC group comprises the countries considered by the IMF and the World Bank for their debt initiative, known as the HIPC Initiative, with the aim of reducing the external debt burdens of all the eligible HIPCs to a "sustainable" level in a reasonably short period of time.[9]

[8]During 2001–05, 51 countries incurred external payments arrears or entered into official or commercial bank debt-rescheduling agreements. This group of countries is referred to as *countries with arrears and/or rescheduling during 2001–05*.

[9]See David Andrews, Anthony R. Boote, Syed S. Rizavi, and Sukwinder Singh, *Debt Relief for Low-Income Countries: The Enhanced HIPC Initiative*, IMF Pamphlet Series, No. 51 (Washington: International Monetary Fund, November 1999).

List of Tables

Output

 1. Summary of World Output   211
 2. Advanced Economies: Real GDP and Total Domestic Demand   212
 3. Advanced Economies: Components of Real GDP   213
 4. Advanced Economies: Unemployment, Employment, and Real Per Capita GDP   215
 5. Other Emerging Market and Developing Countries: Real GDP   217
 6. Other Emerging Market and Developing Countries—by Country: Real GDP   218

Inflation

 7. Summary of Inflation   222
 8. Advanced Economies: GDP Deflators and Consumer Prices   223
 9. Advanced Economies: Hourly Earnings, Productivity, and Unit Labor Costs
      in Manufacturing   224
10. Other Emerging Market and Developing Countries: Consumer Prices   225
11. Other Emerging Market and Developing Countries—by Country: Consumer Prices   226

Financial Policies

12. Summary of Financial Indicators   230
13. Advanced Economies: General and Central Government Fiscal Balances and
      Balances Excluding Social Security Transactions   231
14. Advanced Economies: General Government Structural Balances   233
15. Advanced Economies: Monetary Aggregates   234
16. Advanced Economies: Interest Rates   235
17. Advanced Economies: Exchange Rates   236
18. Other Emerging Market and Developing Countries: Central Government
      Fiscal Balances   237
19. Other Emerging Market and Developing Countries: Broad Money Aggregates   238

Foreign Trade

20. Summary of World Trade Volumes and Prices   239
21. Nonfuel Commodity Prices   241
22. Advanced Economies: Export Volumes, Import Volumes, and Terms of Trade in
      Goods and Services   242
23. Other Emerging Market and Developing Countries—by Region: Total
      Trade in Goods   243
24. Other Emerging Market and Developing Countries—by Source of Export
      Earnings: Total Trade in Goods   246

Current Account Transactions

25. Summary of Payments Balances on Current Account   247
26. Advanced Economies: Balance of Payments on Current Account   248

27. Advanced Economies: Current Account Transactions 250
28. Other Emerging Market and Developing Countries: Payments Balances on
    Current Account 251
29. Other Emerging Market and Developing Countries—by Region: Current
    Account Transactions 253
30. Other Emerging Market and Developing Countries—by Analytical Criteria:
    Current Account Transactions 255
31. Other Emerging Market and Developing Countries—by Country: Balance of
    Payments on Current Account 258

Balance of Payments and External Financing

32. Summary of Balance of Payments, Capital Flows, and External Financing 262
33. Other Emerging Market and Developing Countries—by Region: Balance of
    Payments and External Financing 263
34. Other Emerging Market and Developing Countries—by Analytical Criteria:
    Balance of Payments and External Financing 266
35. Other Emerging Market and Developing Countries: Reserves 269
36. Net Credit and Loans from IMF 271

External Debt and Debt Service

37. Summary of External Debt and Debt Service 272
38. Other Emerging Market and Developing Countries—by Region: External Debt,
    by Maturity and Type of Creditor 274
39. Other Emerging Market and Developing Countries—by Analytical Criteria:
    External Debt, by Maturity and Type of Creditor 276
40. Other Emerging Market and Developing Countries: Ratio of External Debt to GDP 278
41. Other Emerging Market and Developing Countries: Debt-Service Ratios 279
42. IMF Charges and Repurchases to the IMF 280

Flow of Funds

43. Summary of Sources and Uses of World Saving 281

Medium-Term Baseline Scenario

44. Summary of World Medium-Term Baseline Scenario 285
45. Other Emerging Market and Developing Countries—Medium-Term Baseline
    Scenario: Selected Economic Indicators 286

Table 1. Summary of World Output[1]
(Annual percent change)

| | Ten-Year Averages | | 1999 | 2000 | 2001 | 2002 | 2003 | 2004 | 2005 | 2006 | 2007 | 2008 |
	1989–98	1999–2008										
World	**3.2**	**4.4**	**3.7**	**4.8**	**2.5**	**3.1**	**4.0**	**5.3**	**4.9**	**5.4**	**4.9**	**4.9**
Advanced economies	**2.7**	**2.6**	**3.5**	**4.0**	**1.2**	**1.6**	**1.9**	**3.3**	**2.5**	**3.1**	2.5	2.7
United States	3.0	2.8	4.4	3.7	0.8	1.6	2.5	3.9	3.2	3.3	2.2	2.8
Euro area	. . .	2.1	3.0	3.9	1.9	0.9	0.8	2.0	1.4	2.6	2.3	2.3
Japan	2.0	1.6	–0.1	2.9	0.2	0.3	1.4	2.7	1.9	2.2	2.3	1.9
Other advanced economies[2]	3.2	3.5	4.7	5.3	1.7	3.2	2.4	4.1	3.2	3.6	3.3	3.4
Other emerging market and developing countries	**3.8**	**6.4**	**4.1**	**6.0**	**4.3**	**5.0**	**6.7**	**7.7**	**7.5**	**7.9**	**7.5**	**7.1**
Regional groups												
Africa	2.2	4.7	2.7	3.1	4.4	3.7	4.7	5.8	5.6	5.5	6.2	5.8
Central and eastern Europe	1.1	4.4	0.5	4.9	0.2	4.5	4.8	6.6	5.5	6.0	5.5	5.3
Commonwealth of Independent States[3]	. . .	7.0	5.2	9.0	6.3	5.3	7.9	8.4	6.6	7.7	7.0	6.4
Developing Asia	7.3	7.9	6.4	7.0	6.0	7.0	8.4	8.7	9.2	9.4	8.8	8.4
Middle East	4.5	4.8	1.8	5.4	3.0	3.9	6.5	5.6	5.4	5.7	5.5	5.5
Western Hemisphere	3.1	3.2	0.3	3.9	0.5	0.3	2.4	6.0	4.6	5.5	4.9	4.2
Memorandum												
European Union	2.0	2.5	3.0	3.9	2.1	1.4	1.5	2.6	1.9	3.2	2.8	2.7
Analytical groups												
By source of export earnings												
Fuel	–0.3	5.9	3.0	7.1	4.4	4.0	6.9	7.3	6.7	6.7	6.9	6.0
Nonfuel	4.6	6.4	4.2	5.8	4.3	5.2	6.7	7.8	7.6	8.1	7.6	7.2
of which, primary products	2.5	3.7	0.6	1.5	2.9	2.8	3.6	6.1	5.2	4.3	4.8	5.3
By external financing source												
Net debtor countries	3.4	5.0	2.8	4.6	2.5	3.3	4.9	6.4	6.3	6.7	6.3	6.0
of which, official financing	4.1	5.4	3.9	4.6	3.4	3.9	4.7	6.5	7.1	7.0	6.4	6.3
Net debtor countries by debt-servicing experience												
Countries with arrears and/or rescheduling during 2001–05	3.4	4.7	1.1	3.3	2.6	1.6	5.2	6.9	7.2	6.5	6.8	6.1
Memorandum												
Median growth rate												
Advanced economies	3.0	2.9	4.0	4.1	1.9	1.7	1.8	3.7	2.9	3.3	2.9	2.7
Other emerging market and developing countries	3.3	4.6	3.4	4.2	3.6	3.7	4.4	5.4	5.5	5.5	5.5	5.0
Output per capita												
Advanced economies	2.0	2.1	2.9	3.4	0.6	1.0	1.3	2.7	2.0	2.5	2.0	2.2
Other emerging market and developing countries	2.2	5.1	2.6	4.6	2.9	3.7	5.4	6.4	6.2	6.6	6.2	5.8
World growth based on market exchange rates	**2.5**	**3.1**	**3.1**	**4.1**	**1.5**	**1.8**	**2.6**	**4.0**	**3.3**	**3.9**	**3.4**	**3.5**
Value of world output in billions of U.S. dollars												
At market exchange rates	26,238	40,433	30,908	31,759	31,542	32,813	36,853	41,432	44,688	48,144	51,511	54,678
At purchasing power parities	32,232	56,697	42,039	45,010	47,227	49,474	52,510	56,782	61,259	66,229	70,807	75,632

[1]Real GDP.

[2]In this table, "other advanced economies" means advanced economies excluding the United States, euro area countries, and Japan.

[3]Mongolia, which is not a member of the Commonwealth of Independent States, is included in this group for reasons of geography and similarities in economic structure.

Table 2. Advanced Economies: Real GDP and Total Domestic Demand
(Annual percent change)

| | Ten-Year Averages | | 1999 | 2000 | 2001 | 2002 | 2003 | 2004 | 2005 | 2006 | 2007 | 2008 | Fourth Quarter[1] | | |
	1989–98	1999–2008											2006	2007	2008
Real GDP															
Advanced economies	**2.7**	**2.6**	**3.5**	**4.0**	**1.2**	**1.6**	**1.9**	**3.3**	**2.5**	**3.1**	**2.5**	**2.7**	. . .	. . .	. . .
United States	3.0	2.8	4.4	3.7	0.8	1.6	2.5	3.9	3.2	3.3	2.2	2.8	3.1	2.3	2.9
Euro area	. . .	2.1	3.0	3.9	1.9	0.9	0.8	2.0	1.4	2.6	2.3	2.3	3.3	1.9	2.5
Germany	2.5	1.5	1.9	3.1	1.2	—	-0.2	1.2	0.9	2.7	1.8	1.9	3.7	1.0	1.9
France	1.8	2.1	3.0	4.0	1.8	1.1	1.1	2.0	1.2	2.0	2.0	2.4	2.2	2.1	2.6
Italy	1.6	1.4	1.9	3.6	1.8	0.3	—	1.2	0.1	1.9	1.8	1.7	2.8	1.0	2.4
Spain	2.8	3.7	4.7	5.0	3.6	2.7	3.0	3.2	3.5	3.9	3.6	3.4	4.0	3.5	3.4
Netherlands	3.0	2.3	4.7	3.9	1.9	0.1	0.3	2.0	1.5	2.9	2.9	2.7	2.9	2.6	2.5
Belgium	2.3	2.2	3.3	3.9	0.7	1.4	1.0	2.7	1.5	3.0	2.2	2.0	2.9	2.0	2.0
Austria	2.7	2.2	3.3	3.4	0.8	0.9	1.1	2.4	2.0	3.2	2.8	2.4	3.6	2.3	2.6
Finland	1.6	3.3	3.9	5.0	2.6	1.6	1.8	3.7	2.9	5.5	3.1	2.7	5.3	3.4	1.4
Greece	1.9	4.1	3.4	4.5	4.5	3.9	4.9	4.7	3.7	4.2	3.8	3.5	4.3	3.7	3.5
Portugal	3.6	1.7	3.9	3.9	2.0	0.8	-0.7	1.3	0.5	1.3	1.8	2.1	1.7	1.9	2.2
Ireland	6.4	6.1	10.7	9.4	5.8	6.0	4.3	4.3	5.5	6.0	5.0	3.7	5.6	4.1	5.4
Luxembourg	4.9	4.6	8.4	8.4	2.5	3.8	1.3	3.6	4.0	5.8	4.6	4.1	. . .	. . .	. . .
Slovenia	. . .	4.0	5.4	4.1	2.7	3.5	2.7	4.4	4.0	5.2	4.5	4.0	5.5	4.1	3.5
Japan	2.0	1.6	-0.1	2.9	0.2	0.3	1.4	2.7	1.9	2.2	2.3	1.9	2.5	1.9	1.9
United Kingdom	2.0	2.7	3.0	3.8	2.4	2.1	2.7	3.3	1.9	2.7	2.9	2.7	3.0	2.8	2.7
Canada	2.1	3.2	5.5	5.2	1.8	2.9	1.8	3.3	2.9	2.7	2.4	2.9	2.3	2.8	3.0
Korea	5.9	5.4	9.5	8.5	3.8	7.0	3.1	4.7	4.2	5.0	4.4	4.4	4.0	4.7	4.3
Australia	3.3	3.2	4.4	3.4	2.1	4.1	3.1	3.7	2.8	2.7	2.6	3.3	2.8	2.6	3.4
Taiwan Province of China	6.8	4.0	5.7	5.8	-2.2	4.2	3.4	6.1	4.0	4.6	4.2	4.3	4.0	3.5	4.9
Sweden	1.4	3.1	4.5	4.3	1.1	2.0	1.7	4.1	2.9	4.4	3.3	2.5	4.2	4.0	1.8
Switzerland	1.4	1.7	1.3	3.6	1.0	0.3	-0.2	2.3	1.9	2.7	2.0	1.8	2.2	2.0	1.6
Hong Kong SAR	3.8	5.3	4.0	10.0	0.6	1.8	3.2	8.6	7.5	6.8	5.5	5.0	6.9	4.6	5.3
Denmark	2.2	2.1	2.6	3.5	0.7	0.5	0.4	2.1	3.1	3.3	2.5	2.2	3.3	2.9	1.9
Norway	3.5	2.6	2.0	3.3	2.0	1.5	1.0	3.9	2.7	2.9	3.8	2.8	3.0	4.3	1.9
Israel	5.1	3.5	2.9	8.7	-0.6	-0.9	1.5	4.8	5.2	5.1	4.8	4.2	3.7	7.8	2.3
Singapore	7.8	5.6	7.2	10.1	-2.4	4.2	3.1	8.8	6.6	7.9	5.5	5.7	6.6	6.0	4.7
New Zealand	2.1	3.2	4.3	3.6	2.6	4.6	3.2	4.4	2.1	1.5	2.5	2.6	2.0	2.9	2.6
Cyprus	4.7	3.7	4.8	5.0	4.0	2.0	1.8	4.2	3.9	3.8	3.9	4.0	. . .	. . .	. . .
Iceland	1.8	3.4	4.0	4.4	3.6	-0.3	2.7	7.7	7.5	2.9	—	1.9	. . .	. . .	. . .
Memorandum															
Major advanced economies	2.5	2.3	3.1	3.6	1.0	1.2	1.8	3.1	2.3	2.8	2.2	2.5	2.9	2.1	2.6
Newly industrialized Asian economies	6.1	5.0	7.5	7.9	1.2	5.4	3.2	5.8	4.7	5.3	4.6	4.6	4.5	4.4	4.6
Real total domestic demand															
Advanced economies	**2.7**	**2.7**	**4.1**	**4.0**	**1.1**	**1.7**	**2.1**	**3.3**	**2.6**	**2.8**	**2.3**	**2.6**	. . .	. . .	. . .
United States	3.1	3.1	5.3	4.4	0.9	2.2	2.8	4.4	3.3	3.1	1.7	2.7	2.5	2.1	2.9
Euro area	. . .	2.0	3.6	3.4	1.2	0.4	1.5	1.9	1.6	2.3	2.2	2.3	2.3	2.3	2.5
Germany	2.3	0.8	2.7	2.2	-0.5	-2.0	0.6	—	0.5	1.6	1.3	1.8	0.6	2.7	1.5
France	1.5	2.5	3.5	4.5	1.7	1.2	1.9	2.8	2.1	2.3	2.3	2.7	2.1	2.4	2.7
Italy	1.4	1.6	3.2	2.8	1.6	1.3	0.9	1.1	0.3	1.6	1.7	1.7	2.9	1.2	1.9
Spain	2.7	4.5	6.5	6.0	3.7	3.2	3.8	4.8	5.0	4.6	4.0	3.7	4.7	4.0	3.7
Japan	2.0	1.3	—	2.4	1.0	-0.4	0.8	1.9	1.7	1.4	2.1	1.9	2.0	1.9	1.9
United Kingdom	2.0	3.1	4.2	3.9	2.9	3.2	2.7	3.8	1.9	2.9	3.2	2.8	3.2	3.3	2.6
Canada	1.6	3.7	4.2	4.7	1.2	3.3	4.7	4.3	4.8	4.1	2.7	3.2	3.2	3.5	3.0
Other advanced economies	4.2	3.4	5.5	5.4	0.4	3.6	1.3	4.4	3.3	3.6	3.5	3.6	. . .	. . .	. . .
Memorandum															
Major advanced economies	2.4	2.5	3.8	3.7	1.1	1.3	2.2	3.2	2.4	2.6	1.9	2.4	2.3	2.2	2.5
Newly industrialized Asian economies	6.2	3.8	8.0	7.6	—	4.2	—	4.4	2.7	3.5	3.7	4.4	4.1	3.2	5.5

[1]From fourth quarter of preceding year.

Table 3. Advanced Economies: Components of Real GDP

(Annual percent change)

	Ten-Year Averages		1999	2000	2001	2002	2003	2004	2005	2006	2007	2008
	1989–98	1999–2008										
Private consumer expenditure												
Advanced economies	**2.7**	**2.7**	**4.1**	**3.8**	**2.3**	**2.2**	**1.8**	**2.8**	**2.6**	**2.5**	**2.5**	**2.5**
United States	3.0	3.4	5.1	4.7	2.5	2.7	2.8	3.9	3.5	3.2	2.9	2.7
Euro area	...	1.9	3.4	3.1	2.0	0.8	1.2	1.5	1.5	1.9	1.7	2.0
Germany	2.5	0.9	3.0	2.4	1.9	−0.8	−0.1	0.1	0.1	0.8	0.4	1.3
France	1.4	2.6	3.3	3.5	2.5	2.4	2.2	2.5	2.1	2.6	2.2	2.6
Italy	1.8	1.2	2.5	2.4	0.7	0.2	1.0	0.7	0.6	1.5	1.5	1.5
Spain	2.4	3.8	5.3	5.1	3.5	2.8	2.8	4.2	4.2	3.7	3.3	3.2
Japan	2.3	1.2	1.0	0.7	1.6	1.1	0.4	1.6	1.6	0.9	1.6	1.9
United Kingdom	2.2	3.1	4.5	4.6	3.0	3.5	2.9	3.4	1.4	2.1	2.8	2.6
Canada	2.1	3.4	3.8	4.0	2.3	3.6	3.0	3.3	3.9	4.1	3.3	2.8
Other advanced economies	4.2	3.5	5.9	5.6	2.6	3.7	1.0	3.3	3.2	3.3	3.3	3.4
Memorandum												
Major advanced economies	2.6	2.6	3.8	3.5	2.2	2.0	2.0	2.8	2.4	2.4	2.3	2.4
Newly industrialized Asian economies	6.1	3.9	8.2	7.3	3.2	5.0	−0.4	2.2	3.3	3.4	3.3	3.9
Public consumption												
Advanced economies	**1.8**	**2.3**	**2.8**	**2.5**	**2.8**	**3.3**	**2.4**	**2.0**	**1.5**	**1.9**	**1.9**	**1.9**
United States	1.0	2.3	3.1	1.7	3.1	4.3	2.5	2.1	0.9	1.6	2.2	1.9
Euro area	...	1.8	1.9	2.3	2.0	2.4	1.8	1.4	1.4	2.1	1.4	1.6
Germany	1.8	0.8	1.2	1.4	0.5	1.5	0.4	−1.3	0.6	1.8	0.5	1.1
France	1.7	1.7	1.4	2.0	1.1	1.9	2.0	2.2	1.1	1.9	2.0	2.1
Italy	—	1.5	1.3	2.3	3.6	2.1	2.0	1.6	1.5	−0.3	0.3	0.3
Spain	3.7	4.6	4.0	5.3	3.9	4.5	4.8	6.3	4.8	4.4	4.0	3.8
Japan	2.8	2.2	4.2	4.3	3.0	2.4	2.3	1.9	1.7	0.3	1.2	1.0
United Kingdom	1.0	2.9	3.7	3.1	2.4	3.5	3.5	3.2	3.1	1.9	2.3	2.5
Canada	0.9	2.8	2.1	3.1	3.9	2.5	3.5	3.0	2.7	3.4	1.5	2.5
Other advanced economies	4.0	2.5	1.9	2.1	3.1	3.6	2.2	1.7	2.4	3.1	2.5	2.4
Memorandum												
Major advanced economies	1.4	2.1	2.8	2.3	2.7	3.2	2.3	1.9	1.3	1.4	1.7	1.7
Newly industrialized Asian economies	5.9	2.8	0.8	2.4	3.5	4.4	2.5	1.8	2.9	3.7	3.2	2.7
Gross fixed capital formation												
Advanced economies	**3.4**	**2.8**	**5.6**	**5.1**	**−0.8**	**−1.6**	**2.0**	**4.5**	**4.4**	**4.1**	**2.0**	**3.3**
United States	4.6	2.8	8.2	6.1	−1.7	−3.5	3.2	6.1	6.4	3.1	−2.1	3.0
Euro area	...	2.8	6.3	5.0	0.5	−1.5	1.1	2.2	2.5	4.5	4.1	3.6
Germany	2.9	1.1	4.7	3.0	−3.7	−6.1	−0.8	−0.4	0.8	5.6	4.7	4.1
France	1.3	3.4	7.9	7.5	2.3	−1.7	2.3	2.6	3.7	3.5	3.0	3.2
Italy	1.1	2.3	3.6	6.4	2.5	4.0	−1.7	1.6	−0.5	2.3	2.4	2.2
Spain	3.4	6.0	10.4	6.6	4.8	3.4	5.9	5.0	7.0	6.3	5.6	4.8
Japan	0.9	0.8	−0.8	1.2	−0.9	−4.9	−0.5	1.4	2.4	3.5	4.1	2.7
United Kingdom	2.6	3.8	2.8	2.7	2.5	3.7	0.4	6.0	3.4	6.0	7.0	3.6
Canada	1.7	5.3	7.3	4.7	4.0	1.6	6.5	8.0	7.1	6.7	3.6	3.7
Other advanced economies	5.6	3.6	2.9	7.1	−4.6	3.6	2.4	7.1	4.5	4.9	4.7	4.1
Memorandum												
Major advanced economies	3.1	2.5	5.6	4.8	−0.6	−2.5	1.7	4.3	4.4	3.8	1.2	3.1
Newly industrialized Asian economies	8.2	3.4	2.9	10.9	−6.2	2.1	1.7	7.5	2.1	3.4	5.3	5.5

Table 3 *(concluded)*

	Ten-Year Averages		1999	2000	2001	2002	2003	2004	2005	2006	2007	2008
	1989–98	1999–2008										
Final domestic demand												
Advanced economies	**2.5**	**2.6**	**4.1**	**3.7**	**1.8**	**1.5**	**2.1**	**3.0**	**2.7**	**2.7**	**2.2**	**2.5**
United States	3.0	3.1	5.4	4.5	1.8	1.8	2.8	4.0	3.6	2.9	1.9	2.7
Euro area	. . .	2.1	3.7	3.3	1.7	0.6	1.3	1.6	1.6	2.6	2.3	2.3
Germany	2.4	0.9	3.0	2.3	0.4	–1.5	–0.1	–0.3	0.3	1.9	1.3	1.8
France	1.5	2.5	3.7	3.9	2.1	1.5	2.2	2.4	2.2	2.6	2.3	2.6
Italy	1.3	1.5	2.5	3.1	1.6	1.3	0.6	1.1	0.5	1.3	1.4	1.4
Spain	3.2	4.7	6.4	6.8	4.1	3.0	3.8	4.7	4.3	4.9	4.5	4.2
Japan	2.0	1.3	1.1	1.4	1.2	–0.2	0.5	1.6	1.8	1.5	2.1	1.9
United Kingdom	2.0	3.2	4.1	4.0	2.8	3.5	2.6	3.7	2.0	2.7	3.4	2.8
Canada	1.8	3.7	4.2	4.0	2.9	3.0	3.8	4.2	4.3	4.5	3.0	3.0
Other advanced economies	4.4	3.3	4.3	5.4	0.9	3.6	1.5	3.8	3.3	3.6	3.5	3.4
Memorandum												
Major advanced economies	2.4	2.5	4.0	3.6	1.7	1.3	2.0	2.9	2.6	2.5	2.0	2.4
Newly industrialized Asian economies	6.6	3.6	5.5	7.6	0.7	4.1	0.7	3.3	2.9	3.5	3.9	4.2
Stock building[1]												
Advanced economies	**—**	**—**	**–0.2**	**0.1**	**–0.6**	**—**	**0.1**	**0.2**	**–0.1**	**0.1**	**–0.1**	**—**
United States	0.1	—	—	–0.1	–0.9	0.4	—	0.4	–0.3	0.2	–0.2	—
Euro area	. . .	–0.1	–0.1	—	–0.4	–0.3	0.2	0.2	0.1	–0.3	–0.1	—
Germany	—	–0.1	–0.2	–0.1	–0.9	–0.6	0.8	0.3	0.2	–0.2	–0.1	—
France	—	–0.1	–0.2	0.6	–0.4	–0.3	–0.2	0.3	—	–0.3	—	—
Italy	—	0.1	0.1	–0.2	0.1	—	0.1	–0.1	–0.2	1.2	0.2	0.3
Spain	–0.1	—	0.2	–0.1	–0.1	—	–0.1	—	—	0.1	—	—
Japan	—	—	–1.0	1.0	–0.2	–0.3	0.2	0.3	–0.1	0.1	—	—
United Kingdom	—	—	0.2	–0.1	0.1	–0.3	0.2	0.1	–0.1	0.2	–0.2	—
Canada	—	—	0.1	0.8	–1.7	0.3	0.8	0.1	0.3	–0.2	–0.2	0.2
Other advanced economies	–0.1	0.1	0.9	—	–0.4	—	–0.2	0.4	—	–0.1	—	0.1
Memorandum												
Major advanced economies	—	—	–0.2	0.2	–0.6	0.1	0.2	0.3	–0.2	0.2	–0.1	—
Newly industrialized Asian economies	–0.3	0.2	2.1	–0.1	–0.7	0.1	–0.6	0.9	–0.2	0.1	–0.1	0.2
Foreign balance[1]												
Advanced economies	**0.1**	**–0.2**	**–0.6**	**–0.1**	**—**	**–0.2**	**–0.4**	**–0.3**	**–0.3**	**0.1**	**0.2**	**—**
United States	–0.1	–0.4	–1.0	–0.9	–0.2	–0.7	–0.4	–0.7	–0.3	—	0.4	—
Euro area	. . .	0.1	–0.5	0.5	0.7	0.5	–0.7	0.2	–0.2	0.4	0.1	—
Germany	0.2	0.7	–0.8	1.0	1.7	2.0	–0.9	1.2	0.4	1.1	0.6	0.2
France	0.3	–0.4	–0.4	–0.4	0.2	–0.1	–0.8	–0.7	–0.9	–0.4	–0.3	–0.3
Italy	0.2	–0.2	–1.2	0.8	0.2	–1.0	–0.8	0.1	–0.3	0.2	0.2	0.1
Spain	–0.2	–0.9	–1.7	–0.4	–0.2	–0.6	–0.8	–1.7	–1.7	–1.0	–0.8	–0.6
Japan	0.1	0.3	–0.1	0.5	–0.8	0.7	0.7	0.8	0.3	0.8	0.2	—
United Kingdom	0.1	–0.4	–1.0	–0.1	–0.5	–1.1	–0.1	–0.6	—	–0.4	–0.3	–0.2
Canada	0.3	–0.4	1.4	0.6	0.7	–0.1	–2.6	–0.8	–1.6	–1.3	–0.3	–0.2
Other advanced economies	0.1	0.8	0.4	0.8	0.8	0.3	1.3	0.9	0.9	1.1	0.5	0.6
Memorandum												
Major advanced economies	—	–0.2	–0.7	–0.2	—	–0.2	–0.4	–0.2	–0.2	0.1	0.2	—
Newly industrialized Asian economies	–0.2	1.5	0.3	0.5	1.1	1.2	3.1	2.2	2.3	2.3	1.2	0.8

[1]Changes expressed as percent of GDP in the preceding period.

Table 4. Advanced Economies: Unemployment, Employment, and Real Per Capita GDP
(Percent)

	Ten-Year Averages[1]		1999	2000	2001	2002	2003	2004	2005	2006	2007	2008
	1989–98	1999–2008										
Unemployment rate												
Advanced economies	**6.7**	**5.9**	**6.3**	**5.7**	**5.8**	**6.3**	**6.5**	**6.3**	**6.0**	**5.5**	**5.4**	**5.4**
United States[2]	5.9	5.0	4.2	4.0	4.7	5.8	6.0	5.5	5.1	4.6	4.8	5.0
Euro area	...	8.1	9.0	8.1	7.8	8.2	8.7	8.8	8.6	7.7	7.3	7.1
Germany	7.0	7.9	7.5	6.9	6.9	7.7	8.8	9.2	9.1	8.1	7.8	7.6
France	10.6	9.0	10.5	9.1	8.4	8.7	9.4	9.6	9.7	9.0	8.3	7.8
Italy	10.1	8.3	10.9	10.1	9.1	8.6	8.4	8.0	7.7	6.8	6.8	6.8
Spain	19.9	10.7	15.6	13.9	10.6	11.5	11.5	11.0	9.2	8.5	7.8	7.7
Netherlands	5.7	3.4	3.2	2.9	2.2	2.8	3.7	4.6	4.7	3.9	3.2	3.1
Belgium	8.4	7.8	8.5	6.9	6.6	7.5	8.2	8.4	8.4	8.3	7.8	7.6
Austria	3.6	4.3	3.9	3.6	3.6	4.2	4.3	4.8	5.2	4.8	4.5	4.3
Finland	11.2	8.7	10.2	9.8	9.1	9.1	9.0	8.8	8.4	7.7	7.5	7.4
Greece	9.0	10.0	12.1	11.4	10.8	10.3	9.7	10.5	9.9	8.9	8.3	8.5
Portugal	5.6	6.0	4.4	3.9	4.0	5.0	6.3	6.7	7.6	7.7	7.4	7.3
Ireland	13.0	4.5	5.6	4.3	3.9	4.4	4.6	4.4	4.4	4.4	4.5	4.7
Luxembourg	2.3	3.6	2.9	2.5	2.3	2.6	3.5	3.9	4.2	4.4	4.6	4.8
Slovenia	...	6.6	7.6	7.0	6.4	6.4	6.7	6.3	6.5	6.4	6.4	6.4
Japan	2.8	4.6	4.7	4.7	5.0	5.4	5.3	4.7	4.4	4.1	4.0	4.0
United Kingdom	8.3	5.2	6.0	5.5	5.1	5.2	5.0	4.8	4.8	5.4	5.3	5.1
Canada	9.6	6.9	7.6	6.8	7.2	7.6	7.6	7.2	6.8	6.3	6.2	6.2
Korea	2.9	3.9	6.6	4.4	4.0	3.3	3.6	3.7	3.7	3.5	3.3	3.1
Australia	8.5	5.7	6.9	6.3	6.8	6.4	6.1	5.5	5.1	4.9	4.6	4.6
Taiwan Province of China	1.9	4.1	2.9	3.0	4.6	5.2	5.0	4.4	4.1	3.9	3.8	3.7
Sweden	5.8	5.0	5.6	4.7	4.0	4.0	4.9	5.5	5.8	4.8	5.5	5.0
Switzerland	2.8	2.7	2.4	1.7	1.6	2.3	3.4	3.5	3.4	3.4	2.9	2.8
Hong Kong SAR	2.3	5.7	6.3	5.1	4.9	7.2	7.9	6.9	5.7	4.8	4.4	4.2
Denmark	9.9	5.4	5.7	5.4	5.2	5.2	6.2	6.4	5.7	4.5	4.7	4.9
Norway	5.1	3.7	3.2	3.4	3.5	3.9	4.5	4.5	4.6	3.4	2.9	3.0
Israel	8.8	9.0	8.8	8.8	9.4	10.3	10.8	10.3	9.0	8.4	7.5	7.2
Singapore	1.8	3.0	2.8	2.7	2.7	3.6	4.0	3.4	3.1	2.7	2.6	2.6
New Zealand	8.0	4.8	6.8	6.0	5.3	5.2	4.6	3.9	3.7	3.8	4.2	4.4
Cyprus	2.7	4.2	3.6	3.4	3.0	3.3	4.1	4.7	5.3	4.9	4.8	4.7
Iceland	3.3	2.1	1.9	1.3	1.4	2.5	3.4	3.1	2.1	1.3	2.0	2.3
Memorandum												
Major advanced economies	6.4	5.9	5.9	5.5	5.8	6.4	6.6	6.3	6.0	5.6	5.5	5.5
Newly industrialized Asian economies	2.5	4.1	5.4	4.0	4.2	4.2	4.4	4.2	4.0	3.7	3.5	3.3
Growth in employment												
Advanced economies	**1.0**	**1.0**	**1.3**	**2.0**	**0.6**	**0.3**	**0.5**	**0.9**	**1.2**	**1.5**	**1.0**	**0.9**
United States	1.4	1.2	1.5	2.5	—	−0.3	0.9	1.1	1.8	1.9	1.2	1.0
Euro area	...	1.2	2.0	2.3	1.4	0.9	0.7	0.7	0.8	1.4	1.1	0.8
Germany	0.4	0.4	1.3	1.8	0.4	−0.6	−0.9	0.4	−0.2	0.8	0.6	0.3
France	0.4	1.0	2.0	2.7	1.8	0.6	0.1	—	0.5	0.8	0.6	0.5
Italy	−0.2	1.3	1.1	1.8	2.0	1.4	0.9	1.3	0.8	1.8	0.8	0.7
Spain	1.9	3.2	4.6	5.0	3.2	2.3	2.4	2.6	3.1	3.1	2.7	2.4
Japan	0.8	−0.2	−0.8	−0.2	−0.5	−1.3	−0.2	0.2	0.4	0.4	0.1	—
United Kingdom	0.3	0.9	1.4	1.2	0.8	0.8	1.0	1.0	0.9	0.8	0.7	0.6
Canada	1.0	1.9	2.6	2.5	1.2	2.4	2.4	1.8	1.4	2.0	1.4	1.3
Other advanced economies	1.3	1.6	1.6	2.9	1.1	1.6	0.5	1.6	1.5	1.7	1.5	1.5
Memorandum												
Major advanced economies	0.8	0.8	1.1	1.8	0.4	−0.1	0.5	0.8	1.0	1.3	0.8	0.7
Newly industrialized Asian economies	1.7	1.6	1.5	3.6	0.8	2.0	0.3	1.9	1.2	1.5	1.7	1.6

Table 4 *(concluded)*

	Ten-Year Averages[1]		1999	2000	2001	2002	2003	2004	2005	2006	2007	2008
	1989–98	1999–2008										
Growth in real per capita GDP												
Advanced economies	**2.0**	**2.1**	**2.9**	**3.4**	**0.6**	**1.0**	**1.3**	**2.7**	**2.0**	**2.5**	**2.0**	**2.2**
United States	1.8	1.8	3.3	2.5	−0.3	0.6	1.5	2.9	2.2	2.3	1.2	1.7
Euro area	. . .	1.8	2.8	3.5	1.5	0.4	0.2	1.3	0.9	2.2	1.8	1.9
Germany	1.8	1.4	1.8	3.0	1.0	−0.1	−0.2	1.3	0.9	2.9	2.0	2.0
France	1.4	1.5	2.5	3.4	1.1	0.4	0.5	1.4	0.6	1.4	1.5	1.9
Italy	1.5	1.1	1.8	3.3	1.5	0.1	—	1.1	−1.0	1.5	1.6	1.5
Spain	2.5	2.3	3.8	4.3	3.1	1.4	1.2	1.6	1.9	2.1	1.9	1.8
Japan	1.7	1.4	−0.3	2.7	−0.1	0.1	1.2	2.7	1.9	2.2	2.3	1.9
United Kingdom	1.7	2.3	2.7	3.5	2.0	1.7	2.3	2.8	1.3	2.2	2.4	2.4
Canada	0.9	2.1	4.7	4.3	0.7	1.8	0.8	2.3	1.9	1.7	1.1	1.6
Other advanced economies	3.2	3.2	4.5	5.2	0.5	3.0	1.8	4.1	3.2	3.7	3.2	3.2
Memorandum												
Major advanced economies	1.8	1.8	2.5	3.0	0.5	0.6	1.2	2.5	1.8	2.3	1.7	2.0
Newly industrialized Asian economies	4.9	4.4	6.6	7.0	0.5	4.7	2.6	5.3	4.2	4.8	4.1	4.1

[1]Compound annual rate of change for employment and per capita GDP; arithmetic average for unemployment rate.
[2]The projections for unemployment have been adjusted to reflect the survey techniques adopted by the U.S. Bureau of Labor Statistics in January 1994.

Table 5. Other Emerging Market and Developing Countries: Real GDP

(Annual percent change)

	Ten-Year Averages		1999	2000	2001	2002	2003	2004	2005	2006	2007	2008
	1989–98	1999–2008										
Other emerging market and developing countries	**3.8**	**6.4**	**4.1**	**6.0**	**4.3**	**5.0**	**6.7**	**7.7**	**7.5**	**7.9**	**7.5**	**7.1**
Regional groups												
Africa	2.2	4.7	2.7	3.1	4.4	3.7	4.7	5.8	5.6	5.5	6.2	5.8
Sub-Sahara	2.1	4.9	2.7	3.4	4.5	3.7	4.2	6.0	6.0	5.7	6.8	6.1
Excluding Nigeria and South Africa	2.3	5.3	3.2	2.4	5.9	4.0	3.7	6.7	6.5	6.3	7.8	6.9
Central and eastern Europe	1.1	4.4	0.5	4.9	0.2	4.5	4.8	6.6	5.5	6.0	5.5	5.3
Commonwealth of Independent States[1]	...	7.0	5.2	9.0	6.3	5.3	7.9	8.4	6.6	7.7	7.0	6.4
Russia	...	6.6	6.4	10.0	5.1	4.7	7.3	7.2	6.4	6.7	6.4	5.9
Excluding Russia	...	7.7	2.4	6.7	9.1	6.6	9.3	11.0	6.9	9.7	8.3	7.5
Developing Asia	7.3	7.9	6.4	7.0	6.0	7.0	8.4	8.7	9.2	9.4	8.8	8.4
China	9.6	9.4	7.6	8.4	8.3	9.1	10.0	10.1	10.4	10.7	10.0	9.5
India	5.7	7.0	6.7	5.3	4.1	4.3	7.3	7.8	9.2	9.2	8.4	7.8
Excluding China and India	5.1	5.4	3.7	5.8	3.1	4.8	5.8	6.4	6.2	5.9	6.0	6.0
Middle East	4.5	4.8	1.8	5.4	3.0	3.9	6.5	5.6	5.4	5.7	5.5	5.5
Western Hemisphere	3.1	3.2	0.3	3.9	0.5	0.3	2.4	6.0	4.6	5.5	4.9	4.2
Brazil	2.0	3.1	0.3	4.3	1.3	2.7	1.1	5.7	2.9	3.7	4.4	4.2
Mexico	3.4	3.1	3.8	6.6	—	0.8	1.4	4.2	2.8	4.8	3.4	3.5
Analytical groups												
By source of export earnings												
Fuel	−0.3	5.9	3.0	7.1	4.4	4.0	6.9	7.3	6.7	6.7	6.9	6.0
Nonfuel	4.6	6.4	4.2	5.8	4.3	5.2	6.7	7.8	7.6	8.1	7.6	7.2
of which, primary products	2.5	3.7	0.6	1.5	2.9	2.8	3.6	6.1	5.2	4.3	4.8	5.3
By external financing source												
Net debtor countries	3.4	5.0	2.8	4.6	2.5	3.3	4.9	6.4	6.3	6.7	6.3	6.0
of which, official financing	4.1	5.4	3.9	4.6	3.4	3.9	4.7	6.5	7.1	7.0	6.4	6.3
Net debtor countries by debt-servicing experience												
Countries with arrears and/or rescheduling during 2001–05	3.4	4.7	1.1	3.3	2.6	1.6	5.2	6.9	7.2	6.5	6.8	6.1
Other groups												
Heavily indebted poor countries	1.8	4.8	3.6	2.7	4.8	3.5	4.0	6.5	5.9	5.8	5.4	6.0
Middle East and north Africa	4.0	4.8	2.1	4.8	3.3	3.9	6.5	5.5	5.3	5.7	5.5	5.6
Memorandum												
Real per capita GDP												
Other emerging market and developing countries	2.2	5.1	2.6	4.6	2.9	3.7	5.4	6.4	6.2	6.6	6.2	5.8
Africa	−0.5	2.5	0.4	0.8	2.1	1.4	2.5	3.6	3.4	3.3	4.1	3.7
Central and eastern Europe	0.6	3.9	—	4.5	−0.2	4.1	4.4	6.1	5.1	5.6	5.1	4.8
Commonwealth of Independent States[1]	...	7.2	5.4	9.2	6.6	5.6	8.2	8.7	6.8	7.9	7.2	6.6
Developing Asia	5.8	6.7	5.0	5.7	4.8	5.7	7.2	7.6	8.0	8.2	7.7	7.3
Middle East	2.1	2.9	−0.2	3.4	1.0	2.0	4.5	3.7	3.5	3.8	3.6	3.5
Western Hemisphere	1.3	1.8	−1.3	2.4	−1.0	−1.2	0.9	4.6	3.2	4.1	3.5	2.9

[1]Mongolia, which is not a member of the Commonwealth of Independent States, is included in this group for reasons of geography and similarities in economic structure.

Table 6. Other Emerging Market and Developing Countries—by Country: Real GDP[1]

(Annual percent change)

	Average 1989–98	1999	2000	2001	2002	2003	2004	2005	2006	2007	2008
Africa	**2.2**	**2.7**	**3.1**	**4.4**	**3.7**	**4.7**	**5.8**	**5.6**	**5.5**	**6.2**	**5.8**
Algeria	1.7	3.2	2.2	2.6	4.7	6.9	5.2	5.3	2.7	4.5	4.1
Angola	0.3	3.2	3.0	3.1	14.5	3.3	11.2	20.6	15.3	35.3	16.0
Benin	4.1	5.3	4.9	6.2	4.5	3.9	3.1	2.9	4.1	4.7	5.2
Botswana	6.5	7.2	8.3	4.9	5.6	6.3	6.0	6.2	4.2	4.3	4.4
Burkina Faso	4.5	7.4	1.8	6.6	4.7	8.0	4.6	7.1	6.4	6.5	6.3
Burundi	−1.0	−1.0	−0.9	2.1	4.4	−1.2	4.8	0.9	5.1	5.5	6.6
Cameroon[2]	−0.3	4.4	4.2	4.5	4.0	4.0	3.7	2.0	3.5	4.0	4.1
Cape Verde	5.5	11.9	7.3	6.1	5.3	4.7	4.4	5.8	5.8	6.5	7.0
Central African Republic	0.2	3.6	1.8	0.3	−0.6	−7.6	1.3	2.2	3.5	4.0	4.3
Chad	3.5	−0.7	−0.9	11.7	8.5	14.7	33.6	8.6	1.3	−1.2	7.4
Comoros	0.9	1.9	1.4	3.3	4.1	2.5	−0.2	4.2	1.2	3.0	4.5
Congo, Dem. Rep. of	−5.3	−4.3	−6.9	−2.1	3.5	5.8	6.6	6.5	5.1	6.5	6.9
Congo, Rep. of	3.0	−2.6	7.6	3.8	4.6	0.8	3.6	7.7	6.4	3.7	7.3
Côte d'Ivoire	3.8	1.8	−4.6	—	−1.6	−1.7	1.6	1.5	1.4	1.7	3.3
Djibouti	−1.7	3.0	0.4	2.0	2.6	3.2	3.0	3.2	4.5	5.1	5.7
Equatorial Guinea	26.6	24.2	13.7	94.4	24.7	12.5	33.9	6.5	1.0	7.1	9.0
Eritrea	...	—	−13.1	9.2	0.6	3.9	2.0	4.8	2.0	1.3	1.3
Ethiopia	1.9	6.0	5.9	7.7	1.2	−3.5	13.1	10.3	10.6	6.5	6.6
Gabon	4.8	−8.9	−1.9	2.1	−0.3	2.4	1.1	3.0	1.0	4.7	2.2
Gambia, The	4.0	6.4	5.5	5.8	−3.2	6.9	7.0	5.1	6.5	7.0	6.0
Ghana	4.3	4.4	3.7	4.2	4.5	5.2	5.6	5.9	6.2	6.3	6.9
Guinea	4.3	4.7	1.9	4.0	4.2	1.2	2.7	3.3	2.8	2.5	5.0
Guinea-Bissau	0.2	7.6	7.5	0.2	−7.1	−0.6	2.2	3.2	2.7	5.0	4.7
Kenya	2.3	2.4	0.6	4.7	0.3	2.8	4.5	5.8	6.0	6.2	5.8
Lesotho	4.6	−0.6	0.7	2.0	2.8	3.0	3.8	3.7	5.6	5.1	5.2
Liberia	...	34.6	29.3	22.0	31.8	−33.9	−5.2	9.5	9.7	13.3	13.5
Madagascar	1.5	4.7	4.7	6.0	−12.7	9.8	5.3	4.6	4.7	5.6	5.6
Malawi	3.7	3.5	0.8	−4.1	2.1	3.9	5.1	2.1	8.5	5.7	5.5
Mali	5.9	3.0	−3.2	12.1	4.3	7.2	2.4	6.1	4.6	5.9	5.7
Mauritania	2.2	6.7	1.9	2.9	1.1	5.6	5.2	5.4	11.7	1.9	5.0
Mauritius	5.9	4.6	7.2	4.2	1.5	3.8	4.7	3.0	3.7	4.1	4.4
Morocco	2.8	−0.1	1.0	6.3	3.2	5.5	4.2	1.7	7.3	3.5	5.8
Mozambique, Rep. of	5.0	7.5	1.9	13.1	8.2	7.9	7.5	7.8	8.5	6.8	7.6
Namibia	3.7	3.4	3.5	2.4	6.7	3.5	6.6	4.2	4.6	4.8	4.6
Niger	1.9	−0.6	−1.4	7.1	3.0	4.5	−0.7	6.8	3.4	4.1	4.3
Nigeria	3.4	1.5	5.4	3.1	1.5	10.7	6.0	7.2	5.3	8.2	6.7
Rwanda	−1.8	7.6	6.0	6.7	9.4	0.9	4.0	6.0	4.2	4.7	4.9
São Tomé and Príncipe	1.3	2.5	3.0	4.0	4.1	4.0	3.8	6.0	8.0	7.0	7.0
Senegal	2.5	6.3	3.2	4.6	0.7	6.7	5.6	5.5	3.3	5.6	5.6
Seychelles	5.7	1.9	4.3	−2.3	1.2	−5.9	−2.9	1.2	4.5	5.0	4.0
Sierra Leone	−6.6	−8.1	3.8	18.2	27.4	9.5	7.4	7.3	7.4	6.5	6.5
South Africa	1.4	2.4	4.2	2.7	3.7	3.1	4.8	5.1	5.0	4.7	4.5
Sudan	2.6	3.1	8.4	6.2	5.4	7.1	5.1	8.6	12.2	11.1	10.2
Swaziland	4.2	3.5	2.6	1.6	2.9	2.9	2.1	2.3	2.1	1.2	1.0
Tanzania	3.1	3.5	5.1	6.2	7.2	5.7	6.7	6.8	5.9	7.3	7.6
Togo	1.7	2.6	−1.0	−2.3	−0.2	5.2	2.3	1.2	1.8	2.9	3.9
Tunisia	4.6	6.1	4.7	4.9	1.7	5.6	6.0	4.0	5.3	6.0	6.0
Uganda	6.1	8.3	5.3	4.8	6.9	4.4	5.7	6.7	5.4	6.2	6.5
Zambia	−1.2	2.2	3.6	4.9	3.3	5.1	5.4	5.2	6.0	6.0	6.0
Zimbabwe	2.9	−3.6	−7.3	−2.7	−4.4	−10.4	−3.8	−5.3	−4.8	−5.7	−3.6

Table 6 *(continued)*

	Average 1989–98	1999	2000	2001	2002	2003	2004	2005	2006	2007	2008
Central and eastern Europe[3]	**1.1**	**0.5**	**4.9**	**0.2**	**4.5**	**4.8**	**6.6**	**5.5**	**6.0**	**5.5**	**5.3**
Albania	−0.5	10.1	7.3	7.0	2.9	5.7	5.9	5.5	5.0	6.0	6.0
Bosnia and Herzegovina	...	9.5	5.2	3.6	5.0	4.1	5.8	5.0	6.0	6.0	6.0
Bulgaria	−5.6	2.3	5.4	4.1	4.9	4.5	5.7	5.5	6.2	6.0	6.0
Croatia	...	−0.9	2.9	4.4	5.6	5.3	3.8	4.3	4.6	4.7	4.5
Czech Republic	0.0	1.3	3.6	2.5	1.9	3.6	4.2	6.1	6.1	4.8	4.3
Estonia	...	0.3	10.8	7.7	8.0	7.1	8.1	10.5	11.4	9.9	7.9
Hungary	−0.2	4.2	5.2	4.1	4.3	4.1	4.9	4.2	3.9	2.8	3.0
Latvia	...	4.7	6.9	8.0	6.5	7.2	8.6	10.2	11.9	10.5	7.0
Lithuania	...	−1.5	4.1	6.6	6.9	10.3	7.3	7.6	7.5	7.0	6.5
Macedonia, FYR	...	4.3	4.5	−4.5	0.9	2.8	4.1	3.8	4.0	4.5	4.5
Malta	5.3	3.8	−1.0	−1.1	1.9	−2.3	0.8	2.2	2.5	2.3	2.3
Serbia	...	−18.0	4.5	4.8	4.2	2.5	8.4	6.2	5.4	5.0	5.5
Poland	2.5	4.5	4.2	1.1	1.4	3.8	5.3	3.5	5.8	5.8	5.0
Romania	−2.9	−1.2	2.1	5.7	5.1	5.2	8.4	4.1	7.7	6.5	4.8
Slovak Republic	...	0.3	0.7	3.2	4.1	4.2	5.4	6.0	8.2	8.2	7.5
Turkey	4.3	−4.7	7.4	−7.5	7.9	5.8	8.9	7.4	5.5	5.0	6.0
Commonwealth of Independent States[3,4]	**...**	**5.2**	**9.0**	**6.3**	**5.3**	**7.9**	**8.4**	**6.6**	**7.7**	**7.0**	**6.4**
Russia	...	6.4	10.0	5.1	4.7	7.3	7.2	6.4	6.7	6.4	5.9
Excluding Russia	...	2.4	6.7	9.1	6.6	9.3	11.0	6.9	9.7	8.3	7.5
Armenia	...	3.3	6.0	9.6	13.2	14.0	10.5	14.0	13.4	9.0	6.0
Azerbaijan	...	11.4	6.2	6.5	8.1	10.4	10.2	24.3	31.0	29.2	23.1
Belarus	...	3.4	5.8	4.7	5.0	7.0	11.4	9.3	9.9	5.5	3.9
Georgia	...	3.0	1.9	4.7	5.5	11.1	5.9	9.6	9.0	7.5	6.5
Kazakhstan	...	2.7	9.8	13.5	9.8	9.3	9.6	9.7	10.6	9.0	8.1
Kyrgyz Republic	...	3.7	5.4	5.3	−0.0	7.0	7.0	−0.2	2.7	6.5	6.6
Moldova	...	−3.4	2.1	6.1	7.8	6.6	7.4	7.5	4.0	4.5	5.0
Mongolia	−0.3	3.2	1.2	1.1	4.2	6.1	10.8	6.6	8.4	8.0	7.0
Tajikistan	...	3.7	8.3	10.2	9.1	10.2	10.6	6.7	7.0	7.5	8.0
Turkmenistan	...	16.5	18.6	20.4	15.8	17.1	14.7	9.0	9.0	10.0	10.0
Ukraine	...	−0.2	5.9	9.2	5.2	9.6	12.1	2.7	7.1	5.0	4.6
Uzbekistan	...	4.3	3.8	4.2	4.0	4.2	7.7	7.0	7.2	7.7	7.5

Table 6 *(continued)*

	Average 1989–98	1999	2000	2001	2002	2003	2004	2005	2006	2007	2008
Developing Asia	**7.3**	**6.4**	**7.0**	**6.0**	**7.0**	**8.4**	**8.7**	**9.2**	**9.4**	**8.8**	**8.4**
Afghanistan, Rep. of	...	...	...	...	28.6	15.7	8.0	14.0	8.0	12.2	10.8
Bangladesh	4.7	5.4	5.6	4.8	4.8	5.8	6.1	6.3	6.7	6.6	6.5
Bhutan	4.5	7.9	7.6	7.2	10.0	7.6	6.8	6.5	13.7	15.2	8.6
Brunei Darussalam	...	3.1	2.9	2.7	3.9	2.9	0.5	0.4	3.8	2.6	3.0
Cambodia	...	12.6	8.4	7.7	6.2	8.6	10.0	13.4	9.5	7.0	6.0
China	9.6	7.6	8.4	8.3	9.1	10.0	10.1	10.4	10.7	10.0	9.5
Fiji	3.8	9.2	−2.8	2.7	4.3	3.0	5.4	0.7	3.2	2.3	1.7
India	5.7	6.7	5.3	4.1	4.3	7.3	7.8	9.2	9.2	8.4	7.8
Indonesia	4.8	0.8	5.4	3.6	4.5	4.8	5.0	5.7	5.5	6.0	6.3
Kiribati	3.1	9.5	3.9	1.7	5.8	1.4	−2.9	−0.2	5.8	2.5	1.6
Lao PDR	6.6	7.3	5.8	5.7	5.9	6.1	6.4	7.0	7.5	7.1	9.0
Malaysia	7.4	6.1	8.9	0.3	4.4	5.5	7.2	5.2	5.9	5.5	5.8
Maldives	6.7	7.2	4.8	3.5	6.5	8.5	9.5	−4.5	16.1	4.0	3.0
Myanmar	5.3	10.9	13.7	11.3	12.0	13.8	13.6	13.2	7.0	5.5	4.0
Nepal	4.8	4.5	6.1	5.6	−0.6	3.3	3.8	2.7	1.9	3.5	4.5
Pakistan	4.1	3.7	4.3	2.0	3.2	4.9	7.4	8.0	6.2	6.5	6.5
Papua New Guinea	4.2	1.9	−2.5	−0.1	−0.2	2.2	2.7	3.3	3.7	4.3	3.7
Philippines	3.0	3.4	6.0	1.8	4.4	4.9	6.2	5.0	5.4	5.8	5.8
Samoa	2.4	2.1	3.7	7.1	4.4	1.6	3.3	5.4	2.3	3.0	3.5
Solomon Islands	4.8	−0.5	−14.3	−9.0	−1.6	6.4	8.0	5.0	4.8	3.8	3.4
Sri Lanka	5.0	4.3	6.0	−1.5	4.0	6.0	5.4	6.0	7.5	7.0	7.0
Thailand	5.8	4.4	4.8	2.2	5.3	7.1	6.3	4.5	5.0	4.5	4.8
Timor-Leste, Dem. Rep. of	...	...	15.5	16.5	−6.7	−6.2	0.3	2.3	−1.6	32.0	3.6
Tonga	1.4	2.3	5.4	2.6	3.0	3.2	1.4	2.3	1.9	0.6	1.6
Vanuatu	4.4	−3.2	2.7	−2.6	−7.4	3.2	5.5	6.8	5.5	5.0	4.0
Vietnam	7.7	4.8	6.8	6.9	7.1	7.3	7.8	8.4	8.2	8.0	7.8
Middle East	**4.5**	**1.8**	**5.4**	**3.0**	**3.9**	**6.5**	**5.6**	**5.4**	**5.7**	**5.5**	**5.5**
Bahrain	4.8	4.3	5.2	4.6	5.2	7.2	5.6	7.8	7.7	6.9	6.6
Egypt	3.7	6.1	5.4	3.5	3.2	3.2	4.1	4.5	6.8	6.7	6.6
Iran, I.R. of	5.5	1.9	5.1	3.7	7.5	7.2	5.1	4.4	5.3	5.0	5.0
Iraq	...	...	...	...	...	...	...	...	...	...	...
Jordan	2.7	3.4	4.3	5.3	5.8	4.2	8.4	7.2	6.0	6.0	6.0
Kuwait	2.7	−1.8	4.7	0.2	3.0	16.5	10.5	10.0	5.0	3.5	4.8
Lebanon	−0.1	−0.8	1.7	4.5	3.3	4.1	7.0	1.0	—	1.0	3.5
Libya	−1.1	1.1	3.4	5.9	1.4	5.9	5.0	6.3	5.6	7.9	8.1
Oman	5.2	−0.2	5.5	7.5	2.6	2.0	5.4	5.8	5.9	6.0	6.3
Qatar	4.7	4.5	9.1	3.3	7.1	3.5	20.8	6.1	8.8	8.0	11.8
Saudi Arabia	3.1	−0.7	4.9	0.5	0.1	7.7	5.3	6.6	4.6	4.8	4.0
Syrian Arab Republic	5.3	−3.1	2.3	3.7	3.7	1.0	2.4	2.9	3.0	3.3	4.7
United Arab Emirates	6.6	3.1	12.4	1.7	2.6	11.9	9.7	8.5	9.7	8.2	7.2
Yemen, Rep. of	...	3.5	4.4	4.6	3.9	3.1	2.6	3.7	3.8	2.6	2.9

Table 6 *(concluded)*

	Average 1989–98	1999	2000	2001	2002	2003	2004	2005	2006	2007	2008
Western Hemisphere	**3.1**	**0.3**	**3.9**	**0.5**	**0.3**	**2.4**	**6.0**	**4.6**	**5.5**	**4.9**	**4.2**
Antigua and Barbuda	3.5	4.9	3.3	1.5	2.0	4.3	5.2	5.3	8.0	3.8	1.8
Argentina	3.8	−3.4	−0.8	−4.4	−10.9	8.8	9.0	9.2	8.5	7.5	5.5
Bahamas, The	1.6	4.0	1.9	0.8	2.3	1.4	1.8	2.7	4.0	4.5	4.0
Barbados	0.9	0.5	2.3	−2.6	0.5	1.9	4.5	4.1	3.5	4.9	2.0
Belize	6.5	8.7	13.0	5.0	5.1	9.3	4.6	3.5	5.0	3.5	3.3
Bolivia	4.3	0.4	2.5	1.7	2.5	2.9	3.9	4.1	4.5	4.5	5.3
Brazil	2.0	0.3	4.3	1.3	2.7	1.1	5.7	2.9	3.7	4.4	4.2
Chile	7.5	−0.4	4.5	3.5	2.2	4.0	6.0	5.7	4.0	5.2	5.1
Colombia	3.6	−4.2	2.9	1.5	1.9	3.9	4.9	5.3	6.8	5.5	4.5
Costa Rica	5.1	8.2	1.8	1.1	2.9	6.4	4.3	5.9	7.9	6.0	5.0
Dominica	2.0	1.6	1.4	−4.2	−5.1	0.1	3.0	3.4	4.1	3.0	3.0
Dominican Republic	4.2	8.1	8.1	3.6	4.4	−1.9	2.0	9.3	10.7	6.0	4.5
Ecuador	2.9	−6.3	2.8	5.3	4.2	3.6	7.9	4.7	4.2	2.7	2.9
El Salvador	4.6	3.4	2.2	1.7	2.3	2.3	1.8	2.8	4.2	4.0	4.0
Grenada	3.6	7.3	7.0	−4.4	0.8	5.8	−6.9	12.1	2.1	5.0	4.0
Guatemala	4.1	3.8	3.6	2.3	2.2	2.1	2.7	3.2	4.6	4.5	4.0
Guyana	3.9	3.0	−1.3	2.3	1.1	−0.7	1.6	−1.9	4.8	5.2	4.7
Haiti	−0.6	2.6	1.3	−0.6	−0.5	0.2	−2.6	0.4	2.2	3.5	4.0
Honduras	3.4	−1.9	5.7	2.6	2.7	3.5	5.0	4.1	5.5	4.8	3.4
Jamaica	1.2	1.0	0.7	1.5	1.1	2.3	1.0	1.4	2.7	3.0	3.1
Mexico	3.4	3.8	6.6	—	0.8	1.4	4.2	2.8	4.8	3.4	3.5
Nicaragua	2.3	7.0	4.1	3.0	0.8	2.5	5.1	4.0	3.7	4.2	5.0
Panama	5.8	3.9	2.7	0.6	2.2	4.2	7.5	6.9	8.1	6.6	6.8
Paraguay	3.2	−1.5	−3.3	2.1	—	3.8	4.1	2.9	4.0	4.0	4.5
Peru	1.6	0.9	3.0	0.2	5.2	3.9	5.2	6.4	8.0	6.0	5.5
St. Kitts and Nevis	4.3	3.9	6.5	1.7	−0.3	−1.2	7.3	4.1	4.6	6.0	4.3
St. Lucia	3.5	3.9	0.1	−3.7	0.8	2.9	4.8	5.8	4.2	4.0	4.3
St. Vincent and the Grenadines	3.4	3.6	2.0	−0.1	3.2	2.8	6.8	2.2	4.1	5.5	6.3
Suriname	0.8	−0.9	−0.1	6.8	2.6	6.0	8.1	5.5	5.8	5.3	4.0
Trinidad and Tobago	3.0	8.0	6.9	4.2	7.9	13.9	9.1	7.9	12.0	7.0	4.5
Uruguay	3.6	−2.8	−1.4	−3.4	−11.0	2.2	11.8	6.6	7.0	5.0	3.5
Venezuela	2.1	−6.0	3.7	3.4	−8.9	−7.8	18.3	10.3	10.3	6.2	2.0

[1]For many countries, figures for recent years are IMF staff estimates. Data for some countries are for fiscal years.

[2]The percent changes in 2002 are calculated over a period of 18 months, reflecting a change in the fiscal year cycle (from July–June to January–December).

[3]Data for some countries refer to real net material product (NMP) or are estimates based on NMP. For many countries, figures for recent years are IMF staff estimates. The figures should be interpreted only as indicative of broad orders of magnitude because reliable, comparable data are not generally available. In particular, the growth of output of new private enterprises of the informal economy is not fully reflected in the recent figures.

[4]Mongolia, which is not a member of the Commonwealth of Independent States, is included in this group for reasons of geography and similarities in economic structure.

Table 7. Summary of Inflation
(Percent)

	Ten-Year Averages											
	1989–98	1999–2008	1999	2000	2001	2002	2003	2004	2005	2006	2007	2008
GDP deflators												
Advanced economies	**3.3**	**1.7**	**0.9**	**1.5**	**1.9**	**1.6**	**1.7**	**1.9**	**1.9**	**1.9**	**1.4**	**1.7**
United States	2.5	2.2	1.4	2.2	2.4	1.7	2.1	2.8	3.0	2.9	1.7	1.9
Euro area	...	1.9	0.9	1.5	2.7	2.6	2.1	1.9	1.9	1.7	1.8	1.8
Japan	0.9	−1.0	−1.3	−1.7	−1.2	−1.5	−1.6	−1.1	−1.3	−0.9	−0.3	0.6
Other advanced economies[1]	4.0	1.8	1.1	1.9	2.0	1.8	2.0	2.0	1.9	1.7	1.3	2.0
Consumer prices												
Advanced economies	**3.5**	**2.0**	**1.4**	**2.2**	**2.1**	**1.5**	**1.8**	**2.0**	**2.3**	**2.3**	**1.8**	**2.1**
United States	3.3	2.6	2.2	3.4	2.8	1.6	2.3	2.7	3.4	3.2	1.9	2.5
Euro area[2]	...	2.1	1.1	2.1	2.4	2.3	2.1	2.1	2.2	2.2	2.0	2.0
Japan	1.5	−0.2	−0.3	−0.4	−0.8	−0.9	−0.2	—	−0.6	0.2	0.3	0.8
Other advanced economies	4.0	1.9	1.1	1.8	2.1	1.7	1.8	1.7	2.1	2.1	2.0	2.1
Other emerging market and developing countries	**50.3**	**6.2**	**10.3**	**7.1**	**6.7**	**5.8**	**5.8**	**5.6**	**5.4**	**5.3**	**5.4**	**4.9**
Regional groups												
Africa	28.2	10.5	11.8	13.5	12.5	9.7	10.6	7.9	8.4	9.5	10.7	10.4
Central and eastern Europe	63.5	11.2	23.7	23.1	19.7	14.9	8.3	6.1	4.8	5.0	4.8	3.7
Commonwealth of Independent States[3]	...	17.9	69.8	24.7	20.3	13.8	12.0	10.3	12.4	9.5	9.0	8.3
Developing Asia	9.7	3.1	2.5	1.8	2.7	2.0	2.5	4.1	3.6	4.0	3.9	3.4
Middle East	11.4	6.7	6.6	4.0	3.8	5.3	6.2	7.2	7.1	7.9	10.6	8.7
Western Hemisphere	134.2	7.0	8.3	7.6	6.1	8.9	10.6	6.5	6.3	5.4	5.2	5.7
Memorandum												
European Union	11.5	2.4	2.2	3.1	3.0	2.5	2.2	2.3	2.3	2.3	2.2	2.2
Analytical groups												
By source of export earnings												
Fuel	74.1	13.0	36.2	13.9	13.5	11.7	11.3	9.6	9.9	8.9	9.4	8.5
Nonfuel	46.5	5.2	6.7	6.1	5.6	4.9	5.0	5.0	4.7	4.8	4.8	4.3
of which, primary products	73.5	23.9	30.7	35.5	30.9	17.6	19.2	14.7	17.0	22.5	25.5	27.2
By external financing source												
Net debtor countries	55.7	7.3	10.4	8.8	8.1	8.1	7.3	5.7	6.2	6.7	6.4	5.6
of which, official financing	27.7	5.7	5.3	3.8	4.1	3.7	5.9	7.4	7.3	6.9	6.6	5.6
Net debtor countries by debt-servicing experience												
Countries with arrears and/or rescheduling during 2001–05	44.6	11.6	14.1	10.4	11.4	14.2	11.6	8.6	10.7	13.1	11.5	11.2
Memorandum												
Median inflation rate												
Advanced economies	3.1	2.1	1.4	2.7	2.6	2.2	2.1	1.9	2.1	2.2	2.0	2.0
Other emerging market and developing countries	10.3	4.5	3.9	4.0	4.7	3.3	4.0	4.5	5.7	5.5	5.3	4.4

[1]In this table, "other advanced economies" means advanced economies excluding the United States, euro area countries, and Japan.
[2]Based on Eurostat's harmonized index of consumer prices.
[3]Mongolia, which is not a member of the Commonwealth of Independent States, is included in this group for reasons of geography and similarities in economic structure.

Table 8. Advanced Economies: GDP Deflators and Consumer Prices
(Annual percent change)

	Ten-Year Averages		1999	2000	2001	2002	2003	2004	2005	2006	2007	2008	Fourth Quarter[1]		
	1989–98	1999–2008											2006	2007	2008
GDP deflators															
Advanced economies	**3.3**	**1.7**	**0.9**	**1.5**	**1.9**	**1.6**	**1.7**	**1.9**	**1.9**	**1.9**	**1.4**	**1.7**	**. . .**	**. . .**	**. . .**
United States	2.5	2.2	1.4	2.2	2.4	1.7	2.1	2.8	3.0	2.9	1.7	1.9	2.5	1.7	1.9
Euro area	. . .	1.9	0.9	1.5	2.7	2.6	2.1	1.9	1.9	1.7	1.8	1.8	1.5	1.9	1.9
Germany	3.4	0.7	0.4	–0.6	1.2	1.4	1.1	0.9	0.7	0.3	0.8	1.0	0.2	0.8	1.3
France	1.9	1.7	—	1.5	2.0	2.4	1.8	1.7	1.8	2.1	1.8	1.7	2.0	1.7	1.7
Italy	4.9	2.4	1.3	2.0	3.0	3.4	3.1	2.9	2.2	1.8	2.0	1.9	1.2	2.0	1.8
Spain	4.9	3.7	2.6	3.5	4.2	4.3	4.1	4.0	4.1	3.8	3.4	3.1	3.6	3.1	3.0
Netherlands	2.1	2.5	1.8	4.1	5.1	3.8	2.2	0.7	1.7	1.5	2.0	2.2	1.3	2.6	2.1
Belgium	2.6	1.7	0.3	1.9	2.0	1.9	1.6	2.4	2.1	1.8	1.6	1.7	1.5	2.0	1.4
Austria	2.2	1.5	0.6	1.8	1.8	1.4	1.3	1.7	1.9	1.3	1.7	1.7	1.6	1.7	1.7
Finland	2.8	1.1	0.9	2.6	3.0	1.3	–0.4	0.6	0.2	1.3	0.1	1.1	–1.8	4.5	–0.8
Greece	12.3	3.5	3.0	5.7	2.7	3.7	3.6	3.3	3.4	3.1	3.3	3.3	3.1	3.3	3.3
Portugal	7.0	3.1	3.3	3.0	3.7	3.9	3.1	2.7	2.8	2.9	3.0	2.4	3.1	4.3	2.6
Ireland	3.3	3.7	4.0	5.5	5.5	5.0	2.5	1.8	3.5	3.5	3.6	2.4	3.4	3.0	2.4
Luxembourg	2.4	3.1	5.3	2.0	0.1	2.7	4.9	1.7	4.7	3.9	2.8	2.4	. . .	. . .	. . .
Slovenia	. . .	1.9	2.3	–0.5	2.6	3.5	2.4	1.1	1.1	2.3	1.8	2.3	2.1	2.3	3.5
Japan	0.9	–1.0	–1.3	–1.7	–1.2	–1.5	–1.6	–1.1	–1.3	–0.9	–0.3	0.6	–0.6	–0.1	0.8
United Kingdom	4.2	2.4	2.2	1.3	2.2	3.1	3.1	2.6	2.2	2.3	2.7	2.7	2.4	2.5	2.8
Canada	1.9	2.3	1.7	4.1	1.1	1.1	3.4	3.0	3.2	2.1	1.3	2.1	0.5	2.0	1.8
Korea	7.1	1.2	–0.1	0.7	3.5	2.8	2.7	2.7	–0.2	–0.4	–1.0	1.6	–0.5	–1.8	2.9
Australia	2.3	3.2	0.6	4.0	4.0	2.5	3.4	3.4	4.6	4.6	3.2	1.8	4.2	2.2	1.7
Taiwan Province of China	2.9	–0.7	–1.3	–1.6	0.5	–0.8	–2.1	–1.6	–0.5	–0.8	–0.3	1.2	–0.3	–0.2	–10.2
Sweden	3.9	1.5	0.9	1.4	2.1	1.6	2.0	0.2	1.2	1.8	1.8	2.0	2.1	1.8	2.0
Switzerland	2.0	0.9	0.7	0.8	0.6	1.6	1.2	0.6	–0.1	1.0	1.0	1.2	1.0	1.0	1.2
Hong Kong SAR	6.7	–2.5	–5.8	–5.6	–1.8	–3.5	–6.3	–3.6	–0.4	–0.3	1.5	1.0	–0.5	2.0	0.4
Denmark	2.1	2.3	1.7	3.0	2.5	2.3	1.6	2.0	3.2	2.6	1.9	2.0	2.6	2.4	1.8
Norway	2.2	4.8	6.6	15.7	1.7	–1.8	3.0	5.3	8.5	7.4	–1.0	3.6	2.7	–0.4	6.1
Israel	12.9	1.8	6.0	1.3	1.8	4.8	–0.3	–0.1	0.8	2.0	–0.3	2.0	–0.6	1.8	2.1
Singapore	2.5	—	–5.3	3.7	–1.8	–1.2	–1.1	3.7	0.4	0.2	0.8	1.0	0.4	0.8	1.0
New Zealand	2.1	2.3	0.7	2.8	3.9	0.9	2.3	3.4	2.5	1.8	2.0	2.4	1.7	2.3	2.2
Cyprus	4.5	2.8	2.3	3.8	3.4	1.2	5.1	3.3	2.4	2.5	2.1	2.1	. . .	. . .	. . .
Iceland	6.6	4.4	3.2	3.6	8.6	5.6	0.5	2.4	2.9	11.5	6.0	–0.1	. . .	. . .	. . .
Memorandum															
Major advanced economies	2.6	1.6	0.9	1.2	1.6	1.4	1.6	1.9	1.9	1.9	1.4	1.7	1.6	1.4	1.7
Newly industrialized Asian economies	5.5	0.1	–1.5	–0.6	1.6	0.8	—	0.7	–0.3	–0.5	–0.4	1.4	–0.3	–0.6	–1.3
Consumer prices															
Advanced economies	**3.5**	**2.0**	**1.4**	**2.2**	**2.1**	**1.5**	**1.8**	**2.0**	**2.3**	**2.3**	**1.8**	**2.1**	**. . .**	**. . .**	**. . .**
United States	3.3	2.6	2.2	3.4	2.8	1.6	2.3	2.7	3.4	3.2	1.9	2.5	1.9	2.6	2.5
Euro area[2]	. . .	2.1	1.1	2.1	2.4	2.3	2.1	2.1	2.2	2.2	2.0	2.0	1.8	2.0	2.0
Germany	2.6	1.5	0.6	1.4	1.9	1.4	1.0	1.8	1.9	1.8	2.0	1.6	1.3	2.2	1.6
France	2.2	1.8	0.6	1.8	1.8	1.9	2.2	2.3	1.9	1.9	1.7	1.8	1.5	2.7	0.8
Italy	4.5	2.3	1.7	2.6	2.3	2.6	2.8	2.3	2.2	2.2	2.1	2.0	2.0	1.7	2.3
Spain	4.8	3.1	2.2	3.5	2.8	3.6	3.1	3.1	3.4	3.6	2.6	2.7	2.6	2.9	2.6
Japan	1.5	–0.2	–0.3	–0.4	–0.8	–0.9	–0.2	—	–0.6	0.2	0.3	0.8	0.3	0.6	0.8
United Kingdom[2]	3.7	1.6	1.3	0.9	1.2	1.3	1.4	1.3	2.0	2.3	2.3	2.0	2.8	2.0	2.0
Canada	2.5	2.2	1.7	2.7	2.5	2.3	2.7	1.8	2.2	2.0	1.7	2.0	1.3	2.2	2.0
Other advanced economies	4.6	1.9	0.9	2.0	2.4	1.8	1.8	1.9	2.1	2.0	2.0	2.2	. . .	. . .	. . .
Memorandum															
Major advanced economies	2.9	1.9	1.4	2.2	1.9	1.3	1.7	2.0	2.3	2.3	1.7	2.0	1.6	2.1	2.0
Newly industrialized Asian economies	5.3	1.6	—	1.2	1.9	1.0	1.5	2.4	2.3	1.6	2.1	2.1	1.4	2.6	1.7

[1]From fourth quarter of preceding year.
[2]Based on Eurostat's harmonized index of consumer prices.

Table 9. Advanced Economies: Hourly Earnings, Productivity, and Unit Labor Costs in Manufacturing
(Annual percent change)

| | Ten-Year Averages | | 1999 | 2000 | 2001 | 2002 | 2003 | 2004 | 2005 | 2006 | 2007 | 2008 |
	1989–98	1999–2008										
Hourly earnings												
Advanced economies	**4.2**	**3.4**	**3.1**	**5.4**	**3.0**	**4.4**	**4.6**	**2.4**	**3.5**	**3.4**	**3.2**	**3.4**
United States	3.5	4.7	3.9	9.0	2.4	7.3	7.0	2.0	4.7	3.8	3.4	4.0
Euro area	...	3.5	5.2	5.2	4.4	3.3	2.5	2.8	2.6	3.2	2.6	2.8
Germany	5.1	2.3	2.5	3.6	3.5	2.4	2.5	0.7	2.0	2.6	1.5	2.1
France	3.5	2.9	1.0	3.6	1.5	3.3	3.3	3.5	3.0	3.5	3.2	3.0
Italy	4.7	2.6	0.9	1.6	2.5	3.2	2.8	4.0	1.5	3.8	3.1	3.0
Spain	6.1	3.6	2.7	2.9	4.1	5.0	4.9	4.0	3.5	3.5	2.7	2.8
Japan	3.6	0.5	–0.7	–0.1	1.0	–1.3	1.0	0.4	1.2	0.4	2.0	1.7
United Kingdom	6.0	4.1	4.0	4.7	4.3	3.5	3.6	3.7	3.7	5.2	4.8	3.9
Canada	3.4	2.8	2.2	3.2	3.1	3.6	3.1	1.2	3.8	2.4	2.5	2.8
Other advanced economies	7.6	5.3	6.6	6.6	5.6	4.3	4.9	5.3	4.9	5.2	4.8	4.9
Memorandum												
Major advanced economies	4.0	3.4	2.5	5.5	2.4	4.4	4.6	1.9	3.4	3.2	3.1	3.3
Newly industrialized Asian economies	11.6	7.3	9.9	7.9	8.4	5.8	7.2	7.3	6.8	6.5	6.4	6.4
Productivity[1]												
Advanced economies	**2.9**	**3.3**	**4.1**	**5.2**	**0.8**	**4.2**	**4.4**	**3.3**	**3.4**	**3.7**	**3.0**	**2.7**
United States	3.5	4.0	4.4	4.3	1.7	7.0	6.2	1.8	4.8	4.0	3.3	3.0
Euro area	...	3.4	5.6	6.7	2.6	1.5	1.8	3.5	2.9	4.0	2.7	2.4
Germany	3.2	4.0	2.6	5.3	3.0	0.9	3.9	3.8	6.5	6.9	4.0	3.0
France	4.3	3.9	2.9	6.8	1.0	3.1	4.1	4.6	4.9	4.7	3.7	3.5
Italy	0.9	–0.2	–0.7	1.2	–1.2	–1.0	–1.0	1.4	–2.8	1.1	0.5	0.6
Spain	3.5	2.4	4.3	1.9	2.1	2.3	1.9	2.0	0.6	3.9	2.5	2.1
Japan	1.7	3.0	3.2	6.8	–3.0	3.7	5.3	5.3	1.6	3.0	3.0	1.8
United Kingdom	2.4	4.2	4.3	6.1	3.3	2.0	5.8	6.7	2.6	3.8	4.7	3.5
Canada	2.3	1.6	4.3	5.8	–2.2	2.0	–0.6	0.1	3.6	0.1	0.8	2.0
Other advanced economies	3.4	4.2	8.0	7.4	—	4.2	3.9	5.3	3.3	3.9	3.1	3.2
Memorandum												
Major advanced economies	2.9	3.5	3.5	5.0	0.8	4.4	4.8	3.0	3.7	3.8	3.1	2.7
Newly industrialized Asian economies	5.1	6.5	13.3	12.1	–0.3	6.1	5.7	7.7	5.1	6.0	4.8	5.0
Unit labor costs												
Advanced economies	**1.3**	**0.1**	**–1.0**	**0.3**	**2.2**	**0.2**	**0.1**	**–0.8**	**0.1**	**–0.3**	**0.2**	**0.7**
United States	—	0.7	–0.5	4.6	0.7	0.2	0.8	0.2	–0.1	–0.2	0.1	1.0
Euro area	...	0.1	–0.4	–1.4	1.7	1.9	0.7	–0.6	–0.2	–0.8	–0.1	0.4
Germany	1.8	–1.6	–0.2	–1.7	0.5	1.5	–1.3	–2.9	–4.2	–4.0	–2.4	–0.9
France	–0.8	–1.0	–1.8	–3.1	0.5	0.2	–0.7	–1.1	–1.8	–1.2	–0.5	–0.5
Italy	3.8	2.8	1.7	0.5	3.7	4.3	3.8	2.5	4.4	2.6	2.6	2.4
Spain	2.5	1.2	–1.6	1.0	2.0	2.7	3.0	1.9	2.9	–0.3	0.2	0.7
Japan	2.0	–2.4	–3.8	–6.5	4.0	–4.8	–4.1	–4.7	–0.4	–2.6	–0.9	–0.1
United Kingdom[2]	3.5	–0.1	–0.3	–1.3	1.0	1.5	–2.1	–2.8	1.1	1.3	0.1	0.4
Canada	1.0	1.2	–2.0	–2.4	5.3	1.5	3.7	1.1	0.2	2.2	1.7	0.8
Other advanced economies	4.3	0.9	–1.1	–0.9	5.4	—	0.6	–0.4	1.2	1.1	1.4	1.4
Memorandum												
Major advanced economies	1.1	—	–1.0	0.6	1.7	—	–0.2	–1.0	–0.3	–0.6	–0.1	0.6
Newly industrialized Asian economies	6.2	0.3	–2.8	–3.9	8.1	–0.5	0.7	–1.2	0.8	0.1	1.1	1.0

[1]Refers to labor productivity, measured as the ratio of hourly compensation to unit labor costs.
[2]Data refer to unit wage cost.

Table 10. Other Emerging Market and Developing Countries: Consumer Prices
(Annual percent change)

| | Ten-Year Averages | | | | | | | | | | | |
	1989–98	1999–2008	1999	2000	2001	2002	2003	2004	2005	2006	2007	2008
Other emerging market and developing countries	**50.3**	**6.2**	**10.3**	**7.1**	**6.7**	**5.8**	**5.8**	**5.6**	**5.4**	**5.3**	**5.4**	**4.9**
Regional groups												
Africa	28.2	10.5	11.8	13.5	12.5	9.7	10.6	7.9	8.4	9.5	10.7	10.4
Sub-Sahara	33.5	12.9	14.9	17.4	15.5	12.0	13.2	9.5	10.5	11.5	12.7	12.2
Excluding Nigeria and South Africa	52.9	18.7	23.7	28.8	22.2	13.7	18.4	14.1	14.0	16.8	18.6	17.7
Central and eastern Europe	63.5	11.2	23.7	23.1	19.7	14.9	8.3	6.1	4.8	5.0	4.8	3.7
Commonwealth of Independent States[1]	...	17.9	69.8	24.7	20.3	13.8	12.0	10.3	12.4	9.5	9.0	8.3
Russia	...	19.0	85.7	20.8	21.5	15.8	13.7	10.9	12.7	9.7	8.1	7.5
Excluding Russia	...	15.4	37.9	34.5	17.7	9.4	8.4	9.1	11.7	9.2	10.9	10.1
Developing Asia	9.7	3.1	2.5	1.8	2.7	2.0	2.5	4.1	3.6	4.0	3.9	3.4
China	9.4	1.2	−1.4	0.4	0.7	−0.8	1.2	3.9	1.8	1.5	2.2	2.3
India	9.7	4.5	4.7	4.0	3.8	4.3	3.8	3.8	4.2	6.1	6.2	4.3
Excluding China and India	10.4	6.1	8.7	2.6	6.1	6.3	4.6	5.0	7.7	8.5	6.2	5.5
Middle East	11.4	6.7	6.6	4.0	3.8	5.3	6.2	7.2	7.1	7.9	10.6	8.7
Western Hemisphere	134.2	7.0	8.3	7.6	6.1	8.9	10.6	6.5	6.3	5.4	5.2	5.7
Brazil	456.2	6.7	4.9	7.1	6.8	8.4	14.8	6.6	6.9	4.2	3.5	4.1
Mexico	20.4	6.1	16.6	9.5	6.4	5.0	4.5	4.7	4.0	3.6	3.9	3.5
Analytical groups												
By source of export earnings												
Fuel	74.1	13.0	36.2	13.9	13.5	11.7	11.3	9.6	9.9	8.9	9.4	8.5
Nonfuel	46.5	5.2	6.7	6.1	5.6	4.9	5.0	5.0	4.7	4.8	4.8	4.3
of which, primary products	73.5	23.9	30.7	35.5	30.9	17.6	19.2	14.7	17.0	22.5	25.5	27.2
By external financing source												
Net debtor countries	55.7	7.3	10.4	8.8	8.1	8.1	7.3	5.7	6.2	6.7	6.4	5.6
of which, official financing	27.7	5.7	5.3	3.8	4.1	3.7	5.9	7.4	7.3	6.9	6.6	5.6
Net debtor countries by debt-servicing experience												
Countries with arrears and/or rescheduling during 2001–05	44.6	11.6	14.1	10.4	11.4	14.2	11.6	8.6	10.7	13.1	11.5	11.2
Other groups												
Heavily indebted poor countries	56.0	11.9	18.5	25.5	19.5	5.9	9.4	7.0	10.0	9.0	8.8	6.9
Middle East and north Africa	13.3	5.9	5.9	3.6	3.6	4.8	5.4	6.4	6.0	6.9	9.1	7.7
Memorandum												
Median												
Other emerging market and developing countries	10.3	4.5	3.9	4.0	4.7	3.3	4.0	4.5	5.7	5.5	5.3	4.4
Africa	10.3	5.0	3.7	5.7	5.2	4.0	5.5	4.1	6.4	5.1	5.5	4.9
Central and eastern Europe	45.0	3.5	2.9	5.2	5.2	3.0	2.1	3.3	3.0	3.8	3.5	3.2
Commonwealth of Independent States[1]	...	10.7	23.5	18.7	9.8	5.6	5.6	7.2	10.3	8.6	8.8	8.9
Developing Asia	8.5	4.4	4.0	2.4	3.8	3.7	3.5	4.6	5.8	6.1	5.5	5.0
Middle East	5.5	3.1	2.1	0.7	1.4	0.8	1.7	3.4	4.1	5.6	6.2	4.6
Western Hemisphere	12.8	4.5	4.2	4.7	4.5	4.6	5.1	4.4	4.9	5.1	4.5	3.6

[1]Mongolia, which is not a member of the Commonwealth of Independent States, is included in this group for reasons of geography and similarities in economic structure.

Table 11. Other Emerging Market and Developing Countries—by Country: Consumer Prices[1]
(Annual percent change)

	Average 1989–98	1999	2000	2001	2002	2003	2004	2005	2006	2007	2008
Africa	**28.2**	**11.8**	**13.5**	**12.5**	**9.7**	**10.6**	**7.9**	**8.4**	**9.5**	**10.7**	**10.4**
Algeria	18.0	2.6	0.3	4.2	1.4	2.6	3.6	1.6	2.5	5.5	5.7
Angola	397.8	248.2	325.0	152.6	108.9	98.3	43.6	23.0	13.3	10.2	5.9
Benin	7.2	0.3	4.2	4.0	2.4	1.5	0.9	5.4	3.8	3.0	2.8
Botswana	11.3	7.8	8.5	6.6	8.0	9.3	6.9	8.6	11.3	6.0	5.0
Burkina Faso	4.4	−1.1	−0.3	4.7	2.3	2.0	−0.4	6.4	2.4	2.0	2.0
Burundi	14.4	3.4	24.3	9.3	−1.3	10.7	8.0	13.4	2.8	4.2	4.0
Cameroon[2]	4.8	2.9	0.8	2.8	6.3	0.6	0.3	2.0	5.3	1.5	1.9
Cape Verde	7.3	4.3	−2.4	3.7	1.9	1.2	−1.9	0.4	4.9	−0.8	2.6
Central African Republic	3.7	−1.4	3.2	3.8	2.3	4.4	−2.2	2.9	5.1	3.1	2.3
Chad	4.5	−8.4	3.8	12.4	5.2	−1.8	−5.4	7.9	7.9	4.0	3.0
Comoros	2.9	1.1	5.9	5.6	3.6	3.7	4.5	3.0	3.4	3.0	3.0
Congo, Dem. Rep. of	790.1	284.9	550.0	357.3	25.3	12.8	4.0	21.4	13.2	17.4	8.9
Congo, Rep. of	5.9	3.1	0.4	0.8	3.1	1.5	3.6	2.5	4.0	3.5	3.0
Côte d'Ivoire	5.7	0.7	2.5	4.4	3.1	3.3	1.5	3.9	1.6	2.0	3.0
Djibouti	4.5	0.2	1.6	1.8	0.6	2.0	3.1	3.1	3.6	3.5	3.5
Equatorial Guinea	6.7	0.4	4.8	8.8	7.6	7.3	4.2	5.7	4.6	5.4	5.4
Eritrea	...	8.4	19.9	14.6	16.9	22.7	25.1	12.5	17.3	22.7	25.2
Ethiopia	7.6	4.8	6.2	−5.2	−7.2	15.1	8.6	6.8	12.3	17.0	12.9
Gabon	5.7	−0.7	0.5	2.1	0.2	2.1	0.4	—	4.0	4.5	2.0
Gambia, The	5.8	3.8	0.9	4.5	8.6	17.0	14.2	3.2	1.5	3.2	3.5
Ghana	28.1	12.4	25.2	32.9	14.8	26.7	12.6	15.1	10.9	9.4	8.8
Guinea	3.2	4.6	6.8	5.4	3.0	12.9	17.5	31.4	33.9	34.1	25.0
Guinea-Bissau	44.1	−2.1	8.6	3.3	3.3	−3.5	0.8	3.4	1.9	1.9	2.0
Kenya	16.2	5.8	10.0	5.8	2.0	9.8	11.6	10.3	14.1	4.1	3.5
Lesotho	11.6	7.8	4.5	6.9	12.5	7.3	5.0	3.4	6.1	6.0	5.5
Liberia	...	...	5.3	12.1	14.2	10.3	3.6	6.9	7.2	7.0	6.5
Madagascar	16.5	8.1	10.7	6.9	16.2	−1.1	14.0	18.4	10.8	9.6	6.9
Malawi	25.8	44.8	29.6	27.2	14.9	9.6	11.6	12.3	9.0	7.0	6.0
Mali	3.9	−1.2	−0.7	5.2	5.0	−1.3	−3.1	6.4	1.9	2.5	2.5
Mauritania	5.5	3.6	6.8	7.7	5.4	5.3	10.4	12.1	6.2	7.9	6.0
Mauritius	8.5	6.9	5.5	4.8	4.4	5.1	3.9	5.6	5.1	10.4	6.0
Morocco	4.7	0.7	1.9	0.6	2.8	1.2	1.5	1.0	3.3	2.0	2.0
Mozambique, Rep. of	36.2	2.9	12.7	9.1	16.8	13.5	12.6	6.4	13.2	5.9	5.7
Namibia	10.9	8.6	9.3	9.3	11.3	7.2	4.1	2.3	5.1	5.9	5.3
Niger	4.6	−2.3	2.9	4.0	2.7	−1.8	0.4	7.8	0.1	2.0	2.0
Nigeria	33.0	6.6	6.9	18.0	13.7	14.0	15.0	17.8	8.3	7.9	9.1
Rwanda	16.7	−2.4	3.9	3.4	2.0	7.4	12.0	9.2	5.5	5.0	5.0
São Tomé and Príncipe	42.8	11.0	11.0	9.5	9.2	9.6	12.8	16.3	21.4	18.6	11.4
Senegal	4.0	0.8	0.7	3.0	2.3	—	0.5	1.7	2.1	2.8	1.7
Seychelles	1.6	6.3	6.3	6.0	0.2	3.2	3.9	1.0	−0.5	11.0	8.9
Sierra Leone	45.2	34.1	−0.9	2.6	−3.7	7.5	14.2	12.1	9.5	8.4	8.0
South Africa	10.8	5.2	5.4	5.7	9.2	5.8	1.4	3.4	4.7	5.5	4.9
Sudan	81.5	16.0	8.0	4.9	8.3	7.7	8.4	8.5	7.2	9.2	6.0
Swaziland	9.7	5.9	7.2	7.5	11.7	7.4	3.4	4.8	5.1	5.8	4.6
Tanzania	22.5	9.0	6.2	5.1	4.6	4.4	4.1	4.4	5.8	5.5	5.0
Togo	5.9	−0.1	1.9	3.9	3.1	−0.9	0.4	6.8	2.7	2.9	3.0
Tunisia	5.3	2.7	2.3	2.0	2.7	2.7	3.6	2.0	4.5	3.0	2.9
Uganda	26.4	0.2	5.8	4.5	−2.0	5.7	5.0	8.0	6.6	5.8	4.2
Zambia	78.5	26.8	26.1	21.7	22.2	21.4	18.0	18.3	9.1	8.0	4.9
Zimbabwe	23.8	58.0	55.6	73.4	133.2	365.0	350.0	237.8	1,016.7	2,879.5	6,470.8

Table 11 *(continued)*

	Average 1989–98	1999	2000	2001	2002	2003	2004	2005	2006	2007	2008
Central and eastern Europe[3]	**63.5**	**23.7**	**23.1**	**19.7**	**14.9**	**8.3**	**6.1**	**4.8**	**5.0**	**4.8**	**3.7**
Albania	34.6	0.4	—	3.1	5.2	2.3	2.9	2.4	2.2	3.4	3.0
Bosnia and Herzegovina	. . .	3.0	5.1	3.2	0.3	0.6	0.3	1.9	6.0	2.5	1.9
Bulgaria	111.1	2.6	8.2	7.5	5.8	2.3	6.1	5.0	7.3	5.3	3.6
Croatia	. . .	4.0	4.6	3.7	1.7	1.8	2.1	3.3	3.2	2.7	2.8
Czech Republic	13.9	2.3	3.8	4.7	1.8	0.1	2.8	1.8	2.5	2.9	3.0
Estonia	. . .	3.3	4.0	5.8	3.6	1.3	3.0	4.1	4.4	4.8	5.3
Hungary	22.7	10.0	9.8	9.2	5.3	4.6	6.8	3.6	3.9	6.4	3.8
Latvia	. . .	2.4	2.6	2.5	1.9	2.9	6.2	6.7	6.5	7.3	6.5
Lithuania	. . .	1.5	1.1	1.6	0.3	−1.1	1.2	2.7	3.8	3.5	3.4
Macedonia, FYR	. . .	−2.7	5.8	4.8	2.2	1.4	0.1	0.5	3.2	2.5	2.5
Malta	3.0	2.3	3.0	2.5	2.6	1.9	2.7	2.5	2.6	2.4	2.3
Poland	70.4	7.3	10.1	5.5	1.9	0.8	3.5	2.1	1.0	2.2	2.9
Romania	102.7	45.8	45.7	34.5	22.5	15.3	11.9	9.0	6.6	4.5	5.0
Serbia	. . .	41.1	70.0	91.8	19.5	11.7	10.1	17.3	12.7	4.7	6.1
Slovak Republic	. . .	10.6	12.0	7.1	3.3	8.5	7.5	2.8	4.4	2.4	2.3
Turkey	76.2	64.9	54.9	54.4	45.0	21.6	8.6	8.2	9.6	8.0	4.3
Commonwealth of Independent States[3,4]	**. . .**	**69.8**	**24.7**	**20.3**	**13.8**	**12.0**	**10.3**	**12.4**	**9.5**	**9.0**	**8.3**
Russia	. . .	85.7	20.8	21.5	15.8	13.7	10.9	12.7	9.7	8.1	7.5
Excluding Russia	. . .	37.9	34.5	17.7	9.4	8.4	9.1	11.7	9.2	10.9	10.1
Armenia	. . .	0.6	−0.8	3.1	1.1	4.7	7.0	0.6	2.9	4.0	4.5
Azerbaijan	. . .	−8.5	1.8	1.5	2.8	2.2	6.7	9.7	8.4	21.1	17.0
Belarus	. . .	293.7	168.6	61.1	42.6	28.4	18.1	10.3	7.0	11.4	13.7
Georgia	. . .	19.1	4.0	4.7	5.6	4.8	5.7	8.3	9.2	6.3	5.5
Kazakhstan	. . .	8.4	13.3	8.4	5.9	6.4	6.9	7.6	8.6	8.8	6.8
Kyrgyz Republic	. . .	35.9	18.7	6.9	2.1	3.1	4.1	4.3	5.6	5.0	4.0
Moldova	. . .	39.3	31.3	9.8	5.3	11.7	12.5	11.9	12.7	11.4	8.9
Mongolia	. . .	7.6	11.6	8.0	1.1	3.3	8.3	12.1	5.0	5.3	5.0
Tajikistan	. . .	27.5	32.9	38.6	12.2	16.4	7.2	7.3	10.1	11.4	9.2
Turkmenistan	. . .	23.5	8.0	11.6	8.8	5.6	5.9	10.7	8.2	6.5	9.0
Ukraine	. . .	22.7	28.2	12.0	0.8	5.2	9.0	13.5	9.0	11.3	10.0
Uzbekistan	. . .	52.9	49.5	47.5	44.3	14.8	8.8	21.0	19.5	10.4	12.2

Table 11 *(continued)*

	Average 1989–98	1999	2000	2001	2002	2003	2004	2005	2006	2007	2008
Developing Asia	**9.7**	**2.5**	**1.8**	**2.7**	**2.0**	**2.5**	**4.1**	**3.6**	**4.0**	**3.9**	**3.4**
Afghanistan, Rep. of	. . .	. . .	. . .	. . .	. . .	5.1	24.1	13.2	12.3	5.5	5.9
Bangladesh	6.6	6.2	2.5	1.9	3.7	5.4	6.1	7.0	6.3	6.4	5.4
Bhutan	10.0	6.8	4.0	3.4	2.5	2.1	4.6	5.3	5.2	5.5	5.3
Brunei Darussalam	. . .	—	1.2	0.6	−2.3	0.3	0.9	1.1	0.5	1.2	1.2
Cambodia	. . .	4.0	−0.8	0.2	3.3	1.2	3.9	5.8	4.8	3.5	3.5
China	9.4	−1.4	0.4	0.7	−0.8	1.2	3.9	1.8	1.5	2.2	2.3
Fiji	4.6	2.0	1.1	4.3	0.8	4.2	2.8	2.4	3.4	3.7	3.1
India	9.7	4.7	4.0	3.8	4.3	3.8	3.8	4.2	6.1	6.2	4.3
Indonesia	12.2	20.7	3.8	11.5	11.8	6.8	6.1	10.5	13.1	6.3	5.3
Kiribati	3.9	0.6	0.9	7.0	1.6	2.6	−1.9	−0.5	−0.2	0.2	1.0
Lao PDR	18.3	128.4	23.2	7.8	12.1	15.5	10.5	7.2	6.8	4.0	5.0
Malaysia	3.7	2.7	1.6	1.4	1.8	1.1	1.4	3.0	3.6	2.6	2.5
Maldives	8.8	3.0	−1.2	0.7	0.9	−2.8	6.3	3.3	3.5	7.0	6.0
Myanmar	28.3	10.9	−1.7	34.5	58.1	24.9	3.8	10.1	26.3	37.5	35.0
Nepal	9.8	3.4	2.4	2.9	4.7	4.0	4.0	4.5	8.0	7.0	6.1
Pakistan	9.9	5.7	3.6	4.4	2.5	3.1	4.6	9.3	7.9	6.5	6.0
Papua New Guinea	7.6	14.9	15.6	9.3	11.8	14.7	2.1	1.7	3.5	4.3	4.0
Philippines	10.1	6.4	4.0	6.8	2.9	3.5	6.0	7.6	6.2	4.0	4.0
Samoa	5.5	0.8	−0.2	1.9	7.4	4.3	7.9	7.8	3.2	2.6	3.0
Solomon Islands	11.3	8.0	6.9	7.6	9.3	10.0	6.9	7.3	8.0	6.6	8.1
Sri Lanka	11.9	4.0	1.5	12.1	10.2	2.6	7.9	10.6	9.5	14.0	6.5
Thailand	5.5	0.3	1.6	1.7	0.6	1.8	2.8	4.5	4.6	2.5	2.5
Timor-Leste, Dem. Rep. of	. . .	. . .	63.6	3.6	4.8	7.0	3.2	1.8	4.1	5.0	3.7
Tonga	4.4	3.9	5.3	6.9	10.4	11.1	11.7	9.7	6.8	7.9	8.2
Vanuatu	3.8	2.2	2.5	3.7	2.0	3.0	1.4	1.2	1.6	2.5	3.0
Vietnam	26.9	4.1	−1.6	−0.4	4.0	3.2	7.7	8.3	7.5	6.5	6.4
Middle East	**11.4**	**6.6**	**4.0**	**3.8**	**5.3**	**6.2**	**7.2**	**7.1**	**7.9**	**10.6**	**8.7**
Bahrain	1.1	−1.3	−0.7	−1.2	−0.5	1.7	2.3	2.6	3.0	3.0	2.8
Egypt	12.3	3.7	2.8	2.4	2.4	3.2	8.1	8.8	4.2	12.3	10.7
Iran, I.R. of	23.3	20.1	12.6	11.4	15.8	15.6	15.2	12.1	14.6	17.8	15.8
Iraq	. . .	. . .	. . .	. . .	. . .	. . .	. . .	. . .	. . .	. . .	. . .
Jordan	7.4	0.6	0.7	1.8	1.8	1.6	3.4	3.5	6.3	5.7	3.5
Kuwait	3.6	3.1	1.6	1.4	0.8	1.0	1.3	4.1	3.0	2.8	2.6
Lebanon	31.9	0.2	−0.4	−0.4	1.8	1.3	1.7	−0.7	5.6	3.5	2.5
Libya	6.4	2.6	−2.9	−8.8	−9.9	−2.1	−2.2	2.0	3.4	16.2	6.9
Oman	1.7	0.5	−1.2	−0.8	−0.3	0.2	0.7	1.9	3.2	3.8	3.5
Qatar	3.0	2.2	1.7	1.4	0.2	2.3	6.8	8.8	11.8	10.0	8.5
Saudi Arabia	1.4	−1.3	−1.1	−1.1	0.2	0.6	0.4	0.7	2.3	2.8	2.0
Syrian Arab Republic	9.1	−3.7	−3.9	3.4	−0.5	5.8	4.4	7.2	10.0	8.0	5.0
United Arab Emirates	3.6	2.1	1.4	2.8	2.9	3.1	5.0	7.8	10.1	6.2	4.6
Yemen, Rep. of	37.7	8.0	10.9	11.9	12.2	10.8	12.5	11.8	21.6	21.1	17.5

Table 11 *(concluded)*

	Average 1989-98	1999	2000	2001	2002	2003	2004	2005	2006	2007	2008
Western Hemisphere	**134.2**	**8.3**	**7.6**	**6.1**	**8.9**	**10.6**	**6.5**	**6.3**	**5.4**	**5.2**	**5.7**
Antigua and Barbuda	3.8	0.6	−0.6	−0.4	2.4	2.0	2.0	2.1	2.0	3.4	2.0
Argentina	125.4	−1.2	−0.9	−1.1	25.9	13.4	4.4	9.6	10.9	10.3	12.7
Bahamas, The	3.2	1.3	1.6	2.0	2.2	3.0	0.9	2.2	1.9	1.9	2.0
Barbados	3.4	1.5	2.4	2.6	−1.2	1.6	1.4	6.0	7.2	4.9	2.4
Belize	2.1	−1.3	0.7	1.2	2.2	2.6	3.1	3.7	4.3	2.9	2.8
Bolivia	11.7	2.2	4.6	1.6	0.9	3.3	4.4	5.4	4.3	6.5	6.0
Brazil	456.2	4.9	7.1	6.8	8.4	14.8	6.6	6.9	4.2	3.5	4.1
Chile	12.9	3.3	3.8	3.6	2.5	2.8	1.1	3.1	3.4	2.5	3.0
Colombia	23.6	10.9	9.2	8.0	6.3	7.1	5.9	5.0	4.3	4.2	3.7
Costa Rica	17.4	10.0	11.0	11.3	9.2	9.4	12.3	13.8	11.5	8.1	7.0
Dominica	2.9	1.2	0.9	1.6	0.1	1.6	2.4	1.6	1.5	1.5	1.5
Dominican Republic	17.4	6.5	7.7	8.9	5.2	27.4	51.5	4.2	7.6	4.5	4.4
Ecuador	40.6	52.2	96.1	37.7	12.6	7.9	2.7	2.1	3.3	2.8	3.0
El Salvador	12.2	0.5	2.3	3.8	1.9	2.1	4.5	3.7	4.6	4.4	3.5
Grenada	2.8	0.6	2.1	1.7	1.1	2.2	2.3	3.5	3.8	2.7	2.0
Guatemala	15.6	5.2	6.0	7.3	8.1	5.6	7.6	9.1	6.6	6.2	6.0
Guyana	29.4	7.4	6.1	2.7	5.3	6.0	4.7	6.9	6.6	4.5	3.2
Haiti	20.8	8.7	13.7	14.2	9.9	39.3	21.2	15.8	14.2	9.6	9.1
Honduras	19.3	11.6	11.0	9.7	7.7	7.7	8.1	8.8	5.6	6.0	6.6
Jamaica	27.8	6.0	8.1	7.0	7.1	10.5	13.5	15.3	8.6	6.2	6.1
Mexico	20.4	16.6	9.5	6.4	5.0	4.5	4.7	4.0	3.6	3.9	3.5
Nicaragua	154.7	7.2	9.9	4.7	4.0	6.5	9.3	9.6	9.4	6.1	5.2
Panama	1.0	1.3	1.4	0.3	1.0	0.6	0.5	2.9	2.5	2.2	2.4
Paraguay	18.1	6.8	9.0	7.3	10.5	14.2	4.3	6.8	9.6	10.2	3.4
Peru	201.6	3.5	3.8	2.0	0.2	2.3	3.7	1.6	2.0	1.0	2.0
St. Kitts and Nevis	3.7	3.4	2.1	2.1	2.1	2.3	2.2	3.6	6.8	3.2	2.1
St. Lucia	3.3	3.5	4.0	5.4	−0.3	1.0	1.5	3.9	2.5	4.0	3.0
St. Vincent and the Grenadines	3.3	1.0	0.2	0.8	0.8	0.2	3.0	3.7	3.0	3.9	3.7
Suriname	59.7	98.7	58.6	39.8	15.5	23.0	9.1	9.9	11.3	4.6	4.3
Trinidad and Tobago	6.7	3.4	3.6	5.5	4.2	3.8	3.7	6.9	8.3	9.0	9.0
Uruguay	53.1	5.7	4.8	4.4	14.0	19.4	9.2	4.7	6.4	6.0	5.0
Venezuela	52.1	23.6	16.2	12.5	22.4	31.1	21.7	15.9	13.6	21.6	25.7

[1]In accordance with standard practice in the *World Economic Outlook*, movements in consumer prices are indicated as annual averages rather than as December/December changes during the year, as is the practice in some countries. For many countries, figures for recent years are IMF staff estimates. Data for some countries are for fiscal years.

[2]The percent changes in 2002 are calculated over a period of 18 months, reflecting a change in the fiscal year cycle (from July–June to January–December).

[3]For many countries, inflation for the earlier years is measured on the basis of a retail price index. Consumer price indices with a broader and more up-to-date coverage are typically used for more recent years.

[4]Mongolia, which is not a member of the Commonwealth of Independent States, is included in this group for reasons of geography and similarities in economic structure.

Table 12. Summary of Financial Indicators
(Percent)

	1999	2000	2001	2002	2003	2004	2005	2006	2007	2008
Advanced economies										
Central government fiscal balance[1]										
Advanced economies	−1.0	0.1	−0.9	−2.4	−3.1	−2.8	−2.4	−1.8	−1.7	−1.7
United States	1.1	1.9	0.4	−2.6	−3.8	−3.7	−2.9	−1.9	−2.0	−2.1
Euro area	−1.6	−0.4	−1.6	−2.0	−2.3	−2.4	−2.3	−1.5	−1.2	−1.1
Japan	−8.2	−6.6	−6.1	−6.6	−6.7	−5.6	−5.8	−5.9	−5.8	−5.8
Other advanced economies[2]	0.7	1.5	1.0	−0.2	−0.8	−0.2	0.2	0.5	0.4	0.5
General government fiscal balance[1]										
Advanced economies	−1.0	—	−1.4	−3.2	−3.8	−3.3	−2.5	−1.8	−1.6	−1.6
United States	0.9	1.6	−0.4	−3.8	−4.8	−4.6	−3.7	−2.6	−2.5	−2.5
Euro area	−1.4	−1.0	−1.9	−2.6	−3.1	−2.8	−2.4	−1.6	−1.2	−1.1
Japan	−7.4	−7.6	−6.3	−8.0	−8.0	−6.2	−4.8	−4.3	−3.8	−3.5
Other advanced economies[2]	0.2	1.7	0.4	−0.4	−0.7	−0.1	0.6	0.7	0.4	0.6
General government structural balance[3]										
Advanced economies	−1.4	−1.2	−1.8	−3.4	−3.7	−3.4	−2.7	−2.1	−1.8	−1.8
Growth of broad money[4]										
Advanced economies	5.9	4.9	8.1	5.7	5.4	5.5	5.6	. . .	. . .	. . .
United States	6.0	6.0	10.4	6.3	5.0	5.8	4.0	5.3	. . .	. . .
Euro area	5.7	4.1	8.0	6.9	7.1	6.6	7.3	9.8	. . .	. . .
Japan	2.7	1.9	3.3	1.8	1.6	1.8	2.0	0.9	. . .	. . .
Other advanced economies[2]	9.1	6.6	8.1	6.1	7.2	6.5	9.0	. . .	. . .	. . .
Short-term interest rates[5]										
United States	4.8	6.0	3.5	1.6	1.0	1.4	3.2	4.8	5.2	5.1
Euro area	3.0	4.4	4.3	3.3	2.3	2.1	2.2	3.1	3.8	3.7
Japan	0.0	0.2	0.0	0.0	0.0	0.0	0.0	0.3	0.9	1.2
LIBOR	5.5	6.6	3.7	1.9	1.2	1.8	3.8	5.3	5.3	5.1
Other emerging market and developing countries										
Central government fiscal balance[1]										
Weighted average	−3.8	−3.0	−3.1	−3.4	−2.7	−1.6	−0.9	−0.4	−1.1	−0.8
Median	−3.1	−2.7	−3.7	−3.6	−3.2	−2.5	−1.9	−1.2	−1.9	−1.9
General government fiscal balance[1]										
Weighted average	−4.8	−3.5	−3.9	−4.3	−3.4	−1.9	−1.1	−0.5	−1.3	−1.1
Median	−3.4	−3.2	−3.3	−3.6	−3.0	−2.4	−1.9	−0.9	−1.7	−1.9
Growth of broad money										
Weighted average	17.6	15.1	15.7	16.5	15.7	16.9	19.1	20.5	15.9	13.9
Median	13.1	15.1	13.7	13.3	13.0	13.6	14.3	16.2	12.3	11.1

[1]Percent of GDP.

[2]In this table, "other advanced economies" means advanced economies excluding the United States, euro area countries, and Japan.

[3]Percent of potential GDP.

[4]M2, defined as M1 plus quasi-money, except for Japan, for which the data are based on M2 plus certificates of deposit (CDs). Quasi-money is essentially private term deposits and other notice deposits. The United States also includes money market mutual fund balances, money market deposit accounts, overnight repurchase agreements, and overnight Eurodollars issued to U.S. residents by foreign branches of U.S. banks. For the euro area, M3 is composed of M2 plus marketable instruments held by euro-area residents, which comprise repurchase agreements, money market fund shares/units, money market paper, and debt securities up to two years.

[5]Annual data are period average. For the United States, three-month treasury bills; for Japan, three-month certificates of deposit; for the euro area, the three-month EURIBOR; and for LIBOR, London interbank offered rate on six-month U.S. dollar deposits.

Table 13. Advanced Economies: General and Central Government Fiscal Balances and Balances Excluding Social Security Transactions[1]

(Percent of GDP)

	1999	2000	2001	2002	2003	2004	2005	2006	2007	2008
General government fiscal balance										
Advanced economies	**−1.0**	**—**	**−1.4**	**−3.2**	**−3.8**	**−3.3**	**−2.5**	**−1.8**	**−1.6**	**−1.6**
United States	0.9	1.6	−0.4	−3.8	−4.8	−4.6	−3.7	−2.6	−2.5	−2.5
Euro area	−1.4	−1.0	−1.9	−2.6	−3.1	−2.8	−2.4	−1.6	−1.2	−1.1
Germany	−1.5	1.3	−2.8	−3.7	−4.0	−3.7	−3.2	−1.7	−1.3	−1.3
France[2]	−1.7	−1.5	−1.6	−3.2	−4.2	−3.7	−2.9	−2.6	−2.6	−2.4
Italy	−1.7	−0.8	−3.1	−2.9	−3.5	−3.4	−4.1	−4.4	−2.2	−2.4
Spain	−1.1	−0.9	−0.5	−0.3	—	−0.2	1.1	1.8	1.3	1.1
Netherlands	0.6	2.1	−0.3	−2.0	−3.1	−1.8	−0.3	0.5	0.5	0.7
Belgium	−0.5	0.1	0.6	—	—	—	−2.3	—	—	—
Austria[3]	−2.3	−1.6	−0.1	−0.7	−1.8	−1.3	−1.6	−1.2	−1.2	−1.0
Finland	1.6	6.9	5.0	4.1	2.4	2.1	2.5	3.8	3.5	3.7
Greece	−2.7	−3.2	−3.9	−4.1	−4.9	−6.2	−4.2	−2.1	−2.0	−1.9
Portugal	−2.7	−2.7	−4.3	−4.2	−5.2	−5.3	−5.7	−3.9	−3.3	−2.6
Ireland[4]	2.4	4.4	0.7	−0.4	0.3	1.5	1.1	2.1	1.3	0.5
Luxembourg	3.4	6.0	6.1	2.1	0.3	−1.1	−1.0	−1.4	−0.9	−0.8
Slovenia	−0.6	−1.3	−1.3	−1.5	−1.3	−1.4	−1.1	−0.8	−0.9	−0.8
Japan	−7.4	−7.6	−6.3	−8.0	−8.0	−6.2	−4.8	−4.3	−3.8	−3.5
United Kingdom	1.2	1.7	1.1	−1.6	−3.2	−3.1	−3.0	−2.5	−2.4	−2.2
Canada	1.6	2.9	0.7	−0.1	−0.4	0.5	1.4	0.9	0.6	0.7
Korea[5]	−2.5	1.1	0.6	2.3	2.7	2.3	1.9	1.8	1.9	2.1
Australia[6]	1.3	1.8	0.9	1.0	1.6	2.0	1.9	1.0	0.7	1.1
Taiwan Province of China	−5.7	−4.5	−6.4	−4.3	−2.8	−2.9	−0.6	−0.5	−0.9	−1.0
Sweden	2.3	5.0	2.6	−0.5	−0.2	1.6	2.8	2.8	2.3	2.6
Switzerland	−0.6	2.2	—	−1.2	−1.4	−1.0	−0.2	—	−0.1	−0.9
Hong Kong SAR	0.8	−0.6	−4.9	−4.8	−3.3	1.7	1.0	3.9	1.7	3.0
Denmark	1.4	2.3	1.2	0.2	−0.1	1.9	4.6	4.2	3.4	2.5
Norway	6.0	15.4	13.3	9.2	7.3	11.1	15.2	19.3	18.0	19.3
Israel	−4.4	−2.1	−4.2	−4.5	−6.9	−4.8	−2.9	−2.7	−4.0	−3.4
Singapore	4.6	7.9	4.8	4.1	5.8	6.0	7.8	6.4	5.3	5.0
New Zealand[7]	1.5	1.2	1.6	1.7	3.4	4.6	5.8	5.6	3.7	3.2
Cyprus	−4.3	−2.3	−2.2	−4.4	−6.2	−4.0	−2.4	−1.4	−1.6	−0.9
Iceland	2.3	2.4	0.2	−0.8	−2.0	0.3	3.2	2.4	−0.5	−1.1
Memorandum										
Major advanced economies	−1.0	−0.2	−1.7	−4.0	−4.8	−4.2	−3.5	−2.7	−2.4	−2.4
Newly industrialized Asian economies	−2.7	−0.5	−2.0	−0.4	0.5	0.8	1.4	1.7	1.2	1.5
Fiscal balance excluding social security transactions										
United States	−0.2	0.5	−1.3	−4.3	−5.2	−5.0	−4.2	−3.1	−2.9	−3.0
Japan	−8.5	−8.2	−6.5	−7.9	−8.1	−6.6	−5.1	−4.3	−3.8	−3.7
Germany	−1.7	1.3	−2.6	−3.3	−3.7	−3.7	−3.0	−1.6	−0.7	−0.6
France	−2.0	−1.9	−2.0	−2.9	−3.6	−2.7	−2.7	−2.1	−1.8	−1.4
Italy	2.6	3.1	0.8	1.2	0.7	0.8	—	−0.3	1.4	1.4
Canada	3.9	4.8	2.4	1.4	1.0	1.9	2.9	2.4	2.2	2.3

Table 13 *(concluded)*

	1999	2000	2001	2002	2003	2004	2005	2006	2007	2008
Central government fiscal balance										
Advanced economies	**−1.0**	**0.1**	**−0.9**	**−2.4**	**−3.1**	**−2.8**	**−2.4**	**−1.8**	**−1.7**	**−1.7**
United States[8]	1.1	1.9	0.4	−2.6	−3.8	−3.7	−2.9	−1.9	−2.0	−2.1
Euro area	−1.6	−0.4	−1.6	−2.0	−2.3	−2.4	−2.3	−1.5	−1.2	−1.1
Germany[9]	−1.5	1.4	−1.3	−1.7	−1.8	−2.3	−2.6	−1.4	−1.1	−1.1
France	−2.6	−2.5	−2.4	−3.6	−3.9	−3.2	−3.0	−2.6	−2.2	−2.0
Italy	−1.4	−1.0	−2.9	−3.0	−2.9	−3.1	−3.7	−3.3	−1.9	−2.0
Spain	−1.0	−1.0	−0.6	−0.5	−0.3	−1.2	0.4	0.8	0.6	0.5
Japan[10]	−8.2	−6.6	−6.1	−6.6	−6.7	−5.6	−5.8	−5.9	−5.8	−5.8
United Kingdom	1.3	1.8	1.1	−1.8	−3.5	−3.2	−2.9	−2.7	−2.5	−2.1
Canada	0.9	1.9	1.1	0.8	—	0.4	0.1	0.5	0.3	0.2
Other advanced economies	0.2	1.3	0.8	0.3	0.4	1.1	1.7	2.1	1.8	1.9
Memorandum										
Major advanced economies	−1.1	—	−1.2	−3.0	−3.8	−3.5	−3.2	−2.6	−2.4	−2.4
Newly industrialized Asian economies	−0.8	0.2	−0.6	0.3	0.4	1.0	1.0	1.7	1.2	1.5

[1]On a national income accounts basis except as indicated in footnotes. See Box A1 for a summary of the policy assumptions underlying the projections.
[2]Adjusted for valuation changes of the foreign exchange stabilization fund.
[3]Based on ESA95 methodology, according to which swap income is not included.
[4]Data include the impact of discharging future pension liabilities of the formerly state-owned telecommunications company at a cost of 1.8 percent of GDP in 1999.
[5]Data cover the consolidated central government including the social security funds but excluding privatization.
[6]Data are on a cash basis.
[7]Government balance is revenue minus expenditure plus balance of state-owned enterprises, excluding privatization receipts.
[8]Data are on a budget basis.
[9]Data are on an administrative basis and exclude social security transactions.
[10]Data are on a national income basis and exclude social security transactions.

Table 14. Advanced Economies: General Government Structural Balances[1]
(Percent of potential GDP)

	1999	2000	2001	2002	2003	2004	2005	2006	2007	2008
Structural balance										
Advanced economies	**−1.4**	**−1.2**	**−1.8**	**−3.4**	**−3.7**	**−3.4**	**−2.7**	**−2.1**	**−1.8**	**−1.8**
United States	−0.7	—	−1.2	−3.9	−4.6	−4.5	−3.6	−2.7	−2.4	−2.4
Euro area[2,3]	−1.2	−1.6	−2.3	−2.6	−2.7	−2.4	−1.9	−1.3	−1.0	−1.0
Germany[2]	−0.9	−1.2	−2.8	−3.2	−3.4	−3.4	−2.8	−1.8	−1.4	−1.4
France[2]	−1.4	−2.1	−2.2	−3.2	−3.5	−3.0	−2.2	−1.4	−1.4	−1.5
Italy[2]	−1.4	−2.5	−3.8	−3.9	−3.3	−3.4	−3.4	−3.8	−1.8	−2.0
Spain[2]	−1.2	−1.3	−0.9	−0.3	0.1	0.7	1.2	1.8	1.2	1.1
Netherlands[2]	—	0.2	−1.1	−2.2	−2.6	−1.2	0.1	0.9	0.5	0.6
Belgium[2]	−1.0	−0.8	−0.4	−0.5	−0.8	−0.7	0.2	−0.7	−0.4	—
Austria[2]	−3.2	−3.9	−1.2	−0.5	−0.8	−0.9	−1.2	−1.3	−1.6	−1.2
Finland	2.0	6.7	4.8	4.5	3.1	2.7	3.3	3.5	3.3	3.5
Greece	−2.1	−2.9	−4.1	−4.3	−5.4	−7.1	−5.1	−3.1	−2.9	−2.7
Portugal[2]	−3.6	−3.6	−1.4	−0.3	−2.8	−3.0	−5.3	−3.0	−2.5	−2.0
Ireland[2]	2.2	3.8	0.5	−0.7	0.2	1.6	1.2	2.0	1.3	0.7
Slovenia	−0.9	−1.7	−1.4	−2.9	−0.9	−1.2	−1.0	−0.6	−1.1	−1.0
Japan	−6.6	−7.5	−5.8	−7.2	−7.2	−5.8	−4.6	−4.3	−3.9	−3.7
United Kingdom	1.2	1.5	0.6	−1.8	−3.1	−3.4	−3.0	−2.7	−2.2	−2.0
Canada	1.2	1.9	0.3	−0.2	−0.1	0.6	1.3	0.8	0.7	0.8
Other advanced economies	0.2	1.1	0.8	0.1	0.3	0.9	1.3	1.0	0.6	0.7
Australia[4]	0.9	1.6	1.0	1.1	1.4	1.8	1.8	1.0	0.9	1.4
Sweden	1.4	3.1	2.2	−0.3	0.7	1.9	2.9	2.1	1.2	1.8
Denmark	0.1	0.8	1.2	0.4	0.7	1.0	1.3	1.7	1.8	1.6
Norway[5]	−3.6	−2.4	−1.1	−3.4	−5.3	−4.0	−3.6	−2.7	−3.9	−4.1
New Zealand[6]	0.9	1.3	2.2	3.3	4.3	4.9	5.5	5.0	4.2	3.5
Memorandum										
Major advanced economies	−1.5	−1.5	−2.2	−3.9	−4.4	−4.1	−3.3	−2.7	−2.3	−2.2

[1]On a national income accounts basis. The structural budget position is defined as the actual budget deficit (or surplus) less the effects of cyclical deviations of output from potential output. Because of the margin of uncertainty that attaches to estimates of cyclical gaps and to tax and expenditure elasticities with respect to national income, indicators of structural budget positions should be interpreted as broad orders of magnitude. Moreover, it is important to note that changes in structural budget balances are not necessarily attributable to policy changes but may reflect the built-in momentum of existing expenditure programs. In the period beyond that for which specific consolidation programs exist, it is assumed that the structural deficit remains unchanged.

[2]Excludes one-off receipts from the sale of mobile telephone licenses equivalent to 2.5 percent of GDP in 2000 for Germany, 0.1 percent of GDP in 2001 and 2002 for France, 1.2 percent of GDP in 2000 for Italy, 0.1 percent of GDP in 2000 for Spain, 0.7 percent of GDP in 2000 for the Netherlands, and 0.2 percent of GDP in 2001 for Belgium, 0.4 percent of GDP in 2000 for Austria, 0.3 percent of GDP in 2000 for Portugal, and 0.2 percent of GDP in 2002 for Ireland. Also excludes one-off receipts from sizable asset transactions, in particular 0.5 percent of GDP for France in 2005.

[3]Excludes Luxembourg.

[4]Excludes commonwealth government privatization receipts.

[5]Excludes oil.

[6]Government balance is revenue minus expenditure plus balance of state-owned enterprises, excluding privatization receipts.

Table 15. Advanced Economies: Monetary Aggregates[1]
(Annual percent change)

	1999	2000	2001	2002	2003	2004	2005	2006
Narrow money[2]								
Advanced economies	**8.4**	**2.0**	**9.3**	**9.1**	**8.2**	**6.5**	**5.5**	...
United States	2.6	−3.1	8.7	3.2	7.1	5.3	−0.2	−0.6
Euro area[3]	10.6	5.3	6.0	9.9	10.6	8.9	11.4	7.5
Japan	11.7	3.5	13.7	23.5	4.5	4.0	5.6	−0.1
United Kingdom	11.5	4.6	7.6	6.4	7.4	5.7	4.7	3.3
Canada[4]	7.9	14.5	15.3	5.1	10.1	11.0	11.2	14.2
Memorandum								
Newly industrialized Asian economies	19.8	4.6	11.4	13.3	14.1	9.3	7.4	4.8
Broad money[5]								
Advanced economies	**5.9**	**4.9**	**8.1**	**5.7**	**5.4**	**5.5**	**5.6**	...
United States	6.0	6.0	10.4	6.3	5.0	5.8	4.0	5.3
Euro area[3]	5.7	4.1	8.0	6.9	7.1	6.6	7.3	9.8
Japan	2.7	1.9	3.3	1.8	1.6	1.8	2.0	0.9
United Kingdom	4.0	8.4	6.7	7.0	7.2	8.8	12.7	12.7
Canada[4]	5.2	6.7	6.1	5.1	6.2	6.2	5.6	9.3
Memorandum								
Newly industrialized Asian economies	17.2	14.3	7.2	5.7	6.8	3.5	4.5	6.3

[1]End-of-period based on monthly data.

[2]M1 except for the United Kingdom, where M0 is used here as a measure of narrow money; it comprises notes in circulation plus bankers' operational deposits. M1 is generally currency in circulation plus private demand deposits. In addition, the United States includes traveler's checks of nonbank issues and other checkable deposits and excludes private sector float and demand deposits of banks. Canada excludes private sector float.

[3]Excludes Greece prior to 2001.

[4]Average of Wednesdays.

[5]M2, defined as M1 plus quasi-money, except for Japan, and the United Kingdom, for which the data are based on M2 plus certificates of deposit (CDs), and M4, respectively. Quasi-money is essentially private term deposits and other notice deposits. The United States also includes money market mutual fund balances, money market deposit accounts, overnight repurchase agreements, and overnight Eurodollars issued to U.S. residents by foreign branches of U.S. banks. For the United Kingdom, M4 is composed of non-interest-bearing M1, private sector interest-bearing sterling sight bank deposits, private sector sterling time bank deposits, private sector holdings of sterling bank CDs, private sector holdings of building society shares and deposits, and sterling CDs less building society of banks deposits and bank CDs and notes and coins. For the euro area, M3 is composed of M2 plus marketable instruments held by euro-area residents, which comprise repurchase agreements, money market fund shares/units, money market paper, and debt securities up to two years.

Table 16. Advanced Economies: Interest Rates
(Percent a year)

	1999	2000	2001	2002	2003	2004	2005	2006	February 2007
Policy-related interest rate[1]									
United States	5.3	6.4	1.8	1.2	1.0	2.2	4.2	5.2	5.3
Euro area[2]	3.0	4.8	3.3	2.8	2.0	2.0	2.3	3.5	3.5
Japan	0.0	0.2	0.0	0.0	0.0	0.0	0.0	0.2	0.5
United Kingdom	5.5	6.0	4.0	4.0	3.8	4.8	4.5	5.0	5.3
Canada	4.8	5.8	2.3	2.8	2.8	2.5	3.3	4.3	4.3
Short-term interest rate[2]									
Advanced economies	**3.5**	**4.5**	**3.2**	**2.1**	**1.6**	**1.7**	**2.5**	**3.5**	**4.1**
United States	4.8	6.0	3.5	1.6	1.0	1.4	3.2	4.8	5.2
Euro area	3.0	4.4	4.3	3.3	2.3	2.1	2.2	3.1	3.8
Japan	0.0	0.2	0.0	0.0	0.0	0.0	0.0	0.3	0.6
United Kingdom	5.5	6.1	5.0	4.0	3.7	4.6	4.7	4.8	5.6
Canada	4.7	5.5	3.9	2.6	2.9	2.2	2.7	4.0	4.2
Memorandum									
Newly industrialized Asian economies	4.5	4.6	3.6	2.6	2.3	2.2	2.3	2.9	4.4
Long-term interest rate[3]									
Advanced economies	**4.7**	**5.1**	**4.4**	**4.2**	**3.6**	**3.7**	**3.5**	**4.1**	**4.2**
United States	5.6	6.0	5.0	4.6	4.0	4.3	4.3	4.8	4.7
Euro area	4.6	5.5	5.0	4.9	3.9	3.8	3.3	4.0	4.1
Japan	1.7	1.7	1.3	1.3	1.0	1.5	1.4	1.7	1.6
United Kingdom	5.2	5.0	5.0	4.8	4.5	4.8	4.3	4.5	4.9
Canada	5.6	5.9	5.5	5.3	4.8	4.6	4.1	4.2	4.1
Memorandum									
Newly industrialized Asian economies	7.2	7.0	5.5	5.0	3.9	3.7	3.8	4.1	4.9

[1]Annual data are end of period. For the United States, federal funds rate; for Japan, overnight call rate; for the euro area, main refinancing rate; for the United Kingdom, base lending rate; and for Canada, target rate for overnight money market financing.

[2]Annual data are period average. For the United States, three-month treasury bill market bid yield at constant maturity; for Japan, three-month bond yield with repurchase agreement; for the euro area, three-month EURIBOR; for the United Kingdom, three-month interbank offered rate; for the Canada, three-month treasury bill yield.

[3]Annual data are period average. For the United States, 10-year treasury bond yield at constant maturity; for Japan, 10-year government bond yield; for the euro area, a weighted average of national 10-year government bond yields through 1998 and 10-year euro bond yield thereafter; for the United Kingdom, 10-year government bond yield; and for Canada, 10-year government bond yield.

Table 17. Advanced Economies: Exchange Rates

	1999	2000	2001	2002	2003	2004	2005	2006	Exchange Rate Assumption 2007
				U.S. dollars per national currency unit					
U.S. dollar nominal exchange rates									
Euro	1.067	0.924	0.896	0.944	1.131	1.243	1.246	1.256	1.301
Pound sterling	1.618	1.516	1.440	1.501	1.634	1.832	1.820	1.843	1.956
				National currency units per U.S. dollar					
Japanese yen	113.5	107.7	121.5	125.2	115.8	108.1	110.0	116.3	120.4
Canadian dollar	1.486	1.485	1.548	1.569	1.397	1.299	1.211	1.134	1.179
Swedish krona	8.257	9.132	10.314	9.707	8.068	7.338	7.450	7.367	7.046
Danish krone	6.967	8.060	8.317	7.870	6.577	5.985	5.987	5.941	5.724
Swiss franc	1.500	1.687	1.686	1.554	1.346	1.242	1.243	1.253	1.250
Norwegian krone	7.797	8.782	8.989	7.932	7.074	6.730	6.439	6.407	6.323
Israeli new sheqel	4.138	4.077	4.205	4.735	4.548	4.481	4.485	4.450	4.374
Icelandic krona	72.30	78.28	96.84	91.19	76.64	70.07	62.94	70.02	69.43
Cyprus pound	0.542	0.621	0.643	0.609	0.517	0.468	0.464	0.459	0.445
Korean won	1,188.4	1,130.3	1,290.8	1,249.0	1,191.2	1,144.1	1,023.9	954.5	930.0
Australian dollar	1.550	1.717	1.932	1.839	1.534	1.358	1.309	1.327	1.290
New Taiwan dollar	32.263	31.216	33.787	34.571	34.441	33.418	32.156	32.529	32.906
Hong Kong dollar	7.757	7.791	7.799	7.799	7.787	7.788	7.777	7.768	7.808
Singapore dollar	1.695	1.724	1.792	1.791	1.742	1.690	1.664	1.589	1.528
									Percent change from previous assumption[2]
				Index, 2000 = 100					
Real effective exchange rates[1]									
United States	90.0	100.0	103.2	103.0	92.9	88.0	86.1	84.8	1.4
Euro area[3]	114.0	100.0	101.2	107.2	122.2	127.6	127.7	127.7	−0.5
Germany	106.5	100.0	99.1	100.9	104.1	103.3	99.3	97.2	−0.2
France	107.3	100.0	98.2	99.1	107.9	110.9	111.3	112.0	−0.2
Italy	106.5	100.0	101.2	107.9	116.8	121.2	125.0	125.5	−0.2
Spain	100.0	100.0	102.7	105.6	109.2	112.5	113.2	114.3	−0.2
Netherlands	103.7	100.0	103.5	107.3	115.0	117.0	117.2	116.4	−0.2
Belgium	105.9	100.0	102.7	102.9	106.8	108.0	109.1	110.0	−0.2
Austria	110.0	100.0	97.3	98.1	101.2	94.5	95.5	96.5	−0.1
Finland	110.1	100.0	105.8	105.4	110.5	114.9	116.7	116.1	−0.1
Greece	104.3	100.0	99.9	103.1	108.0	116.3	119.8	124.2	−0.1
Portugal	99.5	100.0	102.9	105.8	110.0	113.6	113.2	113.3	−0.1
Ireland	117.7	100.0	99.2	94.1	101.8	109.0	109.0	109.7	−0.5
Luxembourg	104.0	100.0	102.6	102.1	104.5	105.3	106.5	107.5	−0.1
Japan	97.7	100.0	92.3	83.5	80.6	79.7	76.0	70.3	−1.6
United Kingdom	97.8	100.0	96.8	100.2	95.3	98.9	98.6	101.7	1.0
Canada	104.0	100.0	101.3	98.8	108.4	111.3	117.7	127.0	−1.0
Korea	94.3	100.0	93.0	97.1	93.5	93.2	104.4	113.1	−0.3
Australia	103.7	100.0	94.5	99.6	112.5	125.7	134.0	136.6	0.2
Taiwan Province of China	96.3	100.0	106.5	94.3	86.9	82.5	84.8	83.8	−0.3
Sweden	103.0	100.0	96.6	92.7	95.3	90.8	89.9	91.4	−1.4
Switzerland	100.9	100.0	105.9	112.0	112.7	115.1	114.9	114.0	−1.3
Hong Kong SAR	103.0	100.0	103.5	98.8	86.6	77.2	73.8	70.9	0.4
Denmark	105.0	100.0	101.7	104.1	108.5	114.9	114.4	114.0	0.1
Norway	99.2	100.0	102.7	116.4	116.8	114.5	117.1	120.3	1.1
Israel	93.4	100.0	103.3	90.1	81.9	76.7	77.0	78.0	0.1
Singapore	96.4	100.0	105.0	101.3	97.6	98.6	99.8	105.8	1.3
New Zealand	113.0	100.0	96.3	104.1	117.4	125.1	130.1	119.2	0.2

[1]Defined as the ratio, in common currency, of the unit labor costs in the manufacturing sector to the weighted average of those of its industrial country trading partners, using 1999–2001 trade weights.

[2]In nominal effective terms. Average December 7, 2006–January 4, 2007 rates compared with January 26–February 23, 2007 rates.

[3]A synthetic euro for the period prior to January 1, 1999, is used in the calculation of real effective exchange rates for the euro. See Box 5.5 in the *World Economic Outlook*, October 1998.

Table 18. Other Emerging Market and Developing Countries: Central Government Fiscal Balances
(Percent of GDP)

	1999	2000	2001	2002	2003	2004	2005	2006	2007	2008
Other emerging market and developing countries	**−3.8**	**−3.0**	**−3.1**	**−3.4**	**−2.7**	**−1.6**	**−0.9**	**−0.4**	**−1.1**	**−0.8**
Regional groups										
Africa	−3.5	−1.2	−2.1	−2.3	−1.4	−0.2	1.2	3.1	0.4	0.9
Sub-Sahara	−3.8	−2.3	−2.5	−2.4	−2.4	−0.8	0.4	2.6	−0.5	—
Excluding Nigeria and South Africa	−4.9	−4.1	−2.7	−2.9	−2.9	−1.9	−0.7	2.9	−2.2	−1.8
Central and eastern Europe	−5.5	−5.1	−7.5	−8.2	−6.4	−5.2	−3.6	−2.7	−3.1	−2.2
Commonwealth of Independent States[1]	−3.9	0.3	1.8	1.0	1.2	2.6	5.5	5.8	3.0	3.8
Russia	−4.1	0.9	2.7	1.3	1.7	4.3	7.5	7.5	4.0	4.2
Excluding Russia	−3.3	−1.3	−0.8	0.2	−0.2	−1.7	0.2	1.5	0.6	2.8
Developing Asia	−4.2	−4.4	−3.9	−3.7	−3.1	−2.3	−2.1	−1.6	−1.9	−1.7
China	−3.7	−3.3	−2.7	−3.0	−2.4	−1.5	−1.3	−0.7	−1.0	−0.9
India	−6.5	−7.2	−6.6	−6.1	−5.3	−4.4	−4.2	−3.8	−3.6	−3.3
Excluding China and India	−2.8	−3.8	−3.7	−3.1	−2.4	−1.9	−1.8	−1.9	−2.2	−1.9
Middle East	−1.8	2.1	−0.9	−2.1	−0.5	2.2	5.0	6.1	3.5	5.1
Western Hemisphere	−2.7	−2.3	−2.4	−3.5	−3.2	−2.0	−2.1	−2.0	−1.9	−1.9
Brazil	−2.5	−2.1	−1.9	−0.7	−3.7	−1.4	−3.4	−3.2	−2.4	−2.0
Mexico	−1.7	−1.5	−1.0	−2.2	−1.5	−1.3	−1.2	−2.0	−1.9	−1.7
Analytical groups										
By source of export earnings										
Fuel	−2.9	2.8	1.2	0.3	1.8	4.6	7.9	8.0	4.8	6.0
Nonfuel	−3.9	−3.9	−3.8	−4.0	−3.4	−2.5	−2.3	−1.6	−2.0	−1.8
of which, primary products	−3.6	−3.7	−2.6	−2.8	−2.3	−1.3	1.1	6.1	2.0	0.3
By external financing source										
Net debtor countries	−4.1	−4.2	−4.2	−4.5	−3.9	−3.0	−2.7	−2.2	−2.5	−2.2
of which, official financing	−3.8	−4.1	−4.0	−3.3	−2.7	−2.1	−2.4	−1.5	−2.9	−2.7
Net debtor countries by debt-servicing experience										
Countries with arrears and/or rescheduling during 2001–05	−3.1	−3.5	−3.2	−4.7	−2.9	−2.2	−1.5	−0.7	−2.1	−1.7
Other groups										
Heavily indebted poor countries	−4.2	−4.8	−4.0	−4.3	−4.0	−3.1	−2.2	4.3	−2.1	−2.0
Middle East and north Africa	−1.8	2.1	−0.9	−1.9	—	2.0	4.6	5.6	3.2	4.6
Memorandum										
Median										
Other emerging market and developing countries	−3.1	−2.7	−3.7	−3.6	−3.2	−2.5	−1.9	−1.2	−1.9	−1.9
Africa	−3.3	−2.7	−3.4	−3.6	−3.0	−2.9	−1.8	−0.2	−1.9	−2.1
Central and eastern Europe	−3.3	−2.6	−4.2	−5.4	−4.1	−3.7	−3.0	−2.6	−2.4	−2.0
Commonwealth of Independent States[1]	−5.1	−1.2	−1.4	−0.4	−1.0	0.4	−0.2	0.7	1.0	0.5
Developing Asia	−3.2	−3.5	−3.9	−3.8	−3.0	−1.8	−2.2	−1.9	−2.6	−2.6
Middle East	−1.5	3.2	0.3	−0.1	1.2	1.7	1.1	1.6	0.7	3.7
Western Hemisphere	−2.9	−2.6	−4.2	−4.3	−3.7	−2.8	−2.4	−1.7	−1.8	−1.6

[1]Mongolia, which is not a member of the Commonwealth of Independent States, is included in this group for reasons of geography and similarities in economic structure.

Table 19. Other Emerging Market and Developing Countries: Broad Money Aggregates
(Annual percent change)

	1999	2000	2001	2002	2003	2004	2005	2006	2007	2008
Other emerging market and developing countries	**17.6**	**15.1**	**15.7**	**16.5**	**15.7**	**16.9**	**19.1**	**20.5**	**15.9**	**13.9**
Regional groups										
Africa	19.3	19.8	21.0	20.7	21.8	18.6	22.3	25.0	17.2	19.1
Sub-Sahara	21.4	22.4	22.2	23.9	25.3	21.6	26.0	28.5	18.3	21.3
Central and eastern Europe	37.7	24.6	38.0	10.6	10.6	14.3	17.6	16.1	13.7	11.8
Commonwealth of Independent States[1]	53.2	57.5	37.9	34.0	38.7	34.7	36.0	41.7	33.3	23.7
Russia	48.1	57.2	35.7	33.9	39.4	33.7	36.3	40.5	33.9	26.0
Excluding Russia	70.3	58.2	43.2	34.2	36.8	37.7	34.8	45.4	31.2	15.9
Developing Asia	13.9	12.1	14.6	14.0	16.3	13.5	16.2	17.1	15.3	13.0
China	14.7	12.3	17.6	16.9	19.6	14.4	16.6	16.9	15.0	12.0
India	15.9	16.1	14.6	14.6	16.3	13.3	19.2	21.1	20.0	17.8
Excluding China and India	11.7	9.4	9.2	8.2	10.0	12.0	13.1	14.7	12.6	11.7
Middle East	10.6	13.0	13.6	16.8	12.7	18.6	20.3	23.4	16.3	14.4
Western Hemisphere	10.5	7.9	6.8	17.4	11.5	17.4	17.9	18.5	10.8	10.3
Brazil	7.1	3.7	12.6	23.2	3.7	18.6	18.9	15.7	8.0	8.4
Mexico	22.8	16.2	13.7	12.6	11.7	13.5	15.0	18.7	12.4	10.3
Analytical groups										
By source of export earnings										
Fuel	24.7	29.6	20.9	22.1	23.7	25.7	28.3	32.8	22.7	18.9
Nonfuel	16.3	12.5	14.7	15.4	14.1	15.1	17.1	17.7	14.2	12.5
of which, primary products	22.6	24.0	21.8	20.2	31.3	32.9	34.8	30.6	21.0	31.0
By external financing source										
Net debtor countries	16.5	12.8	14.1	15.2	12.1	15.4	17.4	18.3	14.2	12.9
of which, official financing	16.1	14.0	11.9	14.0	14.1	14.8	15.2	16.7	14.0	12.7
Net debtor countries by debt-servicing experience										
Countries with arrears and/or rescheduling during 2001–05	10.6	11.8	1.7	22.3	19.7	19.6	22.3	21.1	18.7	19.4
Other groups										
Heavily indebted poor countries	23.4	29.6	19.9	17.9	17.9	14.5	15.2	19.4	15.6	12.4
Middle East and north Africa	11.1	13.1	14.4	16.2	12.9	17.5	19.2	22.0	16.1	14.3
Memorandum										
Median										
Other emerging market and developing countries	13.1	15.1	13.7	13.3	13.0	13.6	14.3	16.2	12.3	11.1
Africa	12.6	14.1	15.5	18.6	15.5	13.7	14.3	16.4	13.3	11.7
Central and eastern Europe	13.7	19.9	21.1	9.4	11.5	14.6	14.7	18.2	13.0	11.7
Commonwealth of Independent States[1]	32.1	40.1	35.7	34.1	30.7	32.3	26.4	34.9	27.0	19.3
Developing Asia	14.7	12.3	9.1	13.3	13.1	14.4	12.1	15.2	10.3	10.0
Middle East	10.6	10.2	11.6	10.9	8.1	12.3	17.0	20.2	14.7	11.4
Western Hemisphere	10.6	9.2	9.2	8.3	8.1	12.2	13.7	12.4	8.1	8.0

[1]Mongolia, which is not a member of the Commonwealth of Independent States, is included in this group for reasons of geography and similarities in economic structure.

Table 20. Summary of World Trade Volumes and Prices
(Annual percent change)

	Ten-Year Averages		1999	2000	2001	2002	2003	2004	2005	2006	2007	2008
	1989–98	1999–2008										
Trade in goods and services												
World trade[1]												
Volume	6.7	6.8	5.8	12.3	0.2	3.4	5.4	10.6	7.4	9.2	7.0	7.4
Price deflator												
In U.S. dollars	0.3	2.9	−1.5	−0.6	−3.5	1.2	10.4	9.8	5.5	5.4	2.8	0.8
In SDRs	0.2	1.9	−2.3	3.1	—	−0.5	2.1	3.8	5.8	5.9	1.1	0.4
Volume of trade												
Exports												
Advanced economies	6.7	5.6	5.6	11.8	−0.6	2.3	3.3	8.9	5.6	8.4	5.5	5.8
Other emerging market and developing countries	7.6	9.5	3.7	14.7	2.6	6.9	10.8	14.6	11.2	10.6	10.4	9.9
Imports												
Advanced economies	6.4	5.8	8.0	11.7	−0.6	2.6	4.1	9.1	6.1	7.4	4.7	5.7
Other emerging market and developing countries	7.1	10.2	0.8	13.9	3.2	6.3	10.3	16.4	12.1	15.0	12.5	12.2
Terms of trade												
Advanced economies	—	−0.4	−0.3	−2.5	0.3	0.8	0.9	−0.2	−1.4	−1.3	−0.1	—
Other emerging market and developing countries	−0.9	2.0	4.3	5.5	−2.4	0.8	1.1	2.8	5.5	4.1	−2.4	0.9
Trade in goods												
World trade[1]												
Volume	6.7	7.0	5.4	12.8	−0.5	3.7	6.3	11.0	7.4	9.5	7.2	7.7
Price deflator												
In U.S. dollars	0.2	3.0	−1.1	0.3	−3.7	0.6	9.9	9.9	6.2	5.9	2.4	0.8
In SDRs	0.1	2.0	−1.9	3.9	−0.3	−1.1	1.7	4.0	6.4	6.4	0.8	0.4
World trade prices in U.S. dollars[2]												
Manufactures	0.3	2.5	−2.4	−5.9	−3.8	2.3	14.1	9.3	3.4	4.4	4.4	1.1
Oil	−1.2	17.3	37.5	57.0	−13.8	2.5	15.8	30.7	41.3	20.5	−5.5	6.6
Nonfuel primary commodities	−2.2	4.8	−7.2	4.8	−4.9	1.7	6.9	18.5	10.3	28.4	4.2	−8.8
World trade prices in SDRs[2]												
Manufactures	0.2	1.5	−3.2	−2.4	−0.3	0.5	5.5	3.4	3.6	4.9	2.7	0.8
Oil	−1.3	16.2	36.4	62.8	−10.7	0.8	7.1	23.6	41.6	21.0	−7.0	6.2
Nonfuel primary commodities	−2.3	3.8	−7.9	8.6	−1.5	—	−1.2	12.1	10.5	29.0	2.5	−9.1
World trade prices in euros[2]												
Manufactures	0.9	1.0	2.5	8.7	−0.8	−3.0	−4.7	−0.6	3.2	3.6	0.8	0.7
Oil	−0.7	15.6	44.4	81.3	−11.1	−2.8	−3.3	18.9	41.0	19.5	−8.8	6.1
Nonfuel primary commodities	−1.6	3.2	−2.6	20.9	−1.9	−3.5	−10.8	7.8	10.0	27.4	0.6	−9.2

Table 20 *(concluded)*

	Ten-Year Averages		1999	2000	2001	2002	2003	2004	2005	2006	2007	2008
	1989–98	1999–2008										
Trade in goods												
Volume of trade												
Exports												
Advanced economies	6.6	5.6	5.0	12.5	−1.3	2.3	3.9	8.8	5.3	8.9	5.3	6.0
Other emerging market and												
developing countries	7.4	9.5	3.1	14.7	2.0	7.2	11.7	14.7	11.1	11.1	10.5	9.9
Fuel exporters	3.7	5.3	−1.6	10.5	−0.1	2.2	10.1	10.3	6.6	4.6	7.0	4.7
Nonfuel exporters	8.9	11.0	4.4	16.0	2.8	8.9	12.2	16.2	12.7	13.8	12.0	12.2
Imports												
Advanced economies	6.6	6.0	8.2	12.3	−1.6	3.0	5.0	9.4	6.2	7.8	4.9	5.8
Other emerging market and												
developing countries	7.1	10.4	−0.2	14.1	2.9	6.5	12.1	17.6	12.4	13.3	13.5	12.9
Fuel exporters	1.3	11.4	−10.5	10.6	15.2	7.5	9.7	18.0	19.1	17.6	16.8	13.3
Nonfuel exporters	8.9	10.2	1.9	14.7	0.9	6.3	12.5	17.5	11.1	12.4	12.8	12.8
Price deflators in SDRs												
Exports												
Advanced economies	−0.1	1.2	−3.0	0.5	−0.3	−0.8	2.5	3.1	3.8	4.4	1.6	0.4
Other emerging market and												
developing countries	0.9	4.9	4.7	14.2	−0.8	—	1.7	7.4	13.9	10.5	−1.3	0.8
Fuel exporters	0.3	11.6	22.8	40.9	−6.7	1.4	5.6	16.2	31.6	17.1	−6.4	3.4
Nonfuel exporters	1.0	2.7	−0.1	6.0	1.4	−0.5	0.5	4.4	7.6	7.8	1.0	−0.4
Imports												
Advanced economies	−0.4	1.6	−2.9	3.6	−0.6	−1.8	1.3	3.4	5.6	6.0	1.2	0.6
Other emerging market and												
developing countries	1.7	2.6	−0.7	6.9	1.5	−0.7	0.1	4.1	7.3	7.0	0.9	−0.4
Fuel exporters	2.1	2.0	−3.1	1.9	1.0	1.2	—	3.4	7.1	8.5	1.3	−1.0
Nonfuel exporters	1.5	2.7	−0.2	7.8	1.6	−1.1	0.2	4.2	7.3	6.7	0.9	−0.2
Terms of trade												
Advanced economies	0.3	−0.4	−0.2	−3.0	0.3	1.0	1.3	−0.3	−1.6	−1.5	0.4	−0.2
Other emerging market and												
developing countries	−0.8	2.3	5.4	6.9	−2.3	0.7	1.6	3.1	6.2	3.2	−2.2	1.2
Fuel exporters	−1.7	9.4	26.7	38.3	−7.6	0.2	5.6	12.4	22.8	7.9	−7.6	4.5
Nonfuel exporters	−0.5	0.1	0.1	−1.6	−0.1	0.6	0.3	0.1	0.3	1.0	0.1	−0.2
Memorandum												
World exports in billions of U.S. dollars												
Goods and services	5,394	11,227	7,088	7,885	7,614	7,994	9,303	11,283	12,787	14,717	16,139	17,456
Goods	4,309	9,021	5,626	6,345	6,070	6,349	7,418	9,017	10,275	11,920	13,052	14,137

[1]Average of annual percent change for world exports and imports.

[2]As represented, respectively, by the export unit value index for the manufactures of the advanced economies; the average of U.K. Brent, Dubai, and West Texas Intermediate crude oil spot prices; and the average of world market prices for nonfuel primary commodities weighted by their 1995–97 shares in world commodity exports.

Table 21. Nonfuel Commodity Prices[1]
(Annual percent change; U.S. dollar terms)

	Ten-Year Averages		1999	2000	2001	2002	2003	2004	2005	2006	2007	2008
	1989–98	1999–2008										
Nonfuel primary commodities	**−2.2**	**4.8**	**−7.2**	**4.8**	**−4.9**	**1.7**	**6.9**	**18.5**	**10.3**	**28.4**	**4.2**	**−8.8**
Food	−1.5	2.0	−12.6	2.5	0.2	3.4	5.2	14.3	−0.3	9.9	4.4	−4.2
Beverages	0.3	−1.3	−21.3	−15.1	−16.1	16.5	4.9	3.0	21.0	6.3	−1.4	−1.6
Agricultural raw materials	−0.3	2.1	1.2	4.4	−4.9	1.8	3.7	5.5	1.6	10.1	0.1	−2.0
Metals	−4.5	10.3	−1.1	12.2	−9.8	−2.7	12.2	36.1	26.4	56.5	5.8	−14.3
Advanced economies	**−2.5**	**6.0**	**−5.7**	**5.9**	**−6.2**	**1.7**	**8.2**	**21.2**	**13.0**	**36.2**	**4.0**	**−10.3**
Other emerging market and developing countries	**−2.5**	**5.9**	**−6.8**	**5.2**	**−7.1**	**1.9**	**8.7**	**22.2**	**13.5**	**36.3**	**3.6**	**−10.6**
Regional groups												
Africa	−2.4	5.9	−7.4	4.3	−6.8	4.3	8.8	18.9	14.1	36.1	4.3	−9.7
Sub-Sahara	−2.4	6.1	−7.3	4.4	−7.1	4.5	9.1	19.2	14.7	37.3	4.3	−9.9
Central and eastern Europe	−2.8	6.7	4.9	6.7	−7.0	0.9	8.5	24.1	15.7	40.6	3.8	−11.6
Commonwealth of Independent States[2]	...	8.6	−2.5	9.7	−8.3	−0.6	10.3	29.5	20.6	50.0	4.3	−13.3
Developing Asia	−1.9	4.8	−6.5	3.4	−6.8	2.1	7.2	18.7	11.6	30.2	3.2	−9.1
Middle East	−2.5	5.9	−7.1	5.3	−6.5	2.0	9.4	20.2	12.5	34.4	4.9	−9.0
Western Hemisphere	−2.5	5.3	−9.6	5.0	−7.0	2.5	9.5	23.2	11.2	34.1	3.2	−10.6
Analytical groups												
By source of export earnings												
Fuel	−3.3	7.9	−3.3	8.6	−7.9	−0.1	9.8	27.2	18.9	46.3	4.3	−12.5
Nonfuel	−2.4	5.6	−7.3	4.8	−7.0	2.2	8.5	21.5	12.8	34.9	3.5	−10.3
of which, primary products	−3.1	7.5	−6.2	8.7	−8.3	0.8	10.4	31.9	18.7	53.3	−2.0	−15.7
By source of external financing												
Net debtor countries	−2.3	5.3	−7.9	4.3	−7.0	2.5	8.6	21.0	12.2	33.7	3.3	−10.0
of which, official financing	−1.7	4.3	−11.1	−0.4	−8.1	5.3	9.3	17.7	11.5	29.3	3.4	−7.3
Net debtor countries by debt-servicing experience												
Countries with arrears and/or rescheduling during 2001–05	−1.8	3.9	−10.2	2.4	−5.7	5.1	8.2	15.8	6.7	24.2	4.3	−7.5
Other groups												
Heavily indebted poor countries	−1.9	4.6	−10.8	0.8	−7.7	6.7	9.9	16.2	11.0	29.6	3.9	−7.0
Middle East and north Africa	−2.3	5.4	−7.6	4.8	−5.9	2.2	8.8	19.1	11.2	31.8	4.7	−8.6
Memorandum												
Average oil spot price[3]	−1.2	17.3	37.5	57.0	−13.8	2.5	15.8	30.7	41.3	20.5	−5.5	6.6
In U.S. dollars a barrel	18.20	40.53	17.98	28.24	24.33	24.95	28.89	37.76	53.35	64.27	60.75	64.75
Export unit value of manufactures[4]	0.3	2.5	−2.4	−5.9	−3.8	2.3	14.1	9.3	3.4	4.4	4.4	1.1

[1]Averages of world market prices for individual commodities weighted by 1995–97 exports as a share of world commodity exports and total commodity exports for the indicated country group, respectively.
[2]Mongolia, which is not a member of the Commonwealth of Independent States, is included in this group for reasons of geography and similarities in economic structure.
[3]Average of U.K. Brent, Dubai, and West Texas Intermediate crude oil spot prices.
[4]For the manufactures exported by the advanced economies.

Table 22. Advanced Economies: Export Volumes, Import Volumes, and Terms of Trade in Goods and Services
(Annual percent change)

| | Ten-Year Averages | | 1999 | 2000 | 2001 | 2002 | 2003 | 2004 | 2005 | 2006 | 2007 | 2008 |
	1989–98	1999–2008										
Export volume												
Advanced economies	**6.7**	**5.6**	**5.6**	**11.8**	**−0.6**	**2.3**	**3.3**	**8.9**	**5.6**	**8.4**	**5.5**	**5.8**
United States	7.8	4.5	4.3	8.7	−5.4	−2.3	1.3	9.2	6.8	8.9	8.0	7.0
Euro area	6.6	5.3	5.1	12.1	3.7	1.5	1.3	6.7	4.1	8.2	5.7	5.3
Germany	6.3	7.2	5.9	13.5	6.4	4.3	2.4	9.6	6.9	12.5	6.2	4.7
France	6.4	4.2	4.0	12.9	2.7	1.3	−1.1	3.3	3.2	6.2	3.8	6.5
Italy	5.5	1.8	−1.7	9.0	0.5	−4.0	−2.4	3.3	−0.5	5.3	4.9	4.1
Spain	8.9	5.1	7.5	10.2	4.2	2.0	3.7	4.1	1.5	6.2	6.2	6.2
Japan	4.5	6.3	1.8	12.8	−6.8	7.4	9.2	14.0	6.9	9.6	4.5	5.0
United Kingdom	5.7	4.3	3.8	9.1	2.9	1.0	1.7	4.9	7.9	11.2	−3.4	5.1
Canada	6.9	3.0	10.7	8.9	−3.0	1.2	−2.4	5.2	2.1	1.3	2.8	3.5
Other advanced economies	7.6	7.9	8.4	14.8	−1.9	6.4	8.4	13.1	7.4	8.6	7.1	7.1
Memorandum												
Major advanced economies	6.3	4.8	4.1	10.7	−1.1	1.1	1.7	7.9	5.5	8.8	4.6	5.4
Newly industrialized Asian economies	9.4	9.9	9.3	17.3	−3.8	10.2	13.6	17.6	9.4	11.0	7.7	7.9
Import volume												
Advanced economies	**6.4**	**5.8**	**8.0**	**11.7**	**−0.6**	**2.6**	**4.1**	**9.1**	**6.1**	**7.4**	**4.7**	**5.7**
United States	7.6	5.9	11.5	13.1	−2.7	3.4	4.1	10.8	6.1	5.8	2.9	5.0
Euro area	6.0	5.3	7.4	11.1	1.8	0.2	2.8	6.5	5.1	7.6	5.6	5.5
Germany	5.9	5.9	8.6	10.2	1.2	−1.4	5.3	6.9	6.5	11.1	5.7	5.0
France	4.7	5.6	5.8	15.1	2.2	1.6	1.5	5.9	6.4	7.1	4.4	7.0
Italy	4.7	2.4	3.1	5.8	−0.2	−0.5	0.8	2.7	0.5	4.3	4.2	3.8
Spain	9.3	7.8	13.7	10.8	4.5	3.7	6.2	9.6	7.0	8.4	7.3	6.9
Japan	4.7	4.7	3.5	9.2	0.7	0.9	3.9	8.1	5.8	4.6	4.0	6.7
United Kingdom	5.3	5.6	7.9	9.0	4.8	4.8	2.0	6.6	7.0	11.5	−2.0	5.0
Canada	6.0	4.5	7.8	8.1	−5.1	1.7	4.5	8.2	7.1	5.2	3.8	4.3
Other advanced economies	7.3	7.5	7.0	14.2	−3.9	6.3	7.4	13.9	7.7	8.3	7.7	7.2
Memorandum												
Major advanced economies	6.0	5.3	8.1	11.0	−0.4	1.9	3.5	8.0	5.9	7.2	3.2	5.3
Newly industrialized Asian economies	9.5	8.8	8.4	17.7	−5.7	9.0	10.0	16.8	7.8	9.5	7.6	8.4
Terms of trade												
Advanced economies	**—**	**−0.4**	**−0.3**	**−2.5**	**0.3**	**0.8**	**0.9**	**−0.2**	**−1.4**	**−1.3**	**−0.1**	**—**
United States	0.5	−0.6	−1.2	−2.1	2.3	0.5	−1.0	−1.5	−2.6	−1.0	—	0.3
Euro area	−0.4	−0.4	0.2	−3.9	0.7	1.4	1.0	−0.5	−1.2	−1.7	0.1	−0.1
Germany	−1.7	−0.5	0.3	−4.6	0.2	1.4	2.0	−0.2	−1.3	−1.8	−0.3	−0.3
France	−0.6	−0.4	0.2	−3.6	1.0	0.8	0.4	−1.3	−1.3	−1.0	0.4	0.1
Italy	0.5	−0.9	−0.4	−7.1	1.0	2.3	1.7	—	−2.1	−3.5	−0.3	−0.3
Spain	1.0	0.5	−0.1	−2.7	2.6	2.8	1.5	−0.8	0.7	−1.1	1.8	0.5
Japan	−0.3	−2.7	−0.6	−5.2	−0.1	−0.4	−2.0	−4.0	−6.0	−6.4	−0.8	−0.9
United Kingdom	0.8	—	0.7	−0.8	−0.6	2.5	1.0	0.4	−2.5	−0.9	—	−0.1
Canada	−0.6	1.4	1.4	4.0	−1.6	−2.4	6.0	4.1	4.0	0.7	−1.9	0.2
Other advanced economies	0.1	−0.2	−1.0	−0.8	−0.5	0.3	−0.1	0.2	0.2	—	−0.7	0.1
Memorandum												
Major advanced economies	−0.2	−0.5	−0.2	−3.2	0.5	0.9	1.5	−0.3	−2.2	−1.9	−0.2	—
Newly industrialized Asian economies	—	−1.5	−2.4	−3.1	−0.6	—	−1.7	−1.8	−2.2	−1.7	−1.1	—
Memorandum												
Trade in goods												
Advanced economies												
Export volume	6.6	5.6	5.0	12.5	−1.3	2.3	3.9	8.8	5.3	8.9	5.3	6.0
Import volume	6.6	6.0	8.2	12.3	−1.6	3.0	5.0	9.4	6.2	7.8	4.9	5.8
Terms of trade	0.3	−0.4	−0.2	−3.0	0.3	1.0	1.3	−0.3	−1.6	−1.5	0.4	−0.2

Table 23. Other Emerging Market and Developing Countries—by Region: Total Trade in Goods
(Annual percent change)

	Ten-Year Averages		1999	2000	2001	2002	2003	2004	2005	2006	2007	2008
	1989–98	1999–2008										
Other emerging market and developing countries												
Value in U.S. dollars												
Exports	7.8	15.5	8.0	25.4	−2.5	8.6	22.0	29.1	25.3	21.5	10.9	11.0
Imports	8.3	14.0	−0.5	17.6	0.5	7.3	20.5	28.8	20.0	20.4	16.2	12.6
Volume												
Exports	7.4	9.5	3.1	14.7	2.0	7.2	11.7	14.7	11.1	11.1	10.5	9.9
Imports	7.1	10.4	−0.2	14.1	2.9	6.5	12.1	17.6	12.4	13.3	13.5	12.9
Unit value in U.S. dollars												
Exports	1.0	6.0	5.5	10.1	−4.3	1.8	10.0	13.5	13.6	10.0	0.3	1.1
Imports	1.8	3.6	0.1	3.1	−2.0	1.0	8.3	10.1	7.0	6.6	2.6	—
Terms of trade	−0.8	2.3	5.4	6.9	−2.3	0.7	1.6	3.1	6.2	3.2	−2.2	1.2
Memorandum												
Real GDP growth in developing country trading partners	3.1	3.6	3.5	5.0	1.7	2.4	2.9	4.8	3.9	4.4	3.8	3.7
Market prices of nonfuel commodities exported by other emerging market and developing countries	−2.5	5.9	−6.8	5.2	−7.1	1.9	8.7	22.2	13.5	36.3	3.6	−10.6
Regional groups												
Africa												
Value in U.S. dollars												
Exports	3.2	14.2	7.7	28.0	−6.4	2.8	25.5	29.0	28.8	18.1	4.9	10.1
Imports	4.2	12.3	0.6	3.5	1.5	9.6	22.2	26.6	19.0	17.9	14.8	10.4
Volume												
Exports	4.3	5.3	1.7	9.7	1.9	1.6	6.6	7.4	5.3	2.6	10.6	6.4
Imports	4.4	7.9	2.4	1.1	6.7	8.0	6.3	9.7	11.8	11.1	13.0	9.8
Unit value in U.S. dollars												
Exports	−0.8	8.7	6.5	16.6	−8.1	1.4	18.0	20.4	22.4	15.3	−4.6	4.3
Imports	0.3	4.3	−1.5	2.9	−4.8	1.5	15.1	15.5	6.8	6.5	1.8	0.5
Terms of trade	−1.2	4.3	8.0	13.4	−3.6	−0.1	2.5	4.3	14.7	8.2	−6.3	3.8
Sub-Sahara												
Value in U.S. dollars												
Exports	2.8	14.2	6.5	25.5	−6.6	3.2	26.2	30.2	28.4	19.2	5.9	10.2
Imports	3.9	12.6	−0.4	3.2	1.4	9.0	24.9	26.7	22.0	20.4	12.4	10.4
Volume												
Exports	4.4	5.7	−0.4	10.8	1.9	0.6	7.3	7.8	5.8	3.6	13.2	7.4
Imports	4.1	8.2	2.0	0.2	5.7	8.2	7.3	10.1	14.0	14.9	11.0	9.1
Unit value in U.S. dollars												
Exports	−1.5	8.4	7.5	13.1	−8.3	2.9	17.9	21.1	21.5	15.3	−5.6	3.6
Imports	0.3	4.3	−2.0	3.7	−4.0	0.7	16.5	15.2	7.4	5.1	1.2	1.2
Terms of trade	−1.7	4.0	9.7	9.1	−4.4	2.1	1.2	5.1	13.1	9.7	−6.7	2.4

243

Table 23 *(continued)*

	Ten-Year Averages		1999	2000	2001	2002	2003	2004	2005	2006	2007	2008
	1989–98	1999–2008										
Central and eastern Europe												
Value in U.S. dollars												
Exports	6.8	15.9	−2.3	13.9	11.1	14.1	28.9	32.0	16.1	21.6	16.9	11.0
Imports	10.0	14.8	−4.5	16.9	−0.4	14.0	29.5	31.8	16.1	22.8	16.3	10.9
Volume												
Exports	6.3	10.9	1.7	16.4	9.5	7.5	12.3	16.7	10.0	15.0	10.9	9.8
Imports	10.4	9.8	−2.1	16.8	1.3	8.7	12.4	17.7	9.3	13.5	12.3	10.3
Unit value in U.S. dollars												
Exports	1.4	4.7	−3.8	−2.2	2.0	6.2	14.9	13.5	5.7	5.7	5.5	1.1
Imports	2.0	4.6	−2.4	0.1	−1.5	5.2	15.4	12.2	6.4	8.2	3.8	0.6
Terms of trade	−0.6	0.1	−1.4	−2.3	3.6	1.0	−0.4	1.2	−0.6	−2.3	1.7	0.5
Commonwealth of Independent States[1]												
Value in U.S. dollars												
Exports	...	16.4	0.1	36.9	−0.9	6.3	26.8	36.7	28.8	25.0	5.2	8.3
Imports	...	14.0	−25.8	14.6	15.0	9.6	26.5	29.5	23.7	28.4	18.3	12.7
Volume												
Exports	...	6.6	−1.4	9.6	4.1	7.1	12.5	12.8	3.4	6.1	6.1	6.2
Imports	...	11.7	−21.3	13.7	18.1	8.4	23.8	21.8	15.0	18.6	13.9	12.4
Unit value in U.S. dollars												
Exports	...	9.2	1.2	24.3	−4.9	−0.8	12.8	21.6	24.5	17.6	−1.0	1.9
Imports	...	2.3	−5.8	0.8	−2.6	1.6	2.2	6.6	7.9	8.8	3.7	0.4
Terms of trade	...	6.7	7.4	23.3	−2.3	−2.3	10.4	14.1	15.3	8.0	−4.5	1.5
Developing Asia												
Value in U.S. dollars												
Exports	13.5	17.0	8.3	22.2	−1.6	13.8	23.3	27.9	23.8	22.6	17.7	15.1
Imports	10.5	17.2	11.8	25.9	−1.2	12.5	25.6	31.2	20.7	17.8	16.4	15.0
Volume												
Exports	12.7	13.9	5.2	20.4	0.5	13.3	16.3	19.3	17.3	17.3	15.4	15.4
Imports	9.8	13.3	8.3	18.8	1.1	12.6	18.3	19.4	12.6	12.1	14.7	16.2
Unit value in U.S. dollars												
Exports	0.9	3.1	4.8	1.7	−2.1	0.5	6.2	7.5	5.8	4.8	2.0	−0.3
Imports	0.9	3.9	6.2	6.4	−2.1	−0.1	6.2	9.9	7.2	5.3	1.6	−0.8
Terms of trade	—	−0.8	−1.2	−4.5	—	0.7	—	−2.2	−1.3	−0.5	0.4	0.6
Excluding China and India												
Value in U.S. dollars												
Exports	12.5	10.1	10.1	18.6	−9.0	5.7	11.8	18.0	15.0	16.1	9.5	8.5
Imports	10.5	11.3	11.5	21.0	−7.8	5.7	10.9	22.8	19.5	11.5	11.0	10.3
Volume												
Exports	11.2	5.9	3.1	16.1	−6.6	5.5	4.5	8.2	7.4	8.0	6.5	7.9
Imports	9.3	7.4	4.7	16.9	−7.1	6.5	6.4	13.6	10.3	5.9	8.9	9.9
Unit value in U.S. dollars												
Exports	1.3	4.5	10.2	2.5	−2.5	0.4	7.3	9.3	7.2	7.6	2.8	0.5
Imports	1.6	4.3	12.1	3.8	−0.5	−0.8	4.3	8.3	8.2	5.5	2.0	0.4
Terms of trade	−0.3	0.2	−1.6	−1.3	−2.0	1.1	2.9	1.0	−0.9	2.0	0.8	—

Table 23 *(concluded)*

	Ten-Year Averages		1999	2000	2001	2002	2003	2004	2005	2006	2007	2008
	1989–98	1999–2008										
Middle East												
Value in U.S. dollars												
Exports	5.3	18.6	30.0	45.8	−10.8	6.8	25.4	32.8	39.4	20.3	1.2	7.5
Imports	5.6	14.0	−4.8	6.5	7.2	9.0	16.6	29.0	25.1	25.5	18.1	11.6
Volume												
Exports	7.0	6.0	1.0	11.8	−0.3	2.1	10.4	10.7	7.5	6.3	6.9	4.1
Imports	4.8	10.3	−1.8	8.0	10.2	5.7	4.7	17.6	17.3	16.2	15.3	11.8
Unit value in U.S. dollars												
Exports	−0.7	12.6	28.5	33.2	−9.9	5.4	13.6	21.6	30.4	14.0	−5.3	3.7
Imports	1.0	3.4	−2.9	−1.2	−2.5	2.9	11.4	10.0	6.9	8.2	2.6	−0.1
Terms of trade	−1.6	8.9	32.4	34.9	−7.6	2.4	2.0	10.6	22.0	5.4	−7.7	3.8
Western Hemisphere												
Value in U.S. dollars												
Exports	9.6	10.4	6.2	20.1	−4.3	0.9	9.5	23.1	20.6	19.7	6.0	5.5
Imports	13.5	8.4	−3.5	16.0	−2.3	−6.6	3.4	21.4	18.1	18.9	13.7	9.8
Volume												
Exports	8.3	4.9	3.9	8.7	1.5	0.7	3.3	9.8	7.0	4.5	4.1	5.7
Imports	11.6	5.5	−3.6	12.2	−1.0	−7.0	—	14.6	11.5	12.6	10.1	8.6
Unit value in U.S. dollars												
Exports	2.0	5.6	2.0	10.4	−5.6	0.2	7.4	13.5	13.9	15.2	1.2	−0.4
Imports	2.6	2.6	−2.6	2.3	−1.1	−1.1	4.1	7.2	7.1	6.3	3.5	1.2
Terms of trade	−0.6	2.9	4.7	7.9	−4.6	1.4	3.2	5.9	6.3	8.4	−2.2	−1.6

[1]Mongolia, which is not a member of the Commonwealth of Independent States, is included in this group for reasons of geography and similarities in economic structure.

Table 24. Other Emerging Market and Developing Countries—by Source of Export Earnings: Total Trade in Goods
(Annual percent change)

	Ten-Year Averages		1999	2000	2001	2002	2003	2004	2005	2006	2007	2008
	1989–98	1999–2008										
Fuel												
Value in U.S. dollars												
Exports	3.3	18.2	21.3	48.7	−10.3	5.0	25.7	34.3	39.5	21.6	1.6	8.2
Imports	2.8	14.6	−12.2	8.7	12.3	10.6	18.5	28.6	26.8	26.5	20.2	12.5
Volume												
Exports	3.7	5.3	−1.6	10.5	−0.1	2.2	10.1	10.3	6.6	4.6	7.0	4.7
Imports	1.3	11.4	−10.5	10.6	15.2	7.5	9.7	18.0	19.1	17.6	16.8	13.3
Unit value in U.S. dollars												
Exports	0.4	12.7	23.8	35.9	−9.9	3.2	14.2	22.9	31.3	16.6	−4.9	3.8
Imports	2.2	3.0	−2.3	−1.7	−2.5	3.0	8.2	9.4	6.9	8.0	2.9	−0.7
Terms of trade	−1.7	9.4	26.7	38.3	−7.6	0.2	5.6	12.4	22.8	7.9	−7.6	4.5
Nonfuel												
Value in U.S. dollars												
Exports	9.4	14.7	4.6	18.6	0.3	9.8	20.8	27.4	20.4	21.5	14.7	12.0
Imports	9.9	13.9	1.9	19.1	−1.3	6.7	20.9	28.9	18.7	19.2	15.3	12.6
Volume												
Exports	8.9	11.0	4.4	16.0	2.8	8.9	12.2	16.2	12.7	13.8	12.0	12.2
Imports	8.9	10.2	1.9	14.7	0.9	6.3	12.5	17.5	11.1	12.4	12.8	12.8
Unit value in U.S. dollars												
Exports	1.1	3.8	0.7	2.3	−2.1	1.3	8.7	10.4	7.4	7.3	2.6	—
Imports	1.6	3.7	0.6	3.9	−2.0	0.6	8.3	10.2	7.0	6.3	2.5	0.1
Terms of trade	−0.5	0.1	0.1	−1.6	−0.1	0.6	0.3	0.1	0.3	1.0	0.1	−0.2
Primary products												
Value in U.S. dollars												
Exports	2.2	10.7	2.5	8.4	−5.8	−1.5	20.4	42.4	20.8	37.3	0.2	−6.1
Imports	3.3	8.4	−14.5	9.3	−1.0	2.4	12.2	26.3	23.4	14.9	9.3	7.6
Volume												
Exports	6.0	4.8	4.9	1.6	5.9	0.5	5.9	15.4	3.9	0.5	3.6	6.9
Imports	3.9	5.7	−11.3	7.1	4.4	4.6	4.0	15.7	14.1	6.9	8.0	6.1
Unit value in U.S. dollars												
Exports	−1.8	5.9	−2.2	7.0	−10.5	−1.6	13.5	23.8	16.5	36.4	−3.1	−11.4
Imports	—	2.7	−3.6	2.0	−5.2	−2.3	8.7	9.5	8.3	8.0	1.5	1.3
Terms of trade	−1.8	3.1	1.4	4.9	−5.6	0.7	4.4	13.1	7.6	26.3	−4.5	−12.6

Table 25. Summary of Payments Balances on Current Account
(Billions of U.S. dollars)

	1999	2000	2001	2002	2003	2004	2005	2006	2007	2008
Advanced economies	**−114.2**	**−267.9**	**−213.0**	**−229.0**	**−220.6**	**−255.2**	**−473.4**	**−563.2**	**−587.2**	**−637.8**
United States	−299.8	−415.2	−389.0	−472.4	−527.5	−665.3	−791.5	−856.7	−834.6	−866.1
Euro area[1]	22.4	−41.3	3.2	42.2	35.5	97.5	8.1	−29.1	−35.2	−50.6
Japan	114.5	119.6	87.8	112.6	136.2	172.1	165.7	170.4	166.6	159.1
Other advanced economies[2]	48.7	68.9	85.0	88.7	135.1	140.6	144.3	152.2	116.0	119.8
Memorandum										
Newly industrialized Asian economies	57.1	38.9	48.1	55.5	80.0	83.9	79.9	87.0	88.1	89.6
Other emerging market and developing countries	**−21.2**	**85.8**	**39.4**	**77.3**	**147.6**	**212.6**	**428.0**	**544.2**	**455.1**	**470.7**
Regional groups										
Africa	−15.0	7.2	0.5	−7.5	−2.2	0.6	14.6	19.9	0.9	−0.5
Central and eastern Europe	−25.8	−31.8	−16.0	−24.0	−35.8	−58.6	−63.2	−88.9	−98.5	−104.7
Commonwealth of Independent States[3]	23.8	48.3	33.1	30.2	36.0	62.6	87.7	99.0	75.4	76.3
Developing Asia	38.3	38.1	36.6	64.6	82.5	88.5	165.2	253.1	308.9	358.6
Middle East	14.0	72.1	39.2	30.0	59.5	99.2	189.0	212.4	153.0	146.7
Western Hemisphere	−56.4	−48.1	−53.9	−16.1	7.7	20.4	34.6	48.7	15.3	−5.7
Memorandum										
European Union	−22.1	−88.6	−32.1	14.0	15.0	52.3	−49.4	−117.7	−146.8	−172.5
Analytical groups										
By source of export earnings										
Fuel	38.1	150.9	83.7	64.2	110.0	185.9	337.9	395.6	290.0	288.4
Nonfuel	−59.3	−65.1	−44.2	13.1	37.6	26.7	90.1	148.6	165.0	182.3
of which, primary products	−0.9	−1.5	−3.2	−4.3	−2.9	0.4	0.2	9.6	7.7	1.9
By external financing source										
Net debtor countries	−93.1	−95.0	−74.3	−36.0	−29.7	−69.0	−93.5	−111.4	−159.7	−186.6
of which, official financing	−8.7	−6.7	−4.6	−2.3	−0.4	−2.6	−4.6	−7.4	−14.8	−16.6
Net debtor countries by debt-servicing experience										
Countries with arrears and/or rescheduling during 2001–05	−19.8	−9.3	−10.8	7.1	11.0	−2.6	−8.9	−1.2	−15.3	−19.8
Total[1]	**−135.4**	**−182.1**	**−173.5**	**−151.7**	**−73.0**	**−42.6**	**−45.4**	**−19.0**	**−132.1**	**−167.1**
Memorandum										
In percent of total world current account transactions	−0.9	−1.1	−1.1	−0.9	−0.4	−0.2	−0.2	−0.1	−0.4	−0.5
In percent of world GDP	−0.4	−0.6	−0.6	−0.5	−0.2	−0.1	−0.1	—	−0.3	−0.3

[1]Reflects errors, omissions, and asymmetries in balance of payments statistics on current account, as well as the exclusion of data for international organizations and a limited number of countries. Calculated as the sum of the balance of individual euro area countries. See "Classification of Countries" in the introduction to this Statistical Appendix.

[2]In this table, "other advanced economies" means advanced economies excluding the United States, euro area countries, and Japan.

[3]Mongolia, which is not a member of the Commonwealth of Independent States, is included in this group for reasons of geography and similarities in economic structure.

Table 26. Advanced Economies: Balance of Payments on Current Account

	1999	2000	2001	2002	2003	2004	2005	2006	2007	2008
					Billions of U.S. dollars					
Advanced economies	**−114.2**	**−267.9**	**−213.0**	**−229.0**	**−220.6**	**−255.2**	**−473.4**	**−563.2**	**−587.2**	**−637.8**
United States	−299.8	−415.2	−389.0	−472.4	−527.5	−665.3	−791.5	−856.7	−834.6	−866.1
Euro area[1]	22.4	−41.3	3.2	42.2	35.5	97.5	8.1	−29.1	−35.2	−50.6
Germany	−26.9	−32.6	0.4	40.6	46.3	118.0	128.4	146.4	161.9	164.7
France	42.0	18.0	21.5	14.5	7.9	−7.0	−33.6	−46.3	−52.0	−58.5
Italy	5.9	−6.2	−0.9	−8.1	−19.8	−15.5	−28.4	−41.6	−43.3	−46.2
Spain	−18.1	−23.1	−24.0	−22.4	−31.1	−54.9	−83.0	−108.0	−127.5	−142.4
Netherlands	15.6	7.2	9.8	10.9	29.4	54.2	40.0	47.0	55.2	58.0
Belgium	20.1	9.4	7.9	11.7	12.8	12.6	9.2	9.7	10.2	11.1
Austria	−6.7	−4.9	−3.7	0.7	−0.5	0.4	3.8	5.7	6.5	6.0
Finland	7.8	10.6	12.0	12.6	10.6	14.7	9.7	11.2	11.6	12.2
Greece	−8.6	−9.9	−9.5	−9.7	−12.5	−13.3	−18.2	−29.7	−31.8	−31.8
Portugal	−10.3	−11.6	−11.5	−10.4	−9.6	−13.8	−18.0	−18.3	−19.3	−20.1
Ireland	0.2	−0.4	−0.7	−1.2	—	−1.1	−5.2	−9.1	−11.0	−8.0
Luxembourg	2.3	2.7	1.8	2.6	2.2	4.0	4.3	4.8	5.4	5.6
Slovenia	−0.9	−0.6	—	0.2	−0.2	−0.9	−0.7	−0.9	−1.1	−1.1
Japan	114.5	119.6	87.8	112.6	136.2	172.1	165.7	170.4	166.6	159.1
United Kingdom	−35.1	−37.6	−31.5	−24.8	−24.4	−35.4	−53.7	−68.1	−81.4	−88.0
Canada	1.7	19.7	16.2	12.6	10.1	21.3	26.3	21.5	9.4	7.6
Korea	24.5	12.3	8.0	5.4	11.9	28.2	15.0	6.1	3.1	−0.2
Australia	−21.4	−14.9	−7.3	−15.5	−28.3	−38.5	−41.2	−40.9	−46.2	−46.7
Taiwan Province of China	8.0	8.9	18.3	25.6	29.2	18.5	16.0	25.2	25.9	27.9
Sweden	10.6	9.9	9.8	12.5	22.4	24.0	25.2	28.4	28.1	30.1
Switzerland	29.4	30.7	20.0	23.0	42.9	50.4	61.4	69.8	68.5	68.1
Hong Kong SAR	10.3	7.0	9.8	12.4	16.5	15.7	20.3	19.4	19.4	19.9
Denmark	3.3	2.3	5.0	4.3	7.3	7.5	9.3	5.6	5.0	6.1
Norway	8.9	25.3	27.5	24.2	27.7	32.9	46.7	56.1	52.0	58.3
Israel	−1.6	−1.2	−0.7	−0.5	1.8	3.2	3.8	7.3	5.4	6.8
Singapore	14.4	10.7	12.0	12.1	22.3	21.5	28.6	36.3	39.6	41.9
New Zealand	−3.5	−2.7	−1.4	−2.4	−3.5	−6.5	−9.8	−9.1	−9.6	−9.0
Cyprus	−0.2	−0.5	−0.3	−0.4	−0.3	−0.8	−0.9	−1.1	−1.0	−1.1
Iceland	−0.6	−0.9	−0.3	0.1	−0.5	−1.3	−2.6	−4.4	−2.1	−2.0
Memorandum										
Major advanced economies	−197.7	−334.3	−295.5	−325.0	−371.1	−411.8	−586.9	−674.5	−673.4	−727.4
Euro area[2]	−34.0	−91.7	−19.7	53.7	36.9	69.0	−10.3	−21.2	−28.8	−43.7
Newly industrialized Asian economies	57.1	38.9	48.1	55.5	80.0	83.9	79.9	87.0	88.1	89.6

Table 26 *(concluded)*

	1999	2000	2001	2002	2003	2004	2005	2006	2007	2008
					Percent of GDP					
Advanced economies	**−0.5**	**−1.1**	**−0.8**	**−0.9**	**−0.8**	**−0.8**	**−1.4**	**−1.6**	**−1.6**	**−1.6**
United States	−3.2	−4.2	−3.8	−4.5	−4.8	−5.7	−6.4	−6.5	−6.1	−6.0
Euro area[1]	0.3	−0.7	—	0.6	0.4	1.0	0.1	−0.3	−0.3	−0.4
Germany	−1.3	−1.7	—	2.0	1.9	4.3	4.6	5.1	5.3	5.2
France	2.9	1.3	1.6	1.0	0.4	−0.3	−1.6	−2.1	−2.2	−2.3
Italy	0.5	−0.6	−0.1	−0.7	−1.3	−0.9	−1.6	−2.2	−2.2	−2.2
Spain	−2.9	−4.0	−3.9	−3.3	−3.5	−5.3	−7.4	−8.8	−9.4	−9.8
Netherlands	3.8	1.9	2.4	2.5	5.4	8.9	6.3	7.1	7.7	7.6
Belgium	7.9	4.0	3.4	4.6	4.1	3.5	2.5	2.5	2.4	2.5
Austria	−3.2	−2.5	−1.9	0.3	−0.2	0.2	1.2	1.8	1.9	1.6
Finland	5.9	8.7	9.6	9.3	6.4	7.8	4.9	5.3	5.1	5.2
Greece	−5.4	−6.8	−6.3	−5.6	−5.6	−5.0	−6.4	−9.6	−9.3	−8.7
Portugal	−8.5	−10.2	−9.9	−8.1	−6.1	−7.7	−9.7	−9.4	−9.1	−9.1
Ireland	0.2	−0.4	−0.6	−1.0	—	−0.6	−2.6	−4.1	−4.4	−3.0
Luxembourg	10.7	13.2	8.8	11.6	7.5	11.8	11.8	11.7	11.7	11.4
Slovenia	−3.3	−2.8	0.2	1.0	−0.8	−2.7	−2.0	−2.3	−2.6	−2.5
Japan	2.6	2.6	2.1	2.9	3.2	3.7	3.6	3.9	3.9	3.6
United Kingdom	−2.4	−2.6	−2.2	−1.6	−1.3	−1.6	−2.4	−2.9	−3.1	−3.1
Canada	0.3	2.7	2.3	1.7	1.2	2.1	2.3	1.7	0.7	0.6
Korea	5.5	2.4	1.7	1.0	2.0	4.1	1.9	0.7	0.3	—
Australia	−5.3	−3.8	−2.0	−3.8	−5.4	−6.0	−5.8	−5.4	−5.6	−5.5
Taiwan Province of China	2.7	2.8	6.3	8.7	9.8	5.7	4.6	7.1	7.1	7.1
Sweden	4.2	4.1	4.4	5.1	7.3	6.9	7.0	7.4	6.6	6.8
Switzerland	11.1	12.4	8.0	8.3	13.3	14.0	16.8	18.5	17.6	17.1
Hong Kong SAR	6.3	4.1	5.9	7.6	10.4	9.5	11.4	10.2	9.6	9.3
Denmark	1.9	1.4	3.1	2.5	3.4	3.1	3.6	2.0	1.7	1.9
Norway	5.6	15.0	16.1	12.6	12.3	12.7	15.5	16.7	14.9	15.9
Israel	−1.4	−1.0	−0.6	−0.5	1.6	2.6	2.9	5.2	3.6	4.3
Singapore	17.4	11.6	14.0	13.7	24.2	20.1	24.5	27.5	27.1	26.6
New Zealand	−6.2	−5.1	−2.8	−4.0	−4.5	−6.7	−9.0	−8.8	−8.4	−7.6
Cyprus	−1.7	−5.3	−3.3	−3.7	−2.2	−5.0	−5.6	−6.1	−5.2	−5.1
Iceland	−6.8	−10.2	−4.4	1.6	−4.8	−9.9	−16.3	−26.3	−12.0	−11.5
Memorandum										
Major advanced economies	−1.0	−1.6	−1.4	−1.5	−1.6	−1.6	−2.2	−2.4	−2.3	−2.4
Euro area[2]	−0.5	−1.5	−0.3	0.8	0.4	0.7	−0.1	−0.2	−0.3	−0.4
Newly industrialized Asian economies	5.8	3.5	4.7	5.1	6.9	6.6	5.6	5.6	5.3	5.1

[1]Calculated as the sum of the balances of individual euro area countries.
[2]Corrected for reporting discrepancies in intra-area transactions.

Table 27. Advanced Economies: Current Account Transactions
(Billions of U.S. dollars)

	1999	2000	2001	2002	2003	2004	2005	2006	2007	2008
Exports	4,305.0	4,688.7	4,455.6	4,595.6	5,280.1	6,256.9	6,818.0	7,718.3	8,389.8	8,960.9
Imports	4,388.0	4,924.1	4,653.1	4,784.3	5,497.8	6,573.3	7,351.7	8,362.2	9,023.0	9,632.0
Trade balance	−83.1	−235.4	−197.5	−188.7	−217.7	−316.4	−533.7	−643.8	−633.2	−671.1
Services, credits	1,204.4	1,257.3	1,255.6	1,335.9	1,531.4	1,820.6	1,983.1	2,188.3	2,404.6	2,558.6
Services, debits	1,124.1	1,180.8	1,188.6	1,249.6	1,426.0	1,673.3	1,808.1	1,985.6	2,178.1	2,314.6
Balance on services	80.3	76.6	67.1	86.2	105.4	147.3	174.9	202.7	226.5	244.0
Balance on goods and services	−2.7	−158.8	−130.5	−102.5	−112.2	−169.1	−358.7	−441.1	−406.7	−427.1
Income, net	21.7	30.3	45.7	20.4	69.9	121.6	117.0	108.8	80.1	39.7
Current transfers, net	−133.2	−139.4	−128.3	−146.8	−178.3	−207.6	−231.7	−230.9	−260.5	−250.5
Current account balance	**−114.2**	**−267.9**	**−213.0**	**−229.0**	**−220.6**	**−255.2**	**−473.4**	**−563.2**	**−587.2**	**−637.8**
Balance on goods and services										
Advanced economies	**−2.7**	**−158.8**	**−130.5**	**−102.5**	**−112.2**	**−169.1**	**−358.7**	**−441.1**	**−406.7**	**−427.1**
United States	−263.3	−377.6	−362.8	−421.1	−494.9	−611.3	−716.7	−765.3	−725.3	−729.9
Euro area[1]	97.6	35.1	91.6	159.9	177.8	201.9	141.1	114.6	139.3	133.9
Germany	11.8	1.0	34.2	83.6	95.3	136.4	138.0	151.2	170.2	172.0
France	36.3	16.5	21.4	24.7	19.1	2.4	−22.2	−38.3	−43.3	−49.5
Italy	22.4	10.3	15.3	11.8	8.4	12.5	−1.3	−15.2	−14.9	−16.3
Spain	−11.5	−17.7	−14.0	−13.1	−18.7	−39.7	−57.7	−75.9	−82.9	−91.6
Japan	69.2	69.0	26.5	51.7	72.5	94.2	69.8	62.8	62.4	46.9
United Kingdom	−25.0	−29.4	−38.6	−46.4	−48.1	−64.1	−81.2	−101.7	−115.6	−123.1
Canada	23.8	41.3	40.6	31.9	31.8	40.6	42.2	32.8	20.6	18.8
Other advanced economies	95.0	102.6	112.2	121.3	148.6	169.5	186.1	215.6	211.8	226.2
Memorandum										
Major advanced economies	−124.9	−268.8	−263.4	−263.7	−315.9	−389.3	−571.4	−673.6	−645.9	−681.0
Newly industrialized Asian economies	57.5	41.3	46.0	56.4	77.5	84.7	86.8	93.2	89.0	90.6
Income, net										
Advanced economies	**21.7**	**30.3**	**45.7**	**20.4**	**69.9**	**121.6**	**117.0**	**108.8**	**80.1**	**39.7**
United States	13.9	21.1	25.1	12.2	36.6	27.6	11.3	−7.3	−16.3	−64.1
Euro area[1]	−25.2	−29.5	−39.4	−67.5	−73.8	−27.6	−42.2	−54.3	−68.7	−71.1
Germany	−12.2	−7.7	−9.8	−17.0	−17.0	16.3	25.9	28.8	31.8	34.1
France	19.0	15.5	15.0	4.0	8.0	12.6	16.3	14.3	15.4	16.1
Italy	−11.1	−12.1	−10.4	−14.5	−20.1	−18.4	−16.9	−16.7	−18.0	−18.7
Spain	−9.6	−6.9	−11.3	−11.6	−11.8	−15.1	−21.4	−25.7	−33.5	−36.5
Japan	57.4	60.4	69.2	65.8	71.2	85.7	103.5	118.2	113.2	121.2
United Kingdom	2.1	6.9	16.8	35.2	40.3	48.7	49.4	54.0	57.6	60.4
Canada	−22.6	−22.3	−25.4	−19.3	−21.4	−19.1	−15.5	−11.5	−11.0	−11.0
Other advanced economies	−3.9	−6.2	−0.6	−6.0	17.1	6.2	10.5	9.6	5.4	4.4
Memorandum										
Major advanced economies	46.5	61.7	80.5	66.3	97.5	153.4	173.9	179.8	172.5	137.9
Newly industrialized Asian economies	2.6	2.4	8.2	6.3	11.1	8.6	3.2	5.7	11.7	12.1

[1]Calculated as the sum of the individual euro area countries.

Table 28. Other Emerging Market and Developing Countries: Payments Balances on Current Account

	1999	2000	2001	2002	2003	2004	2005	2006	2007	2008
					Billions of U.S. dollars					
Other emerging market and developing countries	**−21.2**	**85.8**	**39.4**	**77.3**	**147.6**	**212.6**	**428.0**	**544.2**	**455.1**	**470.7**
Regional groups										
Africa	−15.0	7.2	0.5	−7.5	−2.2	0.6	14.6	19.9	0.9	−0.5
Sub-Sahara	−14.4	−0.6	−7.3	−12.6	−11.9	−11.0	−7.2	−9.3	−17.3	−19.3
Excluding Nigeria and South Africa	−10.6	−5.8	−9.8	−8.1	−8.5	−7.9	−7.1	−7.0	−12.2	−13.0
Central and eastern Europe	−25.8	−31.8	−16.0	−24.0	−35.8	−58.6	−63.2	−88.9	−98.5	−104.7
Commonwealth of Independent States[1]	23.8	48.3	33.1	30.2	36.0	62.6	87.7	99.0	75.4	76.3
Russia	24.6	46.8	33.9	29.1	35.4	58.6	83.3	95.6	72.9	67.8
Excluding Russia	−0.8	1.4	−0.8	1.1	0.5	4.0	4.4	3.4	2.5	8.5
Developing Asia	38.3	38.1	36.6	64.6	82.5	88.5	165.2	253.1	308.9	358.6
China	15.7	20.5	17.4	35.4	45.9	68.7	160.8	238.5	303.7	358.6
India	−3.2	−4.6	1.4	7.1	8.8	0.8	−6.9	−19.3	−23.8	−24.6
Excluding China and India	25.9	22.2	17.8	22.1	27.8	19.0	11.2	33.9	29.0	24.6
Middle East	14.0	72.1	39.2	30.0	59.5	99.2	189.0	212.4	153.0	146.7
Western Hemisphere	−56.4	−48.1	−53.9	−16.1	7.7	20.4	34.6	48.7	15.3	−5.7
Brazil	−25.3	−24.2	−23.2	−7.6	4.2	11.7	14.2	13.6	8.9	3.3
Mexico	−13.9	−18.7	−17.7	−14.1	−8.9	−6.7	−4.9	−1.5	−9.2	−13.5
Analytical groups										
By source of export earnings										
Fuel	38.1	150.9	83.7	64.2	110.0	185.9	337.9	395.6	290.0	288.4
Nonfuel	−59.3	−65.1	−44.2	13.1	37.6	26.7	90.1	148.6	165.0	182.3
of which, primary products	−0.9	−1.5	−3.2	−4.3	−2.9	0.4	0.2	9.6	7.7	1.9
By external financing source										
Net debtor countries	−93.1	−95.0	−74.3	−36.0	−29.7	−69.0	−93.5	−111.4	−159.7	−186.6
of which, official financing	−8.7	−6.7	−4.6	−2.3	−0.4	−2.6	−4.6	−7.4	−14.8	−16.6
Net debtor countries by debt-servicing experience										
Countries with arrears and/or rescheduling during 2001–05	−19.8	−9.3	−10.8	7.1	11.0	−2.6	−8.9	−1.2	−15.3	−19.8
Other groups										
Heavily indebted poor countries	−9.0	−6.9	−7.3	−8.8	−7.3	−7.7	−9.4	−8.2	−11.2	−13.1
Middle East and north Africa	11.6	77.9	44.7	33.6	67.6	108.8	207.0	236.0	165.7	161.0

Table 28 (concluded)

	Ten-Year Averages		1999	2000	2001	2002	2003	2004	2005	2006	2007	2008
	1989–98	1999–2008										
	Percent of exports of goods and services											
Other emerging market and developing countries	**–7.6**	**6.0**	**–1.3**	**4.4**	**2.1**	**3.7**	**5.9**	**6.6**	**10.7**	**11.3**	**8.5**	**7.9**
Regional groups												
Africa	–8.7	–0.2	–11.7	4.6	0.3	–4.8	–1.1	0.2	4.6	5.4	0.2	–0.1
Sub-Sahara	–10.3	–6.6	–15.1	–0.6	–6.7	–11.1	–8.3	–5.9	–3.1	–3.3	–5.9	–5.9
Excluding Nigeria and South Africa	–21.4	–11.5	–22.1	–10.8	–18.5	–14.1	–12.5	–8.9	–6.3	–5.1	–8.4	–8.1
Central and eastern Europe	–4.1	–11.7	–12.7	–13.7	–6.5	–8.7	–10.2	–12.9	–11.9	–14.0	–13.4	–12.8
Commonwealth of Independent States[1]	...	19.4	19.3	29.3	20.0	16.9	16.0	20.6	22.6	20.5	14.8	13.8
Russia	...	27.6	29.1	40.9	29.9	24.1	23.3	28.8	31.1	28.8	21.2	18.6
Excluding Russia	...	1.8	–2.1	2.8	–1.6	1.9	0.8	3.9	3.6	2.2	1.5	4.5
Developing Asia	–5.1	9.4	6.6	5.5	5.3	8.2	8.7	7.2	10.9	13.6	14.2	14.3
China	7.1	13.9	7.1	7.3	5.8	9.7	9.5	10.5	19.2	22.6	23.6	23.4
India	–16.8	–2.4	–6.3	–7.7	2.3	10.0	10.3	0.7	–4.3	–9.8	–10.1	–9.2
Excluding China and India	–9.7	5.3	8.5	6.2	5.4	6.3	7.3	4.1	2.1	5.6	4.4	3.4
Middle East	–8.1	20.6	7.2	26.7	15.9	11.4	18.2	23.1	32.3	30.5	21.6	19.2
Western Hemisphere	–15.3	–2.6	–16.0	–11.5	–13.4	–4.0	1.8	3.8	5.4	6.4	1.9	–0.7
Brazil	–18.9	–8.7	–45.9	–37.5	–34.4	–10.9	5.0	10.7	10.6	8.7	5.2	1.8
Mexico	–20.4	–5.7	–9.4	–10.4	–10.3	–8.1	–5.0	–3.3	–2.1	–0.6	–3.2	–4.3
Analytical groups												
By source of export earnings												
Fuel	–3.5	22.7	11.7	31.8	19.4	14.1	19.2	24.4	32.1	31.1	22.3	20.5
Nonfuel	–9.1	0.7	–4.7	–4.4	–3.0	0.8	2.0	1.1	3.1	4.2	4.1	4.0
of which, primary products	–9.8	–1.2	–2.3	–3.6	–7.8	–10.5	–6.0	0.5	0.2	8.8	7.0	1.8
By external financing source												
Net debtor countries	–12.6	–5.8	–10.0	–8.8	–6.9	–3.2	–2.3	–4.2	–4.8	–4.8	–6.2	–6.6
of which, official financing	–19.9	–5.2	–11.2	–7.6	–5.3	–2.6	–0.4	–2.1	–3.0	–4.1	–7.6	–7.8
Net debtor countries by debt-servicing experience												
Countries with arrears and/or rescheduling during 2001–05	–17.7	–2.7	–12.3	–4.9	–6.0	3.8	5.2	–1.0	–2.8	–0.3	–3.9	–4.7
Other groups												
Heavily indebted poor countries	–29.2	–23.6	–37.8	–26.5	–27.3	–31.9	–22.6	–18.5	–19.3	–13.8	–18.4	–20.2
Middle East and north Africa	–8.4	19.5	5.1	24.8	15.5	10.9	17.7	21.9	30.7	29.5	20.3	18.3
Memorandum												
Median												
Other emerging market and developing countries	–13.3	–10.0	–10.9	–9.9	–10.3	–9.4	–8.3	–8.3	–9.9	–10.4	–11.4	–11.2

[1]Mongolia, which is not a member of the Commonwealth of Independent States, is included in this group for reasons of geography and similarities in economic structure.

Table 29. Other Emerging Market and Developing Countries—by Region: Current Account Transactions
(Billions of U.S. dollars)

	1999	2000	2001	2002	2003	2004	2005	2006	2007	2008
Other emerging market and developing countries										
Exports	1,320.9	1,656.2	1,614.1	1,753.0	2,138.2	2,760.3	3,457.4	4,201.9	4,662.0	5,175.7
Imports	1,235.2	1,452.3	1,460.0	1,567.1	1,888.3	2,432.9	2,918.5	3,513.3	4,081.2	4,594.9
Trade balance	85.8	204.0	154.1	186.0	249.9	327.3	539.0	688.5	580.8	580.9
Services, net	−48.3	−59.9	−65.8	−66.4	−70.0	−70.1	−76.0	−108.6	−124.9	−129.5
Balance on goods and services	37.5	144.1	88.4	119.5	179.9	257.2	462.9	579.9	455.9	451.4
Income, net	−120.8	−127.2	−126.8	−135.1	−151.9	−183.3	−205.7	−227.4	−198.6	−188.2
Current transfers, net	62.1	68.9	77.9	92.8	119.5	138.6	170.7	191.7	197.8	207.6
Current account balance	**−21.2**	**85.8**	**39.4**	**77.3**	**147.6**	**212.6**	**428.0**	**544.2**	**455.1**	**470.7**
Memorandum										
Exports of goods and services	1,578.2	1,938.9	1,902.6	2,062.4	2,491.0	3,205.9	3,986.3	4,810.3	5,344.8	5,936.1
Interest payments	139.3	139.3	132.1	125.3	138.5	152.4	175.9	211.1	225.4	239.0
Oil trade balance	149.3	241.5	196.5	208.4	265.9	351.2	528.6	609.3	567.4	624.2
Regional groups										
Africa										
Exports	105.7	135.3	126.7	130.2	163.5	210.9	271.7	320.9	336.7	370.6
Imports	101.5	105.1	106.7	116.9	142.9	181.0	215.3	253.9	291.5	321.9
Trade balance	4.2	30.3	20.0	13.3	20.5	29.9	56.4	67.0	45.1	48.7
Services, net	−11.1	−11.2	−11.5	−12.0	−12.6	−16.5	−20.6	−23.4	−28.3	−32.4
Balance on goods and services	−6.8	19.1	8.5	1.3	8.0	13.4	35.8	43.5	16.9	16.3
Income, net	−18.2	−23.3	−20.9	−22.8	−28.2	−35.1	−46.7	−50.2	−44.6	−47.1
Current transfers, net	10.0	11.5	12.9	14.0	18.0	22.3	25.5	26.6	28.7	30.3
Current account balance	**−15.0**	**7.2**	**0.5**	**−7.5**	**−2.2**	**0.6**	**14.6**	**19.9**	**0.9**	**−0.5**
Memorandum										
Exports of goods and services	128.0	157.5	150.1	154.9	194.7	248.8	316.2	371.9	393.0	431.2
Interest payments	14.3	13.6	11.9	10.6	11.3	11.9	12.9	12.5	12.7	13.5
Oil trade balance	25.7	45.8	38.7	38.2	54.0	74.2	112.1	132.9	134.0	151.7
Central and eastern Europe										
Exports	148.9	169.5	188.3	214.7	276.8	365.3	424.1	515.6	602.6	669.1
Imports	189.9	222.0	221.1	252.1	326.4	430.0	499.5	613.1	713.3	791.2
Trade balance	−41.1	−52.5	−32.9	−37.3	−49.6	−64.7	−75.4	−97.5	−110.7	−122.1
Services, net	10.8	16.1	13.5	11.8	15.0	18.5	23.3	22.4	24.3	28.9
Balance on goods and services	−30.3	−36.4	−19.3	−25.5	−34.6	−46.2	−52.0	−75.1	−86.4	−93.2
Income, net	−6.7	−7.2	−7.8	−10.8	−15.0	−29.2	−31.6	−36.5	−37.6	−39.6
Current transfers, net	11.2	11.8	11.2	12.3	13.8	16.8	20.5	22.8	25.5	28.0
Current account balance	**−25.8**	**−31.8**	**−16.0**	**−24.0**	**−35.8**	**−58.6**	**−63.2**	**−88.9**	**−98.5**	**−104.7**
Memorandum										
Exports of goods and services	203.0	231.7	248.3	275.9	352.1	455.8	529.6	633.9	736.0	815.1
Interest payments	11.5	12.5	13.6	13.6	16.4	25.6	27.8	32.4	35.3	37.2
Oil trade balance	−14.0	−22.8	−21.3	−21.8	−27.1	−33.8	−48.2	−63.2	−64.2	−70.3

Table 29 (concluded)

	1999	2000	2001	2002	2003	2004	2005	2006	2007	2008
Commonwealth of Independent States[1]										
Exports	107.5	147.3	145.9	155.1	196.7	268.7	346.1	432.7	455.0	492.6
Imports	73.8	84.6	97.3	106.7	135.0	174.8	216.2	277.6	328.5	370.1
Trade balance	33.7	62.7	48.6	48.4	61.7	94.0	129.9	155.1	126.5	122.5
Services, net	−3.9	−7.0	−10.8	−11.9	−13.3	−18.0	−20.2	−23.7	−24.3	−21.9
Balance on goods and services	29.9	55.6	37.8	36.6	48.3	75.9	109.7	131.4	102.2	100.6
Income, net	−8.4	−9.8	−6.9	−9.0	−16.0	−17.4	−27.5	−40.8	−37.3	−35.0
Current transfers, net	2.4	2.4	2.1	2.7	3.6	4.0	5.4	8.4	10.5	10.6
Current account balance	**23.8**	**48.3**	**33.1**	**30.2**	**36.0**	**62.6**	**87.7**	**99.0**	**75.4**	**76.3**
Memorandum										
Exports of goods and services	123.6	164.7	165.9	178.6	224.0	304.1	388.8	483.6	511.3	555.1
Interest payments	13.0	13.3	12.4	13.4	25.1	25.4	36.9	52.9	51.2	55.2
Oil trade balance	19.6	38.4	36.7	43.2	57.3	84.7	132.4	173.7	174.8	198.6
Developing Asia										
Exports	493.6	603.2	593.6	675.7	833.3	1,065.5	1,319.3	1,617.3	1,903.8	2,191.9
Imports	434.5	546.9	540.2	607.8	763.6	1,001.9	1,209.4	1,424.8	1,658.9	1,908.5
Trade balance	59.1	56.3	53.4	67.9	69.6	63.5	109.9	192.6	244.9	283.4
Services, net	−6.9	−13.0	−14.1	−11.7	−15.8	−6.6	−1.0	−3.3	1.5	8.0
Balance on goods and services	52.2	43.3	39.3	56.2	53.9	56.9	108.9	189.3	246.4	291.4
Income, net	−45.1	−41.1	−43.8	−41.4	−35.1	−36.7	−28.5	−29.2	−30.0	−29.2
Current transfers, net	31.1	36.0	41.1	49.8	63.7	68.2	84.8	93.0	92.5	96.5
Current account balance	**38.3**	**38.1**	**36.6**	**64.6**	**82.5**	**88.5**	**165.2**	**253.1**	**308.9**	**358.6**
Memorandum										
Exports of goods and services	577.3	695.4	689.4	785.0	952.1	1,230.6	1,520.0	1,857.8	2,182.4	2,514.9
Interest payments	33.3	32.3	28.6	28.1	27.5	28.5	33.2	39.4	46.2	50.6
Oil trade balance	−19.3	−37.2	−34.7	−38.7	−50.3	−80.8	−114.6	−157.4	−169.1	−184.4
Middle East										
Exports	163.7	238.7	213.0	227.4	285.1	378.5	527.8	635.2	642.6	690.9
Imports	122.0	130.0	139.3	151.9	177.1	228.5	285.9	358.9	423.8	473.1
Trade balance	41.7	108.8	73.6	75.6	108.0	150.1	241.9	276.3	218.8	217.8
Services, net	−25.2	−32.0	−27.8	−32.9	−34.3	−38.4	−44.6	−64.5	−77.8	−86.7
Balance on goods and services	16.5	76.7	45.8	42.7	73.7	111.7	197.3	211.8	141.0	131.1
Income, net	10.5	10.1	9.4	3.2	1.7	3.7	8.6	18.9	34.1	40.0
Current transfers, net	−13.1	−14.8	−16.0	−15.9	−16.0	−16.2	−16.9	−18.3	−22.1	−24.4
Current account balance	**14.0**	**72.1**	**39.2**	**30.0**	**59.5**	**99.2**	**189.0**	**212.4**	**153.0**	**146.7**
Memorandum										
Exports of goods and services	193.8	270.1	246.4	263.4	326.7	428.5	585.4	697.2	709.2	763.4
Interest payments	11.5	9.3	9.4	9.3	8.2	11.4	13.7	20.5	27.9	29.8
Oil trade balance	115.7	183.0	152.2	159.0	201.0	264.8	386.6	451.7	431.6	467.4
Western Hemisphere										
Exports	301.5	362.2	346.7	349.8	382.9	471.3	568.4	680.2	721.2	760.5
Imports	313.4	363.7	355.3	331.8	343.2	416.7	492.1	585.1	665.1	730.0
Trade balance	−11.9	−1.5	−8.6	18.0	39.7	54.6	76.3	95.1	56.1	30.5
Services, net	−12.1	−12.7	−15.1	−9.8	−9.0	−9.0	−13.0	−16.1	−20.3	−25.4
Balance on goods and services	−24.0	−14.2	−23.7	8.2	30.7	45.5	63.3	79.1	35.8	5.1
Income, net	−53.0	−55.9	−56.8	−54.3	−59.4	−68.5	−80.0	−89.6	−83.2	−77.3
Current transfers, net	20.5	22.0	26.6	30.0	36.4	43.5	51.3	59.2	62.7	66.5
Current account balance	**−56.4**	**−48.1**	**−53.9**	**−16.1**	**7.7**	**20.4**	**34.6**	**48.7**	**15.3**	**−5.7**
Memorandum										
Exports of goods and services	352.5	419.5	402.4	404.7	441.4	538.2	646.2	765.9	812.8	856.4
Interest payments	55.7	58.2	56.2	50.3	50.0	49.7	51.4	53.4	52.1	52.7
Oil trade balance	21.6	34.4	24.8	28.4	31.1	42.1	60.4	71.5	60.3	61.1

[1]Mongolia, which is not a member of the Commonwealth of Independent States, is included in this group for reasons of geography and similarities in economic structure.

Table 30. Other Emerging Market and Developing Countries—by Analytical Criteria: Current Account Transactions
(Billions of U.S. dollars)

	1999	2000	2001	2002	2003	2004	2005	2006	2007	2008
By source of export earnings										
Fuel										
Exports	298.7	444.0	398.3	418.1	525.4	705.8	984.4	1,196.7	1,215.7	1,315.0
Imports	184.0	200.0	224.6	248.3	294.3	378.6	480.1	607.4	730.3	821.4
Trade balance	114.7	244.0	173.7	169.7	231.1	327.2	504.3	589.3	485.4	493.7
Services, net	−48.5	−58.1	−57.5	−62.8	−69.0	−83.7	−97.5	−122.8	−144.2	−158.2
Balance on goods and services	66.2	185.9	116.2	106.9	162.1	243.4	406.8	466.5	341.2	335.4
Income, net	−11.1	−15.9	−11.5	−22.1	−32.9	−38.8	−50.7	−50.9	−28.3	−21.9
Current transfers, net	−16.9	−19.0	−21.0	−20.6	−19.2	−18.8	−18.3	−19.9	−22.8	−25.1
Current account balance	**38.1**	**150.9**	**83.7**	**64.2**	**110.0**	**185.9**	**337.9**	**395.6**	**290.0**	**288.4**
Memorandum										
Exports of goods and services	327.0	474.1	432.2	457.0	571.6	761.5	1,051.3	1,273.6	1,299.0	1,405.6
Interest payments	31.8	29.9	27.9	27.5	38.6	42.2	55.9	76.5	80.6	85.5
Oil trade balance	188.1	309.8	264.0	275.8	349.6	475.8	701.9	840.2	819.4	903.0
Nonfuel exports										
Exports	1,022.3	1,212.2	1,215.8	1,335.0	1,612.8	2,054.5	2,473.0	3,005.2	3,446.2	3,860.7
Imports	1,051.1	1,252.2	1,235.4	1,318.7	1,593.9	2,054.3	2,438.4	2,905.9	3,350.8	3,773.5
Trade balance	−28.9	−40.0	−19.6	16.2	18.8	0.2	34.6	99.2	95.4	87.2
Services, net	0.2	−1.8	−8.3	−3.6	−1.0	13.6	21.5	14.2	19.3	28.7
Balance on goods and services	−28.7	−41.8	−27.8	12.6	17.9	13.8	56.2	113.4	114.7	116.0
Income, net	−109.7	−111.2	−115.3	−113.0	−119.0	−144.4	−155.0	−176.5	−170.3	−166.3
Current transfers, net	79.0	88.0	98.9	113.5	138.8	157.4	189.0	211.7	220.6	232.7
Current account balance	**−59.3**	**−65.1**	**−44.2**	**13.1**	**37.6**	**26.7**	**90.1**	**148.6**	**165.0**	**182.3**
Memorandum										
Exports of goods and services	1,251.2	1,464.8	1,470.4	1,605.4	1,919.4	2,444.4	2,935.0	3,536.7	4,045.8	4,530.4
Interest payments	107.4	109.4	104.2	97.8	99.9	110.2	120.1	134.6	144.8	153.5
Oil trade balance	−38.8	−68.3	−67.5	−67.3	−83.7	−124.6	−173.3	−230.9	−252.1	−278.7
Nonfuel primary products										
Exports	33.6	36.4	34.3	33.8	40.7	57.9	70.0	96.1	96.3	90.4
Imports	29.8	32.6	32.3	33.0	37.1	46.8	57.8	66.4	72.5	78.1
Trade balance	3.8	3.8	2.1	0.8	3.6	11.1	12.2	29.7	23.7	12.3
Services, net	−2.9	−2.8	−2.9	−3.2	−3.3	−4.3	−4.4	−5.2	−5.1	−5.8
Balance on goods and services	0.9	1.0	−0.8	−2.5	0.3	6.8	7.8	24.5	18.6	6.5
Income, net	−4.4	−5.2	−4.9	−5.2	−7.5	−11.7	−14.9	−24.6	−20.8	−14.8
Current transfers, net	2.5	2.6	2.6	3.4	4.2	5.3	7.2	9.7	9.9	10.1
Current account balance	**−0.9**	**−1.5**	**−3.2**	**−4.3**	**−2.9**	**0.4**	**0.2**	**9.6**	**7.7**	**1.9**
Memorandum										
Exports of goods and services	40.1	42.9	41.0	40.9	48.8	67.9	81.8	108.7	110.2	104.3
Interest payments	2.9	3.4	3.1	2.7	2.5	2.6	2.7	2.8	2.6	2.4
Oil trade balance	−1.7	−2.3	−2.6	−3.5	−3.2	−3.0	−3.8	−4.4	−5.2	−6.2

Table 30 *(continued)*

	1999	2000	2001	2002	2003	2004	2005	2006	2007	2008
By external financing source										
Net debtor countries										
Exports	744.4	870.2	865.2	921.3	1,074.3	1,339.3	1,594.8	1,916.0	2,124.1	2,313.8
Imports	826.6	954.7	929.6	959.8	1,116.4	1,415.4	1,700.2	2,027.0	2,304.4	2,539.8
Trade balance	−82.2	−84.5	−64.4	−38.5	−42.1	−76.1	−105.5	−111.1	−180.4	−226.0
Services, net	2.4	1.2	−6.7	−3.0	1.9	14.7	18.8	12.6	16.8	24.2
Balance on goods and services	−79.8	−83.4	−71.1	−41.5	−40.3	−61.5	−86.7	−98.5	−163.6	−201.7
Income, net	−90.1	−96.1	−96.4	−98.1	−112.8	−145.3	−175.4	−202.8	−199.5	−199.7
Current transfers, net	76.7	84.5	93.2	103.6	123.4	137.7	168.7	189.9	203.4	214.8
Current account balance	**−93.1**	**−95.0**	**−74.3**	**−36.0**	**−29.7**	**−69.0**	**−93.5**	**−111.4**	**−159.7**	**−186.6**
Memorandum										
Exports of goods and services	933.7	1,077.2	1,070.4	1,135.3	1,318.8	1,646.2	1,958.6	2,334.3	2,593.5	2,831.2
Interest payments	100.7	103.1	95.3	87.3	89.3	98.0	106.5	118.4	126.5	133.2
Oil trade balance	−21.2	−33.1	−35.2	−31.0	−36.4	−49.6	−67.2	−80.3	−92.8	−93.1
Official financing										
Exports	61.2	71.1	69.7	72.2	84.1	103.8	124.2	150.2	162.2	177.8
Imports	75.6	84.8	83.4	85.6	97.4	118.0	141.9	171.6	194.4	215.7
Trade balance	−14.4	−13.7	−13.7	−13.4	−13.4	−14.3	−17.8	−21.3	−32.1	−37.9
Services, net	−2.7	−2.6	−2.6	−2.5	−2.2	−3.7	−6.0	−7.6	−8.7	−9.9
Balance on goods and services	−17.1	−16.3	−16.3	−15.9	−15.5	−18.0	−23.8	−28.9	−40.9	−47.8
Income, net	−7.5	−8.6	−8.3	−8.9	−11.0	−14.0	−17.0	−19.7	−19.1	−17.5
Current transfers, net	15.8	18.2	20.0	22.5	26.1	29.3	36.2	41.2	45.1	48.7
Current account balance	**−8.7**	**−6.7**	**−4.6**	**−2.3**	**−0.4**	**−2.6**	**−4.6**	**−7.4**	**−14.8**	**−16.6**
Memorandum										
Exports of goods and services	77.8	88.5	87.4	90.3	104.9	127.5	151.6	181.3	195.4	213.8
Interest payments	6.7	7.8	7.2	6.8	7.5	7.9	8.8	9.7	9.7	10.5
Oil trade balance	−1.7	−3.3	−4.6	−3.7	−4.5	−4.6	−6.3	−8.6	−12.2	−12.4
Net debtor countries by debt-servicing experience										
Countries with arrears and/or rescheduling during 2001–05										
Exports	133.7	160.6	151.5	157.1	178.8	212.2	261.8	313.0	334.8	364.1
Imports	127.8	139.7	133.4	127.4	146.5	185.8	239.1	274.0	307.1	336.5
Trade balance	5.8	20.8	18.1	29.7	32.3	26.5	22.7	39.0	27.8	27.6
Services, net	−13.9	−18.7	−20.6	−17.8	−20.7	−21.5	−28.0	−37.3	−42.3	−47.5
Balance on goods and services	−8.0	2.1	−2.5	11.9	11.6	5.0	−5.3	1.7	−14.5	−20.0
Income, net	−27.6	−30.9	−29.4	−28.9	−29.4	−39.4	−45.6	−50.5	−51.5	−54.3
Current transfers, net	15.8	19.4	21.0	24.1	28.8	31.7	42.0	47.5	50.7	54.5
Current account balance	**−19.8**	**−9.3**	**−10.8**	**7.1**	**11.0**	**−2.6**	**−8.9**	**−1.2**	**−15.3**	**−19.8**
Memorandum										
Exports of goods and services	161.0	190.0	180.9	187.9	211.1	255.9	311.5	365.4	390.9	424.8
Interest payments	30.4	30.9	25.0	22.5	21.6	21.9	22.6	22.9	24.0	24.0
Oil trade balance	7.9	13.1	9.6	10.9	13.7	19.5	28.9	42.0	41.1	51.0

Table 30 *(concluded)*

	1999	2000	2001	2002	2003	2004	2005	2006	2007	2008
Other groups										
Heavily indebted poor countries										
Exports	17.7	19.7	20.1	20.5	24.4	31.6	37.5	46.9	47.2	49.9
Imports	26.0	26.1	27.2	30.0	33.4	41.3	49.6	57.1	63.8	69.3
Trade balance	−8.2	−6.4	−7.1	−9.6	−9.1	−9.6	−12.2	−10.2	−16.6	−19.5
Services, net	−3.2	−3.0	−3.4	−3.6	−4.1	−4.9	−5.7	−6.2	−6.2	−6.4
Balance on goods and services	−11.4	−9.4	−10.5	−13.2	−13.2	−14.5	−17.8	−16.4	−22.7	−25.8
Income, net	−3.3	−4.2	−4.5	−3.7	−4.2	−5.1	−6.4	−8.0	−6.1	−6.4
Current transfers, net	5.7	6.7	7.7	8.1	10.0	11.9	14.7	16.2	17.6	19.1
Current account balance	**−9.0**	**−6.9**	**−7.3**	**−8.8**	**−7.3**	**−7.7**	**−9.4**	**−8.2**	**−11.2**	**−13.1**
Memorandum										
Exports of goods and services	23.9	26.1	26.7	27.5	32.5	41.4	49.0	59.7	61.0	64.8
Interest payments	3.1	3.0	2.9	2.7	2.6	2.9	3.1	3.2	2.8	3.1
Oil trade balance	−0.5	−0.1	−1.1	−1.9	−1.2	—	0.1	1.3	−2.1	−2.3
Middle East and north Africa										
Exports	190.6	275.9	247.9	263.2	329.3	434.6	600.8	719.8	730.0	788.6
Imports	151.0	160.4	170.7	186.5	217.2	279.7	344.7	423.7	502.5	559.9
Trade balance	39.6	115.5	77.2	76.6	112.1	154.9	256.1	296.1	227.4	228.7
Services, net	−24.4	−31.3	−26.6	−31.5	−32.4	−36.6	−42.5	−61.8	−76.9	−85.9
Balance on goods and services	15.1	84.3	50.6	45.1	79.7	118.3	213.6	234.3	150.6	142.8
Income, net	5.1	3.8	4.3	−2.0	−4.3	−3.6	−0.7	9.3	25.3	30.2
Current transfers, net	−8.6	−10.1	−10.2	−9.5	−7.8	−5.9	−5.9	−7.5	−10.2	−12.0
Current account balance	**11.6**	**77.9**	**44.7**	**33.6**	**67.6**	**108.8**	**207.0**	**236.0**	**165.7**	**161.0**
Memorandum										
Exports of goods and services	227.6	314.2	289.4	307.7	381.0	496.9	673.3	799.4	815.6	881.7
Interest payments	−16.1	−13.9	−13.3	−12.4	−11.3	−14.6	−16.8	−23.5	−30.6	−32.6
Oil trade balance	126.4	203.3	170.0	176.6	224.3	296.0	431.2	504.8	484.5	527.0

Table 31. Other Emerging Market and Developing Countries—by Country: Balance of Payments on Current Account
(Percent of GDP)

	1999	2000	2001	2002	2003	2004	2005	2006	2007	2008
Africa	**−3.5**	**1.6**	**0.1**	**−1.6**	**−0.4**	**0.1**	**1.8**	**2.2**	**0.1**	**—**
Algeria	—	16.7	12.8	7.6	13.0	13.1	20.7	24.4	15.3	15.2
Angola	−27.5	8.7	−14.8	−2.7	−5.1	3.5	13.5	10.5	4.0	2.8
Benin	−7.3	−7.7	−6.4	−8.4	−8.3	−7.2	−6.2	−6.4	−6.0	−5.8
Botswana	11.0	8.8	9.9	3.3	5.6	3.0	15.4	14.9	14.5	12.2
Burkina Faso	−10.5	−12.3	−11.2	−9.9	−8.9	−10.6	−11.8	−10.3	−10.0	−9.8
Burundi	−5.0	−8.6	−4.6	−3.5	−4.6	−8.1	−10.4	−13.6	−15.3	−13.1
Cameroon	−3.5	−1.4	−3.6	−5.1	−1.8	−3.8	−3.4	−0.5	−2.1	−3.0
Cape Verde	−13.7	−10.9	−10.6	−11.1	−11.1	−14.3	−3.4	−4.6	−8.5	−10.7
Central African Republic	−1.6	−3.0	−2.5	−3.4	−4.7	−4.5	−2.8	−3.3	−2.6	−3.3
Chad	−11.3	−15.4	−33.7	−100.4	−47.4	−4.8	1.1	1.8	5.3	−1.0
Comoros	−6.8	1.7	3.0	−1.4	−3.1	−2.9	−3.4	−5.5	−6.3	−5.9
Congo, Dem. Rep. of	−2.6	−4.6	−4.9	−3.2	−1.8	−3.3	−10.0	−7.5	−10.3	−9.3
Congo, Rep. of	−17.2	7.9	−5.6	0.6	1.0	1.8	10.9	17.5	3.7	6.0
Côte d'Ivoire	−1.4	−2.8	−0.6	6.7	2.1	1.6	−0.1	1.2	1.1	0.7
Djibouti	−4.3	−9.6	−3.4	−1.6	3.4	−1.3	1.2	−8.9	−13.9	−17.0
Equatorial Guinea	−29.9	−15.7	−47.0	−12.7	−38.9	−23.5	−12.0	−4.9	2.2	3.8
Eritrea	−17.9	0.5	4.2	7.4	7.6	5.6	0.4	−2.1	−3.7	−1.9
Ethiopia	−6.7	−4.2	−3.0	−4.7	−2.2	−5.3	−8.6	−11.6	−10.0	−6.6
Gabon	8.4	19.7	11.0	6.8	9.5	8.9	18.7	18.0	11.6	9.4
Gambia, The	−2.8	−3.1	−2.6	−2.8	−5.1	−12.6	−20.2	−14.3	−12.9	−11.7
Ghana	−11.6	−8.4	−5.3	0.5	1.7	−2.7	−7.0	−8.2	−8.4	−7.9
Guinea	−6.9	−6.4	−2.7	−4.3	−3.4	−5.4	−4.0	−3.6	−4.6	−3.0
Guinea-Bissau	−13.3	−5.6	−22.1	−10.7	−2.8	3.1	−3.7	−5.7	−15.6	−17.9
Kenya	−1.8	−2.3	−3.1	2.2	−0.2	−1.3	−3.0	−3.3	−4.1	−3.9
Lesotho	−22.7	−19.0	−14.3	−18.3	−11.1	−3.1	−3.0	6.8	5.1	2.4
Liberia	...	−17.5	−14.9	3.5	−11.4	−2.8	−1.6	−10.8	−8.0	−11.7
Madagascar	−5.6	−5.6	−1.3	−6.0	−4.9	−9.1	−10.4	−8.9	−8.6	−9.5
Malawi	−8.3	−5.3	−6.8	−17.2	−7.9	−10.1	−16.2	−7.1	−1.2	−1.4
Mali	−8.5	−10.0	−10.4	−3.1	−6.2	−8.4	−8.9	−7.4	−5.6	−5.6
Mauritania	−2.5	−9.0	−11.7	3.0	−13.6	−34.6	−47.2	−1.3	−1.5	−8.6
Mauritius	−1.6	−1.5	3.4	5.7	2.4	0.8	−3.5	−5.3	−7.4	−4.9
Morocco	−0.5	−1.4	4.8	4.1	3.6	1.9	1.7	3.9	2.1	0.5
Mozambique, Rep. of	−22.0	−18.2	−19.4	−19.3	−15.1	−8.6	−11.0	−10.4	−11.8	−11.3
Namibia	6.9	10.5	1.5	4.4	5.1	9.5	7.2	16.3	18.3	12.8
Niger	−6.5	−6.2	−4.8	−6.5	−5.6	−7.0	−7.4	−7.5	−10.8	−10.7
Nigeria	−8.4	11.7	4.5	−11.7	−2.7	5.3	9.2	12.2	9.7	7.6
Rwanda	−7.7	−5.0	−5.9	−6.7	−7.8	−3.0	−3.2	−8.1	−9.4	−7.5
São Tomé and Príncipe	−26.0	−30.4	−25.9	−24.1	−22.7	−23.1	−30.7	−62.2	−61.4	−63.8
Senegal	−4.8	−6.6	−4.4	−5.6	−6.2	−6.1	−8.1	−12.0	−9.9	−9.3
Seychelles	−19.8	−7.3	−23.4	−16.3	6.4	−0.3	−30.4	−23.0	−37.8	−32.6
Sierra Leone	−11.0	−15.9	−16.2	−4.8	−7.6	−4.9	−7.7	−4.9	−3.8	−3.6
South Africa	−0.5	−0.1	0.3	0.8	−1.1	−3.2	−3.8	−6.4	−6.4	−6.0
Sudan	−15.9	−14.9	−15.8	−9.9	−7.7	−6.2	−10.5	−14.5	−11.5	−7.0
Swaziland	−2.6	−5.4	−4.5	4.8	6.5	3.1	1.6	0.7	0.7	−0.9
Tanzania	−9.9	−5.3	−5.0	−6.8	−4.7	−3.9	−5.2	−9.3	−11.0	−11.2
Togo	−8.3	−11.8	−12.7	−8.9	−8.9	−9.5	−11.1	−12.1	−8.2	−8.3
Tunisia	−2.2	−4.2	−4.2	−3.5	−2.9	−2.0	−1.0	−2.8	−2.2	−2.1
Uganda	−9.4	−7.1	−3.8	−4.9	−5.8	−1.2	−2.1	−4.1	−4.4	−7.9
Zambia	−13.7	−18.2	−19.9	−15.3	−14.8	−11.8	−10.0	−0.4	−2.1	−6.4
Zimbabwe	2.5	0.4	−0.3	−0.6	−2.9	−8.3	−11.2	−3.9	−0.8	0.2

Table 31 *(continued)*

	1999	2000	2001	2002	2003	2004	2005	2006	2007	2008
Central and eastern Europe	**−4.4**	**−5.3**	**−2.8**	**−3.6**	**−4.3**	**−5.8**	**−5.3**	**−6.7**	**−6.6**	**−6.5**
Albania	2.2	−3.6	−3.6	−7.1	−5.3	−3.9	−6.5	−5.9	−6.2	−6.1
Bosnia and Herzegovina	−9.1	−17.5	−20.1	−26.8	−22.8	−24.9	−27.1	−23.3	−23.1	−21.2
Bulgaria	−5.0	−5.6	−5.6	−2.4	−5.5	−5.8	−11.3	−15.9	−15.7	−14.7
Croatia	−7.0	−2.6	−3.7	−8.3	−6.1	−5.4	−6.4	−8.1	−8.3	−7.8
Czech Republic	−2.4	−4.7	−5.3	−5.7	−6.3	−6.0	−2.6	−4.2	−4.1	−4.2
Estonia	−4.4	−5.4	−5.2	−10.6	−11.6	−12.5	−10.5	−13.8	−12.9	−12.2
Hungary	−7.8	−8.4	−6.0	−7.0	−7.9	−8.4	−6.7	−6.9	−5.7	−4.8
Latvia	−8.9	−4.8	−7.6	−6.6	−8.2	−12.9	−12.7	−21.3	−23.0	−22.7
Lithuania	−11.0	−5.9	−4.7	−5.2	−6.9	−7.7	−7.1	−12.2	−12.3	−11.0
Macedonia, FYR	−2.7	−1.9	−7.2	−9.5	−3.4	−7.7	−1.3	0.4	−3.2	−3.5
Malta	−3.7	−14.2	−5.0	1.6	−4.7	−8.1	−10.5	−11.2	−11.5	−11.0
Poland	−7.4	−5.8	−2.8	−2.5	−2.1	−4.2	−1.7	−2.1	−2.7	−3.6
Romania	−4.1	−3.7	−5.5	−3.3	−5.8	−8.4	−8.7	−10.3	−10.3	−9.8
Serbia	−4.0	0.4	−3.0	−8.6	−8.7	−11.6	−9.5	−12.3	−9.9	−8.9
Slovak Republic	−4.8	−3.3	−8.3	−8.0	−1.1	−3.6	−8.6	−8.0	−5.7	−4.6
Turkey	−0.7	−5.0	2.4	−0.8	−3.3	−5.2	−6.3	−8.0	−7.3	−6.8
Commonwealth of Independent States[1]	**8.2**	**13.6**	**8.0**	**6.5**	**6.3**	**8.1**	**8.8**	**7.7**	**5.0**	**4.3**
Russia	12.6	18.0	11.1	8.4	8.2	9.9	10.9	9.8	6.2	5.0
Excluding Russia	−0.9	1.5	−0.8	1.0	0.4	2.2	1.8	1.1	0.7	2.1
Armenia	−16.6	−14.6	−9.5	−6.2	−6.8	−4.5	−3.9	−5.0	−5.5	−5.3
Azerbaijan	−13.1	−3.5	−0.9	−12.3	−27.8	−29.8	1.3	15.7	27.4	36.2
Belarus	−1.6	−2.7	−3.2	−2.1	−2.4	−5.2	1.6	−4.1	−8.7	−6.4
Georgia	−10.0	−7.9	−6.4	−5.9	−7.3	−8.4	−5.4	−9.5	−15.2	−12.7
Kazakhstan	−0.2	3.0	−5.4	−4.2	−0.9	0.8	−1.3	−1.4	−0.9	−0.4
Kyrgyz Republic	−14.5	−4.3	−1.5	−5.1	−4.4	−3.5	−2.3	−16.8	−12.6	−10.8
Moldova	−5.8	−7.6	−1.7	−4.0	−6.6	−2.0	−8.1	−8.3	−6.2	−5.7
Mongolia	−6.7	−5.7	−7.6	−9.6	−7.7	1.6	1.4	6.1	−1.5	−14.6
Tajikistan	−0.9	−1.6	−4.9	−3.5	−1.3	−3.9	−2.5	−2.5	−15.2	−15.3
Turkmenistan	−14.8	8.2	1.7	6.7	2.7	0.6	5.1	15.3	11.7	11.7
Ukraine	5.3	4.7	3.7	7.5	5.8	10.6	2.9	−1.7	−4.1	−5.5
Uzbekistan	−1.0	1.8	−1.0	1.2	8.7	10.1	14.3	19.4	19.7	18.6

Table 31 *(continued)*

	1999	2000	2001	2002	2003	2004	2005	2006	2007	2008
Developing Asia	**1.8**	**1.7**	**1.5**	**2.4**	**2.7**	**2.5**	**4.1**	**5.4**	**5.8**	**6.1**
Afghanistan, Rep. of	. . .	. . .	. . .	−3.7	3.0	1.8	0.6	−1.7	−3.8	−4.7
Bangladesh	−0.9	−1.4	−0.8	0.3	−0.4	−1.2	−0.3	0.9	0.7	—
Bhutan	2.1	−9.4	−5.4	−8.9	−10.8	−27.3	−3.4	−0.5	−3.2	−3.6
Brunei Darussalam	33.7	48.6	51.5	42.5	49.6	47.9	56.0	58.7	54.8	54.1
Cambodia	−5.0	−2.8	−1.2	−2.4	−3.7	−2.3	−4.3	−4.8	−5.5	−5.1
China	1.4	1.7	1.3	2.4	2.8	3.6	7.2	9.1	10.0	10.5
Fiji	−3.8	−5.8	−3.3	−1.6	−4.7	−16.9	−16.9	−20.4	−16.7	−13.1
India	−0.7	−1.0	0.3	1.4	1.5	0.1	−0.9	−2.2	−2.4	−2.3
Indonesia	3.7	4.8	4.3	4.0	3.5	0.6	0.1	2.7	1.8	1.3
Kiribati	16.5	−1.2	22.0	10.7	12.5	−3.0	−39.9	−37.9	−50.7	−51.7
Lao PDR	−4.0	−10.6	−8.3	−7.2	−8.1	−14.3	−19.9	−14.0	−25.1	−25.6
Malaysia	15.9	9.4	8.3	8.4	12.7	12.6	15.2	15.8	15.3	14.3
Maldives	−13.4	−8.2	−9.4	−5.6	−4.6	−16.0	−34.5	−36.5	−34.3	−30.5
Myanmar	−5.9	−0.8	−2.4	0.2	−1.0	2.3	4.0	4.1	2.7	1.7
Nepal	4.3	3.2	4.8	4.5	2.6	3.0	2.2	2.4	3.4	2.3
Pakistan	−2.6	−0.3	0.5	3.9	4.9	1.8	−1.4	−3.9	−4.0	−3.6
Papua New Guinea	2.8	8.5	6.5	−1.0	4.5	2.2	3.8	7.4	2.5	1.7
Philippines	−3.8	−2.9	−2.5	−0.5	0.4	1.9	2.0	2.9	2.1	1.9
Samoa	2.0	1.0	0.1	−1.1	−1.0	0.5	2.4	−6.2	−6.2	−1.0
Solomon Islands	4.3	−10.6	−12.8	−7.1	−2.5	3.1	−24.2	−22.8	−24.6	−4.1
Sri Lanka	−3.6	−6.5	−1.1	−1.4	−0.4	−3.2	−2.8	−4.1	−4.8	−5.1
Thailand	10.2	7.6	4.4	3.7	3.4	1.7	−4.5	1.6	1.5	0.9
Timor-Leste, Dem. Rep. of	2.1	−60.2	−52.8	−37.2	−25.4	30.4	83.5	116.3	140.8	163.6
Tonga	−0.6	−6.2	−9.5	5.1	−3.1	4.2	−4.8	−7.4	−11.2	−8.4
Vanuatu	−4.9	2.0	2.0	−9.7	−10.7	−7.3	−10.0	−8.0	−13.2	−13.7
Vietnam	4.5	2.3	1.6	−1.9	−4.9	−3.4	0.4	0.3	−1.2	−1.5
Middle East	**2.5**	**11.5**	**6.2**	**4.7**	**8.4**	**12.1**	**18.8**	**18.1**	**12.1**	**10.7**
Bahrain	−0.3	10.6	3.0	−0.4	2.3	4.0	12.0	18.1	12.2	10.6
Egypt	−1.9	−1.2	—	0.7	2.4	4.3	3.2	0.8	0.7	−1.5
Iran, I.R. of	6.3	13.0	5.2	3.1	0.6	1.2	7.4	6.7	6.0	4.7
Iraq	. . .	. . .	. . .	. . .	. . .	. . .	. . .	. . .	. . .	. . .
Jordan	5.0	0.7	−0.1	5.6	11.6	—	−17.8	−16.0	−14.6	−15.0
Kuwait	16.8	38.9	23.9	11.2	19.7	30.6	40.5	43.1	34.4	32.3
Lebanon	−19.1	−17.3	−19.4	−14.3	−13.3	−15.8	−11.7	−6.8	−11.0	−10.0
Libya	14.0	32.2	13.3	3.3	21.5	24.3	41.6	48.5	25.6	25.7
Oman	−2.9	15.5	9.8	6.9	3.9	1.2	8.7	8.4	−0.8	1.4
Qatar	6.8	25.9	23.7	19.7	24.4	23.8	25.2	11.6	5.0	11.2
Saudi Arabia	0.3	7.6	5.1	6.3	13.1	20.7	29.3	27.4	19.7	17.1
Syrian Arab Republic	1.6	5.2	5.7	7.2	4.7	3.0	0.8	−1.2	−3.4	−3.0
United Arab Emirates	1.6	17.3	9.5	5.0	8.6	10.0	15.8	16.3	11.8	8.6
Yemen, Rep. of	2.3	13.2	5.3	5.1	−0.1	1.9	1.6	3.6	−1.8	−4.0

Table 31 *(concluded)*

	1999	2000	2001	2002	2003	2004	2005	2006	2007	2008
Western Hemisphere	**–3.1**	**–2.4**	**–2.8**	**–0.9**	**0.4**	**1.0**	**1.4**	**1.7**	**0.5**	**–0.2**
Antigua and Barbuda	–3.1	–3.2	–8.0	–10.9	–13.4	–9.5	–14.5	–20.2	–15.6	–15.5
Argentina	–4.2	–3.2	–1.4	8.9	6.3	2.1	1.9	2.4	1.2	0.4
Bahamas, The	–5.1	–10.4	–11.6	–7.8	–8.6	–5.4	–8.8	–10.9	–13.4	–11.5
Barbados	–5.9	–5.7	–4.3	–6.8	–6.3	–12.4	–12.6	–8.7	–7.5	–7.8
Belize	–10.1	–20.3	–23.0	–20.3	–18.2	–14.4	–14.3	–8.4	–8.8	–6.6
Bolivia	–5.9	–5.3	–3.4	–4.1	1.0	3.9	6.6	11.3	8.7	6.4
Brazil	–4.3	–3.8	–4.2	–1.5	0.8	1.8	1.6	1.3	0.8	0.3
Chile	0.1	–1.2	–1.6	–0.9	–1.3	1.7	0.6	3.8	2.7	–0.2
Colombia	0.8	0.9	–1.3	–1.7	–1.2	–1.0	–1.6	–2.2	–2.3	–3.3
Costa Rica	–3.8	–4.3	–4.4	–5.6	–5.5	–4.3	–4.8	–4.9	–4.8	–4.7
Dominica	–17.2	–19.7	–18.7	–13.7	–13.0	–17.2	–27.2	–21.3	–20.9	–20.6
Dominican Republic	–2.4	–5.1	–3.4	–3.7	6.0	6.1	–1.5	–2.4	–2.2	–1.6
Ecuador	4.6	5.3	–3.2	–4.8	–0.6	–0.9	1.7	4.5	0.4	0.7
El Salvador	–1.9	–3.3	–1.1	–2.8	–4.7	–4.0	–4.6	–4.8	–4.7	–4.7
Grenada	–14.1	–21.5	–26.6	–32.0	–32.3	–12.7	–25.5	–24.2	–25.3	–22.3
Guatemala	–5.5	–5.4	–6.0	–5.3	–4.2	–4.4	–4.4	–4.4	–4.5	–4.7
Guyana	–11.4	–15.3	–19.2	–15.2	–11.9	–8.9	–19.1	–28.0	–23.0	–21.4
Haiti	–0.7	–1.1	–1.9	–1.4	–1.6	–1.2	0.7	1.4	0.2	–1.0
Honduras	–4.5	–4.0	–4.1	–3.1	–4.0	–5.9	–0.4	–1.2	–2.5	–2.8
Jamaica	–3.9	–4.9	–10.7	–10.3	–9.4	–5.8	–11.2	–10.7	–9.5	–9.3
Mexico	–2.9	–3.2	–2.8	–2.2	–1.4	–1.0	–0.6	–0.2	–1.0	–1.4
Nicaragua	–24.9	–20.1	–19.4	–17.7	–15.7	–13.9	–14.2	–14.2	–13.6	–12.9
Panama	–10.1	–5.9	–1.5	–0.7	–4.5	–7.5	–5.0	–4.3	–5.0	–6.3
Paraguay	–2.3	–2.3	–4.1	1.8	2.3	2.0	–0.3	–1.5	–2.0	–1.8
Peru	–3.4	–2.8	–2.1	–1.9	–1.5	—	1.3	2.6	0.7	0.4
St. Kitts and Nevis	–22.4	–21.0	–31.8	–37.9	–34.4	–25.2	–25.5	–28.2	–27.5	–27.1
St. Lucia	–16.6	–14.1	–16.2	–15.4	–20.4	–13.0	–23.3	–15.8	–10.4	–20.5
St. Vincent and the Grenadines	–20.6	–7.1	–10.4	–11.5	–20.8	–25.1	–24.0	–24.5	–25.1	–26.1
Suriname	–19.0	–3.8	–15.2	–5.6	–10.8	–4.1	–10.8	5.0	2.4	–1.7
Trinidad and Tobago	0.5	6.6	5.5	1.4	9.0	11.5	22.2	28.1	25.2	15.5
Uruguay	–2.4	–2.8	–2.9	3.2	–0.5	0.3	—	–2.4	–3.3	–2.3
Venezuela	2.2	10.1	1.6	8.2	14.1	13.8	17.8	15.0	7.0	6.2

[1]Mongolia, which is not a member of the Commonwealth of Independent States, is included in this group for reasons of geography and similarities in economic structure.

Table 32. Summary of Balance of Payments, Capital Flows, and External Financing
(Billions of U.S. dollars)

	1999	2000	2001	2002	2003	2004	2005	2006	2007	2008
Other emerging market and developing countries										
Balance of payments[1]										
Balance on current account	−21.2	85.8	39.4	77.3	147.6	212.6	428.0	544.2	455.1	470.7
Balance on goods and services	37.5	144.1	88.4	119.5	179.9	257.2	462.9	579.9	455.9	451.4
Income, net	−120.8	−127.2	−126.8	−135.1	−151.9	−183.3	−205.7	−227.4	−198.6	−188.2
Current transfers, net	62.1	68.9	77.9	92.8	119.5	138.6	170.7	191.7	197.8	207.6
Balance on capital and financial account	57.9	−51.4	5.3	−53.8	−136.2	−225.2	−363.7	−509.7	−451.0	−457.1
Balance on capital account[2]	9.5	21.0	1.9	−2.5	7.7	8.3	5.6	44.2	27.2	24.8
Balance on financial account	48.4	−72.4	3.4	−51.3	−144.0	−233.6	−369.4	−553.9	−478.2	−481.9
Direct investment, net	157.6	151.3	172.0	158.0	151.5	193.4	252.3	255.8	275.1	280.7
Portfolio investment, net	2.3	−38.1	−55.1	−46.2	−24.5	15.7	0.5	−97.4	−125.5	−135.1
Other investment, net	−70.2	−98.4	−21.5	−7.7	16.2	−15.5	−87.5	−31.7	26.9	36.2
Reserve assets	−41.3	−87.1	−92.0	−155.4	−287.2	−427.2	−534.7	−680.6	−654.7	−663.7
Errors and omissions, net	−36.8	−34.4	−44.7	−23.5	−11.3	12.7	−64.2	−34.5	−4.1	−13.6
Capital flows										
Total capital flows, net[3]	89.7	14.7	95.4	104.0	143.2	193.6	165.3	126.7	176.5	181.8
Net official flows	40.5	−26.1	18.3	6.5	−30.0	−43.5	−111.8	−130.9	−77.7	−96.4
Net private flows[4]	51.7	42.7	79.7	100.7	175.3	238.8	279.3	281.5	263.4	279.7
Direct investment, net	157.6	151.3	172.0	158.0	151.5	193.4	252.3	255.8	275.1	280.7
Private portfolio investment, net	−1.2	−18.3	−46.7	−39.0	8.4	54.5	63.6	−7.1	−23.8	−13.7
Other private flows, net	−104.7	−90.3	−45.6	−18.3	15.5	−9.1	−36.6	32.8	12.1	12.6
External financing[5]										
Net external financing[6]	230.7	240.3	182.2	173.5	311.0	479.6	607.0	785.5	749.5	810.5
Non-debt-creating flows	184.8	202.1	171.4	151.3	190.0	283.6	371.1	491.0	469.7	489.9
Capital transfers[7]	9.5	21.0	1.9	−2.5	7.7	8.3	5.6	44.2	27.2	24.8
Foreign direct investment and equity security liabilities[8]	175.3	181.1	169.5	153.8	182.3	275.2	365.5	446.7	442.5	465.1
Net external borrowing[9]	45.9	38.2	10.9	22.2	121.0	196.0	235.9	294.5	279.8	320.6
Borrowing from official creditors[10]	34.5	−8.1	24.1	10.6	0.7	−6.4	−50.9	−64.5	14.7	23.6
of which, credit and loans from IMF[11]	−2.4	−10.9	19.0	13.4	1.7	−14.9	−39.9	−30.1	. . .	. . .
Borrowing from banks[10]	−13.0	−10.9	−12.5	−18.0	13.8	30.8	40.1	57.8	41.9	40.5
Borrowing from other private creditors[10]	24.3	57.2	−0.8	29.6	106.4	171.6	246.6	301.2	223.2	256.5
Memorandum										
Balance on goods and services in percent of GDP[12]	0.6	2.3	1.4	1.8	2.4	2.9	4.4	4.7	3.3	3.0
Scheduled amortization of external debt	282.0	323.6	302.3	319.5	356.4	365.7	420.3	501.8	375.9	391.6
Gross external financing[13]	512.7	563.9	484.5	493.1	667.4	845.4	1,027.3	1,287.3	1,125.4	1,202.2
Gross external borrowing[14]	327.9	361.7	313.2	341.8	477.4	561.8	656.1	796.3	655.6	712.2
Exceptional external financing, net	28.9	10.3	28.1	46.9	32.9	13.5	−39.0	22.7	15.7	5.7
Of which,										
Arrears on debt service	8.1	−20.7	0.4	6.9	18.2	9.1	−20.3	7.0	. . .	. . .
Debt forgiveness	2.4	1.9	2.6	3.1	2.1	1.7	2.3	20.9	. . .	. . .
Rescheduling of debt service	13.6	2.5	7.4	10.6	6.7	7.0	5.3	2.4	. . .	. . .

[1]Standard presentation in accordance with the 5th edition of the International Monetary Fund's *Balance of Payments Manual* (1993).

[2]Comprises capital transfers—including debt forgiveness—and acquisition/disposal of nonproduced, nonfinancial assets.

[3]Comprise net direct investment, net portfolio investment, and other long- and short-term net investment flows, including official and private borrowing. In the standard balance of payments presentation above, total net capital flows are equal to the balance on financial account minus the change in reserve assets.

[4]Because of limitations on the data coverage for net official flows, the residually derived data for net private flows may include some official flows.

[5]As defined in the *World Economic Outlook* (see footnote 6). It should be noted that there is no generally accepted standard definition of external financing.

[6]Defined as the sum of—with opposite sign—the goods and services balance, net income and current transfers, direct investment abroad, the change in reserve assets, the net acquisition of other assets (such as recorded private portfolio assets, export credit, and the collateral for debt-reduction operations), and the net errors and omissions. Thus, net external financing, according to the definition adopted in the *World Economic Outlook*, measures the total amount required to finance the current account, direct investment outflows, net reserve transactions (often at the discretion of the monetary authorities), the net acquisition of nonreserve external assets, and the net transactions underlying the errors and omissions (not infrequently reflecting capital flight).

[7]Including other transactions on capital account.

[8]Debt-creating foreign direct investment liabilities are not included.

[9]Net disbursement of long- and short-term credits, including exceptional financing, by both official and private creditors.

[10]Changes in liabilities.

[11]Comprise use of IMF resources under the General Resources Account, Trust Fund, and Poverty Reduction and Growth Facility (PRGF). For further detail, see Table 36.

[12]This is often referred to as the "resource balance" and, with opposite sign, the "net resource transfer."

[13]Net external financing plus amortization due on external debt.

[14]Net external borrowing plus amortization due on external debt.

Table 33. Other Emerging Market and Developing Countries—by Region: Balance of Payments and External Financing[1]
(Billions of U.S. dollars)

	1999	2000	2001	2002	2003	2004	2005	2006	2007	2008
Africa										
Balance of payments										
Balance on current account	−15.0	7.2	0.5	−7.5	−2.2	0.6	14.6	19.9	0.9	−0.5
Balance on capital account	4.6	3.4	4.2	4.8	3.6	5.6	6.6	30.6	13.0	6.4
Balance on financial account	10.7	−10.4	−3.3	1.3	−4.3	−17.3	−27.5	−53.7	−14.5	−7.0
Change in reserves (− = increase)	−0.4	−12.8	−9.7	−5.5	−11.4	−32.7	−42.3	−48.4	−44.9	−56.3
Official flows, net	4.1	7.7	6.5	8.6	6.4	4.3	−1.8	−3.8	10.1	10.8
Private flows, net	9.0	−4.2	2.2	0.9	2.7	12.3	18.3	20.2	28.6	39.9
External financing										
Net external financing	28.5	14.6	22.7	20.3	25.1	34.5	35.7	58.6	65.0	80.0
Non-debt-creating inflows	23.1	15.8	23.3	17.3	21.4	33.3	41.3	77.4	52.5	55.1
Net external borrowing	5.4	−1.2	−0.6	3.0	3.7	1.2	−5.6	−18.8	12.5	24.9
From official creditors	2.1	6.6	4.2	5.9	4.4	3.1	−4.0	−26.2	1.0	8.5
of which, credit and loans from IMF	−0.2	−0.2	−0.4	−0.1	−0.8	−0.7	−1.0	−1.8	. . .	. . .
From banks	0.6	−0.4	—	1.1	0.9	2.1	1.4	0.9	−0.4	1.1
From other private creditors	2.7	−7.4	−4.8	−4.0	−1.6	−4.0	−3.0	6.5	11.9	15.3
Memorandum										
Exceptional financing	8.7	6.5	5.7	19.1	6.6	3.5	−0.9	23.2	6.8	0.3
Sub-Sahara										
Balance of payments										
Balance on current account	−14.4	−0.6	−7.3	−12.6	−11.9	−11.0	−7.2	−9.3	−17.3	−19.3
Balance on capital account	4.3	3.4	4.0	4.6	3.5	5.5	6.5	30.5	12.9	6.3
Balance on financial account	10.0	−2.6	5.1	7.4	6.4	−4.0	−4.9	−22.5	3.5	11.6
Change in reserves (− = increase)	−0.7	−6.2	0.5	−1.1	−2.1	−20.9	−23.2	−26.5	−23.4	−33.7
Official flows, net	6.6	10.6	9.7	11.4	9.3	8.0	2.2	8.3	10.4	11.6
Private flows, net	6.2	−5.9	−2.8	−0.2	1.2	10.1	17.8	17.3	24.9	35.2
External financing										
Net external financing	26.6	13.5	16.3	16.3	21.4	30.6	33.6	61.6	56.0	70.5
Non-debt-creating inflows	21.1	14.2	18.7	14.9	17.9	30.3	37.5	72.7	48.6	51.0
Net external borrowing	5.5	−0.7	−2.5	1.4	3.5	0.3	−3.9	−11.1	7.4	19.5
From official creditors	4.6	9.5	7.5	8.8	7.3	6.8	—	−14.0	1.3	9.3
of which, credit and loans from IMF	−0.1	—	−0.2	0.2	−0.4	−0.3	−0.4	−1.7	. . .	. . .
From banks	−0.9	−0.7	−0.6	0.3	0.1	1.2	1.1	1.2	−0.5	0.7
From other private creditors	1.8	−9.5	−9.3	−7.7	−4.0	−7.7	−4.9	1.7	6.6	9.5
Memorandum										
Exceptional financing	8.0	6.4	5.6	19.0	6.6	3.5	−0.9	23.2	6.8	0.3
Central and eastern Europe										
Balance of payments										
Balance on current account	−25.8	−31.8	−16.0	−24.0	−35.8	−58.6	−63.2	−88.9	−98.5	−104.7
Balance on capital account	0.4	0.6	0.8	0.7	0.5	2.3	3.6	4.2	10.0	15.2
Balance on financial account	21.8	34.4	13.9	27.7	36.0	54.5	60.9	95.0	91.0	92.2
Change in reserves (− = increase)	−12.1	−6.0	−3.0	−18.5	−11.5	−13.6	−48.2	−21.2	−14.9	−22.1
Official flows, net	−2.4	1.6	6.0	−7.5	−5.0	−6.6	−8.3	−4.9	−3.1	−3.3
Private flows, net	36.3	38.7	10.9	54.0	52.5	74.7	117.5	121.1	109.0	117.7
External financing										
Net external financing	46.0	50.5	27.1	44.5	55.4	101.4	132.7	161.6	141.3	149.3
Non-debt-creating inflows	20.7	24.0	23.2	24.6	18.0	42.1	64.6	71.4	76.6	82.2
Net external borrowing	25.4	26.5	4.0	19.9	37.4	59.3	68.1	90.1	64.8	67.1
From official creditors	−2.4	1.7	6.2	−7.6	−5.1	−6.5	−8.4	−4.4	−3.1	−3.3
of which, credit and loans from IMF	0.5	3.3	9.9	6.1	—	−3.8	−5.9	−5.3	. . .	. . .
From banks	1.8	3.9	−7.5	3.2	12.5	14.7	16.9	17.0	13.7	13.7
From other private creditors	26.0	20.9	5.4	24.3	30.0	51.0	59.6	77.5	54.2	56.7
Memorandum										
Exceptional financing	1.1	4.8	11.0	7.0	−0.3	−3.6	−4.9	−3.4	0.2	−0.4

Table 33 (continued)

	1999	2000	2001	2002	2003	2004	2005	2006	2007	2008
Commonwealth of Independent States[2]										
Balance of payments										
Balance on current account	23.8	48.3	33.1	30.2	36.0	62.6	87.7	99.0	75.4	76.3
Balance on capital account	−0.4	10.7	−9.5	−12.5	−1.0	−1.6	−12.8	0.6	0.5	0.5
Balance on financial account	−21.8	−53.7	−12.3	−9.8	−22.8	−53.6	−60.1	−94.0	−74.0	−74.4
Change in reserves (− = increase)	−6.4	−20.3	−14.5	−15.1	−31.8	−53.8	−75.6	−126.9	−108.4	−98.7
Official flows, net	−1.8	−5.8	−4.9	−10.4	−8.9	−7.3	−22.1	−32.6	−3.6	−4.3
Private flows, net	−13.5	−27.6	7.2	15.8	17.9	7.7	37.6	65.7	38.0	28.6
External financing										
Net external financing	0.2	1.1	−2.3	−0.6	41.3	62.0	83.6	120.3	111.9	117.1
Non-debt-creating inflows	4.0	14.4	−5.6	−16.8	14.5	20.9	−1.0	50.7	43.5	49.0
Net external borrowing	−3.8	−13.3	3.3	16.2	26.8	41.1	84.5	69.6	68.4	68.1
From official creditors	−2.0	−5.8	−3.8	−10.5	−3.4	−2.8	−19.2	−24.1	0.5	0.4
of which, credit and loans from IMF	−3.6	−4.1	−4.0	−1.8	−2.3	−2.1	−3.8	−0.7	. . .	. . .
From banks	3.5	1.6	4.2	−1.4	2.3	1.6	8.6	0.2	−0.5	−0.5
From other private creditors	−5.3	−9.1	3.0	28.1	27.9	42.3	95.2	93.5	68.4	68.2
Memorandum										
Exceptional financing	7.4	2.3	−0.1	−0.3	0.8	0.4	0.8	−1.9	—	—
Developing Asia										
Balance of payments										
Balance on current account	38.3	38.1	36.6	64.6	82.5	88.5	165.2	253.1	308.9	358.6
Balance on capital account	0.8	0.9	0.9	0.9	2.3	1.0	6.7	6.4	2.2	2.2
Balance on financial account	−22.4	−25.8	−24.9	−66.7	−95.8	−112.3	−135.8	−233.2	−301.2	−351.5
Change in reserves (− = increase)	−28.9	−16.0	−56.7	−109.9	−163.7	−258.3	−230.6	−311.5	−350.5	−373.4
Official flows, net	26.5	−3.0	−1.3	8.5	—	8.5	11.6	8.7	15.2	14.7
Private flows, net	−20.0	−6.9	33.1	34.7	67.9	137.5	83.2	69.6	34.1	7.2
External financing										
Net external financing	65.2	69.6	54.4	81.5	106.0	174.9	248.8	284.9	261.2	251.9
Non-debt-creating inflows	64.7	71.6	55.2	69.4	84.9	111.5	168.1	180.9	182.2	188.3
Net external borrowing	0.5	−2.0	−0.8	12.1	21.1	63.4	80.7	103.9	79.0	63.6
From official creditors	26.5	−3.0	−1.3	8.5	—	8.5	11.6	8.6	15.2	14.7
of which, credit and loans from IMF	1.7	0.9	−2.2	−2.7	−0.6	−1.9	−1.6	−8.7	. . .	. . .
From banks	−11.7	−13.0	−5.9	−2.9	1.4	16.6	11.0	25.7	13.4	11.9
From other private creditors	−14.3	13.9	6.5	6.5	19.7	38.2	58.1	69.6	50.3	37.0
Memorandum										
Exceptional financing	7.5	7.2	3.5	3.7	3.4	0.3	2.6	−0.2	0.1	—
Excluding China and India										
Balance of payments										
Balance on current account	25.9	22.2	17.8	22.1	27.8	19.0	11.2	33.9	29.0	24.6
Balance on capital account	0.8	1.0	1.0	0.9	2.4	1.1	2.6	2.4	2.3	2.2
Balance on financial account	−25.2	−21.5	−11.7	−16.7	−22.3	−15.3	6.2	−19.0	−21.1	−17.5
Change in reserves (− = increase)	−14.3	0.6	−0.7	−15.6	−21.0	−28.4	−9.1	−37.8	−37.1	−36.3
Official flows, net	19.4	−2.5	−2.3	7.3	4.7	−2.6	−4.3	−5.2	2.9	3.2
Private flows, net	−30.3	−19.6	−8.7	−8.4	−5.9	15.7	19.7	24.1	13.1	15.6
External financing										
Net external financing	11.1	0.9	3.5	17.8	20.2	46.4	76.5	91.4	82.0	82.7
Non-debt-creating inflows	23.7	15.9	5.8	16.7	23.6	38.9	53.7	61.6	63.6	67.5
Net external borrowing	−12.6	−15.0	−2.3	1.1	−3.4	7.5	22.8	29.8	18.4	15.2
From official creditors	19.4	−2.5	−2.3	7.3	4.7	−2.6	−4.3	−5.3	2.9	3.2
of which, credit and loans from IMF	2.1	0.9	−2.2	−2.7	−0.6	−1.9	−1.6	−8.7	. . .	. . .
From banks	−9.8	−6.4	−6.0	−5.0	−5.1	2.3	−4.3	5.4	−3.0	−1.4
From other private creditors	−22.3	−6.1	6.0	−1.2	−3.0	7.9	31.5	29.7	18.6	13.5
Memorandum										
Exceptional financing	7.5	7.2	3.5	3.7	3.4	0.3	2.6	−0.2	0.1	—

Table 33 *(concluded)*

	1999	2000	2001	2002	2003	2004	2005	2006	2007	2008
Middle East										
Balance of payments										
Balance on current account	14.0	72.1	39.2	30.0	59.5	99.2	189.0	212.4	153.0	146.7
Balance on capital account	0.9	2.4	3.0	1.5	1.3	−0.1	—	−0.3	−0.4	−0.5
Balance on financial account	−1.6	−63.6	−30.5	−30.3	−51.3	−85.9	−176.6	−212.2	−152.2	−145.7
Change in reserves (− = increase)	−0.9	−30.3	−11.7	−3.9	−32.6	−45.4	−104.6	−126.1	−78.7	−73.8
Official flows, net	8.1	−20.3	−13.1	−10.0	−26.7	−33.7	−60.6	−80.6	−95.1	−114.0
Private flows, net	−8.6	−12.6	−5.7	−16.3	8.1	−6.7	−11.2	−5.6	21.7	42.1
External financing										
Net external financing	−9.2	26.9	−8.8	−12.1	28.6	51.3	47.6	82.7	79.2	106.2
Non-debt-creating inflows	6.9	6.1	9.3	9.0	12.2	16.7	24.5	34.0	38.2	35.2
Net external borrowing	−16.1	20.8	−18.1	−21.1	16.5	34.6	23.1	48.7	41.1	71.0
From official creditors	3.5	−0.5	−3.8	−1.0	−0.4	0.5	−1.0	−1.2	1.5	2.7
of which, credit and loans from IMF	0.1	−0.1	0.1	—	−0.1	−0.1	−0.1	−0.8	. . .	. . .
From banks	1.7	0.9	−2.1	−4.8	2.3	2.3	9.0	0.9	4.9	1.9
From other private creditors	−21.4	20.3	−12.2	−15.3	14.5	31.8	15.0	49.0	34.7	66.4
Memorandum										
Exceptional financing	0.4	0.4	0.3	0.6	2.5	0.3	0.4	0.3	3.9	1.3
Western Hemisphere										
Balance of payments										
Balance on current account	−56.4	−48.1	−53.9	−16.1	7.7	20.4	34.6	48.7	15.3	−5.7
Balance on capital account	3.3	3.0	2.6	2.2	1.1	1.1	1.5	2.7	1.8	1.0
Balance on financial account	61.7	46.8	60.5	26.4	−5.8	−19.1	−30.2	−55.8	−27.3	4.5
Change in reserves (− = increase)	7.4	−1.8	3.5	−2.4	−36.2	−23.4	−33.4	−46.5	−57.4	−39.3
Official flows, net	6.2	−6.4	25.2	17.4	4.3	−8.7	−30.4	−17.7	−1.2	−0.4
Private flows, net	48.5	55.2	31.9	11.5	26.2	13.3	33.9	10.4	32.0	44.2
External financing										
Net external financing	99.9	77.6	89.0	40.0	54.6	55.5	58.7	77.4	90.8	106.0
Non-debt-creating inflows	65.4	70.2	66.0	47.9	39.0	59.0	73.6	76.5	76.9	80.1
Net external borrowing	34.5	7.5	23.1	−7.9	15.6	−3.5	−14.9	0.9	13.9	25.9
From official creditors	6.8	−7.0	22.7	15.3	5.2	−9.2	−29.9	−17.4	−0.4	0.6
of which, credit and loans from IMF	−0.9	−10.7	15.6	11.9	5.6	−6.3	−27.6	−12.8	. . .	. . .
From banks	−8.9	−4.0	−1.0	−13.2	−5.6	−6.6	−6.8	13.2	10.7	12.4
From other private creditors	36.6	18.5	1.4	−9.9	15.9	12.3	21.8	5.1	3.6	12.9
Memorandum										
Exceptional financing	3.9	−10.9	7.7	16.9	19.8	12.6	−37.1	4.7	4.7	4.4

[1]For definitions, see footnotes to Table 32.
[2]Mongolia, which is not a member of the Commonwealth of Independent States, is included in this group for reasons of geography and similarities in economic structure.

Table 34. Other Emerging Market and Developing Countries—by Analytical Criteria: Balance of Payments and External Financing[1]
(Billions of U.S. dollars)

	1999	2000	2001	2002	2003	2004	2005	2006	2007	2008
By source of export earnings										
Fuel										
Balance of payments										
Balance on current account	38.1	150.9	83.7	64.2	110.0	185.9	337.9	395.6	290.0	288.4
Balance on capital account	1.1	13.6	−6.1	−10.6	—	−1.2	−12.4	0.3	0.2	0.1
Balance on financial account	24.8	−148.2	−56.1	−47.5	−89.0	−171.7	−301.4	−387.0	−289.6	−287.7
Change in reserves (− = increase)	−0.8	−67.1	−29.1	−16.4	−71.1	−118.5	−207.8	−270.9	−206.8	−212.3
Official flows, net	3.4	−23.6	−14.1	−19.9	−30.6	−38.2	−86.6	−113.5	−93.9	−111.7
Private flows, net	−27.2	−57.0	−12.7	−11.2	12.7	−14.9	−6.8	−2.6	11.1	36.4
External financing										
Net external financing	−4.3	24.2	−12.3	−19.5	62.1	91.1	92.0	126.7	143.3	195.2
Non-debt-creating inflows	13.5	26.5	11.6	9.3	30.5	48.6	41.6	77.0	65.5	75.4
Net external borrowing	−17.9	−2.3	−23.9	−28.8	31.6	42.4	50.4	49.7	77.8	119.8
From official creditors	−1.7	−3.3	−5.0	−10.1	−3.6	−3.6	−27.5	−34.6	2.9	5.2
of which, credit and loans from IMF	−4.1	−3.5	−4.1	−1.8	−2.4	−2.2	−4.3	−1.0	. . .	. . .
From banks	3.9	1.6	1.3	−6.9	4.4	2.8	18.9	−2.1	7.4	2.5
From other private creditors	−20.1	−0.6	−20.2	−11.9	30.8	43.2	59.0	86.4	67.6	112.2
Memorandum										
Exceptional financing	12.9	4.6	2.3	2.6	3.3	−0.3	−3.5	3.6	0.4	0.9
Nonfuel										
Balance of payments										
Balance on current account	−59.3	−65.1	−44.2	13.1	37.6	26.7	90.1	148.6	165.0	182.3
Balance on capital account	8.4	7.4	8.0	8.2	7.7	9.6	18.0	44.0	27.0	24.8
Balance on financial account	73.2	75.8	59.5	−3.8	−54.9	−61.9	−68.0	−166.9	−188.6	−194.3
Change in reserves (− = increase)	−40.5	−20.0	−62.9	−138.9	−216.1	−308.7	−326.9	−409.7	−447.9	−451.4
Official flows, net	37.1	−2.4	32.4	26.4	0.6	−5.3	−25.2	−17.4	16.2	15.3
Private flows, net	78.9	99.7	92.4	111.9	162.7	253.7	286.1	284.1	252.3	243.3
External financing										
Net external financing	235.0	216.1	194.5	193.0	248.9	388.5	515.0	658.8	606.2	615.3
Non-debt-creating inflows	171.3	175.6	159.7	142.0	159.5	235.0	329.5	414.0	404.2	414.5
Net external borrowing	63.7	40.5	34.8	51.0	89.4	153.6	185.4	244.8	201.9	200.8
From official creditors	36.2	−4.8	29.1	20.7	4.4	−2.8	−23.4	−29.9	11.9	18.4
of which, credit and loans from IMF	1.7	−7.4	23.1	15.2	4.1	−12.7	−35.6	−29.1	. . .	. . .
From banks	−16.9	−12.5	−13.7	−11.1	9.4	28.0	21.3	59.9	34.4	38.1
From other private creditors	44.4	57.8	19.4	41.5	75.6	128.4	187.6	214.8	155.6	144.3
Memorandum										
Exceptional financing	16.1	5.7	25.9	44.4	29.6	13.8	−35.6	19.2	15.4	4.7
By external financing source										
Net debtor countries										
Balance of payments										
Balance on current account	−93.1	−95.0	−74.3	−36.0	−29.7	−69.0	−93.5	−111.4	−159.7	−186.6
Balance on capital account	9.0	7.7	8.3	8.6	7.6	10.1	14.3	40.0	27.1	24.9
Balance on financial account	90.2	88.9	81.0	50.7	31.0	62.2	95.1	81.3	132.3	170.5
Change in reserves (− = increase)	−27.6	−13.4	−14.9	−61.5	−89.2	−82.0	−111.4	−161.8	−141.7	−124.1
Official flows, net	32.3	2.8	32.9	24.1	6.5	−13.2	−37.2	−24.8	8.3	10.4
Private flows, net	87.9	100.9	65.5	91.2	115.8	159.1	245.8	291.8	274.9	285.6
External financing										
Net external financing	193.3	149.8	153.9	135.1	174.8	256.6	329.1	474.8	426.2	447.3
Non-debt-creating inflows	131.1	116.5	121.1	92.3	106.6	160.3	209.4	292.5	276.0	288.6
Net external borrowing	62.2	33.3	32.9	42.8	68.2	96.3	119.8	182.3	150.2	158.7
From official creditors	31.4	0.4	29.5	18.4	6.2	−13.8	−35.5	−40.4	4.0	13.5
of which, credit and loans from IMF	1.6	−6.7	23.2	15.4	4.3	−12.5	−35.5	−28.9	. . .	. . .
From banks	−15.9	−6.1	−15.1	−12.5	4.6	16.8	8.3	48.8	23.9	30.5
From other private creditors	46.7	39.0	18.5	37.0	57.3	93.3	147.0	173.9	122.3	114.7
Memorandum										
Exceptional financing	18.8	6.1	27.2	46.0	31.1	11.8	−34.4	20.1	15.7	5.6

Table 34 *(continued)*

	1999	2000	2001	2002	2003	2004	2005	2006	2007	2008
Official financing										
Balance of payments										
Balance on current account	−8.7	−6.7	−4.6	−2.3	−0.4	−2.6	−4.6	−7.4	−14.8	−16.6
Balance on capital account	4.0	4.2	5.3	3.6	3.6	4.7	4.5	15.8	8.8	4.3
Balance on financial account	9.7	4.9	4.5	4.6	1.0	1.4	11.4	6.2	16.8	22.0
Change in reserves (− = increase)	2.4	3.6	−1.0	−1.2	−9.4	−6.5	−4.1	−8.9	−5.3	−5.5
Official flows, net	9.8	7.2	9.0	9.5	9.2	4.7	7.0	9.1	10.3	10.9
Private flows, net	−2.0	−5.6	−2.2	−3.2	1.9	3.8	9.3	17.0	17.9	17.7
External financing										
Net external financing	11.7	8.3	14.4	9.5	16.3	15.1	23.6	32.6	32.6	33.6
Non-debt-creating inflows	8.4	9.2	9.6	9.2	8.4	11.1	12.9	27.9	22.8	18.8
Net external borrowing	3.4	−0.9	4.8	0.3	7.9	4.0	10.6	4.7	9.8	14.8
From official creditors	9.4	6.9	7.7	9.0	8.5	4.1	6.2	−1.9	4.2	9.8
of which, credit and loans from IMF	—	−0.4	0.3	1.5	0.4	−0.1	—	−3.8	. . .	. . .
From banks	0.8	0.6	0.6	1.7	0.8	0.2	0.5	0.6	0.8	0.9
From other private creditors	−6.8	−8.4	−3.4	−10.4	−1.4	−0.4	3.9	6.1	4.7	4.1
Memorandum										
Exceptional financing	6.3	5.2	1.4	1.7	1.6	−2.0	0.7	3.7	5.6	1.4
Net debtor countries by debt-servicing experience										
Countries with arrears and/or rescheduling during 2001–05										
Balance of payments										
Balance on current account	−19.8	−9.3	−10.8	7.1	11.0	−2.6	−8.9	−1.2	−15.3	−19.8
Balance on capital account	6.8	5.5	5.6	5.7	4.2	4.9	7.0	20.2	12.3	5.9
Balance on financial account	14.2	−2.0	8.6	−6.6	−9.6	0.1	2.1	−17.3	0.3	11.7
Change in reserves (− = increase)	−2.4	−3.9	12.2	−4.7	−15.7	−13.9	−15.8	−25.2	−23.9	−27.8
Official flows, net	21.4	7.0	18.2	14.5	14.8	0.7	−3.0	−15.4	9.0	8.5
Private flows, net	−2.6	−3.7	−19.5	−13.6	−7.1	14.3	22.3	35.4	23.4	32.1
External financing										
Net external financing	39.5	16.7	9.1	12.8	18.7	29.5	38.5	44.9	55.3	57.2
Non-debt-creating inflows	17.9	12.8	14.2	16.5	18.9	28.1	37.7	60.7	50.6	48.5
Net external borrowing	21.6	3.8	−5.1	−3.8	−0.1	1.4	0.8	−15.8	4.7	8.7
From official creditors	19.1	5.7	15.9	11.7	13.2	−0.3	−4.9	−28.2	—	6.5
of which, credit and loans from IMF	1.1	2.0	8.0	−1.5	−0.2	−3.7	−5.4	−19.7	. . .	. . .
From banks	−0.5	0.7	−2.9	−4.1	−2.2	1.5	−2.5	4.5	3.8	5.7
From other private creditors	3.1	−2.6	−18.1	−11.3	−11.1	0.2	8.1	7.9	0.9	−3.4
Memorandum										
Exceptional financing	13.6	11.0	8.5	27.0	24.5	18.8	−7.0	18.4	11.3	4.6
Other groups										
Heavily indebted poor countries										
Balance of payments										
Balance on current account	−9.0	−6.9	−7.3	−8.8	−7.3	−7.7	−9.4	−8.2	−11.2	−13.1
Balance on capital account	5.2	3.6	4.0	3.3	3.4	5.0	6.3	32.2	13.4	5.9
Balance on financial account	2.6	2.2	4.3	6.5	3.6	3.1	3.6	−20.5	−2.2	6.6
Change in reserves (− = increase)	−0.4	−0.5	−0.3	−1.6	−2.5	−2.7	−2.2	−4.3	−3.1	−3.0
Official flows, net	4.1	8.4	8.6	8.7	8.5	7.6	7.4	7.4	9.2	9.7
Private flows, net	1.0	−4.5	−1.8	0.8	−1.0	−0.6	0.2	−0.2	0.6	1.3
External financing										
Net external financing	8.4	6.3	7.9	11.0	9.9	10.5	10.9	15.2	12.6	13.9
Non-debt-creating inflows	8.6	6.6	7.0	7.6	7.3	9.1	10.1	36.4	17.7	11.1
Net external borrowing	−0.2	−0.3	0.9	3.5	2.5	1.4	0.8	−21.2	−5.1	2.9
From official creditors	2.0	7.3	6.4	7.3	7.0	6.3	5.0	−16.8	−0.5	7.5
of which, credit and loans from IMF	0.3	0.2	—	0.1	−0.2	−0.1	−0.2	−1.9	. . .	. . .
From banks	−0.5	0.1	0.2	1.0	0.3	0.9	0.6	0.9	0.7	−0.1
From other private creditors	−1.7	−7.6	−5.7	−4.9	−4.7	−5.9	−4.8	−5.3	−5.3	−4.5
Memorandum										
Exceptional financing	2.9	2.8	3.3	14.3	3.5	1.6	3.9	16.6	6.9	2.4

Table 34 *(concluded)*

	1999	2000	2001	2002	2003	2004	2005	2006	2007	2008
Middle East and north Africa										
Balance of payments										
Balance on current account	11.6	77.9	44.7	33.6	67.6	108.8	207.0	236.0	165.7	161.0
Balance on capital account	1.2	2.5	3.2	1.7	1.3	—	0.1	0.9	−0.3	−0.4
Balance on financial account	0.5	−70.2	−37.4	−35.2	−60.3	−97.8	−195.6	−239.0	−164.7	−159.9
Change in reserves (− = increase)	−0.6	−37.0	−21.8	−8.5	−42.1	−58.1	−124.5	−147.7	−100.5	−97.9
Official flows, net	6.7	−22.0	−15.6	−12.3	−29.2	−37.0	−63.9	−92.1	−94.1	−113.5
Private flows, net	−5.5	−10.6	—	−14.4	11.0	−2.6	−7.0	1.7	30.1	51.6
External financing										
Net external financing	−6.0	29.2	−1.0	−6.9	34.0	57.6	53.6	84.3	93.5	120.8
Non-debt-creating inflows	9.2	7.9	14.6	12.1	16.9	21.7	31.6	43.7	46.0	43.3
Net external borrowing	−15.2	21.3	−15.6	−19.0	17.1	35.9	22.0	40.6	47.5	77.5
From official creditors	2.2	−2.3	−6.3	−3.3	−2.8	−2.8	−4.3	−13.6	2.5	3.1
of which, credit and loans from IMF	—	−0.3	−0.2	−0.3	−0.6	−0.6	−0.8	−1.0	. . .	. . .
From banks	3.1	1.2	−1.6	−3.9	3.1	3.2	9.5	0.5	4.9	2.3
From other private creditors	−20.5	22.3	−7.7	−11.8	16.8	35.4	16.8	53.7	40.1	72.1
Memorandum										
Exceptional financing	2.4	1.9	1.4	1.5	3.2	1.0	1.2	1.1	4.6	2.2

[1]For definitions, see footnotes to Table 32.

Table 35. Other Emerging Market and Developing Countries: Reserves[1]

	1999	2000	2001	2002	2003	2004	2005	2006	2007	2008
					Billions of U.S. dollars					
Other emerging market and developing countries	**713.3**	**802.5**	**897.7**	**1,075.1**	**1,397.7**	**1,849.4**	**2,338.4**	**3,019.1**	**3,673.8**	**4,337.5**
Regional groups										
Africa	42.1	54.2	64.4	72.0	90.3	126.3	160.3	208.8	253.7	310.0
Sub-Sahara	29.3	35.2	35.6	36.1	40.0	62.4	83.1	109.7	133.1	166.8
Excluding Nigeria and South Africa	17.3	19.0	18.8	22.5	26.1	32.1	36.1	47.4	54.1	65.8
Central and eastern Europe	90.6	92.7	93.0	123.9	151.8	174.7	204.7	225.9	240.8	262.9
Commonwealth of Independent States[2]	16.5	33.2	44.0	58.2	91.6	146.7	211.2	338.2	446.6	545.3
Russia	9.1	24.8	33.1	44.6	73.8	121.5	176.5	284.0	379.9	471.4
Excluding Russia	7.4	8.4	10.9	13.6	17.8	25.2	34.7	54.2	66.7	73.9
Developing Asia	307.7	320.7	379.5	496.2	669.7	933.9	1,155.3	1,466.8	1,817.3	2,190.8
China	158.3	168.9	216.3	292.0	409.2	615.5	822.5	1,062.5	1,352.5	1,672.5
India	33.2	38.4	46.4	68.2	99.5	127.2	132.5	166.2	189.6	206.8
Excluding China and India	116.2	113.4	116.9	136.0	161.1	191.2	200.3	238.1	275.2	311.5
Middle East	113.5	146.1	157.9	163.9	198.6	246.9	351.4	477.4	556.1	629.9
Western Hemisphere	143.0	155.7	158.8	160.7	195.6	220.8	255.5	302.0	359.4	398.7
Brazil	23.9	31.5	35.8	37.7	49.1	52.8	53.6	85.6	122.6	142.8
Mexico	31.8	35.5	44.8	50.6	59.0	64.1	74.1	73.1	80.7	88.9
Analytical groups										
By source of export earnings										
Fuel	125.7	190.3	214.5	230.2	306.1	428.3	619.7	890.6	1,097.4	1,309.7
Nonfuel	587.6	612.2	683.2	844.9	1,091.6	1,421.1	1,718.8	2,128.5	2,576.4	3,027.8
of which, primary products	24.7	25.5	24.5	25.8	26.0	26.5	27.7	29.5	33.9	35.5
By external financing source										
Net debtor countries	404.6	423.1	446.3	529.9	648.8	750.7	832.9	994.7	1,136.5	1,260.6
of which, official financing	28.8	28.4	32.2	36.9	47.9	54.1	60.4	69.3	74.6	80.1
Net debtor countries by debt-servicing experience										
Countries with arrears and/or rescheduling during 2001–05	72.8	76.0	68.0	75.7	89.9	101.8	115.7	140.9	164.8	192.6
Other groups										
Heavily indebted poor countries	9.6	10.2	10.9	13.3	16.0	19.2	20.3	24.6	27.7	30.7
Middle East and north Africa	126.7	165.5	187.1	200.6	249.9	312.7	431.0	578.6	679.1	777.1

Table 35 *(concluded)*

	1999	2000	2001	2002	2003	2004	2005	2006	2007	2008
	Ratio of reserves to imports of goods and services[3]									
Other emerging market and developing countries	**46.3**	**44.7**	**49.5**	**55.3**	**60.5**	**62.7**	**66.4**	**71.4**	**75.1**	**79.1**
Regional groups										
Africa	31.2	39.1	45.5	46.9	48.3	53.6	57.2	63.6	67.4	74.7
Sub-Sahara	28.7	33.6	33.2	31.2	28.0	34.7	38.0	42.1	45.5	51.7
Excluding Nigeria and South Africa	30.2	33.2	31.0	35.3	34.4	34.0	31.1	34.8	35.4	39.0
Central and eastern Europe	38.8	34.6	34.8	41.1	39.3	34.8	35.2	31.9	29.3	28.9
Commonwealth of Independent States[2]	17.6	30.5	34.4	41.0	52.1	64.3	75.7	96.0	109.1	120.0
Russia	17.2	40.6	44.6	52.9	71.5	92.7	107.2	135.2	152.7	170.5
Excluding Russia	18.1	17.5	20.2	23.6	24.5	26.0	30.4	38.1	41.6	41.5
Developing Asia	58.6	49.2	58.4	68.1	74.6	79.6	81.9	87.9	93.9	98.5
China	83.3	67.4	79.7	89.0	91.1	101.5	115.5	124.3	132.2	137.4
India	52.9	52.6	65.0	90.0	107.1	97.0	72.5	70.4	68.6	67.3
Excluding China and India	42.7	34.5	38.0	41.8	45.2	43.9	38.8	41.2	43.3	44.6
Middle East	64.0	75.5	78.7	74.3	78.5	77.9	90.5	98.3	97.9	99.6
Western Hemisphere	38.0	35.9	37.3	40.5	47.6	44.8	43.8	44.0	46.2	46.8
Brazil	37.6	43.5	49.2	61.1	77.2	65.9	54.8	71.3	86.2	88.6
Mexico	20.4	18.6	24.2	27.3	31.4	29.8	30.5	26.2	25.9	26.1
Analytical groups										
By source of export earnings										
Fuel	48.2	66.0	67.9	65.7	74.7	82.7	96.2	110.3	114.6	122.4
Nonfuel	45.9	40.6	45.6	53.0	57.4	58.5	59.7	62.2	65.5	68.6
of which, primary products	62.9	60.8	58.5	59.6	53.6	43.4	37.5	35.1	36.9	36.3
By external financing source										
Net debtor countries	39.9	36.5	39.1	45.0	47.7	44.0	40.7	40.9	41.2	41.6
of which, official financing	30.4	27.1	31.1	34.8	39.8	37.2	34.4	33.0	31.6	30.6
Net debtor countries by debt-servicing experience										
Countries with arrears and/or rescheduling during 2001–05	43.1	40.5	37.1	43.0	45.1	40.6	36.5	38.7	40.6	43.3
Other groups										
Heavily indebted poor countries	27.1	28.6	29.1	32.6	35.1	34.4	30.4	32.4	33.1	33.9
Middle East and north Africa	59.7	72.0	78.4	76.4	82.9	82.6	93.7	102.4	102.1	105.2

[1]In this table, official holdings of gold are valued at SDR 35 an ounce. This convention results in a marked underestimate of reserves for countries that have substantial gold holdings.

[2]Mongolia, which is not a member of the Commonwealth of Independent States, is included in this group for reasons of geography and similarities in economic structure.

[3]Reserves at year-end in percent of imports of goods and services for the year indicated.

Table 36. Net Credit and Loans from IMF[1]
(Billions of U.S. dollars)

	1998	1999	2000	2001	2002	2003	2004	2005	2006
Advanced economies	**5.2**	**−10.3**	**—**	**−5.7**	**—**	**—**	**—**	**—**	**—**
Newly industrialized Asian economies	5.2	−10.3	—	−5.7	—	—	—	—	—
Other emerging market and developing countries	**14.0**	**−2.4**	**−10.9**	**19.0**	**13.4**	**1.7**	**−14.5**	**−39.9**	**−30.1**
Regional groups									
Africa	−0.4	−0.2	−0.2	−0.4	−0.1	−0.8	−0.7	−1.0	−1.3
Sub-Sahara	−0.3	−0.1	—	−0.2	0.2	−0.4	−0.3	−0.4	−1.2
Excluding Nigeria and South Africa	0.1	−0.1	—	−0.2	0.2	−0.4	−0.3	−0.4	−1.2
Central and eastern Europe	−0.5	0.5	3.3	9.9	6.1	—	−3.8	−5.9	−5.3
Commonwealth of Independent States[2]	5.8	−3.6	−4.1	−4.0	−1.8	−2.3	−2.1	−3.8	−1.1
Russia	5.3	−3.6	−2.9	−3.8	−1.5	−1.9	−1.7	−3.4	−0.1
Excluding Russia	0.5	—	−1.2	−0.2	−0.3	−0.4	−0.5	−0.4	−1.0
Developing Asia	6.6	1.7	0.9	−2.2	−2.7	−0.6	−1.9	−1.6	−8.7
China	—	—	—	—	—	—	—	—	—
India	−0.4	−0.3	−0.1	—	—	—	—	—	—
Excluding China and India	7.0	2.1	0.9	−2.2	−2.7	−0.6	−1.9	−1.6	−8.7
Middle East	0.1	0.1	−0.1	0.1	—	−0.1	0.3	−0.1	−1.0
Western Hemisphere	2.5	−0.9	−10.7	15.6	11.9	5.6	−6.3	−27.6	−12.8
Brazil	4.6	4.1	−6.7	6.7	11.2	5.2	−4.4	−23.8	—
Mexico	−1.1	−3.7	−4.3	—	—	—	—	—	—
Analytical groups									
By source of export earnings									
Fuel	4.7	−4.1	−3.5	−4.1	−1.8	−2.4	−1.8	−4.3	−1.2
Nonfuel	9.3	1.7	−7.4	23.1	15.2	4.1	−12.7	−35.6	−28.9
of which, primary products	0.2	−0.1	−0.2	−0.2	0.1	−0.3	−0.3	−0.3	−0.4
By external financing source									
Net debtor countries	8.8	1.4	−6.9	23.3	15.5	4.3	−12.0	−35.1	−28.7
of which, official financing	5.4	0.8	1.7	8.2	—	0.5	−3.3	−4.8	−3.7
Net debtor countries by debt-servicing experience									
Countries with arrears and/or rescheduling during 2001–05	5.3	1.1	1.9	8.1	−1.5	−0.2	−3.4	−5.4	−19.6
Other groups									
Heavily indebted poor countries	0.2	0.3	0.1	—	0.2	−0.2	−0.1	−0.2	−1.4
Middle East and north Africa	−0.1	—	−0.3	−0.2	−0.3	−0.6	−0.1	−0.8	−1.1
Memorandum									
Total									
Net credit provided under:									
General Resources Account	18.811	−12.856	−10.741	13.213	12.832	1.741	−14.276	−39.741	−26.685
PRGF	0.374	0.194	−0.148	0.106	0.567	0.009	−0.179	−0.715	−3.587
IMF credit outstanding at year-end under:[3]									
General Resources Account	84.541	69.504	55.368	66.448	85.357	95.323	84.992	38.859	13.619
PRGF[4]	8.775	8.749	8.159	7.974	9.222	10.108	10.421	8.924	5.725

[1]Includes net disbursements from programs under the General Resources Account and Poverty Reduction and Growth Facility (formerly ESAF—Enhanced Structural Adjustment Facility). The data are on a transactions basis, with conversion to U.S. dollar values at annual average exchange rates.

[2]Mongolia, which is not a member of the Commonwealth of Independent States, is included in this group for reasons of geography and similarities in economic structure.

[3]Data refer to disbursements at year-end correspond to the stock of outstanding credit, converted to U.S. dollar values at end-of-period exchange rates.

[4]Includes outstanding SAF and Trust Fund Loans.

Table 37. Summary of External Debt and Debt Service

	1999	2000	2001	2002	2003	2004	2005	2006	2007	2008
					Billions of U.S. dollars					
External debt										
Other emerging market and developing countries	**2,453.0**	**2,367.6**	**2,379.4**	**2,448.6**	**2,673.0**	**2,924.6**	**3,022.6**	**3,242.9**	**3,492.8**	**3,715.1**
Regional groups										
Africa	298.1	286.8	275.4	284.6	309.2	325.0	298.8	255.5	254.8	266.9
Central and eastern Europe	279.1	301.1	307.5	355.9	445.2	544.9	592.6	701.1	760.5	816.9
Commonwealth of Independent States[1]	218.9	200.4	189.2	199.6	239.6	281.3	335.8	384.5	435.9	489.5
Developing Asia	691.7	652.8	672.7	678.5	711.6	768.8	808.9	895.1	968.7	1,030.9
Middle East	169.6	164.5	160.4	165.6	179.0	208.2	237.1	282.4	318.7	339.7
Western Hemisphere	795.5	762.0	774.2	764.4	788.4	796.3	749.5	724.5	754.2	771.1
Analytical groups										
By external financing source										
Net debtor countries	1,848.7	1,797.1	1,788.5	1,847.4	2,006.3	2,160.9	2,169.7	2,311.5	2,445.4	2,574.1
of which, official financing	182.4	180.8	184.2	198.4	212.6	221.7	217.7	206.7	209.3	218.1
Net debtor countries by debt-servicing experience										
Countries with arrears and/or rescheduling during 2001–05	554.6	531.5	534.1	523.1	550.4	570.1	536.6	526.7	528.2	544.2
Debt-service payments[2]										
Other emerging market and developing countries	**397.0**	**446.7**	**424.7**	**416.1**	**465.4**	**478.3**	**593.7**	**665.2**	**575.0**	**607.6**
Regional groups										
Africa	25.4	26.8	26.0	21.1	25.8	29.4	34.7	46.4	29.6	26.5
Central and eastern Europe	53.6	58.0	66.6	68.2	85.7	98.2	108.0	127.4	140.4	150.4
Commonwealth of Independent States[1]	27.0	61.6	39.9	47.0	63.1	74.4	107.5	130.7	91.2	99.3
Developing Asia	92.6	93.7	100.0	109.7	109.2	99.3	111.6	122.1	128.9	139.5
Middle East	19.4	19.6	22.9	15.5	19.9	22.6	30.2	43.6	36.2	38.4
Western Hemisphere	179.0	187.0	169.4	154.7	161.7	154.4	201.5	195.0	148.7	153.5
Analytical groups										
By external financing source										
Net debtor countries	316.9	333.7	328.7	319.1	344.4	343.4	409.1	433.8	402.8	425.7
of which, official financing	15.6	16.9	16.7	17.1	18.2	19.6	20.2	23.1	18.8	21.1
Net debtor countries by debt-servicing experience										
Countries with arrears and/or rescheduling during 2001–05	68.9	77.6	82.2	67.7	66.5	61.0	83.3	77.1	61.9	59.1

Table 37 *(concluded)*

	1999	2000	2001	2002	2003	2004	2005	2006	2007	2008
	Percent of exports of goods and services									
External debt[3]										
Other emerging market and developing countries	**155.4**	**122.1**	**125.1**	**118.7**	**107.3**	**91.2**	**75.8**	**67.4**	**65.3**	**62.6**
Regional groups										
Africa	232.8	182.0	183.5	183.8	158.8	130.6	94.5	68.7	64.8	61.9
Central and eastern Europe	137.5	129.9	123.9	129.0	126.4	119.6	111.9	110.6	103.3	100.2
Commonwealth of Independent States[1]	177.1	121.7	114.1	111.8	107.0	92.5	86.3	79.5	85.2	88.2
Developing Asia	119.8	93.9	97.6	86.4	74.7	62.5	53.2	48.2	44.4	41.0
Middle East	87.5	60.9	65.1	62.9	54.8	48.6	40.5	40.5	44.9	44.5
Western Hemisphere	225.7	181.6	192.4	188.9	178.6	148.0	116.0	94.6	92.8	90.0
Analytical groups										
By external financing source										
Net debtor countries	198.0	166.8	167.1	162.7	152.1	131.3	110.8	99.0	94.3	90.9
of which, official financing	234.5	204.3	210.6	219.6	202.7	173.9	143.6	114.0	107.1	102.0
Net debtor countries by debt-servicing experience										
Countries with arrears and/or rescheduling during 2001–05	344.5	279.8	295.3	278.3	260.8	222.8	172.2	144.1	135.1	128.1
Debt-service payments										
Other emerging market and developing countries	**25.2**	**23.0**	**22.3**	**20.2**	**18.7**	**14.9**	**14.9**	**13.8**	**10.8**	**10.2**
Regional groups										
Africa	19.9	17.0	17.3	13.6	13.3	11.8	11.0	12.5	7.5	6.1
Central and eastern Europe	26.4	25.0	26.8	24.7	24.3	21.5	20.4	20.1	19.1	18.5
Commonwealth of Independent States[1]	21.8	37.4	24.0	26.3	28.2	24.5	27.7	27.0	17.8	17.9
Developing Asia	16.0	13.5	14.5	14.0	11.5	8.1	7.3	6.6	5.9	5.5
Middle East	10.0	7.3	9.3	5.9	6.1	5.3	5.2	6.2	5.1	5.0
Western Hemisphere	50.8	44.6	42.1	38.2	36.6	28.7	31.2	25.5	18.3	17.9
Analytical groups										
By external financing source										
Net debtor countries	33.9	31.0	30.7	28.1	26.1	20.9	20.9	18.6	15.5	15.0
of which, official financing	20.1	19.0	19.1	18.9	17.3	15.3	13.3	12.7	9.6	9.9
Net debtor countries by debt-servicing experience										
Countries with arrears and/or rescheduling during 2001–05	42.8	40.8	45.4	36.0	31.5	23.8	26.8	21.1	15.8	13.9

[1]Mongolia, which is not a member of the Commonwealth of Independent States, is included in this group for reasons of geography and similarities in economic structure.
[2]Debt-service payments refer to actual payments of interest on total debt plus actual amortization payments on long-term debt. The projections incorporate the impact of exceptional financing items.
[3]Total debt at year-end in percent of exports of goods and services in year indicated.

Table 38. Other Emerging Market and Developing Countries—by Region: External Debt, by Maturity and Type of Creditor
(Billions of U.S. dollars)

	1999	2000	2001	2002	2003	2004	2005	2006	2007	2008
Other emerging market and developing countries										
Total debt	**2,453.0**	**2,367.6**	**2,379.4**	**2,448.6**	**2,673.0**	**2,924.6**	**3,022.6**	**3,242.9**	**3,492.8**	**3,715.1**
By maturity										
Short-term	323.1	301.7	344.6	339.6	414.7	510.3	612.6	702.5	772.9	829.4
Long-term	2,129.9	2,065.9	2,034.9	2,109.0	2,258.3	2,414.3	2,410.1	2,540.4	2,719.9	2,885.6
By type of creditor										
Official	929.2	886.6	882.9	919.5	956.6	958.9	860.4	765.1	772.8	789.0
Banks	700.6	645.9	618.2	615.0	649.1	730.7	756.1	870.2	971.9	1,078.7
Other private	823.2	835.1	878.3	914.1	1,067.4	1,235.0	1,406.1	1,607.6	1,748.0	1,847.4
Regional groups										
Africa										
Total debt	**298.1**	**286.8**	**275.4**	**284.6**	**309.2**	**325.0**	**298.8**	**255.5**	**254.8**	**266.9**
By maturity										
Short-term	34.3	13.7	11.6	14.9	15.8	17.7	15.6	14.9	15.0	15.5
Long-term	263.8	273.1	263.8	269.7	293.4	307.3	283.2	240.6	239.7	251.4
By type of creditor										
Official	205.7	205.4	203.9	217.0	233.1	240.1	209.8	148.5	144.5	149.0
Banks	63.0	55.3	51.5	46.5	51.9	56.9	58.2	70.2	72.1	78.5
Other private	29.4	26.0	20.0	21.1	24.1	28.1	30.8	36.8	38.1	39.4
Sub-Sahara										
Total debt	**238.2**	**232.0**	**225.0**	**232.5**	**252.8**	**270.3**	**250.5**	**218.7**	**217.4**	**229.7**
By maturity										
Short-term	32.5	11.8	9.7	12.6	13.5	14.9	11.7	11.9	12.2	12.5
Long-term	205.7	220.1	215.3	219.9	239.3	255.4	238.9	206.8	205.3	217.2
By type of creditor										
Official	161.7	164.8	166.3	176.8	189.1	197.2	172.2	122.3	118.0	122.8
Banks	50.9	43.9	40.5	35.5	39.6	45.0	47.6	59.6	61.2	67.5
Other private	25.6	23.2	18.2	20.3	24.1	28.1	30.8	36.8	38.1	39.4
Central and eastern Europe										
Total debt	**279.1**	**301.1**	**307.5**	**355.9**	**445.2**	**544.9**	**592.6**	**701.1**	**760.5**	**816.9**
By maturity										
Short-term	57.6	63.5	55.5	62.1	91.6	118.7	140.8	170.2	186.9	201.5
Long-term	221.4	237.6	252.0	293.8	353.6	426.2	451.8	530.8	573.6	615.4
By type of creditor										
Official	75.8	77.5	83.2	76.5	74.4	69.9	61.9	60.3	58.2	55.6
Banks	110.3	122.7	109.4	139.2	177.3	215.9	231.0	270.0	294.2	322.5
Other private	93.0	100.8	114.8	140.3	193.5	259.2	299.8	370.8	408.0	438.8
Commonwealth of Independent States[1]										
Total debt	**218.9**	**200.4**	**189.2**	**199.6**	**239.6**	**281.3**	**335.8**	**384.5**	**435.9**	**489.5**
By maturity										
Short-term	14.4	13.6	16.1	18.8	30.8	36.9	49.3	50.5	51.8	60.8
Long-term	204.5	186.8	173.1	180.9	208.9	244.4	286.4	334.0	384.1	428.7
By type of creditor										
Official	113.5	103.0	91.1	85.2	86.7	85.4	57.4	35.1	35.0	34.6
Banks	49.4	17.8	22.1	20.9	23.0	29.5	48.1	62.1	99.8	141.8
Other private	56.0	79.6	76.1	93.5	129.9	166.4	230.3	287.2	301.1	313.1

Table 38 *(concluded)*

	1999	2000	2001	2002	2003	2004	2005	2006	2007	2008
Developing Asia										
Total debt	**691.7**	**652.8**	**672.7**	**678.5**	**711.6**	**768.8**	**808.9**	**895.1**	**968.7**	**1,030.9**
By maturity										
Short-term	65.1	53.3	105.4	106.7	128.8	167.2	221.2	255.4	275.5	293.1
Long-term	626.6	599.5	567.3	571.8	582.8	601.7	587.6	639.6	693.3	737.8
By type of creditor										
Official	295.9	277.7	271.5	279.4	284.4	293.1	302.9	309.3	322.8	336.1
Banks	195.3	179.5	173.5	167.1	159.8	176.2	188.2	214.6	229.2	242.1
Other private	200.5	195.6	227.7	232.0	267.4	299.5	317.8	371.2	416.8	452.8
Middle East										
Total debt	**169.6**	**164.5**	**160.4**	**165.6**	**179.0**	**208.2**	**237.1**	**282.4**	**318.7**	**339.7**
By maturity										
Short-term	55.5	53.1	56.9	56.9	68.8	86.7	100.5	122.6	140.1	151.0
Long-term	114.1	111.4	103.5	108.7	110.1	121.5	136.6	159.7	178.6	188.8
By type of creditor										
Official	59.9	58.1	55.7	60.8	65.3	67.5	67.3	68.4	69.2	71.8
Banks	52.4	49.6	45.7	40.5	44.2	58.3	68.2	87.8	101.8	110.0
Other private	57.3	56.8	59.0	64.3	69.5	82.4	101.6	126.2	147.7	158.0
Western Hemisphere										
Total debt	**795.5**	**762.0**	**774.2**	**764.4**	**788.4**	**796.3**	**749.5**	**724.5**	**754.2**	**771.1**
By maturity										
Short-term	96.2	104.5	99.1	80.2	78.9	83.2	85.1	88.8	103.6	107.5
Long-term	699.3	657.5	675.1	684.1	709.5	713.2	664.4	635.7	650.6	663.6
By type of creditor										
Official	178.3	164.9	177.5	200.6	212.7	203.0	161.2	143.5	143.2	141.9
Banks	230.2	220.9	216.1	200.7	192.8	193.8	162.4	165.6	174.8	183.9
Other private	387.0	376.2	380.6	363.0	382.9	399.5	425.9	415.4	436.3	445.3

[1]Mongolia, which is not a member of the Commonwealth of Independent States, is included in this group for reasons of geography and similarities in economic structure.

Table 39. Other Emerging Market and Developing Countries—by Analytical Criteria: External Debt, by Maturity and Type of Creditor
(Billions of U.S. dollars)

	1999	2000	2001	2002	2003	2004	2005	2006	2007	2008
By source of export earnings										
Fuel										
Total debt	**454.5**	**422.1**	**402.2**	**413.1**	**459.4**	**516.2**	**572.8**	**606.7**	**686.3**	**751.7**
By maturity										
Short-term	73.8	51.4	56.0	57.9	77.4	98.5	118.6	140.3	162.5	173.2
Long-term	380.7	370.6	346.1	355.2	381.9	417.7	454.3	466.4	523.8	578.5
By type of creditor										
Official	207.5	196.6	182.4	185.7	195.1	197.0	146.4	98.4	98.9	104.0
Banks	106.2	72.3	72.1	63.7	69.7	89.2	119.6	148.2	199.2	250.4
Other private	140.7	153.2	147.7	163.6	194.6	230.0	306.8	360.2	388.2	397.3
Nonfuel										
Total debt	**1,998.5**	**1,945.5**	**1,977.3**	**2,035.5**	**2,213.7**	**2,408.4**	**2,449.8**	**2,636.2**	**2,806.5**	**2,963.4**
By maturity										
Short-term	249.4	250.3	288.6	281.7	337.3	411.8	494.0	562.2	610.4	656.2
Long-term	1,749.1	1,695.3	1,688.7	1,753.9	1,876.4	1,996.6	1,955.8	2,074.0	2,196.1	2,307.2
By type of creditor										
Official	721.7	690.0	700.6	733.8	761.6	762.0	713.9	666.7	673.9	684.9
Banks	594.4	573.6	546.2	551.2	579.4	641.4	636.5	722.0	772.7	828.3
Other private	682.4	681.9	730.5	750.5	872.7	1,005.0	1,099.4	1,247.5	1,359.8	1,450.2
Nonfuel primary products										
Total debt	**82.3**	**85.1**	**87.8**	**96.2**	**100.6**	**103.6**	**101.8**	**84.9**	**89.9**	**93.2**
By maturity										
Short-term	5.9	7.8	6.7	7.5	9.5	10.3	9.7	12.1	12.8	12.8
Long-term	76.3	77.2	81.1	88.8	91.1	93.2	92.0	72.8	77.1	80.4
By type of creditor										
Official	47.1	47.4	48.3	55.6	57.7	57.8	51.3	32.5	33.2	34.5
Banks	19.2	20.1	20.0	20.5	21.6	20.2	1.5	1.2	1.2	1.1
Other private	16.0	17.6	19.5	20.2	21.2	25.5	49.0	51.2	55.6	57.6
By external financing source										
Net debtor countries										
Total debt	**1,848.7**	**1,797.1**	**1,788.5**	**1,847.4**	**2,006.3**	**2,160.9**	**2,169.7**	**2,311.5**	**2,445.4**	**2,574.1**
By maturity										
Short-term	226.9	233.2	217.7	203.8	236.8	277.8	317.3	357.9	385.3	416.0
Long-term	1,621.8	1,563.9	1,570.9	1,643.6	1,769.5	1,883.1	1,852.4	1,953.6	2,060.1	2,158.2
By type of creditor										
Official	695.9	671.7	681.0	714.2	740.9	730.9	666.9	609.8	609.1	616.3
Banks	542.0	522.9	494.7	498.6	528.4	580.6	565.0	639.2	679.1	726.9
Other private	610.8	602.5	612.9	634.6	737.0	849.5	937.9	1062.4	1157.2	1231.0
Official financing										
Total debt	**182.4**	**180.8**	**184.2**	**198.4**	**212.6**	**221.7**	**217.7**	**206.7**	**209.3**	**218.1**
By maturity										
Short-term	15.3	16.2	17.2	10.7	10.3	10.0	11.0	11.3	10.7	10.9
Long-term	167.1	164.7	167.0	187.7	202.4	211.7	206.7	195.4	198.5	207.2
By type of creditor										
Official	120.5	116.4	119.1	136.1	144.2	149.1	142.9	129.1	129.6	135.6
Banks	18.5	19.9	21.6	22.0	24.3	25.6	27.1	27.7	28.1	28.7
Other private	43.4	44.5	43.5	40.3	44.0	47.0	47.8	49.9	51.6	53.8

Table 39 *(concluded)*

	1999	2000	2001	2002	2003	2004	2005	2006	2007	2008
Net debtor countries by debt-servicing experience										
Countries with arrears and/or rescheduling during 2001–05										
Total debt	**554.6**	**531.5**	**534.1**	**523.1**	**550.4**	**570.1**	**536.6**	**526.7**	**528.2**	**544.2**
By maturity										
Short-term	35.1	35.5	30.2	21.5	23.2	26.2	30.2	30.0	30.2	30.7
Long-term	519.5	496.0	503.9	501.6	527.2	543.9	506.4	496.7	498.0	513.5
By type of creditor										
Official	296.3	290.5	291.8	298.1	316.6	316.3	296.7	259.8	253.8	255.2
Banks	104.3	92.0	92.0	81.7	82.2	88.8	86.5	99.4	105.0	114.8
Other private	154.0	149.1	150.3	143.3	151.7	165.0	153.4	167.6	169.3	174.2
Other groups										
Heavily indebted poor countries										
Total debt	**107.9**	**108.7**	**110.1**	**117.5**	**125.6**	**130.2**	**117.3**	**81.0**	**77.5**	**81.8**
By maturity										
Short-term	0.9	0.9	0.6	0.6	0.4	0.6	0.5	0.5	0.6	0.6
Long-term	107.0	107.8	109.5	116.9	125.2	129.6	116.8	80.6	76.9	81.2
By type of creditor										
Official	101.7	103.4	102.4	108.6	115.0	117.8	107.0	69.1	65.2	69.8
Banks	4.1	2.8	6.4	6.9	7.4	8.3	6.1	7.6	8.0	7.8
Other private	2.1	2.5	1.3	1.9	3.2	4.1	4.2	4.2	4.3	4.2
Middle East and north Africa										
Total debt	**255.2**	**242.3**	**234.8**	**244.4**	**264.4**	**292.5**	**316.0**	**350.2**	**388.8**	**412.2**
By maturity										
Short-term	57.4	55.1	58.8	59.3	71.2	89.6	104.6	125.8	143.1	154.1
Long-term	197.8	187.2	176.0	185.1	193.2	202.9	211.3	224.5	245.7	258.1
By type of creditor										
Official	124.1	118.3	113.7	123.9	134.2	135.6	131.0	121.0	123.4	127.9
Banks	68.7	63.6	59.5	54.5	60.0	73.8	82.5	102.0	116.5	125.1
Other private	62.4	60.4	61.6	66.0	70.2	83.2	102.5	127.3	148.8	159.2

Table 40. Other Emerging Market and Developing Countries: Ratio of External Debt to GDP[1]

	1999	2000	2001	2002	2003	2004	2005	2006	2007	2008
Other emerging market and developing countries	**42.0**	**37.3**	**36.9**	**37.0**	**35.7**	**33.0**	**28.7**	**26.3**	**25.3**	**24.4**
Regional groups										
Africa	68.6	64.1	61.9	60.4	54.0	46.9	37.0	28.1	25.5	23.2
Sub-Sahara	72.2	68.3	67.0	65.2	58.1	51.1	40.0	30.9	27.6	25.0
Central and eastern Europe	48.0	50.3	52.9	52.7	53.7	54.0	49.9	52.9	50.9	50.5
Commonwealth of Independent States[2]	75.2	56.4	45.7	43.1	41.8	36.3	33.5	30.0	28.6	27.9
Developing Asia	32.3	28.3	27.7	25.7	23.7	22.1	20.2	19.1	18.2	17.5
Middle East	30.3	26.2	25.4	26.1	25.2	25.3	23.6	24.0	25.3	24.7
Western Hemisphere	43.5	37.9	39.6	44.1	43.7	38.2	29.5	24.6	23.4	22.5
Analytical groups										
By source of export earnings										
Fuel	51.6	40.3	36.0	36.0	34.2	30.4	26.6	23.1	23.1	22.5
Nonfuel	40.3	36.7	37.1	37.2	36.0	33.6	29.2	27.2	25.9	24.9
of which, primary products	61.5	63.4	66.8	64.9	70.1	60.6	50.2	35.0	33.8	29.2
By external financing source										
Net debtor countries	48.6	44.6	45.4	46.7	45.2	42.0	35.8	33.2	31.7	30.7
of which, official financing	53.6	51.7	52.6	56.0	55.3	50.8	43.4	36.3	33.6	32.2
Net debtor countries by debt-servicing experience										
Countries with arrears and/or rescheduling during 2001–05	75.7	70.4	71.4	80.8	74.7	68.0	54.9	45.1	40.0	36.3
Other groups										
Heavily indebted poor countries	100.1	104.4	103.0	104.4	98.7	89.8	70.9	43.3	38.3	37.2
Middle East and north Africa	37.7	32.3	31.0	31.9	30.5	29.0	25.9	24.7	25.5	24.7

[1]Debt at year-end in percent of GDP in year indicated.
[2]Mongolia, which is not a member of the Commonwealth of Independent States, is included in this group for reasons of geography and similarities in economic structure.

Table 41. Other Emerging Market and Developing Countries: Debt-Service Ratios[1]
(Percent of exports of goods and services)

	1999	2000	2001	2002	2003	2004	2005	2006	2007	2008
Interest payments[2]										
Other emerging market and developing countries	**8.7**	**7.4**	**7.2**	**6.1**	**5.7**	**4.6**	**4.4**	**4.4**	**4.2**	**4.0**
Regional groups										
Africa	9.2	7.1	7.1	5.0	4.6	3.6	3.2	3.0	2.6	2.4
Sub-Sahara	6.7	5.7	5.9	3.7	3.9	3.0	3.0	2.7	2.5	2.3
Central and eastern Europe	10.6	10.1	10.2	9.2	8.7	7.4	7.0	6.9	7.1	6.7
Commonwealth of Independent States[3]	10.3	8.0	7.4	7.5	11.0	8.3	9.4	10.9	9.9	9.9
Developing Asia	5.5	4.7	4.2	3.5	2.9	2.3	2.2	2.2	2.1	2.0
Middle East	2.7	2.1	2.0	1.7	2.4	1.9	1.8	1.9	2.2	2.3
Western Hemisphere	15.4	13.7	13.9	11.9	9.8	8.0	7.4	6.5	6.0	5.7
Analytical groups										
By source of export earnings										
Fuel	7.7	5.4	5.6	4.7	6.5	4.9	4.8	5.4	5.2	5.1
Nonfuel	8.9	8.0	7.7	6.5	5.5	4.5	4.2	4.0	3.9	3.7
of which, primary products	5.8	7.5	7.1	5.3	4.2	3.1	2.7	2.1	1.9	1.8
By external financing source										
Net debtor countries	11.0	10.1	9.7	8.2	7.1	5.8	5.5	5.2	5.2	5.0
of which, official financing	8.0	7.6	7.5	6.6	5.7	4.7	4.4	4.1	4.0	3.8
Net debtor countries by debt-servicing experience										
Countries with arrears and/or rescheduling during 2001–05	15.1	14.4	12.6	9.5	6.4	5.2	5.0	4.5	4.6	4.2
Other groups										
Heavily indebted poor countries	6.8	7.0	7.2	4.7	4.7	4.0	3.7	2.5	2.3	2.3
Middle East and north Africa	4.7	3.3	3.2	2.6	3.0	2.3	2.0	2.1	2.3	2.3
Amortization[2]										
Other emerging market and developing countries	**16.5**	**15.7**	**15.1**	**14.0**	**13.0**	**10.3**	**10.5**	**9.4**	**6.6**	**6.2**
Regional groups										
Africa	10.6	9.9	10.2	8.6	8.7	8.2	7.8	9.5	4.9	3.8
Sub-Sahara	9.6	8.9	9.8	7.0	7.4	6.8	7.2	7.6	5.3	3.7
Central and eastern Europe	15.8	15.0	16.6	15.5	15.7	14.2	13.4	13.2	12.0	11.8
Commonwealth of Independent States[3]	11.6	29.3	16.6	18.8	17.2	16.1	18.3	16.1	7.9	8.0
Developing Asia	10.6	8.8	10.3	10.5	8.6	5.7	5.2	4.4	3.8	3.5
Middle East	7.3	5.2	7.3	4.2	3.6	3.4	3.4	4.4	2.9	2.7
Western Hemisphere	35.4	30.9	28.2	26.3	26.9	20.7	23.8	18.9	12.3	12.2
Analytical groups										
By source of export earnings										
Fuel	9.6	13.8	11.1	10.2	9.5	8.5	9.1	9.5	4.5	4.3
Nonfuel	18.2	16.3	16.2	15.1	14.0	10.9	11.0	9.4	7.2	6.9
of which, primary products	13.3	15.7	16.6	19.4	16.6	15.4	9.8	10.2	6.1	7.0
By external financing source										
Net debtor countries	22.9	20.9	21.0	19.9	19.0	15.0	15.4	13.3	10.3	10.0
of which, official financing	12.1	11.4	11.6	12.3	11.6	10.7	8.9	8.7	5.6	6.0
Net debtor countries by debt-servicing experience										
Countries with arrears and/or rescheduling during 2001–05	27.7	26.5	32.9	26.5	25.1	18.6	21.7	16.6	11.2	9.7
Other groups										
Heavily indebted poor countries	11.6	12.9	13.2	8.0	7.4	9.5	5.3	21.2	8.7	5.6
Middle East and north Africa	8.2	6.1	7.9	5.4	4.9	4.6	4.1	5.7	3.0	2.9

[1]Excludes service payments to the International Monetary Fund.

[2]Interest payments on total debt and amortization on long-term debt. Estimates through 2006 reflect debt-service payments actually made. The estimates for 2007 and 2008 take into account projected exceptional financing items, including accumulation of arrears and rescheduling agreements. In some cases, amortization on account of debt-reduction operations is included.

[3]Mongolia, which is not a member of the Commonwealth of Independent States, is included in this group for reasons of geography and similarities in economic structure.

Table 42. IMF Charges and Repurchases to the IMF[1]
(Percent of exports of goods and services)

	1999	2000	2001	2002	2003	2004	2005	2006
Other emerging market and developing countries	**1.2**	**1.2**	**0.7**	**1.1**	**1.2**	**0.7**	**1.2**	**0.7**
Regional groups								
Africa	0.5	0.2	0.3	0.4	0.3	0.2	0.3	—
Sub-Sahara	0.2	0.1	0.1	0.2	—	0.1	0.1	—
Excluding Nigeria and South Africa	0.4	0.3	0.3	0.4	0.1	0.1	0.2	0.1
Central and eastern Europe	0.4	0.3	0.9	2.8	0.8	1.3	1.8	1.4
Commonwealth of Independent States[2]	4.9	3.2	3.1	1.2	1.1	0.7	1.0	0.1
Russia	5.9	3.1	3.8	1.4	1.3	0.9	1.3	—
Excluding Russia	2.9	3.4	1.4	0.7	0.6	0.5	0.4	0.3
Developing Asia	0.2	0.2	0.6	0.6	0.3	0.2	0.1	0.5
Excluding China and India	0.3	0.4	1.2	1.4	0.8	0.5	0.4	1.5
Middle East	0.1	0.1	0.1	—	—	—	-	—
Western Hemisphere	2.7	3.6	0.5	1.7	4.6	2.3	4.6	1.7
Analytical groups								
By source of export earnings								
Fuel	1.9	1.0	1.1	0.5	0.5	0.3	0.4	—
Nonfuel	1.0	1.3	0.6	1.3	1.4	0.9	1.4	0.9
By external financing source								
Net debtor countries	1.3	1.6	0.8	1.7	2.0	1.3	2.1	1.3
of which, official financing	2.2	2.7	4.7	5.3	8.4	6.7	0.6	1.8
Net debtor countries by debt-servicing experience								
Countries with arrears and/or rescheduling during 2001–05	1.3	1.4	2.4	2.6	4.2	3.2	2.0	5.1
Other groups								
Heavily indebted poor countries	0.2	0.1	0.2	0.9	0.1	—	0.1	0.3
Middle East and north Africa	0.3	0.1	0.2	0.2	0.2	0.1	0.1	—
Memorandum								
Total, billions of U.S. dollars[3]								
General Resources Account	18.531	22.863	13.849	22.352	29.425	23.578	46.138	31.664
Charges	2.829	2.846	2.638	2.806	3.020	3.384	3.201	1.586
Repurchases	15.702	20.017	11.211	19.546	26.405	20.193	42.937	30.079
PRGF[4]	0.855	0.835	1.042	1.214	1.225	1.432	1.360	4.360
Interest	0.042	0.038	0.038	0.040	0.046	0.050	0.048	0.028
Repayments	0.813	0.798	1.005	1.174	1.179	1.382	1.312	4.332

[1]Excludes advanced economies. Charges on, and repurchases (or repayments of principal) for, use of IMF credit.
[2]Mongolia, which is not a member of the Commonwealth of Independent States, is included in this group for reasons of geography and similarities in economic structure.
[3]The data are converted to U.S. dollar values at annual average exchange rates.
[4]Poverty Reduction and Growth Facility (formerly ESAF—Enhanced Structural Adjustment Facility).

Table 43. Summary of Sources and Uses of World Saving
(Percent of GDP)

	Averages 1985–92	Averages 1993–2000	2001	2002	2003	2004	2005	2006	2007	2008	Average 2009–12
World											
Saving	22.8	22.1	21.2	20.5	20.8	21.7	22.1	22.8	22.9	23.2	23.9
Investment	23.5	22.5	21.4	20.8	21.1	21.9	22.3	22.8	23.1	23.5	24.4
Advanced economies											
Saving	22.3	21.7	20.4	19.1	19.0	19.5	19.3	19.8	19.5	19.6	19.9
Investment	22.8	21.9	20.8	19.9	19.9	20.4	20.8	21.2	21.1	21.2	21.7
Net lending	–0.5	–0.2	–0.4	–0.7	–0.9	–0.9	–1.5	–1.5	–1.6	–1.6	–1.8
Current transfers	–0.4	–0.5	–0.5	–0.6	–0.6	–0.6	–0.7	–0.6	–0.7	–0.6	–0.6
Factor income	–0.2	—	0.6	0.2	0.1	0.2	0.2	0.4	0.2	0.1	—
Resource balance	—	0.4	–0.5	–0.4	–0.4	–0.5	–1.1	–1.2	–1.1	–1.1	–1.2
United States											
Saving	16.7	16.8	16.4	14.2	13.3	13.2	12.9	13.7	12.9	12.9	13.3
Investment	19.3	19.4	19.1	18.4	18.4	19.3	19.7	20.0	19.0	18.9	19.3
Net lending	–2.6	–2.7	–2.8	–4.2	–5.1	–6.1	–6.8	–6.2	–6.1	–6.0	–6.0
Current transfers	–0.4	–0.6	–0.5	–0.6	–0.6	–0.7	–0.7	–0.6	–0.7	–0.5	–0.5
Factor income	–0.2	–0.2	1.3	0.5	—	0.2	–0.3	0.2	–0.1	–0.4	–0.8
Resource balance	–2.0	–1.9	–3.6	–4.0	–4.5	–5.2	–5.8	–5.8	–5.3	–5.1	–4.7
Euro area											
Saving	...	21.4	21.3	20.8	20.7	21.5	21.0	21.3	21.6	21.9	22.3
Investment	...	21.1	21.0	20.0	20.1	20.4	20.8	21.3	21.7	22.1	22.7
Net lending	...	0.3	0.2	0.8	0.6	1.1	0.2	–0.1	–0.1	–0.2	–0.4
Current transfers[1]	–0.5	–0.7	–0.8	–0.7	–0.8	–0.8	–0.9	–0.8	–0.9	–0.9	–1.0
Factor income[1]	–0.3	–0.3	–0.6	–1.0	–0.9	–0.3	–0.4	–0.5	–0.6	–0.6	–0.6
Resource balance[1]	1.0	1.6	1.4	2.3	2.1	2.1	1.4	1.1	1.2	1.1	1.0
Germany											
Saving	24.0	20.7	19.5	19.3	19.3	21.4	21.7	22.8	23.3	23.5	23.2
Investment	21.5	21.7	19.5	17.3	17.4	17.1	17.1	17.7	18.0	18.4	19.1
Net lending	2.5	–1.0	—	2.0	1.9	4.3	4.6	5.1	5.3	5.2	4.1
Current transfers	–1.6	–1.5	–1.3	–1.3	–1.3	–1.3	–1.3	–1.2	–1.3	–1.3	–1.3
Factor income	0.9	–0.1	–0.5	–0.8	–0.7	0.6	0.9	1.0	1.0	1.1	1.1
Resource balance	3.2	0.5	1.8	4.1	3.9	5.0	4.9	5.2	5.5	5.4	4.3
France											
Saving	20.9	20.2	21.6	20.0	19.4	19.0	18.6	18.4	18.3	18.1	18.4
Investment	21.2	18.5	20.0	19.0	18.9	19.4	20.2	20.5	20.4	20.5	20.4
Net lending	–0.3	1.7	1.6	1.0	0.4	–0.3	–1.6	–2.1	–2.2	–2.3	–2.0
Current transfers	–0.6	–0.8	–1.1	–1.0	–1.1	–1.1	–1.3	–1.0	–1.0	–1.0	–1.0
Factor income	–0.3	0.3	1.1	0.3	0.4	0.6	0.8	0.6	0.6	0.6	0.6
Resource balance	0.6	2.1	1.6	1.7	1.1	0.1	–1.0	–1.7	–1.8	–2.0	–1.6
Italy											
Saving	20.4	20.9	20.5	20.5	19.4	19.9	19.0	19.0	20.0	20.7	21.7
Investment	22.2	19.5	20.6	21.1	20.7	20.8	20.6	21.2	22.2	22.9	23.6
Net lending	–1.8	1.4	–0.1	–0.7	–1.3	–0.9	–1.6	–2.2	–2.2	–2.2	–1.9
Current transfers	–0.3	–0.5	–0.5	–0.4	–0.5	–0.6	–0.6	–0.5	–0.5	–0.5	–0.5
Factor income	–1.7	–1.2	–0.9	–1.2	–1.3	–1.1	–1.0	–0.9	–0.9	–0.9	–0.9
Resource balance	0.2	3.1	1.4	1.0	0.6	0.7	–0.1	–0.8	–0.7	–0.8	–0.5
Japan											
Saving	33.6	30.0	26.9	25.9	26.1	26.8	27.0	28.0	28.5	28.4	28.3
Investment	30.8	27.5	24.8	23.1	22.8	23.0	23.4	24.1	24.7	24.8	25.0
Net lending	2.8	2.5	2.1	2.9	3.2	3.7	3.6	3.9	3.8	3.6	3.3
Current transfers	–0.1	–0.2	–0.2	–0.1	–0.2	–0.2	–0.2	–0.2	–0.2	–0.2	–0.2
Factor income	0.7	1.1	1.7	1.7	1.7	1.9	2.3	2.7	2.6	2.7	2.9
Resource balance	2.3	1.5	0.6	1.3	1.7	2.0	1.5	1.4	1.5	1.1	0.6
United Kingdom											
Saving	16.6	15.8	15.0	15.2	15.1	15.3	14.8	14.9	15.3	15.6	16.1
Investment	19.1	17.1	17.2	16.8	16.5	16.9	17.2	17.8	18.3	18.7	19.4
Net lending	–2.5	–1.3	–2.2	–1.6	–1.3	–1.6	–2.4	–2.9	–3.1	–3.1	–3.3
Current transfers	–0.7	–0.9	–0.7	–0.9	–0.9	–0.9	–1.0	–0.9	–0.9	–0.9	–0.9
Factor income	–0.1	0.4	1.2	2.2	2.2	2.3	2.2	2.3	2.2	2.1	2.0
Resource balance	–1.7	–0.8	–2.7	–2.9	–2.7	–3.0	–3.6	–4.3	–4.3	–4.4	–4.4
Canada											
Saving	18.0	18.7	22.2	21.0	21.2	22.9	23.8	23.7	23.1	23.5	24.3
Investment	21.0	19.4	19.2	19.3	20.0	20.7	21.5	22.0	22.4	22.9	23.8
Net lending	–3.0	–0.7	3.0	1.7	1.2	2.1	2.3	1.7	0.7	0.6	0.5
Current transfers	–0.2	—	0.1	—	—	—	—	—	—	—	—
Factor income	–3.3	–3.4	–2.8	–2.6	–2.5	–1.9	–1.4	–0.9	–0.9	–0.8	–0.8
Resource balance	0.5	2.7	5.7	4.3	3.7	4.1	3.7	2.6	1.6	1.4	1.3

Table 43 *(continued)*

	Averages		2001	2002	2003	2004	2005	2006	2007	2008	Average 2009–12
	1985–92	1993–2000									
Newly industrialized Asian economies											
Saving	35.4	33.5	30.0	29.7	31.4	32.7	31.4	31.3	31.2	31.2	31.0
Investment	29.1	30.7	25.3	24.6	24.5	26.1	25.6	25.7	25.9	26.1	26.8
Net lending	6.3	2.9	4.6	5.1	6.9	6.6	5.8	5.6	5.3	5.1	4.2
Current transfers	0.1	−0.3	−0.6	−0.7	−0.7	−0.7	−0.7	−0.8	−0.8	−0.7	−0.7
Factor income	1.2	0.6	0.8	0.6	1.0	0.7	0.5	0.4	0.7	0.7	0.7
Resource balance	5.0	2.5	4.5	5.2	6.7	6.6	6.1	6.0	5.4	5.1	4.3
Other emerging market and developing countries											
Saving	24.4	24.0	24.6	25.8	27.9	29.6	31.1	31.8	32.0	32.6	33.4
Investment	25.9	25.1	24.0	24.6	25.9	27.2	27.0	27.4	28.7	29.5	30.8
Net lending	−1.6	−1.1	0.6	1.2	2.0	2.4	4.0	4.4	3.3	3.1	2.6
Current transfers	0.4	0.9	1.2	1.4	1.6	1.6	1.6	1.6	1.4	1.4	1.3
Factor income	−1.6	−1.5	−2.0	−2.0	−2.0	−2.0	−2.0	−1.9	−1.4	−1.2	−0.9
Resource balance	−0.4	−0.5	1.4	1.8	2.4	2.9	4.4	4.7	3.3	3.0	2.2
Memorandum											
Acquisition of foreign assets	0.8	3.6	3.2	3.5	5.8	7.2	9.1	9.8	8.1	7.7	6.8
Change in reserves	0.2	1.1	1.4	2.3	3.8	4.8	5.1	5.5	4.7	4.4	3.9
Regional groups											
Africa											
Saving	18.1	17.5	20.4	18.7	20.8	22.1	23.3	24.8	24.0	22.9	22.6
Investment	20.8	19.8	20.2	19.2	20.9	21.9	21.6	22.6	24.0	22.9	23.5
Net lending	−2.7	−2.3	0.2	−0.5	−0.1	0.2	1.7	2.2	0.1	—	−0.9
Current transfers	2.3	2.5	2.9	3.0	3.1	3.2	3.2	2.9	2.9	2.6	2.5
Factor income	−5.1	−4.3	−4.6	−3.8	−4.6	−5.0	−5.9	−5.5	−4.5	−4.1	−3.3
Resource balance	0.1	−0.6	1.9	0.3	1.4	1.9	4.4	4.8	1.7	1.4	−0.1
Memorandum											
Acquisition of foreign assets	0.2	1.7	5.8	2.7	3.6	4.4	5.8	7.6	6.2	6.5	5.7
Change in reserves	0.2	0.8	2.2	1.2	2.0	4.7	5.2	5.3	4.5	4.9	4.0
Central and eastern Europe											
Saving	27.1	20.9	19.2	18.9	18.6	18.8	18.8	18.3	19.2	20.1	21.6
Investment	26.7	23.9	22.0	22.5	22.9	24.5	24.0	24.7	25.3	26.0	27.0
Net lending	0.4	−3.0	−2.8	−3.5	−4.3	−5.7	−5.2	−6.4	−6.2	−6.0	−5.4
Current transfers	1.5	1.9	1.9	1.8	1.7	1.7	1.7	1.7	1.7	1.7	1.7
Factor income	−0.5	−1.0	−1.3	−1.6	−1.8	−2.8	−2.6	−2.4	−2.1	−1.9	−2.0
Resource balance	−0.6	−3.9	−3.3	−3.8	−4.2	−4.6	−4.4	−5.7	−5.8	−5.8	−5.0
Memorandum											
Acquisition of foreign assets	1.0	2.7	1.7	2.8	2.0	3.7	5.1	4.8	2.3	2.3	2.1
Change in reserves	−0.6	2.0	0.5	2.7	1.4	1.3	4.1	1.6	1.0	1.4	1.2
Commonwealth of Independent States[2]											
Saving	...	23.9	29.4	26.4	27.1	29.2	28.9	28.0	26.4	26.4	25.2
Investment	...	20.9	21.1	19.8	20.9	21.1	20.5	20.6	21.6	22.2	23.7
Net lending	...	3.0	8.3	6.6	6.2	8.1	8.5	7.4	4.8	4.1	1.5
Current transfers	...	0.5	0.5	0.6	0.6	0.5	0.5	0.7	0.7	0.6	0.6
Factor income	...	−1.5	−1.4	−1.9	−2.9	−2.2	−3.0	−3.5	−2.6	−2.2	−1.8
Resource balance	...	4.0	9.1	7.9	8.4	9.8	11.0	10.2	6.7	5.7	2.8
Memorandum											
Acquisition of foreign assets	...	4.1	6.8	5.5	11.6	14.3	15.7	16.0	11.4	10.2	7.2
Change in reserves	...	0.9	3.5	3.3	5.6	6.9	7.5	9.9	7.1	5.6	3.6

Table 43 *(continued)*

	Averages		2001	2002	2003	2004	2005	2006	2007	2008	Average 2009–12
	1985–92	1993–2000									
Developing Asia											
Saving	28.0	32.9	31.6	33.6	36.7	38.4	40.7	42.2	44.0	45.6	46.8
Investment	30.9	33.0	30.1	31.2	33.9	35.8	36.6	36.9	38.2	39.5	40.8
Net lending	−2.9	−0.1	1.5	2.4	2.8	2.6	4.1	5.4	5.8	6.1	6.0
Current transfers	0.8	1.2	1.7	1.9	2.1	2.0	2.1	2.0	1.7	1.6	1.4
Factor income	−1.9	−1.3	−1.8	−1.6	−1.1	−1.0	−0.8	−0.7	−0.6	−0.5	−0.3
Resource balance	−1.7	−0.1	1.6	2.1	1.8	1.6	2.7	4.0	4.6	5.0	5.0
Memorandum											
Acquisition of foreign assets	1.5	6.1	3.3	5.2	6.2	7.3	9.9	11.0	10.2	9.7	9.0
Change in reserves	0.6	1.6	2.3	4.2	5.4	7.4	5.8	6.7	6.6	6.3	6.0
Middle East											
Saving	16.8	24.2	27.3	27.5	31.3	34.8	40.8	40.4	37.3	37.0	37.6
Investment	23.2	22.6	21.2	23.0	23.0	22.8	22.2	22.5	25.3	26.5	28.7
Net lending	−6.5	1.5	6.1	4.6	8.3	11.9	18.6	17.9	12.0	10.5	8.9
Current transfers	−3.4	−3.0	−2.5	−2.5	−2.3	−2.0	−1.7	−1.6	−1.8	−1.8	−1.6
Factor income	1.2	2.8	1.4	0.4	0.2	0.3	0.7	1.4	2.6	2.8	3.3
Resource balance	−4.3	1.7	7.2	6.7	10.4	13.6	19.6	18.0	11.2	9.5	7.2
Memorandum											
Acquisition of foreign assets	—	3.5	5.1	2.7	12.9	17.3	22.3	23.5	17.0	17.1	15.3
Change in reserves	−0.4	0.8	1.8	0.6	4.6	5.5	10.4	10.7	6.2	5.4	5.4
Western Hemisphere											
Saving	19.0	17.1	16.5	17.8	18.7	20.8	21.0	21.7	21.2	21.0	20.5
Investment	19.1	20.0	19.5	18.6	18.2	19.8	19.5	20.0	20.7	21.1	21.3
Net lending	−0.1	−2.9	−3.0	−0.8	0.5	1.0	1.5	1.6	0.5	−0.2	−0.8
Current transfers	0.8	0.9	1.4	1.7	2.0	2.1	2.0	2.0	1.9	1.9	2.0
Factor income	−2.6	−2.5	−3.1	−3.1	−3.2	−3.3	−3.1	−3.1	−2.6	−2.2	−1.9
Resource balance	1.7	−1.4	−1.2	0.5	1.7	2.2	2.5	2.7	1.1	0.1	−0.9
Memorandum											
Acquisition of foreign assets	0.5	1.8	1.6	1.1	3.1	2.8	2.9	2.8	2.8	2.3	1.7
Change in reserves	0.4	0.5	−0.2	0.1	2.0	1.1	1.3	1.6	1.8	1.1	0.8
Analytical groups											
By source of export earnings											
Fuel											
Saving	26.9	24.8	30.1	28.3	30.6	33.6	37.5	37.0	33.7	33.1	32.0
Investment	29.1	22.5	22.7	22.8	22.5	22.7	21.9	22.2	24.1	24.7	26.1
Net lending	−2.2	2.3	7.4	5.5	8.1	10.9	15.6	14.8	9.6	8.5	5.8
Current transfers	−1.4	−2.0	−1.9	−1.8	−1.4	−1.1	−0.8	−0.8	−0.8	−0.8	−0.7
Factor income	−0.8	−0.6	−1.1	−2.0	−2.5	−2.3	−2.5	−2.2	−1.1	−0.8	−0.2
Resource balance	—	5.0	10.4	9.3	12.1	14.3	18.9	17.7	11.5	10.1	6.7
Memorandum											
Acquisition of foreign assets	0.6	3.6	6.2	3.3	12.0	14.6	18.5	18.4	13.3	13.3	10.8
Change in reserves	−0.2	0.7	2.6	1.4	5.3	7.0	9.7	10.3	7.0	6.4	5.1
Nonfuel											
Saving	23.2	23.8	23.4	25.3	27.3	28.7	29.4	30.4	31.5	32.5	33.8
Investment	24.7	25.6	24.3	25.0	26.6	28.2	28.3	28.8	30.0	30.9	32.1
Net lending	−1.4	−1.8	−0.9	0.3	0.7	0.4	1.1	1.5	1.6	1.6	1.7
Current transfers	1.1	1.4	1.9	2.1	2.3	2.2	2.3	2.2	2.0	2.0	1.8
Factor income	−1.9	−1.7	−2.2	−2.0	−1.8	−2.0	−1.9	−1.8	−1.5	−1.3	−1.1
Resource balance	−0.7	−1.6	−0.5	0.2	0.3	0.2	0.7	1.2	1.1	1.0	1.0
Memorandum											
Acquisition of foreign assets	0.8	3.6	2.6	3.5	4.5	5.4	6.7	7.5	6.6	6.2	5.7
Change in reserves	0.3	1.1	1.2	2.5	3.5	4.3	3.9	4.2	4.1	3.8	3.6

Table 43 *(concluded)*

	Averages		2001	2002	2003	2004	2005	2006	2007	2008	Average 2009–12
	1985–92	1993–2000									
By external financing source											
Net debtor countries											
Saving	20.7	19.5	18.3	19.4	20.8	21.5	21.4	21.8	22.1	22.4	23.1
Investment	23.1	22.3	20.3	20.3	21.3	22.8	23.0	23.4	24.1	24.5	25.4
Net lending	–2.3	–2.8	–2.0	–0.8	–0.6	–1.3	–1.6	–1.6	–2.0	–2.1	–2.4
Current transfers	1.4	1.8	2.4	2.6	2.8	2.7	2.8	2.7	2.6	2.6	2.4
Factor income	–2.9	–2.9	–2.6	–2.4	–2.4	–2.8	–2.9	–2.9	–2.5	–2.3	–2.1
Resource balance	–0.9	–2.6	–1.8	–1.0	–0.9	–1.2	–1.4	–1.4	–2.1	–2.4	–2.7
Memorandum											
Acquisition of foreign assets	0.6	1.7	1.9	2.3	3.0	3.0	3.3	4.3	3.0	2.6	2.1
Change in reserves	0.3	0.9	0.4	1.6	2.0	1.6	1.8	2.3	1.8	1.5	1.2
Official financing											
Saving	15.1	16.8	19.0	19.9	21.2	21.0	20.8	20.6	20.7	21.0	21.3
Investment	18.2	20.4	20.0	20.4	21.3	21.3	21.7	22.1	22.9	23.2	23.3
Net lending	–3.1	–3.5	–1.1	–0.5	–0.1	–0.3	–0.8	–1.5	–2.2	–2.2	–2.0
Current transfers	3.1	4.5	5.7	6.3	6.8	6.7	7.2	7.2	7.2	7.2	6.8
Factor income	–0.2	–0.2	–2.1	–2.3	–2.9	–2.9	–3.3	–3.7	–2.9	–2.3	–1.4
Resource balance	–6.0	–6.0	–4.7	–4.5	–4.0	–4.1	–4.7	–5.1	–6.6	–7.1	–7.3
Memorandum											
Acquisition of foreign assets	–0.5	0.4	2.4	1.8	4.8	3.1	4.1	4.7	3.2	2.8	1.8
Change in reserves	0.2	0.3	0.3	0.3	2.5	1.5	0.8	1.6	0.8	0.8	0.6
Net debtor countries by debt-servicing experience											
Countries with arrears and/or rescheduling during 2001–05											
Saving	16.2	19.3	16.4	19.2	21.7	20.4	20.5	22.2	22.0	21.5	21.7
Investment	22.5	22.8	18.3	17.1	19.7	20.5	21.2	22.1	22.9	22.6	23.8
Net lending	–6.3	–3.5	–1.9	2.1	2.0	–0.1	–0.7	0.1	–0.9	–1.1	–2.0
Current transfers	1.4	1.9	2.8	3.7	3.9	3.8	4.3	4.1	3.8	3.6	3.3
Factor income	–6.1	–6.1	–4.4	–3.5	–3.5	–4.5	–4.4	–4.1	–3.6	–3.4	–3.0
Resource balance	–1.7	–2.4	–0.3	1.8	1.6	0.6	–0.5	0.1	–1.1	–1.3	–2.4
Memorandum											
Acquisition of foreign assets	0.4	1.9	–0.3	3.1	3.7	2.4	2.4	3.1	2.4	1.9	1.2
Change in reserves	0.2	0.6	–1.6	0.7	2.1	1.7	1.6	2.2	1.8	1.9	1.1

Note: The estimates in this table are based on individual countries' national accounts and balance of payments statistics. Country group composites are calculated as the sum of the U.S. dollar values for the relevant individual countries. This differs from the calculations in the April 2005 and earlier *World Economic Outlooks,* where the composites were weighted by GDP valued at purchasing power parities (PPPs) as a share of total world GDP. For many countries, the estimates of national saving are built up from national accounts data on gross domestic investment and from balance-of-payments-based data on net foreign investment. The latter, which is equivalent to the current account balance, comprises three components: current transfers, net factor income, and the resource balance. The mixing of data source, which is dictated by availability, implies that the estimates for national saving that are derived incorporate the statistical discrepancies. Furthermore, error omissions and asymmetries in balance of payments statistics affect the estimates for net lending; at the global level, net lending, which in theory would be zero, equals the world current account discrepancy. Notwithstanding these statistical shortcomings, flow of funds estimates, such as those presented in these tables, provide a useful framework for analyzing development in saving and investment, both over time and across regions and countries.

[1]Calculated from the data of individual euro area countries.

[2]Mongolia, which is not a member of the Commonwealth of Independent States, is included in this group for reasons of geography and similarities in economic structure.

Table 44. Summary of World Medium-Term Baseline Scenario

	Eight-Year Averages		Four-Year Average 2005–08	2005	2006	2007	2008	Four-Year Average 2009–12
	1989–96	1997–2004						
	Annual percent change unless otherwise noted							
World real GDP	**3.1**	**3.8**	**5.0**	**4.9**	**5.4**	**4.9**	**4.9**	**4.8**
Advanced economies	2.7	2.7	2.7	2.5	3.1	2.5	2.7	2.8
Other emerging market and developing countries	3.7	5.3	7.5	7.5	7.9	7.5	7.1	6.7
Memorandum								
Potential output								
Major advanced economies	2.5	2.5	2.5	2.5	2.5	2.5	2.5	2.5
World trade, volume[1]	**6.6**	**6.5**	**7.8**	**7.4**	**9.2**	**7.0**	**7.4**	**6.8**
Imports								
Advanced economies	6.1	6.2	6.0	6.1	7.4	4.7	5.7	5.6
Other emerging market and developing countries	7.5	7.6	12.9	12.1	15.0	12.5	12.2	9.9
Exports								
Advanced economies	6.6	5.7	6.3	5.6	8.4	5.5	5.8	5.4
Other emerging market and developing countries	7.4	8.6	10.5	11.2	10.6	10.4	9.9	9.0
Terms of trade								
Advanced economies	−0.1	−0.0	−0.7	−1.4	−1.3	−0.1	−0.0	0.1
Other emerging market and developing countries	−0.3	0.7	2.0	5.5	4.1	−2.4	0.9	−0.2
World prices in U.S. dollars								
Manufactures	2.1	−0.2	3.3	3.4	4.4	4.4	1.1	1.5
Oil	4.1	8.0	14.4	41.3	20.5	−5.5	6.6	−0.6
Nonfuel primary commodities	−0.4	−0.1	7.7	10.3	28.4	4.2	−8.8	−5.7
Consumer prices								
Advanced economies	4.0	1.8	2.1	2.3	2.3	1.8	2.1	2.1
Other emerging market and developing countries	62.0	8.0	5.2	5.4	5.3	5.4	4.9	
Interest rates (in percent)								
Real six-month LIBOR[2]	3.2	2.1	2.5	0.7	2.3	3.6	3.2	3.1
World real long-term interest rate[3]	4.1	2.7	2.2	1.3	1.7	2.9	2.7	2.7
	Percent of GDP							
Balances on current account								
Advanced economies	−0.1	−0.5	−1.5	−1.4	−1.6	−1.6	−1.6	−1.8
Other emerging market and developing countries	−1.6	0.5	3.7	4.1	4.4	3.3	3.1	2.6
Total external debt								
Other emerging market and developing countries	33.4	37.2	26.2	28.7	26.3	25.3	24.4	22.9
Debt service								
Other emerging market and developing countries	4.6	6.2	4.8	5.6	5.4	4.2	4.0	3.8

[1]Data refer to trade in goods and services.
[2]London interbank offered rate on U.S. dollar deposits less percent change in U.S. GDP deflator.
[3]GDP-weighted average of 10-year (or nearest maturity) government bond rates for the United States, Japan, Germany, France, Italy, the United Kingdom, and Canada.

Table 45. Other Emerging Market and Developing Countries—Medium-Term Baseline Scenario: Selected Economic Indicators

	Eight-Year Averages		Four-Year Average 2005–08	2005	2006	2007	2008	Four-Year Average 2009–12
	1989–96	1997–2004						
	Annual percent change							
Other emerging market and developing countries								
Real GDP	3.7	5.3	7.5	7.5	7.9	7.5	7.1	6.7
Export volume[1]	7.4	8.6	10.5	11.2	10.6	10.4	9.9	9.0
Terms of trade[1]	–0.3	0.7	2.0	5.5	4.1	–2.4	0.9	–0.2
Import volume[1]	7.5	7.6	12.9	12.1	15.0	12.5	12.2	9.9
Regional groups								
Africa								
Real GDP	2.0	3.8	5.8	5.6	5.5	6.2	5.8	5.4
Export volume[1]	5.3	5.2	6.5	6.2	3.8	10.6	5.7	4.6
Terms of trade[1]	–1.0	1.4	4.7	14.1	7.6	–5.6	3.7	–0.3
Import volume[1]	3.6	6.0	11.7	13.1	11.3	12.9	9.4	5.9
Central and eastern Europe								
Real GDP	0.5	3.6	5.6	5.5	6.0	5.5	5.3	4.8
Export volume[1]	6.0	9.6	10.5	9.6	12.8	10.4	9.5	8.2
Terms of trade[1]	–0.1	0.3	–0.3	–0.2	–2.4	1.1	0.3	0.4
Import volume[1]	8.6	9.6	10.5	9.0	12.1	11.5	9.6	8.1
Commonwealth of Independent States[2]								
Real GDP	. . .	4.9	6.9	6.6	7.7	7.0	6.4	5.6
Export volume[1]	. . .	5.6	6.2	4.6	6.4	6.8	7.2	6.2
Terms of trade[1]	. . .	3.8	4.2	14.9	6.5	–4.5	1.0	–1.5
Import volume[1]	. . .	6.8	13.5	15.3	15.9	12.0	10.8	8.6
Developing Asia								
Real GDP	7.8	6.8	8.9	9.2	9.4	8.8	8.4	8.0
Export volume[1]	13.2	12.2	16.0	17.3	16.5	15.0	15.3	12.2
Terms of trade[1]	0.3	–1.3	0.4	–1.7	3.2	–0.3	0.5	0.4
Import volume[1]	13.0	9.1	14.7	12.1	17.6	13.4	15.7	13.1
Middle East								
Real GDP	4.6	4.3	5.5	5.4	5.7	5.5	5.5	5.4
Export volume[1]	8.5	5.4	5.9	6.3	5.9	7.0	4.3	6.4
Terms of trade[1]	0.4	4.7	5.2	22.2	4.8	–7.4	3.2	–0.5
Import volume[1]	4.8	6.6	14.2	16.1	15.9	14.1	10.9	7.4
Western Hemisphere								
Real GDP	2.9	2.6	4.8	4.6	5.5	4.9	4.2	3.7
Export volume[1]	7.5	5.9	5.4	7.6	4.5	4.1	5.6	5.8
Terms of trade[1]	0.2	0.9	2.1	4.5	7.6	–1.8	–1.5	–1.2
Import volume[1]	10.7	4.8	10.2	11.0	11.8	9.6	8.4	6.1
Analytical groups								
Net debtor countries by debt-servicing experience								
Countries with arrears and/or rescheduling during 2001–05								
Real GDP	3.9	3.0	6.6	7.2	6.5	6.8	6.1	5.7
Export volume[1]	7.9	5.3	8.1	9.6	4.5	10.7	7.6	5.8
Terms of trade[1]	—	–1.5	1.4	1.1	7.6	–4.3	1.6	0.2
Import volume[1]	7.4	2.1	11.1	14.9	10.1	9.8	9.6	7.7

Table 45 *(concluded)*

	1996	2000	2004	2005	2006	2007	2008	2012
	Percent of exports of goods and services							
Other emerging market and developing countries								
Current account balance	−5.5	4.4	6.6	10.7	11.3	8.5	7.9	5.7
Total external debt	142.3	122.1	91.2	75.8	67.4	65.3	62.6	55.5
Debt-service payments[3]	19.7	23.0	14.9	14.9	13.8	10.8	10.2	9.1
Interest payments	8.6	7.4	4.6	4.4	4.4	4.2	4.0	3.6
Amortization	11.1	15.7	10.3	10.5	9.4	6.6	6.2	5.5
Regional groups								
Africa								
Current account balance	−3.9	4.6	0.2	4.6	5.4	0.2	−0.1	−3.1
Total external debt	232.8	182.0	130.6	94.5	68.7	64.8	61.9	61.7
Debt-service payments[3]	22.1	17.0	11.8	11.0	12.5	7.5	6.1	5.3
Interest payments	12.4	7.1	3.6	3.2	3.0	2.6	2.4	2.3
Amortization	9.7	9.9	8.2	7.8	9.5	4.9	3.8	3.0
Central and eastern Europe								
Current account balance	−10.0	−13.7	−12.9	−11.9	−14.0	−13.4	−12.8	−10.5
Total external debt	116.6	129.9	119.6	111.9	110.6	103.3	100.2	88.5
Debt-service payments[3]	20.1	25.0	21.5	20.4	20.1	19.1	18.5	17.4
Interest payments	9.3	10.1	7.4	7.0	6.9	7.1	6.7	6.1
Amortization	10.7	15.0	14.2	13.4	13.2	12.0	11.8	11.3
Commonwealth of Independent States								
Current account balance	3.5	29.3	20.6	22.6	20.5	14.8	13.8	1.2
Total external debt	116.5	121.7	92.5	86.3	79.5	85.2	88.2	114.4
Debt-service payments[3]	10.9	37.4	24.5	27.7	27.0	17.8	17.9	19.4
Interest payments	7.1	8.0	8.3	9.4	10.9	9.9	9.9	11.4
Amortization	3.8	29.3	16.1	18.3	16.1	7.9	8.0	7.9
Developing Asia								
Current account balance	−7.5	5.5	7.2	10.9	13.6	14.2	14.3	12.5
Total external debt	120.3	93.9	62.5	53.2	48.2	44.4	41.0	32.5
Debt-service payments[3]	13.2	13.5	8.1	7.3	6.6	5.9	5.5	4.5
Interest payments	5.9	4.7	2.3	2.2	2.2	2.1	2.0	1.7
Amortization	7.3	8.8	5.7	5.2	4.4	3.8	3.5	2.9
Middle East								
Current account balance	7.6	26.7	23.1	32.3	30.5	21.6	19.2	15.9
Total external debt	71.6	60.9	48.6	40.5	40.5	44.9	44.5	39.6
Debt-service payments[3]	12.7	7.3	5.3	5.2	6.2	5.1	5.0	4.5
Interest payments	4.1	2.1	1.9	1.8	1.9	2.2	2.3	2.0
Amortization	8.6	5.2	3.4	3.4	4.4	2.9	2.7	2.5
Western Hemisphere								
Current account balance	−12.9	−11.5	3.8	5.4	6.4	1.9	−0.7	−3.9
Total external debt	214.3	181.6	148.0	116.0	94.6	92.8	90.0	79.7
Debt-service payments[3]	38.3	44.6	28.7	31.2	25.5	18.3	17.9	16.4
Interest payments	14.7	13.7	8.0	7.4	6.5	6.0	5.7	5.0
Amortization	23.6	30.9	20.7	23.8	18.9	12.3	12.2	11.4
Analytical groups								
Net debtor countries by debt-servicing experience								
Countries with arrears and/or rescheduling during 2001–05								
Current account balance	−17.1	−4.9	−1.0	−2.8	−0.3	−3.9	−4.7	−9.7
Total external debt	295.1	279.8	222.8	172.2	144.1	135.1	128.1	114.4
Debt-service payments[3]	30.2	40.8	23.8	26.8	21.1	15.8	13.9	13.1
Interest payments	12.5	14.4	5.2	5.0	4.5	4.6	4.2	3.6
Amortization	17.7	26.5	18.6	21.7	16.6	11.2	9.7	9.5

[1]Data refer to trade in goods and services.
[2]Mongolia, which is not a member of the Commonwealth of Independent States, is included in this group for reasons of geography and similarities in economic structure.
[3]Interest payments on total debt plus amortization payments on long-term debt only. Projections incorporate the impact of exceptional financing items. Excludes service payments to the International Monetary Fund.

WORLD ECONOMIC OUTLOOK AND STAFF STUDIES FOR THE WORLD ECONOMIC OUTLOOK, SELECTED TOPICS, 1995–2007

I. Methodology—Aggregation, Modeling, and Forecasting

World Economic Outlook

The Difficult Art of Forecasting	October 1996, Annex I
World Current Account Discrepancy	October 1996, Annex III
Alternative Exchange Rate Assumptions for Japan	October 1997, Box 2
Revised Purchasing Power Parity Based Weights for the *World Economic Outlook*	May 2000, Box A1
The Global Current Account Discrepancy	October 2000, Chapter I, Appendix II
How Well Do Forecasters Predict Turning Points?	May 2001, Box 1.1
The Information Technology Revolution: Measurement Issues	October 2001, Box 3.1
Measuring Capital Account Liberalization	October 2001, Box 4.1
The Accuracy of *World Economic Outlook* Growth Forecasts: 1991–2000	December 2001, Box 3.1
On the Accuracy of Forecasts of Recovery	April 2002, Box 1.2
The Global Current Account Discrepancy and Other Statistical Problems	September 2002, Box 2.1
The Global Economy Model	April 2003, Box 4.3
How Should We Measure Global Growth?	September 2003, Box 1.2
Measuring Foreign Reserves	September 2003, Box 2.2
The Effects of Tax Cuts in a Global Fiscal Model	April 2004, Box 2.2
How Accurate Are the Forecasts in the *World Economic Outlook?*	April 2006, Box 1.3
Drawing the Line Between Personal and Corporate Savings	April 2006, Box 4.1

Staff Studies for the World Economic Outlook

How Accurate Are the IMF's Short-Term Forecasts? Another Examination of the *World Economic Outlook* Michael J. Artis	December 1997
IMF's Estimates of Potential Output: Theory and Practice Paula R. De Masi	December 1997
Multilateral Unit-Labor-Cost-Based Competitiveness Indicators for Advanced, Developing, and Transition Countries Anthony G. Turner and Stephen Golub	December 1997

II. Historical Surveys

World Economic Outlook

The Rise and Fall of Inflation—Lessons from Postwar Experience	October 1996, Chapter VI
The World Economy in the Twentieth Century	May 2000, Chapter V
The Monetary System and Growth During the Commercial Revolution	May 2000, Box 5.2

The Great Depression   April 2002, Box 3.2

Historical Evidence on Financial Crises   April 2002, Box 3.3

A Historical Perspective on Booms, Busts, and Recessions   April 2003, Box 2.1

Institutional Development: The Influence of History and Geography   April 2003, Box 3.1

Long-Term Interest Rates from a Historical Perspective   April 2006, Box 1.1

Recycling Petrodollars in the 1970s   April 2006, Box 2.2

*Staff Studies for the
World Economic Outlook*

Globalization and Growth in the Twentieth Century
    Nicholas Crafts   May 2000

The International Monetary System in the (Very) Long Run
    Barry Eichengreen and Nathan Sussman   May 2000

External Imbalances Then and Now   April 2005, Box 3.1

III. Economic Growth—Sources and Patterns

World Economic Outlook

Saving in a Growing World Economy   May 1995, Chapter V

North-South R&D Spillovers   May 1995, Box 6

Long-Term Growth Potential in the Countries in Transition   October 1996, Chapter V

Globalization and the Opportunities for Developing Countries   May 1997, Chapter IV

Measuring Productivity Gains in East Asian Economies   May 1997, Box 9

The Business Cycle, International Linkages, and Exchange Rates   May 1998, Chapter III

The Asian Crisis and the Region's Long-Term Growth Performance   October 1998, Chapter III

Potential Macroeconomic Implications of the Year 2000 Computer Bug   May 1999, Box 1.2

Growth Divergences in the United States, Europe, and Japan:
    Long-Run Trend or Cyclical?   October 1999, Chapter III

How Can the Poorest Countries Catch Up?   May 2000, Chapter IV

Trends in the Human Development Index   May 2000, Box 5.1

Productivity Growth and IT in the Advanced Economies   October 2000, Chapter II

Transition: Experience and Policy Issues   October 2000, Chapter III

Business Linkages in Major Advanced Countries   October 2001, Chapter II

How Do Macroeconomic Fluctuations in the Advanced Countries Affect
    the Developing Countries?   October 2001, Chapter II

Confidence Spillovers   October 2001, Box 2.1

Channels of Business Cycle Transmission to Developing Countries   October 2001, Box 2.2

The Information Technology Revolution   October 2001, Chapter III

Has the IT Revolution Reduced Output Volatility?   October 2001, Box 3.4

The Impact of Capital Account Liberalization on Economic Performance   October 2001, Box 4.2

How Has September 11 Influenced the Global Economy?   December 2001, Chapter II

The Long-Term Impact of September 11   December 2001, Box 2.1

Is Wealth Increasingly Driving Consumption?   April 2002, Chapter II

Recessions and Recoveries   April 2002, Chapter III

Was It a Global Recession?   April 2002, Box 1.1

How Important Is the Wealth Effect on Consumption?   April 2002, Box 2.1

A Household Perspective on the Wealth Effect ..... April 2002, Box 2.2

Measuring Business Cycles ..... April 2002, Box 3.1

Economic Fluctuations in Developing Countries ..... April 2002, Box 3.4

How Will Recent Falls in Equity Markets Affect Activity? ..... September 2002, Box 1.1

Reversal of Fortune: Productivity Growth in Europe and the United States ..... September 2002, Box 1.3

Growth and Institutions ..... April 2003, Chapter III

Is the New Economy Dead? ..... April 2003, Box 1.2

Have External Anchors Accelerated Institutional Reform in Practice? ..... April 2003, Box 3.2

Institutional Development: The Role of the IMF ..... April 2003, Box 3.4

How Would War in Iraq Affect the Global Economy? ..... April 2003, Appendix 1.2

How Can Economic Growth in the Middle East and North Africa
    Region Be Accelerated? ..... September 2003, Chapter II

Recent Changes in Monetary and Financial Conditions in the Major
    Currency Areas ..... September 2003, Box 1.1

Accounting for Growth in the Middle East and North Africa ..... September 2003, Box 2.1

Managing Increasing Aid Flows to Developing Countries ..... September 2003, Box 1.3

Fostering Structural Reforms in Industrial Countries ..... April 2004, Chapter III

How Will Demographic Change Affect the Global Economy? ..... September 2004, Chapter III

HIV/AIDS: Demographic, Economic, and Fiscal Consequences ..... September 2004, Box 3.3

Implications of Demographic Change for Health Care Systems ..... September 2004, Box 3.4

Workers' Remittances and Economic Development ..... April 2005, Chapter II

Output Volatility in Emerging Market and Developing Countries ..... April 2005, Chapter II

How Does Macroeconomic Instability Stifle Sub-Saharan African Growth? ..... April 2005, Box 1.5

How Should Middle Eastern and Central Asian Oil Exporters Use Their
    Oil Revenues? ..... April 2005, Box 1.6

Why Is Volatility Harmful? ..... April 2005, Box 2.3

Building Institutions ..... September 2005, Chapter III

Return on Investment in Industrial and Developing Countries ..... September 2005, Box 2.2

The Use of Specific Levers to Reduce Corruption ..... September 2005, Box 3.2

Examining the Impact of Unrequited Transfers on Institutions ..... September 2005, Box 3.3

The Impact of Recent Housing Market Adjustments in Industrial Countries ..... April 2006, Box 1.2

Awash With Cash: Why Are Corporate Savings So High? ..... April 2006, Chapter IV

The Global Implications of an Avian Flu Pandemic ..... April 2006, Appendix 1.2

Asia Rising: Patterns of Economic Development and Growth ..... September 2006, Chapter 3

Japan's Potential Output and Productivity Growth ..... September 2006, Box 3.1

The Evolution and Impact of Corporate Governance Quality in Asia ..... September 2006, Box 3.2

Decoupling the Train? Spillovers and Cycles in the Global Economy ..... April 2007, Chapter 4

Spillovers and International Business Cycle Synchronization:
    A Broader Perspective ..... April 2007, Box 4.3

***Staff Studies for the
World Economic Outlook***

How Large Was the Output Collapse in Russia? Alternative Estimates and
    Welfare Implications
    Evgeny Gavrilenkov and Vincent Koen ..... September 1995

Deindustrialization: Causes and Implications
    Robert Rowthorn and Ramana Ramaswamy ..... December 1997

IV. Inflation and Deflation; Commodity Markets

World Economic Outlook

The Rise and Fall of Inflation—Lessons from Postwar Experience   October 1996, Chapter VI

World Oil Market: Recent Developments and Outlook   October 1996, Annex II

Inflation Targets   October 1996, Box 8

Indexed Bonds and Expected Inflation   October 1996, Box 9

Effects of High Inflation on Income Distribution   October 1996, Box 10

Central Bank Independence and Inflation   October 1996, Box 11

Recent Developments in Primary Commodity Markets   May 1998, Annex II

Japan's Liquidity Trap   October 1998, Box 4.1

Safeguarding Macroeconomic Stability at Low Inflation   October 1999, Chapter IV

Global Liquidity   October 1999, Box 4.4

Cycles in Nonfuel Commodity Prices   May 2000, Box 2.2

Booms and Slumps in the World Oil Market   May 2000, Box 2.3

Commodity Prices and Commodity Exporting Countries   October 2000, Chapter II

Developments in the Oil Markets   October 2000, Box 2.2

The Decline of Inflation in Emerging Markets: Can It Be Maintained?   May 2001, Chapter IV

The Global Slowdown and Commodity Prices   May 2001, Chapter I, Appendix 1

Why Emerging Market Countries Should Strive to Preserve Lower Inflation   May 2001, Box 4.1

Is There a Relationship Between Fiscal Deficits and Inflation?   May 2001, Box 4.2

How Much of a Concern Is Higher Headline Inflation?   October 2001, Box 1.2

Primary Commodities and Semiconductor Markets   October 2001, Chapter I, Appendix 1

Can Inflation Be Too Low?   April 2002, Box 2.3

Could Deflation Become a Global Problem?   April 2003, Box 1.1

Housing Markets in Industrial Countries   April 2004, Box 1.2

Is Global Inflation Coming Back?   September 2004, Box 1.1

What Explains the Recent Run-Up in House Prices?   September 2004, Box 2.1

Will the Oil Market Continue to Be Tight?   April 2005, Chapter IV

Should Countries Worry About Oil Price Fluctuations?   April 2005, Box 4.1

Data Quality in the Oil Market   April 2005, Box 4.2

Long-Term Inflation Expectations and Credibility   September 2005, Box 4.2

The Boom in Nonfuel Commodity Prices: Can It Last?   September 2006, Chapter 5

Commodity Price Shocks, Growth, and Financing in Sub-Saharan Africa   September 2006, Box 2.2

International Oil Companies and National Oil Companies in a Changing Oil Sector Environment   September 2006, Box 1.4

Has Speculation Contributed to Higher Commodity Prices?   September 2006, Box 5.1

Agricultural Trade Liberalization and Commodity Prices   September 2006, Box 5.2

Recent Developments in Commodity Markets   September 2006, Appendix 2.1

Staff Studies for the World Economic Outlook

Prices in the Transition: Ten Stylized Facts
Vincent Koen and Paula R. De Masi   December 1997

V. Fiscal Policy

World Economic Outlook

Structural Fiscal Balances in Smaller Industrial Countries — May 1995, Annex III

Can Fiscal Contraction Be Expansionary in the Short Run? — May 1995, Box 2

Pension Reform in Developing Countries — May 1995, Box 11

Effects of Increased Government Debt: Illustrative Calculations — May 1995, Box 13

Subsidies and Tax Arrears — October 1995, Box 8

Focus on Fiscal Policy — May 1996

The Spillover Effects of Government Debt — May 1996, Annex I

Uses and Limitations of Generational Accounting — May 1996, Box 5

The European Union's Stability and Growth Pact — October 1997, Box 3

Progress with Fiscal Reform in Countries in Transition — May 1998, Chapter V

Pension Reform in Countries in Transition — May 1998, Box 10

Transparency in Government Operations — May 1998, Annex I

The Asian Crisis: Social Costs and Mitigating Policies — October 1998, Box 2.4

Fiscal Balances in the Asian Crisis Countries: Effects of Changes in the Economic Environment Versus Policy Measures — October 1998, Box 2.5

Aging in the East Asian Economies: Implications for Government Budgets and Saving Rates — October 1998, Box 3.1

Orienting Fiscal Policy in the Medium Term in Light of the Stability and Growth Pact and Longer-Term Fiscal Needs — October 1998, Box 5.2

Comparing G-7 Fiscal Positions—Who Has a Debt Problem? — October 1999, Box 1.3

Social Spending, Poverty Reduction, and Debt Relief in Heavily Indebted Poor Countries — May 2000, Box 4.3

Fiscal Improvement in Advanced Economies: How Long Will It Last? — May 2001, Chapter III

Impact of Fiscal Consolidation on Macroeconomic Performance — May 2001, Box 3.3

Fiscal Frameworks in Advanced and Emerging Market Economies — May 2001, Box 3.4

Data on Public Debt in Emerging Market Economies — September 2003, Box 3.1

Fiscal Risk: Contingent Liabilities and Demographics — September 2003, Box 3.2

Assessing Fiscal Sustainability Under Uncertainty — September 2003, Box 3.3

The Case for Growth-Indexed Bonds — September 2003, Box 3.4

Public Debt in Emerging Markets: Is It Too High? — September 2003, Chapter III

Has Fiscal Behavior Changed Under the European Economic and Monetary Union? — September 2004, Chapter II

Bringing Small Entrepreneurs into the Formal Economy — September 2004, Box 1.5

HIV/AIDS: Demographic, Economic, and Fiscal Consequences — September 2004, Box 3.3

Implications of Demographic Change for Health Care Systems — September 2004, Box 3.4

Impact of Aging on Public Pension Plans — September 2004, Box 3.5

How Should Middle Eastern and Central Asian Oil Exporters Use Their Oil Revenues? — April 2005, Box 1.6

Financial Globalization and the Conduct of Macroeconomic Policies — April 2005, Box 3.3

Is Public Debt in Emerging Markets Still Too High? — September 2005, Box 1.1

Improved Emerging Market Fiscal Performance: Cyclical or Structural? — September 2006, Box 2.1

VI. Monetary Policy; Financial Markets; Flow of Funds

World Economic Outlook

Saving in a Growing World Economy	May 1995, Chapter V
Saving and Real Interest Rates in Developing Countries	May 1995, Box 10
Financial Market Turmoil and Economic Policies in Industrial Countries	October 1995, Chapter III
Financial Liberalization in Africa and Asia	October 1995, Box 4
Policy Challenges Facing Industrial Countries in the Late 1990s	October 1996, Chapter III
Using the Slope of the Yield Curve to Estimate Lags in Monetary Transmission Mechanism	October 1996, Box 2
Financial Repression	October 1996, Box 5
Bank-Restructuring Strategies in the Baltic States, Russia, and Other Countries of the Former Soviet Union: Main Issues and Challenges	October 1996, Box 7
Monetary and Financial Sector Policies in Transition Countries	October 1997, Chapter V
Dollarization	October 1997, Box 6
Interim Assessment (Focus on Crisis in Asia—Regional and Global Implications)	December 1997
Financial Crises: Characteristics and Indicators of Vulnerability	May 1998, Chapter IV
The Role of Hedge Funds in Financial Markets	May 1998, Box 1
International Monetary System: Measures to Reduce the Risk of Crises	May 1998, Box 3
Resolving Banking Sector Problems	May 1998, Box 6
Effective Banking Prudential Regulations and Requirements	May 1998, Box 7
Strengthening the Architecture of the International Monetary System Through International Standards and Principles of Good Practice	October 1998, Box 1.2
The Role of Monetary Policy in Responding to Currency Crises	October 1998, Box 2.3
Summary of Structural Reforms in Crisis Countries	October 1998, Box 3.2
Japan's Liquidity Trap	October 1998, Box 4.1
How Useful Are Taylor Rules as a Guide to ECB Monetary Policies?	October 1998, Box 5.1
The Crisis in Emerging Markets	December 1998, Chapter II
Turbulence in Mature Financial Markets	December 1998, Chapter III
What Is the Implied Future Earnings Growth Rate that Would Justify Current Equity Prices in the United States?	December 1998, Box 3.2
Leverage	December 1998, Box 3.3
The Near Collapse and Rescue of Long-Term Capital Management	December 1998, Box 3.4
Risk Management: Progress and Problems	December 1998, Box 3.5
Supervisory Reforms Relating to Risk Management	December 1998, Box 3.6
Emerging Market Banking Systems	December 1998, Annex
International Financial Contagion	May 1999, Chapter III
From Crisis to Recovery in the Emerging Market Economies	October 1999, Chapter II
Safeguarding Macroeconomic Stability at Low Inflation	October 1999, Chapter IV
The Effects of a Zero Floor for Nominal Interest Rates on Real Output: Selected Simulation Results	October 1999, Box 4.2
Asset Prices and Business Cycle	May 2000, Chapter III
Global Liquidity and Asset Prices	May 2000, Box 3.2
International Capital Flows to Emerging Markets	October 2000, Chapter II
Developments in Global Equity Markets	October 2000, Chapter II
U.S. Monetary Policy and Sovereign Spreads in Emerging Markets	October 2000, Box 2.1

Impact of the Global Technology Correction on the Real Economy — May 2001, Chapter II

Inflation Targeting in Emerging Market Economies: Implementation and Challenges — May 2001, Box 4.3

Financial Market Dislocations and Policy Responses After the September 11 Attacks — December 2001, Box 2.2

Investor Risk Appetite — December 2001, Box 2.3

Monetary Policy in a Low Inflation Era — April 2002, Chapter II

The Introduction of Euro Notes and Coins — April 2002, Box 1.3

Cross-Country Determinants of Capital Structure — September 2002, Box 2.3

When Bubbles Burst — April 2003, Chapter II

How Do Balance Sheet Vulnerabilities Affect Investment? — April 2003, Box 2.3

Identifying Asset Price Booms and Busts — April 2003, Appendix 2.1

Are Foreign Exchange Reserves in Asia Too High? — September 2003, Chapter II

Reserves and Short-Term Debt — September 2003, Box 2.3

Are Credit Booms in Emerging Markets a Concern? — April 2004, Chapter IV

How Do U.S. Interest and Exchange Rates Affect Emerging Markets' Balance Sheets? — April 2004, Box 2.1

Does Financial Sector Development Help Economic Growth and Welfare? — April 2004, Box 4.1

Adjustable- or Fixed-Rate Mortgages: What Influences a Country's Choices? — September 2004, Box 2.2

What Are the Risks from Low U.S. Long-Term Interest Rates? — April 2005, Box 1.2

Regulating Remittances — April 2005, Box 2.2

Financial Globalization and the Conduct of Macroeconomic Policies — April 2005, Box 3.3

Monetary Policy in a Globalized World — April 2005, Box 3.4

Does Inflation Targeting Work in Emerging Markets? — September 2005, Chapter IV

A Closer Look at Inflation Targeting Alternatives: Money and Exchange Rate Targets — September 2005, Box 4.1

How Has Globalization Affected Inflation? — April 2006, Chapter III

The Impact of Petrodollars on U.S. and Emerging Market Bond Yields — April 2006, Box 2.3

Globalization and Inflation in Emerging Markets — April 2006, Box 3.1

Globalization and Low Inflation in a Historical Perspective — April 2006, Box 3.2

Exchange Rate Pass-Through to Import Prices — April 2006, Box 3.3

Trends in the Financial Sector's Profits and Savings — April 2006, Box 4.2

How Do Financial Systems Affect Economic Cycles? — September 2006, Chapter 4

Financial Leverage and Debt Deflation — September 2006, Box 4.1

Financial Linkages and Spillovers — April 2007, Box 4.1

Macroeconomic Conditions in Industrial Countries and Financial Flows to Emerging Markets — April 2007, Box 4.2

Staff Studies for the World Economic Outlook

The Global Real Interest Rate
Thomas Helbling and Robert Wescott — September 1995

A Monetary Impulse Measure for Medium-Term Policy Analysis
Bennett T. McCallum and Monica Hargraves — September 1995

Saving Behavior in Industrial and Developing Countries
Paul R. Masson, Tamim Bayoumi, and Hossein Samiei — September 1995

Capital Structure and Corporate Performance Across Emerging Markets — September 2002, Chapter II

VII. Labor Market Issues

World Economic Outlook

Capital Formation and Employment	May 1995, Box 4
Implications of Structural Reforms Under EMU	October 1997, Annex II
Euro-Area Structural Rigidities	October 1998, Box 5.3
Chronic Unemployment in the Euro Area: Causes and Cures	May 1999, Chapter IV
Labor Market Slack: Concepts and Measurement	May 1999, Box 4.1
EMU and European Labor Markets	May 1999, Box 4.2
Labor Markets—An Analytical Framework	May 1999, Box 4.3
The OECD Jobs Study	May 1999, Box 4.4
The Effects of Downward Rigidity of Nominal Wages on (Un)employment: Selected Simulation Results	October 1999, Box 4.1
Unemployment and Labor Market Institutions: Why Reforms Pay Off	April 2003, Chapter IV
Regional Disparities in Unemployment	April 2003, Box 4.1
Labor Market Reforms in the European Union	April 2003, Box 4.2
The Globalization of Labor	April 2007, Chapter 5
Emigration and Trade: How Do They Affect Developing Countries?	April 2007, Box 5.1

Staff Studies for the World Economic Outlook

Evaluating Unemployment Policies: What Do the Underlying Theories Tell Us? *Dennis J. Snower*	September 1995
Institutional Structure and Labor Market Outcomes: Western Lessons for European Countries in Transition *Robert J. Flanagan*	September 1995
The Effect of Globalization on Wages in the Advanced Economies *Matthew J. Slaughter and Phillip Swagel*	December 1997
International Labor Standards and International Trade *Stephen Golub*	December 1997
EMU Challenges European Labor Markets *Rüdiger Soltwedel, Dirk Dohse, and Christiane Krieger-Boden*	May 2000

VIII. Exchange Rate Issues

World Economic Outlook

Exchange Rate Effects of Fiscal Consolidation	October 1995, Annex
Exchange Rate Arrangements and Economic Performance in Developing Countries	October 1997, Chapter IV
Asymmetric Shocks: European Union and the United States	October 1997, Box 4
Currency Boards	October 1997, Box 5
The Business Cycle, International Linkages, and Exchange Rates	May 1998, Chapter III
Evaluating Exchange Rates	May 1998, Box 5
Determining Internal and External Conversion Rates for the Euro	October 1998, Box 5.4
The Euro Area and Effective Exchange Rates	October 1998, Box 5.5
Recent Dollar/Yen Exchange Rate Movements	December 1998, Box 3.1
International Financial Contagion	May 1999, Chapter III
Exchange Rate Crashes and Inflation: Lessons for Brazil	May 1999, Box 2.1
Recent Experience with Exchange-Rate-Based Stabilizations	May 1999, Box 3.1

The Pros and Cons of Dollarization   May 2000, Box 1.4

Why Is the Euro So Undervalued?   October 2000, Box 1.1

Convergence and Real Exchange Rate Appreciation in the EU Accession Countries   October 2000, Box 4.4

What Is Driving the Weakness of the Euro and the Strength of the Dollar?   May 2001, Chapter II

The Weakness of the Australian and New Zealand Currencies   May 2001, Box 2.1

How Did the September 11 Attacks Affect Exchange Rate Expectations?   December 2001, Box 2.4

Market Expectations of Exchange Rate Movements   September 2002, Box 1.2

Are Foreign Exchange Reserves in Asia Too High?   September 2003, Chapter II

How Concerned Should Developing Countries Be About G-3
    Exchange Rate Volatility?   September 2003, Chapter II

Reserves and Short-Term Debt   September 2003, Box 2.3

The Effects of a Falling Dollar   April 2004, Box 1.1

Learning to Float: The Experience of Emerging Market Countries Since
    the Early 1990s   September 2004, Chapter II

How Did Chile, India, and Brazil Learn to Float?   September 2004, Box 2.3

Foreign Exchange Market Development and Intervention   September 2004, Box 2.4

How Emerging Market Countries May Be Affected by External Shocks   September 2006, Box 1.3

Exchange Rates and the Adjustment of External Imbalances   April 2007, Chapter 3

Exchange Rate Pass-Through to Trade Prices and External Adjustment   April 2007, Box 3.3

Staff Studies for the
World Economic Outlook

Multilateral Unit-Labor-Cost-Based Competitiveness Indicators
    for Advanced, Developing, and Transition Countries
    Anthony G. Turner and Stephen Golub   December 1997

Currency Crises: In Search of Common Elements
    Jahangir Aziz, Francesco Caramazza, and Ranil Salgado   May 2000

Business Cycle Influences on Exchange Rates: Survey and Evidence
    Ronald MacDonald and Phillip Suragel   May 2000

IX. External Payments, Trade, Capital Movements, and Foreign Debt

World Economic Outlook

Trade Among the Transition Countries   October 1995, Box 7

World Current Account Discrepancy   October 1996, Annex III

Capital Inflows to Developing and Transition Countries—Identifying Causes
    and Formulating Appropriate Policy Responses   October 1996, Annex IV

Globalization—Opportunities and Challenges   May 1997

Moral Hazard and IMF Lending   May 1998, Box 2

The Current Account and External Sustainability   May 1998, Box 8

Review of Debt-Reduction Efforts for Low-Income Countries and Status of
    the HIPC Initiative   October 1998, Box 1.1

Trade Adjustment in East Asian Crisis Countries   October 1998, Box 2.2

Are There Dangers of Increasing Protection?   May 1999, Box 1.3

Trends and Issues in the Global Trading System   October 1999, Chapter V

Capital Flows to Emerging Market Economies: Composition and Volatility — October 1999, Box 2.2

The Global Current Account Discrepancy — October 2000, Chapter I, Appendix II

Trade Integration and Sub-Saharan Africa — May 2001, Chapter II

Sustainability of the U.S. External Current Account — May 2001, Box 1.2

Reducing External Balances — May 2001, Chapter I, Appendix 2

The World Trading System: From Seattle to Doha — October 2001, Chapter II

International Financial Integration and Economic Performance: Impact on Developing Countries — October 2001, Chapter IV

Potential Welfare Gains From a New Trade Round — October 2001, Box 2.3

Critics of a New Trade Round — October 2001, Box 2.4

Foreign Direct Investment and the Poorer Countries — October 2001, Box 4.3

Country Experiences with Sequencing Capital Account Liberalization — October 2001, Box 4.4

Contagion and Its Causes — December 2001, Chapter I, Appendix

Capital Account Crises in Emerging Market Countries — April 2002, Box 3.5

How Have External Deficits Adjusted in the Past? — September 2002, Box 2.2

Using Prices to Measure Goods Market Integration — September 2002, Box 3.1

Transport Costs — September 2002, Box 3.2

The Gravity Model of International Trade — September 2002, Box 3.3

Vertical Specialization in the Global Economy — September 2002, Box 3.4

Trade and Growth — September 2002, Box 3.5

How Worrisome Are External Imbalances? — September 2002, Chapter II

How Do Industrial Country Agricultural Policies Affect Developing Countries? — September 2002, Chapter II

Trade and Financial Integration — September 2002, Chapter III

Risks to the Multilateral Trading System — April 2004, Box 1.3

Is the Doha Round Back on Track? — September 2004, Box 1.3

Regional Trade Agreements and Integration: The Experience with NAFTA — September 2004, Box 1.4

Globalization and External Imbalances — April 2005, Chapter III

The Ending of Global Textile Trade Quotas — April 2005, Box 1.3

What Progress Has Been Made in Implementing Policies to Reduce Global Imbalances? — April 2005, Box 1.4

Measuring a Country's Net External Position — April 2005, Box 3.2

Global Imbalances: A Saving and Investment Perspective — September 2005, Chapter II

Impact of Demographic Change on Saving, Investment, and Current Account Balances — September 2005, Box 2.3

How Will Global Imbalances Adjust? — September 2005, Appendix 1.2

Oil Prices and Global Imbalances — April 2006, Chapter II

How Much Progress Has Been Made in Addressing Global Imbalances? — April 2006, Box 1.4

The Doha Round After The Hong Kong SAR Meetings — April 2006, Box 1.5

Capital Flows to Emerging Market Countries: A Long-Term Perspective — September 2006, Box 1.1

How Will Global Imbalances Adjust? — September 2006, Box 2.1

External Sustainability and Financial Integration — April 2007, Box 3.1

Large and Persistent Current Account Imbalances — April 2007, Box 3.2

Staff Studies for the
World Economic Outlook

Foreign Direct Investment in the World Economy
   Edward M. Graham   September 1995

Trade and Financial Integration in Europe: Five Years After the
   Euro's Introduction   September 2004, Box 2.5

X. Regional Issues

World Economic Outlook

Adjustment in Sub-Saharan Africa   May 1995, Annex II

Macroeconomic and Structural Adjustment in the Middle East and North Africa   May 1996, Annex II

Stabilization and Reform of Formerly Centrally Planned Developing
   Economies in East Asia   May 1997, Box 10

EMU and the World Economy   October 1997, Chapter III

Implications of Structural Reforms Under EMU   October 1997, Annex II

The European Union's Stability and Growth Pact   October 1997, Box 3

Asymmetric Shocks: European Union and the United States   October 1997, Box 4

Interim Assessment (Focus on Crisis in Asia—Regional and Global Implications)   December 1997

The Asian Crisis and the Region's Long-Term Growth Performance   October 1998, Chapter III

Economic Policy Challenges Facing the Euro Area and the External
   Implications of EMU   October 1998, Chapter V

Economic Policymaking in the EU and Surveillance by EU Institutions   October 1998, Chapter V, Appendix

Chronic Unemployment in the Euro Area: Causes and Cures   May 1999, Chapter IV

Growth in Sub-Saharan Africa: Performance, Impediments, and
   Policy Requirements   October 1999, Chapter VI

The Regional Economic Impact of the Kosovo Crisis   October 1999, Box 1.5

Counting the Costs of the Recent Crises   October 1999, Box 2.6

Africa and World Trends in Military Spending   October 1999, Box 6.1

The Economic Impact of HIV/AIDS in Southern Africa   October 2000, Box 1.4

Accession of Transition Economies to the European Union:
   Prospects and Pressures   October 2000, Chapter IV

The IMF and the Transition Economies   October 2000, Box 3.1

Previous EU Enlargements   October 2000, Box 4.2

The Enhanced HIPC Initiative in Africa   May 2001, Box 1.4

Large Current Account Deficits in EU Accession Countries   May 2001, Box 1.5

Africa's Trade and the Gravity Model   May 2001, Box 2.2

The Implications of the Japanese Economic Slowdown for East Asia   October 2001, Box 1.4

Relative Euro-Area Growth Performances: Why Are Germany and Italy
   Lagging Behind France?   October 2001, Box 1.5

Economic Growth, Civil Conflict, and Poverty Reduction in Sub-Saharan Africa   October 2001, Box 1.7

Information Technology and Growth in Emerging Asia   October 2001, Box 3.3

The IT Slump and Short-Term Growth Prospects in East Asia   October 2001, Box 3.5

The Effects of the September 11 Attacks on the Caribbean Region   December 2001, Box 3.3

Debt Crises: What's Different About Latin America?   April 2002, Chapter II

Foreign Direct Investment in Africa   September 2002, Box 1.6

Promoting Stronger Institutions and Growth: The New Partnership for
    Africa's Development   April 2003, Box 3.3

How Can Economic Growth in the Middle East and North Africa
    Region Be Accelerated?   September 2003, Chapter II

Gulf Cooperation Council: Challenges on the Road to a Monetary Union   September 2003, Box 1.5

Accounting for Growth in the Middle East and North Africa   September 2003, Box 2.1

Is Emerging Asia Becoming an Engine of World Growth?   April 2004, Box 1.4

What Works in Africa   April 2004, Box 1.5

Economic Integration and Structural Reforms: The European Experience   April 2004, Box 3.4

What Are the Risks of Slower Growth in China?   September 2004, Box 1.2

Governance Challenges and Progress in Sub-Saharan Africa   September 2004, Box 1.6

The Indian Ocean Tsunami: Impact on South Asian Economies   April 2005, Box 1.1

Workers' Remittances and Emigration in the Caribbean   April 2005, Box 2.1

What Explains Divergent External Sector Performance in the Euro Area?   September 2005, Box 1.3

Pressures Mount for African Cotton Producers   September 2005, Box 1.5

Is Investment in Emerging Asia Too Low?   September 2005, Box 2.4

Developing Institutions to Reflect Local Conditions: The Example of
    Ownership Transformation in China Versus Central and Eastern Europe   September 2005, Box 3.1

How Rapidly Are Oil Exporters Spending Their Revenue Gains?   April 2006, Box 2.1

*Staff Studies for the
World Economic Outlook*

The Design of EMU
    David Begg   December 1997

The Great Contraction in Russia, the Baltics, and Other Countries of
    the Former Soviet Union: A View from the Supply Side
    Mark De Broeck and Vincent Koen   May 2000

XI. Country-Specific Analyses

World Economic Outlook

Factors Behind the Financial Crisis in Mexico   May 1995, Annex I

New Zealand's Structural Reforms and Economic Revival   May 1995, Box 3

Brazil and Korea   May 1995, Box 5

The Output Collapse in Russia   May 1995, Box 8

Foreign Direct Investment in Estonia   May 1995, Box 9

September 1995 Economic Stimulus Packages in Japan   October 1995, Box 1

Uganda: Successful Adjustment Under Difficult Circumstances   October 1995, Box 3

Changing Wage Structures in the Czech Republic   October 1995, Box 6

Resolving Financial System Problems in Japan   May 1996, Box 3

New Zealand's Fiscal Responsibility Act   May 1996, Box 4

Deindustrialization and the Labor Market in Sweden   May 1997, Box 7

Ireland Catches Up   May 1997, Box 8

Foreign Direct Investment Strategies in Hungary and Kazakhstan   May 1997, Box 12

China—Growth and Economic Reforms   October 1997, Annex I

Alternative Exchange Rate Assumptions for Japan   October 1997, Box 2

Hong Kong, China: Economic Linkages and Institutional Arrangements   October 1997, Box 9

Russia's Fiscal Challenges   May 1998, Box 9

Japan's Economic Crisis and Policy Options   October 1998, Chapter IV

Brazil's Financial Assistance Package and Adjustment Program   December 1998, Box 1.1

Recent Developments in the Japanese Financial System   December 1998, Box 1.2

Malaysia's Capital Controls   December 1998, Box 2.1

Hong Kong's Intervention in the Equity Spot and Futures Markets   December 1998, Box 2.2

Is China's Growth Overstated?   December 1998, Box 4.1

Measuring Household Saving in the United States   May 1999, Box 2.2

Australia and New Zealand: Divergences, Prospects, and Vulnerabilities   October 1999, Box 1.1

The Emerging Market Crises and South Africa   October 1999, Box 2.1

Structural Reforms in Latin America: The Case of Argentina   October 1999, Box 2.3

Malaysia's Response to the Financial Crisis: How Unorthodox Was It?   October 1999, Box 2.4

Financial Sector Restructuring in Indonesia, Korea, Malaysia, and Thailand   October 1999, Box 2.5

Turkey's IMF-Supported Disinflation Program   May 2000, Box 2.1

Productivity and Stock Prices in the United States   May 2000, Box 3.1

India: Reinvigorating the Reform Process   May 2000, Box 4.2

Risky Business: Output Volatility and the Perils of Forecasting in Japan   October 2000, Box 1.2

China's Prospective WTO Accession   October 2000, Box 1.3

Addressing Barter Trade and Arrears in Russia   October 2000, Box 3.3

Fiscal Decentralization in Transition Economies: China and Russia   October 2000, Box 3.5

Accession of Turkey to the European Union   October 2000, Box 4.3

Japan's Recent Monetary and Structural Policy Initiatives   May 2001, Box 1.3

Japan: A Fiscal Outlier?   May 2001, Box 3.1

Financial Implications of the Shrinking Supply of U.S. Treasury Securities   May 2001, Box 3.2

The Growth-Poverty Nexus in India   October 2001, Box 1.6

Has U.S. TFP Growth Accelerated Outside of the IT Sector?   October 2001, Box 3.2

Fiscal Stimulus and the Outlook for the United States   December 2001, Box 3.2

Argentina: An Uphill Struggle to Regain Confidence   December 2001, Box 3.4

China's Medium-Term Fiscal Challenges   April 2002, Box 1.4

Rebuilding Afghanistan   April 2002, Box 1.5

Russia's Rebounds   April 2002, Box 1.6

Brazil: The Quest to Restore Market Confidence   September 2002, Box 1.4

Where Is India in Terms of Trade Liberalization?   September 2002, Box 1.5

How Important Are Banking Weaknesses in Explaining Germany's Stagnation?   April 2003, Box 1.3

Are Corporate Financial Conditions Related to the Severity of Recessions
  in the United States?   April 2003, Box 2.2

Rebuilding Post-Conflict Iraq   September 2003, Box 1.4

How Will the U.S. Budget Deficit Affect the Rest of the World?   April 2004, Chapter II

China's Emergence and Its Impact on the Global Economy   April 2004, Chapter II

Can China Sustain Its Rapid Output Growth?   April 2004, Box 2.3

Quantifying the International Impact of China's WTO Accession   April 2004, Box 2.4

Structural Reforms and Economic Growth: New Zealand's Experience   April 2004, Box 3.1

Structural Reforms in the United Kingdom During the 1980s   April 2004, Box 3.2

The Netherlands: How the Interaction of Labor Market Reforms and
  Tax Cuts Led to Strong Employment Growth   April 2004, Box 3.3

Why Is the U.S. International Income Account Still in the Black,
  and Will This Last?   September 2005, Box 1.2

Is India Becoming an Engine for Global Growth?   September 2005, Box 1.4

Saving and Investment in China   September 2005, Box 2.1

China's GDP Revision: What Does It Mean for China and
  the Global Economy?   April 2006, Box 1.6

***Staff Studies for the
World Economic Outlook***

How Large Was the Output Collapse in Russia? Alternative Estimates and
  Welfare Implications
  Evgeny Gavrilenkov and Vincent Koen   September 1995

World Economic and Financial Surveys

This series (ISSN 0258-7440) contains biannual, annual, and periodic studies covering monetary and financial issues of importance to the global economy. The core elements of the series are the *World Economic Outlook* report, usually published in April and September, the semiannual *Global Financial Stability Report,* and the semiannual Regional Economic Outlooks published by the IMF's area departments. Occasionally, studies assess international trade policy, private market and official financing for developing countries, exchange and payments systems, export credit policies, and issues discussed in the *World Economic Outlook.* Please consult the IMF *Publications Catalog* for a complete listing of currently available World Economic and Financial Surveys.

World Economic Outlook: A Survey by the Staff of the International Monetary Fund

The *World Economic Outlook,* published twice a year in English, French, Spanish, and Arabic, presents IMF staff economists' analyses of global economic developments during the near and medium term. Chapters give an overview of the world economy; consider issues affecting industrial countries, developing countries, and economies in transition to the market; and address topics of pressing current interest.

World Economic Outlook: Annual subscription: $94

Published twice yearly. Paperback.

ISSN: 0256-6877. **Stock # OPTNEA4**

Available in English, French, Spanish, and Arabic.

Global Financial Stability Report: Market Developments and Issues

The *Global Financial Stability Report,* published twice a year, examines trends and issues that influence world financial markets. It replaces two IMF publications—the annual *International Capital Markets* report and the electronic quarterly *Emerging Market Financing* report. The report is designed to deepen understanding of international capital flows and to explore developments that could pose a risk to international financial market stability.

$57.00 (academic rate: $54.00); paper.

April 2007 ISBN 978-1-58906-637-3. **Stock# GFSREA2007001**
September 2006 ISBN 1-58906-582-4. **Stock# GFSREA2006002**
April 2006 ISBN 1-58906-504-2. **Stock #GFSREA2006001.**
September 2005 ISBN 1-58906-450-X. **Stock #GFSREA2005002.**
April 2005 ISBN 1-58906-418-6. **Stock #GFSREA2005001.**

Regional Economic Outlooks

These in-depth studies of the Asia and Pacific, Middle East and Central Asia, sub-Saharan Africa, and Western Hemisphere regions drill down to specific regional economic and financial developments and trends—bringing the unique resources, experience, and perspective of the IMF to bear. While near-term responses to exogenous shocks, policies for growth, and the effectiveness of financial policies get center-stage examination, the reports also consider vulnerabilities and opportunities developing in the wings.

Regional Economic Outlooks: $31 (academic rate: $26). April 2007
Asia and Pacific: ISBN: 978-1-58906-641-0. **Stock# REOEA2007001**
Middle East and Central Asia: ISBN: 978-1-58906-644-1. **Stock# REOEA2007002**
Sub-Saharan Africa: ISBN: 978-1-58906-639-7. **Stock# REOEA2007003**
Western Hemisphere: ISBN: 978-1-58906-642-7. **Stock# REOEA2007004**

Emerging Local Securities and Derivatives Markets

by Donald Mathieson, Jorge E. Roldos, Ramana Ramaswamy, and Anna Ilyina

The volatility of capital flows since the mid-1990s has sparked an interest in the development of local securities and derivatives markets. This report examines the growth of these markets in emerging market countries and the key policy issues that have arisen as a result.

$42.00 (academic rate: $35.00); paper.

2004. ISBN 1-58906-291-4. **Stock #WEOEA0202004.**

Official Financing: Recent Developments and Selected Issues

by a staff team in the Policy Development and Review Department led by Martin G. Gilman and Jian-Ye Wang

This study provides information on official financing for developing countries, with the focus on low-income countries. It updates the 2001 edition and reviews developments in direct financing by official and multilateral sources.

$42.00 (academic rate: $35.00); paper.
2003. ISBN 1-58906-228-0. **Stock #WEOEA0132003.**
2001. ISBN 1-58906-038-5. **Stock #WEOEA0132001.**

Exchange Arrangements and Foreign Exchange Markets: Developments and Issues

by a staff team led by Shogo Ishii

This study updates developments in exchange arrangements during 1998–2001. It also discusses the evolution of exchange rate regimes based on de facto policies since 1990, reviews foreign exchange market organization and regulations in a number of countries, and examines factors affecting exchange rate volatility.

ISSN 0258-7440
$42.00 (academic rate: $35.00)
March 2003. ISBN 1-58906-177-2. **Stock #WEOEA0192003.**

World Economic Outlook Supporting Studies

by the IMF's Research Department

These studies, supporting analyses and scenarios of the *World Economic Outlook,* provide a detailed examination of theory and evidence on major issues currently affecting the global economy.

$25.00 (academic rate: $20.00); paper.
2000. ISBN 1-55775-893-X. **Stock #WEOEA0032000.**

Available by series subscription or single title (including back issues); academic rate available only to full-time university faculty and students. For earlier editions please inquire about prices.

The IMF *Catalog of Publications* is available on-line at the Internet address listed below.

Please send orders and inquiries to:
International Monetary Fund, Publication Services, 700 19th Street, N.W.
Washington, D.C. 20431, U.S.A.
Tel.: (202) 623-7430   Telefax: (202) 623-7201
E-mail: publications@imf.org
Internet: http://www.imf.org